LIST OF THE OFFICERS
OF THE BENGAL ARMY

1758—1834

*Alphabetically Arranged and Annotated
with Biographical and Genealogical
Notices by*

MAJOR V. C. P. HODSON
INDIAN ARMY (RETIRED LIST)
AUTHOR OF 'HISTORICAL RECORDS OF THE VICEROY'S BODY-GUARD'

S - V

Printed and bound in Great Britain by Antony Rowe Ltd, Eastbourne

LIST OF THE OFFICERS OF
THE BENGAL ARMY

NOTICE

HAVING in the course of compiling this List received much valuable help and advice from a great number of friends and correspondents, my final task—a pleasure no less than a duty—lies in making acknowledgment of the assistance they have so freely rendered. To mention all by name here would be impossible as the number must total many score, but special thanks are due to the following: the late Dr. John Malcolm Bulloch, M.A., LL.D.; Brigadier H. Bullock, O.B.E., J.A.G. in India; Sir Patrick Cadell, C.S.I., C.I.E., V.D.; the late Major F. G. Cardew, O.B.E. (a former brother officer); the late Sir Evan Cotton, C.I.E.; the late Lt.-Col. D. G. Crawford, I.M.S.; Lady Crofton; Sir William Foster, C.I.E., late Historiographer in the India Office (who first suggested to me the idea of this compilation); the late Mr. S. C. Hill, sometime Superintendent of the Calcutta Record Office; Mr. C. Roy Hudleston; the late Mr. W. T. Ottewill, O.B.E., Superintendent of Records in the India Office; Mr. T. U. Sadleir, M.A., M.R.I.A., late Deputy Ulster; and Mr. W. R. Wright, M.B.E., the present Superintendent of Records in the India Office. Nor could I forgo mention of all those members of the Staff of the Record Department in the India Office with whom I have come into contact since 1920, every one of whom I have invariably found to be more than willing to place his specialized knowledge unreservedly at my disposal, thereby easing to a considerable extent the burden of research.

I take this opportunity also of thanking again those authors of privately printed works who have kindly permitted me to quote from their books.

Finally, I must express my gratitude to Messrs. Phillimore & Co., Ltd., the Publishers of Parts III and IV, for the willing and co-operative spirit in which they met and overcame the manifold difficulties and frustrations besetting publisher and author alike in this age of austerity and restriction.

V. C. P. H.

December, 1946.

CONTENTS OF PART IV

	PAGE
NOTICE - - - - - - - - - -	v
SACKVILLE, FREDERICK—SYSONBY, FREDERICK - -	1
TABBY, WILLIAM JAMES—FRASER-TYTLER, GEORGE	229
UNDERWOOD, JAMES—URQUHART, GEORGE - - -	338
VALLÉ, LEWIS (OR LAZARUS)—VYSE, JAMES - - -	340
WADDINGTON, JOHN—WYNNE, JOHN (OR JOSEPH) -	362
XIMENES, HENRY JACKSON - - - - - -	540
YALLAND, JOHN—YULE, WILLIAM - - - - -	541
ZIEGLER, ALEXANDER - - - - - - -	556
APPENDIX A LOCAL OFFICERS - - - - - -	557
— B SUPPLEMENTARY LIST OF CADETS, OFFICERS, AND BREVET ENSIGNS - - - - - -	585
— C MINOR CADETS - - - - - -	592
— D CHANGES OF NAME: ADDITIONAL SURNAMES ASSUMED - - - - - - -	603
— E SCHOOLS, COLLEGES, UNIVERSITIES, AND MILITARY SEMINARIES - - - - - - -	606
— F OFFICERS OF FOREIGN NATIONALITY OR EXTRACTION	608
— G OFFICERS WHO SERVED IN THE ROYAL NAVY -	610
— H OFFICERS WHO HELD COMMISSIONS IN H.M. LAND FORCES - - - - - - -	611
— I OFFICERS WHO SERVED IN THE BOMBAY MARINE, E.I.C.N.S., OR PILOT SERVICE - - -	621
— J OFFICERS WHO SAT AS MEMBERS OF PARLIAMENT	622
— K OFFICERS WHO TOOK HOLY ORDERS - -	622

CONTENTS OF PART IV

	PAGE
APPENDIX L LIST OF AUTHORS, EDITORS, TRANSLATORS, JOURNALISTS, AND POETS	623
— M GLOSSARY	626
CORRIGENDA	627
ADDENDA	631
INDEX TO PAINTERS, ENGRAVERS, MINIATURISTS, AND SCULPTORS MENTIONED	639
INDEX TO REFERENCES TO THE *D.N.B.*	641
GENERAL INDEX NOMINUM	643

S

N.B.—Compound names must be sought under the last element of the compound.
N.B.—An asterisk denotes that the name is omitted from *Dodwell & Miles's List*.
N.B.—The figures in brackets following the word "Artillery" refer to the serial No. as given in *Stubbs's List*.

SACKVILLE, Frederick (1785-1827). Lieut. Colonel, 41st N.I. *b.* 5 Dec. 1785. Cadet 1800. Arrived in India 24 Oct. 1801. Ensign 13 Nov. 1801. Lieut. 30 Sept. 1803. Capt. 19 Feb. 1814. Major 1 May 1824. Lt. Col. 27 Jan. 1826. *d.* Richmond, Surrey, 19 Oct. 1827.
Ed. R.N. Coll., Portsmouth.
Services: Joined 2/18th N.I. Apr. 1802. Second Mahratta War; Bundelkhand 1803-4; Kapsa; Kalpi; Gwalior; Lieut. 2/18th N.I.; siege of fort Bela; defeat of Rajah Ram Singh; storm and capture of Jaitpur; Lieut. 1/18th N.I. Apptd. Surveyor to Bundelkhand Div. May 1805; do. of all ceded and conquered countries S. of Jumna R. Feb. 1806. Operations in Bundelkhand 1805-6; Lieut. 18th N.I., Surveyor. Adjt. 2/18th N.I. 11 Oct. 1808 till 1811; do. 1/18th N.I. 1811-12, during the whole of which time he continued his surveys. Surveyor in Cuttack district Oct. 1809. Capt. Lt. 18th N.I. 13 July 1811. Supt. new Jagannath road Mar. 1813 till 1817. Transfd. to newly-raised 2/28th N.I. 1815. A.Q.M.G. at head of topographical staff in Bengal 1 Jan. 1817 till Mar. 1818. A.Q.M.G. with Sir G. Martindell's force May 1818. D.Q.M.G. Bengal (with official rank of Major) Feb. 1819. Fur. 24 Feb. 1820 till 8 Oct. 1823. Transfd. as Major to 55th N.I. (late 1/28th) May 1824. Agent for Army Clothing 1824-6. Posted Lt. Col. to 41st N.I. 1826. Fur. 1827 till death.
Refs.: E.I.M.C. i. 372-9. *G.M.* 1828, i. 85. Will dated 17 Oct. 1827; proved 20 June 1828.

SACKVILLE, Sackville (1796-?). Cadet. Infantry. *b.* Brampton, Suffolk, 24 Feb. 1796. Cadet 1811. Resigned in India 24 Dec. 1813.
bapt. ptely. Brampton 1 Mar. 1796. Son of Amy Skoulding (who afterwards *m.* Major Philip de Latre, formerly 86th Regt., later Malay Regt. and A.Q.M.G., Ceylon). Ward of George Stone.
Services: N.F.P.

SAGE, Edward (1791-1812). Cadet, Infantry. *bapt.* St. Andrew's, Plymouth, 16 Dec. 1791. Cadet 1808. Arrived in India 24 July 1809. *d.* Berhampore 4 Aug. 1812. Son of John Sage and Elizabeth his wife. Brother of William Sage, *q.v.*
Services : Suspended 21 Nov. 1809 for irregularities committed whilst at Barasat C.C. ; restored by C.D. 20 Aug. 1811, but former rank cancelled. Cadet d.d. 2/9th N.I.

SAGE, Joseph Charles (1803-1839). Lieutenant, Invalid Est. 72nd N.I. *b.* Dinajpur, Bengal, 25 Apr. 1803. Cadet 1818. Admitted 9 Oct. 1819. Ensign 26 May 1819. Lieut. 11 July 1823. Invalided 27 Feb. 1833. *d.* Calcutta 23 Oct. 1839.
bapt. Calcutta 18 Sept. 1803. Eldest son of Joseph White Sage, Senior Merchant, B.C.S., in charge of Radnagore commercial residency, and Elizabeth Allen his 1st wife. Brother of Thomas Edward Sage, *q.v.* Gt. nephew of Colin Shakespear, *q.v. m.* 1st, Ramnagar (? Berhampore) 27 July 1827, Elizabeth, youngest dau. of N. Rabeholm, Danish C.S. (She died Calcutta 18 Feb. 1837, aged 25.) *m.* 2nd, Calcutta 15 Mar. 1837, Marian Ellison, eldest dau. of Henry Methold, *q.v.* Ed. Eton ; in 4th Form in 1817.
Services : Ensign d.d. 18th N.I. 1820 ; posted to 2/2nd N.I. 1820 ; d.d. Hill Rangers 10 Mar. 1821 ; transfd. to newly-formed 31st N.I. July 1823 ; to 61st N.I. (late 1/31st) May 1824 ; to newly-raised 4th Extra Regt. (became 72nd N.I.) May 1825. No record of active service.
Refs. : Family information. *Eton School Lists.* M.I. in S. Park St. cemetery, Calcutta.

SAGE, Thomas Edward (1806-1834). Lieutenant, Artillery. (556) *b.* Agra 8 Apr. 1806. Cadet 1823. Arrived in India 7 Oct. 1824. 2nd Lieut. 18 Dec. 1823. Lieut. 28 Sept. 1827. *d. unm.* Meerut 7 June 1834.
bapt. Cawnpore 2 July 1806. Son of Joseph White Sage, B.C.S., and Elizabeth his 1st wife. Brother of Joseph Charles Sage, *q.v.* Ed. Eton. Addiscombe Cadet 1820-3.
Services : Siege and capture of Bhurtpore ; 2nd Lieut. 2nd Coy. (Field Battery) 3rd Bn. Foot Art. Posted to newly-raised 3rd Troop 1st Bde. H.A. 1826. Leave s.c. 1 yr. to Hills 21 Oct. 1831.
Refs. : Eton School Lists. A.J. N.S. xv. 228.

SAGE, William (1793-1864). Major General. Colonel 22nd N.I. *b.* Hawarden, co. Flint, 7 Feb. 1793. Cadet 1808. Arrived in India 24 July 1809. Ensign 13 Dec. 1809. Lieut. 16 Dec.

1814. Capt. 13 May 1825. Major 1 Oct. 1840. Lt. Col. 19 Feb. 1847. Col. 18 July 1856. Maj. Gen. 13 Mar. 1859. *d.* at his residence, Holcombe House, nr. Dawlish, 25 May 1864.

bapt. Hawarden Oct. 1796. Son of John Sage and Elizabeth his wife. Brother of Edward Sage, *q.v. m.* Hannah. (She died 11 Nov. 1865.)

Services: Operations in Rewah 1812; Ensign 24th N.I. Nepal War 1816; Makwanpur; Lieut. 8th Gren. Bn. (India medal). Lieut. 1/24th N.I. Fur. s.c. 2 Nov. 1816 till 1820, and 12 Dec. 1822 till 4 Oct. 1825. Transfd. to 48th N.I. (late 2/24th) May 1824. Executive Ofr. 3rd (Dinapore) Div. P.W.D. 23 Feb. 1829; do. Benares 12 Oct. 1835; do. Dinapore 29 Aug. 1836. Apptd. Postmr. to Army of Indus 7 Dec. 1838. First Afghan War 1838-40; Ghazni; Bt. Major 48th N.I. (Medal). Fur. s.c. 16 Sept. 1841 till 6 Nov. 1842. Suptg. Engr. S.E. Provs. 11 Apr. 1845; do. C.P. 17 Mar. 1852; do. 2nd Circle N.W.P. 3 May 1854 till 1856. Posted Lt. Col. to 36th N.I. 29 Mar. 1847; transfd. to 69th, 70th, 34th, 9th, 14th, 41st N.I. Posted Col. to 22nd N.I. Sept. 1856; Bdr. 2 cl. comdg. Lucknow 23 Sept. 1856; do. Saugor 12 Jan. till Oct. 1857. Mutiny campaign; Bdr. comdg. at Saugor on outbreak of mutiny, and held the fort for 7 mos. Fur. June 1858 till death.

Refs.: Boase. *G.M.* 1864, ii. 121. *The Times,* 28 May 1864.

ST. CLARE, Francis (1781-?). Lieutenant. 9th N.I. *bapt.* Blackburn, Lancs., 13 May 1781. Cadet 1802. Arrived in India 13 Feb. 1804. Ensign 19 Dec. 1803. Lieut. 25 Aug. 1804. Resigned 13 July 1808.

Son of William St. Clare, M.D., of Preston, and Ann his wife. *Services:* Served in R. Preston Vols. from the raising of that Corps in 1797 till 1798; served in Foot Mil. of Demerara for 3 yrs.; then in the Light Horse Mil. A clerk in firm of Messrs. Bolton & Bell, Demerara. Posted Lieut. to 9th N.I. 1804. (? Second Mahratta War 1804-5; Lieut. 9th N.I.) Fur. 25 Aug. 1805 till resignation.

ST. GEORGE, Thomas Gordon (1812-1874). Lieut. Colonel. 17th N.I. *b.* Ballyshannon 12 Mar. 1812. Cadet 1829. Arrived in India 7 Nov. 1830. Ensign (22 May 1830) 6 Oct. 1830. Lieut. 1 Nov. 1838. Capt. 18 Mar. 1853. Bt. Major 28 Nov. 1854. Retired 31 Dec. 1861. Hon. Lt. Col. 31 Dec. 1861. *d.* Erchfont Manor, Wilts., 22 May 1874.

Eldest son of Acheson St. George, of Wood Park, co. Armagh, and Ellinor his 1st wife, dau. of Robert Gordon, of Clonmel. *m.*

23 Apr. 1861, Sarah Strangham, only child of Lloyd Caldecot, of Plas Llandegwyn, co. Carnarvon. Ed. Armagh Coll.

Services : Cadet d.d. 2nd N.I. 5 Jan. 1831 ; actg. Ensign (having been 2 yrs. in India) 5 Dec. 1832 ; posted Ensign to 17th N.I. 20 Aug. 1833. A.D.C. to G.G. 25 Sept. 1834. Adjt. Talain Corps 14 Mar. 1835. Placed under orders of Resdt. at Gwalior 18 Jan. 1836 ; apptd. Adjt. of Inf., Sindhia's Reformed Contingent ; Adjt. Cav. do. 24 Feb. 1840 till 10 Nov. 1841. Fur. s.c. 3 Feb. 1842 till 27 Jan. 1845, and 16 Feb. 1851 till 1 Dec. 1853. A.D.C. to Bdr.-Gen. G. E. Gowan, *q.v.*, comdg. Lahore Div., 6 Dec. 1853 till 1857. Dy. Paymr. at Jullundur 3 July 1858 ; do. Gwalior Div. 1860. Fur. 6 mos. 16 July 1860.

Refs. : Burke's *Landed Gentry of Ireland*, p. 619, *s.n.* St. George, of Wood Park, co. Armagh. Foster's *Baronetage*, p. 549, *s.n.* St. George, Bart. *The Times*, 27 May 1874.

ST. JOHN, Ellis (1746/47-1783). Lieutenant, Infantry. *b.* Hants 1746/47. Cadet 1780. Ensign 1780. Lieut. 21 June 1781. *d.* Chittagong 31 Dec. 1783.

(*Perhaps* related to Rev. Ellis St. John and Sir Paulet St. John, 1st Bart.)

Services : Sailed for India in the *Earl of Dartmouth* 3 June 1780, aged 33. Posted to 3rd Bengal Eur. Regt. May 1781.

Refs. : (? Burke's *Peerage*, 1923, p. 1562, *s.n.* St. John-Mildmay, Bart.)

SALE, Robert Henry (1815-1876). Lieut. Colonel. 9th N.I. *b.* Mauritius 27 Mar. 1815. Cadet 1830. Arrived in India 29 Dec. 1831. Ensign (9 June 1831) 29 Dec. 1831. Lieut. 8 Oct. 1839. Capt. 3 Oct. 1848. Bt. Major 5 Mar. 1859. Retired 31 Dec. 1861. Hon. Lt. Col. 31 Dec. 1861. *d.* Littlehampton, Sussex, 12 Apr. 1876.

bapt. Port Louis, Mauritius, 12 May 1815. Son of Col. Sir Robert Henry Sale, G.C.B. (*D.N.B.*), and Florentia his wife (*D.N.B.*), dau. of George Wynch, M.C.S. His sister *m.* Frederick Brind, *q.v. m.* Simla 29 Sept. 1846, Matilda Martha, dau. of William Anthony Holmes. (She died 11 Nov. 1889, aged 67.) Addiscombe Cadet 1829-31.

Services : Cadet d.d. 28th N.I. 1 Feb. 1832 ; d.d. H.M. 13th L.I. 18 Mar. 1832 ; d.d. 9th N.I. 20 June 1833 ; posted Ensign to 10th N.I. 18 Oct. 1833 ; transfd. to 9th N.I. 24 Jan. 1834. Adjt. of Inf., Bundelkhand Legion, 2 Dec. 1842 ; actg. Legion Staff at Jhansi 15 May 1843. Rejoined 9th N.I. for a short time at Sukkur, Sind,

THE BENGAL ARMY, 1758-1834 5

1843. Apptd. 2nd in comd. 2nd Cav., Gwalior Contingent, 14 Feb. 1844, but never joined. Leave s.c. 1 yr. to Simla Apr. 1845. Comdt. Cav., Malwa Contingent, 12 Sept. 1846 ; 2nd in comd. 2nd Oudh Local Inf. 29 Apr. 1848 ; do. 6th Inf., Gwalior Contingent, 10 Jan. 1852 ; Comdt. do. 11 Nov. 1853 till 1857, when it mutinied. Mutiny campaign 1857-8 (Medal). Fur. 1 Feb. 1860 till retirement.
Refs.: *The Times*, 20 Apr. 1876.

SALE, Thomas Henry (1814-1903). Colonel. Engineers. *b.* Norfolk St., Strand, London, 8 Dec. 1814. Cadet 1830. Arrived in India 5 July 1832. 2nd Lieut. 10 Dec. 1830. Lieut. 20 May 1839. Capt. 26 Feb. 1850. Major 1 Oct. 1857. Lt. Col. 27 Aug. 1858. Retired 23 Aug. 1859. Hon. Col. 23 Aug. 1859. *d.* London 13 Dec. 1903.

Son of Richard Cowlishaw Sale, of Surrey St., Strand, solicitor to the Grand Junction Canal Coy., and Elizabeth his wife, youngest dau. of George Wye, of Oporto, Portugal. *m.* St. Luke's, Cheetham Hill, 7 Sept. 1848, Maria, 2nd dau. of G. Ravenhill, of Manchester. (She died 13 Jan. 1893, aged 75.) Ed. Westminster ; admitted 7 July 1823. Addiscombe Cadet 6 Feb. 1829 till 10 Dec. 1830 ; Chatham 8 Feb. till 8 Dec. 1831.

Services : d.d. S. & M. Delhi 28 July 1832 ; surveyed Agra and Muttra Cantts. 1834-5. Shekhawat expedn. 1834 ; Asst. Field Engr. Asst. Executive Engr. 6th (Allahabad) Div. P.W.D. 5 Aug. 1835 ; employed in examining Sylhet-Assam road 23 Nov. 1837 till June 1839. Fur. s.c. 27 Oct. 1839 till 10 Sept. 1842. Executive Engr. Jubbulpore Div. 28 Sept. 1842 ; Supt. new road to Nagpur 21 Apr. 1843 ; do. Agra-Bombay road 1 Nov. 1845. Fur. 1847-8. Executive Engr. 6th Div. 30 May 1849 ; do. Peshawar 1 Oct. 1851 till 1856. Fur. p.a. 19 Feb. 1856 till 1857.
Refs. : *Westminster School Register*. *The Times*, 15 Dec. 1903.

SALKELD, Joseph Carleton (1810-1886). Lieut. Colonel. 5th N.I. *bapt.* Penrith 23 Jan. 1810. Cadet 1825. Arrived in India 4 Jan. 1827. Ensign 14 Aug. 1826. Lieut. 21 Dec. 1834. Capt. 10 Jan. 1842. Bt. Major 20 June 1854. Lt. Col. 11 May 1855. Retired 28 Feb. 1855. *d.* at his chambers in St. James's St., London, 14 Apr. 1886.

Of Holm Hill, nr. Carlisle. Son of Joseph Salkeld, of Holm Hill, and Margaret his wife, *née* Wiseman. Nephew of Thomas Salkeld, *q.v.*

Services : Ensign d.d. 67th N.I. 13 Jan. 1827 ; posted to 5th N.I. 10 May 1827 ; actg. Adjt. do. 1 Feb. 1837 ; permanent do.

22 Aug. 1838 till 1841. Fur. s.c. 1 Feb. 1841 till 27 Dec. 1844;
p.a. 3 Mar. 1851 till 5 Jan. 1853. No record of active service.
Refs.: *The Times*, 15 Apr. 1886.

SALKELD, Thomas (1760/61-1820). Lieut. Colonel. 27th
N.I. *b.* Cumberland 1760/61. Cadet 1780. Admitted 10 Jan.
1781. Ensign 1780. Lieut. 16 July 1781. Capt. 14 July
1799. Major 21 Sept. 1804. Lt. Col. 1 Jan. 1810. Retired
2 Jan. 1810. *d.* at his residence in Abbey St., Carlisle, 24 May
1820, aged 59.

Of Holm Hill, Carlisle. J.P. Cumberland and Westmorland;
high sheriff Cumberland 1819. Eldest son of Joseph Salkeld, of
Ranbeck, psh. of Kirkland, Cumberland. Brother of Joseph and
John, and uncle of Joseph Carleton Salkeld, q.v. *m.* Abigail Graves.

Services: Sailed for India in the *Rochford* 3 June 1780, aged 19.
Lieut. 17th Bn. Sepoys in July 1787 and in Dec. 1792. Capt. 1st
N.I. Agent for purchase of cavalry horses 1798-1803. D.Q.M.G.
1803. Second Mahratta War 1803-5; Capt. 1st N.I., D.Q.M.G.
on H.Q. staff, and Supt. of guide and intelligence dept. Posted
Major to newly-raised 27th N.I. 1804. Q.M.G. of Bengal Army
1805-7. Fur. 23 Feb. 1807 till retirement.

Refs.: *E.I.M.C.* iii. 298-9. *Pester*, pp. 201-2. Will dated
2 Dec. 1817; proved 9 July 1829. M.I. Kirkland church.

SALMON, Clare Sewell (1815-1897). Lieut. Colonel. 57th
N.I. *bapt.* Stoke Ferry, Norfolk, 23 Apr. 1815. Cadet 1832.
Arrived in India 7 Mar. 1834. Ensign (11 June 1833) 10 Jan.
1834. Lieut. 8 Oct. 1839. Capt. 31 Dec. 1847. Bt. Major
29 Apr. 1861. Retired 31 Dec. 1861. Hon. Lt. Col. 31 Dec.
1861. *d.* The Woodlands, Isleworth, Middlesex, 25 June 1897.

Son of Thomas Salmon, of Stoke Ferry, merchant, and Elizabeth
his wife. Addiscombe Cadet 12 Aug. 1831 till 11 June 1833.

Services: Supy. Ensign d.d. 24th N.I. 18 Mar. 1834; posted to
57th N.I. 24 May 1834, and passed the whole of his service with
that Regt. Actg. Adjt. 21 May 1841; permanent do. 10 Feb.
1842 till 30 July 1846. Fur. 1846-8, and 1859 till retirement. No
record of active service.

Refs.: *The Times*, 28 June 1897.

SALMON, George Paris (1813-1898). Major. Artillery.
(635) *b.* Benares 17 Sept. 1813. Cadet 1829. Arrived in India
30 May 1830. 2nd Lieut. (11 Dec. 1829) 30 May 1830. Lieut.
22 Aug. 1838. Capt. 1 Nov. 1847. Retired 6 Mar. 1853. Hon.
Major 28 Nov. 1854. *d.* Willanslee, Perth, 2 Mar. 1898.

Son of William Broome Salmon, q.v., and Marian his wife. m. 1st, Jhansi 24 Oct. 1839, Letitia, 6th dau. of William Sandeman, and sister of Robert Turnbull Sandeman, q.v. (She died 1852, aged 33.) m. 2nd, Kennington 11 Apr. 1855, Grace A., dau. of J. W. Hillhouse. Addiscombe Cadet 1827-9.

Services : Actg. 2nd Lieut. (having been 2 yrs. in India) 16 July 1832. Posted to 1st Coy. 3rd Bn. Foot Art. 29 Sept. 1838. Adjt. & Qmr. 3rd Bn. 3 Jan. 1839 ; do. 5th Bn. 7 Dec. 1841 till 1845. Fur. p.a. 23 Mar. 1845 till 1847. Capt. 9th Bn. No record of active service.

Refs. : Burke's *Family Records*, p. 524, s.n. Sandeman. *The Times*, 4 Mar. 1898.

SALMON, William Broome (1787-1843). Lieut. Colonel, 58th N.I. *bapt.* Sandbach, co. Chester, 30 Dec. 1787. Cadet 1803. Arrived in India 3 Dec. 1804. Lieut. 25 Aug. 1804. Capt. 20 Apr. 1818. Major 20 May 1829. Lt. Col. 29 July 1834. *d.* Mirzapur 5 Feb. 1843, aged 56.

Son of George Salmon and Mary his wife. m. (before 1809) Marian, dau. of Andrew Wilson Hearsey, q.v. (*See also* Paris Bradshaw.) (She died Calcutta 12 Jan. 1844, aged 53.) Father of George Paris Salmon, q.v. Marlow Cadet for 18 mos.

Services : Posted Lieut. to 18th N.I. 1805. Operations in Bundelkhand 1805-6 ; Lieut. 18th N.I. Operations in Hariana 1809 ; Bhawani ; Lieut. 2/18th N.I. Actg. Adjt. 2/18th N.I. 1810 ; permanent do. 3 Oct. 1811 till 24 Oct. 1817. Nepal War 1816 ; Lieut. 2/18th N.I. To comd. escort to Major Paris Bradshaw, q.v., 19 Oct. 1816 ; to rejoin 2/18th N.I. in Cuttack 23 May 1817. Capt. Lt. 5 Sept. 1817. A.D.C. to Maj.-Gen. Charles Stuart, q.v., 1820-3. d.d. Dinajpur Local Bn. 22 Mar. 1823 ; tempy. comdg. Resdt.'s escort at Lucknow 3 Nov. 1823 ; permanent do. 15 Jan. 1825 till 26 Sept. 1827, when he rejoined his Regt. Transfd. to 36th N.I. (late 1/18th) May 1824. Posted Lt. Col. to 72nd N.I. 8 Jan. 1835. Fur. p.a. 8 Feb. 1841 till 11 Oct. 1842. Transfd. to 58th N.I. 25 Oct. 1842.

Refs. : *The Hearseys*, p. 37 (where it is incorrectly stated that he " attained the rank of General, retired, and lived in England."). M.I. in Mirzapur cemetery.

SALMOND, James Hanson (1766-1837). Major General. 20th N.I. Mily. Sec. to C.D. *b.* 17 Aug. 1766. Cadet 1782. Admitted 4 Aug. 1784. Ensign 7 Apr. 1783. Lieut. 8 Mar. 1790. Capt. 30 Sept. 1803. Resigned 29 Mar. 1805. Maj. Gen. 10 Jan. 1837. Retired May 1837. *d.* York 31 Oct. 1837.

Of Waterfoot, Cumberland. Eldest son of William Salmond, of Seaforth, Antigua, Agent for Antigua 1776, and Jane his 2nd wife, 2nd dau. of Edward Hasell, of Dalemain, Cumberland. Halfbrother of the mother of James Thorne and cousin-german of the father of Christopher Hasell, qq.v. m. 1st, Marylebone 2 July 1798, Louisa, eldest dau. of David Scott, of Dunninald, M.P., sister of Sir David Scott, Bart., and cousin-german of Archibald Watson, q.v. (She died June 1805, aged 25.) m. 2nd, 17 Aug. 1808, Rachel Mary Ann, eldest dau. of Ven. Thomas Constable, of Beverley, archdeacon of E. Riding, co. York. (She died Feb. 1847, aged 76.)

Services : Apptd. Cadet 1782, but permitted to stay in England till the following year (M.C. 2 May 1782). Adjt. 35th Bn. Sepoys 1787 till 27 Dec. 1791. Second Mysore War 1790-2 ; Lieut. 35th Bn., with Lt.-Col. Cockerell's detachment. Transfd. to 7th Bn. 27 Dec. 1791 ; from 28th to 14th Bn. 26 Mar. 1793. Fur. 14 Mar. 1794 till 1 Apr. 1797. Employed while in England as Adjt. of E.I. Vols. Mily. Sec. to Lord Wellesley, the G.G., 3 Oct. 1799 ; Dy. Mily. Auditor Gen. 4 Sept. 1800 ; Mily. Auditor Gen. 9 Dec. 1800 till 1803. Deputed by G.G. in 1802 to visit Madras and Bombay for the purpose of examining and reporting on the mily. regulations at those Presidencies. Fur. 2 Nov. 1803 till resignation. Mily. Sec. to C.D. " for conducting the Mily. Correspondence with India " 1809 till May 1837. Restored to the Service as Lt. Col. 1816 ; Col. 1836. Author of " A Review . . . of the late decisive war in Mysore," anon., London, 1800.

Refs. : Burke's *Landed Gentry*, 13th edn., p. 1545, *s.n.* Salmond, of Waterfoot. Oliver's *Hist. of Antigua*, iii. 66 (where date of birth is given as 17 Nov. 1766). *List of Mily. Secs. to G.G.* A.J. N.S. xxv. 79. *G.M.* 1838, i. 110. Autotype enlargement of a miniature in the possession of the family is in I.O.

SALT, James (*d.* 1784). Bt. Major. 1st Bengal Eur. Regt. Cadet 1769. Arrived in India Apr. 1770. Ensign 5 Apr. 1770. Lieut. 1 July 1771. Capt. 14 Jan. 1781. Bt. Major 14 Jan. 1782. Pensioned 3 Apr. 1782. *d.* Swansea 9 Oct. 1784.

m. in England 26 Apr. 1783, Miss Huntridge.[1]

Services : Served for 14 yrs. in R.N. as Midshipman and Actg. Lieut. Sailed for India Mar. 1769. Served with G.G.B.G. 1777-81 ; comdd. newly-raised Independent Troop of Cav. 19 Mar. till 30 Sept. 1781, when it was reduced. Campaign against the Rajah of Benares 1781 ; joined Major William Popham, *q.v.*, with his Troop 21 Sept. 1781. Pensd. as Capt. on Lord Clive's fund 26 Feb. 1783.

Refs.: V.B.G. G.M. 1784, ii. 798.
[1] *Note:* Frances, relict of Major Salt, formerly H.E.I.C.S., *d.* Hackney 15 Oct. 1834, aged 89.

SALT, Sampson (*d.* 1770). Lieutenant, Infantry. Cadet 1767. Ensign 2 May 1768. Lieut. 19 Dec. 1769. *d.* Berhampore 27 Sept. 1770.

Services: Sailed for India in the *Lord Holland* 16 Dec. 1766.

SALTER, George (1801-1867). Major. 4th N.I. *b.* 11 June 1801. Cadet 1822. Arrived in India 5 July 1823. Ensign 20 June 1823. Lieut. 13 May 1825. Capt. 2 Jan. 1842. Retired 16 May 1848. Hon. Major 28 Nov. 1854. *d.* Hopetown Lodge, Leamington, 6 Feb. 1867.

bapt. St. Dunstan's, Stepney, 9 July 1801. 2nd son of George Salter, of Poplar, principal clerk to Messrs. Wigrams & Green, Blackwall, and Rebecca his wife. *m.* Barrackpore 19 Feb. 1837, Fanny, widow of Arthur Wortham, *q.v.* (She died Bareilly 27 Nov. 1844.) Glasgow Univ.; matric. 1814.

Services: Posted to 4th N.I. May 1824; Adjt. do. 3 Feb. 1829 till 17 Feb. 1842. Operations against Hill tribes on N. Sind frontier 1844-5; comdd. a detachment of 6th and 9th Irreg. Cav. in action at Uch 15 Jan. 1845 (*Lond. Gaz.* 21 May 1845); Trakki 9 Mar. 1845; Capt. 4th N.I. 2nd in comd. 7th Irreg. Cav. 3 Feb. 1846 till retirement.

Refs.: Cardew, p. 203. *G.M.* 1867, i. 402. *The Times,* 9 Feb. 1867.

SALTER, Henry Fisher (1792-1865). Lieut. General, C.B. 8th L.C. *b.* London 9 Mar. 1792. Cadet 1807. Arrived in India 25 Oct. 1808. Cornet 30 Apr. 1808. Lieut. 1 Sept. 1818. Capt. 1 May 1824. Major 19 May 1838. Lt. Col. 5 Jan. 1844. Col. 27 Sept. 1859. Maj. Gen. 28 Nov. 1854. Lt. Gen. 14 Apr. 1863. *d.* Kingston, nr. Dublin, 21 Aug. 1865.

bapt. Marylebone 7 July 1792. Son of James Salter and Elizabeth Hebbron his wife. *m.* Karnal 21 Oct. 1814, Henrietta F., eldest dau. of Sir David Ochterlony, *q.v.* (She died London 9 Mar. 1872, aged 74.)

Services: Barasat C.C. 8 mos. Posted Cornet to 2nd N.C. 1810. Nepal War 1814-15; Lieut. 2nd N.C., A.D.C. to Sir D. Ochterlony, *q.v.* Actg. Bde. Major Ludhiana 29 Nov. 1815; Bde. Major Karnal 15 Mar. 1816. Third Mahratta War; Lieut. 2nd N.C., D.A.Q.M.G. Reserve Div. Bde. Major 3rd Div. Field Army in 1820. A.A.G., W. Div., 10 Dec. 1821 till Feb. 1826. Fur. p.a. 4 Feb. 1826 till

June 1828. Comdt. Nizam's 5th Cav. 2 Oct. 1834 till May 1839. First Afghan War 1839-40; Ghazni (*Lond. Gaz.* 30 Oct. 1839) (Medal); operations in Kohistan 1840; action at Parwandara, comdg. Advance Column of Sir R. Sale's force (ib. 12 Feb. 1841); Bt. Lt. Col. 2nd L.C. On disbandment of 2nd L.C., d.d. 3rd L.C. 6 May 1841; transfd. to newly-raised 11th L.C. (became 2nd L.C. 24 May 1850) 1842. Gwalior campaign; Paniar; Bt. Lt. Col. 11th L.C. (Bronze star). Posted Lt. Col. to 11th L.C. 3 Apr. 1844. Second Sikh War; Multan; Lt. Col. 11th L.C. (Medal with clasp). Transfd. to 6th L.C. 20 Apr. 1849; to 10th L.C. Jan. 1853; to 8th L.C. 18 June 1853. Bdr. 2 cl. comdg. Peshawar 13 Feb. 1853; 1 cl. comdg. Agra Dec. 1853 till Jan. 1856. Leave s.c. to Cape 31 Jan. 1856. Transfd. to 5th Eur. Bengal L.C. 1 May 1858. Fur. 20 Oct. 1859 till death. C.B. 9 June 1849. Durani 3 cl. 20 Nov. 1840.

Refs.: Boase. G.M. 1865, ii. 528. *The Times,* 24 Aug. 1865.

SAMLER, Frederick (1810-1873). Major. 10th N.I. *b.* London 17 Jan. 1810. Cadet 1826. Arrived in India 12 Oct. 1827. Ensign 8 May 1827. Lieut. 4 Feb. 1833. Capt. 8 May 1842. Invalided 10 Sept. 1845. Retired 1 Oct. 1861. Hon. Major 1 Oct. 1861. *d.* Boulogne 25 Nov. 1873.

bapt. St. Andrew-by-the-Wardrobe, London, 7 Apr. 1810. Son of William Samler, of Blackheath, and Frances his wife. *m.* Calcutta 17 Feb. 1835, Jemima Haldane, posthumous dau. of James Robertson, M.D., Suptg. Surg. Bengal. (*See also* Griffiths Holmes.) (She died Darjeeling 12 Feb. 1852, aged 33.) Ed. Charterhouse; admitted 1822, left same year.

Services: Posted to 10th N.I. 3 Jan. 1828. (? Rising in Cuttack July 1836; Lieut. 10th N.I.) Fur. s.c. 30 Jan. 1837 till 23 Nov. 1839. With Army of Reserve (for Afghanistan) Oct. 1842 till Jan. 1843.

Refs.: Charterhouse School Lists. The Times, 28 Nov. 1873.

SAMPSON, George (1749-1784). Captain, Artillery. (93) *b.* 1749. Fireworker 9 Sept. 1768. Lieut. 16 Mar. 1770. Capt. Lt. 31 Jan. 1774. Capt. 5 Oct. 1778. *d.* 7 Oct. 1784.

3rd son of Rev. Thomas Sampson, of Bosham, and Mary his wife, dau. of William Brown. Brother of George Frederick John Sampson, *q.v.,* Christopher Sampson, E.I.C.N.S., and of Rev. Charles Sampson, rector of Ripley, Yorks.

Services: Gent. Cadet at R.M.A., Woolwich; commissioned as Lieut. F. in England 24 Dec. 1767 (M.C. 1 Sept. 1768). Fur. 10 Feb.

THE BENGAL ARMY, 1758-1834 11

1773 till 22 Aug. 1774. Posted Capt. Lt. to newly-raised Golandaz Coy. 7 Aug. 1777.
Refs. : Family information. Will dated Fatehgarh 11 Dec. 1783 ; filed 27 Oct. 1784.

SAMPSON, George Frederick John (1759-1792). Captain. Artillery. (157) *b.* Brentford, Middlesex, 7 July 1759. Cadet 1778. Ensign (Inf.) 10 Dec. 1778. Lieut. (Art.) 4 Oct. 1778. Capt. Lt. 2 Jan. 1785. Capt. 24 Nov. 1786. Resigned 5 Oct. 1791. *bur.* Madras 4 Jan. 1792 : *d.* from the effects of a wound received 13 Sept. 1790 at Satiyamangalam.
bapt. New Brentford 7 Aug. 1759. 6th and youngest son of Rev. Thomas Sampson and Mary his wife. Brother of George Sampson, *q.v.* Godson of H.R.H. George, Prince of Wales, John, Earl of Bute, and the Duchess of Somerset. Ed. Eton ; K.S. 1772-7.
Services : Sailed for India in the *Calcutta* 27 Apr. 1778. Granted fur. June 1785. Third Mysore War ; Satiyamangalam (s.w.) ; Capt. 5th Coy. 2nd Bn. Permitted at his own request to resign the Service and proceed to Europe 5 Oct. 1791.
Refs. : Family information. *Austen-Leigh.* Will dated 22 Apr. 1789 ; proved 27 Feb. 1792.

SAMPSON, Noah (*d.* 1775). Ensign, Infantry. Cadet 1770. Ensign 25 Sept. 1770. *d.* Chittagong Nov. 1775.
Services : N.F.P.

SAMPSON, Thomas Edmund (1800-1863). Colonel. 38th N.I. *b.* Aughanloo, co. Londonderry, 7 Apr. 1800. Cadet 1817. Admitted 10 Oct. 1818. Ensign (27 Apr. 1818) 30 Sept. 1818. Lieut. 1 Jan. 1819. Capt. 4 June 1829. Major 19 Jan. 1843. Lt. Col. 22 May 1849. Retired 29 Aug. 1851. Hon. Col. 28 Nov. 1854. *d.* Walworth, Londonderry, 14 Oct. 1863.
Son of Rev. (? George) Sampson, rector of Errigal, co. Donegal. Brother of Arthur Alexander Sampson. *m.* Marylebone 4 Apr. 1842, Marion, 2nd dau. of Henry Huey Tyler, of Newtown Limavady. (She died Benares 22 May 1843, aged 29.)
Services : Posted to 1/2nd N.I. 1819. Actg. Adjt. at Lohargaon post 25 Nov. 1822 ; actg. Intr. & Qmr. 1/2nd N.I. 31 Oct. 1823 ; transfd. to 22nd N.I. (late 2/2nd) May 1824 ; Adjt. do. 12 July 1825 ; Intr. & Qmr. do. 29 May 1826 till 28 Sept. 1829. Fur. p.a. 25 Mar. 1829 till 18 Nov. 1833. Shekhawat expedn. 1834 ; Capt. 22nd N.I. Tempy. comdg. 3rd Local Horse 20 Apr. 1835 ; offg. D.J.A.G., W. Div., 20 Nov. 1835 ; do. Saugor Div. 26 Oct. 1838. Fur. s.c. 25 Feb. 1839 till 10 Sept. 1842. Second Sikh War ; no

actions ; Major 22nd N.I. (Medal). Fur. s.c. 10 Apr. 1849 till retirement. Posted Lt. Col. to 49th N.I. in 1849 ; to 38th N.I. 25 Feb. 1851 ; to 43rd N.I. (before a report of his retirement had reached India) Nov. 1851.

Refs. : *A.J.* N.S. xxxviii. 79. *G.M.* 1863, ii. 806.

SANDBY, George Taylor Seton (1799-1828). Lieutenant. 49th N.I. *bapt.* ptely. Old Windsor 15 June 1799. Cadet 1817. Lieut. 2 Dec. 1818. Resigned 18 Nov. 1825. *d.* in India 25 July 1828.

Son of Thomas Sandby, of Gt. Lodge, Old Windsor, professor of drawing at R.M.A., Woolwich, 1797-1828, and Harriot his wife and cousin, dau. of Thomas Sandby (*D.N.B.*). Grandson of Paul Sandby (*D.N.B.*) and cousin of William Francklin, *q.v.* His sisters *m.* George Arthur Brownlow and Joseph William Loder, *qq.v.*

Services : Lieut. 2/25th N.I. ; transfd. to 49th N.I. (late 1/25th) May 1824. First Burma War ; Arakan 1825 ; Lieut. 49th N.I.

SANDEMAN, John (1809-1841). Lieutenant, 17th N.I. *b.* Perth 6 Apr. 1809. Cadet 1827. Arrived in India 11 Oct. 1828. Ensign 10 May 1828. Lieut. 29 Mar. 1836. *d.* Landour, U.P., 18 July 1841.

bapt. Redgorton, co. Perth, 10 Apr. 1809. Son of William John Sandeman, bleacher at Luncarty, and Elizabeth Steuart his wife.

Services : Ensign d.d. 48th N.I. 5 Nov. 1828 ; posted to 47th N.I. 4 Mar. 1829 ; transfd. to 33rd N.I. 12 Apr. 1829 ; to 17th N.I. 16 Sept. 1831. To d.d. at Landour Convalescent Depot 20 Jan. 1841. No record of active service.

Refs. : M.I. Landour.

SANDEMAN, Robert Turnbull (1804-1876). Major General. 33rd N.I. (now 2nd Bn. 7th Rajput Regt.). *b.* Perth 1 Oct. 1804. Cadet 1824. Arrived in India 6 July 1825. Ensign 9 Feb. 1825. Lieut. 8 Apr. 1832. Capt. 12 Feb. 1838. Major 4 Jan. 1847. Lt. Col. 27 Oct. 1852. Bt. Col. 28 Nov. 1854. Retired 31 Dec. 1861. Hon. Maj. Gen. 31 Dec. 1861. *d.* 24 Chepstow Villas, Bayswater, 25 July 1876.

7th son of William Sandeman and Catherine Turnbull his wife. His sister *m.* George Paris Salmon, *q.v.* *m.* Lucknow 2 Feb. 1831, Jane, sister of Andrew Barclay, *q.v.* Father of Sir Robert Groves Sandeman, K.C.S.I. (*D.N.B.*). Ed. Perth Acad.

Services : Posted Ensign to 12th N.I. 1825 ; transfd. to 33rd N.I. 3 Nov. 1828 ; Intr. & Qmr. do. 14 Nov. 1828 till 12 Aug. 1834. Fur. s.c. 4 Aug. 1834 till 9 June 1837. First Sikh War ; Feroz-

THE BENGAL ARMY, 1758-1834

shahr; Sobraon; Capt. comdg. 33rd N.I. (Medal with clasp). Posted Lt. Col. to 33rd N.I. 2 Feb. 1853, and was comdg. the Regt. at Hoshiarpur when the Mutiny broke out; it was disarmed at Phillaur 25 June 1857. Apptd. to comd. at Jullundur 12 July 1857. Bdr. on the Est. 9 Oct. 1860.

Refs.: Burke's *Family Records*, p. 524, *s.n.* Sandeman. *Sandeman Genealogy*, by John Glas Sandeman, Edin., 1895. *The Times*, 28 July 1876.

SANDERS, Arthur (1812-1895). Major General. 5th Bengal Eur. Inf. *b.* Poplar 9 Aug. 1812. Cadet 1830. Arrived in India 16 Oct. 1831. Ensign (10 Dec. 1830) 11 May 1831. Lieut. 12 Mar. 1837. Capt. 24 Aug. 1843. Major 29 Feb. 1852. Lt. Col. 29 May 1857. Col. 1861. Retired 31 Dec. 1861. Hon. Maj. Gen. 31 Dec. 1861. *d.* at his residence, Crooms Hill, Greenwich, 19 Mar. 1895.

Youngest son of Thomas Sanders, of Crooms Hill and Laleham, Comdr. E.I.C.N.S., and Rosetta Fortunata his wife. Brother of Edward Sanders, *q.v.* Addiscombe Cadet 1829-30.

Services: Admitted as Cadet 21 Oct. 1831; d.d. 10th N.I. 23 Nov. 1831; d.d. 60th N.I. 7 Jan. 1832; posted Ensign to 44th N.I. 19 Oct. 1833, and joined Mar. 1834. Expulsion of marauders from Jhabua, C.I., Feb.-Mar. 1836; Ensign 44th N.I. Leave s.c. to Simla 20 Oct. 1837 till 1 Nov. 1838. Offg. D.A.Q.M.G. 2 cl., 2nd Inf. Div., Army of Indus 10 Sept. 1838 till broken up 22 Apr. 1839. In charge of map-drawing branch of Govt. litho. press 24 June 1840; offg. Asst. in Q.M.G. office 10 July 1840; D.A.Q.M.G. 2 cl. 18 Aug. 1841; 1 cl. 17 Jan. 1843; A.Q.M.G. of Army 22 Jan. 1847; D.Q.M.G. at Presdy. 11 June 1852 till Sept. 1858. Posted Lt. Col. to 53rd N.I. June 1857; transfd. to 5th Bengal Eur. Inf. 13 Sept. 1859.

Refs.: *The Times*, 21 Mar. 1895.

SANDERS, Edward (1801-1843). Bt. Lieut. Colonel, C.B., Engineers. Dy. Sec. to Govt. *b.* Ealing 19 Jan. 1801. Cadet 1820. Arrived in India 25 May 1821. Ensign 18 May 1821. Lieut. 1 May 1824. Capt. 23 Jan. 1830. Major 28 Aug. 1841. Bt. Lt. Col. 12 Sept. 1843. *d.* 29 Dec. 1843: kld. in action at battle of Maharajpur.

bapt. Ealing 27 May 1804. Son of Thomas Sanders, Comdr. E.I.C.N.S., and Rosetta Fortunata his wife. Brother of Henry Sanders, *q.v.*, and of Rosetta Hester, wife of James Machell, of Newby Bridge, Lancs. R.M.A. Woolwich; resigned do. Apr. 1818. Addiscombe Cadet 1818-20.

Services : d.d. S. & M. 16 Aug. 1822 ; Bk. Mr. Purnea Div. 7 June 1824 till 18 Aug. 1827. Leave s.c. to Cape 20 Sept. 1828 till 25 Nov. 1830. Executive Engr. 7th (Cawnpore) Div. P.W.D. 21 Apr. 1831 ; do. 10th (Agra) Div. 27 Dec. 1833. Shekhawat expedn. 1834. Offg. Sec. Mily. Board 13 Mar. 1835 ; permanent do. 23 Sept. 1835 till 23 June 1841. To assume comd. of 2 Coys. S. & M. for service in Afghanistan 6 Oct. 1838. First Afghan War 1838-42 ; pol. employ in Herat in May 1840 ; surveyed country Kandahar-Herat ; Tutam-dara (*Lond. Gaz.* 9 Jan. 1841) ; action nr. Kandahar 12 Jan. 1842 (ib. 24 Nov. 1842) ; Ghazni ; Kabul ; Major Engrs. (Medal). Dy. Sec. Govt. of India, Mily. Dept. (with official rank of Major) 9 June 1841 till death. Gwalior campaign ; Maharajpur (kld.) (ib. 8 Mar. 1844) ; Dy. Sec. on H.Q. Staff. Durani 3 cl. 15 Aug. 1840. C.B. 27 Dec. 1842.

Refs. : *The Ritchies in India.* Will dated Kandahar 26 July 1842 ; proved 18 Mar. 1844. M.I. in St. Peter's, Ft. Wm., and on his tomb on the site of the battlefield.

SANDERS, Henry (1808-1835). Lieutenant, Artillery. (574) *b.* Ealing 25 May 1808. Cadet 1825. Arrived in India 2 Aug. 1826. 2nd Lieut. 16 June 1825. Lieut. 19 May 1832. *d.* at sea 31 Jan. 1835, on board the *St. George* on his passage to England.

2nd son of Thomas Sanders, Comdr. E.I.C.N.S., and Rosetta Fortunata his wife. Brother of Arthur Sanders, *q.v.* Addiscombe Cadet 1824-5.

Services : Actg. Adjt. & Qmr. 1st Bn. Foot Art. 18 Feb. 1832 ; posted to 1st Coy. 3rd Bn. 14 Mar. 1833. Fur. s.c. 20 Jan. 1835. No record of active service.

Refs. : *G.M.* 1835, ii. 222.

SANDERS, Thomas (1795-1855). Lieut. Colonel, Invalid Est. Artillery. (439) *b.* 17 Jan. 1795. Cadet 1811. Admitted 4 Aug. 1812. Fireworker 4 Aug. 1812. Lieut. 22 Apr. 1818. Capt. 30 June 1829. Major 16 Dec. 1843. Lt. Col. 1 Apr. 1847. Invalided 1 July 1847. *d.* Lucknow 26 July 1855.

bapt. Enfield 21 Feb. 1795. Son of Richard Francis Sanders and Susannah his wife. Addiscombe Cadet 29 Mar. 1809 till 25 Oct. 1811.

Services : Siege and capture of Hathras 1817 ; Lt. F. 4th Coy. 2nd Bn. Foot Art. Third Mahratta War ; Dhamoni ; Mandala ; Satanwara ; Garhakota ; Lieut. 4th Coy. 2nd Bn. Adjt. 3rd Bn. 22 July 1825 till 22 Sept. 1829. Siege and capture of Bhurtpore ; Adjt. 3rd Bn. (India medal [1]). Comy. of Ord. 1 Nov. 1834. Comdg.

Art. at Delhi in Jan. 1837; to comd. Art. at Ferozepore 7 Dec. 1842. Gwalior campaign; Maharajpur (*Lond. Gaz.* 30 Apr. 1844); Major comdg. 1st Coy. 1st Bn. (No. 10 Light Field Batty.) (Bronze star). To comd. Art. at Ferozepore 25 Apr. 1844.
Refs.: *I.M.* 19 Sept. 1855, p. 518.
¹ *Note*: His name is not in the M.R.

*SANDERSON or SAUNDERSON, John (1753/54-1787). Ensign, Infantry. *b*. London 1753/54. Cadet 1782. Arrived in India Apr. 1783. Ensign 17 Apr. 1783. *d*. Calcutta 27 Apr. 1787.
m. Sarah.
Services: Apptd. Cadet by Order of Court dated 28 Mar. 1782; sailed for India in the *Brilliant* 5 May 1782, aged 28. She was lost on Johanna I. 28 Aug. 1782.
Refs.: Will dated 22 Apr. 1787; filed 1 May 1787.

SANDERSON, John (1787-1818). Lieutenant, 30th N.I. *b.* London 12 Feb. 1787. Cadet 1804. Arrived in India 10 Dec. 1805. Ensign 4 Oct. 1805. Lieut. 5 Nov. 1805. *d.* in England 19 Mar. 1818.
bapt. St. George's, Hanover Sq., London, 26 Mar. 1787. Son of Thomas Sanderson, of Deeping St. James, Lincs., and Mary Buck his wife.
Services: Posted Lieut. to 22nd N.I. 1806. Attached to Champaran L.I. 1814. Nepal War 1814-15; Lieut. Champaran L.I., in 4th Div. Transfd. to newly-raised 2/30th N.I. 1815. Nepal War 1816; Lieut. Champaran L.I., in 2nd Bde. Left Column. Fur. 1816 till death.

SANDERSON, Thomas (1791-1835). Captain. 9th L.C. *b.* Edinburgh 7 Dec. 1791. Cadet 1808. Arrived in India 19 July 1809. Cornet (28 Sept. 1812) 7 July 1813. Lieut. 1 Sept. 1818. Capt. 28 Dec. 1827. Retired 28 Apr. 1832. *d.* 21 Belvedere, Bath, 4 Dec. 1835.
bapt. College Kirk psh., Edinburgh, 28 Dec. 1791. Son of Patrick Sanderson, merchant, and Mary his wife, dau. of Patrick Macqueen, tinsmith. *m.* 1st, Jessie, dau. of Hugh Bremner, accountant in Edinburgh. (She died 11 Oct. 1822.) *m.* 2nd, St. George's, Hanover Sq., London, 11 Aug. 1824, Elizabeth Oswald, eldest dau. of Alexander Anderson, of Chapel St., Grosvenor Sq., London.
Services: Barasat C.C. 8 mos. Cadet d.d. 8th N.C. 1811-12; posted Cornet to 5th N.C. Sept. 1812; transfd. to 8th N.C. July 1813.' Fur. s.c. 15 Aug. 1816 till 30 Jan. 1819. Attached to

G.G.B.G. in 1820. Adjt. 8th L.C. 19 Apr. 1820; Adjt. Native Invalids and Paymr. Native Pensioners at Allahabad 25 Sept. 1820 till 1 Jan. 1823, but never joined this appt. owing to ill health. Leave s.c. to Cape 12 Oct. 1820 till Aug. 1822; fur. s.c. 8 Feb. 1823 till 30 May 1826. Transfd. to newly-raised 1st Extra Cav. (became 9th L.C.) 17 June 1825; actg. Intr. & Qmr. do. 31 Jan. 1828. Fur. s.c. 10 Jan. 1830 till retirement.

Refs.: *V.B.G. Bath Chron.* 17 Dec. 1835. *G.M.* 1836, i. 101.

SANDFORD, Edward (1753-1802). Captain.[1] 21st Bn. Sepoys. *b.* 23 Jan. 1753. Cadet 1769. Admitted 31 Aug. 1769. Ensign 15 Aug. 1769. Lieut. 27 Jan. 1773. Capt. 5 Jan. 1781. Resigned 7 Dec. 1792. *d.* Walcot Bldgs., Bath, 27 Feb. 1802.

3rd son of Humphrey Sandford, of the Isle of Rossall, high sheriff Salop 1787, and Elizabeth his wife, only child of Hugh Jones. Cousin-german of John Scott-Waring, *q.v. m.* 1st, Calcutta 25 Jan. 1787, Miss Mary Nixon. (She died 2 Oct. 1787.) *m.* 2nd, 13 Dec. 1797, Mary Viner. (She died Stepney 9 Nov. 1820.)

Services: Lieut. 2nd Bengal Eur. Regt. in Oct. 1777. Apptd. Adjt. & Qmr. to a corps of 3 Bns. to be raised for Rajah Chet Singh of Benares 31 July 1778; Capt. 1st Eur. Regt. in 1782. Second Mysore War 1782-5; Capt. 24th N.I., with Col. Pearse's detachment. Capt. 5th Bengal Eur. Bn. in July 1787; comdg. 5th Bn. Sepoys in Dec. 1788 and in 1790; comdg. 21st Bn. in 1792; (? Major 3rd Eur. Regt. in 1796).

Refs.: Burke's *Landed Gentry*, 13th edn., p. 1555, *s.n.* Sandford, of the I. of Rossall, Salop. *Bath Chron.* 4 Mar. 1802.

[1] *Note:* According to *Philippart MS.* he was promoted Major 1 Mar. 1794; Lt. Col. 22 July 1796; resigned 14 Mar. 1798. This would appear to be correct. *Burke* styles him Major.

SANDS, Robert. Lieutenant. Artillery. (215) Cadet 1781. Fireworker 17 Sept. 1781. Lieut. 18 Sept. 1788. Struck off 1793.

m. St. Andrew's psh., Edinburgh, 27 July 1787, Jane, dau. of James Shaw, of Preston.

Services: Campaign against the Rajah of Benares 1781; outbreak at Benares 16 Aug.; Cadet with the G.G., "probably in comd. of another brigade of two guns." (*Stubbs.*) Comy. of Ord. at Patna 15 Aug. 1783 till 1786. Fur. 24 Jan. 1786 till struck off.

Refs.: *Stubbs*, i. 66.

SANDS, William (*d.* 1790). Major. Infantry. Cadet 1768. Ensign 13 Jan. 1769. Lieut. 10 Jan. 1773. Capt. 16 July 1778.

THE BENGAL ARMY, 1758-1834   17

Major 4 Feb. 1782. Resigned 28 Jan. 1785. *d.* Hailes, nr. Edinburgh, 14 Nov. 1790.
Son of William Sands, of Edinburgh, bookseller and publisher, and one of the founders of *Scots Mag.*, and Ann, eldest dau. of Rev. Dugald Stewart, minr. of Rothesay 1700-53, and sister of Rev. Matthew Stewart, D.D., the geometrician (*D.N.B.*). *m.* Edinburgh 17 Nov. 1778, Christian Smith (or Smyth), 3rd dau. of Col. Charles Halkett Craigie, of Hall Hill, and aunt of John Craigie-Halkett, *q.v.* (She died Edinburgh 13 Apr. 1807.)
Services: Chaplain to 1st Bde. till 21 Jan. 1774, when he was transfd. to staff of Col. P. Galliez, *q.v.*, comdg. 2nd Bde. First Rohilla War 1774; battle of St. George; Lieut. on staff of Col. Galliez. On fur. in 1778. Was A.D.C. to Warren Hastings in 1780-1; afterwards Regulating Ofr. of Calcutta Mil. till Jan. 1785, when he went home with Hastings.
Refs.: Family information. Burke's *Landed Gentry*, 12th edn., p. 857, *s.n.* Craigie-Halkett, of Cramond. Grier. Macpherson, p. 177. *S.M.* 1778, p. 628; 1790, p. 570. M.I. Greyfriars. Portrait by Raeburn in possession of his gt. grand-dau.

SANDYS, Frederick Hervey (1791-1874). Lieut. General. Colonel 36th N.I. *b.* Bellaghy Glebe House, Ballyscullion, co. Londonderry, 10 Aug. 1791. Cadet 1808. Arrived in India 19 July 1809. Ensign (19 July 1809) 20 Nov. 1809. Lieut. 22 Mar. 1811. Capt. 1 May 1824. Major 1 Feb. 1840. Lt. Col. 30 Jan. 1846. Col. 10 Feb. 1856. Maj. Gen. 15 Oct. 1857. Lt. Gen. 8 Feb. 1870. *d.* at his residence, Douglas Villa, Cheltenham, 28 Dec. 1874.
bapt. Aug. 1791. Son of Rev. Joseph Sandys, rector of Aghadowey. *m.* 1st, Cawnpore 6 Oct. 1821, Miss Jane Culloden, niece of Major John Cathcart Meacham, 24th Ft. His daus. *m.* Samuel John Becher, *q.v.*, and George Timins, *q.v. m.* 2nd, Indore 7 July 1836, Maria Jane Bellasis, youngest sister of William Hewett, *q.v.* (*See also* James William Douglas.) Marlow Cadet.
Services: Barasat C.C. 3 mos. Posted Ensign to 18th N.I. 1809. Nepal War 1816; Lieut. 2/18th N.I., in 2nd Bde. Left Column (India medal). Intr. & Qmr. 2/18th N.I. 1 July 1814 till Oct. 1817; Adjt. 1/18th N.I. 2 Oct. 1817 till 3 Feb. 1821. (? Third Mahratta War 1817-18; Jawad.) D.A.Q.M.G. 3 cl. 21 Jan. 1821; 2 cl. 21 June 1823 till 18 Apr. 1828. Operations in Jodhpur; Lamba; D.A.Q.M.G. Transfd. to 36th N.I. (late 1/18th) May 1824. To take charge of 1st Coy. Pioneers 31 Mar. 1825. Asst. to P.A. at Nemawar, C.I., 25 Jan. 1828, and spent the remainder

of his service in Pol. Dept. On field service in Jan. 1835. P.A. at Mehidpur, C.I., 6 Dec. 1841 till 1856. Posted Lt. Col. to 51st N.I. 1846 ; to 62nd N.I. 1850 ; to 7th N.I. Dec. 1850 ; to 20th N.I. May 1854 ; to 1st Eur. Bengal Fus. May 1855 ; Col. to 36th N.I. Feb. 1856 till 1869. Fur. p.a. 20 May 1856 till death.

Refs. : Boase. *The Times,* 31 Dec. 1874. M.I. in new cemetery, Cheltenham.

SANDYS, Henry Capel (1790-1873). Lieut. Colonel. 28th N.I. *b.* Dublin 27 Dec. 1790. Cadet 1805. Arrived in India 20 July 1807. Ensign 18 July 1807. Lieut. 12 Oct. 1812. Capt. 1 May 1824. Major 9 May 1830. Retired 6 Nov. 1832. Hon. Lt. Col. 28 Nov. 1854. *d.* at his residence, Craig-yr-Halen, Anglesey, 19 Mar. 1873.

bapt. St. Anne's, Dublin, 5 Jan. 1791. Son of Rev. Michael Sandys and Barbara his wife. *m.* Protestant church, Caen, 5 Aug. 1822, Harriet, widow of Hugh Spottiswoode, M.C.S., and dau. of Burton Smith. (She died 20 Dec. 1864, aged 79.) Stepfather of Arthur Cole Spottiswoode, *q.v.*

Services : Barasat C.C. 8 mos. Posted Ensign to 14th N.I. 1808. Surveying embankments in Cuttack Jan. 1813 till Dec. 1814. Nepal War 1815 ; Lieut. 2/14th N.I., in 3rd Div. (India medal). Adjt. 2/14th N.I. Dec. 1814 till 13 Dec. 1816. Leave s.c. 4 mos. to sea 5 Jan. 1816. D.A.Q.M.G. Nagpur Subsdy. Force 29 Nov. 1816 ; do. 1 cl. 1 Jan. 1817 till 24 Oct. 1818. In charge of Guide & Intelligence Dept. in Advanced Div. of Nagpur Subsdy. Force 14 Nov. 1817. Third Mahratta War 1817-18 ; led storming party at capture of Chanda. Bde. Major Nagpur Rajah's Regular Inf. 24 Oct. 1818, and remained in Nagpur service till 1830. Transfd. to 28th N.I. (late 1/14th) May 1824. Fur. s.c. 26 Feb. 1822 till 18 Apr. 1823 ; s.c. 6 July 1830 till retirement.

Refs. : The Times, 24 Mar. 1873.

SANDYS, William (1749-1773). Ensign, Infantry. *b.* Canterbury 29 May 1749. Cadet 1772. Ensign 31 Mar. 1773. *d.s.p.* Calcutta June 1773.

3rd son of Richard Sandys, of Northbourne Court and Canterbury, J.P., and Susan Crayford his wife, dau. of James Taylor. Ed. King's School, Canterbury, 18 July 1757 till Dec. 1759.

Services : N.F.P.

Refs. : The Family of Sandys, by E. S. Sandys (London, privately printed 1930), vol. ii., ped. D.

SANDYS, William (1759-1829). Lieut. Colonel. 15th N.I. *b.* 1759. Cadet 1779. Admitted 30 Mar. 1781. Ensign 29 June

1779. Lieut. 21 Mar. 1781. Capt. 30 Oct. 1797. Major 23 Jan. 1803. Lt. Col. 21 Sept. 1804. Retired 5 June 1805. *d.* Plymouth 21 Aug. 1829, aged 70.

Of Lanarth ; J.P. co. Cornwall. Elder son of William Sandys, of Helston, attorney, and Mary Johns his wife. His sister was mother of Sir William Sampson Whish, *q.v.* *m.* 1st, Madras 10 Jan. 1793, Charlotte, dau. of Rear-Adm. Sir Digby Dent, R.N. (She died Calcutta 22 July 1802, aged 25.) *m.* 2nd, St. Agnes, Cornwall, Dec. 1803, Ellen, 2nd dau. of John James, of Rosemunday. (She died Truro 26 Nov. 1857, aged 74.)

Services : Apptd. Cadet 28 Apr. 1779 and was ordered to sail in *Duke of Kingston* 17 Nov. 1779. Having volunteered, however, to serve without pay in the *Monarch* when the French and Spanish fleets were off Plymouth, he was permitted to defer his departure and eventually embarked for India in the *Earl of Dartmouth* 3 June 1780, aged 20. Arrived Madras in Jan. 1781, and comdd. a Coy. of Cadets then embodied as part of the garr. First Mahratta War 1782-4, with the Bombay detachment. Lieut. 4th Bn. Sepoys in July 1787 ; D.J.A.G. 1788. Apptd. Adjt. & Qmr. to two Vol. Bns. raised for service in Mysore 1790. Third Mysore War 1790-2 ; Seringapatam ; Agent for carriage of public camp equipage. D.J.A.G. at Fatehgarh in Mar. 1793 ; Fort Adjt. & Bk. Mr. of Ft. Wm. 1793-7 ; A.D.C. to actg. G.G. ; Capt. 1st Bengal Eur. Regt. in 1798. Agent for supply of mily. stores 1798 till Jan. 1803. Major 5th N.I. Fur. 19 Jan. 1803 till retirement. Posted Lt. Col. to 15th N.I. 1804.

Refs. : The Family of Sandys, vol. ii., ped. J. *E.I.M.C.* i. 401-5. *G.M.* 1829, ii. 466. *A.J.* xxviii. 382. Will dated 4 Nov. 1823, with various cods. ; proved in London 20 Oct. 1829. M.I. St. Keverne church. Portrait by Robert Home, painted in Bengal in 1799.

Note : An inaccurate ped. of this family will be found in Burke's *Landed Gentry,* 2nd edn., p. 1188, *s.n.* Sandys, of St. Minver, Cornwall.

SANFORD, John Frederick (1789-1816). Lieutenant, 19th N.I. *bapt.* Wimbledon 13 May 1789. Cadet 1803. Arrived in India 17 Mar. 1805. Ensign 3 Apr. 1805. Lieut. 4 Apr. 1805. *d.* suddenly Karnal 16 May 1816, of a ruptured blood vessel, aged 27.

Son of John Smith Sanford and Elizabeth his wife. *m.* Berhampore 18 Oct. 1810, Eliza, dau. of Charles Brietzcke, *q.v.* (She re-*m.* Robert Cauty, *q.v.*) (*See also* William White.)

Services : d.d. 2/22nd N.I. 6 Oct. 1805. Second Mahratta War

1805; pursuit of Holkar; Ensign d.d. 2/22nd N.I. Posted Ensign to 2/19th N.I. 14 Jan. 1806. In charge of timber agency at Moradabad Oct. till 6 Dec. 1814. Nepal War 1814-15; Malaun; Lieut. 2/19th N.I., in 1st Div.
Refs.: De Rhé-Philipe. *A.J.* iii. 197. M.I. at Karnal.

SANKEY, John Henry (1803-1824). Ensign, Bengal Eur. Regt. *b.* Fethard, Tipperary, 27 Apr. 1803. Cadet 1821. Ensign 19 Jan. 1822. *d. unm.* Nagpur 9 Feb. 1824.
2nd son of Matthew Villiers Sankey, of Coolmore, co. Tipperary, and Amelia his wife, sister of Major Elrington, Major of the Tower of London.
Services : Posted Ensign to 25th N.I.; transfd. to Bengal Eur. Regt. 1823. No record of active service.
Refs. : Burke's *Landed Gentry of Ireland*, p. 625, *s.n.* Sankey, of Coolmore, co. Tipperary.

*****SARDELL,**[1] **John** (*d.* 1768). Cornet, Governor's Troop of Body Guard. Cornet 15 Sept. 1766. *d. unm.* Calcutta 21 Dec. 1768.
(*Probably* brother of Richard Sardell, *q.v.*)
Services : Campaign against the Nawabs of Bengal and Oudh 1764; cavalry action nr. the Bunas Nullah 13 Oct.; battle of Buxar; Cadet serving with the Troop of Eur. Dgns. *Probably* comdd. the Govr.'s Eur. Troop of Body Guard from the date of his first Commission as Cornet till death.
Refs. : Broome, p. 469. *V.B.G.* Will dated 6 Nov. 1768; proved 17 Jan. 1769.
[1] *Note :* His name appears thus in his Will and in *B.M. Add. MSS.*, as Surdle in the burial register, as Surdal in *Broome*, and as Sirdel in Caraccioli's *Life of Lord Clive*.

SARDELL, Richard (*d.* 1769). Ensign, Infantry. Cadet (?) Ensign 1768. *d.* 21 Jan. 1769 : kld. in action.
(*Probably* brother of John Sardell, *q.v.*)
Services : N.F.P.

SARGENT, George (1782-1832). Colonel, 29th N.I. *bapt.* Malmesbury, Wilts., 4 Aug. 1782. Cadet 1797. Arrived in India 9 Nov. 1798. Ensign 14 Oct. 1798. Lieut. 1 Nov. 1798. Capt. 24 Oct. 1809. Major 1 Aug. 1818. Lt. Col. 18 Aug. 1823. Lt. Col. Comdt. 2 Apr. 1828. Col. 5 June 1829. *d.* at his residence, Bradford Leigh House, Leigh Frome, Wilts., 25 June 1832. Son of George Sargent and Betty his wife. Brother of Elizabeth Stocker, of Sidmouth.

THE BENGAL ARMY, 1758-1834 21

Services : Lieut. 7th N.I. (? Reduction of Kalinjar 1812 ; Oapt. 1/7th N.I.) Nepal War 1814-15 ; Capt. 1/7th N.I., in 2nd Div. Third Mahratta War 1817-19 ; Major 1/7th N.I. Transfd. to 13th N.I. (late 1/7th) May 1824 ; to 57th N.I. 1825 ; to 13th N.I. 1826. First Burma War ; Assam 1824. Tempy. Bdr. Gen. comdg. Assam Force 10 Nov. 1825 till Apr. 1826. Fur. p.a. 2 Jan. 1827 till death. Posted Col. to 19th N.I. June 1829 ; to 29th N.I. 24 Sept. 1831. *Refs. :* A.J. N.S. ix. 51. G.M. 1832, i. 647 ; ii. 93. Will dated 11 June 1832 ; proved 6 Mar. 1833.

SARGENT, William (1791-1828). Captain, 58th N.I. *bapt.* Ruddington, Notts., 18 Dec. 1791. Cadet 1811. Ensign 9 Aug. 1814. Lieut. 1 Aug. 1818. Capt. 16 Nov. 1827. *d.* Agra 16 July 1828.

Son of George Sargent and Mary his wife. Brother of George and Thomas, both of Nottingham.

Services : Posted to newly-raised 1/29th N.I. Jan. 1815. Siege and capture of Hathras 1817 ; Ensign 1/29th N.I. Third Mahratta War 1817-18 ; Lieut. 1/29th N.I., with Centre Div. of Grand Army. Adjt. 3rd Ceylon Vols. 3 Oct. 1818 till 1819. Leave to N.S.W. 1821-2. Adjt. 2/29th N.I. (became 58th N.I. May 1824) 11 Jan. 1823 till 7 Feb. 1828. Siege and capture of Bhurtpore ; Lieut. 58th N.I.

Refs. : A.J. xxvii. 221. Will dated on board *John Bull* 16 Sept. 1821 ; proved 23 Oct. 1828.

SARNEY, Charles Henry (1741/42-1769). Lieutenant, Infantry. *b.* Oxford 1741/42. Cadet 1764. Ensign 21 Aug. 1765. Lieut. 2 Jan. 1767. *d.* in India 1769.

Ed. Merchant Taylors' Oct. 1751-Oct. 1752.

Services : Fourth Mate of the *Horsenden* East Indiaman 1762-3. Sailed for India as a Cadet in the *Fort William* 17 May 1764, aged 22. Posted to 1st Bengal Eur. Regt. 13 Aug. 1765. Resigned during the " Batta mutiny " ; reinstated 1766.

Refs. : Robinson.

SATCHWELL, John (1793-1838). Major, 29th N.I. A.C.G. *b.* London 17 Nov. 1793. Cadet 1812. Admitted 11 Sept. 1813. Ensign 20 Nov. 1814. Lieut. 2 Aug. 1816. Capt. 3 Mar. 1826. Major 6 Apr. 1838. *d.* Cawnpore 12 Aug. 1838, of cholera.

bapt. St. George's, Hanover Sq., 15 June 1794. Son of Richard Satchwell and Mary Ann Foxlow his wife. *m.* Bareilly 23 Feb. 1827, Eliza Johanna, 5th dau. of Jacob Vanrenen, *q.v.* (*See also* James Blair.) (She died Calcutta 10 Jan. 1833, aged 26.)

22 LIST OF THE OFFICERS OF

Services: Posted Ensign to 2/14th N.I. 1815. Served at Amboyna 1816-18. Intr. & Qmr. 2/14th N.I. 1819-20; S.A.C.G. 15 Nov. 1820; transfd. to 29th N.I. (late 2/14th) May 1824. D.A.C.G. 2 cl. 27 Mar. 1826; 1 cl. 30 Dec. 1826; A.C.G. 2 cl. 11 Dec. 1829; 1 cl. 12 Apr. 1837. Operations against the Kols and Chuars 1832; Capt. 29th N.I., in charge of Comst.

Refs.: De La Ferté. A.J. xxiv. 498; N.S. xxvii. 232.

SAUMAREZ, Nicholas. Bt. Captain. 14th N.I. Cadet 1783. Arrived in India 1 Oct. 1783. Ensign 4 Mar. 1785. Lieut. 2 May 1793. Bt. Capt. 8 Jan. 1798. Retired 7 Nov. 1798.[1]

N.B.—The following is conjectural only: (? 6th and youngest son of Matthew De Saumarez and Carteret his 2nd wife, dau. of James le Marchant. Brother of Sir James De Saumarez, G.C.B., 1st Baron De Saumarez. Became Collector Gen. of revenue in Ceylon.)

Services: Apptd. Cadet 6 Nov. 1782; sailed for India in the *Vansittart* 11 Mar. 1783. Was Adjt. 2nd Bengal Eur. Bn. in Mar. 1787 till after Jan. 1796; posted to 3rd Eur. Regt. June 1796; transfd. to 14th N.I. Fur. 1798.

Refs.: (? Burke's *Peerage*, 1923, p. 707, *s.n.* De Saumarez, B.)

[1] *Note:* His name appears for the last time in *I.A.L.* for Jan. 1866.

SAUNDERS, Henry John (1754-1796). Captain, Infantry. *b.* London 31 Dec. 1754. Cadet 1778. Admitted 10 Dec. 1778. Ensign 1778. Lieut. 14 Oct. 1778. Capt. 7 Jan. 1796. *d.* Chunar 23 July 1796.

Ed. Merchant Taylors' Jan.-Mar. 1769.

Services: Sailed for India in the *Stafford* 27 May 1778. Lieut. 1/2nd Bengal Eur. Regt. in Oct. 1779; in 2nd Bde. in Dec. 1780. Second Mysore War; acted as chaplain to the Bengal detachment 8 Apr. 1782 till 15 May 1783. Lieut. 33rd Bn. Sepoys in July 1787, and in 1792.

Refs.: Robinson. G.M. 1797, i. 356.

SAUNDERS, James (1800-1844). Bt. Major, 50th N.I. *b.* Harwich, Essex, 15 July 1800. Cadet 1819. Admitted 3 Aug. 1820. Ensign 4 Mar. 1820. Lieut. 11 July 1823. Capt. 22 Apr. 1836. Bt. Major 30 Apr. 1844. *d.* Aligarh 15 June 1844.

bapt. St. Nicholas, Harwich, 10 Aug. 1800. 2nd son of Capt. Nathaniel Saunders, of Harwich, Comdr. in the service of the P.M.G., and Maria his wife.

Services: Posted Ensign to 1/23rd N.I. 1820; transfd. to 25th N.I. July 1823; to 50th N.I. (late 2/25th) May 1824; actg.

Intr. & Qmr. do. 26 May 1828 ; permanent do. 3 Feb. 1829 till Dec. 1833. Operations against the Kols and Chuars 1832-3 ; Lieut. 50th N.I. Adjt. 50th N.I. 21 Dec. 1833 till 1 July 1836 ; actg. Intr. & Qmr. do. 17 Jan. 1838.
Refs.: G.M. 1844, ii. 558.

SAUNDERS, Samuel John (1809-1865). Major. 41st N.I. b. Paignton, Devon, 4 June 1809. Cadet 1826. Arrived in India 11 May 1827. Ensign 20 Jan. 1827. Lieut. 22 Apr. 1838. Capt. 28 Dec. 1847. Retired 20 Dec. 1849. Hon. Major 28 Nov. 1854. d. Bedford 27 Sept. 1865.

Youngest son of James Saunders, Purser H.M.S. *St. George* (who was drowned in the wreck of that vessel in Dec. 1811). m. (before 1852) ?

Services : Ensign d.d. 7th N.I. 28 May 1827 ; posted to 41st N.I. 19 June 1827. d.d. Hariana L.I. 18 May 1838 till 25 Feb. 1839. Adjt. 1st Recruit Depot Bn. at Jaunpur 6 Nov. 1839. Fur. s.c. 17 Jan. 1843 till 25 Aug. 1845. Adjt. 41st N.I. 27 Aug. 1846 till 23 Feb. 1848. No record of active service. Lieut. 1st R. Cheshire Mil. 30 Apr. 1855.
Refs.: G.M. 1865, ii. 658. *The Times*, 9 Oct. 1865.

SAURIN, William (1802-1872). Lieut. Colonel. 31st N.I. bapt. Rosenallis, Queen's Co., 28 Nov. 1802. Cadet 1822. Arrived in India 9 July 1823. Ensign 11 July 1823. Lieut. 15 Sept. 1824. Capt. 1 June 1834. Bt. Major 9 Nov. 1846. Retired 10 Feb. 1847. Hon. Lt. Col. 28 Nov. 1854. d. S. Molton St., London, 12 Sept. 1872.

2nd son of Rt. Rev. James Saurin, D.D., bishop of Dromore, and Elizabeth his wife, dau. of William Lyster. m. Esther Davis.

Services : Posted to 15th N.I. ; transfd. to 31st N.I. (late 2/15th) May 1824. Siege and capture of Bhurtpore ; Lieut. 31st N.I. (India medal). Operations against the Bhils 1828 ; against the Chuars 1832 ; Lieut. 31st N.I. Fur. p.a. 9 Jan. 1835 till 15 Dec. 1837. First Afghan War 1838-40 ; Kalat (w.) (*London Gaz.* 13 Feb. 1840) ; Ghazni ; Capt. 31st N.I. (Medal). Gwalior campaign ; Maharajpur ; Capt. 31st N.I. (Bronze star).
Refs.: Burke's *Landed Gentry*, 13th edn., p. 1562, s.n. Saurin, late of Orielton, co. Pembroke. *The Times*, 17 Sept. 1872.

SAVAGE, Charles (1788-1876). Lieut. Colonel. 27th N.I. b. Kilcoo, co. Down, 19 Aug. 1788. Cadet 1804. Arrived in India 10 Sept. 1805. Ensign 14 Nov. 1805. Lieut. 21 Aug. 1806.

Capt. 11 July 1823. Major 3 May 1832. Retired 7 Feb. 1833. Hon. Lt. Col. 28 Nov. 1854. *d.s.p.* 8 Apr. 1876.

2nd son of Francis Savage, of Newcastle, co. Down, and Elizabeth his wife, dau. of Arthur Atkinson, of Mullerstown, Mourne, co. Down.

Services: Posted Lieut. to 13th N.I. 1806. Operations against Dhundia Khan 1807; Komona; Ganauri; Lieut. 1/13th N.I. Nepal War; Lieut. 13th N.I. (India medal). Bareilly insurrection 1816; Lieut. 1/13th N.I. Fur. p.a. 7 Jan. 1823 till 8 Oct. 1824. Transfd. to 27th N.I. (late 2/13th) May 1824. Leave s.c. to Hills 29 Sept. 1831 till retirement.

Refs.: Burke's *Family Records*, p. 532, *s.n.* Savage. *The Times*, 13 Apr. 1876.

SAVAGE, George (1760/61-?). Lieutenant. Infantry. *b.* Antigua 1760/61. Cadet 1781. Ensign 17 May 1781. Lieut. 23 Aug. 1782. Struck off 1788. *d.s.p.*

Only son of George Savage, of Antigua, merchant, and Jane his wife.

Services: Apptd. Cadet 31 Oct. 1781, aged 20. Never arrived in India.

SAVAGE, John (*d.* 1768). Lieutenant, Infantry. Cadet (?) Ensign 20 May 1766. Lieut. 28 May 1767. *d.* in India 1768. *Services:* N.F.P.

SAVARY, John Tanzia (1800-1832). Captain, Pension Est. 24th N.I. *b.* Greenwich 19 May 1800. Cadet 1816. Ensign (?) Lieut. 1 Aug. 1818. Capt. 10 May 1828. Pensioned in India 26 Mar. 1830. *d.* 18 Oct. 1832.

bapt. Greenwich 3 July 1800. Son of William James Tanzia Savary,[1] of Ilfracombe, Devon, formerly of Sevenoaks, Kent, and Catherine his wife, dau. of Philip Oade, and half-sister of Matthew, 5th Baron Aylmer. Brother of William Tanzia Savary, *q.v. m.* Berhampore 18 Jan. 1818, Elizabeth, widow of James McCraken, *q.v.*

Services: Ensign d.d. Bengal Eur. Regt. 1817; posted Lieut. to 2/8th N.I. 1818. Operations in Hariana 1824; Lieut. 2/8th N.I. Transfd. to 24th N.I. (late 2/8th) May 1824.

[1] *Note:* " His ancestors owned the Seigneurie of Tanzia as well as others in the Province of Perigord."—*Genealogist*, N.S. xxiii. 63.

SAVARY, William Tanzia (1802-1855). Bt. Major. 46th N.I. *b.* Wilmington, Kent, 5 July 1802. Cadet 1821. Arrived in India 29 May 1822. Ensign 9 Dec. 1821. Lieut. 17 May 1824.

Capt. 14 Jan. 1833. Bt. Major 9 Nov. 1846. Retired 21 Apr. 1848. *d.* Ilfracombe 14 Apr. 1855.

bapt. Wilmington 3 Aug. 1802. Youngest son of William James Tanzia Savary and Catherine his wife. Brother of John Tanzia Savary, *q.v.*, and cousin-german of Henry Christian Talbot, *q.v.* *m.* 1st, St. George's, Bloomsbury, 11 Mar. 1828, Frances Eliza, only dau. of William Hall Durham, barr.-at-law, of I. of St. Vincent. (She died Gadarwara, C.P., 20 Apr. 1836, aged 29.) *m.* 2nd, Leckhampton, Gloucs., 4 Apr. 1850, Mary Elizabeth, dau. of Allen Dalzell, of Barbados. (She died 21 Dec. 1895, aged 78.)

Services : Posted to 2/3rd N.I. ; actg. Intr. & Qmr. do. 23 Dec. 1823 ; transfd. to 46th N.I. (late 2/23rd) May 1824. (? First Burma War ; Assam 1824 ; Lieut. 46th N.I.) Fur. u.p.a. 19 Sept. 1826 till 1 Aug. 1828 ; leave s.c. 2 yrs. to N.S.W. 27 July 1828.

Refs. : *G.M.* 1828, i. 267 ; 1855, i. 658.

SAVERLAND, Christopher [1] (1786-1805). Cadet, Artillery. (360) *b.* Portsmouth 10 June 1786. Cadet 1804. Never arrived in India. *d.* San Salvador 24 Nov. 1805 : kld. in an affray with natives when a passenger in the *Glory.*

bapt. Portsmouth 14 Apr. 1787. Son of Christopher Saverland, a Surveyor of the Customs, who received a pension from Govt. of £80 *p.a.* on relinquishing the office of Postmr. of Portsmouth in 1802, and Martha his wife.

[1] *Note :* Stubbs gives his name as William Christopher Savarland ; Philippart as Charles Savorland.

SAY, Henry Hirst (1805-1882). Major. 45th N.I. *b.* Boxley, Kent, 22 Mar. 1805. Cadet 1825. Ensign 12 Feb. 1826. Lieut. 6 May 1829. Capt. 24 Jan. 1845. Retired 15 May 1852. Hon. Major 28 Nov. 1854. *d.* The Mount, Braughing, Herts., 22 Jan. 1882.

bapt. ptely. Boxley 29 Mar. 1805. Son of Rev. Henry Morgan Say, vicar of Iwerne Minster, Dorset, and Marianne his wife. *m.* S. Bersted, Sussex, 20 Sept. 1843, Elizabeth, 2nd dau. of Richard Nixon, of Highgate. (She died Ambala 11 Aug. 1845.)

Services : Ensign d.d. 57th N.I. 8 July 1826 ; posted to 45th N.I. 26 Sept. 1826 ; Intr. & Qmr. do. 6 July 1830 till 1842. Fur. s.c. 9 Jan. 1842 till 28 Dec. 1844. First Sikh War ; Mudki ; Ferozshahr ; Sobraon ; Capt. 45th N.I. (Medal with 2 clasps). Fur. 10 Mar. 1847 till 8 Feb. 1850. Actg. Agent army clothing, 1st Div., 22 Mar. 1850.

Refs. : *The Times,* 25 Jan. 1882.

SAYCE, John. (*See* **SAYER, John.**)

SAYER, John (*d.* 1772). Cadet, Infantry. Cadet 1771. *d.* Benares 31 May 1772, " of a pucka fever in a few hours."
Services : Cadet in the Select Picket.
Refs. : Macpherson, p. 94.

SCARLIN, Roger. Captain. 1st Bengal Eur. Regt. Capt. 7 May 1765. Resigned 15 May 1766.
Services : Lieut. H.M. 109th Ft. 24 Oct. 1761 ; h.p. on disbandment 1763-6, and again 1773-80. Apptd. in England 2 Mar. 1764, Capt. on the Bengal Est.; sailed for India in the *Lord Anson* 29 May 1764. Transfd. as Capt. to Bengal Army (G.O. Apr. 1765); posted to 1st Bengal Eur. Regt. 5 Aug. 1765. Resigned his Commission during the " Batta mutiny "; his application in 1769 for reinstatement was refused by C.D.

SCHALCH, John Augustus (1793-1825). Bt. Captain, 29th N.I. *b.* Woolwich 27 Jan. 1793. Cadet 1807. Arrived in India 1 Feb. 1809. Ensign 22 Feb. 1809. Lieut. 16 Dec. 1814. Bt. Capt. 16 Sept. 1823. *d.* 25 Feb. 1825 : kld. in action on board the *Research* at Kiung-pala, Burma.
bapt. St. Mary's, Woolwich, 21 Mar. 1793. Son of Andrew Schalch,[1] Capt. R.A., and Phillis his wife. Brother of Philip Schalch, *q.v. m.* St. John's, Calcutta, 27 Feb. 1822, Mary Ann Catherine, dau. of James Meik, M.D., M.M.B. Bengal. (*See also* F. T. Boyd.) (? She died 15 Dec. 1822.)
Services : Posted Ensign to 14th N.I. 1810 ; Lieut. 2/14th N.I. Surveying in Sundarbans 1816 ; do. Rangpur district 27 June 1817. D.A.Q.M.G. 2 cl. 1819 ; 1 cl. 1822. Surveyor of Calcutta ; erected iron suspension bridge at Kalighat, Calcutta. Supt. Bengal canals 1823. Transfd. to 29th N.I. (late 2/14th) May 1824. First Burma War 1824-5 ; Bt. Capt. 29th N.I., comdg. Pioneers, with official rank of Major (G.O. 16 Sept. 1824).
Refs. : G.M. 1826 i. 180. Will dated 19 May 1823 ; proved 17 Mar. 1825.
[1] *Note :* Of German-Swiss extraction, from Schaffhausen, and nephew of Andrew Schalch, master-founder at Woolwich arsenal (*D.N.B.*).

SCHALCH, Philip (1797-1846). Lieutenant. 2nd L.C. *bapt.* Brentwood, S. Weald, Essex, 19 July 1797. Cadet 1821. Cornet 19 Jan. 1822. Lieut. 1 May 1824. Resigned in England 4 Dec. 1827. *d.* Blagdon, nr. Taunton, 15 May 1846.

3rd son of Capt. Andrew Schalch, R.A., and Phillis his wife. Brother of John Augustus Schalch, q.v. m. Shepton Mallet, Somerset, 11 Sept. 1827, Mary, youngest dau. of W. Purlewent. Woolwich Cadet.

Services: Gent. Cadet R.A. 23 June 1812; 2nd Lieut. do. 11 Dec. 1815; retired on h.p. 14 Dec. 1821. Posted Cornet to 2nd L.C. 1822. Fur. s.c. 5 Jan. 1827 till resignation. No record of active service.

Refs.: Kane, No. 1633. *G.M.* 1846, ii. 109.

SCHNELL, Charles Vaughan (1785-1815). Capt. Lieutenant, Pension Est. 15th N.I. *bapt.* Holborn, Middlesex, 3 Aug. 1785. Cadet 1800. Arrived in India 22 Aug. 1801. Ensign 22 Dec. 1801. Lieut. 2 Jan. 1804. Capt. Lt. 25 June 1813. Pensioned 15 Sept. 1814. *d.* Calcutta 18 Aug. 1815.

Son of John Francis Schnell and Clementina Jacobina Sobieski Stuart his wife, dau. of Col. Allan Macdonald of Kinlochmoidart, co. Inverness, and cousin of Sir John Macdonald, K.C.B., q.v. Brother of John Stewart Schnell, q.v.

Services: Ensign 3rd N.I.; transfd. as Lieut. to 15th N.I. 1804. Second Mahratta War; battle of Deig (w.); Lieut. 1/15th N.I. A.D.C. to Maj.-Gen. Sir John Macdonald, q.v., 1805-10; Adjt. & Qmr. 15th N.I. 1 Aug. 1810 till pensioned; acting Bde. Major at Benares 1811.

Refs.: *G.M.* 1816, i. 564.

SCHNELL, John Stewart (1780-1817). Captain, 3rd N.I. *bapt.* St. Andrew's, Holborn, 12 July 1780. Cadet 1795. Arrived in India 5 Feb. 1797. Ensign 1 Dec. 1796. Lieut. 30 Oct. 1797. Capt. 24 Jan. 1809. *d.* Cawnpore 14 Dec. 1817.

Eldest son of John Francis Schnell, of New Ormond St., London, and Clementina his wife. Brother of Charles Vaughan Schnell, q.v. m. Calcutta 19 Sept. 1801, Miss Eliza Sophia Hogan. (*See also* Robert Morrell.) (She died 22 June 1856, aged 75.)

Services: Lieut. 3rd N.I.; Capt. Lt. 3rd N.I. 19 Feb. 1806; Adjt. 2/3rd N.I. 1805-8; Capt. 1/3rd N.I. S.A.C.G. 3 Apr. 1813.

Refs.: *S.M.* 1818, ii. 103. *G.M.* 1818, i. 568.

SCHOLEY, Godfrey. Dy. Paymr. Resigned 15 Oct. 1781.

Services: Dy. Paymr. to detachment of Nawab-Wazir's troops at Fatehgarh Jan. 1778 till resignation.

Note: Name given in *Dodwell & Miles* as George Scholey. It is doubtful whether he should properly be included here as he does not appear to have been a commissioned officer.

SCOLLAY, William (1789-1813). Cadet, Infantry. *b.* Quebec 7 Sept. 1789. Cadet 1810. *d.* Calcutta 13 Sept. 1813.
Nephew of Samuel Scollay, merchant in Lerwick, and cousin of Ann Scollay Innes, of Bath.
Services: Cornet 25th Light Dgns. 1 Mar. 1812; d.d. 1/12th N.I. at Barrackpore 1812. Admitted as the first mily. student at Coll. of Ft. Wm. May 1812. No record of active service.

SCONCE, John (1790-1820). Lieutenant, Artillery. (400) *bapt.* Ch. Ch., Nicholas Town, I. of St. Kitts, 24 Sept. 1790. Cadet 1807. Arrived in India 21 Mar. 1809. Fireworker 26 Mar. 1809. Lieut. 26 June 1813. *d.* 6 July 1820 : lost in H.M.S. *Carron* off the coast of Jagannath, B. & O.[1]
Son of John Sconce and Harriet his wife. Woolwich Cadet; nominated 29 Jan. 1806.
Services: Lieut. 2nd Troop H.A. 1813-14; 3rd Troop 1815-18. Nepal War 1814-15; Lieut. 3rd Troop, in 2nd Div. Siege and capture of Hathras 1817; Lieut. 3rd Troop. Third Mahratta War 1817-18; Lieut. 3rd Troop, Adjt. H.A. with Centre Div.

[1] *Note:* "He had got nearly safe to the beach, when he was caught by the surf and carried back." (*Stubbs.*)

*****SCOON, Robert** (1727/28-1759). Lieutenant, Infantry. *b.* in Scotland 1727/28. Cadet (Bombay) 1753. Ensign (?) Lieut. (Bombay) 15 Apr. 1757. *d.* Surat 27 Feb. (? 1 Mar.) 1759, of wounds received in action.
Services: Sailed for Bombay in the *Shaftesbury* in 1753, aged 25. Transfd. from Bombay to Bengal Est. 1757; retransfd. to Bombay 1758. Operations against Surat Feb. 1759 (s.w. 26 Feb.).
Refs.: Orme MSS.—India, xiii. p. 3639. Intestate; admon. 25 Apr. 1759.

SCOTLAND, James (*d.* 1772). Captain. Infantry. Capt. 23 Oct. 1763. Resigned 27 Jan. 1766. *d.* nr. Edinburgh 8 June 1772.
Of Easter Dollarbeg, Dunfermline. Brother of William Scotland, merchant in Edinburgh. (*Probably* son of Thomas Scotland, of Wester Dollarbeg.)
Services: Went out to India as Midshipman of an Indiaman and came home 3rd Mate of the *Prince Henry* packet 1757-8. (? Manipur expedn. 1762; Ensign.) Capture of Patna 6 Nov. 1763 (w.). Raised at Jellasore, B. & O., Mar. 1764, 20th Bn. Sepoys. This Bn., which became 14th N.I. in 1824 and mutinied at Jhelum 7 July 1857, was known as "*Escotten-ki-Paltan*" after him.

THE BENGAL ARMY, 1758-1834

Refs.: Williams, p. 142. *S.M.* 1772, p. 333. *London Mag.* 1772, p. 294.

SCOTT, Archibald (*d.* 1781). Lieutenant, 35th N.I. Cadet 1776. Ensign 6 Apr. 1777. Lieut. 1 Sept. 1778. *d.* 16 Aug. 1781 : kld. in action at Sewalah, nr. Benares.[1]

4th son of John Scott, of Malleny, and Susan his wife, dau. of Lord William Hay, of Newhall, 3rd son of John, 2nd Marquess of Tweeddale.

Services: Sailed for India in the *Shrewsbury* 14 Mar. 1776. Ensign 14th Bn. Sepoys in Aug. 1778 ; Lieut. 1/2nd Bengal Eur. Regt. in Oct. 1779. First Mahratta War ; storm and capture of Gwalior 1780. Benares insurrection 16 Aug. 1781 (kld.) ; Lieut. 35th N.I.

Refs.: Burke's *Landed Gentry*, 12th edn., p. 1679, *s.n.* Scott, of Malleny, Midlothian. *Macpherson*, pp. 370, 393. *Grier*, pp. 125-7. *Forrest*, iii. 788. *Cardew*, p. 48. M.I. St. Mary's churchyard, Benares.

[1] *Note:* By a surprise *coup* on the morning of 16 Aug., Hastings, anticipating trouble from Rajah Chait Singh, made him a prisoner in his palace at Sewalah or Shiwala Ghaut under a guard of 2 Gren. Coys. of 35th N.I. These Coys. were comdd. by Scott and Jeremiah Symes, *q.v.*, the whole being under Lieut. John Stalker, *q.v.* Through some mistake the guard had left camp without any ammunition, and was overwhelmed by the Rajah's armed forces who had gained access to the palace. The 2 Coys. were cut down almost to a man, the bodies of the 3 Ofrs. being subsequently found shockingly mangled lying close together.

SCOTT, Benjamin (1803-1824). Lieutenant, 37th N.I. *b.* London 8 Feb. 1803. Cadet 1820. Arrived in India May 1821. Ensign 16 Jan. 1821. Lieut. 11 July 1823. *d.* Cawnpore 18 Aug. 1824.

bapt. 27 Jan. 1804. Son of John Scott, of 63 Cornhill, London, and Anne his wife (? *née* Newman).

Services: Posted Ensign to 1/10th N.I. 1822 ; Intr. & Qmr. do. 1822 ; transfd. to 18th N.I. 1823 ; to 37th N.I. (late 2/18th) May 1824. No record of active service.

SCOTT, Charles (*d.* 1769). Lieutenant, Artillery. (60) Cadet 1763. Ensign (Inf.) 19 Sept. 1763. Fireworker 2 Feb. 1764. 2nd Lieut. Feb. 1767. Lieut. 6 Aug. 1768. *d.* Calcutta 24 May 1769.

Son of Walter Scott and Janet his wife. Brother of Mary and

Elizabeth, spinsters, Alexander, of Virginia, merchant, Robert and William. His exor. was Walter Scott, W.S., father of Sir Walter Scott, the novelist.

Services : (? Comy. of Art. at Ft. Wm. in Dec. 1764.) Lieut. 4th Coy. Art. in 1766. Resigned his Commission 1 May 1766 during the " Batta mutiny " ; readmitted later.

Refs. : Will dated Calcutta 23 May 1769 ; filed and read 30 May 1769.

SCOTT, Charles (*d.* 1802). Lieut. Colonel, Artillery. (129) Country Cadet 1771. Admitted 6 Dec. 1771. Fireworker 10 Jan. 1773. Lieut. (Inf.) 26 Sept. 1777. Struck off to Art. 12 Feb. 1781. Capt. Lt. 15 Apr. 1781. Capt. 31 Jan. 1785. Major 20 Aug. 1794. Lt. Col. 25 Apr. 1797. *d.* nr. Dinapore 14 Nov. 1802.

Son of James Scott, W.S., and Margaret his wife, dau. of Andrew Marjoribanks, of that Ilk. Brother of Thomas Scott (*d.* 1810), *q.v.* Father of Charles Elliot Scott, of London, bookseller.

Services : Was Capt. 3rd Bn. Art. in July 1787 ; comdg. 1st Coy. 3rd Bn. in Dec. 1788 ; posted Major to 2nd Bn. 19 Sept. 1794.

Refs. : Burke's *Landed Gentry*, 5th edn., p. 884, *s.n.* Marjoribanks, of Marjoribanks. *S.M.* 1803, p. 364. Will dated 16 Dec. 1801 ; codicil dated Bankipore, 10 Nov. 1802 ; proved 11 Dec. 1802.

SCOTT, Charles (1814-1847). Captain, 27th N.I. *b.* Rangpur, Bengal, 1814. Cadet 1833. Arrived in India 7 July 1834. Ensign (13 Dec. 1833) 8 May 1834. Lieut. 15 June 1839. Capt. 6 Feb. 1846. *d.* Dacca 3 May 1847, aged 33.

Natural son of David Scott, B.C.S., judge and mgte. at Rangpur (who was younger son of Archibald Scott, of Usan). His father's sister *m.* her cousin Archibald Watson, *q.v. m.* Karnal 21 Sept. 1835, Harriet, only dau. of Richard Becher, B.C.S., of Brighton, formerly salt agent at Tamluk, Bengal. (She died Jessore 23 Feb. 1842.) Addiscombe Cadet 3 Feb. 1832 till 13 Dec. 1833.

Services : d.d. 43rd N.I. 15 July 1834 ; posted to 27th N.I. 5 Nov. 1834 ; d.d. Assam L.I. 14 July 1837 ; transfd. to Assam Sebundy Corps 4 Sept. 1837. Actg. Junr. Asst. to A.G.G., N.E. frontier, 1 Dec. 1838 ; Junr. Asst. to Comr. of Assam 30 May 1840 ; principal do. 22 Feb. 1842 till death.

Refs. : Memorials of Four Old Families, by Capt. D. Wimberley (Inverness, 1893), p. 125. Burke's *Peerage*, *s.n.* Scott, Bart., of Dunninald. Will dated Dacca 29 Apr. 1847 ; proved 17 Sept. 1847. M.I. Dacca cemetery.

SCOTT, Colin Campbell Jackson (1804-1854). Captain, Invalid Est. 32nd N.I. *b.* Port Royal, Jamaica, 29 July 1804. Cadet 1825. Arrived in India 4 May 1826. Ensign 12 Jan. 1826. Lieut. 30 May 1829. Capt. 30 Nov. 1844. Invalided 1 July 1848. *d.* Bordeaux, France, 19 May 1854. Son of —— Scott and Rebecca his wife. *m.* Elizabeth, eldest dau. of George Holden. (She died Brighton 24 Jan. 1860.)
Services : Posted to 32nd N.I. 26 Sept. 1826 ; actg. Intr. & Qmr. do. 12 Mar. 1829 ; Adjt. do. 24 June 1829 ; Intr. & Qmr. do. 5 Jan. 1833. Fur. s.c. 9 Jan. 1835 till 19 May 1837. Actg. Intr. & Qmr. 71st N.I. 18 July 1837 ; do. 39th N.I. 21 Dec. 1838 ; do. 71st N.I. 22 Mar. 1839. Intr. & Qmr. 32nd N.I. 11 Jan. 1840 till 15 Mar. 1841. Fur. s.c. 9 Feb. 1841 till 1843 ; leave s.c. 1 yr. to Hills 15 Sept. 1847 ; fur. s.c. July 1853 till death. No record of active service.
Refs. : I.M. 29 June 1854, p. 372. *G.M.* 1854, ii. 201.

SCOTT, David (1740-1766). Captain, comdg. 20th Bn. N.I. *b.* 1740. Capt. 20 Dec. 1764. *d.* Calcutta 22 Aug. 1766.
Services : Transfd. as Capt. from H.M.S. (*Probably* to be identified with the following :—Ensign 2nd Bn. 4th Ft. 28 Sept. 1757 ; posted Ensign to 2nd Bn. 19th Ft. 5 Oct. 1757 ; formed into 66th Ft. 21 Apr. 1758 ; Lieut. 24 Nov. 1759 ; 108th Ft. 19 Oct. 1761 ; Capt. 17 May 1762.) Transfd. to Bengal Army (?) 1765 ; posted to 2nd Bengal Eur. Regt. 5 Aug. 1765 ; given comd. in 1765 of newly-raised 20th Bn. Sepoys in 2nd Bde. This Bn., known as " *Husseini-ki-Paltan* " owing to its having been raised (at Allahabad in Aug.) during the month of Moharram, became 16th N.I. in 1824 and was disbanded in 1858. Resigned during the " Batta mutiny," May 1766, and ordered down to Calcutta.
Refs. : Officers of the Green Howards, 1688-1931, by Major M. L. Ferrar. *Cardew,* p. 31. *Caraccioli,* iii. 195.

SCOTT, Duncan Gordon (1788-1863). Lieut. General. Colonel 30th N.I. *b.* Auchterhouse, co. Forfar, 5 Dec. 1788. Cadet 1804. Arrived in India 10 Sept. 1805. Ensign 11 Oct. 1805. Lieut. 19 Dec. 1805. Capt. 11 July 1823. Major 7 Dec. 1827. Lt. Col. 29 Oct. 1832. Col. 7 May 1844. Maj. Gen. 20 June 1854. Lt. Gen. 23 July 1858. *d.* Wooden House, co. Roxburgh, 5 Apr. 1863.
Of Wooden. *bapt.* 18 Dec. 1788. 5th son of Rev. James Scott, minister of Auchterhouse 1774-1804, and Margaret his wife, dau. of Rev. James Munro, minister of Kinloss.
Services : Posted Lieut. to 2/5th N.I. Sept. 1806, but to d.d.

with 1/5th till 15 Dec. 1806. Operations in Bundelkhand against Gopal Singh 1810-11; Tirowa; Lieut. 1/5th N.I. Nepal War 1814-15; operations in Kumaon 1815 (s.w.); Lieut. 5th N.I. (India medal). Adjt. 1/5th N.I. 4 May 1815 till 1 Oct. 1823. Operations in Kotah 1821. Fur. p.a. 25 Dec. 1823 till 22 Oct. 1826. Transfd. to 11th N.I. (late 1/5th) May 1824. Actg. Bde. Major to troops in Arakan 22 Nov. 1826. To take charge of 2nd Bengal Eur. Regt. 30 Jan. 1828. Wahabi rising 1831; action at Barasat 19 Nov.; Major comdg. 11th N.I. Posted Lt. Col. to 11th N.I. 9 July 1833. Disturbances in Bundelkhand Dec. 1842; Lt. Col. 11th N.I., comdg. the detachment. Posted Col. to 11th N.I. 2 Aug. 1844. Fur. p.a. 13 Dec. 1844 till death. Col. 30th N.I. 16 July 1849 till death.

Refs.: Scott's *Fasti*, v. 310. Boase. *G.M.* 1863, i. 672. *The Times*, 8 Apr. 1863.

SCOTT, Edward William Smyth (1812-1892). Major General. Artillery. (617) *bapt.* Delgany, co. Wicklow, 15 Dec. 1812. Cadet 1828. Arrived in India 13 Aug. 1829. 2nd Lieut. 12 Dec. 1828. Lieut. 18 Jan. 1837. Capt. 5 July 1846. Major 10 Feb. 1858. Lt. Col. 27 Aug. 1858. Col. 24 Nov. 1862. Retired on special annuity 1 Sept. 1863. Hon. Maj. Gen. 1 Sept. 1863. *d.* 4 Brookside, Cambridge, 1 Jan. 1892, aged 79.

4th son of Rev. John Middleton Scott, of Ballygannon, co. Wicklow, high sheriff co. Wicklow 1805, and Lady Arabella Barbara his wife, 6th and youngest dau. of Anthony (Brabazon), 8th Earl of Meath. *m.* Dum-Dum 11 May 1840, Eliza, dau. of Sir William Sampson Whish, *q.v.* (She died 20 Feb. 1898, aged 76.) His dau. *m.* Robert Cornelis, Baron Napier of Magdala, *q.v.* Addiscombe Cadet 1827-8.

Services : Posted to 4th Coy. 5th Bn. 2 Mar. 1831. Leave s.c. 9 mos. to Singapore 25 Aug. 1832; fur. s.c. 13 Dec. 1835 till 16 May 1839. Adjt. 7th Bn. 12 Aug. 1840; do. 9th Bn. 30 July 1845 till 29 July 1846. 2nd Asst. Sec. Mily. Board 11 Dec. 1846 till 1851. Fur. s.c. 2 Feb. 1851 till Nov. 1853. Mutiny campaign; siege of Delhi; Bt. Major 3rd Coy. 3rd Bn. (Medal with clasp). I.G. of Ord. and Magazines 18 Jan. 1858. Fur. 1862 till retirement.

Refs.: Memorials of Family of Scott, of Scot's Hall, Kent (1876), by J. R. Scott, p. 256. Burke's *Peerage*, 1923, p. 1539, *s.n.* Meath, E. *The Times*, 4 Jan. 1892.

*****SCOTT, George** (1734/35-?). *b.* Fulham, Middlesex, 1734/35. Cadet 1759. (? Resigned Feb. 1767.)

THE BENGAL ARMY, 1758-1834

Services: Apptd. Cadet Jan. 1759; sailed for India in the *Stormont* in 1759, aged 24. N.F.P.

SCOTT, George (1763-1801). Captain, 4th N.I. *b.* in Scotland 1763. Cadet 1781. Arrived in India 30 May 1782. Ensign 24 June 1781. Lieut. 28 Sept. 1782. Capt. 24 Aug. 1800. *d. unm.* Calcutta 3 June 1801.

Son of Charles Scott, of Woodbank, and Helen his wife. Brother of Elizabeth Scott, William, and Charles.

Services: Apptd. Cadet 29 Mar. 1781, aged 17; sailed for India in the *Lord Mulgrave* 26 June 1781, aged 18. Lieut. 35th Bn. Sepoys in July 1787 and in Oct. 1794; posted Bt. Capt. to 1/4th N.I. 1796; Capt. Lt. do. 29 May 1800.

Refs.: S.M. 1802, p. 181. Will dated Jaunpur 12 Oct. 1794; codicil 3 Nov. 1800; proved 29 June 1801.

SCOTT, George (1806-1859). Lieut. Colonel. 6th L.C. *b.* London 2 Mar. 1806. Cadet 1825. Arrived in India 22 Oct. 1826. Cornet 13 June 1826. Lieut. 16 Nov. 1835. Capt. 12 Apr. 1849. Bt. Major 20 June 1854. Retired 20 Nov. 1856. Hon. Lt. Col. 20 Nov. 1856. *d.* Tinarana, Killaloe, co. Clare, 6 Jan. 1859.

Of Fulham. Son of James Scott, of Rotherfield Park, Hants, M.P. for Bridport, and Martha his wife, dau. of Thomas Bradbury Winter, of Shenley, Herts. His sister *m.* Sir Charles Peter Shakerley, 1st Bart., of Somerford Park, co. Chester. Ed. Charterhouse; admitted 1821, left May 1825.

Services: Posted to 4th L.C. 8 Jan. 1827. Fur. s.c. 4 Jan. 1830 till 31 Oct. 1832. Transfd. to 6th L.C. 2 Sept. 1831. Leave s.c. to Hills 1 Apr. 1834 till 13 Jan. 1838; fur. s.c. 18 Nov. 1840 till 19 Jan. 1844. Dy. Paymr. Nasirabad circle 27 June 1845; do. Nimach 1848; do. Rawal Pindi 1850; do. Benares 1851; Pension Paymr. at Dinapore 2 Jan. 1855. Leave s.c. 2 yrs. to sea 17 Jan. 1855 till retirement. No record of active service.

Refs.: Burke's *Landed Gentry*, 13th edn., p. 1572, *s.n.* Scott, of Rotherfield Park, Hants. *Charterhouse School List. G.M.* 1859, i. 221. *The Times*, 14 Jan. 1859. Will dated 18 Aug. 1857; admon. 5 Nov. 1859. M.I. E. Tisted church, Hants.

SCOTT, George Dennistoun (1807-1864). Lieutenant. Artillery. (552) Capt. 1st K.D.G. *b.* Seringapatam, Mysore, 19 Mar. 1807. Cadet 1823. 2nd Lieut. 18 Dec. 1823. Lieut. 28 Sept. 1827. Resigned 24 May 1829. *d.* at his residence, Woodside, Winkfield, 7 Apr. 1864.

Of Lovel Hill, Berks., J.P. *bapt.* Madras 10 Sept. 1807. Only son of Maj.-Gen. James George Scott, Madras Art., by his 1st wife. *m.* Frederica Harriet, 2nd dau. of Edmund Broderip, of Cossington Manor, Somerset. (*See also* Edwin Lovell.) (She died 14 Dec. 1858, aged 52.) Ed. Edin. High School. Addiscombe Cadet 15 Mar. 1822 till 18 Dec. 1823. Trin. Coll., Oxon.; matric. 20 Feb. 1828.

Services : Fur. s.c. 21 Dec. 1826 till resignation. No record of active service. Lieut. 1st K.D.G. 27 Sept. 1831 ; Capt. do. 29 Dec. 1837 ; Capt. 1st Royal Surrey Mil. 6 Oct. 1852 ; Major do.

Refs. : Burke's *Landed Gentry*, 7th edn., p. 216, *s.n.* Broderip, of Cossington Manor, Somerset. *Alumni Oxon.* *G.M.* 1864, i. 677.

SCOTT, George Robertson (1793-1854). Captain. Artillery. (430) *b.* Edinburgh 3 May 1793. Cadet 1810. Admitted 27 Aug. 1811. Fireworker 16 Aug. 1811. Lieut. 25 Sept. 1817. Capt. 28 Sept. 1827. Retired 17 May 1833. *d.* 19 Aug. 1854.

bapt. St. Andrew's, Edinburgh, 27 June 1793. Son of George Robertson Scott, advocate, and Isabella his wife, dau. of Rev. John Pattison, seceding minister.

Services : Operations in Rewah 1813 ; joined battering train under Lt.-Col. George Raban, *q.v.,* Oct. 1813. Siege and capture of Hathras ; Lt. F. 2nd Coy. 2nd Bn. Foot Art. Third Mahratta War ; Asirgarh ; Lieut. 2nd Coy. 2nd Bn., afterwards 3rd Coy. 2nd Bn. Fur. s.c. 2 Feb. 1825 till 23 Nov. 1829 ; p.a. 26 Nov. 1830 till retirement. Retired on h.p., viz., 7/- *p.d.*

SCOTT, Henry (1762-?). Bt. Captain. Infantry. *b.* Shrewsbury 29 June 1762. Cadet 1779. Admitted 16 Nov. 1779. Ensign 20 Aug. 1779. Lieut. 30 Mar. 1781. Bt. Capt. 7 Jan. 1796. Resigned 14 Mar. 1798. (Living in 1829.)

Of Beslow Hall, Salop. *bapt.* St. Chad's, Shrewsbury, 1 July 1762. 5th and youngest son of Jonathan Scott, of Shrewsbury, and Mary his wife, dau. of Humphrey Sandford, of the Isle of Rossal. Brother of Jonathan Scott (1753-1829), *q.v.,* uncle of Jonathan Scott (1788-1838), *q.v.,* cousin-german of Edward Sandford, *q.v.,* and kinsman of Jonathan Scott (1760-1803), *q.v.* *m.* Mary, eldest dau. of his kinsman John Scott, of Eyton, and sister of Jonathan Scott (1785-1824), *q.v.* (She died Cheltenham 16 Aug. 1855, aged 80.)

Services : Sailed for India in the *Ganges* 7 Mar. 1779. Was Fort Adjt. & Bk. Mr. at Chunar from before Mar. 1786 till 16 Nov. 1792, when he went to the Cape on sick leave. He would appear to have returned to Calcutta at the end of 1800.

THE BENGAL ARMY, 1758-1834 35

Refs.: Burke's *Landed Gentry,* 13th edn., p. 1570, *s.n.* Scott, of Betton, Salop. *Misc. Gen. et Her.* 3S. iv. 58-9. *Whinyates Family Records. E.I.M.C.* ii. 243*n.*

SCOTT, James (*d.* 1775). Captain, Infantry. Cadet 1764. Ensign 5 Jan. 1765. Lieut. 9 Dec. 1766. Capt. 18 Apr. 1769. *d.* Dinapore 19 Mar. 1775.

Services: Sailed for India in the *Success* 17 May 1764. First Rohilla War 1774; battle of St. George.

SCOTT, James (*d.* 1772). Cadet, Infantry. Cadet 1772. *d.* Dinapore 19 Jan. 1772.

Services: N.F.P.

SCOTT, James (1778-1820). Lieut. Colonel, 3rd N.I. *b.* Pitarrow, Fordoun, co. Kincardine, 18 Feb. 1778. Cadet 1794. Arrived in India 3 Mar. 1797. Ensign 9 Nov. 1795. Lieut. 20 May 1797. Capt. 19 Feb. 1806. Major 12 Apr. 1815. Lt. Col. 19 Feb. 1820. *d.* at sea 11 Aug. 1820, on board the *Castle Huntley* off P.W.I.

Son of Archibald Scott. *m.* Barrackpore 26 Sept. 1801, Eliza, eldest dau. of Sir Henry White, K.C.B., *q.v.* (*See also* Goodwin Warner.) (She died London 25 Oct. 1860, aged 84.) Father of James Warner Scott and of the wife of John William Ingram, *qq.v.*

Services: Apptd. Cadet 25 May 1796; sailed for India in the *Royal Admiral* 11 Aug. 1796. Lieut. 3rd N.I.; Capt. Lt. do. 21 Sept. 1804; Adjt. 1/3rd N.I. 1805-6. (? Operations in Bundelkhand 1809; Rajaoli; Ajaigarh; Capt. 1/3rd N.I.) Nepal War 1814-15; Major 2/3rd N.I., in 1st Div.

Refs.: Pester, p. 445. *Cal. Gaz.* 1 Oct. 1801.

SCOTT, James Warner (1803-1844). Lieutenant, Pension Est. Artillery. (487) *b.* Calcutta 27 Sept. 1803. Cadet 1818. Admitted 1 Jan. 1820. 2nd Lieut. 14 Apr. 1819. Lieut. 14 Jan. 1821. Pensioned 28 Jan. 1833. *d.* Calcutta 30 Mar. 1844.

Son of James Scott (1778-1820), *q.v.,* and Eliza his wife. Addiscombe Cadet 1818-19.

Services: First Burma War; Chittagong 1824; disaster at Ramu 17 May (s.w.) (*Lond. Gaz.* 27 Nov. 1824).[1] Apptd. to charge of Magh Pioneers 27 Nov. 1824. Fur. s.c. 11 Sept. 1826 till 27 Mar. 1830, and 3 Jan. 1831 till 30 Oct. 1832.

Refs.: I.M. 6 June 1844, p. 433.

[1] *Note:* One of three survivors. After being wounded he was tied on an elephant which took fright at the tumult and bolted, to which fact he owed his life.

SCOTT, John. Lieutenant. Infantry. Lieut. 4 Sept. 1768. Resigned 6 Nov. 1773.
m. (before 1768) Penelope.
Services : Lieut. H.M.S. ; apptd. in England a Lieut. on Bengal Est. 24 Dec. 1767. (*Probably* one or other of the two following : (1) Apptd. an addl. Ensign 79th Ft. 20 Dec. 1759 ; Lieut. do. 18 Sept. 1760 ; ? h.p. on reduction 1763-92 ; not in 1796 *A.L.* (2) Lieut. 66th Ft. 10 Sept. 1762 ; h.p. 1763-98 ; not in 1799 *A.L.*) Was a Lieut. in 3rd Bde. on resignation.

SCOTT, John. Cadet. Infantry. Cadet 1768. Resigned 21 Feb. 1769.
(*Perhaps* identical with the foregoing.)

SCOTT, John (1747-1819). (*See* **SCOTT-WARING, John.**)

SCOTT, John (1772-1808). Captain, 10th N.I. *bapt.* St. Chad's, Shrewsbury, 31 May 1772. Cadet 1794. Arrived in India 23 Feb. 1796. Ensign 7 Dec. 1795. Lieut. 30 Oct. 1797. Capt. 30 Oct. 1806. *d. unm.* at sea 20 Nov. 1808 : lost in the *Experiment*.
Eldest son of John Scott, of Eyton, and Sarah Corall his wife. Brother of Jonathan Scott (1785-1824), *q.v.*, and of Mary, wife of his kinsman Henry Scott, *q.v.*
Services : Apptd. Cadet 22 Apr. 1795 ; sailed for India in the *Earl Fitzwilliam* 9 July 1795. Lieut. 1/9th N.I. in Aug. 1798 ; transfd. to 10th N.I. 1798. Adjt. 2/10th N.I. 1804-6. Second Mahratta War 1805-6 ; Lieut. 2/10th N.I. Fur. 28 Sept. 1808 till death. " Struck off *A.L.* from 24 Jan. 1809, being a passenger on board one of the ships supposed to be lost."
Refs. : Burke's *Landed Gentry*, 2nd edn., p. 1198, *s.n.* Scott, of Betton, Salop. *G.M.* 1810, i. 491. Will dated 18 Oct. 1805 ; proved 21 May 1810.

SCOTT, John (1781-1832). Major. 8th N.I. *b.* Lessudden, co. Roxburgh, 19 Mar. 1781. Cadet 1798. Arrived in India 5 Mar. 1800. Ensign 27 Dec. 1799. Lieut. 29 May 1800. Capt. 22 Aug. 1812. Major 3 Jan. 1820. Retired 8 Apr. 1823. *d. unm.* Ravenswood 28 June 1832.
Of Ravenswood. 5th and youngest son of Walter Scott, of Raeburn, and Jean his wife, 3rd dau. of Robert Scott, of Sandyknowe.
Services : Posted Lieut. to 1/8th N.I. 15 Apr. 1801. Operations in Jumna Doab 1803 ; Sasni ; Bijaigarh ; Lieut. 1/8th N.I.

THE BENGAL ARMY, 1758-1834 37

Second Mahratta War 1804-5 ; capture of Deig ; Bhurtpore ; Lieut. 1/8th N.I. Fur. 1808-12. Capt. 1/8th N.I. S.A.C.G. 5 Aug. 1814 till 1819. Major 2/8th N.I. Fur. 10 Dec. 1820 till retirement.

Refs.: Burke's *Landed Gentry*, 12th edn., p. 1680, *s.n.* Scott, of Raeburn and Lessudden. *A.J.* N.S. viii. 227.

SCOTT, John (1801-1848). Major, 55th N.I. *b.* Dysart, co. Fife, 26 Jan. 1801. Cadet 1817. Admitted 3 Oct. 1818. Ensign (3 May 1818) 28 Sept. 1818. Lieut. 1 Jan. 1819. Capt. 13 Dec. 1830. Major 3 May 1845. *d.* Nowgong 15 June 1848.

Son of Capt. William Scott, H.C.S., and Catherine Reddie his wife. Nephew of Capt. John Reddie, Master Attendant at Madras, and ward of John Barclay. *m.* Calcutta 3 Apr. 1834, Harriet Jenny, eldest dau. of George Hunter (1785-1819), *q.v.* (*See also* E. T. Milner.) (She died Meerut 3 Apr. 1846.)

Services: Posted Lieut. to 1/28th N.I. 1819 ; transfd. to 55th N.I. (late 1/28th) May 1824 ; Adjt. do. 21 Oct. 1825 till 15 Jan. 1831. Bde. Major to troops in Oudh 22 Feb. 1838 till 21 Oct. 1840 ; do. at Ferozepore 9 Mar. 1842 till 30 Mar. 1843. With Army of Reserve (for Afghanistan) at Ferozepore Oct. 1842 till Jan. 1843. (? First Sikh War ; Major 55th N.I.)

Refs.: *I.M.* 22 Aug. 1848, p. 495.

SCOTT, John Augustus (1803-1845). Major, Invalid Est. 1st L.C. *b.* Calcutta 1 July 1803. Cadet 1819. Admitted 22 Aug. 1820. Cornet 3 Apr. 1820. Lieut. 1 May 1824. Capt. 24 Oct. 1828. Major 1 Jan. 1844. Invalided 4 Apr. 1844. *d.* Meerut 2 Dec. 1845.

bapt. Calcutta 26 July 1803. Son of William Scott and Elizabeth his wife. Nephew of Thomas Scott. *m.* Benares 24 May 1823, Julia Frances, eldest dau. of Sir William Ouseley, Kt. (*See also* John Fowler Bradford.) (She died 1869.)

Services: Posted Cornet to 1st L.C. 1820, and served throughout with that Regt. Fur. p.a. 3 Jan. 1831 till 24 Nov. 1832. First Afghan War 1842 ; Tazin (*Lond. Gaz.* 24 Nov. 1842) ; Kabul ; Bt. Major 1st L.C., with Pollock's force (Medal).

Refs.: Foster's *Baronetage*, p. 477, *s.n.* Ouseley, Bart. Burke's *Visitation of Seats & Arms*, ii. 13. Will dated Simla 16 June 1845 ; proved 18 May 1846.

SCOTT, Jonathan (1753-1829). Captain. Infantry. *b.* Shrewsbury 8 Mar. 1753. Cadet 1770. Ensign 27 Dec. 1772. Lieut. 24 Mar. 1777. Capt. 22 Mar. 1781. Resigned 28 Jan.

1785. *d.* at his residence, St. John's Row, Shrewsbury, 11 Feb. 1829.

Of Netley Cottage, Salop. *bapt.* St. Chad's, Shrewsbury, 1 Apr. 1753. 3rd son of Jonathan Scott, of Shrewsbury, and Mary his wife. Brother of Richard Scott, and uncle of Charles Edward Hastings Scott-Waring, *qq.v. m.* his cousin Anne, dau. of Rev. Daniel Austen, rector of Berrington, Salop. Ed. Repton and Shrewsbury.

Services : See *D.N.B.* Posted Ensign to 29th Bn. Sepoys 1772. First Mahratta War 1780-1 ; capture of Gwalior ; action at Mahatpur Mar. 1781 ; Persian Intr. to Major William Popham, *q.v.*, Apr. 1781, and afterwards to Lt.-Col. Jacob Camac, *q.v.* Campaign against the Rajah of Benares 1781 ; outbreak at Benares in Aug. ; capture of Bijaigarh ; Persian Intr. to Popham. Succeeded William Davy, *q.v.*, as Persian Sec. to Warren Hastings 1782-5. Returned to England with Hastings 1785. Professor of Oriental languages at R.M.C. 1802-5, and held a similar position in E.I. Coll., Haileybury, about same time. Pub. translations of various Oriental works, including, 1811, his edn. of the " Arabian Nights Entertainment " in 6 vols. D.C.L., Oxon, 26 June 1805. Hon. LL.D., Cambs., 1808.

Refs. : Burke's *Landed Gentry*, 13th edn., p. 1570, *s.n.* Scott, of Betton, Salop. *Misc. Gen. et Her.* 3S. iv. 58-9. *Repton School Register. Shrewsbury School Register. Alumni Oxon. D.N.B. D.I.B. Grier. A.J.* xxvii. 520. *G.M.* 1829, i. 470.

SCOTT, Jonathan (1760-1803). Major (? Lt. Col.), 10th N.I. *b.* Shrewsbury 21 Feb. 1760. Cadet 1777. Admitted 18 Dec. 1777. Ensign 2 Feb. 1778. Lieut. 13 Sept 1778. Capt. 11 Dec. 1795. Major 24 Feb. 1800. (? Lt. Col. 23 Jan. 1803.) *d. unm.* at sea 6 May 1803, on board the *Lady Burges.*

bapt. St. Chad's, Shrewsbury, 25 Feb. 1760. 3rd son of Richard Scott, of Betton, Salop, and Elizabeth his wife, dau. of Rev. Thomas Gough, rector of Cardington, Salop. Kinsman of Henry Scott, *q.v.*

Services : Apptd. Cadet 13 Nov. 1776 ; sailed for India in the *Ceres* 28 Feb. 1777, aged 17. Second Mysore War 1781-5 ; Lieut. 26th N.I., with Col. Pearse's detachment. Third Mysore War 1790-2 ; Bangalore ; Arikera ; operations before Savandrug ; Utradrug ; Seringapatam ; Lieut. 26th Bn., with Lt.-Col. Cockerell's detachment. Major 10th N.I. Fur. 8 Mar. 1803 till death.

Refs. : Burke's *Landed Gentry*, 12th edn., p. 1677, *s.n.* Scott, of Betton, Salop. *E.I.M.C.* ii. 243 *n. G.M.* 1803, ii. 882.

SCOTT, Jonathan (1785-1824). Captain, 16th N.I. *bapt.* St. Chad's, Shrewsbury, 14 Sept. 1785. Cadet 1800. Arrived in India 23 Aug. 1801. Ensign 25 Sept. 1801. Lieut. 13 July 1803. Capt. 21 July 1818. *d.* Uppington, nr. Shrewsbury, 8 Aug. 1824, aged 38.[1]
3rd son of John Scott, of Eyton, and Sarah his wife. Brother of John Scott (*d.* 1808), *q.v. m.* (?)
Services: Ensign 10th N.I. Second Mahratta War 1805-6; Lieut. 10th N.I. Adjt. 2/10th N.I. 16 July 1808 till Dec. 1816. Operations in Rewah 1813-14; Entauri; Lieut. 2/10th N.I. Capt. Lt. 1/10th N.I. 30 Oct. 1817. Sec. & Persian Intr. to O.C. Nagpur Subsdy. Force 16 Dec. 1816; do. Narbada F.F. 1819-21. Capt. 2/10th N.I. Third Mahratta War 1817-19. 1st A.A.G. of the Army 1821-4. Fur. s.c. 1824 till death.
Refs.: Burke's *Landed Gentry*, 2nd edn., p. 1198, *s.n.* Scott, of Betton, Salop. *A.J.* xviii. 333. Will dated 7 Jan. 1824; proved 2 May 1825.
[1] *Note:* "Long service in the field brought on epilepsy, which occasioned his death." (*A.J.*)

SCOTT, Jonathan (1788-1838). Captain. Artillery. (362) *b.* Rotherhithe, Surrey, 10 July 1788. Cadet 1804. Arrived in India 13 May 1806. Lieut. 1 Apr. 1806. Capt. Lt. 6 May 1817. Capt. 1 Sept. 1818. Invalided 25 July 1832. Retired 19 Feb. 1835. *d.* 7 June 1838.

Son of Folliott Scott and Mary his wife, *née* Brookman. Nephew of Richard Scott and cousin-german of Charles Edward Hastings Scott-Waring, *qq.v. m.* Adelaide. (She died Dum-Dum 8 Oct. 1821, aged 22.)
Services: Present as a Cadet at capture of Cape Jan. 1806. Capture of Java 1811; Cornelis; Adjt. detachment of Bengal Art. Fur. p.a. 27 Jan. 1817 till 3 Sept. 1821. First Burma War; Assam 1824. Posted to 2nd Troop 3rd Bde. H.A. 1825. Siege and capture of Bhurtpore; Capt. comdg. 3rd Bde. H.A. Leave s.c. 12 mos. to Mauritius 31 Mar. 1828. Transfd. to 6th Bn. Foot Art. 10 Nov. 1831. Leave s.c. to Cape and Mauritius 17 Sept. 1832 till retirement.
Refs.: Burke's *Landed Gentry*, 13th edn., p. 1570, *s.n.* Scott, of Betton, Salop.

SCOTT, Patrick (*d.* 1801). Bt. Captain, 5th N.I. Cadet 1782. Arrived in India Mar. 1783. Ensign 12 Mar. 1783. Lieut. 23 Feb. 1790. Bt. Capt. 7 Jan. 1796. *d.* Bond St., London, 29 Oct. 1801.

Services : Apptd. Cadet 19 Dec. 1781 ; sailed for India in H.M.S. *Yarmouth.* Apptd. actg. Adjt. of Invalids at Monghyr 27 May 1788 ; permanent do. 9 July 1793. Transfd. from 1st to 4th Bengal Eur. Bn. 5 Feb. 1790 ; to 6th do. ; to 3rd Eur. Regt. June 1796 ; to 5th N.I. Fur. 14 Jan. 1799 till death.
Refs. : *G.M.* 1801, ii. 1060.

SCOTT, Richard (1750-1824). Lieut. Colonel. 4th N.I. *b.* 24 July 1750. Cadet 1768. Admitted 1 Sept. 1768. Ensign 12 Feb. 1769. Lieut. 15 May 1770. Capt. 26 Aug. 1779. Major 1 Mar. 1794. Lt. Col. 1 June 1796. Retired 9 Sept. 1797. *d.* Welbeck St., London, 21 May 1824.

Of Welbeck St. ; owned land at Bognor. 2nd son of Jonathan Scott, of Shrewsbury, and Mary his wife. Brother of John Scott-Waring, *q.v.* *m.* 1st, Calcutta 24 Sept. 1785, Miss Charlotte Jarret. *m.* 2nd, Woking 19 Aug. 1794, Letitia, 5th dau. of John Camac, of Green Mount, co. Louth, and sister of Jacob Camac, *q.v.* (*See also* William Lane (1753-1814).)

Services : Sailed for India in the *Grenville* 7 Apr. 1768. Joined 3rd Bengal Eur. Regt. Feb. 1769 ; apptd. Adjt. 3rd Sepoy Bde. Nov. 1772 ; Dy. Judge Advocate at Berhampore Jan. 1775. A.D.C. to Col. Ironside, *q.v.,* comdg. 3rd Bde., 1777 ; Bde. Major 3rd Bde. 1778-81. Capt. 2/3rd Bengal Eur. Regt. in Oct. 1779. Posted to newly-formed 24th N.I. Jan. 1781 ; transfd. to 1/26th N.I. at end of 1781. Second Mysore War 1781-5 ; Capt. 26th N.I., comdg. his Bn. from Mar. 1782. Kld. Samuel Kilpatrick, *q.v.,* in a duel at Madras 24 Aug. 1781. For this he was tried by C.M. and acquitted. Third Mysore War 1790-2 ; Bangalore ; Utradrug ; Seringapatam ; Capt. comdg. 26th N.I. Fur. 6 Oct. 1792 till 1796. Posted Lt. Col. to 4th N.I. 1796. Pub. 1808, " The Battle of Maida : an epic Poem."

Refs. : Burke's *Landed Gentry,* 13th edn., p. 1569, *s.n.* Scott, of Betton, Salop. *Misc. Gen. et Her.* 3S iv. 58-9. His private journals pub. in *Naval & Mily. Mag.,* Vols. i-iv (1827-8). *E.I.M.C.* i. 315-20. *G.M.* 1824, i. 645. Will dated 16 July 1823 ; proved 13 Feb. 1827.

SCOTT, Samuel (*d.* 1797). Bt. Captain, Infantry. Country Cadet 1781. Admitted 26 Feb. 1781. Ensign 24 Aug. 1781. Lieut. 8 June 1783. Bt. Capt. 7 Jan. 1796. *bur.* Cawnpore 19 Feb. 1797.

Brother of William Scott (*d.* 1804), *q.v.*

Services : Was Adjt. 34th Bn. Sepoys on 1 Mar. 1787 ; posted to 2nd Cav. Regt. 14 Dec. 1787. Third Mysore War 1790-2 ; Utradrug; Seringapatam; Lieut. 1st Cav. and 26th Bn. Sepoys. From 1st Cav. to d.d. 1st Vol. Bn. 22 Nov. 1791; d.d. 26th Bn. Sepoys 10 Dec. 1791; transfd. to 2nd Cav. 13 Jan. 1792. Apptd. Sec. and Persian Intr. to O.C. troops in the field Dec. 1793; D.A.G. at date of death.

Refs.: Naval & Mily. Mag. iv. 19.

SCOTT, Thomas (*d.* 1810). Major. Infantry. Lieut. 10 Sept. 1768. Capt. 29 Mar. 1777. Major 4 Feb. 1781. Struck off 1793. *d.* 8 July 1810.

Of Lochmalony, co. Fife. Son of James Scott, W.S., and Margaret his wife, dau. of Andrew Marjoribanks, of that Ilk. Brother of Charles Scott (*d.* 1802), *q.v. m.* Calcutta 5 Sept. 1780, Miss Ann Bethune. (She died 10 Nov. 1812.)

Services: Ensign 42nd Ft. 16 Sept. 1760; Lieut. 2/42nd Ft. —; h.p. 1763 till death. Transfd. as Lieut. from H.M.S. (M.C. 1 Sept. 1768). First Rohilla War 1774; battle of St. George; Lieut. 2nd Bn. Sepoys. Apptd. Dy. Judge Advocate at Berhampore 26 Sept. 1777; do. 1st Bde. 20 Sept. 1778; Judge Advocate do. 15 Oct. 1778. Capt. 1st Bengal Eur. Regt. in Oct. 1777; to comd. 1st Bn. Sepoys 16 Aug. 1779. First Mahratta War 1779-81; Capt. 1st Bn. Sepoys. To comd. 3rd N.I. 24 July 1781; comdg. 9th N.I. in Apr. 1786; Major 6th Bengal Eur. Bn. in July 1787. On fur. in Dec. 1788.

Refs.: S.M. 1810, p. 639.

SCOTT, Thomas (1783-1872). Lieutenant. 6th N.I. Subsequently Bde. Major of Yeomanry in Ireland. *b.* 20 Oct. 1783. Cadet 1800. Arrived in India 24 Aug. 1801. Ensign 8 Jan. 1802. Lieut. 30 Sept. 1803. Resigned 12 Feb. 1806. *d.* Jan. 1872.

Of Willsboro', co. Londonderry. J.P. and D.L.; high sheriff 1844. 2nd son and heir of James Scott, of Willsboro', and Catharine Elizabeth his wife, dau. of James Leslie, D.D., bishop of Limerick. *m.* 1st, 1 Dec. 1823, Hannah, widow of John Campbell, of Newtownlimavady. *m.* 2nd, 1827, Anne, 3rd dau. of Rev. Edward Lucas, of Rathconnell, co. Monaghan. (She died 1840.) *m.* 3rd, 1844, Katharine Elizabeth, eldest dau. of Rev. Thomas Richardson, of Somerset, co. Londonderry.

Services: Ensign d.d. 11th N.I. in 1802; posted Ensign to 6th N.I. Second Mahratta War 1803-4; reduction of Cuttack; capture of Balasore; Lieut. 6th N.I., d.d. 1st Vol. Bn.

Refs.: Burke's *Landed Gentry of Ireland*, p. 629, *s.n.* Scott, of Willsboro', co. Londonderry.

SCOTT, Thomas Hare (1805-1851). Bt. Major, C.B., 38th N.I.
b. 24 Nov. 1805. Cadet 1822. Arrived in India 3 May 1823.
Ensign 14 Feb. 1823. Lieut. 13 May 1825. Capt. 25 Sept. 1837.
Bt. Major 23 Dec. 1842. *d.* Lucknow 28 Sept. 1851.

bapt. Helston, Cornwall, 4 May 1806. Son of Charles Scott, of Trevardrevor, Cornwall, atty., and Mary his wife. *m.* Harriet.

Services: Posted to 1/3rd N.I. 22 May 1823; transfd. to 19th N.I.; to 38th N.I. (late 1/19th) May 1824. Fur. s.c. 18 Jan. 1829 till 8 June 1832. Adjt. 38th N.I. 25 Aug. 1832 till 31 Oct. 1837. First Afghan War 1839-42; operations against the Ghilzais under Lt.-Col. G. P. Wymer, *q.v.*; action at Ilmi 29 May 1841, comdg. Wing 38th N.I.; actg. Bde. Major to troops at Kandahar 12 Jan. 1842; action nr. Kandahar 12 Jan. 1842; Goaine (*Lond. Gaz.* 24 Nov. 1842); Bde. Major 1st Inf. Bde. (Medal). Supt. of family money and Paymr. of Native pensioners in Oudh and Cawnpore 25 Nov. 1842 till death. C.B. 27 Dec. 1842.

Refs.: G.M. 1852, i. 105.

SCOTT, William (*d.* 1804). Colonel, Bengal Eur. Regt. Resdt. at Delhi. Cadet 1771. Admitted 14 Oct. 1771. Ensign 5 Jan. 1773. Lieut. 1 Apr. 1777. Capt. 27 Mar. 1781. Major 25 Apr. 1797. Lt. Col. 14 July 1799. Col. 1 May 1804. *d. unm.* Agra 27 Sept. 1804.

Brother of Samuel Scott, *q.v.*, Ann, and Mary. (? Ed. Merchant Taylors' Oct. 1766-Apr. 1767; if so, *b.* 13 Feb. 1754.)

Services: Sec. and Persian Intr. to Maj.-Gen. Giles Stibbert, *q.v.*, 1781-5. A.A.G. of Bengal Army; D.A.G. (with official rank of Major) 16 May 1786; Adjt. Gen. 1796. Third Mysore War 1791-2; on the staff of Lord Cornwallis, the G.G. Apptd. Persian Intr. to Sir Robert Abercromby, the C.-in-C., 6 Oct. 1793. Capt. 3rd Eur. Regt. in 1796; Major 1st N.I. Posted Lt. Col. to 1/10th N.I.; transfd. to 2/13th N.I. 25 Oct. 1799. Resdt. at Lucknow 1799-1804; apptd. Resdt. at Delhi 25 Feb. 1804. Lieut. Col. and Col. Bengal Eur. Regt. The first translator of the Articles of War into Persian.

Refs.: (? *Robinson.*) *Macpherson*, p. 331. *E.I.M.C.* ii. 242 *n.* G.M. 1805, i. 486. Will dated Lucknow 19 Mar. 1802; codicil 16 Apr. 1804; proved 24 Nov. 1804.

SCOTT, William (1763-1808). Lieut. Colonel, 6th N.I. *b.* Jan. 1763. Madras Cadet 1777. Transfd. to Bengal Est. 14 Sept. 1779. Cornet 22 Aug. 1779. Lieut. 10 Apr. 1781. Capt. 25 Dec. 1797. Major 1 Oct. 1803. Lt. Col. 24 Dec. 1806. *d.* at

THE BENGAL ARMY, 1758-1834   43

sea 18 May 1808, on board the *Britannia*, on his passage home from St. Helena.

Son of Charles Scott, of Bavelaw, and Frances his wife, dau. of John Vicaradge. Brother of Primrose Scott, maid of honour to Queen Charlotte. His dau. by a " Persian princess " *m*. David Lester Richardson, *q.v. m*. St. Helena 2 Dec. 1800, Henrietta, 2nd dau. of Col. Francis Robson, Madras Est., Lt. Govr. of St. Helena.

Services: Sailed for Madras in the *Calcutta* 27 Apr. 1778. Cornet on Madras Est. Lieut. 11th Bn. Sepoys in July 1787 and in Dec. 1788. To proceed with Vols. to Madras 9 Aug. 1791; posted to 2nd Vol. Bn. 27 Dec. 1791. Third Mysore War 1791-2; Seringapatam; Lieut. 2nd Vol. Bn. Adjt. 24th Bn. Sepoys in Jan. 1794; Capt. 1/1st N.I. in July 1798; transfd. to 4th N.I. 1798. Second Mahratta War 1803; Capt. 4th N.I. Posted Major to 2/23rd N.I., which he raised at Cawnpore Nov. 1803. Transfd. as Lt. Col. to 6th N.I. Fur. 1 Apr. 1807 till death.

Refs.: *Scott, 1118-1923*, by Keith S. M. Scott, p. 264. *Cal. Gaz.* 22 Nov. 1810. *Misc. Gen. et Her.* 5S. i. 94.

SCOTT, William Lloyd Lewis (1806-1888). Major. 1st L.C. *b*. Kingston-on-Thames 14 Nov. 1806. Cadet 1823. Arrived in India 19 May 1824. Cornet 17 Jan. 1824. Lieut. 13 May 1825. Capt. 27 Aug. 1842. Retired 31 Mar. 1851. Hon. Major 28 Nov. 1854. *d*. Brooklands, Reigate, 27 Sept. 1888.

bapt. 27 Dec. 1806. Son of William Scott and Elizabeth his wife. *m*. Bath Abbey 23 Apr. 1838, Anne Eliza Montague, eldest dau. of Tobias Kirkwood, Col. 40th and 64th Regts. (She died 30 June 1892, aged 88.)

Services: Posted to 1st L.C. 1824, and served throughout with that Regt. Actg. Intr. & Qmr. 11 July 1829, and 5 Aug. 1832. Fur. p.a. 6 Jan. 1836 till 13 Nov. 1838. Actg. Adjt. 6 May 1839, and 7 Sept. 1840; permanent do. 23 Jan. till 17 Feb. 1841. First Afghan War 1842; Capt. 1st L.C., with Pollock's advance on Kabul (Medal). Second Sikh War; passage of Chenab; Chilianwala; Gujerat; Capt. 1st L.C. (Medal with 2 clasps).

Refs.: Burke's *Landed Gentry*, 13th edn., p. 1031, *s.n*. Kirkwood, of Yeo, Devon. *The Times*, 2 Oct. 1888.

CORSE-SCOTT, Alexander (1803-1879). Colonel. 70th N.I. *b*. Synton, co. Selkirk, 15 Dec. 1803. Cadet 1819. Admitted 17 Apr. 1820. Ensign 14 Feb. 1820. Lieut. 11 July 1823. Capt. 25 Sept. 1837. Major 31 Mar. 1853. Bt. Lt. Col. 20 June 1854. Retired 7 Nov. 1857. Hon. Col. 7 Nov. 1857. *d. unm*. Bowland House, Midlothian, 14 June 1879.

44 LIST OF THE OFFICERS OF

bapt. Ashkirk 22 Jan. 1804. 2nd son of John Corse, of Bughtrig (who adopted the name of Scott, of Synton, in addition to his own, on marriage), and Catherine his wife, sister of John Scott, of Synton. Brother of James Corse-Scott, q.v. Ed. Edinburgh.

Services : Posted Ensign to 1/6th N.I. 1820 ; transfd. to Bengal Eur. Regt. July 1823 ; to 37th N.I. 18 Oct. 1824 ; to newly-raised 2nd Extra Regt. (became 70th N.I.) May 1825. Fur. s.c. 4 Aug. 1826 till 24 Nov. 1829. Tempy. comdg. Bhopal Contingent Feb. 1832 till Feb. 1833. Fur. s.c. 6 Mar. 1836 till 25 Oct. 1840. Second Sikh War ; Ramnagar ; passage of Chenab ; Chilianwala ; Gujerat ; Bt. Major 70th N.I. (Medal with 2 clasps). Fur. Jan. 1857 till retirement.

Refs. : Burke's Landed Gentry, 12th edn., p. 1682, s.n. Corse-Scott, of Synton, co. Selkirk. The Times, 18 June 1879.

CORSE-SCOTT, James (1810-1890). Major General. 20th N.I. b. Edinburgh 2 June 1810. Cadet 1825. Arrived in India 22 Oct. 1826. Ensign 27 June 1826. Lieut. 3 Oct. 1828. Capt. 24 Jan. 1845. Major 27 Aug. 1858. Lt. Col. 18 Feb. 1861. Col. 18 Feb. 1866. Retired 1 Sept. 1866. Hon. Maj. Gen. 1 Sept. 1866. d. unm. at his residence, 8 The Royal Terr., Edinburgh, 7 Mar. 1890.

bapt. Tron church, Edinburgh, 13 July 1810. 3rd son of John Corse-Scott, of Synton, and Catherine his wife. Brother of Alexander Corse-Scott, q.v. Ed. Edin. High School and St. Andrews Univ. ; matric. 22 Dec. 1825.

Services : Ensign d.d. 20th N.I. 9 Nov. 1826 ; posted to 20th N.I. 8 Jan. 1827 ; actg. Intr. & Qmr. do. 13 Apr. 1830 ; permanent do. 1 Oct. 1833 till 25 Dec. 1837. S.A.C.G. 1 Mar. 1837. First Afghan War 1839 ; Ghazni ; Lieut. 20th N.I., Comst. Dept. (Medal). Leave s.c. to Cape and N.S.W. 24 Feb. 1841. D.A.C.G. 2 cl. 4 Oct. 1844 ; 1 cl. 13 Sept. 1847 ; A.C.G. 2 cl. 9 Sept. 1850 ; 1 cl. 9 Nov. 1852 ; Dy. Comy. Gen. 29 Oct. 1858 ; offg. Comy. Gen. in 1861 and 1863. Transfd. to Staff Corps 18 Feb. 1861. Leave s.c. 2 yrs. to Aust. and N.Z. Apr. 1851 ; fur. s.c. 11 Mar. 1864 till retirement.

Refs. : Burke's Landed Gentry, 12th edn., p. 1682, s.n. Corse-Scott, of Synton, co. Selkirk. The Times, 19 Mar. 1890.

*SCOTTNEY or SCOTNEY,[1] Bryan. Captain. Infantry. Subsequently a Free Merchant. Capt. 12 Mar. 1758. Resigned 23 Oct. 1758. (Living at Madras in 1787.)

His dau., Mrs. Frances Smith, died Calcutta 30 May 1801, aged 35.

Services : Ensign (Madras) 22 Apr. 1754. On service in Madras under Stringer Lawrence. Served in Bengal under Clive 1757 ; battle of Plassey ; Lieut. & Adjt. of Capt. Edmund Maskelyne's Coy. Transfd. to Bengal Est. as Capt. 1758 ; resigned owing to supersession by John Gowen, q.v., and returned to England. Permitted to return to Bengal as a free merchant 26 Mar. 1760. Alderman of Calcutta 1761, and was trading at Patna in Oct. 1765. C.D. resolved on 8 July 1761 to restore him to the Service, but he wrote on 24 Aug. 1762, declining to accept a comd. inferior to his former rank. In England 1767-73. Apptd. by C.D. in England, Feb. 1777, Mily. Storekeeper at Madras and held this appt. 1778-86.

[1] *Note :* Mr. Brian Scotney d. Lower Clapton 10 Aug. 1885, aged 80.

SCRYMGEOUR, John (1746-1791). Captain, comdg. 28th Bn. Sepoys. bapt. Edinburgh 30 Nov. 1746. Cadet 1769. Ensign 13 Dec. 1769. Lieut. 27 Mar. 1773. Capt. 6 Jan. 1781. d. unm. Ooscotta (Hoskote), Mysore, 3 Mar. 1791.

2nd son of David Scrymgeour, of Birkhill, advocate and sheriff depute of co. Inverness, and Katharine his wife, 6th dau. of Sir Alexander Wedderburn, 4th Bart. of Blackness.

Services : Returned from fur. 1780. Apptd. A.D.C. to Col. Sir John Cumming, q.v., May 1781 ; A.Q.M.G. to detachment under Sir John Feb. 1783. Was Bde. Major at Fatehgarh in Mar. 1786 ; apptd. Bde. Major 4th Bde. 12 June 1786 ; Capt. comdg. 28th Bn. Sepoys in Dec. 1788. Third Mysore War 1790-1 ; Capt. comdg. 28th Bn., with force under Lt.-Col. John Cockerell, q.v.

Refs. : *The Wedderburn Book.* Burke's *Landed Gentry,* 13th edn., p. 1853, s.n. Scrymgeour-Wedderburn, of Wedderburn, co. Forfar. *Williams,* p. 89. *Edin. Evening Courant,* 23 Feb. 1792. Will dated 15 Mar. 1790 ; admon. 6 June 1791. Portrait in youth at Birkhill.

*SEABRIGHT, William (d. 1771). Ensign, Infantry. Cadet 1770. Ensign 20 June 1770. d. in India 1771 : kld.

Services : N.F.P.

*SEAGRAVE, John. Captain. Infantry. Capt. 1 Feb. 1765.

Services : Lieut. H.M. 79th Regt. ; h.p. do. (?) till after 1785. " Lieut. John Seagrave, H.M. 79th Regt., to be a Capt. in H.C.S. and rank from 1 Feb. 1765, agreeable to his engagement with Hon. the Presdt. and Council of Fort St. George, in consequence of raising a Coy. for this (Bengal) Presdy." (G.O. 17 Feb. 1765.) Posted to 3rd Bengal Eur. Regt. 2 Aug. 1765. Not in *A.L.* of 1 Feb. 1767.

Refs.: B.M. Add. MSS. 6050.

Note: One of this name sailed as a Cadet for Madras in the *Essex* 5 Feb. 1762, aged 19. He was *probably* a nephew of Neill Segrave, of Cabra, co. Dublin, and may be identical with the Madras Cadet.

SEALE, Benjamin (1757/58-1793). Ensign. Infantry. Subsequently Lieut. Madras Est. *b.* 1757/58. Cadet 1780. Ensign Apr. 1781. Transfd. to Madras 15 Oct. 1781. *d.* Palamcottah, Madras, 31 Mar. 1793, aged 35.

Of the St. Helena family. Brother of Francis William, John and Sarah. Uncle of Lieut. Stephen Young, St. Helena Regt.

Services: Apptd. a Gent. Vol. in the Coy. of Art. 3 Sept. 1780, and served as such in Col. Pearse's detachment during Second Mysore War. Ensign (Madras) 19 Dec. 1780; Lieut. 17 Apr. 1786.

Refs.: Will dated Dindigul, 2 Jan. 1792; proved (Madras) 1793. M.I. in new burial ground at Palamcottah.

*SEALE, John (*d.* 1761 ?). Ensign, Infantry. Cadet (?) Ensign (?) (? *d.* in India 1761.)

Owned land in St. Helena. Brother of William, George, Frances and Caroline. (*Probably* related to Robert Henry Seale, *q.v.*)

Services: N.F.P.

Refs.: Will undated; admon. 21 Aug. 1761.

SEALE, Robert Henry (1806-1869). Lieut. Colonel. 20th N.I. *b.* St. Helena 6 Jan. 1806. Cadet 1824. Arrived in India 21 May 1825. Ensign 7 Dec. 1824. Lieut. 2 Sept. 1827. Capt. 8 Feb. 1841. Bt. Major 11 Nov. 1851. Retired 31 May 1853. Hon. Lt. Col. 1857. *d.* Dehra Dun 1 Apr. 1869.

Owned landed property at Landour, U.P. *bapt.* St. Helena 27 Oct. 1806. Son of William Seale, Major St. Helena Regt., and Anne his 3rd wife, dau. of Capt. Watkin Greentree, St. Helena Regt. *m.* Delhi 1 Jan. 1836, Sarah Emma, dau. of Joseph Henry Taylor, sometime Dy. Collector of Delhi, formerly a Lieut. in the Mahratta service, and grand-dau. of Joseph Taylor (1765/66-1811), *q.v.* (She died Mussoorie 14 Aug. 1890, aged 70.)

Services: Ensign d.d. 2nd Bengal Eur. Regt. 10 June 1825; posted to 38th N.I. 1825; transfd. to 20th N.I. 1826. Second Sikh War; passage of Chenab; Chilianwala; Gujerat; Capt. 20th N.I. (Medal with 2 clasps). Leave s.c. 1 yr. to Mussoorie 20 Nov. 1849.

Refs.: M.I. Dehra Dun.

SEALY, Charles (1775-1820). Major, Artillery. (286) *b.* 13 Oct. 1775. Cadet 1790. Admitted 19 Sept. 1791. Fireworker 27 Mar. 1791. Lieut. 14 Jan. 1798. Capt. Lt. 23 May 1804. Capt. 13 May 1807. Major 25 Sept. 1817. *d.* Daurutpore, between Nasirabad and Agra 29 June 1820.

bapt. Calcutta 21 Jan. 1776. Eldest son of Charles Sealy, register of the supreme court, Calcutta, and Mary his wife, *née* Hammond. His sister was mother of Francis Thornhill (Baring), 1st Baron Northbrook. *m.* Penang 9 Feb. 1803, Elizabeth Palmer, dau. of John Mannington, Bencoolen C.S. (She *re-m.* 25 June 1824, Bailie Golding, B.C.S.) His dau. *m.* her cousin-german, Rt. Rev. Charles Baring, D.D., bishop of Durham.

Services: Apptd. Cadet 2 Feb. 1791; sailed for India in the *Northumberland* 16 Apr. 1791. On service to Madras for siege of Pondicherry Aug.-Oct. 1793; Lieut. F. 4th Coy. 1st Bn. Bde. Major of Art. 27 Feb. 1809 till 1817.

Refs.: Will dated 11 Dec. 1818; proved 27 Sept. 1820. M.I. in tomb of his brother, John Nathaniel Sealy, B.C.S., in N. Park St. cemetery, Calcutta.

SEALY, John Bellett (1780-1816). Major, 20th N.I. *b.* London 10 Dec. 1780. Cadet 1796. Arrived in India 29 Jan. 1798. Ensign 11 Oct. 1797. Lieut. 10 Sept. 1798. Capt. 9 May 1805. Major 8 Apr. 1816. *d.* Barrackpore 2 June 1816.

bapt. St. Peter-le-Poor, London, 19 Dec. 1780. Son of Benjamin Sealy and Elizabeth his wife.

Services: Posted Ensign to 2nd Bengal Eur. Regt. 1798; Lieut. Marine Regt. (became 20th N.I.). Second Mahratta War 1803-4; surveying with Lt.-Col. E. S. Broughton's detachment. Was serving at P.W.I. in 1807. Capture of Java 1811; Capt. 1/20th N.I. Returned to Bengal Apr. 1814. Nepal War 1816; Capt. 1/20th N.I., comdg. 8th Gren. Bn., in 2nd Bde. Left Column.

Refs.: Will dated Ramnagar, Saran district, 31 Jan. 1816; proved 7 June 1816. M.I. in old cemetery at Barrackpore.

SEARLE, William (1792-1812). Ensign, 14th N.I. *b.* London 18 Aug. 1792. Cadet 1808. Arrived in India 1 June 1810. Ensign 23 Apr. 1811. *d.* Agra 20 Sept. 1812.

Son of Francis Searle.

Services: Barasat C.C. 1810-11. Posted to 2/14th N.I. 1811. No record of active service.

Refs.: M.I. Agra Cantt. cemetery.

SEARS, Samuel (*d.* 1781). Major. Infantry. Subsequently Lt. Colonel Madras Est. Capt. (Madras) 10 July 1765. Transfd.

to Bengal Est. 1766. Major (Bengal) 3 Oct. 1769. Resigned 30 Mar. 1772. *d*. Madras 28 Dec. 1781.

Related to Major Richard Harding, Madras Est. *m*. Mary. (She died Maryland 1787.) Father of Samuel Sears, *q.v.*

Services : Ensign 3rd Bn. 60 Ft. (R. American) 23 June 1758 ; Lieut. do. 4 Oct. 1760 ; h.p. do. 1763 till death. Apptd. in England 2 Nov. 1764, Capt. on the Madras Est. ; sailed in the *Horsenden* 29 Jan. 1765. Transfd. to Bengal Est. owing to the " Batta mutiny " ; retransfd. to Madras Est. after 1773. Fur. to England Mar. 1772 till 1775.

Refs. : Intestate ; admon. 6 Feb. 1782.

SEARS, Samuel (1751-1794). Lieut. Colonel, Artillery. (100) *b*. 1751. Lieut. Fireworker (Bo. Art.) 26 Feb. 1768. Transfd. to Bengal Art. 22 Sept. 1770. Lieut. 8 Mar. (? 18 Sept.) 1770. Capt. Lt. 7 Oct. 1778. Major (1786). Lt. Col. 28 Nov. 1788. *d*. Calcutta 19 Aug. 1794.

Son of Samuel Sears, *q.v. m*. Mary. Father of Samuel Montague Sears (*see* Appendix C). (? Ed. Merchant Taylors' Sept. 1764-Mar. 1766.)

Services : Resigned 22 Sept. 1773 and was granted a passage to England in the *Mercury* ; readmitted Sept. 1776 and returned in the *Duke of Kingston* via Madras. First Mahratta War ; joined the force Mar. 1781 ; returned to Cawnpore with the Bengal detachment Apr. 1784. Fur. 27 Oct. 1785 till 1788.

Refs. : (? Robinson.) *Spring*, No. 84. Will dated 8 Aug. 1794 ; proved 6 Oct. 1794.

SEATON, Douglas (1810-1860). Bt. Colonel, 1st Eur. Bengal Fus. *bapt*. Pontefract, Yorks., 24 Aug. 1810. Cadet 1828. Arrived in India 15 Sept. 1829. Ensign 5 June 1829. Lieut. 29 July 1836. Capt. 6 Feb. 1846. Major 14 Sept. 1856. Lt. Col. 17 Mar. 1860. Bt. Col. 15 Oct. 1857. *d*. Camden Sq., London, 7 Dec. 1860, aged 50.

Son of John Fox Seaton, of Pontefract, afterwards of Clapham, merchant and banker, and Anne his wife, 5th and youngest dau. of Thomas Brown, of Upper Tooting, Surrey, a claimant of the Montagu (Browne) peerage. Brother of Sir Thomas Seaton, *q.v.*

Services : Ensign d.d. 31st N.I. 19 Oct. 1831 ; posted to Left Wing Bengal Eur. Regt. 2 Aug. 1832. Fur. p.a. without pay 27 Feb. 1832 till 10 Jan. 1834. Actg. Adjt. 1st Bengal Eur. L.I. 8 Sept. 1842. With Army of Reserve (for Afghanistan) Oct. 1842 till Jan. 1843. First Sikh War ; Ferozshahr ; Sobraon (comdg. the

THE BENGAL ARMY, 1758-1834

Regt.—horse shot under him); Capt. 1st Eur. Bengal Fus. (Medal with clasp). Fur. s.c. 25 Feb. 1849 till 2 Jan. 1852. Second Burma War 1852-3; relief of Pegu; accompanied Martaban Column under Bdr.-Gen. Steele; comdd. storming party at assault of Gongah stockade 18 Jan. 1853; Bt. Major 1st Eur. Bengal Fus. (Medal). Mutiny campaign; Bt. Col. 1st Eur. Bengal Fus. Fur. 1859 till death.

Refs.: Burke's *Landed Gentry*, 7th edn., p. 1648, *s.n.* Seton, of Cariston, co. Fife. *Family of Seton*, by Geo. Seton (Edin., 1896), ii. 759. *N. & Q.* clxxxviii. 78-80. *G.M.* 1861, i. 114. *The Times*, 11 Dec. 1860.

SEATON, Francis (Lambert [1]**)** (1808-1837). Captain, 66th N.I. *b.* May 1808. Cadet 1824. Arrived in India 12 June 1825. Ensign 25 Jan. 1825. Lieut. 4 Aug. 1827. Capt. 21 Aug. 1834. *d.* Betul, C.P., 15 Nov. 1837.

Ward of Maj.-Gen. John Lambert.[2] *m.* Calcutta 15 July 1833, Eliza, 2nd dau. of Capt. Daniel Ross, and sister of William Hercules Ross, *q.v.* (She died 21 Nov. 1865, aged 51.)

Services: Ensign d.d. 2nd Bengal Eur. Regt. 21 June 1825; posted to 48th N.I. 1825; transfd. to 66th N.I. 1826; Intr. & Qmr. do. 27 Jan. 1830 till 18 Sept. 1834. S.S.O. Arakan 27 Apr. 1831 till 17 Aug. 1832; in charge of bldgs. at Kyaukpyu 1 Apr. 1831 till 1 Mar. 1833. No record of active service.

Refs.: *A.J.* N.S. xxv. 257. M.I. at Betul.

[1] *Note:* The only authority for this second name is his widow's obit. notice.

[2] *Note:* ? Gen. Sir John Lambert, G.C.B. (*D.N.B.*)

SEATON, Sir Thomas (1806-1876). Major General, K.C.B. 1st Eur. Bengal Fus. *b.* Feb. 1806. Cadet 1821. Arrived in India 2 Jan. 1823. Ensign 4 Feb. 1823. Lieut. 1 May 1824. Capt. 2 Apr. 1834. Major 17 Nov. 1852. Lt. Col. 27 June 1857. Bt. Col. 13 Oct. 1857. Retired 3 June 1859. Hon. Maj. Gen. 3 June 1859. *d.* Châtou, Paris, 11 Sept. 1876.

Of Ackworth House, E. Bergholt, Suffolk. *bapt.* 28 May 1806. Eldest son of John Fox Seaton and Anne his wife. Brother of Douglas Seaton, *q.v.* *m.* 1st, 21 Aug. 1831, Caroline, 4th dau. of Charles Corfield, of Knowle Lodge, Taunton. (*See also* John Assey Fairhead.) (She died on the river nr. Kishnaghur 14 Nov. 1835.) *m.* 2nd, Edinburgh 27 July 1838, Elizabeth, only dau. of John Harriman, of Whitehaven (of Tivoli), Cumberland.

Services: See *D.N.B.* Posted to 1/10th N.I.; transfd. to 2/17th N.I. July 1823; to 35th N.I. (late 2/17th) May 1824. Siege and capture of Bhurtpore; Lieut. 35th N.I. (India medal). Fur. p.a. 25 Dec. 1835 till 14 Jan. 1839. First Afghan War 1839-42 ; rejoined 35th N.I. at Kabul 8 Sept. 1839; forcing of Khurd Kabul and Jagdalak Passes ; defence of Jalalabad (Medal) ; action of 7 Apr. 1842; comdd. 35th N.I. from 16 Apr. 1842 during the different engagements leading to reoccupation of Kabul by Pollock's force (*Lond. Gaz.* 11 Feb. & 24 Nov. 1842) (Medal). Bde. Major at Agra 1 Oct. 1844 till 1851. Fur. s.c. 10 Jan. 1852 till Dec. 1854. Comdd. 35th N.I. at Sialkot Jan. 1855 till May 1857 ; took comd. of 60th N.I. at Ambala 15 May 1857. Mutiny campaign 1857-8 ; siege of Delhi (s.w. 23 July 1857); Patiali ; Mainpuri ; Bdr. comdg. at Fatehgarh during siege of Lucknow (Medal with clasp). Transfd. to 35th N.I. 17 Dec. 1857 ; to 1st Eur. Bengal Fus. 14 Jan. 1858. Wrote his autobiog., "From Cadet to Colonel," 1st edn. 2 vols., 1866. C.B. 24 Dec. 1842 ; K.C.B. 24 Mar. 1858.

Refs. : Burke's *Landed Gentry*, 8th edn., p. 1823, *s.n.* Seton, of Cariston, co. Fife. *Walford. D.N.B. D.I.B. Boase. I.L.N.* Vol. xlix. 584 (portrait). *The Times*, 15 Sept. 1876, p. 4. M.I. Winchester cathedral.

SEDGWICK, John (*d*. 1769). Ensign, 2nd N.I. Cadet 1767. Ensign 15 Sept. 1767. *d*. (? Bankipore, B. & O.) 27 Mar. 1769.
Services : Sailed for India in the *Calcutta* 31 Dec. 1766.
Refs. : Will dated 26 Nov. 1768 ; proved 20 Oct. 1769.

SEEDS, John Campbell (1791-1811). Ensign, 17th N.I. *b.* Portsea, Hants, 19 Nov. 1791. Cadet 1807. Arrived in India 14 Aug. 1808. Ensign 25 Sept. 1808. *d*. Plymouth 18 Feb. 1811.
bapt. Portsea 23 Dec. 1791. Son of Thomas Seeds, of Portsea, surgeon, and Mary Ann his wife.
Services : Barasat C.C. Posted to 17th N.I. 1809. Fur. s.c. 17 July 1810. No record of active service.
Refs. : *Hampshire Telegraph*, 4 Mar. 1811.

*****SEGRAVE, John.** (*See* **SEAGRAVE, John.**)

SELLECK or SELLICK, James ($171\frac{4}{5}$-?). Captain. Infantry.

bapt. West Monkton, Somerset, 21 Jan. $171\frac{4}{5}$. Ensign (Madras) 2 Sept. 1759. Lieut. (Madras) 26 Dec. 1762. Capt. (Madras) 12 Nov. 1765. Transfd. to Bengal Est. 1766. Resigned 2 Apr. 1773.

Son of Henry Selleck and Mary his wife. Elder brother ot John Selleck. Ed. Winchester; K.S. 1729; left 1733. Univ. Coll., Oxon.; matric. 11 Mar. $173\tfrac{3}{4}$, aged 18. Barr.-at-law, Middle Temple, 1741.

Services: (? Lieut. in H.M.S.) Sailed for Madras as a Lieut. in the *Duke of Dorset* in 1758, when he gave his age as 35. Transfd. to Bengal Est. in 1766 owing to the "Batta mutiny."

Refs.: *Kirby* (where date of *bapt.* is incorrectly given as 21 Jan. $171\tfrac{6}{7}$). *Alumni Oxon. Wilson,* ii. 336.

SELWYN, George Brydges (1779-1803). Lieutenant. 1st N.I. *b.* Ludgarshall, Wilts., 3 Jan. 1779. Cadet 1799. Admitted 7 Aug. 1800. Ensign 4 Sept. 1800. Lieut. 30 June 1802. Resigned 27 Jan. 1803. *d.* at sea 1 Aug. 1803, on board the country ship *Varuna* on his passage to England.

bapt. Ludgarshall 23 Jan. 1779. Eldest son of Rev. John Selwyn, rector of Ludgarshall, and Bridget his wife, dau. of William Dyer, of Bristol. Nephew of Samuel Dyer, *q.v.* Ed. Charterhouse; admitted scholar 23 Jan. 1789; exhibitioner 7 Apr. 1796. Worcester Coll., Oxon.; matric. 4 May 1796.

Services: Posted Ensign to 2/1st N.I. 17 Apr. 1801. Fur. s.c. 1803. No record of active service.

Refs.: *Alumni Carthusiani. Alumni Oxon. G.M.* 1803, ii. 789.

SEMPILL, Hon. George (*d.* 1779). Lieut. Colonel. Infantry. Lt. Col. 1 Sept. 1768. Resigned 22 Sept. 1773. *d.s.p.* Bishopstown, co. Renfrew, 18 Dec. 1779.

2nd son of Hugh, 12th Lord Sempill, and Sarah his wife, dau. of Nathaniel Gaskell, of Manchester. His niece *m.* Daniel MacGregor, *q.v. m.* 1st, Catherine, dau. of Arthur Gordon, of Wardhouse. (She died 5 Feb. 1762.) *m.* 2nd, Moreton Say 1 Dec. 1764, his cousin Anne, dau. of Richard Clive, of Styche, and sister of Robert, 1st Lord Clive. (? She died Midnapore Mar. 1771, aged 30.) *m.* 3rd, Manchester 15 June 1775, Jane, dau. and heir of Thomas Butterworth, and widow of Francis Jodrell, of Yeardsley.

Services: Ensign 19th Ft. 25 Dec. 1732; Qmr. 25 June 1739; Lieut. 15 Nov. 1740; Capt. Lt. 24 Apr. 1755. Capt. 53rd Ft. 19 Oct. 1755; Major 31 Jan. 1766; sold out as Major 53rd Ft. 13 Apr. 1768. Sailed for India in the *Grenville* 7 Apr. 1768; transfd. as Lt. Col. to Bengal Est. 1 Sept. 1768. Returned to England in the *Northington* Dec. 1773.

52 LIST OF THE OFFICERS OF

Refs.: Burke's *Peerage*, 1923, p. 1993, *s.n.* Sempill, B. *Howard & Crisp (Notes),* xi. 28, *s.n.* Clive. *Officers of the Green Howards,* by Major M. L. Ferrar.

SEMPLE or SEMPILL, James (*d.* 1782). Cadet, Infantry. Cadet 1782. Never arrived in India. *d.* at sea 12 Nov. 1782, on board the *Busbridge,* on the voyage out.
Services: Apptd. Cadet 24 Apr. 1782 ; sailed for India in the *Busbridge* 11 Sept. 1782.

SENIOR, William (1800-1826). Lieutenant, 25th N.I. *b.* Aldenham, Herts., 23 Jan. 1800. Cadet 1816. Lieut. 1 Aug. 1818. *d.* Calcutta 9 Sept. 1826.
bapt. Aldenham 17 Mar. 1800. Son of Rev. John Raven Senior, of Muswell Hill, and Mary his wife, dau. of Henry Duke, of Barbados. Brother of Nassau William Senior (*D.N.B.*). *m.* Calcutta 30 Aug. 1820, Eliza, dau. of Isaac Beardsmore, of Bhowanipore, Calcutta. (She *re-m.* F. B. Lardner, *q.v.*) Addiscombe Cadet 1816-17.
Services: Posted Lieut. to 2/20th N.I. 1818. Fur. s.c. 1822-3. Transfd. to 25th N.I. (late 1/20th) May 1824. No record of active service.
Refs.: Will dated 24 Oct. 1824 ; proved 13 Sept. 1826. M.I. Bhowanipore mily. cemetery, Calcutta.

SEPPINGS, Alworth Merewether (1811-?). Lieutenant. Artillery. (600) *b.* Greenwich 26 July 1811. Cadet 1827. Arrived in India 9 June 1828. 2nd Lieut. 13 Dec. 1827. Lieut. 3 Mar. 1835. Resigned 19 Aug. 1840.
bapt. Greenwich 11 May 1813. Son of John Milligen Seppings, of Chudleigh, formerly surveyor of sloops, Custom House, afterwards (from 1817) surveyor, Marine Dept., Calcutta, and Ann Marshall his wife. Nephew of Sir Robert Seppings, Kt., Surveyor of the Navy (*D.N.B.*). Addiscombe Cadet 1825-7.
Services: d.d. Assam L.I. 3 Mar. 1836 till 26 May 1838. No record of active service.

SEPPINGS, John (1785-1823). Captain, 20th N.I. *b.* Southacre, Norfolk, 28 Dec. 1785. Cadet 1803. Arrived in India 2 Dec. 1804. Ensign 26 Oct. 1804. Lieut. 26 Oct. 1804. Capt. 1 Aug. 1818. *d.* Barrackpore 13 Mar. 1823.
bapt. ptely. Southacre 29 Dec. 1785. Son of William Seppings and Sarah his wife, *née* Martin.
Services: Posted Lieut. to 20th N.I. 1805. Was serving at P.W.I. 1806-7. Capture of Java 1811 ; Lieut. 2/20th N.I. Adjt.

THE BENGAL ARMY, 1758-1834 53

2/20th N.I. 26 Aug. 1813 till 1818. Bde. Major to Bengal detachment in Ceylon 1818. Comdg. at Singapore 1819-21. Capt. 2/20th N.I.
Refs.: M.I. at Barrackpore.

*SERLE or SEARLE, Thomas. Ensign, Infantry. Cadet 1771. Ensign 16 Feb. 1773. *d.* 177–.
Services: Applied on 9 Apr. 1772, to resign his Cadetship and return to Europe in the *Colebrooke*. N.F.P.

*SETON, Robert (1777-1797). Lieutenant, Infantry. *b.* Edinburgh 1 June 1777. Cadet 1794. Admitted 8 Dec. 1794. Ensign 18 Sept. 1794. Lieut. 8 Jan. 1796. *d.* Masulipatam 29 Dec. 1797.
bapt. Edinburgh 18 June 1777. 19th and youngest child of Daniel Seton, of Powderhall, lace merchant in Edinburgh, and Rebecca his 2nd wife, eldest dau. of John Meggat, merchant. Half-brother of Daniel Seton, Bo.C.S., Lt. Govr. of Surat.
Services: Apptd. Cadet 26 Apr. 1794; sailed for India in the *Pitt* 20 June 1794. N.F.P.
Refs.: Burke's *Landed Gentry*, 13th edn., p. 1011, *s.n.* Seton-Karr, *formerly* of Kippilaw, co. Roxburgh. *Family of Seton*, ii. 327. *S.M.* 1798, p. 791.

SEWELL, Thomas (1798-1862). Major General. 25th N.I.
bapt. Madras 24 Jan. 1798. Cadet 1818. Admitted 4 Sept. 1819. Ensign 3 Sept. 1819. Lieut. 2 Dec. 1820. Capt. 7 Dec. 1827. Major 20 Nov. 1845. Lt. Col. 13 Oct. 1851. Bt. Col. 28 Nov. 1854. Retired 31 Dec. 1861. Hon. Maj. Gen. 31 Dec. 1861. *d.* 40 Devonshire St., Portland Pl., London, 18 Sept. 1862, aged 65.
Son of Henry Sewell, sometime H.M. Naval Officer at the port of Madras, later of the firm of Chase, Chinnery & Sewell, Madras, and Rebecca his wife, *née* Chase. *m.* 1st, Calcutta 6 May 1828, Mary Susannah, dau. of Patrick Martin Hay, *q.v.* (He divorced her in 1841, obtaining £2,000 damages.) *m.* 2nd, Calcutta 29 Oct. 1842, Adéle, dau. of John Abbott (? and sister of Henry Abbott, *q.v.*).
Services: Was already in India when apptd. Cadet. Posted Lieut. to 1/5th N.I. 8 Jan. 1821; transfd. to 20th N.I. (late 2/5th) May 1824; Intr. & Qmr. do. 13 July 1824; exchanged to 11th N.I. 16 Aug. 1824; Intr. & Qmr. do. 16 Aug. 1824 till 12 Aug. 1828. Siege and capture of Bhurtpore; Lieut. 11th N.I. (India medal). Offg. Agent for army clothing, 2nd Div., 10 Mar. 1827; permanent do. 31 Mar. 1828 till Oct. 1851. Posted Lt. Col. to 21st N.I. 13 Jan.

1852 ; to 24th N.I. June 1852 ; to 25th N.I. Jan. 1854, and was comdg. this Regt. on outbreak of Mutiny. Though disaffected, and consequently disbanded in 1859, the Regt. did not break into open revolt.

Refs. : *A.J.* xxvi. 487 ; N.S. xxiii. 200. *I.N.* No. 20, p. 469. *The Times,* 24 Sept. 1862.

Note : He called out J. H. Stocqueler (*D.N.B.*), editor of the *Englishman,* at Howrah in Jan. 1837, on account of an article which had appeared in that paper on 24 Jan.

SEYER, Richard Twine (1786-1833). Lieut. Colonel, 41st N.I. *b.* Bristol 9 Jan. 1786. Cadet 1800. Arrived in India 23 Aug. 1801. Ensign 29 Nov. 1801. Lieut. 13 July 1803. Capt. 1 Aug. 1818. Major 27 Jan. 1826. Lt. Col. 2 Jan. 1831. *d. unm.* Aurangabad 20 Apr. 1833.

bapt. St. Michael's, Bristol, 12 May 1786. Son of William Seyer, merchant in Bristol, and Sarah his wife, dau. of Capt. Twine of that port. Brother of Sarah Seyer, of 6 Allen's Terr., Kensington.

Services : Ensign d.d. 16th N.I. in 1802 ; posted Ensign to 6th N.I. Operations in Bundelkhand 1805-6 ; Lieut. 2/6th N.I. With escort to Resdt. with Sindhia 1 May 1811 till 1814. Nepal War 1814-15 ; Kalanga ; Jampta 27 Dec. 1814 (s.w.) ; Lieut. 1/6th N.I., in 2nd Div. Transfd. to newly-raised 1/28th N.I. 1815 ; Capt. Lt. 23 Nov. 1815. Nepal War 1816 ; A.D.C. to Maj.-Gen. Jasper Nicolls, H.M.S., and in charge of Guide and Intelligence Dept. of force assembled at Sitapur from 22 Feb. 1816. Adjt. Native Invalids at Allahabad 1817. Served with Nizam's army June 1817 till death. Third Mahratta War ; operations in Berar 1818. Operations against Umerkhed 20 Jan. 1819 ; comdg. a detachment of 600 horse and 400 inf. Defeated the freebooter Sheikh Dalla 12 Oct. 1824 ; comdg. Ellichpur Bde. Comdg. Aurangabad Div. Apr. 1831, and in charge of Cav. Div. of Nizam's army. Reduction of fort Nandgaon, nr. Mominabad, Apr.-Aug. 1832. Transfd. to 55th N.I. (late 1/28th) May 1824. Posted Lt. Col. to 51st N.I. 10 Sept. 1831 ; to 41st N.I. 16 Oct. 1832.

Refs. : *Burton.* Will dated Aurangabad 16 Apr. 1833 ; proved 23 July 1833. M.I. at Aurangabad and St. Michael's, Bristol.

SEYMER, Edward (*d.* 1776). Ensign, Infantry. Cadet 1772. Ensign 3 Apr. 1773. *d.s.p.* 13 Mar. 1776.

5th son of Henry Seymer, of Hanford, Dorset, and Bridget his wife, dau. of Thomas Haysome, of Weymouth.

Services : Sailed for India in the *Duke of Albany* 18 Feb. 1772,

THE BENGAL ARMY, 1758-1834 55

which was lost on the Long Sand 25 July 1772. First Rohilla War; battle of St. George.

Refs.: Burke's *Landed Gentry*, 13th edn., p. 1586, *s.n.* Seymer, of Hanford.

SEYMOUR, Robert (1789-1868). Colonel. 21st N.I. *b.* British factory, Petrograd, 5 Dec. 1789. Cadet 1803. Arrived in India 30 Sept. 1805. Ensign 21 Aug. 1805. Lieut. 22 Aug. 1805. Capt. 11 July 1823. Major 21 Jan. 1829. Lt. Col. 23 Apr. 1834. Retired 4 Jan. 1841. Hon. Col. 28 Nov. 1854. *d.* Brompton Cresc., London, 3 Dec. 1868.

bapt. Petrograd 30 Dec. 1789. Son of Anthony Seymour and Ann his wife, *née* Piding.

Services: Posted Lieut. to 13th N.I. 1806. d.d. 6th Bn. Bengal Vols. 1811-16. Capture of Java 1811; Lieut. 6th Vol. Bn. (Medal). Expedn. to Palembang 1812; Comy. of provisions. Actg. Fort Adjt. & Paymr. I. of Banca Sept. 1813. Third Mahratta War 1818-19; Mandala; Asirgarh; Lieut. 2/13th N.I. Fur. p.a. 7 Feb. 1821 till 10 Oct. 1824. Transfd. to 26th N.I. (late 1/13th) May 1824. First Burma War; Arakan 1825 (w. 27 Mar.); Capt. 26th N.I. (*Lond. Gaz.* 6 Oct. 1825) (India medal). Siege and capture of Bhurtpore; Bde. Major 4th Bde., 1st Div. (clasp to India medal). Bde. Major on Est. with troops in Cuttack 15 Jan. 1827; D.A.A.G. on Est., Presdy. Div. 28 Jan. 1828 till 11 Apr. 1829. Fur. s.c. 18 Mar. 1833 till 5 Sept. 1835. Posted Lt. Col. to 34th N.I. 10 Sept. 1834; to 74th N.I. 8 Sept. 1835; to 22nd N.I. 7 Nov. 1839; to 21st N.I. 3 Oct. 1840.

Refs.: The Times, 5 Dec. 1868.

SEYMOUR, William Frederick Augustus (1804-1829). Lieutenant, 68th N.I. *b.* Winchester 16 Nov. 1804. Cadet 1820. Arrived in India Sept. 1821. Ensign 5 May 1821. Lieut. 21 Dec. 1823. *d.* in India 8 May 1829.

Son of Maj.-Gen. Richard Augustus Seymour, Govr. of I. of St. Lucia 1816-18, and Anna Maria his wife. Sandhurst Cadet.

Services: Posted to 2/18th N.I. 1821; transfd. to newly-raised 34th N.I. July 1823; to 68th N.I. (late 2/34th) May 1824. First Burma War; Arakan 1825; Lieut. 68th N.I. Adjt. Murshidabad Provl. Bn. 1826; do. Farrukhabad 29 Aug. 1826 till death.

SHADWELL, George John (1786-1840). Lieut. Colonel, Invalid Est. 7th L.C. *b.* London 13 Aug. 1786. Cadet 1806. Arrived in India 1 Aug. 1807. Cornet 27 July 1807. Lieut. 30 June 1818. Capt. 3 Apr. 1822. Major 7 July 1833. Lt. Col.

19 May 1838. Invalided 5 Aug. 1839. *d. unm.* Mussoorie 9 Nov. 1840.

bapt. St. Andrew's, Holborn, 26 Jan. 1787. 5th and youngest son of Lancelot Shadwell, of Beamish, in Albrighton, Salop, and of Lincoln's Inn, London, barr.-at-law, and Elizabeth Sophia his 1st wife, dau. of Charles Whitmore, of Southampton. Brother of Henry Shadwell, *q.v.*, and of Rt. Hon. Sir Lancelot Shadwell, Vice-Chancellor of England (*D.N.B.*).

Services : Barasat C.C. 8 mos. Posted Cornet to 2nd N.C. 1808. Adjt. G.G.B.G. 14 May 1813 till 27 Jan. 1821. Third Mahratta War 1817-18 ; Adjt. G.G.B.G. Bk. Mr. Narbada Div. 29 Jan. 1821 ; do. 9th (Bundelkhand) Div. 1 Oct. 1823 till 18 Apr. 1831. Jodhpur demonstration 1834 ; Major 2nd L.C. Posted Lt. Col. to 7th L.C. 19 Sept. 1838.

Refs. : Howard & Crisp (*Notes*), v. 22, *s.n.* Shadwell. *V.B.G. G.M.* 1841, i. 222. *The Times,* 14 Jan. 1841. Will dated Mussoorie 8 July 1840 ; admon. 3 Aug. 1841.

SHADWELL, Henry (1780-1813). Lieutenant, 7th N.I. *b.* 27 Aug. 1780. Cadet 1802. Arrived in India 17 May 1803. Ensign 18 May 1803. Lieut. 10 June 1804. *d.* Malacca 24 July 1813.

bapt. St. Andrew's, Holborn, 4 Oct. 1780. 2nd son of Lancelot Shadwell and Elizabeth Sophia his 1st wife. Brother of George John Shadwell, *q.v.*, and of the wife of Robert Arding Thomas, *q.v.* Ed. Eton 1793-6. Admitted Lincoln's Inn 22 Jan. 1799.

Services : Apptd. Cadet 25 Aug. 1802. Posted Ensign to 7th N.I. With Java Inf. Vols. in 1813. Adjt. 2/7th N.I.

Refs. : Howard & Crisp (*Notes*), v. 22, *s.n.* Shadwell. *Eton School Lists. G.M.* 1814, ii. 84.

SHADWELL, John Augustus (1783-1830). Lieut. Colonel, Invalid Est. 66th N.I. *b.* London 23 July 1783. Cadet 1798. Arrived in India 25 Nov. 1799. Ensign 10 Jan. 1800. Lieut. 29 May 1800. Capt. 16 Jan. 1814. Major 1 May 1824. Lt. Col. 14 Jan. 1826. Invalided 27 Jan. 1826. *d.* Barrackpore 1 Oct. 1830.

bapt. St. Margaret's, Westminster, Aug. 1783. Son of John Shadwell and Esther his wife. His dau. *m.* William Henry Earle, *q.v.*

Services : Posted Lieut. to 1/1st N.I. 15 Apr. 1801 ; transfd. to 19th N.I. 1803 ; to newly-raised 26th N.I. 1805. Operations in Bundelkhand 1807 ; Sehlehuganj ; Bundelkhand 1809 ; Ajaigarh ;

Lieut. 26th N.I. Capt. Lt. 26th N.I. 1 Jan. 1811. Capt. 2/26th N.I. With 3rd Ceylon Vol. Bn. 1818-19. Transfd. to 1/26th N.I. ; to newly-raised 33rd N.I. July 1823 ; to 66th N.I. (late 2/33rd) May 1824. Comdd. Purnea Provl. Bn. 1826-9 ; do. Burdwan Provl. Bn. 11 Dec. 1829 till death.

Refs.: *G.M.* 1831, i. 285. Will dated 2 Apr. 1828 ; proved 14 Sept. 1831.

SHADWELL, Thomas (1752/53-1785). Lieutenant, Infantry. *b.* London 1752/53. Cadet 1780. Arrived in India Mar. 1781. Ensign 1780. Lieut. 13 Aug. 1781. *d.* Dinajpur 3 Apr. 1785.

Services : Sailed for India in the *Earl of Dartmouth* 3 June 1780, aged 27. N.F.P.

SHAIRP, Charles Mordaunt (1810-1841). Lieutenant, 61st N.I. *b.* Bathgate, co. Linlithgow, 3 Aug. 1810. Cadet 1828. Arrived in India 2 Oct. 1829. Ensign (17 Feb. 1829) 5 June 1829. Lieut. 12 Apr. 1837. *d. unm.* Etawah, U.P., 24 Oct. 1841 : committed suicide.

5th son of Major William Shairp, of Kirkton, late H.M. 29th Regt., collector of customs at Bo'ness, Linlithgow, J.P. and D.L. co. Linlithgow, and Eustatia his wife, 3rd dau. of John Davie, of Orleigh, Devon, and sister of Joseph Davie Bassett, of Watermouth, Devon.

Services : Posted to 61st N.I. 1830. (? Shekhawat expedn. 1834 ; Ensign 61st N.I.) Leave s.c. to Simla 25 July 1835 till 1 Mar. 1837. Was on his way from Agra to Calcutta on sick leave when his death occurred.

Refs. : *Howard & Crisp*, xvii. 143, *s.n.* Shairp. *G.M.* 1842, i. 341.

SHAIRP, George (1811-1838). Lieutenant, 15th N.I. *b.* London 25 June 1811. Cadet 1829. Arrived in India 13 Sept. 1830. Ensign 1 Sept. 1830. Lieut. 10 Jan. 1838. *d.* Boalia, Bengal, 15 Apr. 1838.

Son of Walter Shairp, of London, merchant, and Jane Clare his wife. Brother of Walter Shairp, of Ryde, and of Maria Eleanora, wife of John Hardy, of Cuba.

Services : d.d. 68th N.I. 23 Oct. 1830 ; Actg. Ensign (having been 2 yrs. in India) 1 Oct. 1832 ; posted Ensign to 15th N.I. 20 Aug. 1833. Fur. u.p.a. 9 Jan. 1833 till 23 Feb. 1834.
No record of active service.

Refs. : Will dated 17 Mar. 1837 ; filed 1 May 1838.

SHAIRP, John. (*See* **SHARPE, John.**)

SHAIRP, Norman (1779-1864). Captain. 12th N.I. *b.* Ayrhall 20 Oct. 1779. Cadet 1799. Arrived in India 11 Sept. 1800. Ensign 6 Oct. 1799. Lieut. 28 Oct. 1799. Capt. 26 Oct. 1808. Retired 22 May 1816. *d.* 7 Apr. 1864. Of Houston, co. Linlithgow. J.P. and D.L.; Convener of co. Linlithgow. 2nd son of Thomas Shairp, of Houston, and Mary his wife, youngest dau. of Norman McLeod, of McLeod. *m.* Calcutta 6 Mar. 1808, Elizabeth Binning, 4th dau. of John Campbell, of Kildaloig, co. Argyll, and aunt of Dugald Alexander Campbell, *q.v.*

Services : Posted Lieut. to 1/12th N.I. 15 Apr. 1801. Operations in Jumna Doab 1803; Sasni; Lieut. 12th N.I. Second Mahratta War 1803-5; Koil; Aligarh; battle of Delhi; Agra; Laswari; Monson's retreat; capture of Deig; Bhurtpore (w. in 1st assault 9 Jan. 1805); Lieut. 2/12th N.I., sometime A.D.C. to Lord Lake (India medal). Adjt. & Qmr. 12th N.I. 1805-7. Bde. Major at Berhampore 1807-9; do. at Presdy. 31 Aug. 1809. Capt. 1/12th N.I. Capture of Mauritius 1810. Fur. 9 Mar. 1811 till retirement.

Refs. : Burke's *Landed Gentry*, 13th edn., p. 1589, *s.n.* Shairp, of Houston, co. Linlithgow. Burke's *Peerage*, 1923, p. 429, *s.n.* Campbell, Bart., of Auchinbreck. *Anderson*, iii. 441. *Walford. Pester, passim. History of the Macleods*, p. 154. Burke's *R. Descents*, ped. xxiv.

SHAKESHAFT, John (1746/47-?). Ensign. Infantry. *b.* London 1746/47. Cadet 1780. Never arrived in India. Ensign 17 June 1781. Struck off 1788.

Services : Should have sailed for India in the *Royal George* 27 July 1780, aged 33.

SHAKESPEAR, Colin (1764-1835). Ensign. 1st Bengal Eur. Regt. Subsequently Senior Merchant, B.C.S. *b.* 8 Nov. 1764. Cadet 1782. Ensign 1783. Resigned 20 Feb. 1784. *d.* Berhampore 6 Apr. 1835.

bapt. St. Dunstan's, Stepney, 17 Dec. 1764. 6th son of John Shakespear, of 37 Stepney Causeway, ropemaker, alderman of the Aldgate ward 1767, sheriff 1768-9, and Elizabeth his wife, only dau. of David Currie, of Golden Sq., Crutched Friars. Brother of the wife of Laver Oliver, *q.v.*, and great uncle of Henry John Childe Shakespear and Joseph Charles Sage, *qq.v. m.* Calcutta 18 Mar. 1806, Harriot, younger dau. of William Dawson, Capt. 3rd Buffs. (She was *b.* Bath 7 June 1779; died Brighton 3 Nov. 1880.) Ed. Charterhouse July 1773-Mar. 1780.

Services : Was abroad (? in India) when apptd. Cadet 13 Mar. 1782. Posted Ensign to 1st Eur. Regt. 28 Feb. 1783. Resigned on account of ill health, and engaged in trade in Bengal. Apptd. Writer, B.C.S., 1 Aug. 1790. P.M.G. Bengal 1 Mar. 1821. Commercial Resdt. at Sonamukhi 24 Apr. 1828 till death. The inventor of " Shakespearian bridges," [1] of which he was apptd. Supt. Gen. 19 Apr. 1824.

Refs.: Family information. Pedigree of Shakespear of London, and of Brookwood, Hants, by Sir Thos. Phillipps, Bart., folio page, in Bodleian. *B.*: *P.P.* xiv. 220; xxv. 88. *A.J.* N.S. xviii. 121. M.I. at Berhampore; duplicate tomb and M.I. at Sonamukhi.

[1] *Note*: Suspension bridges constructed of coir rope with stout bamboos laid as roadway.

SHAKESPEAR, Henry John Childe (1814-1884). Lieut. Colonel. 25th N.I. *b*. Berhampore 30 Apr. 1814. Cadet 1832. Arrived in India 11 Aug. 1834. Ensign (5 Feb. 1834) 7 July 1834. Lieut. 5 July 1837. Capt. 26 Dec. 1846. Bt. Major 21 Dec. 1859. Retired 31 Dec. 1861. Hon. Lt. Col. 31 Dec. 1861. *d*. St. Leonards-on-Sea 23 Aug. 1884.

bapt. Berhampore 26 Oct. 1814. Eldest son of Henry Davenport Shakespear, B.C.S., and Louisa Caroline Tobin his wife, dau. of Benjamin Muirson. His sister *m*. Sir J. M. Higginson, *q.v.* Cousin-german of John Dowdeswell Shakespear, *q.v.*, and of Muirson Trower Blake, *q.v. m.* 1st, 24 Nov. 1839, Annie Blanche, eldest dau. of Robert Waller Poë. (She died 2 June 1857.) *m.* 2nd, Borris, co. Carlow, 14 Jan. 1863, Jane, eldest dau. of Francis Boxwell, M.D. (She died 1920.)

Services: d.d. 56th N.I. 23 Aug. 1834; posted to 4th N.I. 5 Nov. 1834; transfd. to 25th N.I. 20 May 1835. Served in Hyderabad Contingent (Nizam's army) 20 Oct. 1837 till Sept. 1854. Siege and capture of Barurgi fort 21-30 Sept. 1841; Lieut. and Adjt. 2nd Cav. Comdd. a Sqdn. of 3rd Cav. against Sikh insurgents at Hingoli Feb. 1850. Action with Arabs at Jeswantpura, nr. Aurangabad, 22 Sept. 1853; led party of dimounted troopers in capture of stockade (s.w.). Comdt. 1st Cav., Hyderabad Contingent, Feb. 1854; Comdt. newly-raised Nagpur Irreg. Force, and Comdt. Cav., 27 Sept. 1854 till retirement. Fur. s.c. 26 Sept. 1856 till 1858.

Refs.: Family information. Burke's *Landed Gentry of Ireland*, p. 568, *s.n.* Poë, of Riverston, co. Tipperary; *Landed Gentry* 13th edn., p. 313, *s.n.* Childe, of Kinlet Hall, Salop. *Burton*, pp. 124, 135, 136-7. *The Times*, 27 Aug. 1884.

SHAKESPEAR, John Dowdeswell (1806-1867). Lieut. Colonel. Artillery. (551) *b*. Bengal 23 June 1806. Cadet 1823.

Arrived in India 17 Aug. 1824. 2nd Lieut. 18 Dec. 1823. Lieut. 28 Sept. 1827. Capt. 13 Jan. 1842. Bt. Major 7 June 1849. Retired 1 Jan. 1852. Hon. Lt. Col. 28 Nov. 1854. d. 58 Warrior Sq., St. Leonards-on-Sea, 6 Apr. 1867.

bapt. Calcutta 18 Nov. 1807. Eldest son of John Talbot Shakespear, B.C.S., Member of the Presdy. Record Committee, and Emily his wife, sister of Thomas Thackeray, *q.v.*, and niece of Jane, wife of James Rennell, *q.v.* Brother of Sir Richmond Campbell Shakespear, cousin-german of Henry John Childe Shakespear, and 1st cousin once removed of Thomas Perring Moore, *qq.v. m.* St. James's, Paddington, 12 May 1853, Marianne Elizabeth, dau. of Joseph Hodgson, F.R.C.S. (*D.N.B.*). (She *re-m.* Col. William Brumell.) Ed. Harrow. Addiscombe Cadet 2 Mar. 1821 till 18 Dec. 1823.

Services : Posted to 2nd Troop 2nd Bde. H.A. 5 Aug. 1833 ; to 4th Coy. 6th Bn. Foot Art. Aug. 1836. Extra Asst. to Resdt. at Lucknow 21 Jan. 1835. Leave s.c. to Cape 6 Feb. 1839 till 27 Nov. 1840. 1st Asst. to Resdt. at Lucknow 30 Nov. 1840 till 1845. Fur. s.c. 1845-8. Second Sikh War ; Gujerat ; Capt. comdg. two 18-pdrs. and two 8-in. howitzers (Medal with clasp).

Refs. : Family information. *G.M.* 1867, i. 690. *The Times,* 10 Apr. 1867.

SHAKESPEAR, Sir Richmond Campbell (1812-1861). Bt. Colonel, Kt., C.B., Artillery. (613) *b.* in India 11 May 1812. Cadet 1827. Arrived in India 10 Feb. 1829. 2nd Lieut. 12 June 1828. Lieut. 14 May 1836. Capt. 1 May 1846. Major 14 Jan. 1858. Lt. Col. 27 Aug. 1858. Bt. Col. 28 Nov. 1854. *d.* Indore 29 Oct. 1861.

bapt. Kishnagore 13 Apr. 1813. Youngest son of John Talbot Shakespear, B.C.S., and Emily his wife. Brother of William Makepeace Shakespear, *q.v. m.* Agra 5 Mar. 1844, Marion Sophia, 3rd dau. of George Powney Thompson, B.C.S., and niece of Henry Fendall, *q.v.* (She died Bournemouth 16 Dec. 1899.) Ed. Charterhouse Sept. 1823-1825/6. Addiscombe Cadet 1827-8.

Services : See *D.N.B.* First Afghan War 1838-9 ; to Kandahar and to Girishk ; Pol. Asst. to Elliott D'Arcy Todd, *q.v.*, in his mission to Herat ; to Khiva ; obtained the release from slavery of 416 Russian subjects and escorted them to Orenburg ; carried despatches from Petrograd to London ; returned to India 1841. Afghan War 1842 ; forcing of Khyber ; Mamu Khel ; Jagdalak ; Tazin ; Mily. Sec. to Gen. Pollock 23 Feb. till 31 Dec. 1842 (Medal). D.C. Saugor 28 Mar. 1843 ; Pol. charge of Gwalior Oct. 1843 till June 1848. Gwalior campaign ; Maharajpur (*Lond. Gaz.* 8 Mar.

THE BENGAL ARMY, 1758-1834 61

1844); A.D.C. to Sir Hugh Gough (Bronze star). Second Sikh
War; Chilianwala; Gujerat (w.) (ib. 7 Mar. 1849); comdg. a
battery of 6 heavy guns (Medal with 2 clasps). P.A. Jodhpur 2 Aug.
1851; Resdt. at Baroda 13 Mar. 1857 till 1 May 1859. Pol. Comr.
of Baroda district Feb. 1858, and actg. comd. of N. Div. Bombay
Army with rank of Bdr. Gen. July 1859. A.G.G., C.I., 30 Apr.
1859 till death. Author of " A Journey from Herat to Orenburg."
Kt. 21 Aug. 1841. C.B. 18 May 1860.

Refs.: Family information. *D.N.B. D.I.B. Boase. Vibart.
Walford. Charterhouse School List. G.M.* 1862, i. 225-6. *The
Times,* 12 Dec. 1861. *B.: P.P.* vi. 297-317 (portrait). M.I.
Indore old cemetery.

SHAKESPEAR, William Makepeace (1807-1835). Lieutenant, Artillery. (565) *b.* Calcutta 29 July 1807. Cadet 1824.
Arrived in India 21 Dec. 1825. 2nd Lieut. 16 Dec. 1824. Lieut.
27 Aug. 1828. *d.* Lucknow 28 Sept. 1835.

bapt. Calcutta 16 Nov. 1807. 2nd son of John Talbot Shakespear,
B.C.S., and Emily his wife. Brother of John Dowdeswell Shakespear, *q.v.*, and of the wife of Archibald Irvine, *q.v.* Ed. Harrow.[1]
Addiscombe Cadet 1822-4.

Services: Lieut. 4th Troop 3rd Bde. H.A. 1828; 3rd Troop 2nd
Bde. 1829-35. Wahabi rising 18 and 19 Nov. 1831; comdg.
detachment H.A. (both he and his horse were contused by brickbats
at Barasat 18 Nov.). Adjt. & Qmr. 3rd Bde. H.A. 20 Aug. 1835.

Refs.: Family information. *A.J.* N.S. xix. 206.
[1] *Note:* Name not given in *Harrow School Register.*

SHAND, Charles (*d.* 1806). Captain, Pension Est. 8th N.I.
Country Cadet 1779. Admitted 19 Aug. 1779. Ensign 6 Sept.
1779. Lieut. 24 Apr. 1781. Capt. 11 July 1798. Pensioned
9 June 1803. *d.* Calcutta 5 Oct. 1806, in the Insane Hospital.

Services: Apptd. Cadet 19 Aug. 1779. Lieut. 33rd Bn. Sepoys
in July 1787 and in 1792; Capt. 8th N.I. in 1798. Was insane for
several years before his death.

SHAND, Robert. Lieutenant, Infantry. Cadet 1763. Ensign 24 Feb. 1764. Lieut. 9 Aug. 1765. Resigned 10 Aug. 1767.

Services: Campaign against the Nawabs of Bengal and Oudh
1764-5. Lieut. of Sepoys in 3rd Bde. in May 1766, when he resigned
during the " Batta mutiny "; subsequently readmitted.

Refs.: Caraccioli, ii. 473-4.

SHAPLAND, John (1776-1835). Colonel, C.B., 27th N.I. *b.*
Marshfield, Gloucs., 14 Feb. 1776. Cadet 1794. Arrived in

India 26 Oct. 1794. Ensign 20 Oct. 1794. Lieut. 3 Oct. 1796. Capt. 21 Sept. 1804. Major 11 Sept. 1811. Lt. Col. 24 Apr. 1816. Lt. Col. Comdt. 1 May 1824. Col. 5 June 1829. *d.* in England 9 (or 11) Nov. 1835.

Son of John Shapland, of Marshfield, and Martha his wife. *m.* in England Apr. 1814, Elizabeth, elder sister of Gilbert Nicholetts, *q.v.* (She died Chittagong 25 Oct. 1824.)

Services : Posted to 1st Bengal Eur. Regt. June 1796 ; Lieut. 12th N.I. in 1798 ; with 1st Bn. Vols. 1799-1800. Fur. s.c. 15 Mar. 1804 till 30 Nov. 1807. Operations in Oudh 1808 ; Capt. 12th N.I. Fur. s.c. 12 Feb. 1812 till 9 Dec. 1814. Nepal War 1816 ; Makwanpur (*Lond. Gaz.* 12 Aug. 1816) ; Major 2/12th N.I., in 3rd Bde. Centre Column. Posted Lt. Col. to 1/25th N.I. 1816 ; to 2/13th N.I. 1821. Tempy. charge of Invalid Tannah Ests. at Chittagong Nov. 1822. To comd. Chittagong frontier 2 Mar. 1824. First Burma War ; Chittagong 1824. Transfd. as Lt. Col. Comdt. to 27th N.I. (late 2/13th) May 1824. To comd. 1st Bde. on Chittagong frontier 25 Oct. 1824. Fur. p.a. 15 Jan. 1825 till death. Posted Col. to 27th N.I. 1829. C.B. 3 Feb. 1817.

SHARD, Stephen (*d.* 1773). Cadet, Infantry. Cadet 1772. *d.* Calcutta 27 Jan. 1773.

Services : N.F.P.

SHARP, David (1786-1809). Lieutenant, 15th N.I. *b.* Perth 6 Aug. 1786. Cadet 1804. Arrived in India 10 July 1805. Ensign 16 Aug. 1805. Lieut. 17 Aug. 1805. *d.* 12 Apr. 1809 : drowned on his passage from Calcutta to Barrackpore owing to the upsetting of his *paunchway* [1] in a sudden squall.

bapt. Perth 27 Aug. 1786. Son of William Sharp, merchant in Perth, and Helen Ford his wife.

Services : Posted Lieut. to 2/15th N.I. 1806. No record of active service.

Refs. : Calcutta Monthly Journal, Apr. 1809, p. 478.

[1] *Note :* A large sailing dinghy.

SHARP, Hamilton (*d.* 1771). Fireworker, Artillery. (109) Cadet (?) Fireworker 8 Apr. 1770. *d.* Dacca 15 Oct. 1771.

Services : N.F.P.

SHARP, John Nixon [1] (1811-1856). Bt. Major, Engineers. *bapt.* St. Michael's, Coventry, 19 Nov. 1811. Cadet 1829. Arrived in India 24 Sept. 1830. 2nd Lieut. 12 Dec. 1828. Lieut.

THE BENGAL ARMY, 1758-1834 63

20 May 1839. Capt. 19 Aug. 1847. Bt. Major 20 June 1854. *d.* Mian Mir 17 Aug. 1856, of cholera.

Son of Thomas Sharp, of Coventry, hat manufacturer, and Charlotte his wife. Brother-in-law of Thomas Dyer Edwards, of Worthing, and of Alexander Beattie, of London. *m.* Allahabad 24 Feb. 1840, Sophia, dau. of William Watson. (She died 5 Feb. 1890.) Addiscombe Cadet 1827 till 12 Dec. 1828.

Services: d.d. S. & M. at Delhi 23 Oct. 1830 till Apr. 1834; Asst. to Executive Engr. Allahabad Div., P.W.D., 1 May 1834; do. Cawnpore Div. 5 Aug. 1835. Suptg. repairs to Allahabad fort 1839-40; tempy. charge of Allahabad Div. 1841; permanent do. Jan. 1843. Offg. Executive Ofr. Agra Div. Aug 1843; permanent do. 27 Oct. 1843 till Nov. 1846. Gwalior campaign; Maharajpur (Bronze star). Fur. 19 Jan. 1847 till 17 Jan. 1851. Offg. Garr. Engr. Ft. Wm. and Civil Architect at Presdy. Feb. 1851; offg. Executive Engr. Mian Mir Div. 17 Oct. 1851; permanent do. May 1854. Architect of church of St. Mary Magdalene at Mian Mir. Offg. Suptg. Engr. 1st circle P.W.D. (Punjab) 13 June 1856 till death.

Refs.: De Rhé-Philipe. *G.M.* 1856, ii. 780. M.I. St. Mary Magdalene, Lahore Cantt., and R.A. cemetery, Lahore. Will dated 4 May 1852; admon. 6 Jan. 1857.

¹ *Note:* "Nickson (commonly spelt Nixon)." (Will).

SHARP(E), James (1778-1825). Major. 21st N.I. *b.* Edinburgh 25 Dec. 1778. Cadet 1794. Arrived in India 6 Jan. 1796. Ensign 24 Nov. 1795. Lieut. 30 Oct. 1797. Capt. 6 June 1805. Major 16 Mar. 1814. Retired 6 May 1815. *d.* Hastings 4 Feb. 1825.

Of Kincarrathie or Kincarrochy, co. Fife. (*Perhaps* son of Lt.-Col. James Sharp, of Kincarrochy, to whom he was served heir 16 June 1813.) *m.* Richmond, Surrey, 2 Jan. 1808, Clarissa, 5th dau. of Sir Lionel Darell, 1st Bart., Chairman E.I.Co. (She died Heavitree, Devon, 29 Aug. 1812, aged 32.)

Services: Apptd. Cadet 1 Apr. 1795; sailed for India in the *Prince William Henry* 24 May 1795. Lieut. 1/13th N.I. in Aug. 1798. Adjt. 2/1st N.I. 29 May 1800 till 1804. Transfd. to newly-raised 1/21st N.I. 1804; Adjt. do. 1804-5. Second Mahratta War 1805-6; pursuit of Holkar to Punjab; Capt. 1/21st N.I. Fur. 23 Feb. 1807 till 11 Sept. 1810, and 4 Sept. 1811 till retirement. Major 1/21st N.I.

Refs.: Burke's *Peerage*, 1923, p. 662, *s.n.* Darell, Bart., of Richmond Hill, Surrey. Howard & Crisp (*Notes*), xii. 82, *s.n.* Darell. *G.M.* 1825, i. 381.

SHARPE, James Petrie (1806-1825). Ensign, 54th N.I. *b.* Lambeth 22 May 1806. Cadet 1823. Ensign 20 May 1824. *d.* 17 Oct. 1825 : drowned nr. Ghazipur, U.P.
bapt. Jevington, Sussex, 29 July 1806. Son of Rev. John Sharpe, P.C. of Shipley, afterwards rector of Castle-Eaton, Wilts., and Clara his wife. Brother of John Grove Sharpe, *q.v.*
Services : Posted to 60th N.I. 31 Mar. 1825 ; transfd. to 54th N.I. 1825. No record of active service.

SHARPE, John (*d.* 1776). Ensign, Infantry. Cadet 1771. Ensign 26 Feb. 1773. *d.* Calcutta 12 Apr. 1776.
Services : N.F.P.

SHARPE, John Grove (1803-1833). Lieutenant, 24th N.I. *b.* Ninfield, Sussex, 14 Feb. 1803. Cadet 1822. Arrived in India 5 July 1823. Ensign 11 July 1823. Lieut. 28 Nov. 1824. *d.* at the Sandheads, Bengal, 16 July 1833, on board the *Juliana*. on his passage home.
bapt. 9 Apr. 1803. Eldest son of Rev. John Sharpe, curate ol Elsted, Sussex, and Clara his wife. Brother of James Petrie Sharpe, *q.v. m.* Mary Knight. (She died 17 Sept. 1861.)
Services : Posted to 8th N.I. ; transfd. to 24th N.I. (late 2/8th) May 1824. Leave s.c. 8 mos. to Singapore 22 Apr. 1825 ; fur. s.c. 8 Mar. 1826 till 24 Mar. 1829. Operations against the Chuars 1832-3 ; Lieut. 24th N.I., with Jungle Mehals F.F. Fur. s.c. 9 July 1833.
Refs. : A.J. N.S. xiii. 67. *G.M.* 1834, i. 231.

SHAW, David (1809-1842). Bt. Captain, 54th N.I. *b.* Calcutta 10 Mar. 1809. Cadet 1824. Arrived in India 9 Aug. 1825. Ensign 11 Apr. 1825. Lieut. 3 Sept. 1827. Bt. Capt. 11 Apr. 1840. *d.* 10 Jan. 1842 : kld. in action nr. Kabul during the retreat.
Son of Lt.-Col. William Shaw, H.M. 22nd Ft., and Ann his wife. Brother of William Shaw, *q.v.*, cousin-german of Robert Shaw, *q.v.*, and 1st cousin once removed of Sir James Shaw, 1st Bart. of Kilmarnock, chamberlain of London (*D.N.B.*); and kinsman of James Woodburn, *q.v. m.* Calcutta 11 Sept. 1833, Alicia, 2nd dau. of Simeon Henry Boileau, Register in the Persian office.
Services : Posted to 54th N.I. 1825, and served throughout with that Regt. First Afghan War 1840-2 ; outbreak at Kabul ; retreat to Butkhak 7 Jan. 1842 (s.w. in thigh) ; retreat to Tazin 10 Jan. (kld.) ; Bt. Capt. 54th N.I.

THE BENGAL ARMY, 1758-1834

Refs.: Burke's *Peerage*, 1859, p. 900, *s.n.* Shaw, Bart., of Kilmarnock. M.I. Afghan Memorial Church, Bombay.

SHAW, Francis (1773-1811). Captain, 13th N.I. *b.* I. of Dominica 4 July 1773. Cadet 1794. Arrived in India 29 Feb. 1796. Ensign 22 Oct. 1795. Lieut. 25 Apr. 1797. Capt. 23 Sept. 1804. *d. unm.* Java 28 Sept. 1811, of wounds received in action.

Son of —— Shaw and Amaranthe his wife. Brother of Lewis Simeon Shaw, *q.v.*

Services: Apptd. Cadet 28 Apr. 1795; sailed for India in the *Henry Dundas* 9 July 1795. Posted Ensign to 3rd Bengal Eur. Regt. June 1796. Lieut. 1/13th N.I. in Aug. 1798. (? Second Mahratta War 1803-4; occupation of Bundelkhand; Lieut. 1/13th N.I.) Capture of Java 1811 (s.w.); Capt. 2/13th N.I., 6th Vol. Bn.

Refs.: Will dated 1 July 1811; proved 7 May 1812. Name on cenotaph in Barrackpore park.

SHAW, George (1765/66-1786). Lieutenant, Infantry. *b.* 1765/66. Country Cadet 1778. Ensign 1778. Lieut. 21 Sept. 1780. *d.* Calcutta 1 Nov. 1786, aged 20.

Services: Apptd. Cadet 27 Feb. 1778. Ensign 1/3rd Bengal Eur. Regt. in Oct. 1779.

Refs.: M.I. Bhowanipore mily. cemetery, Calcutta.

SHAW, John (1811-1840). Lieutenant, 2nd N.I. *b.* Greenock 26 July 1811. Cadet 1827. Arrived in India 5 Oct. 1828. Ensign 11 May 1828. Lieut. 11 Feb. 1835. *d.* Kabul 3 Oct. 1840: assassinated by a *Ghazi*.

Son of John Shaw, of Wigtown, collector of customs, and Harriet his wife.

Services: Ensign d.d. 5th N.I. 5 Nov. 1828; posted to 61st N.I. 4 Mar. 1829; transfd. to 5th N.I. 1829; to 2nd N.I. 1 Oct. 1831, but remained with 5th N.I. till end of 1832. Adjt. 1st Inf., Oudh Auxy. Force, 29 Jan. 1838; rejoined 2nd N.I. for service Sept. 1838. First Afghan War 1838-40; apptd. Asst. to Paymr. and Comst. Ofr., Shah Shuja's force, 27 Nov. 1838.

Refs.: *I.N.* 11 Jan. 1841, p. 176. *A.J.* Jan. 1841. M.I. Afghan Memorial Church, Bombay.

SHAW, Joseph (*d.* 1786). Ensign, Infantry. Cadet 1782. Ensign 18 Jan. 1783. *d.* Chittagong June 1786.

Services: Apptd. Cadet 6 June 1782, but permitted to stay in England till the following year; sailed from Denmark in 1783; arrived in India Oct. 1783. N.F.P.

SHAW, Lewis Simeon (1784-1823). Captain, 31st N.I. *b.* psh. of St. George, I. of Dominica, 31 July 1784. Cadet 1802. Arrived in India 21 July 1803. Ensign 27 July 1803. Lieut. 4 June 1804. Capt. 5 Sept. 1817. *d.* 21 July 1823.

bapt. 12 Jan. 1785. Son of —— Shaw and Amaranthe his wife. Brother of Francis Shaw, *q.v. m.* Ft. Wm. 1 Oct. 1814, Miss Aurora Madgett. (His widow, Sophia A., died Jersey 25 Dec. 1894, aged 97.) His dau. *m.* Sir Albert John de Hochpied Larpent, 2nd Bart.

Services: Ensign d.d. 1/14th N.I. 1803-4. Second Mahratta War; Monson's retreat (w.) [1]; Lieut. d.d. 1/14th N.I. Posted to 18th N.I. 1805. Operations in Bundelkhand 1805-6; Lieut. 18th N.I. Capt. Lt. 1 Oct. 1815. Nepal War 1816; Capt. Lt. 2/18th N.I., in 2nd Bde. Left Column. Capt. 2/18th N.I. With 1st Ceylon Vol. Bn. 1818-19. Transfd. to newly-raised 31st N.I. July 1823.

Refs.: E.I.M.C. ii. 554.

[1] *Note:* "At about 11 p.m. (24 Aug. 1804) a horseman galloped up to the square. His horse was shot and he fell to the earth, stunned and slightly wounded. He proved to be Lieut. Shaw of the 14th N.I., who, in consequence of a previous wound, had been placed on a camel, and had so fallen into the hands of the enemy. The Marathas had put him on a pony, and he had taken this opportunity to escape." (*Viscount Lake*, by Col. H. Pearse, p. 287.)

SHAW, Robert (1813-1873). Major. 23rd N.I. *b.* Irvine, co. Ayr, 5 Feb. 1813. Cadet 1828. Arrived in India 9 Feb. 1830. Ensign (29 Aug. 1829) 9 Feb. 1830. Lieut. 27 Mar. 1840. Capt. 10 Oct. 1853. Retired 1 Apr. 1854. Hon. Major 28 Nov. 1854. *d.* Hertford 4 Mar. 1873.

Son of James Shaw, of Irvine and London, merchant. Cousin-german of David Shaw, *q.v. m.* Blytheswood Sq., Glasgow, 20 July 1841, Sophia, 2nd dau. of Walker Pearson, of Glasgow. (*See also* R. R. W. Ellis.) (She died Ambala 12 Nov. 1851, aged 31.)

Services: Ensign d.d. 63rd N.I. 10 Apr. 1830; Cadet d.d. 52nd N.I. 17 July 1830. Apptd. Actg. Ensign (having been 2 yrs. in India) 12 Mar. 1832. Posted to 23rd N.I. 14 Mar. 1833; Intr. & Qmr. do. 6 June 1834 till Dec. 1839. Fur. s.c. 23 Dec. 1839 till 30 Dec. 1841. Intr. & Qmr. 23rd N.I. 9 Mar. 1842 till 10 Dec. 1853. Operations against Afridis in Kohat Pass Feb. 1850; Bt. Capt. 23rd N.I. (Medal).

Refs.: Burke's *Peerage*, 1859, p. 900, *s.n.* Shaw, Bart., of Kilmarnock. *The Times*, 6 Mar. 1873.

SHAW, Samuel (1786-1861). Lieut. General, Artillery (336) *bapt.* ptely. Haverfordwest 22 Apr. 1786. Cadet 1803. Arrived in India 14 Aug. 1804. Lieut. 25 Aug. 1804. Capt. Lt. 31 Mar. 1808. Capt. 6 May 1817. Major 1 May 1824. Lt. Col. 31 May 1833. Lt. Col. Comdt. 25 Mar. 1840. Col. 26 Dec. 1844. Maj. Gen. 20 June 1854. Lt. Gen. 5 Mar. 1859. *d.* St. Helier, Jersey, 28 Apr. 1861, aged 75.

bapt. St. Thomas, Haverfordwest, 16 July 1786. Son of Thomas Shaw and Mary his wife. Brother of Thomas Shaw (1782-1801), *q.v. m.* (before 1814) Katherine. His dau. *m.* H. F. Dunsford, *q.v.*

Services : Served in Bencoolen 1810 ; in Java 1813 till Mar. 1817. Expedn. to Palembang 1813 ; to Bali under Gen. Sir M. Nightingale 1815. Comy. of Stores in Java 13 Feb. 1813. To comd. Art. at Karnal 23 Dec. 1823 ; do. Saugor 24 Sept. 1824 ; do. 1st Bn. Art. at Agra 4 Sept. 1826. Posted Lt. Col. to 5th Bn. 29 Nov. 1833 ; as Lt. Col. Comdt. to 7th Bn. 13 Apr. 1840. Actg. Comdt. of Art. 5 Jan. 1842. Fur. p.a. 5 Mar. 1844 till 1846. Comdt. of Art. 1847 till 1 July 1852. Bdr. 2 cl. comdg. Rohilkhand & Kumaon district 7 Apr. 1848 till 14 July 1851. M.M.B. 24 May 1851. Bdr. Gen. comdg. Presdy. Div. 26 July 1852 till 1 Aug. 1856. Fur. s.c. 6 Jan. 1855 till death.

Refs. : Boase. The Times, 1 May 1861.

SHAW, Thomas (1761-1841). Lieut. Colonel. 23rd N.I. *b.* in Ireland 1761. Cadet 1778. Admitted 2 Oct. 1778. Ensign Oct. 1778. Lieut. 19 Oct. 1778. Capt. 1 June 1796. Major 29 May 1800. Lt. Col. 13 July 1803. Retired 22 Feb. 1809. *d.* at his residence, 10 Widcombe Cresc., Bath, 10 Feb. 1841, aged 79.

Owned lands at Bannvale and Kilmore, co. Down. Eldest son of Capt. Thomas Shaw, of Lurgan, co. Armagh, of the Lurgan Yeomanry, and Jane Maria his wife, dau. of Simon McVeagh, and sister of Joseph McVeagh, *q.v.* Brother of Richardson Shaw, Ensign h.p. H.M.S., of Jane Maria, wife of Richard Blood, of Corcoolduren, co. Clare, and of Mrs. Cumming, in India. Cousin-german of Ezekiel Davys Wilson, *q.v. m.* (before Nov. 1793) Edith, reputed dau. of John Lumsden, B.C.S., and niece of David Lumsden, *q.v.* (She died Buxton 21 Oct. 1851.)

Services : Sailed for India in the *Shrewsbury* 7 Mar. 1778, aged 17. Ensign 3rd Bengal Eur. Regt. Oct. 1778 ; 2/3rd do. in Oct. 1779. First Mahratta War 1780-1 ; Lahar ; Gwalior ; Lieut. 2nd " Bombay Bn.," with Major William Popham's detachment ; later Qmr. to the detachment under Camac and Grainger Muir, *qq.v.*

Granted leave s.c. to sea 1 Sept. 1783. Apptd. in 1785 to discipline the Corps of Bhagulpur Hill Rangers; Adjt. do. 1786; comdd. do. 1793 till Dec. 1804. Capt. 1st N.I.; Major 2/1st N.I.; posted Lt. Col. to newly-raised 23rd N.I. in 1804. Fur. 31 Jan. 1805 till retirement.

Refs.: Burke's *Landed Gentry of Ireland*, p. 446, *s.n.* M'Veagh, of Drewstown, co. Meath; p. 57, *s.n.* Blood, late of Cranagher. *E.I.M.C.* i. 228-30. *G.M.* 1841, i. 333. *Bath Chron.* 11 Feb. 1841. Will dated 27 Nov. 1823; codicils dated 6 Feb. 1836, 17 Dec. 1838; proved 14 Dec. 1841.

SHAW, Thomas (1782-1801). Ensign, 14th N.I. *bapt.* Coventry 16 July 1782. Cadet 1799. Arrived in India 7 Jan. 1801. Ensign 19 Sept. 1800. *d. nr.* Cawnpore Sept. 1801, when proceeding to join his Regt. at Bahraich.

Son of Thomas Shaw and Mary his wife. Brother of Samuel Shaw, *q.v.*

Services: Posted to 2/14th N.I. 17 Apr. 1801. No record of active service.

Refs.: *G.M.* 1802, ii. 785.

SHAW, William (1810-1837). Lieutenant, 52nd N.I. *b.* Berhampore 24 June 1810. Cadet 1825. Arrived in India 19 Nov. 1826. Ensign 9 July 1826. Lieut. 4 June 1828. *d.* Mhow 8 Aug. 1837.

Son of William Shaw, of Irvine, Lt. Col. 22nd Ft. Brother of David Shaw, *q.v.*

Services: Ensign d.d. 54th N.I. 13 Jan. 1827; d.d. 52nd N.I. 27 Jan. 1827; posted to 52nd N.I. 10 May 1827. Leave s.c. 18 mos. to Mauritius and N.S.W. 18 Dec. 1828. Actg. Intr. & Qmr. 44th N.I. 14 Mar. 1837 till death. No record of active service.

Refs.: Burke's *Peerage*, 1859, p. 900, *s.n.* Shaw, Bart., of Kilmarnock. *A.J.* N.S. xxiv. 277.

SHAW, William Alexander (1760/61-?). Lieutenant. Infantry. *b.* in Ireland 1760/61. Cadet 1781. Ensign 19 Apr. 1781. Lieut. 8 Aug. 1782. Struck off 1788.

(? Of Kentstown, co. Meath.) 3rd son of William Jocelyn Shaw, of Kentstown, and Mary his wife, elder dau. of William Alexander, of Dublin, and sister of Sir William Alexander, 1st Bart.

Services: Apptd. Cadet 27 Apr. 1781, aged 20; should have sailed for India in the *Nassau* 8 Feb. 1782, but never arrived in India.

THE BENGAL ARMY, 1758-1834

SHEA, Robert Percy (1754/55-1783). Ensign, Infantry. *b.* in Ireland 1754/55. Cadet 1782. Arrived in India 27 Feb. 1783. Ensign 1783. *d.* Berhampore 29 Apr. 1783.

(*Probably* brother of Stephen Shea, *q.v.*)
Services: Sailed for India in the *Morse* 6 Feb. 1782, aged 27.

SHEA, Stephen. Ensign. Infantry. Country Cadet 1781. Ensign 1783. Resigned 8 May 1783.

(*Probably* brother of Robert Percy Shea, *q.v.*)
Services: Apptd. Asst. & Intr. to J. P. Auriol, Sec. to the Board in Calcutta, Dec. 1780. Apptd. Cadet Oct. 1781. Was Portuguese translator to the Bengal Govt. in 1782.

SHEARER, John Alexander (1803-1823). Lieutenant, 1st N.I. *bapt.* Kensington 23 May 1803. Cadet 1819. Ensign 20 Sept. 1819. Lieut. 1823. *d.* Bhagulpur 7 Sept. 1823.

Son of Alexander Shearer, of Swanmore House, Hants, and Elizabeth his wife, *née* Battye.

Services: Posted to 1/23rd N.I. 1820 ; transfd. to 1st N.I. July 1823. No record of active service.

SHEE, John (*d.* 1804). Ensign. Engineers. Afterwards Lt. Col. 33rd Ft. Cadet (Inf.) 1783. Arrived in India 27 Sept. 1783. Ensign (Engrs.) 1 Apr. 1785. Struck off 1792. *d.* Dover Mar. 1804.

m. (?)

Services: Apptd. Cadet 3 Jan. 1783 ; sailed for India in the *Pigot* 11 Mar. 1783. Transfd. as Cadet from Inf. to Engrs. 26 Jan. 1784. Apptd. addl. A.D.C. to Mr. Wheler during absence of the G.G. 1 Mar. 1784. Was on fur. in 1790. Cornet 13th Light Dgns. 31 May 1789 ; Lieut. 38th Ft. 30 July 1791 ; Capt. 33rd Ft. 30 Sept. 1793 ; Major do. 1 Dec. 1794 ; Lt. Col. in the Army 1 Jan. 1800 ; sold his Commission in 33rd Ft. 20 Mar. 1802. In the Cinque Port Vols. at death. Siege and capture of Seringapatam May 1799 ; Major 33rd Ft.

Refs.: M.M. xvii. 303.

SHEIL, Sir Justin (1803-1871). Lieut. General, K.C.B. 17th N.I. *b.* Rathpatrick, Kilkenny, 2 Dec. 1803. Cadet 1819. Admitted 29 July 1820. Ensign 4 Mar. 1820. Lieut. 11 July 1823. Capt. 13 Apr. 1830. Local Lt. Col. in Persia 2 June 1837. Major 17 Apr. 1841. Lt. Col. 11 Mar. 1847. Col. 28 Nov. 1856. Maj. Gen. 26 Apr. 1859. Lt. Gen. 25 June 1870. *d.* 13 Eaton Pl., London, 17 Apr. 1871.

Son of Edward Sheil, merchant, and Catherine MacCarthy his wife, of Spring House, co. Tipperary. *m.* 1847, Mary Leonora, only dau. of Rt. Hon. Stephen Woulfe, Chief Baron of the Irish Exchequer. (She died 1869.) Ed. Stoneyhurst.
Services : See *D.N.B.* Posted to 1/3rd N.I. ; transfd. to 35th N.I. 12 July 1824. Siege and capture of Bhurtpore ; Lieut. 35th N.I. (India medal). Adjt. 35th N.I. 16 May 1828 till 24 Feb. 1829. Fur. s.c. 3 Jan. 1830 till 15 Nov. 1832. Apptd. 2nd in comd. of disciplined troops in Persia under Major William Pasmore, *q.v.*, 4 July 1833, and sailed 20 Nov. 1833. Sec. to Brit. Legation in Persia 16 Feb. 1836 till 1844 ; Brit. Envoy and Minister in Persia 17 Sept. 1844 till 3 Sept. 1854. Fur. s.c. 1854 till death. Posted Lt. Col. to 19th N.I. 1847 ; to 15th N.I. 12 June 1850 ; to 73rd N.I. Mar. 1853 ; Col. 17th N.I. Feb. 1857 till 1869. C.B. (Civil) 27 Apr. 1848 ; K.C.B. (Civil) 3 Feb. 1855. Persian Order of Lion & Sun, 2 cl., 27 Aug. 1841 ; 1 cl. 19 July 1842. Contributed to Vol. iii. of *Journal of Royal Geog. Soc.*
Refs. : Burke's *Landed Gentry of Ireland,* p. 779, *s.n.* Woulfe, of Tiermaclane, co. Clare. *D.N.B. Boase. D.I.B. Walford. I.L.N.,* lviii. 427. *The Times,* 21 Apr. 1871.

SHELDON, Richard (1778-1802). Lieutenant, 14th N.I. *bapt.* Shinfield, Berks., 15 Jan. 1778. Cadet 1795. Arrived in India 16 Feb. 1797. Ensign 28 Oct. 1796. Lieut. 30 Oct. 1797. *d.* Bahraich, U.P., 6 Oct. 1802.
Son of William Sheldon and Susannah his wife.
Services : Lieut. 2/14th N.I. No record of active service.

SHEPHERD, Augustus Howell (1804-1894). Major. 14th N.I. *b.* London 8 June 1804. Cadet 1824. Arrived in India 29 June 1825. Ensign 8 Jan. 1825. Lieut. 5 Oct. 1825. Capt. 10 June 1842. Retired 1 July 1848. Hon. Major 28 Nov. 1854. *d.* Oak House, Surbiton, 1 Mar. 1894.
bapt. Marylebone 12 July 1804. Son of Edward Charles Howell Shepherd, Capt. 1st Life Gds., and Eliza his wife, dau. of Edmund Pepys, of Braywick, Berks.[1] *m.* Marylebone 12 July 1856, Harriet, dau. of Frederick R. Coore. (She died 17 Jan. 1892, aged 73.)
Services : Posted to 14th N.I. 1825, and served throughout with that Regt. Fur. p.a. 9 Feb. 1837 till 26 Dec. 1839. Gwalior campaign ; Maharajpur ; Capt. 14th N.I. (Bronze star). First Sikh War ; Ferozshahr ; Capt. 14th N.I. (Medal).
Refs. : The Times, 5 Mar. 1894 (where his name is given as Augustus Howell-Shepherd.)
[1] *Note :* She signs " Elizabeth Howell Shepherd, widow " in 1824.

Although his father and an elder brother called themselves Howell-Shepherd, his name invariably appears officially without the hyphen.

SHEPLEY, John (1789-1812). Lieutenant, 23rd N.I. *b.* Wandsworth 19 Jan. 1789. Cadet 1803. Arrived in India 1 Dec. 1804. Ensign 11 Nov. 1804. Lieut. 11 Nov. 1804. *d.* Agra 19 July 1812.

bapt. Wandsworth 14 Feb. 1790. Son of Richard Shepley and Eleanor his wife.

Services : Posted Lieut. to 23rd N.I. 1805. Settlement of Hariana 1809 ; Bhawani ; Lieut. 2/23rd N.I.

Refs. : M.I. Agra Cantt. cemetery.

SHEPPARD or SHEPHEARD, Robert (1754/55-?). Ensign. Infantry. *b.* Dublin 1754/55. Cadet 1781. Ensign 1 Apr. 1783. Struck off 1788.

Services : Apptd. Cadet 5 Oct. 1781 ; should have sailed for India in the *Nottingham* 6 Feb. 1782, aged 27. Never arrived in India.

SHEPPARD, William (1789-1812). Lieutenant, 25th N.I. *bapt.* St. Patrick's, Waterford, 20 Mar. 1789. Cadet 1804. Arrived in India 10 Sept. 1805. Ensign 20 Oct. 1805. Lieut. 13 Mar. 1806. *d.* Java 12 Nov. 1812.

Son of Rev. Thomas Sheppard and Susannah his wife.

Services : Posted to 25th N.I. 1806. A.D.C. to Maj.-Gen. Sir Ewen Baillie, Bart., *q.v.*, comdg. at the Presdy. 1807-8. Shot Lieut. Henry Phillips, *q.v.*, in a duel at Calcutta Oct. 1808 ; tried before the Supreme Court Dec. 1808 and convicted of manslaughter.[1] Capture of Java 1811 ; Lieut. 2/25th N.I., attached 5th Vol. Bn.

Refs. : A.A.R. x. 109-17.

[1] *Note :* After the verdict had been recorded, three of the jury announced in court that they dissented, being of opinion that the prisoner ought to have been acquitted, and they further declared that they had not been asked to vote on the question. The judges decided unanimously " that a verdict once recorded could not be touched by any subsequent declaration of a juror."

SHERER, Sir George Moyle (1800-1870). Major General, K.C.S.I. 26th N.I. *b.* Blandford, Dorset, 4 Sept. 1800. Cadet 1821. Arrived in India 13 May 1822. Ensign 20 Dec. 1821. Lieut. 23 Aug. 1824. Capt. 8 July 1836. Major 12 Aug. 1847. Lt. Col. 11 July 1853. Bt. Col. 28 Nov. 1854. Retired 31 Dec. 1861. Hon. Maj. Gen. 31 Dec. 1861. *d.* 31 Inverness Rd., Hyde Pk., London, 5 Nov. 1870.

bapt. Blandford 5 Sept. 1800. 2nd son of Rev. Joseph Godfrey Sherer, of Godmersham, Kent, and Margaret his wife. *m.* Barrackpore 1 Feb. 1827, Jane Baillie, 5th dau. of Sir Joseph O'Halloran, *q.v.* (*See also* George Cuninghame.) (She died 22 Nov. 1887, aged 79.) Ed. Wye Coll. Queen's Coll., Oxon. ; matric. 15 June 1820. *Services :* d.d. 1/20th N.I. 1 Aug. 1822 ; posted to 2/20th N.I. 24 Dec. 1822 ; transfd. to 29th N.I. 1823 ; to 57th N.I. (late 1/29th) May 1824. Fur. s.c. 27 Dec. 1825 till 23 Oct. 1826. Actg. Supt. of Cadets in Ft. Wm. 16 June 1827 ; Asst. Executive Engr., suptg. works at Sulkea, 26 Dec. 1827 ; Adjt. Calcutta Native Mil. 22 June 1829 till 5 June 1830. Sub-Asst. in Stud Dept. 17 Apr. 1830 ; 2nd Asst. Central Stud 30 Dec. 1840 ; 1st do. 4 Aug. 1841 ; Supervisor of Hissar Stud 30 Jan. 1843 ; Supt. C.P. Div. of Stud 7 July 1843 till 16 Aug. 1853. Fur. s.c. 23 Feb. 1854 till Dec. 1856. Posted Lt. Col. to 71st N.I. Sept. 1853 ; to 2nd Eur. Bengal Fus. 19 Apr. 1854 ; to 59th N.I. Feb. 1855 ; to 16th N.I. Sept. 1855 ; to 73rd N.I. 2 Jan. 1857, and was comdg. this Regt., the greater part of which remained loyal, when the Mutiny broke out. Transfd. to 26th N.I. 1860. Fur. s.c. 16 Dec. 1859 till retirement. K.C.S.I. 24 May 1866. Hon. A.D.C. to the Queen 22 Feb. 1861.

Refs. : Burke's *Colonial Gentry*, p. 83, *s.n.* O'Halloran. Boase. *Alumni Oxon. I.L.N.* Vol. lvii. 531. *The Times*, 10 Nov. 1870.

SHERRIFF,[1] **David** (1794-1838). Captain, 48th N.I. *b.* Calcutta 1 Jan. 1794. Cadet 1808. Admitted 6 Mar. 1811. Ensign 1 Oct. 1812. Lieut. 10 Aug. 1816. Capt. 18 July 1829. *d.* Alipore, Calcutta, 29 June 1838.

3rd and youngest son of Robert Sherriff, of Calcutta, and Euphemia his wife, dau. of Surg.-Major David Urquhart, Bengal Est. Cousin-german of Francis Sherriff, *q.v. m.* 1st, Mary, sister of David Pringle, *q.v. m.* 2nd, Craig Lodge, Haddington, 31 Mar. 1823, Catherine, only dau. of Ker Richardson. (She died Cape Town 20 Sept. 1823.) *m.* 3rd, Barrackpore 18 June 1832, Miss Harriet Pickersgill. (She *re-m.* Henry Cope 2 Apr. 1840.)

Services : Captured by the French on the way out to India ; present at capture of Mauritius Dec. 1810. Barasat C.C. 1811. Cadet d.d. 9th N.I. 1811-12. Posted Ensign to 1/24th N.I. 1812. (? Nepal War 1816 ; Ensign 8th Gren. Bn., in 2nd Bde. Left Column.) Third Mahratta War ; Lieut. 1/24th N.I. 2nd in comd. 1st Rampura Local Cav. 1819. Fur. s.c. 21 Sept. 1820 till 24 Mar. 1824. Transfd. to 48th N.I. (late 1/24th) May 1824. Leave s.c. 2 yrs. to Cape 16 May 1837.

Refs. : Memorials of Four Old Families, by Capt. Douglas

Wimberley (Inverness, 1893), p. 139. *S.M.* 1823, i. 646; 1824, i. 127. *A.J.* N.S. ix. 186; xxvii. 208. M.I. in Bhowanipore cemetery.

[1] *Note:* Other spellings are, Shirriff, Shirreff, Sheriff, and Shirref.

SHERRIFF,[1] **Francis** (1811-1857). Bt. Major, 65th N.I. *bapt.* Inverness 21 Oct. 1811. Cadet 1830. Arrived in India 29 Aug. 1831. Ensign (25 Apr. 1831) 29 Aug. 1831. Lieut. 16 Mar. 1838. Capt. 24 Jan. 1845. Bt. Major 28 Nov. 1854. *d.* Morar, nr. Gwalior, 14 June 1857 : kld. by mutineers of the Gwalior Contingent on the parade ground.

4th and youngest son of David Sherriff, tacksman of Kinmylies, Inverness, and Anne Farquharson his wife, eldest dau. of Lachlan Mackintosh, Balnespick. Cousin-german of Henry Mackintosh and David Sherriff, *qq.v. m.* Coventry 6 Jan. 1846, Ann, only dau. of Capt. Archibald Erskine Pattullo, Madras Est., and niece of Elizabeth, last Duchess of Gordon.

Services: Cadet d.d. 2nd N.I. 6 Sept. 1831; posted Ensign to 65th N.I. 18 Oct. 1833. Fur. s.c. 12 Feb. 1844 till 4 Oct. 1847. 2nd in comd. 1st Inf., Gwalior Contingent, 23 May 1849; Comdt. 4th Inf. do. 20 May 1856, and was comdg. the Regt. at Gwalior when it mutinied. No record of active service.

Refs.: Memorials of Four Old Families, by Capt. D. Wimberley, p. 139. M.I. Jarerua cemetery, Morar.

[1] *Note:* His name appears as Shirreff in official documents and *A.L.*

SHERWILL, Markham Eeles (1814-1865). Major General. 2nd Eur. Bengal Fus. *b.* 12 Jan. 1814. Cadet 1829. Arrived in India 6 Sept. 1830. Ensign (7 Apr. 1830) 1 Sept. 1830. Lieut. 3 Oct. 1840. Capt. 12 June 1847. Major 1 May 1858. Bt. Lt. Col. 28 Nov. 1854. Bt. Col. 4 June 1860. Retired 31 Dec. 1861. Hon. Maj. Gen. 31 Dec. 1861. *d.* Kirkby Lonsdale, Westmorland, 25 Sept. 1865.

bapt. Kew Green 11 Feb. 1814. Eldest son of Markham Eeles Sherwill, Capt. Stafford Mil., and Lucy Maria his wife, eldest dau. of James Lind, M.D., F.R.S., Physician to George III (*D.N.B.*). Brother of Walter Stanhope Sherwill and of the wife of Hugh Troup, *qq.v. m.* Bedhampton 17 July 1845, Sarah Jane, 2nd dau. of Rev. Thomas Hesketh Biggs, rector of Whitbourne, co. Hereford. (She died Cleeve, Somerset, 30 Dec. 1894, aged 74.)

Services: Cadet d.d. 16th N.I. 30 Sept. 1830; Actg. Ensign (having been 2 yrs. in India) 1 Oct. 1832; posted Ensign to 3rd N.I. 20 Aug. 1833. Shekhawat expedn. 1834; Ensign 3rd N.I. Transfd.

to 64th N.I. 24 Sept. 1835 ; to 69th N.I. 4 Aug. 1837 ; Intr. & Qmr. do. 10 Aug. 1839. Transfd. to newly-raised 2nd Bengal Eur. Regt. 8 Oct. 1839 ; Intr. & Qmr. do. 13 Dec. 1839 till 18 Apr. 1843. Fur. s.c. 12 Feb. 1843 till 1846. Intr. & Qmr. 2nd Eur. Regt. Mar. 1847 till 1848. Second Sikh War ; Ramnagar ; passage of Chenab ; Chilianwala ; Gujerat ; Capt. 2nd Eur. Fus., Bde. Major (Medal with 2 clasps). Bde. Major at Ferozepore 9 May 1849 ; do. Ambala Jan. 1852 ; do. Lucknow 21 Mar. 1855 till 1859. Leave s.c. 2 yrs. to Cape Mar. 1854.

Refs.: Foster's *Families of Royal Descent*, ii. 787. *G.M.* 1865, ii. 658. *The Times*, 29 Sept. 1865.

SHERWILL, Walter Stanhope (1815-1890). Lieut. Colonel. 66th N.I. *b.* 31 Aug. 1815. Cadet 1832. Arrived in India 8 Jan. 1834. Ensign (11 June 1833) 8 Jan. 1834. Lieut. 3 Oct. 1840. Capt. 22 Feb. 1847. Major 2 Apr. 1859. Retired 31 Dec. 1861. Hon. Lt. Col. 31 Dec. 1861. *d.* 20 Mar. 1890.

bapt. Old Windsor 25 Sept. 1815. 2nd son of Markham Eeles Sherwill and Lucy Maria his wife. Brother of Markham Eeles Sherwill, *q.v. m.* Ghazipur 24 Feb. 1845, Cecilia, dau. of John Montgomery Hill, Comr. of Port Elizabeth, S.A., and ward and sister-in-law of Alexander Charles Heyland, B.C.S., judge at Ghazipur. (*See also* George Newbolt.) Ed. Christ's Hospital. Addiscombe Cadet 5 Aug. 1831 till 11 June 1833.

Services: Ensign d.d. 72nd N.I. 15 Jan. 1834 ; posted to 66th N.I. 24 May 1834. Asst. Revenue Surveyor at Cawnpore 27 July 1838. Leave s.c. to Cape and Aust. 10 Mar. 1840 till 14 Nov. 1841. Bengal Revenue Survey 16 May 1842 till Nov. 1856. Leave s.c. 2 yrs. to Cape and Aust. 3 Mar. 1848. Santhal revolt 1855 ; D.A.Q.M.G. to F.F. under Maj.-Gen. G. W. A. Lloyd, *q.v.* Professor of surveying in civil engineering coll., Calcutta, 22 Nov. 1856 till retirement. Boundary Comr. of Bengal. Fellow of Calcutta Univ.

Refs.: Foster's *Families of Royal Descent*, ii. 789. Burke's *Landed Gentry*, 6th edn., p. 780, *s.n.* Heyland, of Glendaragh and Tamlaght.

Note: A coloured litho. of a drawing by him of Darjeeling in 1852 is in I.O.

SHERWOOD, James Dodington (*d.* 1837). Major General, Artillery. (253) Cadet 1783. Admitted 11 July 1784. Fireworker 13 Feb. 1785. Lieut. 12 Nov. 1791. Capt. Lt. 16 Feb. 1802. Capt. 28 May 1804. Major 6 Dec. 1809. Lt. Col. 18 Jan. 1816. Lt. Col. Comdt. 1 May 1824. Col. 5 June 1829. Maj.

Gen. 10 Jan. 1837. *d.* at his house in Gt. Cumberland St., London, 18 Jan. 1837.

m. 1st, Calcutta 15 Dec. 1795, Mary, sister of David Thomas Richardson, *q.v.* (*See also* Peter Littlejohn.) (She died Calcutta 22 Aug. 1819, aged 49.) His dau. *m.* Sir William Russell, 1st Bart., of Charlton Park (uncle of John Russell, *q.v.*); their dau. *m.* George Roydes Birch, *q.v.* *m.* 2nd, St. Luke's, Cheltenham, 30 Apr. 1823, Miss E. A. Howell.

Services: Apptd. Cadet 26 Nov. 1783. 3rd Bn. Art. in July 1787. To Madras Aug.-Oct. 1793 for siege of Pondicherry; Lieut. 5th Coy. 3rd Bn., transfd. tempy. from 3rd Coy. 1st Bn. To Madras June-Oct. 1794 for the projected expedn. against French Is. off E. coast of Madagascar; Lieut. 3rd Coy. 2nd Bn., Adjt. Qmr. 1st Bn. 14 Dec. 1795; Adjt. & Qmr. do. 1799-1803. Tempy. charge of gun carriage agency 24 Nov. 1803. On command in the field in 1805. Actg. 1st Asst. to Comy. of Stores, Presdy., 12 Nov. 1807; Comy. of Stores 9 Jan. 1809 till 6 Aug. 1821. Fur. s.c. 27 Dec. 1821 till death.

Refs.: *A.J.* N.S. xxii. 135.

SHEWEN, Edward (1749-1776). Captain, Infantry. A.D.C. to Warren Hastings. *b.* 1749. Cadet (?) Ensign 2 Aug. 1766. Lieut. 10 Sept. 1767. Capt. 2 Dec. 1772. *d. unm.* Calcutta 27 Nov. 1776.

3rd son of William Shewen, of Swansea, by a dau. of —— Howel.

Services: Apptd. A.D.C. to Col. Alexander Champion, *q.v.*, 19 Jan. 1774. First Rohilla War 1774; battle of St. George; A.D.C. Was A.D.C. to Warren Hastings 1775 till death.

Refs.: *Genealogies of Morgan and Glamorgan*, by G. T. Clark, p. 504, *s.n.* Shewen, of Thistleboom. *Macpherson*, p. 176. Will proved 1778.

SHICKLE, John (1787-1819). Lieutenant, Pension Est. 9th N.I. *b.* 19 Nov. 1787. Cadet 1805. Arrived in India 7 Apr. 1807. Ensign 10 Apr. 1807. Lieut. 5 Jan. 1810. Pensioned 15 Aug. 1814. *d.* Monghyr 19 Nov. 1819.

bapt. Chalfont St. Giles, Bucks., 17 Dec. 1787. Son of John Hayle Shickle and Anne his wife.

Services: Barasat C.C. Posted Ensign to 9th N.I. 1808, and served throughout with that Regt.

*****SHIPP, John** (1784-1834). Cadet. Infantry. Afterwards Lieut. H.M. 87th Ft. *bapt.* Saxmundham, Suffolk, 16 Mar. 1784. Cadet 1809. Did not take up his appt. *d.* Liverpool 27 Feb. 1834, aged 50.

2nd son of Thomas Shipp, a marine, and Laetitia his wife. m. 1st, Cawnpore 4 July 1816, Anne, dau. of Conductor Humphreys. (*See also* Charles Arthur Morris.) (She died 1824.) m. 2nd, Mary. (She died Blackheath 12 Apr. 1891, aged 88.)

Services: See *D.N.B.* " Performed the unique feat of twice winning a commission from the ranks before he was 32." Enlisted as a boy in H.M. 22nd (Cheshire) Regt. 17 Jan. 1797. For his bravery at Bhurtpore was given by Lord Lake a Commission as Ensign in H.M. 65th Ft.; promoted Lieut. in 76th Ft. a few weeks later, both Commissions being dated 10 Mar. 1805. Returned to England with 76th Ft. 1807; sold out to pay his debts 19 Mar. 1808. Re-enlisted in 1808 in 24th Light Dgns. and returned to India 1809. Apptd. Cadet of Inf. on the Bengal Est. " on account of his Singular Bravery and peculiar circumstances." (M.C. 17 Feb. 1809.) Won a Commission in H.M. 87th Ft. 4 May 1815. Served in Second Mahratta, Nepal and Pindari campaigns. Sentenced by G.C.M. July 1823 to be discharged from the Service; was permitted to retire, and sold out 3 Nov. 1825. Granted a special pension of £50 *p.a.* by E.I. Co. with effect from Dec. 1825, on account of, " the conspicuous gallantry displayed by him on many occasions, and to the wounds received by him in the course of his service in India." (M.C. 24 Jan. 1826.) Became Master of the Liverpool Workhouse. Pub. 1829, " Memoirs of the Extraordinary Military Career of John Shipp; " 1831, " The Military Bijou, . . ."

Refs.: *D.N.B.* *D.I.B.* His *Autobiog.* (portrait), ed. H.M. Chichester, London, 1890. *A.J.* N.S. xiii. 304. Portrait by J. Buchanan, engraved by W. T. Fry.

SHIPTON, John (1757/58-1789). Lieutenant, Artillery. (173) *b.* 1757/58. Country Cadet 1778. Fireworker 29 Sept. 1778. Lieut. 2 July 1782. *d.* Dum-Dum 15 Jan. 1789, aged 31.

Son of Rebecca Shipton, of Watford, Herts. Brother of William Shipton, *q.v.*, of Isaac, of Sarah, wife of James Hammond, *q.v.*, and of Mary, wife of Joseph Thomas Brown, of Calcutta. Cousin of William Nicholl, *q.v.* m. Calcutta 17 Dec. 1788, Miss Juliana Barker, dau. of Sir Robert Barker, *q.v.* (She *re-m.* 1 Mar. 1790, C. R. Crommelin, B.C.S.; became mother of John Dethick Crommelin, *q.v.*; and died June 1833, aged 60.)

Services: Apptd. Cadet 11 Aug. 1778. Lieut. 2nd Bn. Art. in July 1787.

Refs.: Will dated 10 Jan. 1788; proved 20 Jan. 1789. M.I. at Dum-Dum.

THE BENGAL ARMY, 1758-1834 77

SHIPTON, William (1764/65-1804). Captain, Artillery. (208)
b. 1764/65. Country Cadet 1779. Admitted 19 Aug. 1779. Fireworker 4 Oct. 1780. Lieut. 5 Sept. 1786. Capt. Lt. 8 Jan. 1796. Capt. 15 Feb. 1802. *d.* Barrackpore 28 Dec. 1804, aged 39. Son of Rebecca Shipton, of Watford, Herts. Brother of John Shipton, *q.v.*
Services : Campaign against the Rajah of Benares 1781 ; capture of Bijaigarh, C.I. ; Lt.F. Art., with force under Major William Popham, *q.v.* Lieut. 3rd Bn. in July 1787. Third Mysore War 1790-2 ; storm of Utradrug ; Lieut. 5th Coy. 2nd Bn. Second Rohilla War ; battle of Bitaurah. Operations in Jumna Doab 1803 ; Sasni ; Bijaigarh ; Kachaura ; Capt. 3rd Coy. 2nd Bn. Second Mahratta War 1803-4 ; storm of Aligarh (w.) ; Capt. 3rd Coy. 2nd Bn.
Refs. : Will dated camp, Biana, 1 Feb. 1804 ; proved 14 Jan. 1805. M.I. at Dum-Dum.

SHOOLBRED, Thomas (1775-1800). Lieutenant, 3rd N.I.
b. Brixton Causeway, Lambeth, 25 May 1775. Cadet 1795. Arrived in India 3 Mar. 1797. Ensign 16 Oct. 1796. Lieut. 30 Oct. 1797. *d.* Fatehgarh 6 Oct. 1800.
bapt. 6 July 1775. Son of John Shoolbred, of Mark Lane, and Jane his wife, dau. of Francis Hislop, of Bradford, Wilts.
Services : Served throughout with 3rd N.I.
Refs. : G.M. 1801, i. 275.

SHORE, Charles (1785-1811). Lieutenant, 20th N.I. *bapt.* Upper Chapel, Sheffield, 13 July 1785. Cadet 1804. Arrived in India 10 Sept. 1805. Ensign 11 Sept. 1805. Lieut. 12 Sept. 1805. *d.* P.W.I. 4 Aug. 1811.
3rd son of John Shore, banker at Sheffield, afterwards of Scarborough, and Gertrude his wife, dau. of George Binks, of Sheffield.
Services : Posted Lieut. to 20th N.I. 1806. No record of active service.
Refs. : Burke's *Landed Gentry*, 12th edn., p. 1709, *s.n.* Shore, late of Norton Hall, co. Derby. *History of Sheffield*, by Joseph Hunter (1819), p. 219. *G.M.* 1832, i. 464.

SHOREDICHE, Robert (1785-?). Lieutenant. 10th N.I. *bapt.* Gt. Stanmore 28 Sept. 1785. Cadet 1805. Arrived in India 13 Nov. 1806. Ensign 30 Dec. 1806. Lieut. 13 Sept. 1809. Struck off in England 16 Sept. 1814.
Son of Michael Shorediche,[1] of Ickenham Hall, Middlesex, and Anne his wife.

Services : Posted Ensign to 10th N.I. 1807, and served throughout with that Regt. Fur. 16 Mar. 1812 till 1817, when he was struck off with effect from 16 Sept. 1814, *i.e.*, 2½ yrs. from the date of his quitting India.

Refs. : G.M. 1809, ii. 1081.

[1] *Note :* Matric. Pembroke Coll., Oxon., 1767, as Shoredicke; *cr.* M.A. 1771 as Shorditch.

*SHORT, Charles (*d.* 1785). Ensign. Infantry. Subsequently a Free Merchant. Ensign 9 May 1766. Resigned (?) *d. unm.* Russapuglah, Calcutta, 2 July 1785.

Nephew of Miss Ann Short. Ed. Merchant Taylors' Jan.-Sept. 1755.

Services : Permitted to proceed to India as a free mariner 2 Nov. 1764. Probably commissioned owing to the " Batta mutiny." Became a free merchant in Calcutta where he owned much house property and land, and was one of the Comrs. of Police in Calcutta at death. Short St. in Calcutta is named after him.

Refs. : Robinson. B.M. Add. MSS. 6050. Will dated Calcutta, 10 Nov. 1782; proved 5 July 1785. M.I. in S. Park St. burial ground, Calcutta.

SHORT, George (1808-1847). Bt. Major, 45th N.I. *bapt.* Kenn, Devon, 14 Mar. 1808. Cadet 1824. Arrived in India 23 July 1825. Ensign 12 Feb. 1825. Lieut. 29 Jan. 1829. Capt. 1 May 1844. Bt. Major 3 Apr. 1846. *d.* Kasauli 8 May 1847, aged 39.

Son of George Short, formerly of Exeter, solicitor, later of Sydenham, Kent, and Elizabeth his wife. *m.* Agra 15 Sept. 1835, Lucy, younger dau. of Charles Parker, *q.v.* Ed. Christ's Hospital.

Services : Posted Ensign to 45th N.I. 23 July 1825; actg. Adjt. 5th Local Horse 7 Jan. 1828 till Apr. 1829; do. 45th N.I. Sept.-Dec. 1841, and July 1843 till Jan. 1844. First Sikh War; Mudki; Ferozshahr; Sobraon; Capt. comdg. 45th N.I. (Medal with 2 clasps). Was on leave at Kasauli when he died.

Refs. : (? Burke's *Landed Gentry*, 13th edn., p. 1599, *s.n.* Short (*now* Fradgley), of Bickham, Devon.) *De Rhé-Philipe. I.M.* 3 Aug. 1847, p. 453. Will dated 20 Dec. 1845; proved 28 Sept. 1847. M.I. at Kasauli.

SHORT, William (1777-1826). Lieut. Colonel, 2nd N.I. *b.* 17 Aug. 1777. Cadet 1798. Arrived in India 16 Dec. 1799. Ensign 26 Oct. 1799. Lieut. 28 Oct. 1799. Capt. 31 Aug. 1810. Major 7 Nov. 1822. Lt. Col. 1 May 1824. *d.* Barrackpore 23 Aug. 1826.

m. Calcutta 14 June 1820, Miss Emily Stewart, niece of Lewis Wiggens, *q.v.* (She died London 10 Nov. 1875.)

Services : Posted to 1/11th N.I. 15 Apr. 1801. Second Mahratta War ; Lieut. 11th N.I. Reduction of Kalinjar 1812 ; Capt. 1/11th N.I. With 3rd Gren. Bn. 1815-16. Posted Lt. Col. to 37th N.I. May 1824 ; to newly-raised 5th Extra Regt. 21 May 1825 ; to 2nd N.I. 1826.

Refs. : Will dated 7 Aug. 1824 ; proved 7 Sept. 1826. M.I. at Barrackpore.

SHORTES,[1] **Walter** (*d.* 1782). Lieutenant, Infantry. Country Cadet 1779. Ensign 5 Sept. 1779. Lieut. 23 Apr. 1781. *d.* 1782.

Services : Apptd. Cadet 19 Aug. 1779. N.F.P.

[1] *Note :* His name also appears as Shortess and Shortless.

SHORTLAND, Vincent (1803-1880). Lieutenant. 36th N.I. Subsequently Archdeacon of Madras. *b.* 10 May 1803. Cadet 1818. Admitted 16 Sept. 1819. Ensign 20 May 1819. Lieut. 20 Aug. 1821. Resigned 12 June 1832. *d.* St. Helier, Jersey, 6 Nov. 1880.

bapt. Kidlington, Oxon., 15 May 1803. Son of Vincent John Shortland and Mary Maria Wentworth his wife. *m.* 1st, Barrackpore 8 Nov. 1823, Charlotte Estelle, 4th dau. of Jacques Grand-Jean de Fouchy, of Chandernagore. (*See also* Henry Hodgson.) (She died Vizagapatam 16 Aug. 1838.) *m.* 2nd, Newington, Surrey, 3 Dec. 1840, Anne, dau. of —— Middleton, of Cheltenham, and widow of Capt. Richard James Nixon, 25th Madras N.I. Ed. Winchester ; Scholar 1815. St. Catherine's Coll., Camb. ; entered as a " Ten Year Man " in 1832 ; B.D. 19 Nov. 1841.

Services : Ensign d.d. Bengal Eur. Regt. 1819 ; posted Ensign to 1/18th N.I. 1820 ; actg. Adjt. 5 Coys. 1/18th N.I. 13 Dec. 1822. Leave u.p.a. 6 mos. to Calcutta 27 Jan. 1823. d.d. 1/23rd N.I. 2 Aug. 1823. Suptg. construction of N. Div. of Cuttack road 15 Oct. 1823 till 31 Oct. 1825. Transfd. to 36th N.I. (late 1/18th) May 1824. Fort Adjt. of Ft. Wm. 31 Oct. 1825 till 17 Apr. 1826. Siege and capture of Bhurtpore ; Lieut. 36th N.I.[1] Supt. S. Div. of Cuttack road 17 Apr. 1826 ; do. N. Div. 18 Aug. 1826 ; do. N. Div. Jagannath road till 19 Sept. 1829, when he returned to regtl. duty. Fur. p.a. 2 Feb. 1830 till resignation. Apptd. Chaplain on Madras Est. (Mily. Despatch of 28 Aug. 1833). Archdeacon of Madras 1846. Retired 19 Dec. 1859.

Refs. : Burke's *Royal Families,* ped. lxii. *Kirby. Graduati Cantab. The Times,* 16 Nov. 1880.

[1] *Note :* His name is not in India M.R.

SHORTREED, Pringle (1808-1878). Lieut. Colonel. 17th N.I. b. Jedburgh 16 Nov. 1808. Cadet 1825. Arrived in India 4 Oct. 1826. Ensign 2 Mar. 1826. Lieut. (16 Nov. 1827) 15 Feb. 1830. Capt. 8 Sept. 1843. Bt. Major 20 June 1854. Retired 15 Jan. 1856. Hon. Lt. Col. 15 Jan. 1856. d. Fleet, Hants, 24 June 1878.

Youngest son of Robert Shortreed, writer in Jedburgh, sheriff substitute co. Roxburgh, and Margaret his wife, dau. of James Fair, of Langlee, writer. Brother of William Shortreed, q.v. m. Calcutta 16 Nov. 1844, Miss Isabella Thompson. Ed. Edin. High School.

Services: Posted to 58th N.I. 26 Sept. 1826; exchanged to 17th N.I. 15 Feb. 1830. Fur. p.a. 17 Jan. 1838 till 3 Feb. 1840. Second Sikh War; Capt. 17th N.I., with Army of Reserve at Jagraon.

Refs.: Tancred's *Annals of a Border Club*, p. 443. *The Times*, 1 July 1878.

SHORTREED, William (1804-1846). Captain, 1st Bengal Eur. L.I. b. Jedburgh 25 Jan. 1804. Cadet 1819. Arrived in India 17 July 1820. Ensign 14 Feb. 1820. Lieut. 2 July 1822. Capt. 15 Nov. 1836. d. Alnwick, Northumberland, 14 May 1846.

5th son of Robert Shortreed, of Jedburgh, writer, and Margaret his wife. Brother of Pringle Shortreed, q.v. m. Alnwick 7 Jan. 1846, Mary Juliana, eldest dau. of John Lambert, of Alnwick, solicitor, and niece of Anthony Lambert (1785-1803), q.v. (She died Carlisle 31 Mar. 1858, aged 45.)

Services: d.d. Bengal Eur. Regt. 17 July 1820; d.d. 1/19th N.I. Oct. 1820. Posted Ensign to 1/22nd N.I. Jan. 1821; transfd. to Bengal Eur. Regt. Sept. 1823; to 2nd Bengal Eur. Regt. May 1824. Served with his Regt. at Cheduba I., off coast of Arakan, 1825-6, during First Burma War. Offg. Adjt. 2nd Bengal Eur. Regt. Mar.-Oct. 1827 and Jan.-Aug. 1829; do. Bengal Eur. Regt. Aug.-Oct. 1834. d.d. Assam L.I. Jan. till 28 Sept 1835. Adjt. Bengal Eur. Regt. 26 Apr. till 26 Dec. 1836. First Afghan War 1838-40; Ghazni 1839 (Medal); occupation of Kabul; Bde. Major 4th Inf. Bde. Oct. 1839 till Nov. 1840; Bamian (*Lond. Gaz.* 19 Nov. 1840). Bde. Major at Karnal Apr. till 1 Oct. 1842; do. 4th Inf. Bde., Army of Reserve (for Afghanistan), 14 Oct. 1842 till Jan. 1843; do. N.W.F. district 22 Dec. 1843. A.D.C. to Maj.-Gen. G. Hunter, q.v., comdg. troops at Sukkur, 12 Apr. 1844. Operations against Hill tribes in Sind 1844-5; capture of Trakki; A.D.C. Fur. s.c. 12 May 1845 till death.

Refs.: *De Rhé-Philipe*. M.I. at Sabathu.

THE BENGAL ARMY, 1758-1834

SHORTT, Henry Palmer (1789-1817). Lieutenant, 20th N.I.
b. (? Opherlane,) Queen's Co. 7 Mar. 1789. Cadet 1804. Arrived in India 10 Sept. 1805. Ensign 10 Sept. 1805. Lieut. 17 Sept. 1806. *d.* Malacca 26 Mar. 1817.
Eldest son of James Shortt, of Newtown, Queen's Co. *m.* Calcutta 26 Jan. 1811, Miss Julia Mulder. (She died nr. Ballygunge, Calcutta, 26 June 1832.)
Services: Posted Lieut. to 20th N.I. 1806. Capture of Java 1811; Lieut. 1/20th N.I.

SHOWERS, Charles Lionel (1780-1815). Captain, 19th N.I.
b. in India 1780. Cadet 1795. Arrived in India 22 Oct. 1796. Ensign 23 Oct. 1796. Lieut. 30 Oct. 1797. Capt. 14 May 1806. *d.* Malaun 15 Apr. 1815 : kld. in action.
bapt. Calcutta 5 Aug. 1783, "near 3 years of age." Godson of Warren Hastings. Eldest son of Samuel Howe Showers, *q.v.*, and Melian his 2nd wife. Brother of Howe Daniel Showers, *q.v.*
Services: Apptd. a Minor Cadet Nov. 1781; struck off 2 May 1786. Posted Ensign to 3rd Bengal Eur. Regt. 1796; Lieut. 10th N.I. in 1798. Expedn. to Egypt 1801-2; Lieut. Bengal Vols. Second Mahratta War 1803-4; reduction of Cuttack; capture of Balasore; Lieut. 19th N.I., d.d. 1st Vol. Bn. Nepal War 1814-15; Malaun (kld.); Capt. 1/19th N.I., in 1st Div.
Refs.: Grier. B.: P.P., passim. A.J. xiv. 232. *S.M.* 1815, p. 958. Will dated 19 Oct. 1813; proved 20 Sept. 1815. White marble tablet (with portrait), by Joseph Bonomi, in S. gallery of St. John's, Calcutta.

SHOWERS, Charles Lionel (1816-1895). General. 14th N.I.
b. Barrackpore 5 Feb. 1816. Cadet 1834. Arrived in India 8 June 1835. Ensign 21 Jan. 1835. Lieut. 8 Oct. 1839. Capt. 27 Oct. 1848. Major 1 Jan. 1862. Lt. Col. 7 Feb. 1866. Bt. Col. 18 Feb. 1866. Maj. Gen. 1 Oct. 1877. Lt. Gen. 1 July 1881. Gen. 22 Jan. 1889. *d.* Geneva 13 Sept. 1895.
Son of Howe Daniel Showers, *q.v.*, and Harriet his wife. Brother of Edward Henry Showers, *q.v. m.* Wargrave, Berks., 9 Feb. 1856, Frederica Helen, only dau. of George P. Hurst, and widow of Manby Nightingale, Asst. Surg. Bengal. (She died 20 Mar. 1895.)
Services: d.d. 58th N.I. 19 June 1835; posted to 45th N.I. 24 Sept. 1835; transfd. to 14th N.I. 5 Nov. 1835. Leave s.c. to Hills 10 Mar. 1838 till 5 Apr. 1839. Fur. s.c. 18 Feb. 1844 till 1845. Capture of Kot Kangra June 1846. Campaign in W. Rajputana 1847; comdd. in attack and reduction of Garsesur. Asst. to Agent

in Rajputana 4 Feb. 1848 till 1860. Second Sikh War; Gujerat; on Sir H. Gough's staff (Medal with clasp). Fur. s.c. May 1855 till Aug. 1856. Actg. P.A. Meywar Mar. 1857. Mutiny campaign; C.I. 1857-8; pursuit of Nimach mutineers; cavalry affair before Fort Nimach; action of Partabgarh (Medal with clasp). Fur. 18 mos. 30 Apr. 1860. Resdt. at Gwalior 1868. Transfd. to u.s.l. 1 July 1881. Author of " A Missing Chapter of the Indian Mutiny," 1888, &c. Contested Devonport 3 July 1886.

Refs.: Burke's *Peerage*, 1923, p. 1667, *s.n.* Nightingale, Bart. Boase. *The Times*, 20 Sept. 1895, p. 8; 26 Sept. p. 7.

SHOWERS, Edward Henry (1811-1834). Ensign, 72nd N.I. *b.* Calcutta 20 July 1811. Cadet 1827. Arrived in India 12 Dec. 1828. Ensign 12 June 1828. *d.* Berhampore 10 Mar. 1834, of cholera.

Son of Howe Daniel Showers, *q.v.*, and Harriet his wife. Brother of St. George Daniel Showers, *q.v.* Addiscombe Cadet 1826-8.

Services: Ensign d.d. 72nd N.I. 14 Jan. 1829; posted to do. 3 June 1829. Leave s.c. 7 mos. to Madras 26 Dec. 1832. No record of active service.

Refs.: *A.J.* N.S. xiv. 305; xv. 32. *G.M.* 1834, ii. 335.

SHOWERS, Howe Daniel (1786-1829). Lieut. Colonel, 72nd N.I. *b.* Fatehgarh 28 Jan. 1786. Cadet 1800. Arrived in India 24 Aug. 1801. Ensign 10 Oct. 1801. Lieut. 13 July 1803. Capt. 1 Oct. 1815. Major 13 May 1825. Lt. Col. 20 May 1829. *d.* in his father-in-law's house, London, 31 May 1829.

2nd son of Samuel Howe Showers, *q.v.*, and Melian his 2nd wife. Brother of Charles Lionel Showers, *q.v. m.* Etawah 27 July 1806, Harriet, dau. of St. George Ashe, *q.v.*, and widow of John Lumsdaine, *q.v.* (She died 17 Oct. 1826, aged 37.) Father of Charles Lionel Showers, Edward Henry Showers, and St. George Daniel Showers, *qq.v.*

Services: Ensign d.d. 5th N.I. in 1802. Second Mahratta War 1803-5; Agra; Laswari; Gwalior; Monson's retreat; Bhurtpore (w. in 2nd assault on 21 Jan. 1805); Lieut. 2/9th N.I. Adjt. 1/9th N.I. 16 Dec. 1807 till 1810; do. 2/9th 1810 till 6 Nov. 1815. Capt. Lt. 9th N.I. 1 Oct. 1814. Capt. 1/9th N.I. Bde. Major in Rohilkhand 28 June 1816; do. Meerut Div. 1819 till Feb. 1825. Dy. Postmaster Bareilly 30 Sept. 1817. Transfd. to 8th N.I. (late 1/9th) May 1824. D.A.A.G. Meerut Div. 22 Feb. till May 1825. Transfd. as Major to newly-raised 4th Extra Regt. (became 72nd N.I.) May 1825. Fur. 1828 till death.

Refs.: *E.I.M.C.* iii. 525. *G.M.* 1829, i. 572; ii. 180. *A.J.* xxviii. 27.

SHOWERS, St. George Daniel (1808-1865). Major General, C.B. 2nd Eur. Bengal Fus. *b.* Karnal 21 Oct. 1808. Cadet 1824. Arrived in India 8 May 1825. Ensign 9 Jan. 1825. Lieut. 25 June 1826. Capt. 22 Feb. 1836. Major 24 Apr. 1847. Lt. Col. 10 May 1853. Bt. Col. 18 Mar. 1856. Maj. Gen. 14 Jan. 1864. *d.* Calcutta 8 Oct. 1865.

Son of Howe Daniel Showers, *q.v.*, and Harriet his wife. Brother of Charles Lionel Showers (1816-1895), *q.v. m.* Calcutta cathedral 25 Jan. 1841, Julia, dau. of James Atkinson. (She died 26 Nov. 1886.)

Services: Ensign d.d. 16th N.I. 23 May 1825; posted to 4th Extra Regt. (became 72nd N.I.) 1825; actg. Intr. & Qmr. do. 16 Feb. and 24 Aug. 1829. Leave p.a. 6 mos. to Madras 5 Jan. 1830. A.D.C. to Bdr.-Gen. W. Richards, C.B., *q.v.*, 6 Apr. 1836; do. on personal staff of G.G. 6 Oct. 1838 till 3 Feb. 1841. Actg. Sec., Coll. of Ft. Wm., and Examiner in Persian 5 June 1840; actg. Examiner in Hindi 1 July 1840; Supt. of education of Nawab Nazim of Bengal 10 Feb. 1841 till 1847. Fur. s.c. 8 Feb. 1848 till 1850. Posted Lt. Col. to 72nd N.I. July 1853; to 40th N.I. 1854; to 2nd Eur. Bengal Fus. May 1855 till 1863. Mutiny campaign 1857-8; Badli-ki-Serai; operations before Delhi; comdg. 1st Inf. Bde. (s.w. 12 Aug. 1857); comdd. Moveable Column in Delhi district after capture of the city (Medal with clasp). Bdr. 1 cl. comdg. Agra 22 Jan. 1858; comdd. Presdy. Div. 12 Apr. 1861 till death. C.B. 21 Jan. 1858.

Refs.: Howard & Crisp, iv. 8, *s.n.* Chisenhale-Marsh. Boase. *The Times*, 1 Dec. 1865.

SHOWERS, Samuel Howe (1745-1827). Lieut. Colonel. Infantry. *b.* New England 1745. Cadet 1764. Ensign 27 Dec. 1764. Lieut. 4 Dec. 1766. Capt. 14 Apr. 1769. Major 5 Jan. 1781. Lt. Col. 28 May 1786. Dismissed by C.D. 1 Sept. 1793. *d.* Windsor 12 Oct. 1827, aged 82.

Of Woodside, nr. Windsor. *m.* 1st, Calcutta 15 Jan. 1772, Miss Ann Hammond (*probably* aunt of Charles Sealy, *q.v.*). (She died Patna 4 May 1778, aged 25.) *m.* 2nd, Calcutta 13 Nov. 1779, Melian, widow of William Dare, *q.v.* (She died 1 Jan. 1834, aged 87.) Father of Charles Lionel Showers, *q.v.*, and of Howe Daniel Showers, *q.v.*[1]

Services: Sailed for India in the *Devonshire* 20 Feb. 1764, aged

18. Posted to 1st Bengal Eur. Regt. 13 Aug. 1765. Was comdg. 7th Bn. Sepoys at Monghyr in Sept. 1777. First Mahratta War 1778-9; Capt. comdg. 7th Bn. till Aug. 1779. Apptd. to comd. 2nd Bn. Sepoys 3 Sept. 1780; do. 21st N.I. 1 Jan. 1781; comdg. at Chandernagore in 1783; comdg. 4th Eur. Bn. and Comdt. at Fatehgarh in July 1787. Fur. on h.p. 29 Oct. 1788 till 1790.
Refs.: *Grier*, pp. 315-16. *B.:* *P.P. passim.* *Hickey*, iv. 21. *G.M.* 1827, ii. 380. Will proved (England) 24 Dec. 1827.

[1] *Note :* He obtained Minor Cadetships for no fewer than six of his sons. (*See* Appendix C.) Pub. (London, 1796) the Proceedings of his trial.

SHRIMPTON, John. Captain. Infantry. Lieut. 29 Oct. 1764. Capt. May 1767. Resigned 14 Sept. 1767.

Brother of Edward Shrimpton, protonotary of the High Court in Calcutta.

Services : Ensign 64th Ft. 1 Oct. 1761; Lieut. 106th Ft. 22 Oct. 1761; h.p. do. 1763. Apptd. in England 9 Mar. 1764, Lieut. for Bengal; sailed in the *Lord Anson* 29 May 1764; transfd. as Lieut. to Bengal Army (G.O. Apr. 1765). Posted to 1st Bengal Eur. Regt. 13 Aug. 1765; resigned his commission during the ' Batta Mutiny.' [1] Dismissed in Jan. 1767 for signing, 23 Oct. 1766, an Address in favour of Sir Robert Fletcher, *q.v.*; readmitted shortly afterwards. [Lieut. 62nd Ft. (22 Oct. 1761) 3 June 1767; Capt. do. 17 Sept. 1773; left the Regt. 18 Mar. 1782. (? *d.* 15 Oct. 1783.)]

N.B.—It is not certain that the last portion, in brackets, of the above refers to this man. One J. Shrimpton was apptd. Major of the Tower of London 1785. Maj.-Gen. John Shrimpton (*d.* 1707) was Govr. of Gibraltar 1704; afterwards M.P. for Whitchurch.

Refs.: *Broome*, p. lxxii.

[1] *Note :* Sir Robert Fletcher, writing to Lord Clive under date Monghyr, 14 May 1766, adds a P.S. : " Lieut. Shrimpton is still here sick, and has agreed to stay. He is the best of the whole [of the 1st Bde.], and is much of a gentleman."

SHUBRICK, Henry (1780-?). Captain. 4th N.C. *b.* Enfield 15 June 1780. Cadet 1795. Arrived in India 1 Mar. 1797. Cornet (7 Nov. 1796). Lieut. 29 May 1800. Capt. 29 Aug. 1810. Struck off 17 May 1816. (? Living at Brighton in 1842.)

bapt. Enfield 22 July 1780. Son of Richard Shubrick and Sarah his wife. Brother of Thomas Shubrick, *q.v.*

Services : Posted Cornet to newly-raised 4th N.C. 1797; Qmr. do. 29 May 1800 till 1810. Operations in Jumna Doab 1803;

Sasni; Bijaigarh; Kachaura; Lieut. 4th N.C. Second Mahratta War; Laswari; Lieut. 4th N.C. Capt. Lt. 11 Mar. 1805. Fur. 14 Feb. 1813 till struck off.

SHUBRICK, Thomas (1781-1863). General. Colonel 2nd Eur. L.C. *b*. Enfield 8 Sept. 1781. Cadet 1796. Arrived in India 22 Sept. 1798. Cornet (22 Sept. 1798) 1 Nov. 1798. Lieut. 29 May 1800. Capt. 18 Aug. 1814. Major 4 May 1823. Lt. Col. 26 June 1826. Col. 19 Apr. 1836. Maj. Gen. 23 Nov. 1841. Lt. Gen. 11 Nov. 1851. Gen. 6 Apr. 1862. *d*. 5 York St., St. James's, London, 5 Jan. 1863.

bapt. Enfield 6 Oct. 1781. Son of Richard Shubrick and Sarah his wife. Brother of Henry Shubrick, *q.v.*

Services: Posted Ensign to 3rd Bengal Eur. Regt. Oct. 1798; transfd. to Cav. and posted Cornet to 1st N.C. Dec. 1798. Operations in Jumna Doab 1803; Sasni; Bijaigarh; Kachaura; Lieut. 1st N.C. Second Mahratta War; Koil; Aligarh; Laswari; capture of Deig; Bhurtpore; Lieut. 1st N.C. (India medal). Capt. Lt. 1st N.C. 1 Feb. 1806. Operations in Bundelkhand 1810-11; Bichaund; Capt. Lt. 1st N.C. Fur. s.c. 15 Feb. 1811 till 7 Nov. 1815. Third Mahratta War 1817-18; Capt. 1st N.C., in Rt. Div. Operations against the Bhattis of Hariana 1818. Posted Lt. Col. to 1st L.C. 11 Aug. 1826. Fur. s.c. 15 Jan. 1829 till 2 Oct. 1833. Transfd. to 7th L.C. 13 Oct. 1830; to 2nd L.C. 18 Oct. 1833; to 7th L.C. 24 Dec. 1833. Leave s.c. 2 yrs. to Cape 8 Jan. 1834. Posted Col. to 7th L.C. 10 Sept. 1836. Fur. p.a. 21 Jan. 1838 till death. Transfd. to 3rd, 11th, 2nd L.C. Col. 2nd Bengal Eur. L.C. 1 May 1858 till death.

Refs.: Boase. *The Times*, 8 Jan. 1863.

SHUCKBURGH, Henry Adolphus (1800-1860). Colonel. 40th N.I. *b*. Chester 25 Nov. 1800. Cadet 1824. Arrived in India 20 Oct. 1825. Ensign 9 Feb. 1825. Lieut. 18 Aug. 1825. Capt. 1 Jan. 1844. Major 8 Aug. 1857. Bt. Lt. Col. 4 Feb. 1859. Retired 1 Sept. 1859. Hon. Col. 1 Sept. 1859. *d*. Weston-super-Mare 22 Dec. 1860.

bapt. Chester 10 Nov. 1801. 4th and youngest son of Sir Stewkley Shuckburgh, 7th Bart., and Charlotte Catherine his wife, dau. of Thomas Tydd, of Airdworth, Worcs. *m*. 1st, St. Mary's, Cheltenham, 16 Nov. 1843, Sarah Elizabeth, eldest dau. of William Dwarris, of Golden Grove, Jamaica. (She died Cheltenham 1 Feb. 1846, aged 54.) *m*. 2nd, 5 May 1854, Catharine Dorothy, eldest dau. of Daniel Johannes Cloete, high sheriff of Cape Town, S.A., and great-niece of Jacob Vanrenen, *q.v.* (She died Weston-super-Mare 17 Apr. 1866, aged 35.)

Services: Ensign Northants Mil. 4 July 1823. Posted to 40th N.I. 1825; actg. Adjt. do. 11 Apr. 1827 and 31 Mar. 1830; do. Arakan Local Bn. 16 June 1835 till 13 July 1836. Operations against dacoits Jan.-May 1836. Leave s.c. to China 30 Aug. 1836 till 23 Jan. 1837. Insurrection in Bundelkhand 1842-3; Bt. Capt. 40th N.I. Fur. p.a. 8 June 1843 till 1846. Second Burma War 1852-3; Pegu; Bt. Major 40th N.I. (Medal). Leave 6 mos. to Cape Mar. 1854. Santhal insurrection 1855-6; Major 40th N.I.

Refs.: Burke's *Peerage*, 1923, p. 2024, *s.n.* Shuckburgh, Bart., of Shuckburgh, co. Warwick. *De La Ferté*, ped. 36. *G.M.* 1861, i. 229. *The Times*, 27 Dec. 1860. M.I. Upper Shuckburgh church.

SHULDHAM, Arthur (1786-1835). Lieut. Colonel, 31st N.I. *b.* York 16 Nov. 1786. Cadet 1805. Arrived in India 11 July 1806. Ensign 22 Aug. 1806. Lieut. 27 July 1808. Capt. 29 Mar. 1822. Major 13 Apr. 1827. Lt. Col. 14 May 1832. *d.* Bankura, Bengal, 23 Feb. 1835.

bapt. St. Michael-le-Belfrey, York, 13 Dec. 1786. 5th son of Arthur Lemuel Shuldham, of Dunmanway, co. Cork, and of Pallas Green, co. Limerick, late K.D.G., D.L. co. Devon, Lt. Col. E. Devon Yeomanry Cav., and Katherine Maria his 1st wife, dau. of Sir William Anderson, 6th Bart., of Broughton, and Lea Hall, Lincs. Nephew of Thomas Shuldham, *q.v.* *m.* 1st, Calcutta 3 July 1812, Eliza, sister of Henry Sibley, *q.v.* (*See also* Broadfield Sissmore.) *m.* 2nd, Berhampore 29 Jan. 1823, Charlotte, dau. of Innis Delamain, *q.v.* (*See also* John William Gibbs.)

Services: Barasat C.C. Posted Ensign to 15th N.I. Adjt. 2/15th N.I. 26 Dec. 1810 till July 1814; Intr. & Qmr. do. 1 July 1814 till 1818. Nepal War 1814-15. Nepal War 1816; Lieut. 2/15th N.I., in 4th Bde. Centre Column. Siege and capture of Hathras 1817; Lieut. 2/15th N.I. d.d. Murshidabad Provl. Bn. 1819; Adjt. do. 1820 till 19 July 1822. Transfd. to 31st N.I. (late 2/15th) May 1824. Tempy. D.A.A.G., E. Div., 26 July 1824. To join troops under Bdr.-Gen. Thomas Shuldham, *q.v.*, on Sylhet frontier Nov. 1824. First Burma War; operations in Cachar 1825; D.A.A.G. Bde. Major on Est. at Barrackpore 18 June 1825; D.A.A.G. on Est., R. Div., 9 July 1825; do. Sirhind Div. 12 June 1826; do. Presdy. Div. 4 Sept. 1826 till 11 Jan. 1828. To take charge of 22nd N.I. 16 Sept. 1829; to join 31st N.I. 25 Nov. 1830. Operations against the Chuars 1832. Posted Lt. Col. to 31st N.I. 1 Dec. 1832.

Refs. : Burke's *Landed Gentry of Ireland*, p. 638, s.n. Shuldham, of Ballymulvey, co. Longford. Foster's *Families of Royal Descent*, p. 614. *A.J.* N.S. xvii. 240.

SHULDHAM, Thomas (1756/57-1833). Major General. Colonel 15th N.I. *b.* 1756/57.[1] Cadet 1780. Admitted 27 Apr. 1781. Ensign 1780. Lieut. 1 June 1781. Capt. 1 Nov. 1798. Major 10 May 1804. Lt. Col. 19 May 1808. Col. 4 June 1814. Maj. Gen. 27 May 1825. *d.* London 14 Mar. 1833.
3rd son of Edmund Shuldham and Judith his wife, 2nd dau. of Capt. Arthur Ussher, of Cappagh, co. Waterford. Uncle of Arthur Shuldham, *q.v. m.* Sophia, dau. of Rt. Rev. John Hume, D.D., bishop of Salisbury. (She died Cheltenham 8 Feb. 1855, aged 88.) Father of Thomas Henry Shuldham, *q.v.*
Services : Ensign H.M. 55th Regt. 1 May 1776 ; Lieut. 7th Regt. 4 Oct. 1777. Sailed for India in the *Neptune* 3 June 1780, aged 23. Lieut. 30th Bn. Sepoys in July 1787. Adjt. & Qmr. 4th Bde. in 1790. Fur. s.c. 15 Feb. 1791 till 27 Sept. 1793. Transfd. from 1st to 3rd Bengal Eur. Bn. 7 Sept. 1793 ; A.D.C. to C.-in-C. 2 Jan. 1794 ; posted to 3rd Eur. Regt. June 1796. Bk. Mr. at Berhampore in 1795 ; do. Barrackpore 7 June 1800 till Oct. 1804. Capt. Marine Regt. (became 20th N.I.). Comdt. Burdwan Provl. Bn. 4 Oct. 1804 till 28 Feb. 1808. Posted Lt. Col. to 2/20th N.I. 1808. Comdd. troops at P.W.I. 1810-15 ; at Barrackpore 1817. To comd. troops under orders to proceed to Ceylon, with rank of Bdr., 3 July 1818. Served in Ceylon 25 Sept. 1818 till 1 Apr. 1819. Bdr. 26 June 1819. Comdg. at P.W.I. till 24 Aug. 1820. To comd. Agra and Muttra frontier, with tempy. rank of Bdr. Gen. 6 Mar. 1820. Transfd. to 25th N.I. 1820 ; to 46th N.I. May 1824 ; to 10th N.I. 2 Apr. 1827 ; to 15th N.I. 22 Mar. 1829. Bdr. Gen. 3 June 1824. First Burma War ; operations in Cachar Feb.-Mar. 1825 ; comdg. the force. Comdd. Sirhind Div. 10 Dec. 1826 till 3 May 1828. Fur. p.a. 8 Mar. 1829 till death.
Refs. : Burke's *Landed Gentry of Ireland*, p. 638, s.n. Shuldham, of Ballymulvey, co. Longford. *A.J.* N.S. x. 178. M.I. St. Giles-in-the-Fields, London.
[1] *Note :* M.I. gives age at death as 73, but his own statement of age on embarkation is more likely to be correct.

SHULDHAM, Thomas Henry (1801-1875). Lieut. General. 15th N.I. *bapt.* Calcutta 29 Dec. 1801. Cadet 1822. Arrived in India 6 Oct. 1823. Ensign 6 Oct. 1823. Lieut. 16 May 1824. Capt. 1 Jan. 1837. Major 30 Sept. 1845. Lt. Col. 15 Sept. 1851. Bt. Col. 28 Nov. 1854. Maj. Gen. 18 Mar. 1863. Lt. Gen.

15 Nov. 1871. *d.* at his residence, 6 Park Villas, The Park, Cheltenham, 5 Feb. 1875, aged 73.

2nd son of Thomas Shuldham, *q.v.*, and Sophia his wife. Cousin-german of Arthur Shuldham, *q.v. m.* 1st, St. Cross, psh. of St. Faith, Hants, 31 May 1834, Frances Anne Hamilton, dau. of Levitt Broadley Parkyns, of co. Notts. (He divorced her Jan. 1845, and she *re-m.* David Downing, *q.v.*, and died 7 Aug. 1892, aged 84.) *m.* 2nd, Pakpattan 3 July 1850, Charlotte, widow of Major Harry Hall Watts, 26th Madras N.I., and dau. of James Kempthorne. (She died Meerut 13 Sept. 1856.) Ch. Ch., Oxon.; matric. 31 Jan. 1821.

Services : Posted to 26th N.I.; transfd. to 52nd N.I. (late 2/26th) May 1824. Apptd. A.D.C. to his father 3 Dec. 1824. First Burma War; Cachar 1825; Lieut. 52nd N.I., A.D.C. (India medal). Intr. & Qmr. 52nd N.I. 30 June 1828 till 18 Feb. 1832. Fur. s.c. 21 Nov. 1831 till 13 Nov. 1835. Adjt. 52nd N.I. 2 Apr. 1836 till 19 Feb. 1837. First China War Feb. 1842 till Mar. 1843; Capt. 2nd Vol. Regt. (Medal). Fur. s.c. 19 Feb. 1846 till Dec. 1849. Posted Lt. Col. to 52nd N.I. 18 Nov. 1851; to 15th N.I. 1 Nov. 1854, and was comdg. this Regt. when it mutinied at Nasirabad 28 May 1857. Fur. 3 yrs. 14 Apr. 1859 till death.

Refs. : Burke's *Landed Gentry of Ireland*, p. 638, *s.n.* Shuldham, of Ballymulvey, co. Longford. *Alumni Oxon. The Times*, 13 Feb. 1875.

SHUTE, Thomas Bowman (1790-1818). Lieutenant, 26th N.I. *b.* Bothal, Northumberland, 26 Apr. 1790. Cadet 1806. Arrived in India 1 Aug. 1807. Ensign 4 Aug. 1807. Lieut. 23 Mar. 1809. *d.* in camp nr. Burseah 19 Oct. 1818.

bapt. Bothal 4 July 1790. Son of Rev. Thomas Shute, of Morpeth (of Shipwash), Northumberland, and Mary his wife, dau. of Mr. Bowman, of Crossthwaite, mariner.

Services : Barasat C.C. Posted Ensign to 26th N.I. 1808. Operations in Bundelkhand 1809; Ajaigarh; Ensign 26th N.I. Adjt. 1/26th N.I. 10 July 1810 till death. Third Mahratta War 1818; Dhamoni; Satanwara.

Refs. : Will dated camp 13 Oct. 1818; proved 21 Nov. 1818.

SIBBALD, Hugh (1791-1857). Colonel, C.B., 41st N.I. Bdr. comdg. in Rohilkhand. *b.* 28 Feb. 1791. Cadet 1805. Arrived in India 7 Feb. 1807. Ensign (24 May 1806) 1 Jan. 1807. Lieut. 1 June 1811. Capt. 1 May 1824. Major 28 Feb. 1840. Lt. Col. 27 Feb. 1846. Col. 2 Apr. 1856. *d.* Bareilly 31 May 1857 : kld. by mutineers.

THE BENGAL ARMY, 1758-1834

bapt. Leith 15 Mar. 1791. Son of William Sibbald, of Gladswood, "Admiral of Leith," and Katherine Grieve, of Branxholme Park, his 1st wife. *m.* Calcutta 21 Apr. 1835, Mary Ann Sarah, only dau. of James Tichborne, indigo planter, and widow of Capt. Thomas Howard. (She died 24 Mar. 1887, aged 81.)

Services : Barasat C.C. 16 mos. Posted Ensign to 21st N.I. 1808. Capture of Java 1811 ; Cornelis ; Lieut. 4th Bengal Vol. Bn. (Medal). Served in Java with 4th Vol. Bn. till Nov. 1816 ; Adjt. 1/21st N.I. 12 June 1823 till 17 June 1824 ; transfd. to 41st N.I. (late 1/21st) May 1824. Siege and capture of Bhurtpore ; Capt. Rt. Wing 41st N.I. (India medal). Fur. s.c. 4 June 1826 till 14 July 1829. Comdd. 3rd L.I. Bn. at Cawnpore from its formation Oct. 1840 till broken up 1 Nov. 1842. First Sikh War ; Ferozshahr ; Sobraon ; Major 41st N.I. (Medal with clasp). Posted Lt. Col. to 41st N.I. 1846 ; transfd. to 15th N.I. 1847. Second Sikh War ; passage of Chenab ; Chilianwala ; Gujerat ; Lt. Col. 15th N.I. (Medal with 2 clasps). Assumed comd. of escort to Maharajah Dulip Singh 24 Dec. 1849 ; transfd. to 56th N.I. 23 Mar. 1850 ; to 70th N.I. June 1852. Bdr. 2 cl. comdg. Benares 23 Nov. 1855 ; Bdr. on Est. Jan. 1856 ; comdg. Rohilkhand district 21 Mar. 1856 till death. Col. 41st N.I. June 1856 till death. C.B. 9 June 1849.

Refs. : Burke's *Landed Gentry*, 4th edn., p. 1372, *s.n.* Sibbald, of Westcott. *Memoirs of Susan Sibbald*, by F. P. Hett, London, 1926 (portrait). *Boase*. *G.M.* 1857, ii. 466. M.I. in new cemetery, Bareilly.

SIBBALD, William (*d.* 1800). Major, 9th N.I. Cadet (Art.) (III.-9) 1772. Admitted 1 Aug. 1772. Ensign (Inf.) 17 July 1776. Lieut. 5 July 1778. Capt. 16 Jan. 1793. Major 31 Aug. 1798. *d.* Cawnpore 3 Mar. 1800.

Brother of John Sibbald. *m.* 1st, (?) *m.* 2nd, Cawnpore 23 Aug. 1788, Mary Reed, widow. (She *re-m.* John Williams (1741/42-1809), *q.v.*) Stepfather of Eleanor Reed, the mother of Charles Hutton, *q.v.*

Services : First Rohilla War 1774 ; battle of St. George ; Cadet in Art. Transfd. to Inf. as Ensign 1776. Lieut. 35th Bn. Sepoys in July 1787 ; Capt. d.d. 4th Bengal Eur. Bn. 10 Nov. 1794 ; Major 9th N.I. in 1798.

Refs. : Will dated 30 July 1796 ; proved 25 July 1800.

SIBLEY, Henry (1778-1815). Captain, 15th N.I. *b.* London 11 May 1778. Cadet 1798. Arrived in India 24 Feb. 1800. Ensign 20 Sept. 1799. Lieut. 28 Oct. 1799. Capt. 2 Jan. 1806. *d.* Parsa 1 Jan. 1815 : kld. in action.

bapt. St. John's, Wapping, 4 June 1778. Son of Thomas Sibley, cooper, in the Orchard, Wapping St., and Catharine his wife. Brother of William Sibley, *q.v.*, and of the wives of Arthur Shuldham, *q.v.*, and Broadfield Sissmore, *q.v. m.* Azamgarh 3 Jan. 1801, Lucy Elizabeth Melian, dau. of William Bedell, *q.v.* (*See also* Archibald Dickson.) (She died Calcutta 18 June 1837, aged 53.)
Services : Posted to 1/15th N.I. 15 Apr. 1801. Operations in Jumna Doab 1803 ; Sasni ; Bijaigarh ; Kachaura ; Lieut. 1/15th N.I. Second Mahratta War 1803-5 ; battle of Delhi ; Agra ; Laswari ; battle of Deig (w.) ; Bhurtpore (w. in 3rd assault 20 Feb. 1805) ; Lieut. 1/15th N.I. Nepal War 1814-15 ; Barhawa 25 Nov. 1814 ; Parsa (kld.) ; Capt. 2/15th N.I., in 4th Div.

SIBLEY, William (1782-1803). Lieutenant, 15th N.I. *b.* Wapping 8 Sept. 1782. Cadet 1798. Arrived in India 24 Feb. 1800. Ensign 11 Oct. 1799. Lieut. 28 Oct. 1799. *d.* Calcutta 29 May 1803.
bapt. St. John's, Wapping, 30 Sept. 1782. Son of Thomas Sibley, cooper, and Catharine his wife. Brother of Henry Sibley, *q.v.*
Services : Posted to 1/15th N.I. 15 Apr. 1801. (? Operations in Jumna Doab 1802-3 ; Sasni ; Bijaigarh ; Kachaura ; Lieut. 1/15th N.I.)

SIBTHORPE, Thomas. Lieutenant. Infantry. Country Cadet 1777. Ensign 22 Feb. 1778. Lieut. 28 Sept. 1778. Struck off 1793.
Services : Was already in India when apptd. Cadet 9 Apr. 1777· Arrived at Fort Marlbro' for service in that settlement in Sept· 1780, and was promoted Local Capt. Fur. on h.p. 2 Oct. 1786 till struck off.

SIDDONS, George Richard (1809-1857). Lieut. Colonel. 1st L.C. *b.* Fort Marlbro', Sumatra, 21 Dec. 1809. Cadet 1825. Arrived in India 11 May 1827. Cornet (20 Jan. 1827) 26 Oct. 1827. Lieut. 12 Jan. 1834. Capt. 8 May 1849. Major 17 Sept. 1855. Retired 1 Jan. 1857. Hon. Lt. Col. 1 Jan. 1857. *d.* at sea 7 Jan. 1857, of apoplexy, on board the *Sir Frederick Currie.*
Eldest son of George John Siddons (who was 2nd son of Sarah Siddons, the actress), Head Asst. to Resdt. at Fort Marlbro', afterwards P.M.G. Bengal, and Mary his wife, dau. of John Fombelle, B.C.S., "who, on one side, derived her blood from the Kings of Delhi." (*See also* Henry Templer.) Brother of William Young Siddons, *q.v.*, and cousin-german of Henry Siddons, *q.v. m.* Benares

THE BENGAL ARMY, 1758-1834

18 July 1850, Elizabeth, dau. of Philip Vander Byl. Haileybury 1826.
Services : d.d. 1st L.C. 28 May 1827 ; posted to do. 28 Dec. 1827. Offg. Intr. & Qmr. 10th L.C. 1 Jan. 1832 ; do. 7th L.C. 6 Oct. 1832 ; Adjt. 3rd Local Horse 9 Mar. 1835 ; 2nd in comd. do. 16 Mar. 1835 till 26 June 1837. Fur. p.a. 7 Jan. 1838 till 5 Jan. 1841. Adjt. 1st L.C. 17 Feb. 1841 till 6 Mar. 1844 ; Intr. & Qmr. do. 6 Mar. 1844 till 1849. First Afghan War 1842 ; reoccupation of Kabul ; Bt. Capt. 1st L.C., with Pollock's force (Medal). Gwalior campaign ; Maharajpur ; Bt. Capt. 1st L.C. (Bronze star). First Sikh War ; Aliwal ; Bt. Capt. 1st L.C. (Medal). Second Sikh War ; passage of Chenab ; Chilianwala ; Gujerat ; Bt. Capt. 1st L.C. (Medal with 2 clasps). Bde. Major Barrackpore 8 Mar. 1851 ; do. Agra Jan.-Sept. 1855. Fur. s.c. Jan. 1857. Translated, 1851, the *Vichitra Natak*.
Refs. : The Incomparable Siddons, by Mrs. Clement Parsons. *N. & Q.* 7S. iii. 4. *I.M.* 3 Mar. 1857, p. 142.

SIDDONS, Henry (1812-1850). Bt. Major, Engineers. *bapt.* Edinburgh 9 Aug. 1812. Cadet 1830. Arrived in India 3 June 1831. 2nd Lieut. (11 Dec. 1829) 3 June 1831. Lieut. 20 May 1839. Capt. 1 May 1849. Bt. Major 7 June 1849. *d.* Portobello, Edinburgh, 26 Feb. 1850.

Son of Henry Siddons (who was eldest child of Mrs. Sarah Siddons), of the Theatre Royal (*D.N.B.*), and Harriet his wife, dau. of Charles Murray (*D.N.B.*). Cousin-german of William Young Siddons, *q.v. m.* Calcutta 7 July 1834, Harriot Emma, 2nd dau. of his uncle George John Siddons, B.C.S., P.M.G., Bengal. (She died Edinburgh 16 Mar. 1856.) Addiscombe Cadet 1 Aug. 1828 till 11 Dec. 1829 ; Chatham 8 Feb. till 29 Nov. 1830.
Services : d.d. S. & M. at Delhi 14 July 1831. Apptd. Actg. 2nd Lieut. 13 June 1833, with effect from 3 June 1831. Apptd. to Survey Dept. Jan. 1833 ; Revenue Surveyor at Chittagong 13 Oct. 1834 till 1840. Fur. p.a. 8 Feb. 1841 till 11 Oct. 1842. Adjt. Engrs. and Asst. Field Engr. Bundelkhand F.F. 25 Nov. 1842. Executive Engr. Arakan Div., P.W.D., 22 May 1843. Adjt. S. & M. 29 Aug. 1845. First Sikh War ; Sobraon ; Lieut. Engrs. (Medal). Supt. canals W. of Jumna 30 Oct. 1846. Second Sikh War ; Multan ; Gujerat ; Bt. Capt. Engrs., comdg. Sappers & Pioneers (Medal with 2 clasps). Fur. s.c. 10 Sept. 1849 till death.
Refs. : The Incomparable Siddons. *N. & Q.* 7S. iii. 4. *I.M.* 22 Mar. 1850, p. 176.

*SIDDONS, William Young (1815-1851). Bt. Captain, 63rd N.I. *b.* Fort Marlbro' 14 Aug. 1815. Cadet 1832. Admitted

10 Jan. 1834. Ensign (11 June 1833) 10 Jan. 1834. Lieut. 10 Sept. 1838. Bt. Capt. 11 June 1848. *d.* Bhopawar, C.I., (? Indore) 21 Sept. 1851.

bapt. Fort Marlbro' 20 Oct. 1815. 3rd son of George John Siddons, B.C.S., and Mary his wife. Brother of George Richard Siddons, *q.v. m.* Mussoorie 16 Feb. 1843, Susan Mary, eldest dau. of John Lucas Earle, *q.v.* (*See also* Robert Christopher Tytler.) Addiscombe Cadet 5 Aug. 1831 till 11 June 1833.

Services: Supy. Ensign d.d. 7th N.I. 13 Jan. 1834; posted Ensign to 63rd N.I. 5 Nov. 1834. Actg. Intr. & Qmr. 11th L.C. 3 Mar. 1842; do. 42nd N.I. 24 Jan. 1843; do. 64th N.I. 11 Sept. 1843. Offg. D.C. 3 cl., Saugor Div., 18 Feb. 1845; Asst. to P.A. Bhopal 13 Jan. 1849; Bhil Agent at Indore 2 Jan. 1851. No record of active service.

Refs.: The Incomparable Siddons. N. & Q. 7S. iii. 4. *I.M.* 19 Nov. 1851, p. 674. *G.M.* 1852, i. 105. M.I. Indore.

SIDNEY, Charles (1793-1822). Lieutenant, 7th L.C. *b.* Bingham, Notts., 22 Sept. 1793. Cadet 1810. Cornet 31 Dec. 1815. Lieut. 21 Dec. 1818. *d.* at sea 14 Aug. 1822, on board the *Abberton,* on his passage to England.

bapt. Kensington 1 Apr. 1811. Son of John Sidney and Mary his wife. Nephew of the House Steward to H.R.H. the Princess of Wales.

Services: Cadet d.d. 2nd N.C. 1811-12; posted to 7th N.C. 1816. Siege and capture of Hathras 1817; Cornet 7th N.C. Third Mahratta War 1817-18; Dhamoni; Mandala; Multai; Harna; Cornet 7th N.C. Adjt. 7th L.C. 14 Jan. 1819 till 7 Mar. 1822. Fur. s.c. 1822 till death.

SIM, James Milne (1787-1827). Captain, 1st Extra N.I. *b.* Barry, co. Forfar, 21 Mar. 1787. Cadet 1807. Arrived in India 16 Nov. 1808. Ensign 1 Nov. 1808. Lieut. 20 Aug. 1813. Capt. 13 June 1825. *d.* Westhaven 3 July 1827.

Eldest son of Rev. David Sim, minister of Barry 1776-1823, and Agnes Maule his wife.

Services: Barasat C.C. 1808-9. Posted to 1/11th N.I. 1809. Reduction of Kalinjar 1812; Ensign 1/11th N.I. Adjt. 1/11th N.I. 28 Jan. 1822 till May 1824. Transfd. to 15th N.I. (late 1/11th) May 1824. (? Action at Patan, nr. Kotah, 7 Nov. 1824; Lieut. 15th N.I.) Transfd. to newly-raised 1st Extra Regt. May 1825. Fur. 1825 till death.

Refs.: Scott's *Fasti,* v. 431. *A.J.* xxiv. 270.

SIMMONDS, John Henry (1790-1869). Lieut. Colonel. 55th N.I. *b.* 1790. Cadet 1807. Arrived in India 16 Nov. 1808. Ensign 6 Nov. 1808. Lieut. 31 May 1813. Capt. 13 May 1825. Major 3 Oct. 1842. Invalided 2 May 1845. Retired 12 Oct. 1846. Hon. Lt. Col. 28 Nov. 1854. *d.* Southstoke, nr. Bath, 7 May 1869, aged 79.

bapt. Leixlip, co. Kildare, 6 Jan. 1791. Son of John Simmonds and Catherine his wife. *m.* Calcutta 15 Feb. 1838, Elizabeth Susannah, eldest dau. of Sir Robert Graham, 8th Bart., of Esk. (*See also* John Hore Hatchell.)

Services : Barasat C.C. 10 mos. Posted Ensign to 6th N.I. 1810. Fur. s.c. 6 Mar. 1812 ; do. 28 Jan. 1814 till 30 Apr. 1816. Transfd. to newly-raised 2/28th N.I. 1815. Third Mahratta War 1818 ; Dhamoni ; Lieut. 2/28th N.I. Intr. & Qmr. 3rd Ceylon Vols. 3 Oct. 1818 till 1819. Transfd. to 55th N.I. (late 1/28th) May 1824. Asst. Revenue Surveyor 12 Feb. 1824 till June 1835. Sec. to Clothing Board 21 Feb. 1835 till 30 Mar. 1841. Leave s.c. to Cape 15 Mar. 1836 till 9 Dec. 1837. Agent for Army Clothing, 1st Div., 31 Mar. 1841 till May 1845.

Refs. : Burke's *Peerage*, 1923, p. 1017, *s.n.* Graham, Bart., of Esk, Cumberland. *The Times*, 12 May 1869.

SIMONDS, William (1786-1865). Lieut. Colonel. 21st N.I. *b.* Wigton, Cumberland, 19 Sept. 1786. Cadet 1807. Arrived in India 14 Sept. 1808. Ensign 30 Sept. 1808. Lieut. 16 Aug. 1814. Capt. 13 May 1825. Major 15 Mar. 1841. Invalided 1 Sept. 1841. Retired 10 Jan. 1845. Hon. Lt. Col. 28 Nov. 1854. *d.* at his residence, 39 Fitzroy Sq., London, 4 Oct. 1865.

bapt. Wigton 31 Aug. 1787. Son of James Simonds, of Wigton, brandy merchant, and Bellinda his wife, *née* Robinson. *m.* Cawnpore 24 Aug. 1822, Cecilia Emma Cromey, sister of John Angelo, *q.v.* (*See also* G. R. Pemberton.) (She died London 27 Feb. 1848, aged 49.) His dau. *m.* John Butler (1809-1874), *q.v.*

Services : Barasat C.C. 6 mos. Posted Ensign to 9th N.I. 1809. Nepal War 1816 ; Makwanpur ; Lieut. 2/9th N.I., in 4th Bde. Centre Column (India medal). Intr. & Qmr. 2/9th N.I. 17 Aug. 1819 till 29 July 1825. Transfd. to 21st N.I. (late 2/9th) May 1824. Siege and capture of Bhurtpore ; Capt. 21st N.I. (clasp to India medal). Fur. p.a. 9 Nov. 1826 till 15 Jan. 1830. Comdt. Magh Sebundy Corps (designation changed to " Arakan Local Bn." from 5 Nov. 1832) 5 Dec. 1831 till 16 Mar. 1835 ; do. newly-raised Lower Assam Sebundy Corps 19 Mar. 1835 till Sept. 1841.

Refs. : *The Times*, 6 Oct. 1865.

SIMONS, Edward (1780-1830). Lieut. Colonel, 12th N.I. bapt. West Drayton 5 Mar. 1780. Cadet 1799. Arrived in India 24 Oct. 1800. Ensign 23 Sept. 1800. Lieut. 19 Dec. 1802. Capt. 23 Mar. 1814. Major 30 Jan. 1824. Lt. Col. 8 Sept. 1825. d. Guernsey 26 Nov. (? Dec.) 1830.

Eldest son of Rev. John Simons, LL.D., rector of St. Paul's Cray, Kent, and Mary Anne his wife, dau. of William Sturges, of Datchet, and of Bradford, Yorks., J.P. m. Guernsey 31 July 1820, Maria, sister of H. C. A. Browne, q.v.

Services: Posted Ensign to 1/1st N.I. 17 Apr. 1801. Second Mahratta War 1803-4 ; reduction of Cuttack ; capture of Balasore ; Lieut. 1st Vol. Bn. Operations in Bundelkhand 1805-6 ; Lieut. 1st N.I. Third Mahratta War 1817-18 ; Rampur ; Jawad ; Capt. 1/1st N.I., in Left Div. Fur. 11 Mar. 1819 till 1822. Transfd. to 2nd N.I. (late 1/1st) May 1824 ; to 2nd Extra Regt. May 1825. To comd. 9th Extra Regt. 21 May 1825. Transfd. to 2nd N.I. 1826 ; to 5th Extra Regt. ; to 48th N.I. 7 July 1826 ; to 56th N.I. 1827 ; to 12th N.I. 1827. Fur. s.c. 11 Jan. 1830 till death.

Refs.: Burke's *Landed Gentry*, 4th edn., p. 1470, s.n. Symons, of Hatt, Cornwall. *A.J.* N.S. iv. 114. *G.M.* 1830, ii. 648. Will dated Nasirabad, 8 Oct. 1828 ; proved 7 Apr. 1832.

SIMPSON, Charles [1] (d. 1794). Lieutenant, Infantry. Cadet 1782. Admitted 15 Aug. 1783. Ensign 6 Feb. 1783. Lieut. 18 Jan. 1790. d. at sea c. Aug. 1794 : lost on his passage to Bencoolen ; struck off from 31 July 1795.

Services: Apptd. Cadet 22 May 1782 ; sailed for India in the *Francis* 11 Sept. 1782. Ensign 2nd Bengal Eur. Bn. in July 1787 ; transfd. to 1st Eur. Bn. 29 Jan. 1790 ; to 11th Bn. Sepoys 16 Mar. 1792.

[1] *Note:* His name sometimes appears as Charles Leighton Simpson.

SIMPSON, David (1801-1887). General. 54th N.I. b. Minto, co. Roxburgh, 25 Sept. 1801. Cadet 1818. Admitted 9 Feb. 1820. Ensign 16 Aug. 1819. Lieut. 16 Aug. 1822. Capt. 24 Apr. 1833. Major 22 Dec. 1844. Lt. Col. 15 Mar. 1851. Col. 13 Apr. 1860. Maj. Gen. 2 Oct. 1862. Lt. Gen. 3 Sept. 1871. Gen. 1 Oct. 1877. d. Harrogate 1 Sept. 1887.

Of Leinster Gdns., Hyde Pk., London. bapt. Minto 31 Oct. 1801. Youngest son of David Simpson, of Teviotbank, co. Roxburgh (of Know), and Margaret his wife, dau. of John Elliot of Borthwickbrae. Brother of Gen. Sir James Simpson, G.C.B. (*D.N.B.*). m. 1st, Margaret, dau. of James Hill, of Busbie, writer in Glasgow, and

THE BENGAL ARMY, 1758-1834   95

cousin-german of Lawrence Hill, *q.v.* (She died Banda 24 July 1836.) *m.* 2nd, Allahabad 11 Feb. 1840, Maria, youngest dau. of George Birrell, *q.v.* (She died London 10 Apr. 1902, aged 88.)

Services : Posted Ensign to 2/14th N.I. ; transfd. to 29th N.I. (late 2/14th) May 1824 ; actg. Adjt. do. 24 Aug. 1824 ; permanent do. 10 Aug. 1825 till 13 Aug. 1832. Fur. p.a. 14 Jan. 1833 till 30 Nov. 1835. Actg. Paymr. & Supt. of Native Pensioners at Allahabad 13 Sept. 1838 ; permanent do. 9 June 1842 till Dec. 1844. Second Sikh War ; Jullundur Doab 1848-9 ; Amb ; Oonah ; Major comdg. force of 5 Coys. 29th N.I., under Capt. Alexander Park, *q.v.* (Medal). Posted Lt. Col. to 29th N.I. 20 May 1851. Fur. s.c. 17 Feb. 1852 till 23 Jan. 1856. Transfd. to 28th N.I. 18 June 1853 ; to 6th N.I. 28 Mar. 1855, and was comdg. this Regt. at Allahabad when it mutinied 6 June 1857. He managed to escape to the fort. Transfd. to 54th N.I. (which had mutinied at Delhi 11 May) 24 June 1857. Fur. s.c. 6 May 1858 till death.

Refs. : Burke's *Landed Gentry*, 11th edn., p. 1034, *s.n.* Elliot-Lockhart, of Cleghorn. *Boase. The Times*, 9 Sept. 1887.

SIMPSON, Edward Henry (1784-1845). Major General, comdg. Dinapore Div. Colonel 24th N.I. *b.* 3 Sept. 1784. Cadet 1799. Arrived in India 8 Dec. 1800. Ensign 17 Jan. 1800. Lieut. 29 May 1800. Capt. 3 June 1814. Major 5 Mar. 1823. Lt. Col. 3 June 1824. Col. 29 Aug. 1833. Maj. Gen. 28 June 1838. *d.* Darjeeling 30 Sept. 1845.

Eldest son of Noah Simpson, Major 31st Regt., of Boyle, co. Roscommon, and Alicia his wife, 4th dau. of Richard Sheffield Cassan, of Sheffield, Queen's Co. *m.* Chilla Tarra 20 Feb. 1817, Christina, dau. of —— Boyd, of co. Armagh. (She died Lee 15 Dec. 1880.)

Services : Posted Ensign to 2/8th N.I. 15 Apr. 1801. (? Operations in Jumna Doab 1803 ; Sasni ; Bijaigarh ; Kachaura ; Lieut. 8th N.I.) Second Mahratta War 1804-5 ; Monson's retreat (w. 28 July 1804 at Lakeri Pass) ; Lieut. 2/8th N.I. Adjt. 1st L.I. Bn. 1808-9. Capt. Lt. 8th N.I. 23 Aug. 1812. Nepal War 1814-15 ; Capt. 1/8th N.I., in 4th Div. Nepal War 1816 ; Capt. 1/8th N.I., in 2nd Bde. Left Column. Third Mahratta War 1817-19 ; Capt. 1/8th N.I. Transfd. to 9th N.I. (late 1/8th) May 1824 ; Lt. Col. 33rd N.I. 1826 ; 56th 24 Dec. 1827 ; 22nd 24 Sept. 1831 ; 67th 11 June 1832 ; 25th 14 Sept. 1833. Fur. p.a. 21 Jan. 1831 till 1 June 1833. Col. 25th N.I. 15 Oct. 1833 ; 24th 18 Dec. 1834 ; 19th 11 Dec. 1837 ; comdd. Shah Shuja's Force 2 Oct. 1838 till 1 Apr. 1840. First Afghan War 1838-40 ; Ghazni (Medal).

96 LIST OF THE OFFICERS OF

Transfd. to 24th N.I. 28 May 1841. Bdr. 2 cl. comdg. Agra 26 Jan. 1843; apptd. to Gen. Staff of Army, comdg. Benares Div. 17 Mar. 1843; do. Dinapore Div. 1 Oct. 1844 till death. Durani 2 cl. 15 Aug. 1840.

Refs.: Burke's *Landed Gentry*, 7th edn., p. 1671, *s.n.* Simpson, of Cloncorick Castle, co. Leitrim. *G.M.* 1846, i. 110. Will dated Darjeeling 1 July 1845; proved 15 Dec. 1845.

SIMPSON, Frederick John (1800-1869). Lieut. Colonel. 55th N.I. *b.* Marylebone, Middlesex, 19 May 1800. Cadet 1817. Admitted 1818. Ensign 14 Mar. 1818. Lieut. 1 Aug. 1818. Capt. 23 May 1828. Bt. Major 23 Nov. 1841. Retired 3 May 1845. Hon. Lt. Col. 28 Nov. 1854. *d.* Milford, nr. Lymington, Hants, 8 Oct. 1869.

bapt. Marylebone 27 June 1800. Son of John Simpson, of Begsbrook, Armagh, and Jane his wife. Brother of Thomas Simpson and stepson of William Popham, *qq.v.* Ed. Westminster; admitted 2 June 1812.

Services: Posted Lieut. to 2/28th N.I. 1819; d.d. Rangpur L.I. 14 Nov. 1823; transfd. to 55th N.I. (late 1/28th) May 1824; Intr. & Qmr. do. 24 Nov. 1824 till 2 Oct. 1827. Fur. p.a. 17 Jan. 1836 till 15 Aug. 1839. With Army of Reserve (for Afghanistan) Oct. 1842 till Jan. 1843. No record of active service.

Refs.: *Westminster School Register*. *The Times*, 12 Oct. 1869.

SIMPSON, James (1761/62-1793). Lieutenant, 15th Bn. Sepoys. *b.* in Ireland 1761/62. Cadet 1781. Arrived in India 30 May 1782. Ensign 2 July 1781. Lieut. 5 Oct. 1782. *d.* Barrackpore 12 Feb. 1793.

Services: Apptd. Cadet 9 May 1781, aged 19; sailed for India in the *Lord Mulgrave* 26 June 1781. Lieut. 15th Bn. Sepoys in July 1787.

SIMPSON, John (1781-1836). Colonel, 58th N.I. *b.* New North Kirk psh., Edinburgh, 3 Jan. 1781. Cadet 1798. Arrived in India 24 Feb. 1800. Ensign 25 Jan. 1800. Lieut. 31 July 1800. Capt. 12 Oct. 1812. Major 11 July 1823. Lt. Col. 13 May 1825. Col. 23 June 1835. *d.* Edinburgh 30 June 1836.

Son of Edward Simpson, perfumer and hairdresser, and Margaret his wife, dau. of Peter Ogilvy (or Ogilvie), smith in Stirling. *m.* Edinburgh 2 Mar. 1815, Janet (Jessy) Eckford. (She died Versailles 4 Jan. 1882.)

Services: Posted Lieut. to 2/14th N.I. 15 Apr. 1801. Second Mahratta War 1803-5; taken prisoner by a party of Pindaris

Sept. 1803 ; Lieut. 14th N.I. Adjt. 1/14th N.I. 8 Sept. 1804 till Oct. 1812. Capt. Lt. 14th N.I. 6 July 1811. Fur. p.a. 24 Oct. 1812 till 26 Aug. 1815. Capt. 2/14th N.I. Operations against insurgents at Sitamau, C.I., Dec. 1822 ; comdg. 5 Coys. 2/14th N.I. and a small battering train. Transfd. to 28th N.I. (late 1/14th) May 1824. To comd. newly-raised 2nd Extra Regt. (became 70th N.I.) 21 May 1825 ; transfd. to 4th N.I. 7 Sept. 1829 ; to 22nd 11 June 1832 ; to 69th 23 Sept. 1834. Comdg. troops in Oudh territory 1834. Fur. s.c. 8 Jan. 1835 till death. Posted Col. to 58th N.I. 11 Dec. 1835.

Refs. : G.M. 1836, ii. 222.

SIMPSON, John James (d. 1769). Captain, Infantry. Lieut. 6 Jan. 1766. Capt. 1768. d. 1769.

Services : N.F.P.

SIMPSON,[1] **John Mackenzie** (1782-1804). Lieutenant, 17th N.I. b. Dingwall 13 Oct. 1782. Cadet 1799. Arrived in India 9 Dec. 1800. Ensign 22 Sept. 1800. Lieut. 17 July 1801. d. Delhi 14 Oct. 1804 : mortally wounded in defending his post during the last assault of the enemy that day.

bapt. Dingwall 20 Oct. 1782. Son of John Simpson, writer in Dingwall, and Catharine Hay his wife. Brother of Charles Simson, writer in Dingwall.

Services : Posted Ensign to 2/17th N.I. 17 Apr. 1801. Operations in Jumna Doab 1802-3 ; Lieut. 2/17th N.I. Second Mahratta War 1803-4 ; defence of Delhi Oct. 1804 (s.w.) ; Lieut. 2/17th N.I.

Refs. : Calcutta Monthly Journal, Nov. 1804, p. 793. Will dated Delhi 1 Sept. 1804 ; proved 3 Dec. 1804.

[1] Note : Simson in his Will.

SIMPSON, John Matthew (1805-?). Ensign. 17th N.I. bapt. Richmond, Yorks., 14 Nov. 1805. Cadet 1825. Ensign 15 Mar. 1826. Resigned in India 13 Apr. 1830. (Dead in 1839.)

Son of Thomas Simpson, mayor, and Elizabeth his wife.

Services : Ensign d.d. 5th Extra Regt. 27 July 1826 ; posted to 17th N.I. 26 Sept. 1826. No record of active service. Pensd. on Lord Clive's fund 5 Sept. 1832.

SIMPSON, Leonard (1757/58-1806). Lieut. Colonel, 2nd N.I. b. 1757/58. Cadet 1776. Admitted 1776. Ensign 1 Apr. 1777. Lieut. 26 Aug. 1778. Capt. 10 Jan. 1795. Major 31 July 1799. Lt. Col. 16 Nov. 1802. d. unm. Fatehgarh 7 June 1806, aged 48. Brother of John Simpson.

Services : Apptd. Cadet 13 Dec. 1775 ; sailed for India in the *Nassau* 9 Jan. 1776. Campaign against the Rajah of Benares 1781. Lieut. 15th Bn. Sepoys in July 1787 ; transfd. to 2nd Bengal Eur. Bn. 5 Jan. 1792 ; Capt. 1/9th N.I. in Aug. 1798 ; transfd. to 5th N.I. 1798. Operations in Jumna Doab 1803 ; Sasni ; Bijaigarh ; Kachaura ; Lt. Col. 2/2nd N.I. Second Mahratta War 1803-5 ; Aligarh ; battle of Delhi ; pursuit of Holkar ; Bdr. comdg. 4th Bde. 1804-5.

Refs. : Will dated Fatehgarh 1 June 1806 ; proved 25 June 1806. M.I. in Fatehgarh fort cemetery.

SIMPSON, Richard Salisbury (1810-1888). Colonel. 27th N.I. *b.* Lancaster 19 Mar. 1810. Cadet 1827. Arrived in India 16 Oct. 1828. Ensign 1 May 1828. Lieut. 7 Feb. 1833. Capt. 24 Jan. 1845. Major 11 Nov. 1856. Lt. Col. 4 June 1860. Retired 31 Dec. 1861. Hon. Col. 31 Dec. 1861. *d.* Moffat 1 June 1888.

Son of John Simpson, of Lancaster, merchant, and Maria his wife. *m.* Karnal 3 Dec. 1835, Emily Ann, widow of Thomas Richardson, B.C.S., and dau. of Charles William Hamilton, *q.v.* (*See also* T. V. Lysaght.)

Services : Ensign d.d. 55th N.I. 20 Nov. 1828 ; posted to 27th N.I. 22 Apr. 1829 ; transfd. to 68th N.I. 27 Aug. 1831 ; to 27th N.I. 18 Feb. 1832 ; actg. Adjt. do. 31 May 1834 ; do. Nassiri Bn. 5 Nov. 1835. S.A.C.G. 4 Sept. 1837 ; apptd. Comst. Ofr. 1st Bde., Army of Indus, 18 Sept. 1838. First Afghan War 1839 ; Ghazni ; Lieut. 27th N.I., Comst. Dept. (Medal). Returned sick to India Nov. 1839 ; leave s.c. to Cape 25 Mar. 1840 till 28 Feb. 1842. D.A.C.G. 2 cl. 16 May 1845 ; 1 cl. 10 Feb. 1848 ; A.C.G. 2 cl. 14 May 1852 ; 1 cl. 9 May 1853. Second Sikh War ; D.A.C.G. (Medal). Against Afridis in Kohat Pass Feb. 1850 ; D.A.C.G. (N.W.F. medal). Second Burma War 1852 ; capture of Rangoon ; A.C.G. (Medal). Fur. s.c. 29 Feb. 1856 till Sept. 1858. Permanently attached to Comst. Dept. as A.C.G. 1 cl. 29 Oct. 1858 till 27 July 1860.

Refs. : *The Times*, 7 June 1888.

SIMPSON, Robert (1789-?). Ensign. Infantry. *b.* Hoxton, London, 18 June 1789. Cadet 1805. Arrived in India 19 Sept. 1806. Ensign 1 Oct. 1806. Resigned in India 1 Jan. 1807.

bapt. St. Leonard's, Shoreditch, 17 July 1789. Son of Robert Simpson, of Hoxton, and Catherine his wife.

Services : N.F.P.

THE BENGAL ARMY, 1758-1834 99

SIMPSON, Thomas (1811-1890). Colonel. 57th N.I. *bapt.* Tamlaght Finlagan, co. Londonderry, 5 Apr. 1811. Cadet 1827. Arrived in India 20 June 1828. Ensign (10 Jan. 1828) 4 Nov. 1828. Lieut. 17 July 1832. Capt. 24 Jan. 1845. Bt. Major 20 June 1854. Bt. Lt. Col. 24 Mar. 1858. Retired 31 Dec. 1861. Hon. Col. 31 Dec. 1861. *d.* 30 Nov. 1890.

Son of John Simpson, of Armagh, and Jane his wife. Brother of Frederick John Simpson, *q.v. m.* Gaya, B.&O., 19 May 1853, E. Mary, dau. of Rev. Fulwar Craven Fowle (? and niece of Charles Fowle, *q.v.*).

Services: Ensign d.d. 6th Extra Regt. 17 July 1828; posted to 57th N.I. 4 Nov. 1828. Fur. s.c. 10 Feb. 1830 till 16 July 1832. Attached to Ramgarh Bn. 8 Jan. 1834 till Feb. 1836. Operations against the Chuars Nov. 1835. Offg. Junr. Asst. to A.G.G., S.W. frontier, 17 Feb. 1836 till 24 Oct. 1837. Operations against the Kols Dec. 1837; Lieut. 57th N.I., attached to Ramgarh Bn. Junior Asst. to A.G.G., S.W. frontier, 11 Dec. 1837; Principal do. 17 Feb. 1841; do. to Comr. of Chota Nagpur 1 Sept. 1854 till retirement. Fur. s.c. 15 mos. Apr. 1855. Mutiny campaign 1857-8 (Medal).

SIMSON, Connell (1774-1811). Captain, 14th N.I. *b.* Glasgow 6 Dec. 1774. Cadet 1794. Arrived in India 26 Sept. 1796. Ensign 23 Oct. 1795. Lieut. 25 Apr. 1797. Capt. 21 Sept. 1804. *d.* Port Louis, Mauritius, 5 July 1811.

Son of John Simson and Elizabeth Nasmith his wife.

Services: Apptd. Cadet 29 Mar. 1796; sailed for India in the *Europa* 17 May 1796. Posted to 2nd Bengal Eur. Regt. 1796; Lieut. 14th N.I. in 1798; at P.W.I. in 1803. Second Mahratta War; Capt. 14th N.I. Fur. 23 Feb. 1807 till 2 Aug. 1810. Expedn. to Mauritius 1810-11; Capt. 2nd Vol. Bn.

SINCLAIR, George (*d.* 1782). Major, Infantry. Cadet 1766. Ensign 7 Jan. 1767. Lieut. 1 Apr. 1769. Capt. 1 Apr. 1777. Major 7 May 1781. *bur.* Bombay 17 May 1782.

Brother of James Sinclair (1757/58-1804), *q.v. m.* Katharine. (She died 10 May 1788.)

Services: Sailed for India in the *Speaker* 21 Feb. 1766. Fur. s.c. 1774-7; employed on recruiting duty in Scotland in 1777. Confirmed in comd. of 6th Bn. Sepoys 13 Nov. 1780. First Mahratta War 1778-82; Capt. and Major comdg. 6th Bn. N.I.

Refs.: Will undated; admon. (Bombay) 10 June 1782.

SINCLAIR, James (1746-1788). Lieutenant, Infantry. *b.* 1746. Cadet 1773. Ensign 10 July 1776. Lieut. 30 June 1778. *d.s.p.* Whitcomb St., London, 11 Jan. 1788, aged 41.

In Reiss, Caithness. Elder son of David Sinclair and Margaret More or McKay his wife. *m.* Reiss 17 Dec. 1763, Catherine Rosie. Unsuccessfully claimed the earldom of Caithness in 1766 and 1768.[1]

Services: Sailed for India in the *Anson* Feb. 1772. Apptd. Qmr. to Select Picket 4 Sept. 1773. First Rohilla War 1774; battle of St. George; Cadet in Select Picket. Lieut. 2/3rd Bengal Eur. Regt in Oct. 1779. Apptd. actg. Adjt. of Mil. at Ft. Wm. 18 Sept. 1781. Fur. 2 Nov. 1785 till death.

Refs.: Burke's *Peerage*, 1923, p. 419, *s.n.* Caithness, E. *G.E.C. Complete Peerage,* ii. (1912) 482, note (a). *The St. Clairs of the Isles.* Macpherson, p. 146. *S.M.* 1788, p. 50. *G.M.* 1788, i. 84. Will (Somerset House) dated 1785 and 1787.

[1] *Note:* " Would have been successful but for his sudden death, without issue."—*Genealogist,* N.S. xv. 67.

SINCLAIR, James (1757/58-1804). Major, 2nd N.I. *b.* in Scotland 1757/58. Cadet 1779. Admitted 12 Feb. 1780. Ensign 13 Aug. 1779. Lieut. 5 Apr. 1781. Capt. 6 Dec. 1797. Major 30 Sept. 1803. *d.* Sikandra 24 Aug. 1804: kld. in action during Monson's retreat.

Brother of George Sinclair, *q.v. m.* a sister of Capt. William Geddes, of Dundee.

Services: Sailed for India in the *Walpole* 16 June 1779, aged 21. Adjt. 23rd Bn. Sepoys in July 1787 till after 1794. Capt. 2/1st N.I. in July 1798; transfd. to 2nd N.I. 1798. Operations in Jumna Doab 1802-3; Sasni; Capt. 1/2nd N.I. Second Mahratta War 1803-4; Aligarh; Agra; battle of Delhi; Laswari; Capt. 1/2nd N.I.; capture of Hinglaisgarh fort 2 July 1804; Major comdg. the detachment; Monson's retreat (kld.) [1]; Major comdg. 2/2nd N.I.

Refs.: Pester, pp. 312-13. *E.I.M.C.* ii. 552-3. Col. H. Pearse's *Lake,* pp. 275, 286. Will dated camp, 22 July 1804; proved 4 Apr. 1805.

[1] *Note:* " The river had risen so high that he could not cross, and rather than surrender himself and his officers and men into the hands of so sanguinary a butcher as Holcar, he took the colours of his Corps in his own hands, and most gallantly stormed the enemy's guns, the greater part of which he had actually gained possession of when an unhappy grape shot killed him on the spot." (*Pester.*)

SINCLAIR, Hon. Patrick Campbell (1800-1834). Bt. Captain, 70th N.I. *b.* Barrogill Castle, Canisbay, Caithness, 14 Feb. 1800.

Cadet 1817. Admitted 15 Jan. 1819. Ensign 18 July 1818. Lieut. 20 Jan. 1820. Bt. Capt. 18 July 1833. d. Banda 13 Mar. 1834.

4th son of Sir James Sinclair, of Mey, Bart., 12th Earl of Caithness, and Jane his wife, 2nd dau. of Gen. Alexander Campbell, of Barcaldine. Brother of Charlotte Anne, mother of A. N. M. MacGregor, q.v. m. St. John's, Calcutta, 11 Mar. 1822, Isabella Dunbar, eldest dau. of James Murray MacGregor, q.v. (See also John Graham (1777-1816), and John Samuel Henry Weston.) (She died Portobello 3 Mar. 1853.) Ed. Edin. High School.

Services : Ensign d.d. Bengal Eur. Regt. 1819. Leave s.c. 10 mos. 14 Aug. 1819. Posted to 1/22nd N.I. 1820 ; transfd. to 43rd N.I. (late 1/22nd) May 1824 ; to newly-raised 2nd Extra Regt. (became 70th N.I.) May 1825. Bde. Qmr. to O.C. Nagpur Subsdy. Force 29 July 1822 till 24 Sept. 1824, and served with the Force 1825 till June 1830, when it was broken up. d.d. 64th N.I. 24 Jan. 1831 ; do. 53rd N.I. 7 Jan. till Nov. 1832.

Refs. : Burke's *Peerage*, 1923, p. 420, *s.n.* Caithness, E. Burke's *Landed Gentry*, 2nd edn., iii. 216, *s.n.* Rob Roy Macgregor, of Craigrostan. M.I. at Banda.

SINCLAIR, Thomas (*d.* 1770). Ensign, Engineers. Cadet 1769. Ensign 13 Dec. 1769. *d.* Calcutta 18 Dec. 1770.

Services : N.F.P.

SINGER, Alexander Stewart (1803-1845). Captain, 24th N.I. *b.* Kirkpatrick Juxta, nr. Moffat, Dumfries, 4 Dec. 1803. Cadet 1821. Arrived in India 4 May 1822. Ensign 3 Dec. 1821. Lieut. 2 Nov. 1823. Capt. 19 Sept. 1833. *d.* Simla 20 Sept. 1845.

6th son of Rev. William Singer, D.D., minister of Kirkpatrick Juxta 1799-1840, and Ann his wife, dau. of Duncan Stewart, Comdt. of Fort William, co. Inverness, of the Fasnacloich family. *m.* Clara, 4th dau. of Rev. John Johnstone, minister of Crossmichael. (She died Moffat 21 Oct. 1856.)

Services : Posted Ensign to 2/23rd N.I. 31 May 1822 ; transfd. to 2/22nd N.I. 23 Oct. 1822 ; to 2/8th N.I. Sept. 1823 ; to 24th N.I. (late 2/8th) May 1824. Operations in Hariana 1824 ; Lieut. 24th N.I. Adjt. 24th N.I. 4 May 1825 till 14 Jan. 1830. Leave s.c. 1 yr. to Mussoorie Jan. 1829 ; fur. s.c. 31 Jan. 1830 till 3 Dec. 1832. Operations against the Kols and Chuars in Chota Nagpur 1832-3 ; Lieut. 24th N.I. Adjt. 24th N.I. 22 May 1833 till 5 Mar. 1834. Fur. 19 Mar. 1838 till 9 Feb. 1841. Actg. A.D.C. to Maj.-Gen. J. W. Fast, *q.v.*, comdg. Saugor Div., afterwards Sirhind Div.,

8 June 1841; permanent do. 29 Jan. 1842. Rejoined 24th N.I. 8 Oct. 1842. Insurrection in Bundelkhand 1842-3; Capt. 24th N.I. A.D.C. to Maj.-Gen. Fast Apr. 1843 till Jan. 1845, when he rejoined 24th N.I. Leave to Simla Apr. 1845 till death.
Refs.: Scott's *Fasti*, ii. 212. De Rhé-Philipe. M.I. in cart road cemetery, Simla.

SINNOCK, Henry (1785-1862). Lieut. Colonel. 3rd N.I. *bapt.* Hailsham, Sussex, 10 May 1785. Cadet 1800. Ensign 9 Nov. 1801. Lieut. 13 July 1803. Capt. 1 Oct. 1815. Major 13 May 1825. Retired 13 July 1827. Hon. Lt. Col. 28 Nov. 1854. *d.* at his residence, 32 Queen's Rd., Brighton, 28 Nov. 1862, aged 79.

Son of John Sinnock and Mary his wife.

Services: Ensign d.d. 7th N.I. in 1802; posted Ensign to 6th N.I. 1802. Attached to Ramgarh Bn. 1807-24, during which period he took part in a number of minor operations, mostly in Chota Nagpur. Supt. Irreg. Cav. with Maj.-Gen. Sir William Toone, *q.v.*, 15 Oct. 1817 till 1 Apr. 1818, during Third Mahratta War. Capt. 1/6th N.I. Leave s.c. to Cape 1822; fur. s.c. 1824 till retirement. Transfd. to 3rd N.I. (late 1/6th) May 1824.

Refs.: *E.I.M.C.* iii. 230-5. *G.M.* 1863, i. 130. *The Times*, 4 Dec. 1862.

SISSMORE, Broadfield (1783-1858). Colonel. 3rd N.I. *b.* Rowner, Hants, 15 Apr. 1783. Cadet 1803. Arrived in India 17 Mar. 1805. Ensign 31 Mar. 1805. Lieut. 1 Apr. 1805. Capt. 1 Aug. 1818. Major 21 Dec. 1827. Lt. Col. 14 Nov. 1832. Retired 25 July 1839. Hon. Col. 28 Nov. 1854. *d.* 13 Ladbrooke Terr., Notting Hill, London, 25 Nov. 1858.

bapt. 7 Aug. 1794. Son of Broadfield Sissmore and Ann his wife. *m.* Calcutta 26 Nov. 1808, Caroline, sister of Henry Sibley, *q.v.* (*See also* Arthur Shuldham.) (She died London 17 Dec. 1855, aged 70.) Father of Edmund, James, and Thomas Henry Sissmore, *qq.v.*

Services: Posted Lieut. to 12th N.I. 1806. Operations in Oudh 1808; Lieut. 12th N.I. Adjt. Purnea Provl. Bn. 1810. Adjt. & Qmr. 12th N.I. 29 May 1810 till July 1814; Intr. & Qmr. 1/12th N.I. 1 July 1814 till 1816. Nepal War 1814-15; Bde. Major to Reserve (India medal). Leave s.c. 6 mos. to sea 5 Dec. 1815. Capt. Lt. 29 Sept. 1816. Third Mahratta War; Dy. Field Paymr. Centre Div., Grand Army, Sept. 1817 till 1 Apr. 1820. Actg. Dy. Paymr. Narbada F.F. 20 Oct. 1820 till 5 May 1821; Agent for

army clothing, 2nd Div.; Executive Engr. 12th (Karnal) Div. P.W.D. 17 Apr. 1822 till 13 June 1828. Transfd. to 1st N.I. (late 2/12th) May 1824. Fur. p.a. 17 Feb. 1829 till 29 Aug. 1831. Posted Lt. Col. to 41st N.I. 22 July 1833; to 12th N.I. 29 Oct. 1834, and comdd. till 23 Sept. 1836. Fur. s.c. 25 Jan. 1837 till retirement. Transfd. to 3rd N.I. 23 Mar. 1836.
Refs.: *I.M.* 6 Dec. 1858, p. 984.

SISSMORE, Edmund (1813-1870). Colonel. 69th N.I. *b.* Calcutta 2 June 1813. Cadet 1833. Arrived in India 8 Dec. 1834. Ensign (5 Aug. 1834) 1 Nov. 1834. Lieut. 22 Apr. 1840. Capt. 29 July 1848. Major 11 July 1857. Lt. Col. 8 Dec. 1861. Retired 31 Dec. 1861. Hon. Col. 31 Dec. 1861. *d.* at his residence, 2 Auckland Pl., St. Helier, Jersey, 19 June 1870.

Son of Broadfield Sissmore, *q.v.*, and Caroline his wife. Brother of James Sissmore, *q.v.* *m.* 1st, Berhampore 9 Feb. 1841, Amelia, 2nd dau. of Lt.-Col. William Wilkinson, H.M. 49th Regt. (She died Kaithal, Punjab, 13 Jan. 1844, aged 24.) *m.* 2nd, Mussoorie 7 Oct. 1850, Marian Antoinette, dau. of John Angelo, *q.v.* (*See also* John Abercrombie (1814-1860).) (She died 25 Nov. 1902, aged 74.)

Services: Ensign d.d. 12th N.I. 17 Dec. 1834; d.d. 41st N.I. 27 Mar. 1835; posted to 69th N.I. 24 Sept. 1835. Actg. Adjt. Nassiri Bn. 1 Oct. 1842; offg. 2nd in comd. do. 31 Oct. 1842; actg. Adjt. Sirmoor Bn. 23 Mar. 1843; S.S.O. at Kaithal 18 Nov. 1843. Rejoined 69th N.I. in Sind Feb. 1844; Adjt. do. 3 July 1845 till 24 Oct. 1848. Second Sikh War; Chilianwala; Gujerat; Capt. 69th N.I. (Medal with 2 clasps). Junr. Asst. to Comr. in Chota Nagpur 9 Sept. 1856; Senior do. 5 Jan. till 24 Aug. 1857. Fur. s.c. Jan. 1859 till retirement.

Refs.: *The Times,* 30 June 1870.

SISSMORE, James (1808-?). Bt. Captain. 23rd N.I. *b.* Dinapore 3 Sept. 1808. Cadet 1825. Arrived in India 18 Mar. 1826. Ensign 28 Sept. 1825. Lieut. 17 Jan. 1829. Bt. Capt. 28 Sept. 1840. Cashiered by G.C.M. 2 May 1843.

bapt. Dinapore 28 Jan. 1810. Son of Broadfield Sissmore, *q.v.* Brother of Thomas Henry Sissmore, *q.v.* *m.* Calcutta 24 Nov. 1835, Sophia Jane, dau. of George Dick, *q.v.* (*See also* John Thomas.)

Services: Posted to 35th N.I. 1826; transfd. to 23rd N.I. 16 July 1829. Leave p.a. to Fatehgarh 23 Mar. 1833 till 22 Sept. 1834. Attached to 2nd Vol. Regt. for China 1 Feb. 1842 till 1 Mar. 1843. First China War 1842; Bt. Capt. 23rd N.I., 2nd Vol. Regt.

Refs.: *I.M.* 4 July 1843, p. 80.

SISSMORE, Thomas Henry (1811-1872). Lieut. Colonel. Artillery. (593) b. Barrackpore 24 Apr. 1811. Cadet 1826. 2nd Lieut. 28 Sept. 1827. Lieut. 7 June 1834. Capt. 3 July 1845. Major 30 May 1857. Retired 28 Sept. 1857. Hon. Lt. Col. 28 Sept. 1857. d. St. Leonards-on-Sea 19 Nov. 1872. Son of Broadfield Sissmore, q.v., and Caroline his wife. Brother of Edmund Sissmore, q.v. m. Datchet 21 Mar. 1857, Sarah, youngest dau. of John Fowler, of Datchet. (She died 4 Sept. 1893, aged 75.) Addiscombe Cadet 1825-7.

Services: Posted to H.A. 14 Mar. 1833. Served in Sind 1844-5; Lieut. 4th Troop 1st Bde. H.A. Fur. s.c. 10 Apr. 1845 till 10 Apr. 1848. Transfd. to 1st Troop 2nd Bde. May 1845. Second Sikh War; Jullundur Doab 1848-9; Rangar Nagal, comdg. 4 guns No. 15 Light Field Batty.; heights of Dalla; Capt. 6th Coy. 8th Bn., with Bdr. Wheeler's force (Medal). Fur. p.a. 19 Dec. 1856 till retirement. Posted Major to 2nd Bde. H.A. 14 Sept. 1857.

Refs.: *The Times*, 21 Nov. 1872.

SIVERIGHT, William (d. 1771). Ensign, Infantry. Cadet 1769. Ensign 14 June 1770. d. Calcutta 20 Apr. 1771: kld. in a duel.

Services: N.F.P.

SIVRIGHT, William (1783-1812). Lieutenant, 8th N.C. bapt. Bridekirk, Cumberland, 28 Aug. 1783. Cadet 1798. Arrived in India 26 Aug. 1799. Cornet 19 June 1800. Lieut. 11 Mar. 1805. d. Kaitha, U.P., 6 Dec. 1812.

Only son of David Sivright, of Blyth, Northumberland, and of Papcastle, Cumberland, and Elizabeth his wife, eldest dau. of William Dallas, of N. Newton, and half-sister of the father of Charles Dallas, q.v. m. Kaitha 12 Dec. 1810, Ann, dau. ("and heir"— *Burke*) of Sir Gabriel Martindell, q.v. (*See also* Henry Finch.)

Services: Ensign R. Edin. Regt. of Vols. 26 Dec. 1798. Cornet 5th N.C. (? Second Mahratta War 1803-4; Cornet 5th N.C.) Transfd. as Lieut. to newly-raised 8th N.C. Mar. 1805.

Refs.: Burke's *Landed Gentry*, 13th edn., p. 1608, s.n. Sivright, of South House and Meggatland, co. Edinburgh. *Family of Dallas*, by James Dallas (Edin., 1921), p. 371.

SKARDON, Charles Ramsay (1785-1857). Lieut. General. Colonel 44th N.I. b. Fatehgarh 23 July 1785. Cadet 1804. Arrived in India 6 Apr. 1806. Ensign 10 Sept. 1805. Lieut. 25 Nov. 1805. Capt. 9 Apr. 1822. Major 13 May 1825, Lt.

Col. 13 Apr. 1830. Col. 14 June 1842. Maj. Gen. 20 June 1854. Lt. Gen. 22 Aug. 1855. d. Hastings 29 May 1857, suddenly. Of Lansdown Terr., Notting Hill, London. Son of Samuel Skardon, q.v., and Mary his wife. m. Calcutta 31 Aug. 1811, Anna Priscilla, dau. of Isaac Binns, q.v., by his 2nd wife.
Services : Posted Lieut. to 20th N.I. 1806. Served in Chittagong 1811 ; Ft. Marlbro' 1814-18 ; Ceylon 1818-19 ; Lieut. 2/20th N.I. Capt. 2/20th N.I. Fur. p.a. 6 Dec. 1821 till 13 Oct. 1824. Transfd. to 40th N.I. (late 2/20th) May 1824. First Burma War ; Ramree I. Feb. 1825 (Lond. Gaz. 9 Aug. 1825) ; Capt. 40th N.I., comdg. Reserve (India medal). To take charge of 5th N.I. 10 July 1828. Posted Lt. Col. to 68th N.I. 18 Nov. 1830 ; to 49th N.I. 16 May 1834 ; to 47th 15 Dec. 1838. Comdd. a detachment of Nimach F.F. against the Bhils 1837-8. Fur. s.c. 22 Feb. 1839 till 22 Oct. 1841. Transfd. to 45th N.I. 30 Oct. 1841 ; posted Col. do. 1 July 1842 ; transfd. to 44th N.I. 1 Dec. 1843. To comd. troops in Oudh 19 Dec. 1842. Fur. p.a. 9 Jan. 1844 till death.
Refs. : Boase. I.M. 9 June 1857, p. 387. G.M. 1857, ii. 101.

SKARDON, Samuel (1730/31-1788). Bt. Lieut. Fireworker, Artillery. (240) b. 1730/31. Dy. Comy. Ord. (?) Comy. 1780. Bt. Lieut. F. 1 Sept. 1783. d. Fatehgarh 30 Oct. 1788, aged 57. m. Bombay 7 Nov. 1768, Miss Mary Woodson. (She re-m. 1st, John Lowis, and became mother of John Thornton Lowis, q.v. She m. 3rdly, Lawrence O'Hara.) Father of Charles Ramsay Skardon, q.v., of the wives of Richard Ramsay and Thomas Wharton, qq.v., and of the mother of Samuel Lowis Thornton, q.v.
Services : Sailed for India as a free merchant in the Harcourt 9 May 1765. Posted as Comy. of Ord. to Fatehgarh 3 Dec. 1780.
Refs. : M.I. Fatehgarh fort cemetery.
Note : One Samuel Skardon entered Merchant Taylors' School in 1738.

SKELTON, Arnoldus Jones (1750-1793). Lieutenant. Infantry. Subsequently in 3rd Ft. Gds. b. 1750. Cadet 1767. Ensign 15 Sept. 1767. Lieut. 23 Apr. 1769. Resigned 3 Feb. 1771. d. Whitehaven 23 Mar. 1793, aged 43.
Of Branthwaite Hall and Papcastle, Cumberland. Assumed the surname of Skelton 24 Nov. 1772. Son of Capt. James Jones, 3rd Gds., of Branthwaite, and Jemima his wife, dau. of Col. Tulleken. (See James Jones Tulliken.) His sister m. Charles, 1st Marquis Cornwallis. m. Oct. 1775, Elizabeth, eldest dau. of William Hicks, of Whitehaven and Papcastle. (She died Papcastle July 1812.)

Grandfather of Charles Cornwallis Skelton, q.v. Ed. Eton 16 May 1759 till 1765.

Services : Sailed for India in the *Calcutta* 31 Dec. 1766. Ensign 3rd (Coldstream) Gds. 20 Oct. 1772 ; Lieut. & Capt. do. 12 Feb. 1776. M.P. for Eye 1780-2.

Refs. : Burke's *Landed Gentry,* 4th edn., p. 1380, *s.n.* Skelton, of Papcastle, Cumberland. Whellan's *Hist. of Cumberland & Westmorland. Austen-Leigh. G.M.* 1793, i. 376.

SKELTON, Charles Cornwallis (1812-1836). Ensign, 47th N.I. *b.* Colchester 22 Oct. 1812. Cadet 1830. Arrived in India 29 Dec. 1831. Ensign (9 June 1831) 29 Dec. 1831. *d.* Lucknow 28 May 1836.

Elder son of Daniel Jones Skelton, of Papcastle, Cumberland, late Capt. R.A., and Mary Anne his wife, dau. of Thomas Theed, of London. Grandson of Arnoldus Jones Skelton, *q.v.* Addiscombe Cadet 1829-31.

Services : Cadet d.d. 2nd N.I. 1 Feb. 1832 ; posted Ensign to 47th N.I. 18 Oct. 1833. No record of active service.

Refs. : Burke's *Landed Gentry,* 4th edn., p. 1380, *s.n.* Skelton, of Papcastle, Cumberland.

SKENE, George (1811-1831). Ensign, 63rd N.I. *b.* Aberdeen 8 May 1811. Cadet 1828. Arrived in India 22 May 1829. Ensign 7 Feb. 1829. *d.* Berhampore 4 June 1831.

Eldest son of Charles Skene, M.D. (of the family of Skene, of Drumbeck), Professor of Medicine in Marischal Coll., Aberdeen, 1823-39, and Margaret Ann his wife, dau. of —— Anderson, of Linkwood, Elgin. Nephew of William Skene, *q.v.* Ed. Aberdeen Grammar School 1820-4 ; Aberdeen Univ.

Services : Ensign d.d. 5th N.I. 13 July 1829 ; d.d. 43rd N.I. 13 Aug. 1829 ; posted to 63rd N.I. 14 Sept. 1829. No record of active service.

Refs. : Memorials of family of Skene of Skene, by W. F. Skene, p. 74. W. Wood's *E. Neuk of Fife,* 2nd edn., p. 74.

SKENE, William (1784-1854). Lieut. Colonel. 73rd N.I. *b.* Aberdeen 26 Feb. 1784. Cadet 1800. Arrived in India 4 Feb. 1802. Ensign 1 Sept. 1801. Lieut. 26 Dec. 1802. Capt. 1 Aug. 1818. Major 13 May 1825. Lt. Col. 21 May 1829. Retired 14 May 1832. *d.* 12 Brighton Cresc., Portobello, 6 May 1854.

bapt. Aberdeen 27 Feb. 1784. 5th and youngest son of Dr. George Skene, physician, Professor at Marischal Coll., Aberdeen, and Margaret his wife, dau. of Charles Gordon, of Abergeldie.

Uncle of George Skene, *q.v.* *m.* 1st, Calcutta 8 Jan. 1807, Miss Emma Eliza Neville Birch. (She died Jubbulpore 8 Sept. 1828, aged 37.) *m.* 2nd, Aberdeen 3 Nov. 1831, Jane, 2nd dau. of Archibald Campbell (of Lochnell), of the Mount, Harrow. Ed. Aberdeen Grammar School 1795-98.

Services : Ensign H.M. 56th Ft. ; Qmr. 109th Ft. ; h.p. do. in 1801. Posted Ensign to 7th N.I. 1802. Adjt. 2/7th N.I. 1806-10 ; do. 1/7th N.I. 23 Jan. 1810 till 4 May 1815. Reduction of Kalinjar 1812. Capt. Lt. 7th N.I. 16 Dec. 1814. Nepal War 1814-15 ; Capt. Lt. 1/7th N.I., in 2nd Div. (India medal). Transfd. to newly-raised 2/29th N.I. 1815 ; d.d. 3rd Ceylon Vol. Bn. 1818-19. Operations in Jodhpur 1823 ; Lamba ; Capt. 2/29th N.I. Transfd. to newly-raised 33rd N.I. July 1823 ; to 66th N.I. (late 2/33rd) May 1824 ; as Major to newly-raised 5th Extra Regt. (became 73rd N.I.) May 1825 ; as Lt. Col. to 22nd N.I. 1829 ; to 73rd N.I. 31 Mar. 1830. Fur. s.c. 31 Dec. 1829 till retirement.

Refs. : Memorials *of family of* Skene *of* Skene, p. 74. W. Wood's *E. Neuk of Fife*, 2nd edn., p. 74. *G.M.* 1854, i. 670.

SKENE, formerly SMITH, William Abraham (1803-1875). Captain. 57th N.I. *bapt.* Killaghtee, co. Donegal, 22 Sept. 1803. Cadet 1820. Admitted 5 June 1821. Ensign 16 Jan. 1821. Lieut. 11 July 1823. Capt. 13 Jan. 1834. Retired 8 July 1836. *d.* Leamington 7 Mar. 1875, aged 74.

Of Lethenty, co. Aberdeen ; J.P. and D.L. Assumed the surname of Skene in lieu of Smith in 1834.[1] Son of Capt. John Skene, C.B., R.N., formerly Smith, and Frances his wife, *née* McDowel. Cousin-german of William Smith (1805-1856), *q.v.* *m.* (before 1837) Elizabeth, dau. of Hugh Gordon, of Manar, co. Aberdeen. Ed. Marischal Coll., Aberdeen.

Services : Posted to 2/25th N.I. 1821 ; transfd. to 29th N.I. July 1823 ; to 57th N.I. (late 1/29th) May 1824. First Burma War ; Assam 1824 ; Lieut. 57th N.I. (India medal). Actg. Adjt. 57th N.I. 12 July 1826. d.d. Assam L.I. 8 Nov. 1828 till 13 Feb. 1830. Actg. Adjt. 57th N.I. 20 Dec. 1830 ; permanent do. 5 Mar. 1831 till 30 July 1833. Fur. p.a. 8 Jan. 1834 till retirement. Retired on h.p. of Lieut. (viz. 7/– *p.d.*).

Refs. : Memorials *of family of* Skene *of* Skene, by W. F. Skene, p. 88. *Walford* (1900 edn.), p. 945. *The Times*, 10 Mar. 1875.

[1] *Note :* This change of name appears for the first time in *E.I.R.* for May 1851, although his father had changed his name in 1830.

SKINNER, Alexander. Ensign. Infantry. Cadet 1765. Ensign (?) Threw up his Commission and was sent home in 1766.

Services : Apptd. Cadet in India 15 May 1765. Resigned his Commission during the " Batta mutiny " in May 1766.

SKINNER, Alexander Macgregor (1804-1824). Ensign, 9th N.I. *b.* Knockbreda, co. Down, 25 July 1804. Cadet 1822. Ensign 11 July 1823. *d.* at sea 1 Mar. 1824, on board the *Marquis Wellington*, on the voyage home.

Son of Cortland Skinner, of the Customs, Belfast, and Isabella his wife, dau. of Capt. Macartney, R.N.

Services : Posted to 2/9th N.I. 1823. Fur. s.c. 1824. No record of active service.

Refs. : Burke's *Landed Gentry*, 2nd edn., p. 1362, *s.n.* Van Cortlandt. *Hist. of the Clan Gregor*, ii. 297.

SKINNER, Hercules (*d.* 1803). Lieut. Colonel, 19th N.I. Country Cadet 1771. Admitted 31 Oct. 1771. Ensign 26 Mar. 1773. Lieut. 23 May 1778. Capt. 17 Jan. 1784. Major 30 Oct. 1797. Lt. Col. 29 May 1800. *d.* Baragaon, U.P., 12 July 1803.

Son of David Skinner, provost of Montrose 1733-46, and Margaret his wife, dau. of Alexander Beattie, burgess of Montrose and master of the ship *Hopeful Jean of Montrose*. Brother of James Skinner (1733-1773), *q.v.*, and of David Skinner, of Bordeaux. Cousin-german of William Anne Skinner, *q.v.*, and of Alexander Wight, advocate in Edinburgh. Father (by " Jeany," a native) of James Skinner, C.B. (Appendix A), Robert Skinner (Appendix A), Mary, wife of William Ridley, Elizabeth Jane, mother of James Oldham Oldham, *qq.v.*, and Margaret, wife of Thomas Templeton, of Calcutta, atty.

Services : Served with 20th Bn. Sepoys 1777-80 ; posted to 1/12th N.I. Jan. 1781 ; transfd. to newly-raised 1/36th N.I. 4 Apr. 1781. Capt. 32nd Bn. Sepoys in July 1787 ; brought on full pay from Supy. Capt. and posted to 6th Eur. Bn. 16 Mar. 1792 ; Capt. do. in Feb. 1796 ; Major 2nd Eur. Regt. Posted Lt. Col. to 2/19th N.I.

Refs. : De Rhé-Philipe. Will dated Burragong 27 June 1803 ; proved 14 Oct. 1803.

SKINNER, James (1733-1773). Captain, comdg. 6th N.I. *b.* 1733. Lieut. 13 Oct. 1763. Capt. Lt. 1 Aug. 1765. Capt. 8 July 1766. *d.* Berhampore 15 Dec. 1773, aged 40.

Son of David Skinner, of Montrose, and Margaret his wife. Brother of Hercules Skinner, *q.v.*

Services : Ensign H.M. 84th Ft. 25 Aug. 1762 ; h.p. do. 25 Dec. 1764 till death. Transfd. as Lieut. to Bengal Army Oct. 1763.

THE BENGAL ARMY 1758-1834 109

Assault and capture of Patna 6 Nov. 1763. Shared Buxar prize money 1764, though not actually present at the battle, having been detained elsewhere on service. Lieut. comdg. 1st Rissalah of Cav. in 1765. On fur. s.c. in England c. 1769-71. Comdd. 6th Bn. Sepoys 24 May 1773 till death.
Refs.: Williams, p. 110. Will dated 18 July 1773; codicil 22 Aug. 1773; proved 22 Mar. 1774. M.I. at Berhampore.

SKINNER, James. Lieutenant. Infantry. Ensign 14 May 1766. Lieut. 15 Sept. 1767. Resigned 20 June 1769.
Services: Apptd. by Sir Robert Fletcher, *q.v.*, from Vol. to act as Ensign 14 May 1766, owing to the " Batta mutiny."

SKINNER, James (1803-1842). Captain, 61st N.I. *b.* Kinsale, co. Cork, 20 Sept. 1803. Cadet 1824. Arrived in India 6 May 1825. Ensign 8 Jan. 1825. Lieut. 2 May 1826. Capt. 16 July 1839. *d.* Jagdalak Pass, Afghanistan, 12 Jan. 1842; kld. in action during retreat from Kabul,[1]
3rd son of Lt.-Gen. John Skinner (of the ancient family of Skinner, of Knapp, co. Hereford) and Ann his wife, 2nd dau. of Charles Maclean (of Borreray), of Ardgour House, co. Argyll. Brother of Lt.-Col. Thomas Skinner, C.B., 31st Regt. (*D.N.B.*)
Services: Ensign d.d. 28th N.I. 23 May 1825; posted to 61st N.I. 1825; actg. Adjt. do. 14 Oct. 1829, 18 Mar. 1830, 10 July 1832. S.A.C.G. 16 Apr. 1833; D.A.C.G. 2 cl. 14 Aug. 1837. Apptd. Comst. Ofr. 2nd Div., Army of Indus, 13 Sept. 1838; to proceed from Karnal to Jalalabad 1839. First Afghan War 1839-42; apptd. to executive charge of Comst. duties in Afghanistan 16 Apr. 1840; Kabul insurrection and retreat (kld.); Capt. 61st N.I.[2] " Accounted one of the best linguists in India."
Refs.: Robinson's *Mansions of co. Hereford*, p. 235, *s.n.* Skinner, of Ledbury and Pixley. *An Account of the Clan Maclean*, p. 280. Eyre's *Journal*. Litho. portrait (L. Dickinson) pub. *c.* 1843. M.I. Afghan Memorial Church, Bombay.
[1] *Note:* He was shot through the face by a Ghilzai and died the same day.
[2] *Note:* He was seized by the rebels in the shop of a seller of wood, where he had been concealed some days, and was forced to translate English letters.

SKINNER, William Anne. Ensign. Infantry. Cadet 1771. Ensign 1 Jan. 1773. Resigned 20 Jan. 1775.
Cousin-german of Hercules Skinner, *q.v. m.* Eleanor ——.

LIST OF THE OFFICERS OF

Services : Was Ensign in 3rd Bde. on resignation. (The following may perhaps refer to him or to his father :—Lieut. H.M. 35th Ft. 27 July 1759 ; Lieut. 1 Feb. 1762, in a Corps of German Vols., composed of prisoners of war, raised on that date. This Corps " broke " in 1763, and the officers were placed on h.p. He is shown as on h.p. in *A.L.* for 1766.)

SKIPTON, Thomas (Kennedy) (1789-1827). Lieutenant, 10th L.C. bapt. Londonderry 29 Jan. 1789. Cadet 1810. Cornet 23 Nov. 1815. Lieut. 1 Sept. 1818. *d.s.p.* Meerut 21 Dec. 1827 : kld. by his horse falling on him.

4th son of George Crookshank Kennedy, Dy. Govr. of co. Derry (who assumed by Sign Manual the name of Skipton 13 Feb. 1802), and Sarah his wife, dau. of Conolly M'Causland, of Fruit Hill. Uncle of George Dysart and cousin-german of Alexander Thomas Lecky, *qq.v.*

Services : Barasat C.C. 1810-11. d.d. 8th N.I. 1811-13 ; posted to 8th N.C. 1815. Third Mahratta War 1817-18 ; Jubbulpore 19 Dec. 1817 ; Cornet 8th N.C., actg. Dy. Postmr. to Bdr.-Gen. F. Hardyman's Div. Intr. & Qmr. 8th L.C. 24 May 1819 till 12 July 1825. Transfd. to newly-raised 10th L.C. 17 June 1825 ; Intr. & Qmr. do. 12 July 1825 till death. Siege and capture of Bhurtpore ; Lieut. 10th L.C.

Refs. : Burke's *Landed Gentry*, 7th edn., p. 1678, *s.n.* Skipton, of Beech Hill, co. Londonderry. *A.J.* xxv. 825. Will dated Bhurtpore, 6 Jan. 1826 ; proved 22 Jan. 1828.

SKIRVING,[1] Robert (*d.* 1843). Captain. 4th N.I. Cadet 1783. Admitted 22 Oct. 1783. Ensign 19 Apr. 1785. Lieut. 6 June 1793. Capt. 30 Sept. 1803. Retired 20 July 1808. *d.* 26 July 1843.

Of Croys, Galloway. Son of Adam Skirving (*D.N.B.*). Brother of Archibald Skirving, Scottish portrait-painter (D.N.B.). *m.* Spottes Hall, Dalbeattie, co. Kirkcudbright, 10 June 1816, Jane, only dau. of Rev. Dr. James Muirhead of Logan, minister of Urr (*D.N.B.*). (She died 15 Jan. 1847.)

Services : Apptd. Cadet 18 Dec. 1782 ; sailed for India in the *Earl of Oxford* 11 Mar. 1783. Unposted Supy. Ensign till 15 Feb. 1790, when he was brought on full pay and posted to 6th Bengal Eur. Bn. Transfd. from 4th Eur. Bn. to 7th N.I. 9 July 1793 ; to 4th N.I. 1798 ; Adjt. 2/4th N.I. in 1802. Second Mahratta War 1803-4 ; Aligarh ; defence of Delhi ; Capt. 2/4th N.I. Fur. 22 Dec. 1805 till retirement.

THE BENGAL ARMY, 1758-1834

Refs.: Scott's *Fasti*, ii. 306. *S.M.* 1816, p. 638. *Hobson-Jobson*, *s.v.* Bunow.

[1] *Note :* His name also appears in early MS. *A.L.* as Skirvin and Sherwin.

SKIRWIN or SHIRWIN, Alexander (d. 1769). Lieutenant, Infantry. Cadet (?) Ensign 26 Aug. 1765. Lieut. 7 June 1767. d. 1769.

Nephew of James Ramsay.

Services : Resigned his Commission May 1766 during the " Batta mutiny " and went home ; restored to the Service 22 Feb. 1769, without prejudice to his rank, and returned to India.

SKRINE, Thomas Henry (1792-1815). Ensign, 5th N.I. *b.* London 30 May 1792. Cadet 1809. Arrived in India 3 Oct. 1810. Ensign 24 Feb. 1812. *d. unm.* Muttra 3 Aug. 1815.

bapt. Marylebone 28 June 1792. 3rd and youngest son of Henry Skrine, of Warleigh, Somerset, and Letitia Sarah Maria his 2nd wife, dau. of John Harcourt, of Dan-y-Park, Crickhowell, Brecon. Ed. Winchester Coll. ; Scholar 1805-9.

Services : Barasat C.C. 1810-11. Cadet d.d. 15th N.I. 1811 ; posted Ensign to 1/5th N.I. 1812. Operations in Baghelkhand 1813-14 ; Entauri ; Ensign 1/5th N.I.

Refs.: Burke's *Landed Gentry*, 12th edn., p. 1722, *s.n.* Skrine, of Warleigh and Claverton Manors, Somerset. *Skrine of Warleigh*, by F. W. A. Walker, M.D. (Taunton, 1936). *Kirby. G.M.* 1816, i. 473. *Bath Chron.*, 24 Apr. 1816.

SLACKE, Charles (1810-1828). Ensign, 43rd N.I. *bapt.* Dublin 4 Aug. 1810. Cadet 1826. Ensign 14 June 1827. d. Benares 31 July 1828, of cholera.

Son of John Slacke and Agnes his wife.

Services : Ensign d.d. 43rd N.I. 22 Jan. 1828 ; posted to 43rd N.I. 20 Feb. 1828. No record of active service.

Refs. : A.J. xxvii. 249. M.I. Benares.

SLADE, John (1780-1802). Lieutenant, 18th N.I. *bapt.* Shelford, Notts., 28 Oct. 1780. Cadet 1794. Arrived in India 6 Mar. 1797. Ensign 18 Nov. 1796. Lieut. 30 Oct. 1797. d. Sherghati, B. & O., 29 July 1802.

Son of William Slade and Elizabeth his wife.

Services : Transfd. from 2nd Bengal Eur. Regt. to 2/2nd N.I. 27 July 1798 ; to 11th N.I. ; to 2/18th N.I. 29 May 1800. Adjt. 1/18th N.I. at death.

SLAUGHTER, Thomas (1748/49-?). Lieutenant. Infantry. *b.* Cheshire 1748/49. Cadet 1780. Never arrived in India. Ensign 1781. Lieut. 19 July 1781. Struck off 1788. *Services:* Apptd. Cadet 7 Feb. 1781, aged 32; was to have sailed for India in the *Valentine* 13 Mar. 1781.

*SLEATH, Joseph Barnabas. Cadet. Artillery. (III.-15) Cadet 1783. Never commissioned. *Services:* Apptd. Cadet for Art. 17 Dec. 1783; declined to proceed to India Apr. 1784.
Refs.: Stubbs's *List* (where the name is wrongly given as Heath). (*See also* Vol. ii. 424; iii. 727.)

SLEEMAN, James (1807-1889). Colonel. 73rd N.I. Gen. Supt. for suppression of *thagi* in India. *b.* 31 July 1807. Cadet 1826. Arrived in India 15 Aug. 1827. Ensign 7 Jan. 1827. Lieut. 21 May 1829. Capt. 24 Jan. 1845. Major 18 July 1856. Lt. Col. 25 Oct. 1859. Retired 26 Dec. 1859. Hon. Col. 26 Dec. 1859. *d.* Weir End, Ross, co. Hereford, 15 Oct. 1889.

Elder son of Thomas Sleeman, of Tenby, merchant, twice mayor of Tenby, and Elizabeth Morgan his wife. Nephew of Sir William Henry Sleeman, *q.v. m.* Clifton 28 Sept. 1854, Jane Georgina, 3rd dau. of Rev. Charles Penry Bullock, P.C. of St. Paul's, Bristol. (She died Ross 31 Dec. 1899.)

Services: Posted to 46th N.I. 19 June 1827; transfd. to 73rd N.I. 1827; d.d. 56th N.I. 20 Mar. 1831 till 20 Feb. 1832; Intr. & Qmr. 73rd N.I. 15 Feb. 1832 till 8 Feb. 1836. Asst. in *Thagi* Dept. 12 Jan. 1836; do. at Berhampore 1 Jan. 1840; Supt. do., and D.C. 3 cl. Saugor Div., 25 Jan. 1845; Gen. Supt. *Thagi* Dept. 26 Mar. 1849 till 1859. (? Mutiny campaign—Medal.) Fur. 6 mos. May 1854; s.c. 19 Feb. 1859 till retirement. Posted Lt. Col. to late 41st N.I. 14 Jan. 1860, but had already retired.

Refs.: Burke's *Landed Gentry*, 15th edn., p. 2069, *s.n.* Sleeman, *formerly* of Pool Park. *The Times*, 18 Oct. 1889.

SLEEMAN, Sir William Henry (1788-1856). Major General, K.C.B. Colonel 16th N.I. *b.* Stratton, Cornwall, 18 Aug. 1788. Cadet 1808. Arrived in India 2 Oct. 1809. Ensign 23 Sept. 1810. Lieut. 16 Dec. 1814. Capt. 23 Dec. 1826. Major 1 Feb. 1837. Lt. Col. 26 Feb. 1843. Col. 24 Nov. 1853. Maj. Gen. 28 Nov. 1854. *d.* at sea 10 Feb. 1856, on board the *Monarch*, off Ceylon.

bapt. Stratton 19 Sept. 1788. 8th and youngest son of Philip

Sleeman, of Pool Park, St. Tudy, Cornwall, Supervisor of Excise, and Mary his wife, dau. of John Spry, of Boyton. Uncle of James Sleeman, *q.v. m.* Jubbulpore 21 June 1829, Amélie Josephine, dau. of Comte Blaudin de Fontenne de Chalon, of a noble French house. (She died Southsea 19 Oct. 1882, aged 72.)
Services : See *D.N.B.* Posted Ensign to 12th N.I. 1810. Nepal War 1814-15 and 1816 ; Lieut. 2/12th N.I. (India medal). Intr. & Qmr. 1/12th N.I. 13 Dec. 1816 till 7 Mar. 1822. Apptd. in 1820 Junior Asst. to A.G.G., Saugor & Narbada territories, and never reverted to mily. duty. Transfd. to 1st N.I. (late 2/12th) May 1824. Leave s.c. 18 mos. to N.S.W. 5 Apr. 1825. Posted to Jubbulpore district 1828 ; to Saugor 1831. Gen. Supt. of operations for suppression of *thagi* 5 Mar. 1835. Resdt. at Gwalior 30 Sept. 1843 ; do. Lucknow 11 Jan. 1849 till Jan. 1856. Posted Lt. Col. to 47th N.I. 17 Aug. 1843 ; to 69th N.I. 16 Oct. 1845 ; to 36th N.I. Nov. 1851. Posted Col. to 16th N.I. 2 Feb. 1854. Fur. s.c. 3 yrs. Jan. 1856. K.C.B. (Civil) 6 Feb. 1856. Author of " Rambles and Recollections of an Indian Official," 1844, etc.

Refs. : Burke's *Landed Gentry,* 15th edn., p. 2069, *s.n.* Sleeman, *formerly* of Pool Park. *D.N.B. Ency. Brit. D.I.B. Boase. Thug,* by Col. James L. Sleeman, C.M.G., 1933 (portrait). *I.M.* 3 June 1856, p. 333. *G.M.* 1856, ii. 243. Portrait in oils, by Beechey, sometime in possession of Mrs. L. Brooke. M.I. Christ Church, Jubbulpore.

SLESSOR, William (1778-1810). Captain, 7th N.I. *b.* Portugal 29 Oct. 1778. Cadet 1793. Arrived in India 27 Sept. 1795. Ensign 13 Oct. 1794. Lieut. 27 July 1796. Capt. 10 June 1804. *d.* Kishanganj, B. & O., 7 Jan. 1810 : kld. by the accidental discharge of his fowling-piece.

Son of John Slessor, of Portugal. (*Possibly* son of Gen. (? John) Slessor, govr. of Oporto, and Harriet his wife, 7th dau. of John Bristow, of Quidenham Hall, Norfolk, and great-aunt of Cerjat Michael Bristow, *q.v.*)
Services : Sailed for India in the *Francis* 24 May 1795. Lieut. 2nd Bengal Eur. Regt. in 1796. Capt. Lt. 7th N.I. 26 Dec. 1802. Second Mahratta War 1803-4 ; reduction of Cuttack ; capture of Balasore ; Lieut. 1st Vol. Bn. Was serving at P.W.I. in 1805. Capt. 2/7th N.I.

SLOANE, Andrew (*d.* 1770). Ensign, Infantry. Cadet 1769. Ensign 6 Oct. 1769. *d.* 12 Aug. 1770 : drowned.
Services : N.F.P.

SLOAN(E), Anthony (d. 1770). Captain, Infantry. Country Cadet 1763. Ensign 25 Oct. 1763. Lieut. 27 Sept. 1764. Capt. May 1767. d. Berhampore 31 July 1770.

Services : Permitted to proceed to India as a free merchant 18 Feb. 1763. Served as a Vol. in the campaign against the Nawab of Bengal 1763 ; Lieut. in 2nd Bengal Eur. Regt. in 1766. Requests permission to resign the Service 2 Feb. 1767 ; fur. s.c. 1767-9.

Refs. : Cal. Gaz. 31 Aug. 1786.

SLOANE, Davi(e)s (d. 1813). Major, 17th N.I. Cadet 1782. Admitted 12 Nov. 1782. Ensign 19 Apr. 1783. Lieut. 18 Mar. 1790. Capt. 1 July 1803. Major 30 Oct. 1811. d. Bombay 27 June 1813.

Eldest surviving son of John Sloane, of Lisabuck (? Sissabush), co. Monaghan. m. 1788, Ann ———. (She died Dinapore 7 Nov. 1826, aged 56.) His dau. m. William Clinton Baddeley, q.v.

Services : Posted to 2nd Bengal Eur. Regt. 28 Feb. 1783 ; to 1st Eur. Bn. 5 Feb. 1790. Transfd. to 20th Bn. Sepoys 26 Feb. 1790 ; to 2nd Eur. Bn. 6 Oct. 1792 ; to 5th do. 25 Oct. 1792 ; to 33rd Bn. Sepoys 9 Nov. 1792. Lieut. 17th N.I. in 1798 ; Adjt. 1/17th N.I. 1802-3 ; tempy. comdg. Hill Rangers 1 May-5 June 1805. Major 1/17th N.I.

Refs. : Will dated Calcutta 22 Oct. 1812 ; proved 16 Sept. 1813. M.I. Sonapur cemetery, Bombay.

SLOANE, George (1760/61-1781). Ensign, Infantry. b. in Ireland 1760/61. Cadet 1780. Never arrived in India. Ensign 20 Apr. 1781. d. St. Helena 10 Nov. 1781 : drowned by the upsetting of the *Northumberland's* boat at the landing place.

Services : Apptd. Cadet 5 Dec. 1780 ; sailed for India in the *Deptford* 26 June 1781, aged 20.

SLOANE, William (1769-1795). Fireworker, Artillery. (285) b. Newry, co. Down, 18 July 1769. Cadet (Inf.) 1790. Fireworker 25 Dec. 1790. d. Cawnpore 21 Aug. 1795.

bapt. Newry 19 July 1769. m. (?) (She was pensioned on Lord Clive's fund 4 Jan. 1797.) His dau. m. George Blacker, q.v.

Services : Apptd. Inf. Cadet 11 Mar. 1791 ; sailed for India in the *Northumberland* 16 Apr. 1791. Transfd. as Cadet from 4th Bengal Eur. Bn. to Art. 6 Oct. 1791. To Madras Aug.-Oct. 1793 for siege of Pondicherry ; Lt.F. d.d. 4th Coy. 3rd Bn. Transfd. from 3rd Coy. 2nd Bn. to 4th Coy. 3rd Bn. 28 Oct. 1793.

SLYE, Charles (1783-1819). Captain, 28th N.I. b. Carlton, Northants, 2 Jan. 1783. Cadet 1798. Ensign 10 Nov. 1799.

THE BENGAL ARMY, 1758-1834 115

Lieut. 21 Apr. 1800. Capt. 30 Aug. 1809. d. nr. Colgong, B. & O., 4 Jan. 1819.

bapt. Carlton 30 Jan. 1783. Son of Rev. Matthias Slye,[1] rector of Carlton, and Mary his wife.

Services: Posted Lieut. to 1/5th N.I. 15 Apr. 1801. Second Mahratta War 1803-4 ; operations in Cuttack ; capture of Balasore ; Lieut. 1/5th N.I., with 1st Vol. Bn. (? Operations against Gopal Singh 1810 ; Tirowa ; Capt. 1/5th N.I.) Fur. 2 Jan. 1815 till 1818. Transfd. to newly-raised 2/28th N.I. 1815.

[1] *Note:* A.B. from Peterhouse, Camb., 1769, as Sly ; A.M. 1778 as Slye.

SMALL, John (1787-?). Lieutenant. 3rd N.I. Afterwards a merchant in Calcutta. *b.* Newtyle, co. Forfar, 6 Jan. 1787. Cadet 1803. Arrived in India 18 Mar. 1805. Ensign 22 Apr. 1805. Lieut. 23 Apr. 1805. Resigned 22 May 1815.

Of Foodie. 3rd and youngest son of Rev. Alexander Small, minister of Newtyle 1778-91, and Jean his wife, dau. of Rev. Alexander Stewart, of Strathgarry, minister of Blair-Atholl. *m.* in England 16 Apr. 1824, Mary Anne, youngest dau. of William Lindesay, of Balmungie, co. Fife.

Services: Posted Lieut. to 2/3rd N.I. Fur. 1812 till resignation. No record of active service. In business in Calcutta 1817-24, in the firm of J. Small & Co., merchants and agents. (? Sometime purser in an East Indiaman.)

Refs.: Scott's *Fasti*, v. 210.

SMALPAGE, Francis (1788-1838). Bt. Major, 8th L.C. *b.* Wakefield 4 Nov. 1788. Cadet (Inf.) 1807. Arrived in India 17 Sept. 1808. Transfd. to Cav. 15 Aug. 1809.[1] Cornet 1 Mar. 1812. Lieut. 1 Sept. 1818. Capt. 13 May 1825. Bt. Major 28 June 1838. *d.* 24 July 1838 : drowned in attempting to cross the Balund Nadi about 22 miles from Mirzapur, U.P.

bapt. Wakefield 13 Dec. 1788. Son of Daniel Smalpage, Capt. 3rd W. Yorks. Mil., and Frances his 1st wife. Brother of Sarah Power, and cousin-german of James Bell, of Angel Court, Throgmorton St., London, merchant. *m.* Whitby, Yorks., 15 Oct. 1820, Esther, eldest dau. of Thomas Hunter, of Whitby. (She died 6 June 1858.)

Services: Barasat C.C. 14 mos. Cadet d.d. 8th N.C. 1811-12 ; posted Cornet to 8th N.C. 1812. Third Mahratta War ; Nagpur ; Cornet 8th N.C. Fur. s.c. 7 Mar. 1819 till 12 Nov. 1822. Bde. Major on Est., with troops in Oudh 10 May 1823 till 11 Aug. 1829.

Volunteered for active service with his Regt. at Bhurtpore. Siege and capture of Bhurtpore ; Capt. 8th L.C. Fur. p.a. 6 Nov. 1829 till 1 Oct. 1834. Apptd. Comdt. 3rd Local Horse 29 June 1838, and was on his way to join at Saugor when drowned.

Refs. : A.J. N.S. xxvii. 232. *G.M.* 1839, i. 333. Will dated 13 June 1822 ; codicil, Lucknow 14 Dec. 1825 ; admon. 11 Dec. 1838. Litho. portrait (M. Gauci-W. Whitaker) pub. *c.* 1840. M.I. St. Mary's, Benares.

[1] *Note :* Commenced the Service afresh when apptd. a Cadet for Cav. (Letter from C.D. 25 Aug. 1824.)

SMELT, Arthur (1789-1849). Lieutenant. 23rd N.I. Subsequently B.C.S. *b.* 8 June 1789. Cadet 1803. Arrived in India 13 Aug. 1805. Ensign 13 Aug. 1805. Lieut. 14 Aug. 1805. Resigned 23 July 1807. *d.* Calcutta 26 Nov. 1849.

Youngest son of Rev. William Smelt, rector of Gedling, Notts., and Margaret his wife, only sister of Philip Stanhope, 5th Earl of Chesterfield, K.G. (*D.N.B.*). *m.* 21 July 1811, Frances Georgina, widow of James Richard Mockler, *q.v.* (She died London 19 July 1881, aged 89.) His dau. *m.* Frederick Lloyd, *q.v.* Ed. Repton ; admitted Jan. 1802.

Services : Posted Lieut. to 23rd N.I. 1806. No record of active service. Transfd. to B.C.S. with rank as Writer from 29 July 1805. Admitted to Coll. of Ft. Wm. Nov. 1807. Was Civil & Sessions Judge E. Burdwan (Champaran) at death.

Refs. : Burke's *Peerage*, 1923, p. 494, *s.n.* Chesterfield, E. *Repton School Register.* *I.M.* 22 Jan. 1850, p. 40. *G.M.* 1850, i. 340. Will dated 21 Nov. 1849 ; proved 5 Dec. 1849.

SMITH, Adoniah [1] (1791-1829). Captain, 50th N.I. *b.* 19 Dec. 1791. Cadet 1806. Arrived in India 30 July 1807. Ensign 29 Aug. 1807. Lieut. 15 June 1813. Capt. 1 May 1824. *d.* Azamgarh, U.P., 10 Jan. 1829, from the effects of a fall from his horse the previous month at Allahabad.[2]

bapt. St. Budeaux, Devon, 8 Mar. 1792. 2nd son of Rev. William Smith, rector of Meavy, Devon, and Amy his wife. *m.* Cawnpore 9 July 1818, Charlotte, 6th sister of Edmund Swetenham, *q.v.* (*See also* James Parsons.) (She died 20 Sept. 1825.)

Services : Barasat C.C. 1807-8. Posted to 2/25th N.I. 1808. Capture of Mauritius 1810; Ensign 1st Vol. Bn. Nepal War 1814-15; Lieut. 2/25th N.I., in 4th Div. Nepal War 1816 ; Chirriaghati ; Makwanpur ; Lieut. 2/25th N.I., in 3rd Bde. Centre Column. Third Mahratta War 1817-18 ; Lieut. 2/25th N.I. Adjt. Farrukha-

THE BENGAL ARMY, 1758-1834 117

bad Provl. Bn. 1819-24. Transfd. to 1/25th N.I. ; to 50th N.I. (late 2/25th) May 1824. Fur. 1826 till June 1828.

Refs. : *Bath Chron.*, 18 June 1829. *A.J.* xxvii. 755. Will dated Fatehgarh, 19 May 1823 ; proved 1 July 1829. M.I. at Azamgarh.

¹ *Note* : Name given as Adonijah in all *E.I.R.*

² *Note* : " Returning from chasing a jackal one evening, it was very dark, and as Capt. A—— S—— was cantering his Arab across the parade-ground, the animal put his foot into a deep hole and fell ; our friend thought nothing of it, and refused to be bled ; a few days afterwards the regiment quitted Allahabad, and he died the second day, on the march to Benares." (Fanny Parkes' *Wanderings of a Pilgrim* . . ., i. 97.)

SMITH, Andrew (1757-1782). Lieutenant, Infantry. *b.* in Ireland 1757. Cadet 1777. Ensign 10 Feb. 1778. Lieut. 20 Sept. 1778. *d.* Bombay 1782.

Services : Sailed for India in the *Egmont* 1 Jan. 1777, aged 19 2/1st Bengal Eur. Regt. in Oct. 1779. Leave s.c. to sea 30 Aug. 1779 and Feb. 1782.

*****SMITH or SMYTH, Blakeney.** Cadet. Infantry. Country Cadet 1781. Resigned 5 Apr. 1782.

Services : Apptd. Cadet 30 June 1781. Fought a duel on Calcutta race-course 13 Aug. 1781. Granted a charter-party passage to Europe in the *Hinchinbrooke* 27 Feb. 1785.

Refs. : *India Gazette*, 18 Aug. 1781.

*****SMITH, Charles** (1783-1814). Lieutenant, Bengal Eur. Regt. *b.* Chiswick, Middlesex, 28 Feb. 1783. Cadet 1803. Arrived in India 11 Aug. 1804. Ensign 21 Aug. 1804. Lieut. 21 Sept. 1804. *d.* Amboyna 30 June 1814.

bapt. Chiswick 25 Apr. 1783. Son of William Edward Smith, of the Treasury, and Jane Tenison his wife.

Services : Posted Lieut. to Bengal Eur. Regt. 1805. Was serving at Amboyna 1811 ; at Banda I., latterly as Asst. Comr., 1812-13.

Refs. : *G.M.* 1815, i. 470.

SMITH, Charles (1786-1821). Bt. Captain, 15th N.I. *b.* London 26 May 1786. Cadet 1804. Arrived in India 13 May 1806. Ensign 25 Mar. 1806. Lieut. 1 Feb. 1807. Bt. Capt. 1 Jan. 1819. *d.* Bareilly 16 Dec. 1821.

bapt. St. Pancras 30 Apr. 1789. Son of John Smith and Mary his wife (who *re-m.* —— Culliford). *m.* Calcutta 26 May 1809, Miss Laurette Françoise L'Elant.

118 LIST OF THE OFFICERS OF

Services : Barasat C.C. Posted Lieut. to 15th N.I. 1807. Nepal War 1814-15 ; Parsa (w.) ; Lieut. 2/15th N.I., in 4th Div. Nepal War 1816 ; Lieut. 2/15th N.I., in 4th Bde. Centre Column. Siege and capture of Hathras 1817 ; Lieut. 2/15th N.I. Acting Bk. Mr. at Cawnpore 30 Sept. 1817 till 1818. Third Mahratta War 1819 ; Asirgarh ; Bt. Capt. 2/15th N.I.

SMITH, Charles (1787-1826). Captain, Artillery. (406) *b.* London 23 May 1787. Cadet 1808. Arrived in India 19 July 1809. Fireworker 2 Apr. 1809. Lieut. 17 Feb. 1815. Capt. 21 Apr. 1824. *d.* Dum-Dum 30 Aug. 1826.

bapt. Marylebone 18 June 1787. Son of John Smith and Elizabeth his wife.

Services : Nepal War 1814-15 ; Kalanga ; Jaithak ; Lieut. 5th Coy. 3rd Bn., in 2nd Div. Siege of Hathras 1817 ; Lieut. 6th Coy. 1st Bn., d.d. 4th Coy. 3rd Bn. Third Mahratta War ; Taragarh ; Madhurajpura ; siege of Nasridah 25-29 Oct. 1818 ; Lieut. 6th Coy. 1st Bn., d.d. 7th Coy. 3rd Bn., afterwards with Reserve Div. First Burma War ; Cachar Mar.-Dec. 1824 ; comdg. Art. with force under Lt.-Col. W. Innes, C.B., *q.v.*

Refs.: E.I.M.C. iii. 525.

SMITH, Charles (1798-1826). Lieutenant, 27th N.I. *b.* 25 Mar. 1798. Cadet 1817. Ensign (?) Lieut. 8 Aug. 1818. *d.* Calcutta 19 Feb. 1826.

bapt. Brechin 30 Mar. 1798. Son (twin with John) of James Smith, of Brechin, merchant, and Margaret Irvine his wife.

Services : Posted Lieut. to 2/13th N.I. 1818 ; transfd. to 26th N.I. (late 1/13th) May 1824 ; to 27th N.I. 3 June 1825. (? First Burma War ; Arakan 1825 ; Lieut. 26th N.I.)

Refs.: M.I. in S. Park St. cemetery, Calcutta.

SMITH, Charles Corner (1786-1827). Captain, 6th Extra N.I. *bapt.* Upwey, Dorset, 3 Sept. 1786. Cadet 1802. Arrived in India 13 Feb. 1804. Ensign 17 Dec. 1803. Lieut. 21 Sept. 1804. Capt. 1 Aug. 1818. *d.* Berhampore 6 Nov. 1827, aged 41.

Son of John B. Smith and Rachel his wife. Nephew of Major Hughes. *m.* Dinapore 10 Mar. 1811, Miss Emily Prospère de Panouilhère. (She was pensd. on Lord Clive's fund 20 Jan. 1833 ; living in 1860.)

Services : Posted Lieut. to Bengal Eur. Regt. 1805. Expedn. to Macao 1808-9 ; Lieut. Eur. Regt. Served with his Regt. in Java 1812-15, at Macassar 1815-16. Transfd. to newly-raised 6th Extra Regt. May 1825 ; suspended 13 July 1827.

Refs.: A.J. xxv. 518. Naval & Mily. Mag., iii, p. cxii.

SMITH, Daniel (1733/34-?). Cadet. Infantry. b. I. of Man 1733/34. Cadet 1758. Ensign (Madras) 26 May 1759. Lieut. 3 June 1761.

Services: Apptd. Cadet for Bengal 1758; sailed for India in the Bombay Castle 1758, aged 24. Transfd. to Madras Est.; returned to England 1761-2.

Refs.: Will dated in England 29 Apr. 1758 and 22 July 1762; proved at Madras 21 May 1765.

SMITH, Daniel (1791-1815). Lieutenant, 21st N.I. b. London 23 Apr. 1791. Cadet 1807. Arrived in India 24 Aug. 1808. Ensign 29 Aug. 1808. Lieut. 16 Dec. 1814. d. Chittagong 2 Feb. 1815.

bapt. Temple church, Middlesex, 7 May 1791. Son of Rev. Haddon Smith and Hester his wife. Brother of Michael Smith.

Services: Barasat C.C. Posted Ensign to 21st N.I. 1809. Operations in Bundelkhand 1809-12; in Rewah 1811; attack on Bhapwai fort; Ensign 1/21st N.I. Lieut. 1/21st N.I.

SMITH, David (1746/47-1779). Captain, Infantry. 2nd Bde. b. 1746/47. Country Cadet 1768. Ensign 9 May 1768. Lieut. 25 Dec. 1769. Capt. 7 July 1778. d. unm. Calcutta 15 Sept. 1779, aged 32.

Son of Elizabeth Moor. Brother of Mungo, James, Peter, Jennet, Elizabeth, Jean and Christian.

Services: Apptd. Cadet 3 Feb. 1768. First Rohilla War 1774; battle of St. George; Lieut. in 2nd Bde. Adjt. of Sepoys in Barrackpore detachment of 2nd Bde. 24 July 1777 till 17 July 1778.

Refs.: S.M. 1780, p. 447. Will dated camp in Rohilla country, 21 Apr. 1774; codicil 23 Aug. 1779; proved 9 Aug. 1780. M.I. in S. Park St. cemetery, Calcutta.

SMITH, David (1764/65-1794). Lieutenant, Infantry. b. 1764/65. Cadet 1782. Arrived in India 15 Nov. 1782. Ensign 13 Feb. 1783. Lieut. 4 Feb. 1790. d. Calcutta 19 July 1794.

A native of Scotland. Son of William Smith (? 1726/27-1767), q.v., and Isabella Anderson his wife. Brother of William Smith (? 1763/64-?), q.v., and of Bernard Smith. Nephew of Mrs. Ann Mackenzie.

Services: Sailed for India in the Worcester 6 Feb. 1782, aged 17. Posted to 3rd Bengal Eur. Regt. 28 Feb. 1783. Ensign 2nd Eur. Regt. in July 1787; transfd. to 29th Bn. Sepoys 5 Feb. 1790.

Refs.: Will dated Barrackpore, 20 Jan. 1794; proved 24 July 1794.

SMITH, Edward (*d.* 1772). Capt. Lieutenant, Artillery. (64) Cadet (Inf.) 1763. Fireworker 1 June 1764. 2nd Lieut. Feb. 1767. Lieut. 1 Apr. 1769. Capt. Lt. 4 Mar. 1770. *d.* May 1772: drowned in the Hooghly R.

Services: Whilst a Cadet served as Conductor of Art; promoted Ensign in Inf. by mistake 1 June 1764; reposted to Art. 17 Feb. 1765, and posted as Conductor to the magazine.

SMITH, Edward Fleetwood (1809-1872). Colonel. 23rd N.I. *b.* Calcutta 16 May 1809. Cadet 1825. Arrived in India 25 June 1826. Ensign 16 Feb. 1826. Lieut. 28 July 1833. Capt. 1 Apr. 1846. Bt. Major 20 June 1854. Lt. Col. 29 Apr. 1861. Retired 31 Dec. 1861. Hon. Col. 31 Dec. 1861. *d.* at his residence, 101 Hereford Rd., Bayswater, 12 Mar. 1872.

bapt. Calcutta 10 June 1809. Son of (Capt.) Mathew Smith, of Howrah, ship-builder, and Alice his wife, *née* Hennes. Brother of Mathew Smith, *q.v. m.* Dibrugarh, Assam, 14 July 1853, Catherine ——, spinster. (She died 4 Oct. 1883.)

Services: Ensign d.d. 28th N.I. 8 July 1826; posted to 23rd N.I. 26 Sept. 1826. 2nd in comd. Assam L.I. 14 Mar. 1843; do. 1st Assam L.I. 1844-53. Supt. of Dacca elephant *keddahs* June 1853 till retirement.

Refs.: The Times, 15 Mar. 1872.

SMITH, Edward James (1797-1846). Lieut. Colonel, C.B., Engineers. *bapt.* Bideford, Devon, 17 Nov. 1797. Cadet 1815. Admitted 5 Sept. 1818. Ensign 1 Sept. 1818. Lieut. 18 May 1821. Capt. 28 Sept. 1827. Major 4 Sept. 1839. Lt. Col. 19 Feb. 1844. *d.* Sabathu 11 Nov. 1846.

Son of James Smith, of Bideford, lawyer, and Mary his wife.[1] Brother of James Smith (1781-1804), *q.v.* Addiscombe Cadet 20 July 1814 till 14 Oct. 1816.

Services: Leave to P.W.I. 12 Sept. 1818 till 18 Nov. 1819. Posted to S. & M. at Saugor 1 June 1822. Siege and capture of Bhurtpore; volunteered to accompany the storming party (w.); Lieut. S. & M. (*Lond. Gaz.* 5 July 1826). Executive Engr. Allahabad Div. 27 Jan. 1827; offg. Suptg. Engr. P.W.D., C.P., 11 June 1830. Shekhawat expedn. 1834. Suptg. Engr. C.P. 16 Dec. 1837. Field Engr. with force for service in Marwar 5 Aug. till 14 Oct. 1839. Chief Engr. with Army of Reserve (for Afghanistan) 10 Jan. 1843. Chief Engr. with Army of Exercise 20 Oct. 1843. Gwalior campaign; Maharajpur (ib. 8 Mar. 1844) ; Chief Engr. (Bronze star). First Sikh War ; Lt. Col. Engrs. (Medal). C.B. 1 Nov. 1844.

Refs. : Will dated camp, Hingonah, 29 Dec. 1843 ; admon. 19 Apr. 1847.

[1] *Note* : In the original register at Bideford, and in the copy of his baptismal certificate attached to his Cadet Papers, his mother's name is given as Jane. In the former, however, a footnote in a later handwriting asserts that her name 'should be Mary.'

SMITH, Francis (*d*. 1770). Ensign, Infantry. Cadet 1769. Ensign 26 Sept. 1769. *d*. Calcutta 18 July 1770.

Services : N.F.P.

SMITH, Francis Edward (1804-1859). Bt. Captain. 69th N.I. *bapt*. Julianstown, co. Meath, 19 Nov. 1804. Cadet 1823. Arrived in India 25 June 1824. Ensign 14 Jan. 1824. Lieut. 13 May 1825. Bt. Capt. 14 Jan. 1839. Retired 24 Aug. 1840. *d.s.p.* 12 Oct. 1859.

2nd son of Henry Smith, D.L., of Beabeg, and Annesbrook, co. Meath, high sheriff 1819, and Margaret his 1st wife, dau. of Henry Osborne, of Dardistown Castle, co. Meath. *m*. (before 1828) ?

Services : Posted to 56th N.I. 1824 ; transfd. to newly-raised 1st Extra Regt. (became 69th N.I.) May 1825 ; actg. Adjt. do. 11 July 1827 ; permanent do. 20 Feb. 1828 till 28 Mar. 1838. Operations against the Bhils 1827. Leave s.c. to Simla 6 Sept. 1835 till Feb. 1838 ; fur. s.c. 24 Feb. 1838 till retirement.

Refs. : Burke's *Landed Gentry of Ireland*, p. 643 *s.n.* Smith, of Annesbrook, co. Meath.

SMITH, Frederick. Cadet. Infantry. Cadet 1770. Resigned 23 Nov. 1770.

Services : N.F.P.

SMITH, Frederick Coape (1798-1882). Bt. Captain. 48th N.I. *b*. Little Parndon, Essex, 14 Feb. 1798. Cadet 1818. Admitted 4 Sept. 1819. Ensign 17 Apr. 1819. Lieut. 6 May 1822. Bt. Capt. 17 Apr. 1834. Resigned 1 Aug. 1838. *d*. Melbourne, Aust., 13 Oct. 1882.

4th and youngest son of William Smith, of Parndon, M.P. for Sudbury, Camelford and Norwich, and Frances his wife, dau. of John Coape. Uncle of Florence Nightingale (*D.N.B*.) and of the wife of John Ludlow (1801-1882), *q.v. m*. Margaret Yates. (She died 1883, aged 84.)

Services : Ensign d.d. Bengal Eur. Regt. 1819 ; posted to 1/24th N.I. 1820 ; d.d. Gorakhpur L.I. 25 Apr. 1820. Adjt. 1/24th N.I. 18 Sept. 1823 ; do. 48th N.I. (late 2/24th) 17 June 1824 till 1 Jan. 1836. Siege and capture of Bhurtpore ; Lieut. 48th N.I., d.d. 60th N.I. (India medal). Leave s.c. to N.S.W. 20 May 1826 till 29 Jan. 1828 ; s.c. to Tasmania 6 Feb. 1830 till 8 June 1832 ; fur. s.c. via Tasmania 5 Feb. 1836 till resignation.

Refs. : *The Smith Family*, by Rev. Compton Reade (London, 1902), p. 174, *s.n.* Smith, of I.W. and Parndon. *The Times*, 23 Oct. 1882.

SMITH, Frederick Thomas (*d.* 1770). Major, Infantry. Comdg. Patna *Pargannah* Bn. Capt. 20 Dec. 1764. Major 3 Apr. 1768. *d.* Patna 21 Sept. 1770.

Brother of Joseph Nicholas Smith, of London. *m.* Calcutta 24 Nov. 1768, Miss Elizabeth Hamilton. (She was *bur.* Calcutta 16 Aug. 1769.)

Services : Ensign 3rd Ft. Gds. 9 Nov. 1749 ; Lieut. & Capt. do. 17 Dec. 1756 ; exchanged to Capt. of 104th Coy. Marines 2 Oct. 1757 ; resigned 20 Apr. 1758, but rejoined (in war time) as Capt. of 122nd Coy. Marines 20 Jan. 1759 ; renewed 27 Oct. 1760 by George III. Arrived in Bengal with the fleet from Madras 9 Sept. 1763. Transfd. as Capt. to Bengal Est. 20 Dec. 1764. Apptd. A.D.C. to Col. John Carnac, *q.v.*, 13 Feb. 1765. Town Major of Ft. Wm. *c.* 1767-9.

Refs. : *Williams*, p. 23*n*. *Broome*, p. lviii. *Forrest's Clive*, ii. 321. *S.M.* 1771, p. 558 (where he is incorrectly called " Major Frederick Thomas "). Will dated 10 Feb. 1770 ; proved 9 Oct. 1770.

SMITH, George Acklom (1797-1857). Bt. Colonel, 10th N.I. *b.* Petworth, Sussex, 15 May 1797. Cadet 1813. Admitted 9 Dec. 1814. Ensign (16 Dec. 1814) 5 June 1815. Lieut. 31 Aug. 1816. Capt. 6 Aug. 1832. Major 15 Feb. 1842. Lt. Col. 3 Oct. 1848. Bt. Col. 28 Nov. 1854. *d.* Cawnpore 15 July 1857 : kld. by mutineers.

bapt. Petworth 10 July 1797. Son of Rev. Richard Smith, of Sutton, Surrey, and Mary Edith his wife. *m.* 1st, St. Luke's, Chelsea, 10 Sept. 1839, Anna Maria, only dau. of Major Chalmers, H.M. 55th Regt. (She died Benares 5 Sept. 1841.) *m.* 2nd, Ambala, 6 Mar. 1850, Mary, sister of H. J. Piercy, *q.v.* (She was kld. with him, aged 41.)

Services : Nepal War 1816 ; Makwanpur ; Ensign 2/8th N.I., in 4th Bde. Centre Column (India medal). Third Mahratta War 1817-19 ; Nagpur ; Mandala ; Lieut. 2/8th N.I. Transfd. to 9th

THE BENGAL ARMY, 1758-1834 123

N.I. (late 1/8th) May 1824. Fur. p.a. 30 Jan. 1837 till 3 Feb. 1840. Comdd. 2nd L.I. Bn. 23 Aug. 1842 till broken up Jan. 1843. To comd. escort of C.-in-C. 29 Nov. 1844. Posted Lt. Col. to 9th N.I. 1849; to 47th N.I. 21 Sept. 1852; to 10th N.I. 21 June 1854, and was comdg. this Regt. at Fatehgarh on outbreak of Mutiny. Apptd. Bdr. on the Est. 30 May 1857; posted to Lucknow 23 July 1857, a week after his death.
Refs.: Boase. *A.J.* N.S. xxx. 169. *G.M.* 1857, ii. 685. M.I. All Sts. Memorial Church, Cawnpore.

SMITH, George Stacey. Cadet. Artillery. (III.-19) Cadet 1783. Declined coming out.

SMITH, Henry (*d.* 1774). Ensign, Infantry. Cadet 1772. Ensign 16 Jan. 1773. *d.* Midnapore 17 Dec. 1774.
Services: N.F.P.

SMITH, Henry (1761/62-?) Lieutenant. Infantry. *b.* Norfolk 1761/62. Cadet 1778. Never arrived in India. Ensign 12 Feb. 1780. Lieut. 3 Apr. 1781. Struck off 1788.
Services: Should have sailed for India in the *Ganges* 7 Mar. 1779, aged 17.

SMITH, Henry (1785-1805). Cornet, 6th N.C. *b.* Dublin " on or about 16 May 1785." Cadet 1800. Arrived in India 24 Aug. 1801. Cornet 26 July 1803. *d.* Cawnpore 22 Nov. 1805.
Son of Anna Smith, of Bath.
Services: Ensign d.d. 7th N.I. in 1802; transfd. from Inf. to Cav. Second Mahratta War 1803-5; Laswari; relief of Delhi; Shamli; pursuit of Holkar; Cornet 6th N.C.

SMITH, Henry (1803-1830). Lieutenant, 2nd N.I. *b.* Newcastle-on-Tyne 26 Mar. 1803. Cadet 1821. Arrived in India 20 Aug. 1822. Ensign 16 Apr. 1822. Lieut. 1 May 1824. *d.* Barrackpore 9 Oct. 1830.
bapt. All Sts., Newcastle-on-Tyne, 27 Dec. 1803. 4th son of Thomas Smith, of Newcastle-on-Tyne, shipowner, and Mary his wife, dau. of William Carss, shipowner.
Services: Posted to 4th N.I. 1822; transfd. to 1st N.I. 1823; to 4th N.I. (late 2/1st) May 1824; to 2nd N.I. 21 July 1824; Adjt. do. 29 July 1825 till death. No record of active service.
Refs.: M.I. at Barrackpore.

SMITH, Henry Bowden (1799-1833). Captain, 37th N.I. *b.* Brockenhurst, Hants, 25 June 1799. Cadet 1820. Admitted

31 May 1820. Ensign 13 Jan. 1821. Lieut. 11 July 1823. Capt. 4 Apr. 1833. d. Nimach 14 Nov. 1833, of wounds received in an engagement with the Bhils 21 Oct.

bapt. Brockenhurst 6 July 1800. Son of Robert Smith, of Carey's, Brockenhurst, and Ann Bowden his wife. m. (?)

Services: Posted to 1/16th N.I.; transfd. to 2/18th N.I. July 1823; to 37th N.I. (late 2/18th) May 1824. Siege and capture of Bhurtpore; Lieut. 37th N.I. Intr. & Qmr. 37th N.I. 2 Oct. till 21 Dec. 1827. Fur. s.c. 20 Feb. 1830 till 11 Oct. 1832. On service with Meywar F.F. against the Bhils Oct. 1833 (w.).

Refs.: The Smith Family, by Rev. Compton Reade, p. 59. A.J. N.S. xiv. 49. M.I. Nimach.

SMITH, Henry Tipper (1787-1836). Lieut. Colonel, Invalid Est. 73rd N.I. bapt. ptely. Southampton 17 Aug. 1787. Cadet 1803. Arrived in India 17 Mar. 1805. Ensign 28 Apr. 1805. Lieut. 29 Apr. 1805. Capt. 11 June 1822. Major 22 May 1829. Lt. Col. 18 Dec. 1834. Invalided 11 July 1836. d. Serampore 7 Dec. 1836.

Received into Church at Southampton 16 Oct. 1787. 3rd and youngest son of Nicholas Tipper Smith, solicitor in Southampton, and Elizabeth his wife, dau. of —— Forder, lord of the manor of Silkstead, Hants. (Probably related to Thomas Paterson Smith, q.v.) m. Cawnpore 9 June 1806, Jane Louisa, née Carlisle, widow of Lieut. William Meulh, Adjt. H.M. 76th Ft. (She died Dinapore 7 Mar. 1835, aged 45.)

Services: Posted Lieut. to 25th N.I. 1806. Nepal War 1814-15; actg. Qmr. 2/25th N.I., in 4th Div. Intr. & Qmr. 1/25th N.I. 20 June 1815 till June 1822. Siege and capture of Hathras 1817; Lieut. 1/25th N.I. Third Mahratta War 1817-18; Bde. Qmr. 4th Inf. Bde., 2nd Div. Transfd. to newly-raised 34th N.I. July 1823, but continued to d.d. for some months with 1/25th. Transfd. to 67th N.I. (late 1/34th) May 1824. 2nd in comd. newly-raised 11th Extra Regt. 21 May 1825 till its reduction 1 Apr. 1826. Posted Lt. Col. to 54th N.I. 11 Mar. 1835; to 17th N.I. 7 Apr. 1835; to 73rd N.I. 8 June 1835.

Refs.: Misc. Gen. et Her. N.S. iv. 242. A.J. N.S. xxii. 268. Will dated 3 Dec. 1836; proved 30 Dec. 1836. M.I. Serampore Mission burial ground.

SMITH, James (d. 1792). Major, 8th Bn. Sepoys. Cadet 1768. Ensign 25 Jan. 1769. Lieut. 24 May 1770. Capt. 19 Sept. 1778. Major 7 Feb. 1784. d. Barrackpore 22 June 1792.

Cousin of Susannah Smith, 18 Bennet St., Westminster.

THE BENGAL ARMY, 1758-1834 125

Services: Capt. 2/3rd Bengal Eur. Regt. in Oct. 1779. Fur. 1782 till Oct. 1788. 1st Bengal Eur. Bn. in 1790; comdg. 8th Bn. Sepoys in 1792.

Refs.: Will dated 15 June 1792; proved 27 June 1792.

SMITH, James (1757/58-1791). Captain, Artillery. (164) *b.* 1757/58. Country Cadet 1778. Fireworker 20 Sept. 1778. Lieut. 20 Mar. 1780. Capt. 6 Feb. 1789. *d.* Bangalore 24 Oct. 1791, aged 33.

Services: Apptd. Cadet 17 July 1778. Lieut. 3rd Bn. Art. in July 1787. Third Mysore War 1790-1; Bangalore; Capt. 4th Coy. 2nd Bn.

Refs.: *S.M.* 1792, p. 258. Will dated 27 Oct. 1785; proved 16 May 1792. Name on cenotaph erected by Mysore Govt. in Bangalore fort.

*SMITH, James (*d.* 1783). Ensign, Infantry. Cadet 1782. Ensign 8 Mar. 1783. *d.* Madras Harbour 19 Apr. 1783 : blown up in the *Duke of Athol.*[1]

Services: Apptd. Cadet 29 May 1782; sailed for India in the *Duke of Athol* 11 Sept. 1782.

[1] *Note:* See note to James Barnes.

SMITH, James (1781-1804). Lieutenant, Bengal Eur. Regt. *b.* Calcutta 10 Oct. 1781. Cadet 1795. Arrived in India 9 Oct. 1797. Ensign 13 Aug. 1797. Lieut. 9 Aug. 1798. *d.* Bilhaur, nr. Cawnpore, U.P., 10 Oct. 1804 : " kld. in action on the Frontiers." (M.I.)

Of Bideford, Devon. (*Probably* son of James Smith, of Bideford, lawyer, formerly of Calcutta, and brother of John Smith (1783-1846), *q.v.*)

Services: Lieut. 1st Bengal Eur. Regt. in 1798. Served in Ceylon with 2nd Vol. Bn. 1803-4.

Refs.: M.I. nr. Bilhaur rly. stn.

SMITH, James (1786-1844). Captain. 67th N.I. *b.* Edinburgh 11 Nov. 1786. Cadet 1805. Arrived in India 19 Sept. 1806. Ensign 3 Oct. 1806. Lieut. 16 June 1811. Capt. 1 May 1824. Retired 10 Jan. 1832. *d.* 9 July 1844.

bapt. S. Leith 26 Nov. 1786. Son of Thomas Smith, in Calton Hill, Edinburgh, writer, and Margaret Gow his wife, relict of Alexander Taylor.

Services: Barasat C.C. Posted Ensign to 5th N.I. 1807. Reduction of Kalinjar 1812; Lieut. 2/5th N.I. To take charge of

8th Coy. Pioneers 13 Feb. 1812. With 6th Gren. Bn. in 1816. Third Mahratta War 1817-19; Lieut. 2/5th N.I. Adjt. 2/5th N.I. 28 May 1818 till 1823; transfd. as Adjt. to newly-raised 1/34th N.I. 1 Oct. 1823. Fur. p.a. 21 Nov. 1823 till 23 Oct. 1826. Transfd. to 67th N.I. (late 1/34th) May 1824.

SMITH, James Willis (1800-1830). Captain, 35th N.I. *b.* Calcutta 20 Jan. 1800. Cadet 1817. Ensign (?) Lieut. 1 Aug. 1818. Capt. 20 Nov. 1827. *d.* at sea 13 Apr. 1830, on board the *Robarts*.

bapt. Calcutta 24 May 1801. Son of Joseph Barnard Smith, Senior Merchant B.C.S., and Rose his wife, *née* Morrow (? Moreau). Brother of Joseph Barnard Smith and uncle of Charles Corfield, *qq.v.*

Services: Posted Supy. Lieut. to 2/17th N.I. 1818; transfd. to 34th N.I. (late 1/17th) May 1824; to 35th N.I. 1825. Siege and capture of Bhurtpore; Lieut. 35th N.I. Adjt. 35th N.I. 21 May 1827 till 16 May 1828. Leave s.c. 10 mos. to Mauritius 15 Mar. 1830.

Refs.: Will dated on board *Robarts*, 8 Apr. 1830; proved 19 June 1830.

SMITH, John (1738/39-1777). Major, Infantry. *b.* 1738/39. Cadet (Madras) 1761. Arrived at Madras June 1762. Vol. 1 June 1762. Ensign 1 Dec. 1762. Lieut. 1 June 1764. Capt. (Bengal) 10 June 1766. Major 31 Dec. 1772. *bur.* Calcutta 6 Sept. 1777.

Of Eardisland, co. Hereford. Brother of Richard Smith, *q.v. m.* Madras 24 Aug. 1776, Susannah Sophia Selina, dau. of John Debonnaire, of Madras. (She *re-m.* 18 Apr. 1782, Sir Thomas Theophilus Metcalfe, Bart., *q.v.*, and died 10 Sept. 1815.)

Services: Sailed for Madras in the *Tilbury* 5 Feb. 1762, aged 23. Saw active service in Madras, including siege and capture of Madura 1764. Transfd. to Bengal Est. 4 July 1766, owing to the "Batta mutiny." Returned to England Jan. 1773, and came out again with G. F. Grand, *q.v.*, in the *Greenwich* which sailed in Jan. 1776.

SMITH or SMYTHE, John. Ensign. 3rd Bengal Eur. Regt. Cadet 1771. Ensign 30 Jan. 1773. Resigned 8 Feb. 1773.

Services: Sailed for India in the *Ponsborne* 15 Jan. 1771. Remained in India after resignation.

SMITH, John (1761-1803). Captain, 6th N.C. *b.* 1761. Cadet 1782. Admitted 21 Aug. 1783. Ensign (?) Lieut. 25 Oct.

THE BENGAL ARMY, 1758-1834 127

1782. Capt. 17 July 1801. *d. unm.* Nehmeda, U.P., 21 Dec. 1803.

Natural son of John Wilkes, the demagogue (*D.N.B.*), by his housekeeper, Catherine Smith. Ed. Harrow *c.* 1768-9.

Services : Clerk in an office in Hamburgh. Sailed for India in the *Duke of Athol* 11 Sept. 1782. Lieut. 31st Bn. Sepoys in July 1787 ; transfd. to Cav. ; Lieut. and Bt. Capt. 4th N.C. ; transfd. as Capt. Lt. to newly-raised 6th N.C. 29 May 1800. Operations in Jumna Doab 1802-3 ; Sasni ; Bijaigarh ; Kachaura ; Capt. 6th N.C.

Refs. : Life of John Wilkes, by Horace Bleackley. Will dated 3 Feb. 1803 ; proved 11 Feb. 1804.

SMITH, John (1783-1846). Lieut. Colonel. 19th N.I. *b.* Bengal 5 June 1783. Cadet 1798. Arrived in India 26 Nov. 1799. Ensign 12 Jan. 1800. Lieut. 29 May 1800. Capt. 19 Aug. 1814. Major 1 May 1824. Lt. Col. 3 Mar. 1826. Retired 26 Feb. 1829. *d.* 21 June 1846.

Son of James Smith, of Bideford, lawyer, formerly of Calcutta. Brother of Robert Smith (1787-?), *q.v.*

Services : Posted to 2/3rd N.I. 15 Apr. 1801 ; Adjt. do. 5 Oct. 1809 till 1812. Capt. Lt. 2 Sept. 1812. A.D.C. to Lt.-Gen. Samuel Watson, *q.v.*, 1812-13. Capt. 1/3rd N.I. Fur. 2 Jan. 1815 till 1817. D.A.Q.M.G. 2 cl. 1819 ; 1 cl. 1823. Transfd. to 19th N.I. (late 2/3rd) May 1824 ; posted Lt. Col. to do. 30 Oct. 1826.

SMITH, John (1813-1892). Colonel. 49th N.I. *b.* 24 Apr. 1813. Cadet 1828. Arrived in India 25 Sept. 1829. Ensign (7 June 1829) 25 Sept. 1829. Lieut. 8 Jan. 1835. Capt. 7 July 1845. Major 18 May 1856. Lt. Col. 11 Oct. 1859. Retired 31 Dec. 1861. Hon. Col. 31 Dec. 1861. *d.* 25 Feb. 1892.

bapt. Lambeth 21 Sept. 1813. Son of Edward Smith, of Vauxhall, brewer, and Sarah his wife (? *née* Morfett).

Services : Apptd. Actg. Ensign (having been 2 yrs. in India) 27 Oct. 1831. Posted Ensign to 49th N.I. 23 Dec. 1832. Jodhpur demonstration 1834-5 ; Lieut. 49th N.I. Actg. Intr. & Qmr. 1st L.C. 26 Aug. 1835 till 1838 ; Adjt. 49th N.I. 1 Nov. 1839 till 29 Aug. 1845. Fur. s.c. 14 Nov. 1847 till 1849. Comdt. Sialkot Depot 12 Dec. 1856. Posted Lt. Col. to 49th N.I. Oct. 1859. Fur. 27 Mar. 1860 till retirement.

Refs. : The Times, 26 Feb. 1892.

SMITH, John David (1785-1813). Captain, Artillery. (324) *bapt.* Wimbledon 14 Apr. 1785. Cadet 1801. Arrived in India

15 Dec. 1803. Lieut. 4 Sept. 1803. Capt. Lt. 28 Feb. 1806. Capt. 28 Apr. 1812. d. Java 25 Mar. 1813.

Son of Thomas Smith and Jane Meliora his wife. Brother of Thomas Paterson Smith, *q.v.* Woolwich Cadet.

Services : Second Mahratta War ; capture of Deig (w.) ; Bhurtpore ; Lieut. 4th Coy. 2nd Bn. Capture of Java 1811 ; Capt. Lt. 7th Coy. 1st Bn.

Refs. : Will dated 20 May 1808 ; codicil 23 Jan. 1813 ; proved 10 Sept. 1813.

SMITH, John Fairlie (or Farley) (*d.* 1803). Captain, 18th N.I. Cadet 1779. Admitted 18 Feb. 1780. Ensign 10 July 1779. Lieut. 2 Mar. 1781. Capt. 30 Oct. 1797. *d.* Kapsa, Bundelkhand, 12 Oct. 1803 : kld. in action.

Services : Apptd. Cadet 28 Oct. 1778 ; sailed for India in the *True Briton* 16 June 1779. Lieut. 21st Bn. Sepoys. Qmr. to Sepoy Corps in 2nd Bde. 24 Oct. 1781 till 1786 ; Lieut. 6th Bn. Sepoys in July 1787 and in 1792 ; Lieut. in Cav. in 1795. Capt. 1/9th N.I. ; transfd. to 1/18th N.I. 29 May 1800. Second Mahratta War ; occupation of Bundelkhand 1803 ; Kapsa (kld. by the first cannon-shot from the enemy) ; Capt. 1/18th N.I.

Refs. : Thorn's *Memoir of the War in India, 1803-6*, p. 242.

SMITH, John Hamilton (*d.* 1789). Lieutenant, Infantry. Country Cadet 1778. Ensign 1778. Lieut. 29 Aug. 1779. *d. unm.* Ghazipur 12 Sept. 1789.

Son of John Smith, surgeon at Greenock, and Ursilla Hamilton. Brother of Ursilla Beamish.

Services : Apptd. Cadet 27 Feb. 1778. Lieut. 2/1st Bengal Eur. Regt. in Oct. 1779 ; apptd. Adjt. 38th Bn. Sepoys 22 Mar. 1780 ; transfd. to 31st Bn. Was Adjt. & Qmr. of Sepoy Corps in 5th Bde. in July 1787 and at death.

Refs. : Will dated Chunar 10 Sept. 1789 ; proved 5 Oct. 1789. M.I. at Buxar.

SMITH, John Nicholas (1758-1842). Major General. Colonel 59th N.I. *b.* in Ireland 1758. Cadet 1782. Admitted 22 Jan. 1783. Ensign 10 Mar. 1783. Lieut. 21 Feb. 1790. Capt. 5 Jan. 1801. Major 18 Feb. 1808. Lt. Col. 17 Feb. 1814. Lt. Col. Comdt. 11 July 1823. Col. 5 June 1829. Maj. Gen. 10 Jan. 1837. *d.* Cheltenham 22 Oct. 1842, aged 83.

m. Kilmurry, Limerick, Feb. 1817, Miss Ellen Theresa Dodd, of Richmond Pl. (She died 12 June 1871, aged 75.) His daus. *m.* Allan Ronald Macdonald and Mathew Smith, *qq.v.*

THE BENGAL ARMY, 1758-1834

Services: Posted to 3rd Bengal Eur. Regt. 28 Feb. 1783. Ensign 6th Bengal Eur. Bn. in Dec. 1788; reposted to do. 5 Feb. 1790. Adjt. 1/15th N.I. in 1800; transfd. as Adjt. to 1/18th N.I. 29 May 1800. Second Mahratta War; operations in Bundelkhand 1803-4; detached in May 1804 with 7 Coys. 1/18th and 50 Art. against Fort Bela. In consequence of the disaster which overwhelmed his force, was placed in arrest until subsequently exonerated by a Court of Inquiry. (? Fur. p.a. June 1806.) Operations in Hariana 1809; Bhawani (where he led 2 Coys. to the attack and greatly distinguished himself); Major 2/18th N.I. Lt. Col. 2/18th N.I. Fur. s.c. 19 Jan. 1816 till 5 Sept. 1818. Transfd. to 12th N.I. 1819; to 1/21st N.I. 1820; to 1/4th N.I. 24 Aug. 1821; as Lt. Col. Comdt. to 18th N.I. July 1823; to 36th N.I. (late 1/18th) May 1824; to 40th 3 Oct. 1831; to 59th 18 Apr. 1834. Comdt. Saugor Force. Fur. p.a. 24 Jan. 1824 till 25 Sept. 1829. Bdr. on the Est. and comd. troops in Rohilkhand 15 Nov. 1829; Bdr. Gen. comdg. Saugor Div. 22 Nov. 1831 till 22 Nov. 1836. Fur. p.a. 27 Jan. 1837 till death.

Refs.: E.I.M.C. i. 373-4. *Stubbs,* i. 207. A.J. N.S. xxxix. 347. *The Times,* 25 Oct. 1842 and 6 Jan. 1843.

SMITH, Joseph Barnard (1790-1849). Lieut. Colonel, 60th N.I. *b.* Calcutta 29 Nov. 1790. Cadet 1807. Arrived in India 19 Aug. 1808. Ensign 2 Sept. 1808. Lieut. 13 Aug. 1813. Capt. 13 May 1825. Major 20 Jan. 1835. Lt. Col. 14 Oct. 1841. *d.* Wazirabad, Punjab, 22 May 1849.

bapt. Calcutta 18 Mar. 1791. Son of Joseph Barnard Smith, B.C.S., and Rose his wife. Brother of Samuel Smith (1783-1852), *q.v. m.* Bloomsbury 24 May 1832, Maria, eldest dau. of Thomas Baylis. (She died 21 Nov. 1872.)

Services: Barasat C.C. 7 mos. Posted Ensign to 2/17th N.I. 1 Aug. 1809. Nepal War 1814-15; Jitpur; Lieut. 2/17th N.I., in 3rd Div. Actg. Adjt. and Intr. & Qmr. 2/17th N.I. Apr.-July 1819. Transfd. to newly-formed 2/32nd N.I. Sept. 1823; to 63rd N.I. (late 1/32nd) May 1824. Siege and capture of Bhurtpore; Lieut. 63rd N.I. Fur. s.c. 3 Mar. 1831 till 7 Mar. 1834. Posted Lt. Col. to 63rd N.I. 23 Nov. 1841; to 60th N.I. 27 Mar. 1844. Second Sikh War; Lt. Col. comdg. 60th N.I., in Reserve Div.

Refs.: De Rhé-Philipe. M.I. in Saroke cemetery, nr. Wazirabad.

SMITH, Joseph Hendy (1798-1841). Captain, 62nd N.I. *b.* in Ireland 13 Mar. 1798. Cadet 1819. Admitted 9 Oct. 1820. Ensign 17 Apr. 1820. Lieut. 11 July 1823. Capt. 2 Nov. 1835. *d.* Landour, U.P., 30 Mar. 1841.

bapt. Jeffreston, co. Pembroke, 7 Feb. 1813. Son of Alexander Smith and Mary his wife. *m.* Rondebosch, S.A., 4 Sept. 1833, Julia Anne, eldest dau. of Major Charles Cornwallis Michell, K.H., late R.A., H.M. Surveyor Gen. and Civil Engr. to that Colony. (She died Boulogne 3 Aug. 1878, aged 63.)
Services : Posted to 24th N.I. 1820 ; transfd. to 1/16th N.I. 1821 ; to newly-formed 2/31st N.I. (became 62nd N.I.) July 1823 ; Adjt. do. 1 Oct. 1823 till 16 Aug. 1833. First Burma War ; Arakan 1825 ; Lieut. 62nd N.I. Actg. S.A.C.G. in Arakan 26 July 1825. Leave s.c. 2 yrs. to Cape and N.S.W. 3 Feb. 1832 ; s.c. to Landour 1 Mar. 1839 till death.
Refs. : A.J. N.S. xiii. 123.

SMITH, Lewis [1] (*d.* 1794). Major, Infantry. Cadet 1768. Ensign 1 Jan. 1769. Lieut. 29 Dec. 1769. Capt. 11 July 1778. Major 28 Jan. 1784. *d.* Thakurdwara (? nr. Fatehgarh) 13 Dec. 1794.
Grandfather of Lucius Horton Smith, *q.v.*
Services : Granted fur. s.c. Mar. 1770 ; sailed for India in the *Anson* 5 Feb. 1772. Capt. 1/2nd Bengal Eur. Regt. in Oct. 1779. Leave s.c. to sea Mar. 1783. To comd. 11th N.I. Nov. 1783 ; Major 14th Bn. Sepoys in July 1787 ; to comd. 21st Bn. 3 Feb. 1790. Transfd. from 5th Eur. Bn. to 4th Sepoy Bde. 7 Dec. 1793 ; apptd. 2nd in comd. of 3rd Bde. of Army on service in Rohilkhand 17 Oct. 1794.
[1] *Note :* Or Lucius, *or* Lewis Lucius.

SMITH, Llewellyn (1807-1848). Captain. Artillery. (605) *b.* Llandulas, co. Denbigh, 23 Nov. 1807. Cadet 1827. Arrived in India 9 Aug. 1828. 2nd Lieut. 13 Dec. 1827. Lieut. 13 Oct. 1835. Capt. 3 Oct. 1845. Retired 1 Sept. 1848. *d.* at sea nr. Madras 28 Sept. 1848.
bapt. Llandulas 13 Dec. 1807. Son of Benjamin Smith, Lieut. (afterwards Comdr.) R.N., by his 1st wife, Sophia, formerly Wills. Addiscombe Cadet 1825-7.
Services : Lieut. 1st Troop 2nd Bde. H.A. in 1833. Leave s.c. 2 yrs. to Hills 15 Oct. 1834. First Afghan War 1842 ; reoccupation of Kabul ; action at Ali Masjid 3 Nov. 1842 ; Lieut. 2nd Coy. 2nd Bn. Foot Art., with Pollock's force (Medal).

SMITH, Lucius Horton (1793-1858). Lieut. Colonel, Invalid Est. 5th L.C. *b.* Lucknow 18 Oct. 1793 (*or* Fatehgarh 28 Sept. 1793). Cadet 1808. Arrived in India 21 Oct. 1809. Cornet

(24 Apr. 1809) 28 Sept. 1813. Lieut. 1 Sept. 1818. Capt. 1 May 1824. Major 12 Apr. 1849. Lt. Col. 4 Nov. 1854. Invalided 1 Apr. 1854. *d.* Kasauli 29 Sept. 1858.

Eldest son of Lewis Ferdinand Smith, Major in Daulat Rao Sindhia's service, and Anna Mitchell his wife. Grandson of Lewis Smith, *q.v.*, stepson of Samuel Middleton, junr., B.C.S., and cousin-german of Charles Terraneau, *q.v. m.* Mhow 2 Oct. 1822, Emma Lydia, widow of William Scott Kennedy, *q.v.* (She died Ambala 13 Aug. 1856, aged 56.)

Services : Barasat C.C. till Jan. 1811. Transfd. from Inf. to Cav. by C.D. 12 Dec. 1809. d.d. 1/12th N.I. Jan. 1811. Supy. Cornet d.d. 3rd N.C. July 1811 ; do. 8th N.C. Oct. 1811 ; posted Cornet to 7th N.C. 3 July 1813 ; transfd. to 6th N.C. 9 Oct. 1813. Third Mahratta War 1817-18 ; Sitabaldi ; Nagpur ; storm of Chanda ; Cornet 6th N.C. (India medal). d.d. Nagpur Auxy. Horse 1820. Intr. & Qmr. 6th L.C. 10 Apr. 1819 till 7 Nov. 1823. Post Adjt. at Lohargong 19 Jan. till 21 June 1824. Siege and capture of Bhurtpore ; Capt. 6th L.C. (clasp to India medal). Tempy. comdg. 4th L.C. June-Oct. 1830. Offg. A.D.C. to Bdr.-Gen. Robert Stevenson, *q.v.*, comdg. Cawnpore Div., 7 Nov. 1833 till Nov. 1838. Jodhpur demonstration 1834-5 ; A.D.C. Rejoined 6th L.C. Nov. 1838. Reduction of Jhansi 1838-9. Comdt. 1st Irreg. Cav. (Skinner's Horse) 23 Feb. 1842 till Nov. 1849. Posted Lt. Col. to 6th L.C. Jan. 1853 ; transfd. to 5th L.C. Oct. 1853.

Refs.: De Rhé-Philipe. I.M. 19 Nov. 1858, p. 935. Will dated 20 July 1857 ; admon. 18 June 1859. M.I. at Ambala.

SMITH, Mathew [1] (1805-1840). Bt. Captain, 23rd N.I. *b.* Calcutta 17 Apr. 1805. Cadet 1820. Admitted 8 Oct. 1821. Ensign 5 May 1821. Lieut. 31 Jan. 1824. Bt. Capt. 5 May 1836. *d.* at sea nr. the Cape 27 Mar. 1840, on board the *Robert Small*, of spleen.

bapt. Calcutta 1 June 1805. Son of Capt. Mathew Smith, of Howrah, ship-builder, and Alice his wife, *née* Hennes. Brother of Edward Fleetwood Smith, *q.v.*, and nephew of Robert Lemon, the archivist (*D.N.B.*). *m.* Saugor 6 Oct. 1836, Margaret Ellen, youngest dau. of John Nicholas Smith, *q.v.* (*See also* A. R. Macdonald.) (She *re-m.* 5 Jan. 1853, Richard Fort, of Read Hall, Lancs., and died 2 Feb. 1909.)

Services : Posted to 1/13th N.I. 1821 ; d.d. 1/10th N.I. 1822 ; transfd. to 4th N.I. 1823 ; to 7th N.I. (late 1/4th) May 1824 ; to 23rd N.I. 1824. Tempy. Asst. to P.A. Chittagong 30 Oct. 1824. First Burma War 1824-6 ; acted as A.D.C. to Sir A. Campbell on advance from Prome and actions of 1 and 2 Dec. 1825, nr. Prome. Comdd. Arakan Police Bn. 18 Feb. till 5 July 1828. Junr. Asst. to A.G.G., Saugor & Narbada, 1 June 1828 ; 1st Junr. Asst. at Betul Nov. 1835 ; Principal Asst. in Saugor district 10 Oct. 1837 till death. Leave s.c. to sea 31 Mar. till Dec. 1838 ; s.c. 15 mos. to Tasmania 5 Feb. 1840.

Refs.: *A.J.* N.S. xxxii. 291. *I.N.* June 1840, p. 22. M.I. St. Peter's, Saugor.

[1] *Note*: His christian name usually appears thus, but sometimes with two 't' s.

*SMITH, Pooley Molyneux (1773-?). Cadet. Artillery. Afterwards Capt. 36th Ft. *b*. 31 Oct. 1773. Cadet 1791. Resigned 13 July 1792.

bapt. in his grandfather's house, co. Westmeath, Nov. 1773.[1]

Services: Apptd. Cadet for Bengal Art. 5 Jan. 1791 ; was to have sailed in the *Deptford* 16 Apr. 1791, but did not proceed to India. Ensign H.M. 36th Ft. 8 Feb. 1792 ; Lieut. do. 11 Jan. 1795 ; Capt. do. 25 June 1803. His name is in *A.L.* for Jan. 1811, not Jan. 1813.

[1] *Note*: Pooley Molineaux Smith, son of James Smith, of Mayore, co. Westmeath, was admitted Lincoln's Inn 21 Aug. 1762.

Note: Pooley Molyneux, of Ballymulvey, co. Longford, *d.s.p.* 1772. (cf. Burke's *Landed Gentry*, 2nd edn., p. 1234, *s.n.* Shuldham, of Ballymulvey.)

SMITH, Ralph (1806-1845). Bt. Major, 28th N.I. *b*. Southwark 21 Oct. 1806. Cadet 1822. Arrived in India 20 Jan. 1824. Ensign 11 July 1823. Lieut. 13 May 1825. Capt. 8 Oct. 1839. Bt. Major 30 Apr. 1844. *d*. Barrackpore 10 Aug. 1845.

bapt. St. Saviour's, Southwark, 18 Nov. 1806. Son of Joseph Smith, of Southwark, hosier, later of Cheam, and Anne his wife. His sister *m*. Andrew Thomas Alexander Wilson, *q.v.*

Services: Posted to 28th N.I. May 1824 ; Intr. & Qmr. do. 29 July 1825 till 1836. Fur. s.c. 27 Feb. 1836 till 7 Feb. 1839. Actg. Adjt. Bhagulpur Hill Rangers 23 Apr. 1839. Attached to 1st Vol. Regt. 15 Feb. 1840 till 1 June 1841. First China War 1840-1 ; Capt. 1st Vol. Regt., and actg. Asst. in Comst. Dept. from 1 Feb. 1841 (Medal). A.D.C. to Sir Hugh Gough, C.-in-C., 22 Aug. 1843 till death. Gwalior campaign ; Maharajpur (*Lond. Gaz.* 8 Mar. 1844) ; Capt. 28th N.I., A.D.C. (Bronze star).

Refs.: *G.M.* 1845, ii. 664. Will dated Bhagulpur 6 May 1839 ; proved 29 Sept. 1845.

SMITH, Richard (*d.* 1803). Bdr. General. C.-in-C. Bengal. Col. 3 May 1764. Bdr. Gen. 2 Nov. 1768. Resigned Mar. 1770. *d.* in England 3 July 1803.

Of Chiltern Lodge, nr. Hungerford, Berks. High Sheriff of Berks. 1779. Brother of John Smith (1738/39-1777), *q.v. m.* Madras 25 Sept. 1756, Amelia, dau. of Capt. Charles Hopkins, a master-mariner, afterwards M.C.S.

Services: Commissioned from Purser's Mate as Ensign on Madras Est. 9 Dec. 1752; Lieut. 2 Nov. 1753; Capt. 2 June 1756. Comdg. at Arcot in Jan. 1758; afterwards comdg. at Chingleput; resigned and returned to England 1761. Apptd. by C.D., on recommendation of Lord Clive, Col. 2nd Bengal Eur. Regt. 9 May 1764; granted H.M. Commission as Col., in E. Indies only, 11 May 1764. Sailed for India with Clive in the *Kent* June 1764; arrived Madras 10 Apr. 1765. Col. 2nd Bengal Eur. Regt., and comdg. 2nd Bde. at Allahabad in 1765. C.-in-C. Bengal, as Bdr. Gen., 29 Jan. 1767 till resignation. Was a candidate for the governorship of Madras 1780; M.P. for Wendover 1780-4 [1]; M.P. for Wareham 1790-6. Prominent on the turf and a member of the Jockey Club.

Refs.: Holzman. Hickey. Love. *Narrative of a Gentleman long resident in India,* by G. F. Grand, *q.v. G.M.* 1803, ii. 696. Portrait in *Town and Country Mag.* No. xx.

[1] *Note:* He may have been of the family of Samuel Smith, of Ashfordby and London, great-uncle of 1st Lord Carrington, for Wendover was a Carrington borough.

SMITH, Robert (1787-1873). Colonel, C.B. Engineers. *bapt.* Nancy, Lorraine, 13 Sept. 1787.[1] Cadet 1803. Admitted 27 June 1805. Ensign 29 Apr. 1805. Lieut. 17 Sept. 1807. Capt. 6 May 1817. Major 28 Sept. 1827. Lt. Col. 25 June 1830. Retired 10 July 1832. Hon. Col. 28 Nov. 1854. *d.* Torquay 16 Sept. 1873.

Of Redcliff Tower, Paignton. 3rd son of James Smith, of Bideford, and Mary his wife. Brother of Edward James Smith, *q.v.*

Services: Transfd. from Inf. to Engrs. 27 June 1805. Suptg. works of gun-carriage agency 1807-8; do. construction of lighthouse at Kedgeree 1 Aug. 1808. Adjt. Engrs. 1809-16. Apptd. Field Engr. with Bengal Div. 15 Sept. 1810. Capture of Mauritius 1810-11; Field Engr. Suptg. Engr. at P.W.I. 11 Nov. 1814. Nepal War 1815; Asst. Field Engr. 2nd Div. (India medal). Returned to P.W.I. Fur. s.c. 24 July 1819 till 30 Oct. 1822. Garr. Engr. and Executive Ofr. at Delhi 16 Dec. 1822. Siege and capture of Bhurtpore (w. 26 Dec. 1825); Capt. S. & M. (*Lond. Gaz.* 10 June

1826) (clasp to India medal). Repaired Jumma Masjid at Delhi. Leave s.c. 8 mos. to Cape 6 Feb. 1830; fur. s.c. 26 Nov. 1830 till retirement. C.B. 26 Sept. 1831. Bt. Major from 19 Jan. 1826 for services at Bhurtpore. Author of a set of views of P.W.I., pub. 1820.

[1] *Note :* From the Bideford psh. register.

SMITH, Robert (1802-?). Ensign. 21st N.I. *b.* Aberdeen 16 Nov. 1802. Cadet 1821. Ensign Aug. 1822. Resigned in India 14 Feb. 1823.

bapt. St. Nicholas, Aberdeen. Son of Alexander Smith, of Aberdeen, merchant, and Ann Aiken his wife. Ed. Aberdeen Grammar School, 1810-14.

Services : Posted Ensign to 21st N.I. 1822. No record of active service.

SMITH, Robert Wood (1789-1835). Major, 6th L.C. *bapt.* Chelmsford 15 Apr. 1789. Cadet 1805. Arrived in India 1 Aug. 1807. Cornet 25 July 1807. Lieut. 15 Apr. 1816. Capt. 1 Jan. 1819. Major 1 Dec. 1829. *d.* Mandleshwar, Holkar State, 19 Nov. 1835, aged 47.

Son of Andrew Smith, linendraper. Related to (? nephew by marriage of) Sir George Hilaro Barlow, 1st Bart., G.G. (*D.N.B.*). *m.* Nagpur 10 Jan 1818, Miss Maria Josephine Monneruit. (She died Pondicherry 16 Jan. 1844, aged 43.)

Services : Barasat C.C. 1807-8. Posted Cornet to 6th N.C. 1808. Third Mahratta War 1817-18; Sitabaldi (s.w.—*Cal. Gaz.* 5 Mar. 1818); Nagpur; Chanda; Lieut. 6th N.C. Fur.;p.a. 7 Mar. 1823 till 24 Feb. 1826; leave s.c. 14 mos. to Cape 3 Oct. 1828; do. 14 Jan. 1833 till 10 Nov. 1834.

Refs. : The Hearseys, p. 323. *A.J.* N.S. xx. 47. Will dated Cawnpore 1 Oct. 1832; proved 9 Mar. 1836. M.I. Mhow old cemetery and Mhow church.

SMITH, Samuel (1783-1852). Lieut. General. Colonel 8th L.C. *bapt.* Calcutta 27 Nov. 1783. Cadet 1800. Arrived in India 22 Aug. 1801. Cornet 2 Jan. 1802. Lieut. 11 Mar. 1805. Capt. 23 Oct. 1818. Major 4 Feb. 1825. Lt. Col. 24 July 1828. Col. (22 Jan. 1834) 15 Nov. 1837. Maj. Gen. 3 Nov. 1841. Lt. Gen. 11 Nov. 1851. *d.* Lyncroft House, nr. Lichfield, 21 Oct. 1852.

Son of Joseph Barnard Smith, B.C.S., and Rose his wife. Brother of James Willis Smith, *q.v. m.* Partabgarh 26 Aug. 1811, Miss Mary

THE BENGAL ARMY, 1758-1834 135

Eliza Hyde. (She died 1 Jan. 1816.) His daus. m. Charles Garrett and William Binfield Wemyss, qq.v.
Services: Ensign d.d. 7th N.I. in 1802. Operations in Jumna Doab 1803; Sasni; Bijaigarh; Kachaura; Cornet 3rd N.C. Second Mahratta War 1803-6; Aligarh; battle of Delhi; Laswari; Rampura; battle and capture of Deig; pursuit of Holkar; Lieut. 3rd N.C. (India medal). (? Operations in Bundelkhand 1809; Rajaoli; Ajaigarh; Lieut. 3rd N.C.) Siege and capture of Hathras 1817; Bt. Capt. 3rd N.C. Third Mahratta War 1817-18; Jawad; Bt. Capt. 3rd N.C., in Centre Div. (? Operations in Jodhpur 1823; Lamba; Capt. 3rd L.C.) Siege and capture of Bhurtpore; Major 3rd L.C. (clasp to India medal). Posted Lt. Col. to 8th L.C. 4 Sept. 1828; to 9th L.C. 31 July 1829; to 3rd L.C. 26 Dec. 1833; to 8th L.C. 30 Sept. 1834, and comdd. till 12 Feb. 1839. Col. 8th L.C. 26 Feb. 1838 till death. Fur. p.a. 23 Mar. 1840 till death.
Refs.: Boase. *G.M.* 1852, ii. 658. M.I. Christ Church, Lichfield.

SMITH, Samuel (1805-1858). Captain, Invalid Est. 9th L.C. *bapt.* Seend, Melksham, Wilts., 8 Sept. 1805. Cadet 1827. Arrived in India 8 Apr. 1828. Cornet (13 Oct. 1827) 24 Oct. 1828. Lieut. 28 Apr. 1832. Capt. 24 Mar. 1843. Invalided 16 Oct. 1846. d. Mussoorie 29 Nov. 1858.

Of Warminster and Mussoorie. Son of Joseph Smith and Ann his wife. Ward of Mr. Tilby, of Devizes. Brother of Sidney Smith, and uncle of John Scott, of Warminster, seedsman and corn dealer.
Services: Posted Cornet to 9th L.C. 26 Jan. 1829. Leave s.c. 2 yrs. to Cape and Tasmania 20 Feb. 1834; fur. s.c. 6 Feb. 1836 till 19 Dec. 1838. Conquest of Sind 1843; Miani (w.) (*Lond. Gaz.* 11 Apr. 1843); Hyderabad; Capt. 9th L.C. (Medal). First Sikh War; occupation of Lahore 1846; Capt. 9th L.C. Fur. Feb. 1853 till 1854.
Refs.: Will dated Warminster, 7 Oct. 1853; admon. 25 July 1860. M.I. old cemetery, Mussoorie.

SMITH, Thomas (*d.* 1774). Captain, Infantry. Lieut. 20 July 1765. Capt. 10 Sept. 1767. *d.* Banjarra (? Bangar, Rohilkhand) 26 Sept. 1774.

Brother of William Smith. m. Calcutta 22 Dec. 1769, Elizabeth, widow of Norcross Dunstall, q.v.
Services: Apptd. Lieut. in England 1764; sailed for India in the *Tilbury* 6 Dec. 1764. First Rohilla War 1774; battle of St. George; Capt. comdg. 8th Bn. Sepoys.

Refs.: Williams, p. 140. Will dated 22 Apr. 1774; proved 18 May 1775.

SMITH, Thomas (*d.* 1783). Lieutenant, Infantry. Cadet 1778. Ensign 11 June 1778. Lieut. 15 Nov. 1780. *bur.* Calcutta 22 Oct. 1783.

Services: Apptd. Cadet 1 Dec. 1778; sailed for India in the *Walpole* 16 June 1779. Ensign 1/3rd Bengal Eur. Regt. in Oct. 1779. Received a nomination for B.C.S. in 1782 from John Smith, the Dir., afterwards Sir John Smith-Burges, Bart., but died before news of his appt. reached India.

SMITH, Thomas (1750/51-1788). Lieutenant, Infantry. *b.* Hants 1750/51. Cadet 1779. Ensign 7 July 1779. Lieut. 27 Feb. 1781. *d.* Jaunpur 13 Dec. 1788.

m. Eleanor, dau. of Robert Catts, Dy. Comy. of Ord. (*See also* Joseph Fletcher.) (She *re-m.* John Carige, *q.v.*)

Services: Apptd. Cadet 10 Nov. 1779; sailed for India in the *Ponsborne* 3 Apr. 1780, aged 29. Lieut. 4th Bn. Sepoys in July 1787; 6th Bn. in Dec. 1788.

SMITH, Thomas (1799-1827). Lieutenant, 67th N.I. *b.* Cupar, co. Fife, 20 July 1799. Cadet 1819. Ensign 20 May 1820. Lieut. 11 July 1823. *d.* Dinapore 2 Oct. 1827.

bapt. Cupar 27 July 1799. 3rd son of James Smith, of Cupar, merchant, and Jane Galloway his wife.

Services: Posted Ensign to 2/15th N.I. 1820; transfd. as Lieut. to newly-raised 34th N.I. July 1823; to 67th N.I. (late 1/34th) May 1824. First Burma War; Arakan 1825; Lieut. 67th N.I. Adjt. 67th N.I. 5 Aug. 1825 till death.

SMITH, Thomas (1808-?). Captain, Pension Est. 15th N.I. *b.* Shoreditch, Middlesex, 13 Apr. 1808. Cadet 1828. Arrived in India 15 Sept. 1829. Ensign 5 June 1829. Lieut. 29 Sept. 1835. Capt. 5 Oct. 1846. Pensioned 9 Aug. 1848. (In *A.L.* Oct. 1852, not Jan. 1853.)

Son of Robert Smith, of Margam, co. Glam., ironmaster. Ed. Mill Hill.

Services: Fur. s.c. 21 May 1830 till 16 July 1832. Posted to 49th N.I. 17 Jan. 1831; transfd. to 15th N.I. 2 Aug. 1832. Leave s.c. to Simla 26 Oct. 1833 till 25 Dec. 1836; fur. s.c. 16 Aug. 1837 till 29 June 1840. Apptd. extra A.D.C. to Maj.-Gen. G. B. Brooks, Bo. Est., comdg. in Upper Sind. First Afghan War; operations in Sind against Brahuis 1840; served with Irreg. Horse under Lt.-Col. T. Marshall, Bo. Est., in attack on Nasir Khan's camp at Kotra 1 Dec. (*Cal. Gaz.* 1 Apr. 1841).[1] Rejoined his Regt. Aug. 1841. Asst. to Resdt. in Nepal and comdg. his escort 26 Feb. 1842 till 3 Aug. 1844. Fur. s.c. 1847 till pensioned. Author of "Narrative of a Five Years' Residence in Nepaul (1841-45)," 2 vols, cr. 8vo, 1852.

[1] *Note:* He left Gen. Brooks on 28 Nov. with a detachment and marched 150 miles in 38 hours to join Col. Marshall, being frequently attacked by the enemy on the way. Gen. Brooks wrote of him, ' A braver young soldier and more active zealous officer I never met.'

SMITH, Thomas Paterson (1783-1852). Lieut. General. Colonel 17th N.I. *b.* 16 Apr. 1783. Cadet 1798. Arrived in India 20 Aug. 1799. Ensign 4 Nov. 1799. Lieut. 8 Feb. 1800. Capt. 10 Dec. 1811. Major 1 Jan. 1821. Lt. Col. 1 May 1824. Col. 15 Oct. 1832. Maj. Gen. 28 June 1838. Lt. Gen. 11 Nov. 1851. *d.* Paris 27 Sept. 1852, suddenly.[1]

bapt. St. Clement Danes, London, 27 May 1783. Son of Thomas Smith and Jane Meliora his wife. Brother of John David Smith, *q.v. m.* (?) Father of Walter Tipper Smith. (*See* Henry Tipper Smith.)

Services: Posted Ensign to 1st Bengal Eur. Regt. 15 Apr. 1801. Second Mahratta War; battle and capture of Deig; Lieut. Eur. Regt. (India medal). Transfd. to newly-raised 25th N.I. 1805. Capt. Lt. 25th N.I. 16 Aug. 1809. Nepal War 1814-15; Capt. 2/25th N.I., in 4th Div. Nepal War 1816; Chirriaghati; Makwanpur; Capt. comdg. 2/25th N.I., in 3rd Bde. Centre Column (clasp to India medal). Third Mahratta War 1817-18; Capt. 2/25th N.I. Major 2/25th N.I.; Comdt. newly-raised 1st (Fatehgarh) Inf. Levy 1819-22.[2] Transfd. as Lt. Col. to 49th N.I. (late 1/25th) May 1824. First Burma War; Arakan 1825 (*Lond. Gaz.* 1 Oct. 1825); Lt. Col. 49th N.I. (clasp to India medal). Removed from 49th N.I. 9 May 1825; posted to 2nd Eur. Regt. 9 Aug. 1825; to 8th N.I. 1828; to 18th N.I. 7 Sept. 1829. Col. 18th N.I. 2 Mar. 1833; Left Wing Eur. Regt. 21 Dec. 1833; 29th N.I. 1 July 1837; 17th N.I. 28 Nov. 1837 till death. (? Second Sikh War; with Army of Reserve at Jagraon; Col. 17th N.I.) Fur. 10 Feb. 1850 till death.

Refs.: Boase. *G.M.* 1852, ii. 659.

[1] *Note:* Both *G.M.* and *I.M.* give date of death as 27 Oct.

[2] *Note:* Became 63rd N.I. in 1824, and is now represented by 9th Gurkha Rifles.

SMITH, Thomas Sidney (*d.* 1777). Lieutenant, Infantry. Country Cadet 1767. Ensign 19 Aug. 1767. Lieut. 7 Oct. 1769. *d. unm.* Monghyr 4 June 1777 : shot in a duel by Surgeon James Ford.[1]

Son of Mrs. Sidney Williams Smith, of West Chester. Brother of Edward Smith and Eleanor Arrowsmith.

Services : Was Dy. Judge Advocate at Dinapore in Oct. 1771.

Refs. : Crawford, ii. 239. Will dated Monghyr 5 May 1777 ; proved 21 June 1777.

[1] *Note :* Ford was tried before the Supreme Court in Calcutta in Dec. 1777 and honourably acquitted.

SMITH, Walter. Fireworker. Artillery. (241) Country Cadet 1782. Fireworker 12 May 1783. Struck off 1791.

Services : Apptd. a Vol. of Art. by Col. Charles Morgan 13 Sept. 1782, and served with Bengal detachment during First Mahratta War. Fur. on h.p. 20 Oct. 1786 till struck off.

SMITH, William (1727/28-1767). Lieut. Colonel, Infantry. *b.* in Scotland 1727/28. Cornet 11 Feb. 1761. 2nd Lieut. (Cav.) 1 May 1761. Capt. (Inf.) 10 Oct. 1763. Major 9 Dec. 1765. Lt. Col. Sept. 1767. *d.* Nov. 1767.

Brother of Charles Smith. (? *m.* Isabella Anderson, and was father of David Smith and William Smith (1763/64-?), *qq.v.*)

Services : Apptd. in England 11 Feb. 1761, Cornet in the Troop of Light Horse being raised for Madras ; promoted 2nd Lieut. do. 1 May 1761 ; sailed in the *Chesterfield* May 1761, aged 33. Transfd. to Bengal Est. Raised at Burdwan in 1763 the 9th Bn. Sepoys (" *Chota Burdwan-ki-Paltan* "), which became 8th N.I. in 1824, and mutinied at Dinapore in July 1857. Battle of Buxar Oct. 1764 ; Capt. comdg. 8th (late 9th) Bn.

Refs. : Williams, p. 139. Nuncupative Will dated 1 Nov. 1767 ; proved 1767.

*SMITH, William (1739/40-?). Fireworker. Artillery. (41) *b.* London 1739/40. Fireworker 14 Mar. 1763.

Services : Apptd. in England 27 Jan. 1762, Lieut. F. on Bencoolen Est. ; sailed in the *Valentine* 24 June 1762, aged 22. Out of the Service before 1 Feb. 1767.

Note : Although he appears in *Stubbs's List,* it seems doubtful whether he ever belonged to the Bengal Art.

SMITH, William (*d.* 1783). Lieutenant, Infantry. Country Cadet 1778. Ensign 1778. Lieut. 2 Jan. 1781. *d.* 17 July 1783, on active service with the Bombay detachment.

THE BENGAL ARMY, 1758-1834 139

Son of Elizabeth Smith, of Middlesex. Brother of Miles Smith, of Bengal, George, Walter, and Elizabeth Ann Claydon.
Services: Apptd. Cadet 4 June 1778. First Mahratta War; capture of fort Arnalla Jan. 1781; forcing of Bhor Ghaut Feb. 1781; Lieut. with Col. Goddard's detachment to Bombay.
Refs.: Will dated 3 Jan. 1780; codicils 5 Jan. 1781, 10 Apr. 1783; admon. 14 Oct. 1785.

SMITH, William (1763/64-?). Lieutenant. Infantry. Subsequently B.C.S. *b.* 1763/64. Cadet 1780. Ensign 1780. Lieut. 9 July 1781. Resigned 1781.
A native of Scotland. (*Probably* brother of David Smith (1764/65-1794), *q.v.*
Services: Sailed for India in the *Hinchinbrooke* 13 Mar. 1781, aged 17; captured by the enemy on the voyage out; arrived in India June 1782. Writer, B.C.S., 7 Aug. 1783; Asst. in Mily. Paymr.'s office 1785; Dy. Paymr. at Fatehgarh May 1786; Junior Merchant 1795; Senior do. 1800. No trace after 1800.

SMITH, William (1805-1856). Captain, Invalid Est. 19th N.I. *bapt.* 16 Mar. 1805. Cadet 1826. Arrived in India 17 June 1827. Ensign 5 Jan. 1827. Lieut. 6 Jan. 1832. Capt. 8 Aug. 1838. Invalided 1 Mar. 1850. *d.* Meerut 4 Aug. 1856.
Son of Andrew Smith, of Skene.[1] Cousin-german of William Abraham Skene, *q.v.*
Services: Posted to 19th N.I. 19 June 1827; actg. Adjt. do. 7 Nov. 1829; permanent do. 14 Apr. 1830 till 28 Mar. 1838. Rising in Cuttack 1836; Lieut. 19th N.I. Leave s.c. to Cape 3 Feb. 1838 till 25 Feb. 1839. Suspended by G.C.M. from rank and pay 20 Aug. 1839 till 22 Feb. 1840.
Refs.: *Skene of Skene*, by W. F. Skene, p. 88. *I.M.* 6 Oct. 1856, p. 578.

[1] *Note:* He was eldest son of William Smith by Margaret Skene his wife, natural dau. of John Skene, VIII of Dyce. He became Skene of Lethentie.

SMITH, William Abraham. (*See* **SKENE, William Abraham.**)

*****SMITH, ——.** Volunteer. Volunteer 22 Feb. 1758.
Services: N.F.P. *Possibly* identical with William Smith (1727/28-1767), *q.v.*
Refs.: *Orme MSS.*—India, xiii. 3639.

SMOULT, James Temple (1796-1830). Lieutenant. Artillery. (452) *b.* Newcastle-on-Tyne 9 May 1796. Cadet 1813. Fireworker 10 June 1816. Lieut. 1 Sept. 1818. Resigned 1 Feb. 1820. d. Torrington Sq., London, 6 Apr. 1830.

Son of William Smoult, atty. in Calcutta, sealer and clerk to Mr. Justice Chambers, and Charlotte his wife, dau. of William Hardcastle, of Masham, Yorks. His sister m. William Paterson (1791-1819), q.v. Addiscombe Cadet 1812-14.

Services : Posted to 2nd Troop H.A. 1820. No record of active service. After resigning the Service he joined his brother, William Hunter Smoult, atty. in the Supreme Court of Calcutta, as an assistant. He returned to England 1826.

Refs. : G.M. 1830, i. 475.

SMYTH, Christopher (d. 1799). Captain, 5th N.I. Country Cadet 1780. Admitted 28 Apr. 1780. Ensign 23 Feb. 1781. Lieut. 18 Oct. 1781. Bt. Capt. 7 Jan. 1796. Capt. 1799. d. Fatehgarh 4 Sept. 1799.

Brother of Eleanor, wife of —— Sheridan, of Dublin.

Services : Apptd. a Gent. Vol. in the Coy. of Art. 3 Apr. 1780. First Mahratta War 1781-4. Lieut. 21st Bn. Sepoys in July 1787 ; Bt. Capt. 2/13th N.I. in Aug. 1798 ; transfd. to 5th N.I.

Refs. : Will dated Fatehgarh 4 Sept. 1799 ; proved 7 Nov. 1799.

SMYTH, John Hall (1814-1894). Major General, C.B. Artillery. (653) b. Swettenham, co. Chester, 5 Oct. 1814. Cadet 1831. Arrived in India 24 Apr. 1832. 2nd Lieut. (9 June 1831) 24 Apr. 1832. Lieut. 11 Apr. 1840. Capt. 5 May 1849. Bt. Major 19 Jan. 1858. Lt. Col. 12 Mar. 1860. Col. 24 Jan. 1865. Retired 1 Aug. 1872. Hon. Maj. Gen. 1 Aug. 1872. d. Frimhurst, Frimley, 31 Mar. 1894.

4th son of Edward Smyth, manager of the Leeds branch of Bank of England, and of the Fence, Macclesfield, formerly 25th Light Dgns., and Sarah his wife. Related to Rev. Thomas Scott Smyth, of St. Anstell, Cornwall, who m. a sister of Sir Charles Theophilus Metcalfe, G.C.B., G.G. Brother of William Mathew Smyth, q.v. m. 1st, Rackheath, Norfolk, 4 Jan. 1849, Emma, only dau. of Charles Struth, and niece of Sir Edward Strachey, Bart. m. 2nd, Nina. (She died 12 Jan. 1891, aged 67.) Ed. Leeds Grammar School July 1827-June 1828. Addiscombe Cadet 1829-31.

Services : A.D.C. to V.P. and Dy. Govr. of Ft. Wm. 6 Feb. 1834 ; offg. A.D.C. to Govr. of Agra 12 Nov. 1834 ; A.D.C. to G.G. 21 Mar. 1835. d.d. 1st Troop 2nd Bde. H.A. 16 Nov. 1835. Apptd. to Sindhia's Contingent 12 Jan. 1836. Operations in Bundelkhand 1837-8 and 1839-43 ; Chirgaon 21 Apr. 1841 ; comdg. Art. of

Sindhia's Reformed Contingent. Gwalior campaign; Paniar; Lieut. comdg. Field Batty., Sipri Contingent (Bronze star). Capt. Comdt. 1st Bn. Gwalior Contingent 13 Jan. 1844. Fur. 4 May 1845 till 1849. Capt. 3rd Bn. Foot Art.; transfd. to 5th Troop 1st Bde. H.A. 1853. Mutiny campaign; operations nr. Cawnpore; Rohilkhand 1859; minor operations; Bt. Lt. Col. 5th Troop 1st Bde. (Medal). Fur. 1 yr. 11 June 1859. Lt. Col. 2nd Horse Bde. 1862; C. Bde. H.A. 1867 till retirement. C.B. 28 Feb. 1861.

Refs.: Walford (1900 edn.). *G.M.* 1849, i. 311. *The Times,* 2 and 3 Apr. 1894.

Note: He was father of Dame Ethel Smyth (1858-1944), D.B.E., D.Mus., D.Litt., composer and writer.

SMYTH, Ralph (1812-1886). Lieut. Colonel. Artillery. (619) *b.* 27 Aug. 1812. Cadet 1828. 2nd Lieut. 12 Dec. 1828. Lieut. 5 Apr. 1837. Capt. 19 Aug. 1846. Bt. Major 20 June 1854. Retired 20 May 1858. Hon. Lt. Col. 20 May 1858. *d.* Ilfracombe, Devon, 7 Feb. 1886.

Of St. George's Lodge, Southampton. *bapt.* Bradford 11 Sept. 1812. 3rd son of Ralph Smyth, Capt. 7th D.G., Major Cumberland Mil., and Amelia St. George his wife, 2nd dau. of Rev. Thomas Adderley Browne and niece of Sir George Sackville Browne, *q.v.* Cousin-german of Adderley Thomas Browne, *q.v.* His sister *m.* a brother of John Turton, *q.v. m.* 1st, Dinapore 29 Apr. 1834, Ann, 4th dau. of James Gibbon, indigo planter. (*See also* William Nisbett.) (She died Ootacamund 15 Oct. 1855, aged 41.) *m.* 2nd, Harriett, dau. of Campbell Cameron. Addiscombe Cadet 1826-8.

Services: Apptd. to Revenue Survey in Cuttack 20 Nov. 1837. Fur. p.a. 13 May 1843 till 25 Aug. 1845. Employed on the Revenue Survey of Bengal 11 June 1847 till 1857. Fur. s.c. Sept. 1857 till retirement. No record of active service.

Refs.: Burke's *Landed Gentry of Ireland,* p. 648, *s.n.* Smyth, of Gaybrook, co. Westmeath. *The Times,* 10 Feb. 1886.

SMYTH, William Mathew (1810-1851). Major, Engineers. *b.* Poynton, co. Chester, 19 Jan. 1810. Cadet 1826. Arrived in India 25 Sept. 1827. 2nd Lieut. 16 Dec. 1825. Lieut. 28 Sept. 1827. Capt. 20 May 1839. Major 1 May 1849. *d.* Danson, Kent, 7 Oct. 1851.

bapt. Poynton 30 Apr. 1810. Son of Edward Smyth, of Swettenham, banker at Macclesfield, and Sarah his wife. Brother of John Hall Smyth, *q.v.* Addiscombe Cadet 27 Aug. 1824 till 16 Dec. 1825; Chatham 7 Mar. till 19 Dec. 1826.

Services : Posted to S. & M. at Aligarh 15 Dec. 1827. A.D.C. to V.P. and Dy. Govr. of Ft. Wm. 11 Nov. 1830. Executive Engr. 17th (Burdwan) Div., P.W.D., 17 Jan. 1835. A.D.C. and Mily. Sec. to Sir Charles T. Metcalfe, offg. G.G., 20 Mar. 1835 till 4 Mar. 1836. Fur. p.a. 27 Jan. 1837 till 1 Apr. 1840. Executive Engr. Karnal Div. 24 Feb. 1840 ; do. 2nd (Berhampore) Div. 9 Feb. 1843 ; Supt. Nadia Rivers 17 Sept. 1845 till 1849. Fur. 10 Sept. 1849 till death. No record of active service.

Refs. : List of Mily. Secs. to G.G. I.M. 18 Oct. 1851, p. 627. *G.M.* 1851, ii. 559. Will undated ; proved 14 May 1852.

CARMICHAEL-SMYTH, George Monro (1803-1890). Major General. 5th Eur. L.C. *b.* London 1 Sept. 1803. Cadet 1819. Admitted 21 Aug. 1820. Cornet 14 Aug. 1820. Lieut. 3 Oct. 1821. Capt. 24 July 1828. Major 21 Oct. 1852. Lt. Col. 3 May 1856. Bt. Col. 22 Aug. 1855. Retired 31 Dec. 1861. Hon. Maj. Gen. 31 Dec. 1861. *d.* 12 Royal Cresc., London, 29 Apr. 1890.

bapt. St. George's, Bloomsbury, 22 Mar. 1804. 8th and youngest son of James Carmichael Smyth, M.D., of Aithernie (*D.N.B.*), who assumed the additional name of Smyth, and Mary his wife, dau. of Thomas Holyland, of Bromley. Brother of Henry William Carmichael-Smyth and of the wife of William Forrest, *qq.v. m.* 1st, Mussoorie 4 June 1838, Miss Jane Ross. *m.* 2nd, 7 Oct. 1879, Celia Black, only child of James Martin Hamilton, of Halifax, N.S. (She died 3 Dec. 1891.)

Services : Posted Cornet to 3rd L.C. ; Intr. & Qmr. do. 13 Oct. 1823 till 23 Aug. 1825 ; Bde. Major Rajputana F.F. 12 July 1825. Siege and capture of Bhurtpore ; Lieut. 3rd L.C. (India medal). d.d. 9th L.C. 8 Feb. 1826. Fur. s.c. 8 Dec. 1827 till 1 Dec. 1831 ; leave s.c. 18 mos. to Cape 30 Mar. 1832. First Afghan War 1838-9 ; Ghazni ; Capt. 3rd L.C. (Medal). First Sikh War ; Badhowal ; Aliwal ; Sobraon ; Bt. Major 3rd L.C. (Medal with clasp). Was comdg. 3rd L.C. when it mutinied at Meerut 10 May 1857. Posted to newly-raised 1st Eur. Bengal L.C. 1 May 1858 ; transfd. to 5th do. 28 Dec. 1859. Author of "A History of the Reigning Family of Lahore, . . ." (Calcutta, 1847.)

Refs. : Burke's *Landed Gentry*, 12th edn., p. 328, *s.n.* Carmichael, of Balmedie. *Scots Peerage*, (ed. Sir J. Balfour Paul), iv. 571, *s.n.* Carmichael, E. of Hyndford. *The Times*, 1 May 1890.

CARMICHAEL-SMYTH, Henry William (1779-1861). Major. Engineers. *b.* London 30 July 1779. Cadet 1793. Arrived in

India 14 Feb. 1797. Ensign 15 Sept. 1794. Lieut. 21 Feb. 1801. Capt. 10 May 1807. Major 19 July 1821. Retired 5 July 1822. *d.* Alloway Pl., Ayr, 9 Sept. 1861.

bapt. St. George's, Bloomsbury, 19 Aug. 1779. 2nd son of James Carmichael Smyth, M.D., and Mary his wife. Brother of Charles Montauban Carmichael, *q.v. m.* Cawnpore 13 Mar. 1817, Anne, 2nd dau. of John Harman Becher, B.C.S., and widow of Richmond Makepeace Thackeray, B.C.S. (She died 31 Dec. 1864.) Stepfather of William Makepeace Thackeray, the author (*D.N.B.*). Ed. Charterhouse ; admitted Sept. 1790.

Services : Second Mahratta War 1803-5 ; Aligarh ; Delhi ; Laswari ; Rampura ; battle and capture of Deig ; Bhurtpore (India medal). Capture of Gohad 1806. Fur. s.c. 10 Oct. 1807 till 15 Dec. 1810. Garr. Engr. at Agra 12 June 1809 till 1819. Java 1811 ; Weltervreden ; Cornelis (Medal). Reduction of Kalinjar 1812 ; Field Engr. (*Cal. Gaz.* Mar. 1812). Nepal War 1814-15 ; with 2nd Div. (clasp to India medal). Capture of Hathras 1817. Third Mahratta War 1817-18 ; Field Engr., Centre Div. of Grand Army. Fur. s.c. 15 Feb. 1820 till retirement. Apptd. in 1822 *pro. tem.* Resdt. Supt. at Addiscombe, and held this post till 6 Apr. 1824.

Refs. : Burke's *Landed Gentry*, 12th edn., p. 328, *s.n.* Carmichael, of Balmedie. *Scots Peerage*, iv. 569. *Boase. E.I.M.C.* ii 337-40. *Thackeray. G.M.* 1861, ii. 457. *The Times*, 14 Sept. 1861. M.I. Holy Trinity church, Ayr.

SNEADE (SNEYD or SNEED), Henry (*d.* 1769). Lieutenant, Infantry. Cadet 1765. Ensign 12 Nov. 1765. Lieut. 17 Jan. 1767. *d.* Sept. 1769.

Services : Ensign 2nd Bengal Eur. Regt. in 1766 ; resigned during the " Batta mutiny " ; readmitted later.

SNEIDER, Thomas Peter (1783-1804). Lieutenant, 2nd N.I. *b.* London 16 Jan. 1783. Cadet 1800. Arrived in India 18 July 1802. Ensign 7 Sept. 1801 (? 6 July 1802). Lieut. 15 Feb. 1804. *d.* Sikandra 24 Aug. 1804 : kld. in action during Monson's retreat.

bapt. St. Pancras 9 May 1788. Son of Thomas Peter Sneider and Abigail his wife.

Services : Barasat C.C. till Apr. 1803. Posted Ensign to 2/2nd N.I. Second Mahratta War 1803-4 ; battle of Delhi ; Hinglaisgarh ; Monson's retreat (kld.) ; Lieut. 2/2nd N.I.

Refs. : E.I.M.C. ii. 559.

LIST OF THE OFFICERS OF

SNEYD, Anthony (1789-1807). Lieutenant, 9th N.I. *bapt.* Castleknock, co. Dublin, 14 Feb. 1789. Cadet 1804. Arrived in India 6 Apr. 1806. Ensign 16 Apr. 1806. Lieut. 3 June 1807. *d.* 18 Nov. 1807 : kld. in action at the assault of Komona.

Eldest son of Henry Sneyd, of Elm Green, Major R. Irish Art., and Eliza Malone his wife. Ed. Rugby; admitted 1797.

Services : Operations against Dhundia Khan 1807 ; Komona (kld.) ; Lieut. 1/9th N.I.

Refs. : Ormerod's *Cheshire*, iii. 493. *Rugby School Register. A.A.R.* x. 21.

SNEYD, Edward Carncross [1] (1790-1826). Captain, 6th N.I. *b.* Belleek, co. Fermanagh (*sic*), 1 Apr. 1790. Cadet 1805. Arrived in India 13 Dec. 1806. Ensign 17 Dec. 1806. Lieut. 2 Oct. 1810. Capt. 1 May 1824. *d.* Akyab, Burma, 24 Feb. 1826 : drowned.

3rd son of Rev. Wetenhall Sneyd (a cadet of the family of Sneyd, of Ashcombe, Staffs.), vicar of Newchurch and Ryde, I.W., and Margaret his 1st wife, 2nd dau. of Patrick Cullen, of Skreeny. Brother of Nathaniel Sneyd, *q.v.*, and of Harriet, wife of Major Turner Macan, of Cariff, whose dau. *m.* Mark, 5th Earl of Antrim. *m.* Agra 3 June 1820, Elizabeth, sister of George Halhed, *q.v.* (She died London 5 June 1878.)

Services : Barasat C.C. Posted Ensign to 3rd N.I. 1807. Adjt. 2/3rd N.I. 1812-13 ; Intr. & Qmr. do. 1814 till 26 Mar. 1816. Nepal War 1814-15 ; Lieut. 2/3rd N.I., in 1st Div. Offg. in Comst. Dept. 1816 ; D.A.Q.M.G. 2 cl. 1 Jan. 1817 ; actg. S.A.C.G. 17 Sept. 1817 ; permanent do. 1818 ; D.A.C.G. 1824 till death. Transfd. to 6th N.I. (late 1/3rd) May 1824.

Refs. : Family information. Burke's *Landed Gentry*, 2nd edn., p. 294, *s.n.* Cullen, of Glenade, co. Leitrim ; 7th edn., p. 1701, *s.n.* Sneyd, of Basford Hall, Staffs. Will dated 25 Feb. 1824 ; proved 31 May 1826.

[1] *Note :* There is some doubt as to whether his 2nd name was Carncross or Cairncross.

*SNEYD, Nathaniel [1] (*d.* 1821). Lieutenant (8th Light Dgns.), d.d. G.G.B.G. *d.* Ballygunge, Calcutta, 26 May 1821, of fever.

4th son of Rev. Wetenhall Sneyd and Margaret his 1st wife. Brother of Ralph Henry Sneyd, *q.v.*

Services : Cornet H.M. 8th Light Dgns. 17 Feb. 1809 ; Lieut. do. 17 May 1812. Second in comd. Sneyd's Frontier Horse Feb. 1818 till Aug. 1819. To d.d. with G.G.B.G. 16 Mar. 1821.

THE BENGAL ARMY, 1758-1834

Refs.: Burke's *Landed Gentry*, 7th edn., p. 1701, *s.n.* Sneyd, of Basford Hall, Staffs. *V.B.G.*
[1] *Note:* As he never actually held a Commission in H.E.I.C.S. he should, perhaps, not be included in this List.

SNEYD, Ralph Henry (1784-1840). Major. 9th L.C. *b.* Dec. 1784. Cadet 1800. Arrived in India 19 Aug. 1801. Cornet 5 Jan. 1802. Lieut. 11 Mar. 1805. Capt. 1 Jan. 1819. Major 2 Oct. 1828. Retired 9 Sept. 1829. *d.* at his residence, Mattingley Lodge, Hants, 16 Dec. 1840.

bapt. Bray, co. Wicklow, 11 Dec. 1784. Eldest son of Rev. Wetenhall Sneyd and Margaret his 1st wife. Brother of Edward Carncross Sneyd, *q.v. m.* St. George's, London, 29 May 1817, Jane Rabina, youngest dau. of William Dunbar. (She died London 15 Dec. 1878, aged 87.) His dau. *m.* Sir George Glynn Petre, K.C.M.G. (*D.N.B.*).

Services: Ensign d.d. 11th N.I. in 1802. Operations in Jumna Doab 1803; Sasni; Bijaigarh; Kachaura; Cornet 1st N.C. Second Mahratta War 1803; Laswari; Cornet 1st N.C. Qmr. 1st N.C. 16 Aug. 1803 till 1811, and 1812 till 12 Feb. 1813. Operations in Bundelkhand 1810-11; Bichaund; Lieut. 1st N.C. Fur. 31 July 1814 till 1817. Raised in Feb. 1818, and comdd. till its disbandment Sept. 1819, a body of Frontier Horse known as "Sneyd's Frontier Horse," or 4th Rohilla Cav. Comdt. Agra Najib Bn. 1819-20; do. G.G.B.G. 14 Oct. 1820 till 3 Mar. 1827. Transfd. to newly-raised 1st Extra Cav. (became 9th L.C.) 17 June 1825. First Burma War 1824-6; operations in Burma; Donabyu; Prome; Capt. comdg. G.G.B.G., with Bdr.-Gen. Sir A. Campbell's force. Fur. s.c. 3 Mar. 1827 till retirement.

Refs.: Family information. Burke's *Landed Gentry*, 7th edn., p. 1702, *s.n.* Sneyd, of Basford Hall, Staffs. *V.B.G.* (portrait). *N. & Q.* 12S. xii. 507; 13S. i. 355. *G.M.* 1841, i. 107.

SNEYD, William (1764/65-1824). Major. 14th N.I. *b.* London 1764/65. Cadet 1780. Admitted 12 Nov. 1782. Ensign 1780. Lieut. 25 June 1781. Capt. 1 Nov. 1798. Major 21 Sept. 1804. Retired 23 Feb. 1807. *d.* London 23 Aug. 1824.

Services: Apptd. Cadet 9 Feb. 1780; sailed for India in the *Worcester* 6 Feb. 1782, aged 17. Lieut. 19th Bn. Sepoys in July 1787. Fur. 22 Feb. 1794 till 1 Mar. 1797. Second Mahratta War; Capt. 14th N.I.

SNODGRASS, George (1785-1825). Captain, 23rd N.I. *b.* Abbey of Paisley 12 Mar. 1785. Cadet 1805. Arrived in India

11 July 1806. Ensign 20 July 1806. Lieut. 20 July 1808. Capt. 1 May 1824. d. Benares 11 Jan. 1825.

bapt. 24 Mar. 1785. Son of Hew Snodgrass, writer in Paisley, and Henrietta Somerville his wife. Brother of Francis, of Edinburgh, W.S.; Campbell, of Johnstone, nr. Paisley; Harriot, of Helensburgh, nr. Greenock; and Ann, wife of Duncan Kennedy, accomptant in Glasgow.

Services: Barasat C.C. Posted Ensign to 4th N.I. 1807. Nepal War 1816; Lieut. 2/4th N.I., in 4th Bde. Centre Column. Fur. 1817-19. Transfd. to 1/4th N.I.; as Capt. to 23rd N.I. (late 2/4th) May 1824. Dy. Paymr. at Benares 1824 till death.

Refs.: *N. & Q.* 108 x. 10. Will dated Calcutta 31 Aug. 1822; proved 18 Feb. 1825. M.I. at Benares.

SNOOK, John Violett (1806-1853). Bt. Major, 23rd N.I. *bapt.* ptely. Seaton, Devon, 29 Mar. 1806. Cadet 1824. Arrived in India 13 Sept. 1825. Ensign 11 Apr. 1825. Lieut. 29 Apr. 1826. Capt. 24 Jan. 1845. Bt. Major 11 Nov. 1851. *d.* Hapur, U.P., 10 Oct. 1853.

Son of John Snook, of Creech, Somerset, farmer, and Sarah his wife, dau. of John Violett.

Services: Posted to 23rd N.I. 1825, and served throughout with that Regt. Demonstration against Jodhpur 1834; Lieut. 23rd N.I. Adjt. 23rd N.I. 31 Oct. 1840 till 12 June 1844. Fur. s.c. 24 June 1851 till 4 Oct. 1852.

Refs.: Intestate; admon. 13 Feb. 1855.

Note: " He is a little man, about 5 ft. high, and is supposed to have called out three people for calling him Snooks instead of Snook." (*Up the Country*, by Hon. Emily Eden, 3rd edn. (1866), ii. 200.)

SOADY, Thomas Eales (1788-1860). Major. 3rd N.I. *bapt.* ptely. Talland, Cornwall, 1 Nov. 1788. Cadet 1809. Arrived in India 2 Aug. 1810. Ensign 27 Nov. 1811. Lieut. 16 Dec. 1814. Capt. 13 May 1825. Retired 1 Jan. 1837. Hon. Major 28 Nov. 1854. *d.* Edrington House, co. Berwick, 31 Mar. 1860, aged 72.

bapt. Liskeard, Cornwall, 25 Feb. 1789. Only son of Thomas Soady and Eliza his wife, sister of John Eales, *q.v. m.* (before 1842) ?

Services: Exempted by his age from going to Barasat C.C.; d.d. Bengal Eur. Regt. 6 Aug. 1810; do. 25th N.I. 1811; posted to 1/6th N.I. 1812. Convicted of manslaughter at the Supreme

Court of Calcutta 22 June 1812, and sentenced to pay a fine of 200 rupees and to be imprisoned in the common gaol of Calcutta for the space of one year. Served with 6th Vol. Bn. in Java 1813-16. Third Mahratta War; Lieut. 1/6th N.I., in Reserve Div. Offg. Intr. & Qmr. 1/6th N.I. 7 Oct. 1822 till 24 Mar. 1824; transfd. to 3rd N.I. (late 1/6th) May 1824; Adjt. do. 22 June 1824 till 14 July 1825. Shekhawat expedn. 1834; Capt. 3rd N.I.
Refs.: The Pedigree Register, i. (Dec. 1909), 317. Cal. Gaz. 25 June 1812. *I.M.* 5 Apr. 1860, p. 261. The Times, 4 Apr. 1860.

SOMERS,[1] **Henry** (*d.* 1763). Captain, Bengal Eur. Regt. Cadet (?) Ensign 8 June 1757. Lieut. 1 Aug. 1758. Capt. 1761. *d.* 5th, 6th or 11th Oct. 1763 : massacred at or near Patna by order of Nawab Mir Muhammad Kasim.[2]

Services: A sea-faring man; in the Mil. during siege of Calcutta 1756; Mate of a ship, and fled to Fulta; Volunteer in list of 28 Feb. 1757. Expedn. to the N. Circars 1758-9; storm of Masulipatam 8 Apr. 1759 (w.); Lieut. Bengal Eur. Regt. Assault of Patna city 25 June 1763.
Refs.: Broome, pp. 53, 73. *Innes*, p. 169. *Hill. Hill's Calcutta.*

[1] *Note:* The name appears also as Summers and Sommers.
[2] *Note:* "... On the nights of the 5th or 6th and 11th of October 1763, brutally massacred near this spot by the troops of Mir Kasim, Nawab Subahdar of Bengal, under command of Walter Reinhardt *alias* Samru, a base renegade." (M.I. in Patna City.)

SOMERVILLE, James (1788-1831). Captain, 16th N.I. *b.* Haddington 14 Nov. 1788. Cadet 1806. Arrived in India 3 Oct. 1807. Ensign 12 Oct. 1807. Lieut. 5 Mar. 1813. Capt. 1 May 1824. *d.* Kumarkhali, Bengal, 19 Dec. 1831.

bapt. 30 Nov. 1788. Son of Robert Somerville, surgeon, and Margaret Cunningham his wife. *m.* 4 Dec. 1808, Miss N. Blake. (She died Kumarkhali 23 Apr. 1828.)
Services: Lieut. Berwick Mil. Barasat C.C. 8 mos. Posted Ensign to 10th N.I. 1808. With 3rd Gren. Bn. 1815-16. Third Mahratta War 1817-18; Lieut. 1/10th N.I. Actg. Bde. Major 1st Inf. Bde., Nagpur Subsdy. Force, 1 June 1818. Actg. District Bk. Mr. Benares Div. 27 Apr. 1820. Executive Ofr., P.W.D., at Kumarkhali 14 June 1822 till death. Suptg. erection of bldgs. and steam apparatus at Kumarkhali. Transfd. to 16th N.I. (late 1/10th) May 1824.
Refs.: Will dated 7 Dec. 1831; proved 25 Jan. 1832.

SOMERVILLE, John (*d.* 1784). Captain, Infantry. Cadet 1771. Ensign 12 Feb. 1773. Lieut. 9 Mar. 1778. Capt. 5 Oct. 1781. *d.* Cawnpore 24 Nov. 1784.
Services: Capt. 3rd Bengal Eur. Regt. in 1782.

SOMERVILLE, John Townsend (1799-1861). Major. 51st N.I. *bapt.* Castlehaven, co. Cork, 19 Aug. 1799. Cadet 1815. Admitted 12 July 1816. Ensign 7 May 1816. Lieut. 1 Aug. 1818. Capt. 3 Nov. 1831. Retired 1 May 1843. Hon. Major 28 Nov. 1854. *d.* at his residence, Point House, Castle Townsend, 19 Aug. 1861.

2nd son of Thomas Townsend Somerville, of Drishane and Castlehaven, co. Cork, J.P., and Elizabeth Becher his wife, dau. of John Townsend, M.P., of Shepperton. Brother of Richard Somerville, cousin-german of J. B. D. Gahan, and 1st cousin once removed of W. N. Cameron, *qq.v.* *m.* 1st, Cawnpore 25 Mar. 1825, Miss Henrietta Kingston. (*See also* Samuel Stapleton.) (She died Meerut 9 June 1832.) *m.* 2nd, 19 May 1836, Frances Margaret, dau. of Rev. Arthur Herbert, rector of Myross Wood, co. Cork. Addiscombe Cadet 1814-15.

Services: Ensign d.d. 2/22nd N.I. 1817-18; posted to 1/26th N.I. 1819; transfd. to 51st N.I. (late 1/26th) May 1824; Intr. & Qmr. do. 26 June 1824 till 13 Apr. 1831; d.d. 52nd N.I. 4 Apr. till 1 Oct. 1832. Fur. p.a. 6 Feb. 1834 till 9 Nov. 1836. Posted to Vol. Regt. for China 15 Feb. 1840. First China War 1840-2; Capt. 51st N.I., 1st Vol. Regt. (Medal). Actg. Comdt. 2nd Inf. Levy 29 Sept. 1842.

Refs.: Burke's *Landed Gentry of Ireland*, p. 653, *s.n.* Somerville, of Drishane, co. Cork. *The Times*, 23 Aug. 1861.

SOMERVILLE, Richard (1800-1823). Lieutenant, 26th N.I. *b.* Castlehaven, co. Cork, 10 Sept. 1800. Cadet 1819. Ensign 10 July 1820. Lieut. 11 July 1823. *d.* Dinapore 15 Dec. 1823.

3rd son of Thomas Townsend Somerville and Elizabeth his wife. Brother of John Townsend Somerville, *q.v.*
Services: Posted Ensign to 2/21st N.I.; transfd. as Lieut. to 26th N.I. July 1823. No record of active service.
Refs.: Burke's *Landed Gentry of Ireland*, p. 653, *s.n.* Somerville, of Drishane, co. Cork.

SOTHEBY, Frederick Samuel (1792-1870). Lieut. Colonel, C.B. Artillery. (424) *b.* London 3 July 1792. Cadet 1809. Admitted 24 Nov. 1810. Fireworker 10 Nov. 1810. Lieut.

THE BENGAL ARMY, 1758-1834   149

25 Sept. 1817. Capt. 14 Jan. 1826. Major 23 Nov. 1841. Retired 1 Mar. 1844. Hon. Lt. Col. 28 Nov. 1854. *d.* at his residence, 47 Park St., Grosvenor Sq., London, 21 Oct. 1870.

bapt. St. George's, Hanover Sq., 9 Aug. 1792. 5th son of William Sotheby, of Sewardstone (*D.N.B.*), and Mary his wife, dau. of Ambrose Isted, of Ecton, Northants. Woolwich Cadet; nominated 13 Aug. 1806.

Services: Apptd. to comd. guns attached to Nizam's Bde. of regular inf. 17 May 1816, and served with Hyderabad Contingent till 1838. Third Mahratta War 1817-19; battle of Mahidpur 21 Dec. 1817 (*Lond. Gaz.* 9 June 1818); siege of Nowah 8-31 Jan. 1819; Lieut. 1st Coy. 3rd Bn. Art., comdg. Golandaz of Russell's Bde., Nizam's Contingent (India medal). Actg. Comy. of Stores 10 Jan. 1818. Placed tempy. at disposal of C.-in-C. 24 Sept. 1824. Siege and capture of Bhurtpore (clasp to India medal). Comdd. 1st Coy. Nizam's Art. Principal Comy. Ord. Bdr. 1 cl. comdg. Hingoli Div. of Nizam's army 21 Aug. 1837. Fur. p.a. 5 Jan. 1838 till 6 Jan. 1841. First Afghan War 1841-2; action of 12 Jan. 1842 (*Lond. Gaz.* 24 Nov. 1842); Major 2nd Bn., comdg. Art. of Nott's force (Medal). To comd. Art. at Ferozepore 30 Dec. 1842; do. Art. of Ludhiana Div. 15 Apr. 1843. C.B. 24 Dec. 1842.

Refs.: Burke's *Landed Gentry*, 12th edn., p. 1747, *s.n.* Sotheby, of Sewardstone, Northants. *Burton*, pp. 30, 59, 60. *Calcutta Review*, xi. 161, 171. *The Times*, 24 Oct. 1870.

SOUTER, William (1801-1835). Captain, Pension Est. 66th N.I. *b.* 11 Sept. 1801. Cadet 1821. Arrived in India 13 Dec. 1822. Ensign 2 Jan. 1823. Lieut. 13 May 1825. Capt. 8 May 1832. Pensioned 23 July 1832. *d.* Calcutta 16 Oct. 1835.

bapt. Walton-on-Thames 11 Aug. 1811. Son of Thomas Souter, of Ashbourne, co. Derby, Major h.p. 5th Ft., and Sarah his wife. *m.* St. John's, Calcutta, 11 Mar. 1823, Harriet, youngest dau. of Ralph Uvedale, prothonotary and sealer of the Supreme Court, Calcutta. (She *re-m.* 13 Jan. 1838, M. Charnier.)

Services: Posted to 5th N.I.; transfd. to 1/20th N.I. 31 May 1823; to newly-raised 33rd N.I. July 1823; to 66th N.I. (late 1/33rd) May 1824. Served at Natal, Sumatra, with his Regt. 1823-4. Actg. Adjt. Purnea Provl. Bn. 1 July 1826; Intr. & Qmr. 66th N.I. 25 July 1827 till 27 Jan. 1830. No record of active service.

Refs.: *A.J.* N.S. xix. 206. M.I. Bhowanipore mily. cemetery, Calcutta.

SOWERBY, John (1791-?). Captain. 25th N.I. *bapt.* St. Mary's, Carlisle, 15 Dec. 1791. Cadet 1809. Arrived in India 2 Aug. 1810. Ensign 25 Aug. 1811. Lieut. 16 Dec. 1814. Capt. 1 May 1824. Struck off in England 2 Oct. 1823.

Son of Wasdale Sowerby, of Low Cummersdale, Cumberland, farmer, and Ann his wife, late Scott. Ed. Carlisle Grammar School.

Services: Barasat C. C. 1810-11. Posted to 1/20th N.I. 1811, and served at Malacca with his Regt. Fur. 3 Feb. 1821 till struck off. Transfd. as Capt. to 25th N.I. (late 1/20th) May 1824, before it was known in India that he had been struck off. This promotion, presumably, was cancelled subsequently.

SPAN, Oliver William (1802-1842). Bt. Captain. 53rd N.I. *b.* Bristol June 1802. Cadet 1820. Admitted 31 May 1821. Ensign 13 Jan. 1821. Lieut. 11 July 1823. Bt. Capt. 13 Jan. 1836. Retired 21 Apr. 1837. *d.* 13 Jan. 1842.

bapt. St. Stephen's, Bristol, 27 Apr. 1803. 3rd son of Samuel Span, of Union I., Grenadines, and Harriet Elizabeth his wife, youngest dau. of Rev. Oliver McCausland, of Letterkenny, rector of Finlagan, co. Londonderry. *m.* Clifton 1 June 1824, Katherine Elizabeth, dau. of Martin Whish, late chairman of board of excise. (*See also* A. A. L. Corri.)

Services: Posted to 1/6th N.I.; transfd. to 27th N.I. July 1823; to 53rd N.I. (late 1/27th) May 1824. Fur. p.a. 13 July 1822 till 9 Nov. 1824. Actg. Adjt. 53rd N.I. 18 Feb. 1829; permanent do. 11 June 1830 till 21 Nov. 1834. Offg. Bde. Major at Dacca 25 Feb. 1832. Fur. s.c. 21 Oct. 1834 till Feb. 1839, when he retired on h.p. of Lieut. (viz. 4/- *p.d.*) with effect from 21 Apr. 1837. Promotion to rank of Capt. cancelled 11 Mar. 1839. No record of active service. Admitted a Burgess of Bristol 7 July 1823.

Refs.: *Bath Chron.*, 16 Mar. 1824. M.I. Union I., W.I.

SPARKES, Henry (1783-1818). Captain, 10th N.I. *bapt.* Bromley, Kent, 7 July 1783. Cadet 1799. Admitted 23 Oct. 1800. Ensign 13 Sept. 1800. Lieut. 3 Jan. 1802. Capt. 1 Oct. 1815. *d.* nr. Multai, C.P., 20 July 1818 : kld. in action.

Son of Joseph Sparkes and Mary his wife. Brother of Harriet Heapy, of Goodge St., Tottenham Court Rd., and of George, of the General Bank, Exeter.

Services: Posted Ensign to 1/10th N.I. 17 Apr. 1801. Second Mahratta War 1805-6; pursuit of Holkar; Lieut. 10th N.I. Fur. 5 Oct. 1812 till 1815. Third Mahratta War 1817-18; Chanda; Multai (kld.) [1]; Capt. 2/10th N.I.

THE BENGAL ARMY, 1758-1834 151

Refs. : Cardew, pp. 134-5. Will dated Hussingabad 25 Dec. 1817 ; proved 31 Dec. 1818. M.I. Betul bazar.

[1] *Note :* " A body of Arabs assembled at Mailgha, on the Tapti R., and seized the town of Maisdi ; Capt. Sparkes, with a coy. of 2/10th N.I., marched against them from Baitul ; near Multai, immediately after crossing the Tapti, he encountered the enemy, who were in force (20 July) ; his detachment was surrounded, but fought gallantly until their ammunition was exhausted, when the whole party was destroyed, except two naicks and seventeen sepoys, of whom ten were wounded, those killed being Capt. Sparkes, one subadar, one jemadar, 4 havildars, 2 naicks, 82 sepoys and 7 followers." (*Cardew.*)

SPARKS,[1] **Thomas** (*d.* 1808). Captain. 3rd Bengal Eur. Regt. Cadet 1769. Ensign 3 Nov. 1769. Lieut. 7 Mar. 1773. Capt. 18 Sept. 1780. Resigned 4 Nov. 1782. *d.* Randolphfield, nr. Stirling, 28 July 1808.

Son of Patrick Spark(s), writer in Edinburgh, and Sarah his wife, dau. of George Manson, wigmaker in Edinburgh.

Services : First Rohilla War 1774 ; battle of St. George ; D.J.A.G. Apptd. Chaplain to 2nd Bde. 14 Mar. 1779 ; actg. D.J.A.G. at Berhampore in Oct. 1779. Campaign against the Rajah of Benares 1781 ; Bijaigarh ; Capt. comdg. 1/35th N.I. Transfd. to 3rd Eur. Regt. Apr. 1782, on the disbandment of 35th Regt. for mutiny.

Refs. : G.M. 1808, ii. 755.

[1] *Note :* The name frequently appears as Spark.

*SPEAR(S),[1] **James** (1724/25-1761). Captain. Bengal Eur. Regt. *b.* in Ireland 1724/25. Capt. (Madras) 22 Apr. 1754. Transfd. to Bengal Est. Nov. 1759. Dismissed by C.M. *d. unm.* Calcutta Nov. 1761.

Brother of Robert, of Strahany, co. Fermanagh, gent., and of Ann Buchanan, of Abbey St., Dublin. Uncle of Ralph and Ann Buchanan.

Services : Arrived at Madras July 1748 as a Midshipman in the fleet under Hon. Edward Boscawen. Commissioned as Ensign in Madras Army ; as Lieut. in Swiss Coy. for Madras 26 July 1752. Dismissed in 1756 for accepting a present of Rs. 600 from some Sepoy Subadars on taking comd. at the station to which he had been posted. Returned to England ; reinstated on appeal to C.D. ; sailed for Bengal in the *Prince George* in 1758 as Capt., aged 32. Posted to Bengal Eur. Regt. Nov. 1759. War with Shah Alam 1760 ; Capt. Bengal Eur. Regt. Again dismissed 1760 or 1761.

Refs. : Dodwell's *The Nabobs of Madras*, p. 68. *Innes*, p. 109.

Broome, p. 289, etc. Will dated 14 Nov. 1761; proved 19 Jan. 1762; proved P.C. Dublin 1763.

[1] *Note:* His name usually appears with a final 's', but this is believed to be incorrect.

SPECK, Samuel (Smith) [1] (1789-1854). Colonel, 14th N.I. *b.* Southwark 25 Feb. 1789. Cadet 1805. Arrived in India 13 Dec. 1806. Ensign 11 Dec. 1806. Lieut. 21 Aug. 1811. Capt. 11 July 1823. Major 23 Aug. 1831. Lt. Col. 21 Jan. 1838. Col. 6 Nov. 1848. *d.* Glos. Gdns., Hyde Pk., London, 16 Dec. 1854.

Of Pitville Lawn, Cheltenham. *bapt.* St. John's, Horsleydown, Surrey, 1 Apr. 1789. Son of Henry Smith Speck, atty., and Ann his wife, née Hollingworth. Brother of Harriet, wife of Henry Deacon.

Services: Barasat C.C. 8 mos. Posted Ensign to 1st N.I. 1807. Operations in Bundelkhand against Lachman Dawa 1809; Rajaoli (w.); Ensign 2/1st N.I. Nepal War 1814-15 (w.); Lieut. 2/1st N.I., in 1st Div. (India medal). Adjt. 2nd Nassiri Bn. 27 July 1815 till 1 Oct. 1823. Transfd. to 4th N.I. (late 2/1st) May 1824. 2nd in comd. 2nd Nassiri Bn. 5 Mar. 1825; do. 1st Nassiri Bn. 8 Mar. till 19 Nov. 1828. Leave s.c. 12 mos. to N.S.W. 8 Jan. 1827; fur. p.a. 29 Mar. 1829 till 14 Sept. 1832. Posted Lt. Col. to 4th N.I. 20 Sept. 1838; to 17th N.I. 19 Jan. 1842. Fur. s.c. 18 Aug. 1846 till death. Posted Col. to 70th N.I. 1849; 14th N.I. 14 July 1853 till death.

Refs.: Boase. *G.M.* 1855, i. 220. Will dated 10 Aug. 1850; admon. 22 May 1855.

[1] *Note:* The name Smith is given in his bapt. certificate, but not in his Will or in any other official document.

*SPEKE, Edward. Cadet. Artillery. (III.-20) Cadet 1783. Declined coming out.

SPELISSY, George (1785-1828). Captain, 10th N.I. *b.* Drumcliff, co. Clare, 26 Sept. 1785. Cadet 1803. Arrived in India 29 Apr. 1805. Ensign 8 May 1805. Lieut. 9 May 1805. Capt. 7 Oct. 1821. *d.* Nimach 5 Nov. 1828.

bapt. Drumcliff 28 Sept. 1785. Son of (? John Spelissy, M.D., of Ennis, co. Clare) and Anne his wife. Brother of Anne and Ellen, of Ennis; uncle of Anne, dau. of Edward Coplin Langford, of Stone Hall, co. Limerick, and of James Molony, *q.v.*

Services: Posted Lieut. to 7th N.I. 1806. Nepal War 1814-15; Malaun; Lieut. 2/7th N.I., in 1st Div. Fur. 1817-20. Transfd.

THE BENGAL ARMY, 1758-1834   153

as Capt. to 1/7th N.I. ; to 10th N.I. (late 2/7th) May 1824. Apptd. to tempy. charge and formation of Orissa Bn. at Balasore 31 July 1823 ; comdg. Patna Provl. Bn. 1825 ; Pol. employ in Nemawar, C.I., 1826-7.
Refs.: Will dated 26 Oct. 1828 ; proved 25 Nov. 1828. M.I. at Nimach.

SPELMAN, Henry (1718/19-1765). Captain, Cavalry. *b.* 1718/19. Ensign (Madras) 10 Aug. 1755. Lieut. (?) Capt. (Bengal) 19 May 1759. *d.* Calcutta 19 Apr. 1765.
Described in embarkation roll as a native of Wandsworth, Surrey. (*Probably* son of Henry Spelman, Recorder of Norwich.[1])
Services : Sailed for Madras in the *Duke of Dorset* in 1755, aged 36. Apptd. Qmr. (being then a Lieut.) to the newly-raised Troop of Horse at Madras, comdd. by Capt. Baron de Vasserot, 15 Aug. 1758 ; transfd. to Bengal Est. 1759 ; comdd. 1st Troop of newly-raised Eur. Dgns. (M.C. 22 Sept. 1760) till disbanded in July 1764.
Refs.: Will dated Calcutta 6 Apr. 1765 ; proved 14 May 1765.

[1] *Note :* His Will contains the following bequests :—£100 to Sir Horatio Pettus, 6th and last Bart., of Rackheath, Norfolk, and small sums each to Elizabeth, wife of John Domville, of St. Martin-in-the-Fields, and to Stephen Hoare, of the Broadway, Westminster. The residue of his estate he left to " The Most Noble the Marchioness of Annandale, of Turnham Green," with £50 each to her sons, Charles and George Johnston, and her dau. Charlotte.

SPENCE, James Knox (1810-1890). General, C.B. 20th N.I. *b.* Camus, co. Tyrone, 16 Jan. 1810. Cadet 1825. Arrived in India 21 Sept. 1826. Ensign 21 May 1826. Lieut. 6 Aug. 1834. Capt. 3 Sept. 1849. Major 18 Feb. 1861. Lt. Col. 18 Feb. 1863. Col. 18 Feb. 1866. Maj. Gen. 1 Oct. 1877. Lt. Gen. 20 Aug. 1878. Gen. 22 Jan. 1889. *d.* 30 Colville Terr., Bayswater, 14 June 1890.
Son of John Spence, of Strabane, co. Tyrone. Brother of Letitia K. Ogilvie. *m.* Saugor 5 Feb. 1844, Sophia Helen, dau. of Michael Ramsay, *q.v.* (She died 27 Oct. 1893, aged 70.)
Services : Posted to 28th N.I. 9 Nov. 1826 ; transfd. to 20th N.I. 4 Nov. 1828 ; actg. Adjt. do. 15 Apr. 1835. Apptd. Adjt. Shah Shuja's 5th Inf. 17 Aug. 1838. First Afghan War 1838-40 ; Ghazni ; offg. Asst. Comst. Ofr. with Shah's force in Ghilzai country May-Aug. 1840 ; Lieut. 20th N.I., Shah's 5th Inf. (Medal). D.C. 1 cl. Saugor Div. 1 May 1843 till 1854 ; do. Nagpur Div. 14 Aug. 1854 till 1862 ; Comr. Nagpur Div., C.P., 7 Jan. 1862 ; do. Jubbul-

pore Div. 1864-71. Transfd. to Staff Corps 18 Feb. 1861. Fur.
s.c. 8 May 1856 till Oct. 1857; fur. 25 Feb. 1871 till retirement.
Retired under R. Warrant of 25 June 1881. C.B. (Civil) 18 May
1860.
Refs.: Boase. *The Times*, 17 June 1890. M.I. Nagpur cathedral.

SPENCER, Edward Frowd (1797-1827). Lieutenant, Invalid
Est. 32nd N.I. *b.* Wells 11 Dec. 1797. Cadet 1818. Ensign
16 Aug. 1819. Lieut. 11 July 1822. Invalided 30 Dec. 1825.
d. Monghyr 23 June 1827.
bapt. St. Cuthbert's, Wells, 24 Mar. 1798. Son of Edward
Spencer, of Wells, surgeon, and Mary his wife.
Services: Ensign d.d. Bengal Eur. Regt. 1819; posted to 2/3rd
N.I. 1820; transfd. to 16th N.I. July 1823; to 32nd N.I. (late
1/16th) May 1824. No record of active service.
Refs.: *A.J.* xxv. 103. M.I. at Monghyr.

SPENCER, Robert (1812-1857). Bt. Major, 26th N.I. *b.*
London 14 May 1812. Cadet 1827. Arrived in India 27 Oct.
1828. Ensign 19 May 1828. Lieut. 19 Sept. 1834. Capt.
22 Nov. 1843. Bt. Major 20 June 1854. *d.* Mian Mir 30 July
1857: murdered by mutineers of his Regt.
Son of Robert Spencer, of Calcutta, barr.-at-law, and Anne
Matilda his wife. Ward of R. Spankie.
Services: Ensign d.d. 13th N.I. 20 Nov. 1828; posted to 26th
N.I. 4 Mar. 1829; Intr. & Qmr. do. 30th Jan. 1837; Adjt. do.
24 Feb. 1837 till Nov. 1843. First Afghan War 1842; forcing of
Khyber; Mamu Khel; Jagdalak; Tazin; Haft Kotal; reoccupation of Kabul; capture of Istalif (w.) (*Lond. Gaz.* 6 Dec.
1842); Lieut. 26th N.I., with Pollock's force (Medal). First Sikh
War; Mudki; Ferozshahr; Sobraon; Capt. 26th N.I. (Medal with
2 clasps). Offg. Cantt. Joint Mgte. at Dinapore Mar. 1852 till
1854, when he rejoined his Regt. at Delhi. Was comdg. 26th N.I.
at Mian Mir when it was disarmed 13 May 1857. On 30 July the
Regt. broke out into open mutiny, and on his going down, unarmed,
to their lines, he was felled with a hatchet and hacked to pieces.
Refs.: *De Rhé-Philipe*. M.I. in St. Mary Magdalene, Lahore.

SPENDER, Thomas (1777-1800). Lieutenant, 2nd Bengal
Eur. Regt. *bapt.* Burton-on-Trent 19 Dec. 1777. Cadet 1797.
Arrived in India 20 Oct. 1798. Ensign 30 Sept. 1798. Lieut.
1 Nov. 1798. *d.* Calcutta 15 Nov. 1800.
Son of John Spender and Ellen his wife.
Services: Served throughout with 2nd Bengal Eur. Regt.

SPENS, Andrew (1801-1859). Major General. Colonel 14th N.I. *b.* Edinburgh 23 Dec. 1801. Cadet 1817. Admitted 13 Feb. 1819. Ensign 15 July 1818. Lieut. 27 Dec. 1819. Capt. 27 Apr. 1833. Major 1 Mar. 1838. Lt. Col. 21 Dec. 1844. Col. 11 Nov. 1854. Maj. Gen. 18 July 1856. *d.* Edinburgh 25 Apr. 1859.
2nd son of Thomas Spens, M.D., of Edinburgh, and Bethia his wife, dau. of Andrew Wood, surgeon. Brother of James Spens, *q.v.* *m.* Calcutta 14 June 1832, Diana Frances, dau. of Henry Wadham Diggle, Bo. C.S. Ed. Edin. High School.
Services: Ensign d.d. 23rd N.I. 1819; posted to 1/2nd N.I. 1820; transfd. to 5th N.I. (late 1/2nd) May 1824. Adjt. Sirmoor Bn. 30 Jan. 1824; do. newly-raised 7th Extra Regt. 21 May 1825 till 1 Apr. 1826, when reduced. Transfd. to 6th Extra Regt. (became 74th N.I.) 1826; actg. Intr. & Qmr. do. 13 June 1827 and 23 June 1828. Offg. Bde. Major in Rohilkhand and Kumaon 31 Oct. 1835. Shot in the thigh by a sepoy in Sept. 1842 : his assailant was hanged. Fur. p.a. 13 Mar. 1843 till 25 Oct. 1845. Posted Lt. Col. to 29th N.I. Jan. 1845; to 67th N.I.; to 11th N.I. 1846. Capture of Kot Kangra Apr. 1846; Lt. Col. 11th N.I. Transfd. to 2nd Eur. Bengal Fus. 12 Nov. 1850; Col. 14th N.I. Feb. 1855 till death. Bdr. 2 cl. comdg. Ferozepore 22 Dec. 1854; comdd. Lucknow Bde. Nov. 1855 till July 1856. Fur. Jan. 1857 till death.
Refs.: Burke's *Landed Gentry*, 13th edn., p. 1641, *s.n.* Spens (*now* Dunning), of Craigsanquhar, co. Fife. *Boase. G.M.* 1859, i. 654. *The Times*, 28 Apr. 1859.

SPENS, James (1811-1856). Captain, Engineers. *b.* Edinburgh 28 Nov. 1811. Cadet 1832. Arrived in India 15 Dec. 1833. 2nd Lieut. 8 Dec. 1831. Lieut. 20 May 1839. Capt. 7 Oct. 1851. *d.* Ambala 21 Nov. 1856, of heart disease.
5th son of Thomas Spens, M.D., and Bethia his wife. Brother of Andrew Spens, *q.v.* *m.* St. Luke's, Cork, 1849, Penelope Clarine, 4th dau. of Bt. Lt.-Col. Lionel John Westropp, 58th Regt. (She *re-m.* 31 Dec. 1863, Rev. Edward James Rhoades, and died 14 Apr. 1897.) Ed. Edin. Acad.; in Rector's class 1824-7. Addiscombe Cadet 2 Feb. 1830 till 8 Dec. 1831; Chatham 13 Feb. till 26 Dec. 1832.
Services: d.d. S. & M. at Delhi Jan. 1834. Offg. Supt. new Benares-Burdwan road Apr. 1835; Asst. to Supt. of Doab canal 8 Feb. 1839; Executive Engr. at Kasauli 17 Nov. 1842; Supt. of canals W. of Jumna Sept. 1845 till Oct. 1846. First Sikh War;

Sobraon (Medal). Fur. 10 Feb. 1847 till 8 Feb. 1850. Executive Engr. at Midnapore 19 Apr. 1850; do. Meerut 17 Oct. 1851; do. Ferozepore 27 Sept. 1853. Leave s.c. May 1855 till death.

Refs.: Burke's *Landed Gentry*, 13th edn., p. 1641, *s.n.* Spens (now Dunning), of Craigsanquhar, co. Fife. *Howard & Crisp's Ireland*, ii. 61, *s.n.* Westropp, of Ballyvolane, co. Cork. *De Rhé-Philipe. Edin. Acad. Register. I.M.* 17 Jan. 1857, p. 40. M.I. at Ambala.

SPETTIGUE, Stephen William (1795-1815). Lieutenant, 12th N.I. *bapt.* St. Mary Magdalen, Launceston, 30 Apr. 1795. Cadet 1810. Ensign 13 Nov. 1813. Lieut. July 1815. *d.* Natpur, Bengal, 15 July 1815.

Son of Stephen Spettigue, of Launceston, surgeon and apothecary, and Sibella his wife. Ed. Exeter Grammar School.

Services: Barasat C.C. 1810-11. Cadet d.d. 12th N.I. 1811-12; posted Ensign to 1/12th N.I. 1813. No record of active service.

SPIERS, Alexander (1788-1847). Colonel, 50th N.I. Resdt. at Nagpur. *b.* Paisley 17 Dec. 1788. Cadet 1804. Arrived in India 5 Aug. 1805. Ensign 25 Aug. 1804. Lieut. 25 Aug. 1804. Capt. 1 Mar. 1818. Major 1 Apr. 1828. Lt. Col. 29 Aug. 1833. Col. 1 Jan. 1845. *d.* Jalna, Hyderabad, 18 Mar. 1847.

Son of Archibald Spiers. *m. c.* 1846, Bibi Bunnoo. Marlow Cadet.

Services: Posted Lieut. to 23rd N.I. 1806. Operations against Dhundia Khan 1807; Komona; Ganauri; Lieut. 1/23rd N.I. Actg. Adjt. 5 Coys. 1/23rd N.I. at Etawah in May 1813. Intr. & Qmr. 1/23rd N.I. 1 July 1814 till 22 Apr. 1817. Capt. Lt. 19 Sept. 1816. Capt. 1/23rd N.I. Third Mahratta War; Bde. Major 8th Inf. Bde., 4th Div. Bde. Major Advanced Corps Rajputana (Nimach) Force 23 June 1818 till 13 July 1824. Operations in Kotah 1821; Mangrol; Bde. Major (*Lond. Gaz.* 20 Mar. 1822). Transfd. to 46th N.I. (late 2/23rd) May 1824. P.A. in Sirohi 10 July 1824, and spent the remainder of his service on Pol. duty. Supt. of Ajmer 18 June 1832; Resdt. at Gwalior 24 Feb. 1841; do. at Nagpur 30 Sept. 1843 till death. Posted Lt. Col. to 14th N.I. 24 Dec. 1833; as Col. to 43rd N.I. 15 Mar. 1845; to 50th N.I. 1846.

Refs.: Will dated Nagpur 25 Nov. 1845; codicil 17 Mar. 1847; admon. 27 Aug. 1847. M.I. Jalna.

SPILLER, Francis John (1784-1836). Major, 8th L.C. *b.* Norfolk St., Strand, London, 13 Dec. 1784. Cadet 1804.

THE BENGAL ARMY, 1758-1834   157

Arrived in India 21 June 1806. Cornet 10 Sept. 1805. Lieut. 31 Mar. 1809. Capt. 1 Sept. 1818. Major 17 May 1829. *d.* Sultanpur, U.P., 5 [1] Oct. 1836, of apoplexy.

bapt. St. Clement Danes 1785. Son of George Price Spiller (descendant of Spiller, of Shevoike, Cornwall), Comy. Gen., and Caroline his wife, *née* Tinker, representative of the family of Bladen, of Ketton Hall, co. Rutland. His sister was mother of Bdr.-Gen. James George Smith-Neill *(D.N.B.)*. *m.* Ghazipur 7 Feb. 1807, Miss Louisa Grant.

Services: Ensign York Fuzileers; Lieut. Warwick Mil. Present as Cadet at capture of Cape Jan. 1806. Posted Cornet to 8th N.C. 1806. S.A.C.G. 11 July 1812; A.C.G. 27 Dec. 1816 till 8 Mar. 1822. Nepal War; S.A.C.G. Third Mahratta War; A.C.G. 3rd Div. A.C.G. to Malwa F.F. Apr. 1820. Siege and capture of Bhurtpore; Capt. 8th L.C. Leave s.c. to Hills 11 Oct. 1828 till 1 Jan. 1831.

Refs.: Burke's *Landed Gentry*, 13th edn., p. 1303, *s.n.* Smith-Neill, of Barnweil, co. Ayr. *A.J.* N.S. xxii. 212. *G.M.* 1837, i. 558. M.I. Chunar (Sultanpur) old cemetery.

[1] *Note:* E.I.R. and M.I. give date of death as 5th, *A.J.* as 10th, *G.M.* as 15th Oct.

SPILSBURY, Edgar Richard (1806-1828). Lieutenant, 37th N.I. *b.* London 11 Feb. 1806. Cadet 1823. Ensign 17 Jan. 1824. Lieut. 13 May 1825. *d.* in India 22 Nov. 1828.

bapt. St. Anne's, Westminster, 22 Mar. 1806. Son of Edgar Ashe Spilsbury, of Stafford, surgeon, and Emma Gybbon his wife.

Services: Posted to 5th N.I. 1824; d.d. 51st N.I. 12 Jan. 1825; transfd. to 37th N.I. 1826; actg. Adjt. Bareilly Provl. Bn. 6 Feb. 1828. No record of active service.

SPITTA, Charles Lewis (1814-1846). Lieutenant, Engineers. *b.* Dec. 1814. Cadet 1832. Arrived in India 5 Feb. 1834. 2nd Lieut. (14 June 1832) 5 Feb. 1834. Lieut. 4 Sept. 1839. *d.* Berhampore 18 Oct. 1846.

bapt. Camberwell 31 Mar. 1815. Son of Charles Lewis Spitta,[1] of Camberwell, merchant, and Mary his 2nd wife. Brother of Robert John Spitta, and nephew of Henry Arthur Spitta and Rev. Francis John Spitta. *m.* Calcutta 16 Aug. 1841, Harriet, only dau. of Frederick Brett (? Surg. Frederick Harrington Brett). (She *re-m.* 1849, Edwin Morton, 9th Ft.) Ed. Christ's Hospital. Addiscombe Cadet 28 May 1830 till 14 June 1832; Chatham 3 Aug. 1832 till 22 Aug. 1833.

Services : d.d. S. & M. at Delhi 5 Feb. 1834. Shekhawat expedn. 1834. d.d. S. & M. at Hazaribagh 7 May 1835 ; actg. Asst. to Supt. canals W. of Jumna 19 Feb. 1838 ; Executive Engr. Upper Assam 12 Aug. 1840 ; do. 2nd (Berhampore) Div. 1845.
Refs. : G.M. 1847, i. 110. Will dated 8 Mar. 1842 ; admon. 7 Sept. 1847.
¹ *Note :* John Spitta naturalized 1758 ; Charles Louis Spitta naturalized 1774.

SPOONER, John (*d.* 1781). Ensign, Infantry. Cadet 1777. Ensign 12 Feb. 1778. *d.* Calcutta 17 Oct. 1781.
Services : N.F.P.

SPOONER, Thomas (*d.* 1791). Lieutenant, Invalid Est. Infantry. Cadet 1770. Ensign 29 Mar. 1771. Invalided 1776. Lieut. 13 Dec. 1779. Resigned on pension 30 Dec. 1779. *d.* in England 26 Apr. 1791.
Services : Lieut. H.M. Marines, and served during war in W.I. Lost his money by the failure of his Agent and was obliged, at a very advanced age, to come out to Bengal as a Cadet. Served as Cadet in the Select Picket. Apptd. Adjt. & Qmr. of Chunargarh fort 30 Apr. 1777. Pensioned in England on Lord Clive's fund from 9 Feb. 1781, owing to age and infirmity.

SPOTTISWOOD, Robert (1755/56-1828). Major, Invalid Est. 10th N.I. *b.* 1755/56. Cadet 1783. Admitted 22 Oct. 1783. Ensign 23 Feb. 1785. Lieut. 21 Mar. 1793. Capt. 21 Sept. 1804. Major 16 Dec. 1814. Invalided 1 Oct. 1815. *d.* Portobello, Edinburgh, 31 Aug. 1828, aged 72.
Services : Apptd. Cadet 3 Jan. 1783 ; sailed for India in the *Vansittart* 11 Mar. 1783. Brought on full pay from Supy. Ensign and posted Ensign to 28th Bn. Sepoys 8 Feb. 1790. Third Mysore War 1790-1 ; Arikera ; operations before Savandrug ; Ramgiri ; Shivanagiri ; Ensign 28th Bn., with Lt.-Col. Cockerell's detachment. Posted to 1st Eur. Bn. 26 Jan. 1792 ; to 26th Bn. Sepoys 16 Apr. 1793. Lieut. 10th N.I. in 1798 ; comdg. at Vishnupur, Bengal, in Feb. 1799. Capt. Lt. 10th N.I. 27 Jan. 1804. Asst., Tannah Ests. 1803 ; Regulating Ofr. do. in Bihar 1807 till Jan. 1828. Fur. p.a. 25 Jan. 1828 till death.
Refs. : A.J. xxvi. 517.

SPOTTISWOODE, Arthur Cole (1808-1874). Major General. 37th N.I. *b.* Ganjam, Madras, 9 Jan. 1808. Country Cadet 1823. Admitted 9 Sept. 1824. Ensign 25 Feb. 1824. Lieut. 13 May 1825. Capt. 14 Nov. 1833. Major 17 Mar. 1851. Lt.

THE BENGAL ARMY, 1758-1834 159

Col. 22 May 1856. Bt. Col. 23 July 1858. Retired 31 Dec. 1861. Hon. Maj. Gen. 31 Dec. 1861. d. Hastings 23 Mar. 1874.
bapt. 28 Mar. 1809. Eldest son of Hugh Spottiswoode, M.C.S., Collector in the zillah of Ganjam, and Harriet his wife, dau. of Burton Smith. Brother of Henry Spottiswoode, *q.v.* m. Nimach 29 July 1834, Jessy Eliza, dau. of Lambert Loveday, *q.v.* (*See also* John Herring.) (She died 28 Jan. 1898, aged 80.)
Services : Was at Patna when apptd. Cadet 11 Feb. 1824. Posted to 37th N.I. 1824. Siege and capture of Bhurtpore ; Lieut. 37th N.I., d.d. Sirmoor Bn. (India medal). Rejoined 37th N.I. Feb. 1826. d.d. 4th Coy. Pioneers 19 Oct. 1829 ; d.d. Pioneers 30 Dec. 1830. Adjt. 37th N.I. 6 May 1831 till 14 Dec. 1833. Sub-Asst. in Stud Dept. 25 June 1835 ; rejoined his Regt. for service Sept. 1838. First Afghan War 1838-9 ; Ghazni ; Capt. 37th N.I. (Medal). Rejoined Stud Dept. Dec. 1839 ; 2nd Asst. at Central Stud 30 Jan. 1843 ; 1st do. 7 July 1843 till 1853. Fur. p.a. 15 July 1853 till 3 Jan. 1856. Posted Lt. Col. to 37th N.I. Aug. 1856, and was comdg. the Regt. when it was disarmed and mutinied at Benares 4 June 1857. Leave s.c. 2 yrs. to Aust. and N.Z. 20 Nov. 1858.
Refs. : Burke's *Landed Gentry*, 15th edn., p. 2110, *s.n.* Spottiswoode, *late* of Spottiswoode. *The Times*, 27 Mar. 1874.

SPOTTISWOODE, Henry (1809-1857). Lieut. Colonel, 55th N.I. b. Madras 4 Mar. 1809. Cadet 1824. Arrived in India 19 Jan. 1826. Ensign 9 Aug. 1825. Lieut. 1 Aug. 1828. Capt. 1 Sept. 1841. Major 1 Dec. 1849. Lt. Col. 13 Apr. 1855. d. Nowshera (? Peshawar) 25 May 1857 : committed suicide.[1]
bapt. Madras 28 Mar. 1809. 2nd son of Hugh Spottiswoode, M.C.S., and Harriet his wife. Brother of Arthur Cole Spottiswoode and stepson of Henry Capel Sandys, *qq.v.*
Services : Posted Ensign to 21st N.I. 1826. Leave s.c. 6 mos. to Bombay 26 Feb. 1830. Adjt. 21st N.I. 7 Jan. 1832 till 7 Oct. 1841. Offg. Asst. Sec. to Govt., Mily. Dept., 30 June 1843 ; Mily. Sec. to Presdt. of Council of India (Hon. W. W. Bird) 12 Jan. 1844. Sub-Asst. in Stud Dept. 12 July 1844 till Feb. 1850. Posted Lt. Col. to 55th N.I. 1855. No record of active service.
Refs. : Burke's *Landed Gentry*, 15th edn., p. 2110, *s.n.* Spottiswoode, *late* of Spottiswoode. *I.M.* 17 Sept. 1857, p. 593.
[1] *Note* : He was comdg. 55th N.I. at the outbreak of the Mutiny, and on the discovery of their treachery he shot himself in despair during the night of 24/25 May.

SPRY, Edmund Trant (1806-1838). Lieutenant, 24th N.I. b. London 11 Sept. 1806. Cadet 1824. Arrived in India 21 May

1825. Ensign 7 Dec. 1824. Lieut. 10 May 1828. *d*. Midnapore 7 Aug. 1838.

bapt. St. Botolph's, Aldersgate, 7 Jan. 1807. 2nd son of James Hume Spry, of London, for 24 yrs. one of the surgeons to H.C.S. Home Dept., medical ofr. to Charterhouse, and Frances his wife, dau. of William Robinson, of Charterhouse Sq., London, merchant. *m*. 1st, Cawnpore 2 July 1830, Sophia Maria, only dau. of Adam Maxwell. (She died Barrackpore 1 Feb. 1835, aged 24.) *m*. 2nd, Midnapore 7 Aug. 1837, Harriet Augusta Hayes, eldest dau. of Thomas Ephraim Monsell, B.C.S. (*See also* Frederick William Cornish.) Ed. Charterhouse; admitted 1814, left May 1823.

Services: Ensign d.d. 28th N.I. 10 June 1825; posted to 28th N.I. 1825; transfd. to 24th N.I. 1826; actg. Adjt. do. 23 Jan. 1829; actg. Intr. & Qmr. do. 30 Jan. 1830; permanent do. 4 Mar. 1830 till death. Operations against the Chuars 1832; attack on stockade at Cooknoocoon 20 Dec. (s.w.); Lieut. 24th N.I., with Jungle Mehals F.F. Rising in Cuttack 1836; Lieut. 24th N.I.

Refs.: *Charterhouse School List. A.J.* N.S. xi. 64; N.S xxvii. 232. Family information.

SPUNNER, Benjamin (1733/34-1763). Lieutenant, Infantry. *b.* in Ireland 1733/34. Cadet 1761. Ensign 1 Dec. 1761. Lieut. 24 July 1763. *d.* 5th, 6th or 11th Oct. 1763: massacred at or near Patna by order of Nawab Mir Muhammad Kasim. (See note to Henry Somers.)

Services: Sailed for India in the *Earl of Holderness* 30 Mar. 1761, aged 27. Was taken prisoner in 1763 by the Nawab's people at Cossimbazar, whither he had gone for the recovery of his health.

Refs.: Bengal Letter of 29 Sept. 1763. MS. list at I.O., dated Ft. Wm. 20 Feb. 1764, signed by John Graham, Sec., entitled " List of Persons kld. in the Massacre at Patna, and at other places during the Troubles, 1763." *Firminger,* p. 71.

*SPUNNER, John (1726/27-?). (? Ensign. Infantry.) *b.* in Ireland 1726/27. Cadet 1759. Ensign (Madras) 5 Oct. 1760. *d.* (?)

Brother of Benjamin Spunner, who was granted permission in 1773 (M.C. 19 Feb.) " to proceed to Bengal and reside two years to settle the affairs of his deceased brother, John Spunner, late an Ofr. in the Coy.'s service."

Services: Sailed for India as a Bengal Cadet in the *Latham* in 1759, aged 32. Transfd. to Madras Est.; apparently retransfd. later to Bengal Est.

THE BENGAL ARMY, 1758-1834 161

SQUIBB, Edward (1802-1824). Lieutenant, 55th N.I. *b.* London 23 Mar. 1802. Cadet 1819. Ensign 14 Feb. 1820. Lieut. 11 July 1823. *d.* Mhow 29 Aug. 1824.

bapt. St. James's, Westminster, 28 Mar. 1802. 5th son of George Squibb, of Savile Row, London, auctioneer, and Mary Ann his wife, dau. of John Fladgate, of Conduit St., London. Ed. Harrow 1816-18.

Services : Posted to 1/8th N.I. 1820 ; transfd. to 28th N.I. July 1823 ; to 55th N.I. (late 1/28th) May 1824. No record of active service.

Refs. : Some Account of the Clark Family, by G. W. Clark (n.d.), p. 36. *Harrow School Register.*

SQUIRE, Arnot(t) (*d.* 1792). Lieutenant. Infantry. Cadet 1769. Ensign 26 July 1769. Lieut. 30 June 1771. Resigned 2 Dec. 1776. *d.* 21 Jan. 1792.

Of Thrapston, Northants. *m.* Anna.

Services : Resigned and returned to England owing to ill health. Lieut. Northants Mil. 18 Nov. 1779. Pensd. on Lord Clive's fund Dec. 1784.

SQUIRE, William Hill (1786-?). Lieutenant. 11th N.I. *bapt.* St. Paul's, Covent Garden, 27 July 1786. Cadet 1804. Arrived in India 13 May 1806. Ensign 20 Mar. 1806. Lieut. 1 Jan. 1807. Resigned in India 2 Feb. 1808.

Son of Thomas Squire and Frances Dinah his wife.

Services : Barasat C.C. Posted Lieut. to 11th N.I. 1807. No record of active service.

STABLES, John (*c.* 1742/43-1795). Captain. Infantry. Afterwards Member of the Supreme Council at Calcutta. *b.* Westmorland *c.* 1742/43. Cadet (Madras) 1759. Ensign (Madras) 23 Oct. 1759. Lieut. 12 July 1762. Capt. 22 Oct. 1763. Resigned 1766. *d.* Wonham, nr. Reigate, Surrey, 21 Jan. 1795, aged 51.

Related to Anthony Robinson, *q.v.*, and to John Robinson, Sec. to the Treasury and manager of Indian affairs under the North ministry (*D.N.B.*). *m.* (?)

Services : Sailed for India in the *Prince Henry* in 1759, when he gave his age as 18. Went to Bengal from Madras as an Ensign with Col. Caillaud Nov. 1759. Comdd. a detachment at Monghyr Dec. 1760, when he attacked and defeated the Kharakpur Rajah. Manipur expedn. 1762. Campaign of 1763 under Major Thomas Adams ; battles of Gheria and Udhua Nullah. Battle of Buxar

Oct. 1764; Capt. comdg. 15th Bn. Sepoys, A.D.C. to Munro. Member of the Supreme Council 11 Nov. 1782 till Jan. 1787 ; Presdt. of the Board of Revenue. Purchased Wonham from Charles, 3rd Baron Romney, 1793.

Refs. : *D.I.B. Caraccioli,* iii. 273. *Broome,* pp. 320-2. Dodwell's *Letters of Warren Hastings. Grier. B.: P.P.* No. 78, p. 171. *G.M.* 1795, i. 171, 252. Portrait in Zoffany's "Tiger hunt near Chandernagore," seated on the elephant to the left.

STACEY, John (*d.* 1789). Captain, Invalid Est. 5th Bengal Eur. Bn. Cadet 1769. Ensign 30 Aug. 1769. Lieut. 4 Feb. 1771. Capt. 11 Sept. 1779. Invalided 1 Mar. 1789. *d.* Moradbag, Murshidabad, 17 Mar. 1789.

Services : Capt. 2/3rd Bengal Eur. Regt. in Oct. 1779 ; 5th Eur. Bn. in July 1787.

STACK, Thomas (1757/58-?). Lieutenant. Infantry. *b.* Cumberland 1757/58. Cadet 1781. Never arrived in India. Ensign 22 July 1782. Lieut. 20 Oct. 1783. Struck off 1788.

Services : Apptd. Cadet 21 Nov. 1781, aged 24 ; was to have sailed for India in the *Morse* 6 Feb. 1782, aged 24. Shown as on fur. in Mar. 1787.

STACY, Henry Peter (1783-1804). Lieutenant, 2nd N.I. *bapt.* St. Martin's, Salisbury, 17 Dec. 1783. Cadet 1800. Arrived in India 9 Feb. 1802. Ensign 21 Dec. 1801. Lieut. 15 Aug. 1803. *d.* Sikandra 24 Aug. 1804 : kld. in action during Monson's retreat.

Son of Rev. Henry Peter Stacy, LL.D., chaplain Bengal Est., and Ann his 1st wife. Brother of Lewis Robert Stacy, *q.v.,* of the mother of George Abbott, *q.v.,* and of the wife of Robert Hornby, *q.v.* Ed. Winchester ; scholar 1797.

Services : Second Mahratta War 1803-4 ; battle of Delhi ; Hinglaisgarh ; Monson's retreat (kld.) ; Lieut. 2/2nd N.I.

Refs. : *Kirby. E.I.M.C.* ii. 559.

STACY, Lewis Robert (1788-1848). Colonel, C.B., 43rd N.I. (now 1st Royal Bn. (L.I.) 9th Jat Regt.). *bapt.* Oxford 11 Jan. 1788. Cadet 1804. Arrived in India 14 June 1806. Ensign 21 Sept. 1805. Lieut. 22 Sept. 1805. Capt. 5 May 1821. Major 30 May 1829. Lt. Col. 23 Feb. 1835. Col. 1 Mar. 1846. *d.* Nimach 18 July 1848.

Son of Rev. Henry Peter Stacy and Ann his 1st wife. Brother of Henry Peter Stacy, *q.v. m.* Allahabad 28 May 1824, Miss Sophia Maria Grimes, sister of his father's 2nd wife.

THE BENGAL ARMY, 1758-1834

Services : Present as Cadet at capture of Cape Jan. 1806. Posted Lieut. to 16th N.I. 1806. (? Operations in Bundelkhand 1807 ; Chamir ; Sehlehuganj ; Lieut. 1/16th N.I.) Postmr. at Muttra 1 Dec. 1810. Adjt. 1/16th N.I. Oct. 1810 till July 1814. Leave s.c. 6 mos. to sea 8 Aug. 1812. Intr. & Qmr. 1/16th N.I. 1 July 1814 till 10 June 1820. Capt. 1/16th N.I. A.D.C. to Maj.-Gen. Sir William Toone, *q.v.*, in 1822. Transfd. to 32nd N.I. (late 1/16th) May 1824. 2nd in comd. 7th Extra Regt. 21 May 1825 till 1 Apr. 1826. d.d. 1st Nassiri Bn. 29 Sept. 1826. (? Shekhawat expedn. 1834 ; Major 32nd N.I.) Posted Lt. Col. to 43rd N.I. 9 June 1835 ; to 5th N.I. 20 Oct. 1838 ; to 43rd N.I. 15 Dec. 1838. First Afghan War 1839-42 ; Ghazni (Medal) ; selected to comd. troops to remain at Kandahar 27 Aug. 1839 ; operations in Baluchistan 1840 ; reoccupation of Kalat ; against Nasir Khan of Kalat July 1841 ; fighting around Kandahar 1842 ; Bdr. comdg. 2nd Inf. Bde. 21 July 1842 ; Ghazni ; Kabul ; Istalif ; Lt. Col. 43rd N.I., with Nott's force (*Lond. Gaz.* 12 Feb. 1841, 6 Sept. & 6 Dec. 1842) (Medal). Gwalior campaign ; Maharajpur ; Bdr. comdg. 4th Bde., 2nd Div. (Bronze star). First Sikh War ; Sobraon ; Lt. Col. 43rd N.I., Bdr. comdg. 7th Bde. (Medal). Posted Col. to 43rd N.I. 1846. Comdd. Meywar F.F. 11 Mar. 1846 till death. C.B. 24 Dec. 1842. Durani 3 cl. 3 Nov. 1843. A.D.C. to the Queen. Pub. Serampore, 1841, " Narrative of the Operations of Gen. Nott's Army . . ." ; London, 1848, " Narrative of Services in Beloochistan and Afghanistan, in the years 1840, 1841, and 1842."

Refs.: *I.M.* 26 Sept. 1848, p. 548. Will dated 18 July 1848 ; proved 25 Oct. 1848. M.I. Nimach.

STAFFORD, Hugh (1751/52-1819). Lieut. General. Colonel 21st N.I. *b.* 1751/52. Cadet 1769. Admitted 12 June 1770. Ensign 10 Nov. 1771. Lieut. 25 July 1776. Capt. 18 Feb. 1781. Major 1 Mar. 1794. Lt. Col. 1 July 1798. Col. 1 Jan. 1803. Maj. Gen. 25 July 1810. Lt. Gen. 4 June 1814. *d.* Calcutta 13 Jan. 1819, aged 67.

3rd son of Hugh Stafford, of Maine, co. Louth, and Mary his 1st wife, dau. and heir of Edward Smith, of Maine. *m.* 1st (before 1783), Thomasine, dau. of Rev. H. Sullivan, of Clonakilty, co. Cork. (She died Buxar 15 Sept. 1803, aged 41.) His daus. *m.* James Caulfeild, *q.v.*, and John Forbes Paton, *q.v. m.* 2nd, in England 12 Apr. 1810, Harriet, only child of Lt.-Col. William Spencer, of Hinton, Dorset.

Services : Was on fur. 21 Oct. 1776 till Apr. 1783. Capt. 6th Bengal Eur. Bn. in July 1787 and Dec. 1788. To comd. 5th Bn.

Sepoys 16 Dec. 1793 ; apptd. early in 1798 to comd. newly-raised 1/14th N.I. This Bn., which became 28th N.I. in 1824, and mutinied at Shahjahanpur 31 May 1857, was called after him " *Stupper-ki-Paltan.*" Posted Lt. Col. to 2/9th N.I. 27 July 1798 ; comdg. at Buxar in 1802 ; Col. newly-raised 21st N.I. 1803 till death. Fur. 19 Sept. 1806 till 8 Feb. 1811. Maj. Gen. comdg. at Cawnpore 1811-13 ; comdg. 1st Div. 1814 ; struck off Gen. Staff 28 Jan. 1815 ; afterwards unemployed in India till death.

Refs. : Burke's *Landed Gentry of Ireland,* p. 656, *s.n.* Stafford, of Maine, co. Louth. Burke's *Colonial Gentry,* i. 36, *s.n.* Stafford. Will dated 6 Jan. 1819 ; proved 28 Jan. 1819. M.I. in S. Park St. cemetery, Calcutta.

STAIG, William (1779-1806). Lieutenant, 3rd N.I.
bapt. Dumfries 15 Oct. 1779. Cadet 1798. Arrived in India 8 Apr. 1800. Ensign 7 Sept. 1799. Lieut. 28 Oct. 1799. *d.* 1 July 1806, on board his budgerow on the Jalangi R.

Youngest son of David Staig, of Dumfries, banker.

Services : Posted to 2/3rd N.I. 15 Apr. 1801. On fur. in 1802. No record of active service.

Refs. : S.M. 1807, p. 317.

STAINFORTH, Francis John (1797-1866). Captain. 1st L.C. Subsequently P.C. of All Hallows, Staining. *bapt.* St. Peter-le-Poor, London, 19 Dec. 1797. Cadet 1817. Cornet 15 Aug. 1818. Lieut. 24 Nov. 1819. Capt. 13 May 1825. Resigned 7 Dec. 1827. *d.* Mark Lane, London, 3 Sept. 1866.

Son of Richard Stainforth, of Clapham, merchant, and Maria his wife, 2nd dau. of Sir Francis Baring, 1st Bart., of Larkbeer, Devon, Dir. E.I. Co. 2nd cousin of James Drummond Baring, *q.v. m.* Benares 23 Jan. 1823, Elizabeth, youngest dau. of Dr. Fraser, of London. St. John's Coll., Camb. ; B.A. 1830 ; M.A. 1 July 1833.

Services : Posted to 1st L.C. 1819 and served throughout with that Regt. (? Operations in Oudh 1822 ; capture of Bardgaon.) Took holy orders ; Deacon 1830 ; Priest 1834. P.C. of All Hallows, Staining, Middlesex, 1851.

Refs. : Burke's *Peerage,* 1923, p. 1683, *s.n.* Earl of Northbrook. *Graduati Cantab. G.M.* 1866, ii. 560. *The Times,* 5 Sept. 1866.

STAINFORTH, John (*d.* 1781). Lieut. Colonel, 2nd Bengal Eur. Inf. Capt. 5 Aug. 1765. Cashiered Sept. 1766. Restored to the Service 1 Dec. 1770. Major 2 Nov. 1774. Lt. Col. 18 Nov. 1780. *d.* Cawnpore 27 Oct. 1781.

Son of William Stainforth, of Stillington, nr. York, and Judith his wife, one of the co-heiresses of Sir Walter Hawkesworth, of Hawkesworth, 2nd and last Bart. Brother of William, George, and Mary, wife of Rev. Henry Greene, preby. of Oxted, in St. Paul's Cathedral.

Services : Ensign H.M. 57th Ft. (at Gibraltar) 27 Feb. 1759 ; Lieut. 68th Ft. 4 May 1761 ; Lieut. h.p. of Addl. Ofrs. 68th Ft. on reduction 1763 till death. Apptd. in England 2 Nov. 1764, Capt. on Bengal Est. ; sailed in the *Speke* 14 Apr. 1765. Cashiered for uttering threatening expressions against Lord Clive and proposing to assassinate him. Reinstated by C.D. in England 10 Jan. 1770 ; sailed for India in the *Morse* 9 Apr. 1770. Major 1/2nd Bengal Eur. Regt. in Oct. 1779.

Refs. : Burke's *Landed Gentry*, 4th edn., p. 599, *s.n.* Greene, of Rolleston, Leics. *Broome*, pp. 607-8. Will dated camp nr. Illahabad, 21 Sept. 1781 ; proved 31 July 1782. M.I. in Kachahri cemetery, Cawnpore.

STALKART, George (1794-1814). Ensign, 13th N.I. *b.* 28 Mar. 1794. Cadet 1808. Admitted 16 Apr. 1810. Ensign 13 Aug. 1811. *d.* nr. Jampta, Nahan, 27 Dec. 1814 : kld. in action.

bapt. St. Mary's, Rotherhithe, Surrey, 27 Apr. 1794. Son of Marmaduke Stalkart, of Ghusri, nr. Howrah, Calcutta, shipwright, and Mary his 1st wife.

Services : Was already in India when apptd. Cadet. d.d. 1/13th N.I. May 1810 ; posted Ensign to 1/13th N.I. 20 Sept. 1811. Mily. student at Coll. of Ft. Wm. 7 July till 30 Nov. 1814. Nepal War 1814 ; repulse at Jaithak (kld.) ; Lieut. 1/13th N.I., in 2nd Div.

Refs. : De Rhé-Philipe. M.I. at Nahan.

STALKER, John (*d.* 1781). Lieutenant, 27th N.I. Cadet 1771. Ensign 19 Feb. 1773. Lieut. 14 Mar. 1779. *d.* Sewalah, nr. Benares, 16 Aug. 1781 : kld. in action.

Brother of Mrs. Stewart.

Services : Apptd. Adjt. 34th Bn. Sepoys 22 Mar. 1780 ; apptd. 19 Feb. 1781 to comd. 2 Coys. Sepoys as a guard for Mr. William Markham, Resdt. at Benares. (See note to Archibald Scott.)

Refs. : M.I. St. Mary's churchyard, Benares.

STAMFORD, Bryan I'Anson. Lieutenant. 23rd Bn. Sepoys. Afterwards Lieut. 76th Ft. Cadet 1781. Ensign 30 Aug. 1781. Lieut. 13 June 1783. Resigned 1788.

(*Probably* brother of Thomas Stamford, *q.v.*) *m.* Madras 25 June 1792, Miss Anne Smith Manoury, dau. of Capt. Isaac Manoury, Madras Art.[1] Ed. Westminster ; admitted 8 Nov. 1773.

Services : Transfd. to H.M.S. ; Lieut. in Army 9 July 1783 ; Lieut. 76th Ft. 4 Nov. 1788 till 8 Feb. 1793. Was an indigo planter in Oudh in 1796, and continued as such till after 1837.[2]
Refs. : Westminster School List.
[1] *Note :* This marriage had previously been celebrated by a R.C. missionary padre at Tripasore, 5 May 1791.
[2] *Note :* His name appears in the *Bengal & Agra Directory* for 1850 ; but this may have been a son.

STAMFORD, Thomas (*d.* 1790). Ensign. Infantry. Subsequently Ensign 76th Ft. Cadet 1784. Ensign 10 Apr. 1785. Resigned before July 1787. *d.* 1790.

(*Probably* brother of Bryan I'Anson Stamford, *q.v.*, and apparently related in some manner to Sir Thomas Stamford Raffles (*D.N.B.*).)
Ed. Westminster ; admitted 8 Nov. 1773.
Services : Ensign H.M. 65th Ft. 22 Mar. 1780 ; Lieut. (new) 102nd Ft. 24 Sept. 1781 ; h.p. of Lieut. do. on disbandment 1783. Exchanged with Joseph Griffiths, *q.v.*, 28 Dec. 1784. Retransfd. to H.M.S. ; Ensign 76th Ft. 5 Nov. 1788.
Refs. : Westminster School List.

STAMFORD, William (1751/52-1786). Ensign, Infantry. *b.* Berwick-on-Tweed 1751/52. Cadet 1782. Ensign 9 Jan. 1783. *d.* Calcutta 24 Nov. 1786.
Brother of Thomas Stamford, of Berwick-on-Tweed, carpenter. *m.* (?)
Services : Held a Warrant as Qmr. Queen's Regt. of Dgns. 25 Dec. 1777. Sailed for India in the *Worcester* 6 Feb. 1782, aged 30. N.F.P.
Refs. : Will dated 23 Nov. 1786 ; proved 6 Jan. 1787.

STAMPER, Henry (1775-1805). Lieutenant, 5th N.I. *bapt.* Bolton, Cumberland, 12 Mar. 1775. Cadet 1795. Arrived in India 1 Feb. 1797. Ensign 18 Oct. 1796. Lieut. 30 Oct. 1797. *d.* Jagannath, B. & O., 15 Oct. 1805.
Son of Jacob Stamper, of Bolton Hall, and Bellah his wife. Brother of William Benson Stamper and of Capt. Richard Stamper, Bombay Est.
Services : Lieut. 5th N.I., d.d. Marine Bn. in 1802. (? Second Mahratta War 1804 ; reduction of Cuttack ; capture of Khurda ; Lieut. 2/5th N.I.)

STANDLEY, William (1792-?). Ensign. 9th N.I. *bapt.* Little Paxton, Hunts., 29 Jan. 1792. Cadet 1805. Arrived in

India 17 Mar. 1808. Ensign 28 Mar. 1808. Resigned 19 Sept. 1810.

Son of Henry Pointer Standley, of Paxton Place, nr. St. Neots, and Persis his wife. Ed. Charterhouse Jan.-June 1806.

Services : Barasat C.C. 1808-9. Posted Ensign to 2/9th N.I. Fur. 29 Apr. 1809 till resignation.

STANFORD, George (*d.* 1769). Fireworker, Artillery. (78) Cadet 1765. Fireworker 1766. *d.* Calcutta 18 Dec. 1769.

Services : Apptd. Conductor of Art. stores 1 Feb. 1765, when a Cadet. Lieut. F. 1st Coy. Art. Resigned his Commission 1 May 1766 during the " Batta mutiny " ; readmitted 19 Oct. 1766.

STANLEY, James (1790-1822). Lieutenant, Pension Est. 2nd N.I. *bapt.* Wallasey, co. Chester, 7 Feb. 1790. Cadet 1804. Arrived in India 11 July 1805. Ensign 19 Aug. 1805. Lieut. 20 Aug. 1805. Pensioned 1 Apr. 1812. *d.* Calcutta 20 Nov. 1822.

Son of Gerrard Stanley and Mary his wife. *m.* (?) (She died 2 Apr. 1817.) Ed. Merchant Taylors' Oct. 1802-Mar. 1804.

Services : Posted Lieut. to 2nd N.I. 1806. No record of active service.

Refs. : Robinson.

STANLEY, William (1788-1806). Cadet, Cavalry. *bapt.* Workington, Cumberland, 21 July 1788. Cadet 1805. Never arrived in India. *d.* Dec. 1806, on his passage to India, in the wreck of the *Skelton Castle.* Struck off with effect from 5 Nov. 1806. (See note to David Allan.)

Son of Edward Stanley and Julia his wife, dau. of John Christian, of Unerigg.

Refs. : Burke's *Landed Gentry,* 13th edn., p. 1652, *s.n.* Stanley, of Ponsonby Hall, Cumberland.

STANSBURY, Daniel (1815-1877). Major. 60th N.I. *b.* Bristol 15 July 1815. Cadet 1834. Arrived in India 21 July 1835. Ensign 12 Dec. 1834. Lieut. 13 Mar. 1837. Capt. 15 Nov. 1853. Retired 31 Dec. 1861. Hon. Major 31 Dec. 1861. *d.* at his residence, Woodfield Villa, Weston-super-Mare, 5 Nov. 1877, very suddenly, of heart disease.

bapt. St. James's, Bristol, 2 June 1816. Son of John Adolphus Stansbury, of 13 James's Pl., Bristol, and Elizabeth his wife. *m.* Cawnpore 30 Jan. 1851, Eliza Mary, eldest dau. of William Beckett, *q.v.* (*See also* Thomas Riddell.) (She died 27 Dec. 1851.) Addiscombe Cadet 1 Feb. 1833 till 12 Dec. 1834.

Services: d.d. 57th N.I. 8 Aug. 1835; posted to 60th N.I. 24 Sep. 1835. First Afghan War 1842; Lieut. 60th N.I., with Gen. Pollock's force (Medal). Adjt. 60th N.I. 3 Mar. 1848 till 16 Jan. 1854. Second Sikh War; Lieut. 60th N.I., with Reserve Div. Fur. p.a. 14 Dec. 1855 till 5 Nov. 1857, and 1860 till retirement. *Refs.:* The Times, 9 Nov. 1877.

STAPLES, John (1756/57-1794). Lieutenant, Infantry. *b.* Wilts. 1756/57. Cadet 1780. Arrived in India Mar. 1781. Ensign 1780. Lieut. 20 July 1781. *d.* at sea 19 Apr. 1794.

Services: Sailed for India in the *Rochford* 3 June 1780, aged 23. Lieut. 2nd Bn. Sepoys in July 1787. Transfd. from 5th Eur. Bn. to 11th Bn. Sepoys 26 Oct. 1793.

STAPLES, John (1816-1857). Captain, 7th L.C. *b.* Lissan, co. Londonderry, 14 Mar. 1816. Cadet 1831. Arrived in India 18 Oct. 1832. Cornet (5 June 1832) 18 Oct. 1832. Lieut. 23 Apr. 1839. Capt. 8 May 1849. *d.* Lucknow 10 June 1857: kld. in action against mutineers.

Eldest son of Rev. John Molesworth Staples, rector of Lissan and Upper Moville, and Annie his wife, eldest dau. of Nathaniel Alexander, D.D., bishop of Meath. Brother of Sir Nathaniel Alexander Staples, Bart., *q.v. m.* (?)

Services: Cadet d.d. 10th L.C. 26 Oct. 1832; do. 3rd L.C. 27 Dec. 1832. Leave s.c. to Hills 1 May till 1 Dec. 1835. Posted to 7th L.C. 9 June 1836. Fur. s.c. 11 June 1837 till 19 Nov. 1840. Second Sikh War; operations in Jullundur and Bari Doabs 1848-9; Bt. Capt. 7th L.C., with Bdr. Wheeler's force (Medal). Operations against the Afridis in Kohat Pass Feb. 1850; Capt. 7th L.C. Asst. Supt. Karnal Remount Depot Dec. 1850 till 1851.

Refs.: Burke's *Peerage*, 1923, p. 2083, *s.n.* Staples, Bart., of Lissan, co. Tyrone.

STAPLES, Sir Nathaniel Alexander, tenth baronet (1817-1899). Captain. Artillery. (664) *b.* Lissan 1 May 1817. Cadet 1834. Arrived in India 11 Feb. 1835. 2nd Lieut. (13 June 1834) 11 Feb. 1835. Lieut. 1 Mar. 1841. Capt. 21 July 1851. Resigned 3 Sept. 1853. *d.* at his residence, Lissan, Cookstown, co. Tyrone, 12 Mar. 1899.

10th Bart., of Lissan, J.P. and D.L. *s.* his uncle, Sir Thomas Staples, 9th Bart., Q.C., 14 May 1865. 2nd son of Rev. John Molesworth Staples and Annie his wife. Brother of John Staples, *q.v. m.* 22 Oct. 1844, Elizabeth Lindsay, only dau. of Capt. James Head, H.E.I.C.S., elder brother of Sir Francis Bond Head, 1st Bart.

(She died 1 Dec. 1907.)   Addiscombe Cadet 1 Aug. 1832 till 13 June 1834.
Services: Postmr. at Dacca 21 May 1838 till 2 Sept. 1839; d.d. Assam L.I. 5 Aug. 1839 till 29 Apr. 1840; actg. Intr. & Qmr. 6th Bn. Foot Art. 13 Apr. 1840; permanent do. 12 Mar. 1841 till 20 Jan. 1843. Fur. s.c. 12 Jan. 1843 till 25 Oct. 1845. Lieut. 9th Bn. Fur. s.c. 3 Mar. 1851 till resignation. No record of active service.
Refs.: Burke's *Peerage*, 1923, p. 2083, *s.n.* Staples, Bart., of Lissan, co. Tyrone. Boase. *The Times*, 13 Mar. 1899, p. 6. *I.L.N.*, 25 Mar. 1899, p. 413 (portrait).

STAPLETON, Samuel (1803-1827). Lieutenant, 52nd N.I. *b.* Eling, Hants, 14 July 1803. Cadet 1821. Ensign 2 Aug. 1822. Lieut. 1 May 1824. *d.* Chittagong 13 Sept. 1827, of a bilious fever.

bapt. Eling 18 Sept. 1803. Son of Samuel Stapleton and Mary Burnett his wife. Nephew of John Stapleton, of Thorpe Lee. *m.* Chittagong 29 Mar. 1826, Miss Barbara Kingston. (*See also* John Townsend Somerville.) (She died 27 May 1827, aged 27.)

Services: Posted to 15th N.I. 1822; transfd. to 26th N.I. July 1823; to 52nd N.I. (late 2/26th) May 1824. (? First Burma War; Cachar 1825; Lieut. 52nd N.I.) Was actg. Adjt. 52nd N.I. at death.

Refs.: *A.J.* xxv. 378.

STAPLETON, Hon. William (1797-1826). Lieutenant, 5th Extra N.I. *b.* London 5 Dec. 1797. Cadet 1818. Ensign 11 July 1819. Lieut. 4 July 1821. *d. unm.* Barrackpore 26 Sept. 1826.

bapt. Marylebone 11 Jan. 1798. 2nd son of Sir Thomas Stapleton, 6th Bart., Lord Le Despencer (in whose favour the abeyance of the Barony of Le Despencer terminated in 1788), and Elizabeth his wife, dau. of Samuel Eliot, of Antigua. Ed. Harrow 1812-13.

Services: Posted to 2/8th N.I. 1820; transfd. to 28th N.I. July 1823; to 55th N.I. (late 1/28th) May 1824; to newly-raised 5th Extra Regt. May 1825. Extra Asst. to Resdt. in Malwa and Rajputana 1824-5; extra A.D.C. to Lord Combermere, C.-in-C., Oct. 1825 till death. Siege and capture of Bhurtpore; Lieut. 5th Extra Regt., A.D.C.

Refs.: Burke's *Peerage*, 1923, p. 2085, *s.n.* Stapleton, Bart., of the Leeward Is. Oliver's *Hist. of Antigua*, iii. 102. *Harrow School Register*. *G.M.* 1827, i. 478.

STARK, Harry (1775-1830). Bt. Colonel, Artillery. (307) *b.* 1775. Cadet 1794. Fireworker 28 Sept. 1794. Lieut. 16 Feb.

1802. Capt. Lt. 21 Sept. 1804. Capt. 30 Sept. 1808. Major 1 Sept. 1818. Lt. Col. 1 May 1824. Bt. Col. 5 June 1829. *d. unm.* Cawnpore 26 Sept. 1830, aged 55.

Natural son of Harry Stark, of Teasses, nr. Cupar, Dy. Sheriff of Calcutta 1779. Nephew of the wife of Charles Russell Deare, *q.v.*, and cousin-german of Thomas Barron, Thomas Wilson (1779-1856), and the mother of James Hunter (1808-1867), *qq.v.*

Services : Apptd. Cadet 30 Apr. 1794 ; sailed for India in the *Rockingham* 2 May 1794. Capture of Ceylon 1795-6 ; Lieut. F. 5th Coy. 1st Bn. Foot Art. Served in Ceylon till 1799. Expedn. to Egypt 1801-2 ; Lieut. with Experimental Troop H.A. Second Mahratta War 1803-5 ; capture of Deig ; Bhurtpore ; Afzalgarh ; Lieut. 1st Troop H.A. Served with 1st Troop 1803-5 ; 2nd Troop 1809-18. Operations against Dhundia Khan 1807 ; Komona (w.) ; Ganauri ; Capt. Lt. & Adjt. 2nd Coy. 2nd Bn. Operations in Bundelkhand under Col. G. Martindell, *q.v.*, 1812 ; Baghelkhand under Lt.-Col. J. W. Adams, *q.v.*, 1813 ; Entauri. Third Mahratta War 1817-18 ; Major comdg. 2nd Troop H.A. Siege and capture of Bhurtpore ; Lt. Col. comdg. 2nd Bde. H.A. Transfd. to 1st Bde. 5 Oct. 1826.

Refs. : *Bengal Obit.*, p. 362. *A.J.* N.S. iv. 145. Will dated 18 May 1829 ; proved 8 Oct. 1830. M.I. at Cawnpore.

STARK, John. Lieutenant, Artillery. (162) Asst. Surg. 1 July 1774. Cadet (Art.) 1778. Fireworker 18 Sept. 1778. Lieut. 16 Sept. 1779. Struck off the list of Asst. Surgs. 3 Nov. 1780. *d.* Calcutta (?)

Services : Surg. Mate of *Morse* 1771-2 ; Surg. of *Mercury* 1773-4. Apptd. Art. Cadet 7 July 1778. First Mahratta War 1778-81 ; Lieut. Art., with detachment to Bombay under Col. Goddard. Was Lieut. in 7th Coy. Art. in May 1784 when granted leave s.c. to sea. Not in MS. *A.L.* of 1 July 1787.

Refs. : *Crawford*, i. 243. *Roll of I.M.S.*, No. B.201.

CROSS-STARKEY, Samuel (1807-1888). Major. 7th N.I. *b.* St. Pancras, London, 3 Mar. 1807. Cadet 1827. Ensign 13 Oct. 1827. Lieut. 1 Sept. 1833. Capt. 6 Nov. 1848. Retired 10 Apr. 1852. Hon. Major 28 Nov. 1854. *d.* Wrenbury Hall, co. Chester, 28 Mar. 1888.

Of Wrenbury Hall, J.P. *bapt.* St. Pancras 3 June 1809. 2nd son of John Cross (who assumed by R.L. 23 Sept. 1811, the surname and arms of Starkey) and Susan Warren his 1st wife. *m.* 1st, Cawnpore 2 Apr. 1839, Henrietta Suft, dau. of James Manson, *q.v.*

THE BENGAL ARMY, 1758-1834 171

(She died Simla 13 Aug. 1850, aged 30.) *m.* 2nd, Sephton, Lancs., 3 Nov. 1853, Eleanor, dau. of Charles Robert Simpson, of Waterloo, Liverpool. Lincoln's Inn; admitted 13 June 1825.

Services: Posted to 7th N.I. 9 May 1828; actg. Intr. & Qmr. do. 14 Mar. 1838; do. 10th N.I. 8 Mar. 1839; do. 45th N.I. 1843. Intr. & Qmr. 7th N.I. 16 Sept. 1843 till Dec. 1846. 2nd in comd. 3rd Regt. Inf., N.W.F. Bde. (became 3rd Regt. Sikh Inf.), 14 Dec. 1846; Comdt. do. 1 Apr. 1848 till 16 Dec. 1851.

Refs.: Burke's *Landed Gentry*, 13th edn., p. 1660, *s.n.* Starkey, of Wrenbury Hall, co. Chester. *Walford. The Times*, 31 Mar. 1888.

STARKIE, Nicholas. Cadet. Infantry. Cadet 1768. Resigned 1768.

Services: Sailed for India in the *Salisbury* 21 Mar. 1768. Resigned in India owing to ill health and returned to England; sought permission to return to India Oct. 1770.

(*N.B.*—One Nicholas Starkie became Lieut. H.M. 57th Ft. (in America) 28 Aug. 1775; Capt. 21st Ft. (in America) 18 Oct. 1778; Capt. h.p. 72nd Ft. (disbanded in 1783) in A.L. for 1803.)

Refs.: (? Burke's *Landed Gentry*, 13th edn., p. 1661, *s.n.* Starkie, of Huntroyde, Lancs. ? *Howard & Crisp* (*Notes*), vi. 189.)

STARLING, Parlett (1779-1854). Lieut. Colonel. 21st N.I. *bapt.* Wood Dalling, Norfolk, 16 Feb. 1779. Cadet 1799. Arrived in India 12 Jan. 1801. Ensign 31 Oct. 1800. Lieut. 19 May 1803. Capt. 19 May 1815. Major 11 July 1823. Lt. Col. 13 May 1825. Retired 4 June 1831. *d.* Norwich 16 Aug. 1854.

(*N.B.*—John Parlett Starling (living in 1781) was elder son of Matthew Starling, of Hellesdon, afterwards of Cawston, both in Norfolk, by Mary his wife.)

Services: Posted Ensign to 2/16th N.I. 17 Apr. 1801. Second Mahratta War 1803-4; Agra; Laswari; Gwalior; Lieut. 2/16th N.I. (India medal). Adjt. 2/16th N.I. 12 July 1804 till 1812. Capture of Gohad 1806. Reduction of Kalinjar 1812. Adjt. & Qmr. 16th N.I. 1812-14; Adjt. 1/16th N.I. till 4 May 1815. Capt. 1/16th N.I. Fur. s.c. 4 Feb. 1819 till 27 Dec. 1823. Transfd. to 32nd N.I. (late 1/16th) May 1824. Siege and capture of Bhurtpore (w.[1]); Lt. Col. 32nd N.I. (clasp to India medal). Transfd. to 21st N.I. 1828. Fur. p.a. 20 Sept. 1828 till 14 Aug. 1833, when he retired on pension of £1 *p.d.* with effect from 4 June 1831.

Refs.: (? Carthew's *Hundred of Launditch*, iii. 375.) *I.M.* 30 Aug. 1854, p. 498. *G.M.* 1854, ii. 410.

[1] *Note:* He was wounded in the leg by a stray shot after the action was supposed to be concluded.

STAUNTON, John (*d*. 1786). Ensign, Infantry. Cadet 1783. Ensign 12 Feb. 1785. *d*. Calcutta 24 Aug. 1786.

Brother of Philip Staunton, *q.v.*
Services : Was abroad at St. Helena when apptd. Cadet 10 Jan. 1783. Granted fur. on h.p. 24 July 1786.

STAUNTON, Philip (*d*. 1836). Lieutenant. Infantry. Country Cadet 1779. Ensign 26 Sept. 1779. Lieut. 4 May 1781. Pensd. on Lord Clive's fund Jan. 1789. *d*. Brighton 29 Nov. 1836.

Brother of John Staunton, *q.v. m.* Anne.
Services : Apptd. Cadet 19 Aug. 1779, from Dy. Paymr. Dy. Paymr. 3rd Bde. 23 Nov. 1778 till 1784. Fur. for 3 yrs. 10 Oct. 1785. (According to the Will of Edward Clayton, *q.v.*, whose residuary legatee he was, he was a Capt. in H.M.S. in 1799. The only one of this name traceable in H.M.S. appears to have been apptd. an addl. Paymr. to 2nd Bn. 17th Ft. *c.* 1805.)
Refs. : A.J. N.S. xxii. 68.

STAUNTON, Thomas (*d*. 1805). Captain, 2nd N.I. Country Cadet and Asst. Surg. Oct. 1781. Admitted Aug. 1781. Ensign 11 July 1782. Lieut. 8 Jan. 1785. Capt. 17 July 1801. *d*. Fatehgarh 21 Nov. 1805.

m. Catherine (before Jan. 1803).

Services : Was bred a surgeon and served as such with the Sepoy Corps of 1st and 3rd Bdes. Oct. 1781 till 1783, when he resigned the medical service. Was Lieut. in 8th Bn. Sepoys in May 1787, when he unsuccessfully applied to return to the Medical Dept. as Regtl. Mate to his Bn., and on 19 Nov. 1791, when he was apptd. A.D.C. to Col. C. Morgan, *q.v.* He was still holding this appt. in Jan. 1794. Returned from fur. 12 July 1798. Lieut. & Bt. Capt. 2nd N.I. ; Capt. Lt. do. 4 Sept. 1800. Operations in Jumna Doab 1803 ; Sasni ; Bijaigarh ; Kachaura ; Capt. 2nd N.I. Second Mahratta War 1803-4 ; Capt. 2nd N.I. Dy. Paymr. at Fatehgarh 27 Dec. 1804.
Refs. : Crawford, i. 229. *Roll of I.M.S.*, No. B.268.

STEDMAN, Robert Adrian (1789-1849). Lieut. Colonel, C.B., 1st L.C. *b.* Tiverton 3 Oct. 1789. Cadet 1808. Arrived in India 20 Oct. 1809. Cornet 3 Feb. 1813. Lieut. 1 Sept. 1818. Capt. 1 May 1824. Major 13 Apr. 1837. Lt. Col. 10 Mar. 1841. *d.* at sea 12 Apr. 1849, on board the *Haddington*, between Calcutta and Madras.

Of Ernieside, co. Kinross ; a Count of the Holy Roman Empire.

bapt. Protestant Dissenters' chapel, Tiverton, 29 Oct. 1789. 2nd son of John Gabriel Stedman,[1] Lt. Col. in Scots Bde., Dutch service, and Adriana Wiertz van Coehoorn his 2nd wife, grand-dau. of Baron Menno van Coehoorn, the famous mily. engr. *m.* Meerut 11 Oct. 1821, Miss Anne Hennessy. (She died 14 May 1875.)
Services: Barasat C.C. Cadet d.d. 25th N.I. 1811-13. Posted Cornet to 7th N.C. Feb. 1813. Nepal War 1814-15; Cornet 7th N.C., in 2nd Div. Leave s.c. 6 mos. to sea 5 July 1816. Third Mahratta War 1817-18; Dhamoni; Mandala; Multai; Harna; Lieut. 7th N.C. Intr. & Qmr. 7th L.C. 4 Dec. 1820 till 17 June 1824. Operations against the Bhils 1822-3. Shekhawat expedn. 1834; Capt. 7th L.C. Posted Lt. Col. to 7th L.C. 18 June 1841. With Army of Reserve (for Afghanistan) Oct. 1842 till Jan. 1843. Transfd. to 1st L.C. 20 Mar. 1844. First Sikh War; Aliwal; Lt. Col. 1st L.C. (Medal). Second Sikh War; Multan; Lt. Col. 1st L.C. (Medal). Fur. s.c. 1849. C.B. 27 June 1846.
Refs.: Family information. *Anderson,* iii. 508. M.I. in St. Paul's cathedral, Calcutta, and at Cawnpore.
[1] *Note:* For his services, see *G.M.* 1797, i. 435.

STEEL, Charles Edward (1811-1842). Lieutenant, 61st N.I. *b.* Apr. 1811. Cadet 1827. Arrived in India 8 Nov. 1828. Ensign 16 June 1828. Lieut. 13 Oct. 1834. *d.* Calcutta 7 Feb. 1842.
bapt. Lamesley, co. Durham, 3 Nov. 1811. 9th child of Edward Steel, of Gateshead, co. Durham, civil engr. and mine surveyor, and Isabella Rutter his wife.
Services: Ensign d.d. 42nd N.I. 14 Jan. 1829; posted to 57th N.I.; transfd. to 61st N.I. 29 June 1829. (? Shekhawat expedn. 1834; Lieut. 61st N.I.) Fur. s.c. 28 Feb. 1839 till 31 Dec. 1841.
Refs.: M.I. in Bhowanipore mily. cemetery, Calcutta.

STEEL, George Crawford (1781-1805). Lieutenant, 13th N.I. *bapt.* Tring, Herts., 22 Mar. 1781. Cadet 1796. Arrived in India 30 Sept. 1797. Ensign 3 Oct. 1797. Lieut. 10 Sept. 1798. *d.* in camp nr. Jhansi 1 Oct. 1805.
Son of Andrew Steel and Ann his wife.
Services: Lieut. 13th N.I. in 1798. Second Mahratta War; Bundelkhand 1803-4; Lieut. 1/13th N.I.

STEEL, James (1792-1859). Colonel, C.B., 67th N.I. *bapt.* Cockermouth, Cumberland, 30 July 1792. Cadet 1806. Arrived in India 17 Mar. 1808. Ensign (4 Sept. 1807) 29 Mar. 1808.

Lieut. 16 Mar. 1814. Capt. 15 Dec. 1824. Major 15 Aug. 1842. Lt. Col. 8 Mar. 1849. Col. 9 Oct. 1858. *d.* Brighton 18 Aug. 1859.

3rd and youngest son of Joseph Steel, of Cockermouth, and Dorothy his wife, dau. of John Ponsonby, of Haile, Cumberland. *m.* Fatehgarh 27 Nov. 1821, Adelaide Charlotte Christine, dau. of A. A. M. Tremamondo, *q.v.* (*See also* George Richard Pemberton.) (She died Dumfries 11 Oct. 1884, aged 80.) His dau. *m.* William MacGeorge, *q.v.*

Services: Barasat C.C. 7 mos. Ensign d.d. 15th N.I. 1809-11. Operations against the Garrows 1810 (w.). Posted to 21st N.I. 1811. Served in Java with (7th) L.I. Vol. Bn. as Intr. & Qmr. 1812 till 1 Nov. 1816. Lieut. 1/21st N.I. With 2/21st N.I. in Oudh 1817. Adjt. Muttra Levy 1819-23. Intr. & Qmr. 2/21st N.I. 1 Oct. 1823 till 20 July 1824. Transfd. to 41st N.I. (late 1/21st) May 1824. Adjt. 1st L.I. Bn. 14 Sept. 1824 till 8 June 1825. First Burma War; Arakan 1825; Capt. L.I. Bn. (India medal). Offg. D.J.A.G. Dinapore and Benares Divs. 26 May 1825. Siege and capture of Bhurtpore; Capt. 41st N.I. (clasp to India medal). D.J.A.G. on Est., Dinapore and Benares, 2 Dec. 1826; Supt. of Police in Calcutta 20 Dec. 1830 till 1835. Fur. s.c. 17 June 1836 till 26 Jan. 1839. Tempy. comdg. Ramgarh L.I. Bn. 8 Apr. 1839. Transfd. to newly-raised 2nd Eur. Regt. Oct. 1839. Fur. p.a. 10 Mar. 1840 till 6 Nov. 1842. Apptd. Insp. new Police Bn. 29 May 1844; Supt. Cantt. Police N.W.P. 30 June 1847 till June 1857. Rejoined his Regt. for service 4 Oct. 1848. Second Sikh War; Ramnagar; passage of Chenab; Chilianwala; Gujerat; pursuit of Sikhs; Major comdg. 2nd Bengal Eur. Regt. (Medal with 2 clasps). Posted Lt. Col. to 2nd Eur. Bengal Fus. 1849; to 71st N.I. 19 Apr. 1854; to 4th N.I. Nov. 1855. Bdr. on Est. comdg. Benares 17 July 1857; do. Ambala 15 Dec. 1857 till 1859. Col. 67th N.I. 24 July 1858 till death. Fur. 1859. C.B. 9 June 1849.

Refs.: Burke's *Landed Gentry*, 4th edn., p. 1427, *s.n.* Steel, of Derwent Bank, Cumberland. *Boase. G.M.* 1859, ii. 430. *The Times*, 23 Aug. 1859. M.I. Christ Church, Mussoorie.

STEELE, Charles (1801-1828). Ensign, 26th N.I. *b.* Forfar 7 Dec. 1801. Cadet 1825. Ensign 21 June 1826. *d.* Cawnpore 8 June 1828.

bapt. Forfar 13 Dec. 1801. Son of John Steele, of Forfar, merchant, and Catherine Gray his wife. Ed. Montrose Grammar School and Dundee Acad.

Services: Ensign 2nd Regt. Surrey Mil. 7 May 1825. Ensign d.d.

40th N.I. 9 Nov. 1826; posted to 26th N.I. 8 Jan. 1827. No record of active service.

STEELL, George (1781-1840). Captain. Engineers. *b.* Tokenhouse Yard, St. Margaret, Lothbury, London, 20 Aug. 1781. Cadet 1795. Arrived in India 31 Jan. 1798. Ensign 28 May 1798. Lieut. 6 Oct. 1803. Capt. 4 Oct. 1808. Resigned 6 May 1817. *d.* London 18 May 1840; *bur.* St. Mary's churchyard, Lambeth.

Son of Robert Steell and Mary his wife, dau. of Gilbert Man. *m.* Ann. (She died 11 Apr. 1880, aged 70; *bur.* Tooting cemetery.)
Services: Campaign in Egypt 1801; Ensign Engrs., attached to Sir D. Baird's staff. Served in Cuttack 1805-7; at Agra 1807-13. Operations against Dhundia Khan 1807; Komona; Ganauri; Lieut. Engrs. Fur. 25 July 1813 till resignation.
Refs.: A.J. N.S. xxxii. 186. *I.N.* No. 1, p. 22. *N. & Q.* 11S. xii. 397.

STEER, Sulivan Harington (1817-?). Captain. 56th N.I. *b.* 4 Nov. 1817. Cadet 1833. Arrived in India 4 Nov. 1834. Ensign (14 June 1834) 13 Oct. 1834. Lieut. 3 Oct. 1840. Capt. 4 July 1845. Cashiered 27 Jan. 1849.

bapt. Calcutta 23 Nov. 1817. Son of Charles William Steer, B.C.S., Collector of Bhagulpur, and Jane Woodburn his wife, dau. of Samuel Watson (1748/49-1814), *q.v.* Brother of William Watson Steer, cousin-german of James John M'Clary Morgan, and nephew of William Frederick Steer, *qq.v. m.* Mullye, B. & O., 27 Nov. 1841, Sarah Jane, dau. of William John Baldwin, of Tirhut.
Services: d.d. 56th N.I. 10 Nov. 1834; posted to 5th N.I. 2 Mar. 1835; transfd. to 56th N.I. 31 Mar. 1835. Fur. s.c. 19 Jan. 1843 till 1845. No record of active service.
Refs.: Hunter's *Familiæ Minorum Gentium* (Harl. Soc. xxxviii), ii. 819.

STEER, William Frederick (1789-1871). Lieut. Colonel. 32nd N.I. *b.* Middlesex 19 Aug. 1789. Cadet 1809. Arrived in India 3 Oct. 1810. Ensign 6 Sept. 1811. Lieut. 13 Aug. 1815. Capt. 13 May 1825. Bt. Major 28 June 1838. Retired 28 Oct. 1839. Hon. Lt. Col. 28 Nov. 1854. *d.* Marazion, Cornwall, 12 June 1871.

bapt. Christ Church, Middlesex, 5 Dec. 1789. Son of Charles Steer, of Church St., London, merchant, and Mary Wood his wife, of Jamaica. Brother of the wives of 5th Earl of Albemarle and Sir James Harington, 9th Bart., and uncle of William Watson Steer, *q.v. m.* Cawnpore 3 Jan. 1825, Lucy, widow of Cosmo Macdonald, *q.v. Ed.* Charterhouse Jan. 1803-Dec. 1805.

Services : Having attained age of 21, was exempted from going to Barasat C.C. d.d. 2/14th N.I. 9 Oct. 1810 ; posted Ensign to 2/16th N.I. 1811. Reduction of Kalinjar 1812 ; Ensign 2/16th N.I. Nepal War 1814-15 ; Ensign Light Coy. 2/16th N.I., with 2nd Div. (India medal). Actg. Intr. & Qmr. 2/16th N.I. 20 Dec. 1820 ; permanent do. 1 Jan. 1822. Transfd. to 32nd N.I. (late 1/16th) May 1824 ; Adjt. do. 17 June 1824 till 23 Aug. 1825. Siege and capture of Bhurtpore ; Capt. 32nd N.I. (clasp to India medal). Shekhawat expedn. 1834 ; Capt. 32nd N.I. Fur. s.c. 7 Jan. 1836 till 19 Dec. 1838.

Refs. : Hunter's *Familiæ Minorum Gentium*, ii. 819. *Charterhouse School List. The Times,* 14 June 1871.

STEER, William Watson (1813-1842). Lieutenant, 37th N.I. *b.* Ghazipur 19 June 1813. Cadet 1829. Arrived in India 1 May 1830. Ensign (11 Dec. 1829) 23 Mar. 1830. Lieut. 27 Oct. 1838. *d.* Jagdalak Pass 12 Jan. 1842 : kld. in action during the retreat from Kabul.

bapt. Monghyr 31 Oct. 1813. Son of Charles William Steer, B.C.S., and Jane Woodburn his wife. Brother of Sulivan Harington Steer, *q.v.* Addiscombe Cadet 1828-9.

Services : d.d. 63rd N.I. 10 May 1830 ; do. 72nd N.I. 17 Dec. 1831 ; Actg. Ensign 16 July 1832 ; posted to 25th N.I. 20 Aug. 1833 ; transfd. to 37th N.I. 11 Oct. 1833. Leave s.c. to Simla 20 Jan. 1835 till 29 Jan. 1836. First Afghan War 1838-42 ; Ghazni 1839 (Medal) ; action in Khyber Pass 22 Nov. 1839 ; actg. Adjt. Left Wing 37th N.I. 8 Apr. 1840 ; outbreak at Kabul ; comdd. a Coy. 37th N.I. in storm and capture of Kila-i-Muhammad Sharif, nr. Kabul, 6 Nov. 1841 ; retreat from Kabul (kld.) ; Lieut. 37th N.I.

Refs. : Hunter's *Familiæ Minorum Gentium*, ii. 819. *M.I.* in Afghan Memorial Church, Bombay.

STEIN, Robert (1807-1850). Captain, 49th N.I. *b.* London 15 Jan. 1807. Cadet 1827. Arrived in India 10 Jan. 1829. Ensign 19 July 1828. Lieut. 26 Apr. 1833. Capt. 13 Apr. 1848. *d.* Phillaur, Punjab, 10 June 1850.

bapt. St. Giles-in-the-Fields 22 Feb. 1807. Son of James Stein, of Fenchurch St., London, merchant, and Wilhelmina Bushby his wife. *m.* Cawnpore 29 Mar. 1841, Elizabeth, youngest dau. of Henry Hopper. (*See also* A. N. M. MacGregor.)

Services : Ensign d.d. 49th N.I. 11 Feb. 1829 ; posted to 49th

THE BENGAL ARMY, 1758-1834

N.I. June 1829, and served throughout with that Regt. Demonstration against Jodhpur 1839 ; Lieut. 49th N.I., with Marwar F.F. Adjt. 49th N.I. 29 Aug. 1845 till July 1848. Second Sikh War ; both sieges of Multan ; action of Suraj-khund 7 Nov. 1848 ; Capt. 49th N.I. (Medal with clasp).
Refs.: De Rhé-Philipe. M.I. at Phillaur.

*STENYER, ——. Lieutenant. Infantry. Lieut. 14 May 1758.
Services: N.F.P. Not in List of 1760.
Refs.: Orme MSS.—India, xiii. 3639.

STEPHEN, Henry Virtue (1811-1858). Major. 19th N.I. *b.* Chelsea 1 Jan. 1811. Cadet 1827. Arrived in India 12 Nov. 1828. Ensign 27 June 1828. Lieut. 18 June 1835. Capt. 9 Aug. 1843. Retired 30 Apr. 1851. Hon. Major 28 Nov. 1854. *d.* 12 The Grove, Clapham Common, 21 May 1858.
bapt. Chelsea 23 Apr. 1811. Son of John Stephen, chief clerk to Messrs. Greenwood, Cox & Co., Chelsea, and Harriet his wife. Brother of James Stephen, *q.v.*
Services: Ensign d.d. 19th N.I. 14 Jan. 1829; posted to do. 3 June 1829. Apptd. tempy. to Revenue Survey at Allahabad Nov. 1834. (? Rising in Cuttack July 1836 ; Lieut. 19th N.I.) Apptd. to Revenue Survey Dept. 25 Nov. 1837 ; Field Surveyor do. 9 Aug. 1841. Served with his Regt. at Sukkur, Sind, Apr. 1842 till Mar. 1843, when he rejoined Survey Dept. Fur. 17 Mar. 1844 till 1846. Surveyor, N.W.F., 10 Oct. 1846 till Feb. 1851. Author of " Handbook to the Maps of India," London, 1856.
Refs.: G.M. 1858, ii. 91. *The Times*, 25 May 1858.

STEPHEN, James (1806-1833). Captain, 19th N.I. *b.* Chelsea 27 Apr. 1806. Cadet 1821. Arrived in India 21 Dec. 1822. Ensign 29 Oct. 1822. Lieut. 13 May 1825. Capt. 18 July 1831. *d.* Landaur, U.P., 3 Sept. 1833, of fever.
bapt. St. Luke's, Chelsea, 24 Sept. 1809. Son of John Stephen and Harriet his wife. Brother of James William Virtue Stephen, *q.v.*
Services: Posted to 5th N.I. 1823 ; transfd. to 11th N.I. (late 1/5th) May 1824 ; to 19th N.I. 1825 ; Intr. & Qmr. do. 27 Nov. 1826 till 19 Aug. 1830 ; offg. do. 25 Apr. 1831. Leave s.c. to Mussoorie 22 Feb. 1832 till death. No record of active service.
Refs.: A.J. N.S. xiii. 123.

STEPHEN, James William Virtue (1804-1847). Captain, 41st N.I. *b.* Chelsea 26 Oct. 1804. Cadet 1822. Arrived in

India 22 Aug. 1823. Ensign 11 July 1823. Lieut. 15 Dec. 1824. Capt. 28 Feb. 1840. d. Kangra 28 Dec. 1847.
bapt. St. Luke's, Chelsea, 27 Dec. 1804. Son of John Stephen and Harriet his wife. Brother of Henry Virtue Stephen, *q.v.*
Services : Posted to 21st N.I. ; transfd. to 41st N.I. (late 1/21st) May 1824. Adjt. Saharanpur Provl. Bn. 29 July 1825. Siege and capture of Bhurtpore ; Lieut. 41st N.I. Actg. Intr. & Qmr. 19th N.I. 15 Sept. 1834 ; do. 43rd N.I. 29 July 1835 ; do. 41st N.I. 28 Aug. 1835 ; permanent do. 11 Jan. 1836 till 23 July 1840. First Sikh War ; Sobraon ; Capt. 41st N.I. (Medal). Comdt. newly-raised 2nd Hill Regt. of Inf., N.W.F. Bde. (now 2/12th F.F. Regt.), 14 Dec. 1846 till death.
Refs.: *I.N.* 6 Mar. 1848, p. 102.

STEPHEN, William George (1792-1823). Captain, Engineers. *bapt.* St. Augustine, Bristol, 17 July 1792. Cadet 1807. Arrived in India 21 Mar. 1809. Ensign 25 Mar. 1809. Lieut. 10 Dec. 1814. Capt. 1 Sept. 1818. *d.* Puri, B. & O., 10 May 1823.
Only son of William Stephen, M.D., of the W.I., and Mary Forbes his wife. Uncle of Major W. S. R. Hodson (*D.N.B.*). *m.* Calcutta 26 Aug. 1817, Esther, dau. of Rev. Thomas Truebody Thomason, of Calcutta, senior chaplain, and sister of James Thomason, Lt. Govr. of N.W.P. (*D.N.B.*). (*See also* George Hutchinson (1793-1852).) (She died Westbury-on-Trym 4 June 1880, aged 80.) Woolwich Cadet ; nominated 13 Aug. 1806.
Services : Served in Cuttack 1810-11 ; at Benares 1812-14. Nepal War ; operations in Kumaon 1815 ; Asst. Field Engr. Apptd. Surveyor N. district of Benares 10 May 1817 ; at Ghazipur 1817 ; Garr. Engr. and Executive Ofr. at Allahabad ; suptg. construction of lighthouse on Palmyras Point, Cuttack, 1822 till death.
Refs.: Burke's *Colonial Gentry*, i. 42, *s.n.* Stephen, of Sydney. Family information. Will dated Calcutta 26 Aug. 1817 ; proved 19 June 1823. M.I. at Puri.

*STEPHENS, Alexander. Cadet. Infantry. Cadet 1779. Declined going out.
Services : Apptd. Cadet 31 Mar. 1779 ; under orders to embark in the *Duke of Kingston* which sailed 17 Nov. 1779.

STEPHENSON or STEVENSON,[1] **James** (1744/45-1797). Lieutenant, Invalid Est. Infantry. *b.* 1744/45. Cadet 1769. Ensign 7 Nov. 1771. Lieut. 22 July 1776. Invalided 21 Aug. 1778. *d.* Chunar 18 Oct. 1797, aged 52.
Services : N.F.P.

Refs.: M.I. in old cemetery nr. Chunar fort.
[1] *Note:* Stephenson in MS. *A.L.* of the period and in the official casualty list; Stevenson on M.I., where date of death is given as 14 Sept. 1797. He was *bur.* in the same tomb as Anthony Hartle, *q.v.,* who died ten days later. *D.&M.* incorrectly gives two separate individuals, James Stevenson and Thomas Stephenson: they are in reality one and the same person.

*STEUART, Archibald (1774-1823). Cadet. Infantry. Subsequently Maj. Gen. H.M.S. *b.* Edinburgh 28 June 1774. Cadet 1791. Resigned in India 14 Dec. 1791. *d. unm. v.p.* 18 Apr. 1823.

Eldest son of David Steuart, of Steuart Hall, nr. Stirling, W.S., and Margaret his wife, dau. of Robert Ramsay, of Camno and Arthurstone, co. Fife.

Services: Apptd. Cadet 23 Feb. 1791; sailed for India in the *Phœnix* 4 Apr. 1791. Ensign 14th Ft. 1791; do. 18th Ft. 1793; Lieut. do. 1794; Capt. Scots Bde. 5 Oct. 1795; Major 1st Ft. 16 July 1800; Lt. Col. do. 25 Mar. 1802; Col. 4 June 1811; Maj. Gen. 4 June 1814.

Refs.: Burke's *Peerage,* 1923, p. 2091, *s.n.* Shaw-Stewart, Bart. *R. Mily. Calendar,* iii. 338.

*STEUART, Robert (1806-1876). Major. 20th N.I. *b.* Logierait, co. Perth, 7 Jan. 1806. Cadet 1824. Arrived in India 6 May 1825. Ensign 8 Jan. 1825. Lieut. 4 Sept. 1825. Capt. 23 July 1837. Retired 25 Mar. 1850. Hon. Major 28 Nov. 1854. *d. unm.* Ballechin House, co. Perth, 8 Apr. 1876.

Of Ballechin House, J.P. *bapt.* Logierait 4 Feb. 1806. Eldest son of Hope Steuart, of Ballechin, J.P. and D.L. co. Perth, Lt. Col. comdg. R. Athole Vols., and Louisa his wife, 2nd dau. of James Morley, of Kempshott Park, Hants, Bo.C.S., and cousin-german of Abraham Stoneham, *q.v.*

Services: Ensign d.d. 68th N.I. 23 May 1825; posted to 20th N.I. 1825; actg. Adjt. do. 14 Nov. 1829. Fur. p.a. 1 Aug. 1845 till 1846. Second Sikh War; passage of Chenab; Chilianwala; Gujerat; Capt. 20th N.I. (Medal with 2 clasps).

Refs.: Burke's *Landed Gentry,* 13th edn., p. 1667, *s.n.* Steuart, of Ballechin, co. Perth. *Walford. The Times,* 20 Apr. 1876.

STEUART, Thomas David (1782-1836). Bt. Colonel, 1st L.C. *b.* Edinburgh 3 Aug. 1782. Cadet 1798. Arrived in India 14 Dec. 1799. Cornet 15 June 1800. Lieut. 11 Mar. 1805.

Capt. 1 Sept. 1818. Major 13 May 1825. Lt. Col. 3 May 1829.
Bt. Col. 22 Jan. 1834. d. Nimach 10 Oct. 1836.

bapt. St. Giles's, Edinburgh, 20 Aug. 1782. 3rd son of David
Steuart, of Edinburgh, merchant and banker, lord provost 1778,
and Anne his wife, dau. of Robert Fordyce, of Broadford. m.
Glasgow 1 Sept. 1823, Mary, eldest dau. of George Pinkerton.

Services: Second Mahratta War 1803-5; battle of Delhi;
Laswari; battle of Deig; Cornet 1st N.C. Capt. Lt. 1st N.C.
18 Aug. 1814. Nepal War 1814; Capt. Lt. 1st N.C., in 1st Div.
Third Mahratta War; Persian Intr. to Maj.-Gen. Rufane Shaw
Donkin, H.M.S., comdg. Rt. Div. Apptd. actg. Asst. under Sir
John Malcolm 9 Oct. 1820. Actg. A.A.G. 15 Feb. 1821. Fur. p.a.
2 Dec. 1821 till 1825. To comd. newly-raised 2nd Extra Regt.
(became 10th L.C.) 17 June 1825. Siege and capture of Bhurtpore;
Major comdg. 2nd Extra Regt. Transfd. to 1st L.C. 24 Nov. 1834.
To comd. Meywar F.F. tempy. Mar. 1836.

Refs.: Burke's *Landed Gentry*, 10th edn., p. 1497, s.n. Durrant-
Steuart, of Dalguise, co. Perth. *Bengal Obit.*, p. 396. Will dated
13 Feb. 1832; proved 7 Aug. 1837. M.I. at Nimach.

STEUART, William (1762/63-1795). (*See* **STEWART, William.**)

STEVENS, Alexander (d. 1770). Cadet, Infantry. Cadet
1769. d. Burdwan 18 Dec. 1770.
Services: N.F.P.

STEVENS, James (1801-1868). Major, Invalid Est. 6th N.I.
b. London 31 Jan. 1801. Cadet 1818. Admitted 11 Sept. 1819.
Ensign 20 May 1819. Lieut. 28 June 1821. Capt. 18 July 1831.
Major 6 Apr. 1850. Invalided 31 Dec. 1850. d. Mussoorie
4 July 1868.

bapt. St. Olave's, Jewry, 2 Dec. 1805. Of Bitchett House, Seal,
Kent. Son of William Stevens, of 6 Frederick Pl., Old Jewry,
surveyor, and Lucy his wife.

Services: Posted Ensign to 1/3rd N.I.; transfd. to 6th N.I.
(late 1/3rd) May 1824. Siege and capture of Bhurtpore; Lieut.
6th N.I. (India medal). Actg. Intr. & Qmr. 6th N.I. 15 June 1826,
and 21 Aug. 1827. Fur. s.c. 3 Jan. 1837 till 20 Jan. 1840. First
Afghan War 1842; Capt. 6th N.I., with Pollock's force (Medal).
Fur. s.c. 16 Feb. 1844 till 1846.

STEVENSON, Sir Robert (d. 1839). Major General, K.C.B.,
comdg. Cawnpore Div. Colonel 1st N.I. Cadet 1783. Arrived

in India 20 Sept. 1783. Ensign 7 Apr. 1785. Lieut. 7 Oct. 1793. Capt. 21 Sept. 1804. Major 23 Sept. 1810. Lt. Col. 14 June 1815. Lt. Col. Comdt. 1 May 1824. Col. 5 June 1829. Maj. Gen. 10 Jan. 1837. d. at sea 30 July 1839, on board the *Moira*, on the voyage home.

An Anglo-Indian.[1]

Services: Apptd. Cadet 14 Jan. 1783; sailed for India in the *Barwell* 11 Mar. 1783. Posted to 2nd Bengal Eur. Bn. 15 Feb. 1790; from 4th to 3rd do. 26 Jan. 1792; to 6th do. 18 Aug. 1794. Adjt. 2/12th N.I. 1799-1804. Capt. Lt. 12th N.I. 15 Jan. 1804. Operations in Jumna Doab 1803; Bijaigarh. Second Mahratta War 1803-6; Aligarh; Agra; battle of Delhi (comdg. 2/12th); Laswari (comdg. 1/12th); Bhurtpore. Bde. Major to Reserve of Grand Army 1805-6. To comd. escort of Resdt. at Delhi 30 Jan. 1806. Bde. Major at Fatehgarh 19 Feb. till June 1807. Agent for purchase of cavalry horses. A.C.G. 1 Feb. 1810; do. 2nd Div. for Nepal 15 Nov. 1814. Nepal War 1814-15; Kalanga; Jaithak. Posted Lt. Col. to 2/12th N.I. 1815. Dy. Comy. Gen. 4 Oct. 1816. Siege and capture of Hathras 1817; Dy. Comy. Gen. (*Lond. Gaz.* 12 Oct. 1818). Third Mahratta War 1817-18; Dy. Comy. Gen. Transfd. to 2/29th N.I. 1816; to 27th N.I. 1818; to 2/18th 1819. Offg. Q.M.G. of the Army 18 Nov. 1820; M.M.B. 18 Jan. 1821; Q.M.G. 2 July 1821 till 29 Nov. 1833. Transfd. as Lt. Col. Comdt. to 1st N.I. (late 2/12th) May 1824. Siege and capture of Bhurtpore; Q.M.G. (*Lond. Gaz.* 7 Oct. 1826). Posted Col. to 1st N.I. 1829. To Gen. Staff of Army with rank of Bdr. Gen. 7 Nov. 1833. Comdd. Cawnpore Div. 7 Nov. 1833 till 7 Nov. 1838. Demonstration against Jodhpur and Shekhawat expedn. 1834; comdg. the force. Fur. s.c. 17 May 1839 till death. C.B. 2 Jan. 1827; K.C.B. 10 Mar. 1837.

Refs.: *A.J.* N.S. xxx. 263, 292.

[1] *Note:* See the evidence of Mr. J. W. Ricketts before the House of Lords, 31 Mar. 1830.

STEVENSON, Thomas. (*See* **STEPHENSON or STEVENSON, James.**)

STEWARD, Robert (1811-1855). Bt. Major, 16th N.I. *b.* 19 Aug. 1811. Cadet 1827. Arrived in India 10 Feb. 1829. Ensign 31 July 1829. Lieut. 4 June 1834. Capt. 23 Dec. 1845. Bt. Major 20 June 1854. *d.* Mian Mir 11 June 1855, of fever.

bapt. Birmingham 9 Oct. 1813. Son of Samuel Edward Steward, of Myton House, nr. Warwick, late Lt. Col. Warwick Mil., and Catherine his wife. Addiscombe Cadet 1826-8.

Services : d.d. 44th N.I. Mar. 1829 ; posted to 16th N.I. 31 July 1829. First Afghan War 1839-42 ; capture of Ghazni 1839 (Medal) ; against Ghilzais 1839-41 ; operations around Kandahar 1842 ; Goaine ; recapture of Ghazni ; reoccupation of Kabul ; Lieut. 16th N.I., with Nott's force (Medal). Campaign in Sind 1843 ; battle of Hyderabad ; attached to army under Sir Charles Napier (*Lond. Gaz.* 4 Aug. 1843) (Medal). Fur. from Bombay 26 May 1843 till Dec. 1846. With force assembled nr. Titalia, Bengal, 1849-50, for service against Rajah of Sikkim.

Refs. : De Rhé-Philipe. *G.M.* 1855, ii. 440. M.I. in R.A. cemetery, Lahore.

STEWART, Alexander (1778-1835). Colonel, 58th N.I. *b.* Balquhidder, co. Perth, 27 Dec. 1778. Cadet 1798. Arrived in India 6 Sept. 1799. Ensign 29 Nov. 1799. Lieut. 29 May 1800. Capt. 25 Aug. 1811. Major 27 May 1820. Lt. Col. 1 May 1824. Col. 3 Nov. 1831. *d.* in U.K. 23 June 1835.

V of Strathgarry, co. Perth. *bapt.* 6 Jan. 1779. Eldest son of Rev. Duncan Stewart, IV of Strathgarry, minister at Balquhidder, and Arabella his wife, dau. of Duncan Campbell, of Auchline. Brother of Robert Stewart (1787-1867), *q.v.*, and of Louisa, mother of Robert Duncan Kay, *q.v. m.* 1st (before 1810), Sarah Harriet, dau. of Rev. P. Dart, curate of St. James's, Bath, later of Dover. (She died Benares 4 Feb. 1813.) *m.* 2nd, Portobello 20 Apr. 1830, Janetta, 5th dau. of Ralph Allen Daniell, of Trelissick, Cornwall, high sheriff 1795, and sister of Capt. Sir William Daniell, Kt., R.N. (She died London 26 Feb. 1885, aged 80.) St. Andrews Univ. ; matric. 21 Feb. 1793.

Services : Lieut. 3rd (or Strathern Highrs.) Regt. of Perthshire Bde. 14 Aug. 1799. Posted to 1/1st N.I. 15 Apr. 1801. Operations in Bundelkhand 1804-6 ; Lieut. 1/1st N.I. Fur. s.c. 10 July 1806 till 9 Oct. 1810. Capt. Lt. 1st N.I. 1 July 1810. Translator to Resdt. at Delhi 30 Oct. 1810. Nepal War 1814-15 ; Capt. 2/1st N.I., in 1st Div. Siege and capture of Hathras 1817 ; Capt. 2/1st N.I. Third Mahratta War 1817-18 ; Dhamoni ; actg. Bde. Major 5th Bde., with Bdr. Watson's Div., 1818 ; Capt. 2/1st N.I. (*Lond. Gaz.* 7 Dec. 1818). Posted Lt. Col. to 4th N.I. (late 2/1st) May 1824. Fur. s.c. 15 Jan. 1829 till death. Transfd. to 70th N.I. 7 Sept. 1829 ; to 59th N.I. 1 Mar. 1831. Col. 58th N.I. 21 Nov. 1831 till death.

Refs. : Stewarts of Appin, p. 180. Burke's *Landed Gentry,* 2nd edn., p. 305, *s.n.* Daniell, of Trelissick, Cornwall. Scott's *Fasti,* iv. 338. *A.J.* N.S. xvii. 279.

THE BENGAL ARMY, 1758-1834

STEWART, Alexander (1785-1826). Captain, 28th N.I. *b.* Appin, Lorne, 3 Aug. 1785. Cadet 1804. Arrived in India 21 June 1806. Ensign 5 Oct. 1805. Lieut. 14 Nov. 1805. Capt. 11 July 1823. *d.* Calcutta 28 Aug. 1826.

Son of Alexander Stewart, Appin, and Margaret his wife. Brother of Allan Stewart, Capt. R.N., Charles Stewart, Capt. H.M.S., and Jane, wife of John Campbell, Capt. H.M.S. *m.* C.G.H. 17 Apr. 1819, Miss Johanna Anna Kohstein. (She died Douglas, I. of Man, 13 July 1852.)

Services: Posted Lieut. to 14th N.I. Capture of Java 1811; Lieut. 5th Vol. Bn. Expedn. to Palembang 1812; Lieut. 5th Vol. Bn. Adjt. 5th Vol. Bn. 1 Mar. 1814 till 1816. Lieut. 2/14th N.I. Leave to Cape 1819. Transfd. to 28th N.I. (late 2/14th) May 1824. Fur. s.c. 25 Aug. 1826.

Refs.: Will dated Calcutta 26 Aug. 1826; proved 1 Sept. 1826. M.I. S. Park St. cemetery, Calcutta.

STEWART, Alister (1804-1846). Captain, 1st Bengal Eur. L.I. *b.* Kinneff, co. Kincardine, 23 Feb. 1804. Cadet 1823. Arrived in India 7 June 1824. Ensign 21 Feb. 1824. Lieut. 13 May 1825. Capt. 5 Mar. 1838. *d.* at sea 31 Mar. 1846, on board the *Queen.*

10th son of Rev. Patrick Stewart, minister of Kinneff, and Christian Leslie his wife. *m.* Allahabad 17 May 1838, Harriette, 2nd dau. of George Hamilton, of Hamilton Lodge, Staffs., Lieut. 16th Lancers. (*See also* William Stuart-Menteth.) (She *re-m.* 23 Aug. 1848, Lieut. (afterwards Lt.-Gen.) John Douglas Campbell, Bengal Engrs.) Ed. Aberdeen Univ.

Services: Ensign d.d. 2nd Bengal Eur. Regt. 26 June 1824; posted to do. Aug. 1824. Served with his Regt. at Cheduba I., off coast of Arakan, 1825-6, during First Burma War. Posted to Bengal Eur. Regt. Oct. 1829, on amalgamation of 1st and 2nd Eur. Regts. Fur. 23 Jan. 1835 till 15 Dec. 1837. First Afghan War 1838-9; Ghazni (Medal); returned sick to India Sept. 1839; Capt. Bengal Eur. Regt. Comdd. depot of his Regt. at Agra 9 Dec. 1839 till 1841. With Army of Reserve (for Afghanistan) Oct. 1842 till Jan. 1843. Fur. s.c. Feb. 1846 till death.

Refs.: Scott's *Fasti*, v. 474. *The House of Hamilton*, p. 997. De Rhé-Philipe. *Patrician*, i. 398. M.I. at Sabathu.

STEWART, Andrew (*d.* 1780). Lieutenant, 35th Bn. Sepoys. Cadet 1771. Ensign 22 Feb. 1773. Lieut. 17 Mar. 1778. *d.* 1780.

Services: Apptd. Adjt. 35th Bn. Sepoys 22 Mar. 1780.

STEWART, Archibald (*d.* 1772). Capt. Lieutenant, Artillery. (40) Cadet 1762. Fireworker 19 July 1763. 2nd Lieut. 5 Oct. 1763. Lieut. 13 Mar. 1765. Capt. Lt. 31 Mar. 1767. *d.* Monghyr 12 Aug. 1772.

Services: Apptd. Adjt. of Art. 3 Jan. 1765. Resigned his Commission during the " Batta mutiny " 14 May 1766 ; readmitted 1 Aug. 1766.

***STEWART, Archibald** (1774-1823). (*See* ***STEUART, Archibald.**)

STEWART, Archibald Henry (1790-?). Ensign. 18th N.I. *b.* Lancs. 1790.[1] Cadet 1807. Arrived in India 16 Nov. 1808. Ensign 21 Nov. 1808. Suspended 10 Apr. 1809. Restored by C.D. 20 Aug. 1811, but former rank cancelled. Dismissed by G.C.M. 29 Nov. 1813. (? Living in Dec. 1861.)

" Under the patronage of Sir Sidney Smith's family." (? *m.* Ann Catherock, who died 15 Dec. 1861, aged 69.[2])

Services : Served in the Mil. at home. Suspended for irregularities committed whilst an Ensign at Barasat C.C. Posted Ensign to 18th N.I. (? Afterwards served in H.M. 59th Regt.) Capture of Java 1811 ; Lieut. in Intelligence Dept. (India medal).

[1] *Note :* Aged 18 when passed for Cadet on 23 Mar. 1808. " Nursed in the town of Uxbridge by Mrs. Mary Dee ; not more than 5 weeks old in 1791."

[2] *Note :* " Ann Catherock, wife of Archibald H. S. Stewart, formerly Bengal Army and Lieut. H.M. 59th Regt."

STEWART, Benjamin (*d.* 1829). Lieut. Colonel. 26th N.I. Cadet 1782. Admitted 15 Aug. 1783. Ensign 25 Mar. 1783. Lieut. 2 Mar. 1790. Capt. 30 Sept. 1803. Major 29 Nov. 1809. Lt. Col. 16 Dec. 1814. Invalided 12 Apr. 1815. Retired 30 July 1823. *d.* in Ireland 25 Oct. 1829.

Brother of Maj.-Gen. Robert Stewart, late R.I. Art., and of Martha Maria Magee.

Services: Apptd. Cadet 22 Jan. 1782 ; sailed for India in the *Montagu* 11 Sept. 1782. Posted Lieut. to 1st Bengal Eur. Bn. 5 Feb. 1790 ; transfd. to 5th Bn. Sepoys 26 Feb. 1790. Lieut. 9th N.I. Transfd. as Capt. to newly-raised 23rd N.I. 1803 ; to 26th N.I. 1805. Operations in Bundelkhand 1807 ; Sehlehuganj ; Capt. 26th N.I. Comdd. Bareilly Provl. Bn. 1815-21. Fur. 16 Mar. 1821 till retirement.

Refs. : Will dated Lurgan 1 Apr. 1826 ; proved 4 Dec. 1830.

STEWART, Bowyer (1805-?). Lieutenant. 3rd Extra N.I.
b. Ratho, Edinburgh, 31 July 1805. Cadet 1821. Ensign 13 Sept.
1822. Lieut. 29 July 1824. Struck off in India 13 Sept. 1827.
bapt. Ratho 4 Aug. 1805. 4th son of Alexander Stewart, M.D.,
physician at Gogar, Midlothian, sometime surgeon 60th Foot, and
Elizabeth Edmonston(e) his wife. Nephew of Sir Walter Scott's
great friend, Alexander Stewart, VIII of Invernahyle. Ed. Edin.
High School.
Services : Posted to 13th N.I. 1822 ; transfd. to 27th N.I. July
1823 ; to 54th N.I. (late 2/27th) May 1824 ; to newly-raised 3rd
Extra Regt. May 1825. Fur. 1824 till struck off. No record of
active service.
Refs. : Stewarts of Appin, p. 176, *s.n.* Invernahyle.

STEWART, Charles (1764-1837). Major. 11th N.I. *b.* 1764.
Cadet 1781. Admitted 29 May 1782. Ensign 8 Oct. 1781.
Lieut. 11 July 1782. Capt. 31 July 1799. Major 12 June 1807.
Retired 4 Sept. 1808. *d.* at his residence, Royal Cresc., Bath,
9 Apr. 1837, aged 72.
Eldest son of Poyntz Stewart, Capt. The Buffs, and Magdalen
his wife, dau. of Rev. P. Gayer. *m.* 1st, Barrackpore 27 Jan. 1795,
Amelia, sister of Sir John Gordon, Bart., *q.v.* (*See also* William
Neville Cameron.) (She died Bath 21 Feb. 1827.) *m.* 2nd, All
Souls, Langham Pl., London, 2 June 1828, Anne, dau. of Rev.
Nicholas Holland, rector of Stifford, sister of Thomas Holland,
q.v., and widow of John Reid, of Bedford and of Kingswood
Lodge, Surrey, formerly of Calcutta. (She died Bath 17 Feb. 1848,
aged 79.)
Services : See *D.N.B.* Orientalist. Ensign Warwickshire Mil.
1 Sept. 1779. Apptd. Cadet 4 Jan. 1781 ; sailed for India in the
Hinchinbrooke 13 Mar. 1781, aged 17. Posted Ensign to 2nd Bengal
Eur. Regt. May 1782 ; transfd. as Lieut. to 34th Bn. Sepoys 1783 ;
to 4th N.I. 1784 ; Adjt. do. 1784-96. Transfd. as Bt. Capt. to
2/5th N.I. 1796 ; to 1/6th N.I. 1797 ; Adjt. & Qmr. 6th N.I. 1797.
Transfd. as Capt. to 1/11th N.I. July 1799. Second in comd. of
embassy to Amarapura under Col. Michael Symes, *q.v.,* May 1802
till Feb. 1803. Asst. Professor of Persian at Coll. of Ft. Wm. Mar.
1804 till Feb. 1806. Fur. 21 Feb. 1806 till retirement. Professor
of Arabic, Persian and Hindustani at Haileybury 1807-27. Pub.
" The History of Bengal from the First Muhammadan Invasion
until 1757," 4to, London, 1813, and various other works on Oriental
subjects.
Refs. : Burke's *Landed Gentry,* 13th edn., p. 1677, *s.n.* Poyntz-

Stewart, of Chesfield Park, Herts. *D.N.B. D.I.B. E.I.M.C.* i. 200-3. *Bath Chron.* 13 Apr. 1837. Portrait, painted in his old age, in Victoria Memorial Hall, Calcutta.

STEWART, Charles (1813-1842). Lieutenant, Artillery. (630)
b. Woolwich 19 May 1813. Cadet 1828. Arrived in India 11 Dec. 1829. 2nd Lieut. 12 June 1829. Lieut. 20 Feb. 1838. *d.* Gandamak 13 Jan. 1842 : kld. in action during the retreat from Kabul.

Eldest son of Peter Desbrisay Stewart, Lt. Col. R.A., and Dorcas his wife. *m.* Calcutta 10 Jan. 1832, Margaret, natural dau. of Sir Alexander Macleod, *q.v.* Addiscombe Cadet 1827-9.

Services : Apptd. Actg. 2nd Lieut. 12 Mar. 1832 ; d.d. Foot Art. at Cawnpore 7 Jan. 1832 ; d.d. 1st Bde. H.A. 4 Sept. 1832 ; posted to 1st Troop 1st Bde. H.A. 23 May 1838 Offg. Comy. Ord. at Agra 29 July till 5 Oct. 1840. First Afghan War 1840-2 ; Kabul insurrection ; retreat from Kabul (kld.) ; Lieut. 1st Troop 1st Bde.

Refs. : M.I. Afghan Memorial Church, Bombay.

STEWART, Charles Forbes (1781-1815). Captain, 28th N.I.
b. 17 May 1781. Cadet 1798. Arrived in India 23 Nov. 1799. Ensign 2 Nov. 1799. Lieut. 13 Dec. 1799. Capt. 30 Oct. 1811. *d.* Diamond Harbour, Bengal, 22 Nov. 1815, on board the *Carnatic.*

bapt. Montrose 21 May 1781. 3rd son of Thomas Stewart, town clerk of Montrose, and Elizabeth his wife, dau. of Capt. John Guise, 6th Foot.

Services : Posted to 2/17th N.I. 15 Apr. 1801. Operations in Jumna Doab 1803 ; Lieut. 2/17th N.I. Second Mahratta War 1803-6 ; Lieut. 2/17th N.I. Adjt. 2/17th N.I. 14 Mar. 1804 till 1812. Capt. Lt. 15 Feb. 1808. Fur. 1812 till Nov. 1815. Posted whilst on fur. to newly-raised 28th N.I., but never joined.

Refs. : Family information. Burke's *Colonial Gentry,* i. 337, *s.n.* Cumbrae-Stewart, of Montrose, nr. Melbourne, etc. Will dated 3 Feb. 1812 ; proved 9 Dec. 1815.

STEWART, Duncan (1756-1784). Lieutenant, 10th N.I. *b.* in Scotland 1756. Cadet 1772. Ensign 7 Aug. 1776. Lieut. 24 July 1778. *d.* 15 Jan. 1784, in camp at " Kohaary Nullah " with the Bombay detachment.

Cousin of Mr. Campbell and Mrs. Watson. His exor. was William Stewart, the brother of John Stewart (1750-1795), *q.v.*

Services : Left England as a Midshipman on board the *Duke of Albany,* East Indiaman (Capt. John Stewart), 18 Feb. 1772 ; wrecked at the Sandheads, mouth of Hooghly R., July 1772. A.D.C.

THE BENGAL ARMY, 1758-1834 187

to Sir Archibald Campbell, *q.v.*, 1772 ; apptd. Inf. Cadet 1772, and Asst. Engr., Bengal Engrs. Joined 17th Bn. Sepoys as a Vol. in 1774, and served with that Corps on service in the Midnapore district 1774-5. Leave s.c. to Bombay 1775. Posted Ensign to 10th Bn. Sepoys 1776 ; apptd. Surveyor to the Field Army 1777. First Mahratta War 1778-84. Apptd. Surveyor to Col. Goddard's force Mar. 1779.

Refs. : *E.I.M.C.* iii. 450*n*. (Left, by way of a Will, a rough memo. for the information of the " Court of Enquiry.")

STEWART, Francis (*d.* 1773). Cadet, Infantry. Asst. Engr. Cadet 1770. *d.* Dinapore 19 July 1773 (? Nov. 1770).
m. Euphemia.
Services : N.F.P.

STEWART, George Augustus Chichester (1804-1826). Lieutenant, 1st Bengal Eur. Regt. *b.* Belfast 23 Mar. 1804. Cadet 1819. Ensign 20 May 1820. Lieut. 11 June 1822. *d.* Agra 7 Aug. 1826.

Son of —— (? T. Ludford) Stewart, of Dublin and Belfast, solicitor. *m.* Nagpur 1 May 1824, Mrs. Ann Corbett.

Services : Posted to 22nd N.I. 1820 ; transfd. to Bengal Eur. Regt. 1821 ; to 1st Bengal Eur. Regt. May 1824. Siege and capture of Bhurtpore ; Lieut. 1st Bengal Eur. Regt.

STEWART, Henry Shaw (1811-1846). Bt. Captain, 29th N.I. *b.* Carrickfergus 11 Sept. 1811. Cadet 1829. Arrived in India 23 Apr. 1830. Ensign (3 Jan. 1830) 23 Apr. 1830. Lieut. 6 Apr. 1838. Bt. Capt. 3 Jan. 1845. *d.* at sea 29 Mar. 1846, on board the *Queen.*

Son of Richard Stewart, chief mgte. of Belfast. Brother of Robert Stewart (1800-1829), *q.v. m.* Barrackpore 15 May 1843, Sophia, dau. of Major Robert Joseph Debnam, H.M. 13th L.I. (*See also* Perceval Bridgman.)

Services : d.d. 4th N.I. 7 June 1830 ; actg. Ensign (having been 2 yrs. in India) 2 July 1832 ; d.d. 52nd N.I, 16 Jan. 1833 ; posted to 29th N.I. 20 Aug. 1833 ; Intr. & Qmr. do. 30 Dec. 1837 till 1846. Fur. s.c. 1846. No record of active service.

*STEWART, James (1748/49-1768). Ensign, Infantry. Cadet 1767. Ensign (?) *d.* Pirpahar, 3 m. below Monghyr, 5 June 1768, aged 19.

Brother of John Stewart (*d.* 1769), *q.v.*
Services : N.F.P.
Refs. : M.I. at Monghyr, B. & O.

STEWART, James. Ensign. Infantry. Cadet 1771. Ensign 19 Mar. 1773. Resigned 5 Feb. 1776.[1]
Services : Was an Ensign in 3rd Bde. on resignation.
[1] *Note :* Permitted to resign in order to avoid dismissal. " A needy adventurer, who had practiced so many deceits and impositions both in the Army and elsewhere as to become obnoxious to Society." (Memorial from Col. G. Ironside, *q.v.*—M.C. 1 June 1778.)

STEWART, James (*c.* 1788-1833). Bt. Captain. 14th N.I. *b.* Bombay Presdy. *c.* 1788. Cadet 1804. Arrived in India 10 Sept. 1805. Ensign 6 Nov. 1805. Lieut. 18 July 1806. Bt. Capt. 10 Jan. 1819. Resigned in India 4 Oct. 1822. *d.* Burdwan, Bengal, 20 Mar. 1833, aged 45.
Son of Charles Stewart, of Bengal, " then Lieut. in H.M.S."[1] *m.* Calcutta 19 Jan. 1820, Miss Frances Jones.
Services : Posted to 14th N.I. 1806. Lieut. 1/14th N.I. With 4th L.I. Bn. 1810. Adjt. Burdwan Provl. Bn. 30 May 1811 till resignation. Transfd. as Bt. Capt. to 2/14th N.I. No record of active service.
Refs. : *A.J.* N.S. xii. 113.
[1] *Note :* Either Lt. & Qmr. H.M. 75th (Highland) Ft., and Anne his wife, or Lt. & Qmr. H.M. 77th Ft., and Jane his wife.

STEWART, John (*d.* 1769). Lieutenant, Invalid Est. Infantry. Cadet (?) Ensign 21 Oct. 1763. Lieut. 15 July 1764. Invalided (?) *d.* Calcutta 4 Jan. 1769.
Brother of James Stewart,* *q.v.*
Services : Posted to 1st Bengal Eur. Regt. 13 Aug. 1765.
Refs. : Will dated 28 Apr. 1768 ; proved 31 Jan. 1769.

STEWART, John (1759/60-1785). Lieutenant, 21st Bn. Sepoys. *b.* 1759/60. Cadet 1778. Ensign 1778. Lieut. 10 Dec. 1778. *bur.* Bombay 11 Jan. 1785.
Services : Apptd. Cadet 19 Dec. 1777 ; sailed for India in the *Grosvenor* 9 Feb. 1778, aged 18. 1/1st Bengal Eur. Regt. in Oct. 1779. Granted leave s.c. to sea 13 Oct. 1784.

STEWART, John (1750/51-1795). Lieutenant, Invalid Est. Artillery. (186) *b.* 1750/51. Country Cadet 1778. Fireworker 2 Nov. 1778. Lieut. 15 Feb. 1784. Invalided (?) *d. unm.* Dinapore 1 Jan. 1795, aged 44.
4th son of Charles Stewart, purse bearer to Prince Charles Edward in " the 45," and Elizabeth his wife, dau. of Johnstone, of Redacres.

THE BENGAL ARMY, 1758-1834   189

Brother of William Stewart, at Hillhead, co. Dumfries, and of Duncan Stewart, Bk. Mr. of Fort William, Inverness.
Services: Apptd. Cadet 10 Sept. 1778. Lieut. 1st Bn. Art. Apptd. Actg. Comy. of Ord. to the magazine with the detachment under Col. Ironside 23 Jan. 1781. With Art. Invalids at Chunar in July 1787. Apptd. Dy. Comy. of Ord. 19 Sept. 1791, and posted to the expense magazine at Patna.
Refs.: Stewarts of Appin, p. 159. *S.M.* 1795, p. 749. Will dated Patna, 21 Oct. 1793; proved 12 Jan. 1795. M.I. Dinapore.

STEWART, John (1762/63-1819). Lieut. Colonel. 14th N.I.
b. in Ireland 1762/63. Cadet 1780. Admitted 13 July 1781. Ensign 13 July 1781. Lieut. 1 Sept. 1781. Capt. 21 Apr. 1800. Major 19 Nov. 1804. Lt. Col. 6 Aug. 1810. Retired 4 Dec. 1812. *d.* Kingston, nr. Taunton, 20 Dec. 1819, of apoplexy, aged 56. *m.* Bhagulpur 23 Oct. 1801, Miss Harriet Wainwright.
Services: Sailed for India in the *Bellmont* 2 Apr. 1780, aged 17. Lieut. 23rd Bn. Sepoys in Dec. 1788; posted to 6th Eur. Bn. 5 Feb. 1790; from 4th do. to 25th Bn. Sepoys 9 Sept. 1791; to 23rd Bn.; Adjt. 32nd Bn. 17 Dec. 1793. Posted Capt. to 2/16th N.I. 21 Apr. 1800; A.D.C. to Maj.-Gen. H. Briscoe, *q.v.*, in 1802. (? Second Mahratta War 1803; Agra; Laswari; Capt. 2/16th N.I.) Comdg. Patna Provl. Bn. 1804-10; posted Lt. Col. to 14th N.I. 1810. Fur. 8 Jan. 1811 till retirement.
Refs.: Bath Chron. 30 Dec. 1819. M.I. Kingston church.

STEWART, John MacLean (1767-1816). Bt. Major, Invalid Est. 21st N.I. *b.* 14 Feb. 1767. Country Cadet 1782. Admitted 14 Feb. 1782. Ensign 1 May 1783.[1] Lieut. 2 May 1790. Capt. 27 Jan. 1804. Bt. Major 25 July 1810. Invalided 1 June 1811. *d.* Dinapore 16 Feb. 1816.
Son of John Stewart, Sec. to G.G. and Council at Ft. Wm., J.A.G. Bengal, 1772-5, and Johanna Maria his wife (whom he *m.* 11 Dec. 1777), dau. of William Murray, of Jamaica.
Services: Apptd. Minor Cadet 12 Nov. 1781. Transfd. from 2nd Bengal Eur. Regt. on its reduction in May 1802, to newly-constituted Marine Regt.; transfd. as Capt. to newly-raised 21st N.I. 1804. Second Mahratta War 1804-5; Capt. 21st N.I.
[1] *Note:* Apptd. Ensign 24 Feb. 1785; subsequently antedated.

STEWART, Neil (*d.* 1794). Captain, Infantry. Cadet 1769. Ensign 9 Oct. 1769. Lieut. 31 Mar. 1773. Capt. 27 Jan. 1781. *d.* Fatehgarh 1 Sept. 1794.
Services: Apptd. Adjt. 14th Bn. Sepoys 22 Mar. 1780; Capt.

comdg. 2/8th N.I. in Aug. 1781 ; Capt. 2nd Bengal Eur. Bn. in July 1787 and Dec. 1792.
Refs.: Macpherson, p. 401. *S.M.* 1795, p. 545. *G.M.* 1795, ii. 703.

STEWART, Neil (1791-1842). Captain. 72nd N.I. *bapt.* Fortingall, Perth, 10 Apr. 1791. Cadet 1808. Arrived in India 24 July 1809. Ensign 14 Feb. 1810. Lieut. 16 Dec. 1814. Capt. 19 Oct. 1826. Retired 1 Dec. 1836. *d.* 29 Sept. 1842.

Son of John Stewart, of Crossmount, co. Perth (a cadet of the Stewarts of Garth), and Jean Menzies his wife.

Services: Barasat C.C. 1809-10. Posted Ensign to 5th N.I. 1810. (? Reduction of Kalinjar 1812 ; Ensign 2/5th N.I.) Nepal War 1815 ; operations in Kumaon ; Lieut. 2/5th N.I., with detachment under Robert Patton (*d.* 1837), *q.v.* Third Mahratta War 1817-19 ; Lieut. 2/5th N.I. Intr. & Qmr. 2/5th N.I. 16 Oct. 1823 ; do. 11th N.I. (late 1/5th) 17 June 1824 ; do. 20th N.I. 16 Aug. 1824 ; do. newly-raised 4th Extra Regt. (became 72nd N.I.) 12 July 1825 till 28 Dec. 1826. Retired on pension of a Major.

STEWART, Patrick [1] (*d.* 1792). Lieutenant, Engineers. Country Cadet 1780. Ensign 30 Sept. 1781. Lieut. 1 Nov. 1782. *d. unm.* Seringapatam 6 Feb. 1792 : kld. in action.

2nd son of William Stewart, of Loinmaristock, lord provost of Perth, and Christian his wife, only child of Patrick Cree, also sometime lord provost of that city. Brother of Robert Stewart, of St. Fort (1746-?), *q.v.*

Services: Campaign against the Rajah of Benares 1781 ; Bijaigarh ; Cadet, Inf. Transfd. from Inf. to Engrs. Apptd. Draughtsman in Surveyor Gen.'s office, Calcutta, 1 Aug. 1787 ; Dy. Paymr. of King's Troops in Dec. 1788. Employed suptg. bldgs. at new gaol in Calcutta 1789-90 ; do. at Old Fort 1790. Ordered to proceed to the Coast and join the army under Earl Cornwallis 15 Aug. 1791. Third Mysore War 1791-2 ; Seringapatam (kld.) ; Lieut. Engrs.

Refs.: Burke's *Landed Gentry*, 2nd edn., p. 1303, *s.n.* Stewart, of St. Fort. Will dated Calcutta, 16 Aug. 1790 ; proved 20 Mar. 1792. Name on cenotaph in Bangalore fort.

[1] *Note:* Also known as Peter.

STEWART, Robert (1744-1820). (*See* **STUART, Robert.**)

STEWART, Robert (*d.* 1780). Captain, 21st Bn. Sepoys. Country Cadet 1765. Ensign 3 Sept. 1765. Lieut. 7 Jan. 1767. Capt. 20 Sept. 1770. *d.* Berhampore 5 Sept. 1780.

A cadet of the Stewarts of Garth. Brother of Donald Stewart, of Shierglas, co. Perth, and of Malcolm Stewart.
Services: Apptd. Cadet by G.O. of 24 May 1765. N.F.P.
Refs.: Will dated 4 May 1779; filed 7 Nov. 1780.

STEWART, Robert (1746-?). Captain. 2nd Bengal Eur. Regt. *b.* 1746. Country Cadet 1770. Ensign 4 Mar. 1771. Lieut. 12 July 1776. Capt. 8 Feb. 1781. Resigned 22 Jan. 1784. Of St. Fort, co. Fife, and Castle Stewart, co. Wigtown, which estates he purchased on his return from India. Eldest son of William Stewart, merchant, lord provost of Perth, and Christian his wife. Brother of Patrick Stewart, *q.v. m.* 1st, before 1775, (?) *m.* 2nd, 1792, Ann Stewart, dau. of Henry Balfour, of Dunbog, co. Fife. Was exor. of the Will of Robert Stewart (*d.* 1780), *q.v.*
Services: Went out to India in a private capacity (? as an Engr.). Was an Asst. Engr. in Mar. 1774, when C.D. wrote to Bengal recommending his appt. as Supt. of their gunpowder works nr. Calcutta, which post he held from Dec. 1774 till Oct. 1782. "Served on the staff of Gen. Clavering." (*Anderson.*) Returned to England in the *Talbot* Feb. 1784. Author of "Narrative of a Transaction which passed in Bengal 1782-3, between James Fraser, Esq. and the Executors of the late Lt. Col. Hannay," London and Edin., 1787.
Refs.: Burke's *Landed Gentry*, 7th edn., p. 1742, *s.n.* Stewart, of St. Fort, co. Fife. *Anderson*, iii. 516. *E.I. Co.'s Arsenals & Manufactories*, by Bdr.-Gen. H. A. Young, C.I.E., 1937.

STEWART, Robert (1776-1800). Lieutenant, 10th N.I. *b.* Dull, co. Perth, 9 Dec. 1776. Cadet 1797. Admitted 24 Dec. 1798. Ensign 19 Oct. 1798. Lieut. 1 Nov. 1798. *d.* Calcutta 16 May 1800.
bapt. Dull 13 Dec. 1776. Son of Adam Stewart, of Cluny, co. Perth (a cadet of Garth), and Helen his wife, dau. of John Hepburn, of Colquhalzie, co. Perth.
Services: Posted Lieut. to 10th N.I. in 1798.
Refs.: Burke's *Landed Gentry*, 2nd edn., p. 560, *s.n.* Hepburn, of Colquhalzie, co. Perth.

STEWART, Robert (1787-1867). Major General. Colonel 41st N.I. *b.* Balquhidder, co. Perth, 7 Mar. 1787. Cadet 1805. Arrived in India 19 Nov. 1806. Ensign (29 Mar. 1806) 11 Oct. 1806. Lieut. 31 Oct. 1808. Capt. 1 May 1824. Major 11 Oct. 1838. Lt. Col. 26 Dec. 1844. Col. 16 Dec. 1854. Maj. Gen. 15 Sept. 1856. *d.* 9 Drummond Pl., Edinburgh, 30 Oct. 1867.
bapt. Balquhidder 14 Mar. 1787. 3rd son of Rev. Duncan Stewart,

IV of Strathgarry, minister at Balquhidder, and Arabella his wife. Brother of Alexander Stewart (1778-1835), q.v. m. 1st, Glenbuckie House, co. Perth, 8 Jan. 1831, Ann, eldest dau. of Duncan Stewart, of Glenbuckie. (She died 1833.) m. 2nd, Mirzapur 25 Aug. 1834, Grace, 3rd dau. of Robert Menzies, of Dalreoch, co. Perth. (*See also* Henry Le Mesurier.) (She died Edinburgh 12 Feb. 1874.)

Services: Barasat C.C. 1806-8. Posted Ensign to 26th N.I. 1808. Operations in Bundelkhand 1809-11; Sehlehuganj; Hirapur; Rajaoli; Ajaigarh; against Gopal Singh; Lieut. 2/26th N.I. On service in Bikanir 1813. (? Nepal War 1814-15.) Intr. & Qmr. 2/26th N.I. 27 Aug. 1818 till Sept. 1823. Transfd. to newly-formed 1/31st N.I. 1823; Intr. & Qmr. do. 1 Oct. 1823 till 17 June 1824. Transfd. to 61st N.I. (late 1/31st) May 1824. Tempy. charge of Magh Levy in Arakan 18 Mar. 1826. Fur. s.c. 15 Jan. 1829 till 31 Oct. 1832. Shekhawat expedn. 1834. On service in Bundelkhand 1843-4. Fur. s.c. 10 Mar. 1845 till 1846. Posted Lt. Col. to 56th N.I. 13 Mar. 1845; to 26th N.I. Sept. 1845; to 10th N.I. 1847; to 65th N.I. 19 July 1851; to 20th N.I. 1 Mar. 1853. Fur. s.c. 10 Mar. 1850 till Mar. 1853; 12 Aug. 1853 till death. Posted Col. to 49th N.I. 22 Mar. 1855; 41st N.I. 6 Aug. 1857 till death.

Refs.: Burke's *Landed Gentry*, 13th edn., p. 1675, *s.n.* Stewart, of Coll. *Stewarts of Appin*, p. 179. Scott's *Fasti*, iv. 338. *Boase*. *The Times*, 1 Nov. 1867.

STEWART, Robert (1800-1829). Lieutenant, 6th N.I. *b.* Clare 13 June 1800. Cadet 1817. Ensign (?) Lieut. 1 Aug. 1818. *d.* Tor Hill cottage, Devon, 16 Jan. 1829.

bapt. Ramoan, co. Antrim, 20 June 1800. Son of Richard Stewart, chief mgte. of Belfast, and Catherine his wife. Brother of Henry Shaw Stewart, q.v. Addiscombe Cadet 1816-18.

Services: Posted Supy. Lieut. to 2/3rd N.I. 1818; transfd. to 6th N.I. (late 1/3rd) May 1824; Intr. & Qmr. do. 5 Aug. 1825 till May 1826. Fur. s.c. 1826 till death.

Refs.: *A.J.* xxvii. 253. *G.M.* 1829, i. 92.

STEWART, Robert (1802-1831). Lieutenant, 69th N.I. *b.* Avondale, co. Lanark, 17 Nov. 1802. Cadet 1820. Admitted 31 May 1821. Ensign 16 Jan. 1821. Lieut. 11 July 1823. *d.* Kalpi 16 Sept. 1831, of a bilious fever.

Youngest son of John Stewart, of Overtoun (a cadet of Stewart of Allanton, co. Lanark), and Margaret Sword his wife. Brother of John Stewart, Capt. H.M. 53rd Regt., and of Mary, wife of James

THE BENGAL ARMY, 1758-1834

Sword, of Westthorn. Cousin of Robert Stewart, of Alderston, co. Haddington. Ed. Peebles Grammar School.

Services: Posted to 1/12th N.I.; transfd. to 21st N.I. July 1823; to 42nd N.I. (late 2/21st) May 1824; actg. Intr. & Qmr. do. 23 July 1825. First Burma War; Arakan 1825; Lieut. 42nd N.I. Transfd. to newly-raised 1st Extra Regt. (became 69th N.I.) 1826. Operations against the Bhils 1827; Lieut. 1st Extra Regt. Was on his way to Calcutta on leave, prior to going home on fur., when his death occurred.

Refs.: A.J. N.S. vii. 159. Will dated Muttra 14 Mar. 1830; proved 22 Nov. 1832.

*STEWART or STUART, William (d. 1763). Lieutenant, Infantry. Cadet (?) Ensign (?) Lieut. (?) d. 5th, 6th or 11th Oct. 1763: massacred at or near Patna by order of Nawab Mir Muhammad Kasim. (See note to Henry Somers.)

Services: Was at Kasim Bazar on sick leave in 1763 when he was taken prisoner by the Nawab's people. N.F.P.

Refs.: Bengal Letter of 29 Sept. 1763. MS. list in I.O.

STEWART or STEUART, William (1763-1795). Lieutenant, Infantry. Asst. Resdt. at Hyderabad. *bapt.* Moulters Hill, Edinburgh, 10 June 1763. Cadet 1780. Ensign 1780. Lieut. 2 Sept. 1781. *d. unm.* Hyderabad 14 Sept. 1795.

3rd son of James Steuart, writer in Edinburgh, and Alison his wife, only dau. of Thomas Ruddiman, the philologist (*D.N.B.*), Keeper of the Advocates' Library. Brother of Thomas Ruddiman Stewart, physician, Charles Steuart, of Edinburgh, W.S., Anna, Cecilia, Frances and Mary. Nephew of Charles Stewart.

Services: Sailed for India in the *Neptune* 3 June 1780, aged 17. Transfd. as Practitioner Engr. to Madras Est. May 1781, but never joined. Was serving with guard to Resdt. with Sindhia in July 1787 till middle of 1790; Asst. Resdt. at Hyderabad 1 Apr. 1790 till death. Third Mysore War; Lieut. with Nizam's detachment; surveyed country around Bangalore 1791-2. Sometime Dy. Postmr. at Hyderabad.

Refs.: Scottish Antiquary, xi. 189. *G.M.* 1796, i. 439. Will dated Sindhia's camp nr. Muttra, 10 Apr. 1790; another dated Hyderabad, 18 Aug. 1795; proved 11 Dec. 1800.

STEWART, William Douglas (1800-1824). Lieutenant, 19th N.I. *b.* Liverpool 14 Apr. 1800. Cadet 1820. Ensign 24 Mar. 1821. Lieut. 11 July 1823. *d.* at sea 1824, on board the *Albion.*

bapt. Liverpool 29 Apr. 1800. Son of John Stewart, of Liverpool, merchant. Ed. Repton; admitted Aug. 1814.

Services : Posted to 1/7th N.I. 1821 ; transfd. to 3rd N.I. July 1823 ; to 19th N.I. (late 2/3rd) May 1824. Fur. s.c. 1824. No record of active service.

Refs. : Repton School Register.

STEWART, William Murray (1804-1853). Major, 22nd N.I. P.A. at Benares. *b.* 11 Mar. 1804. Cadet 1820. Admitted 8 Oct. 1821. Ensign 5 May 1821. Lieut. 15 Feb. 1824. Capt. 26 Nov. 1836. Major 22 May 1849. *d.* Benares 22 July 1853, of cholera.

bapt. Comrie, co. Perth, 20 Mar. 1804. 4th son of William Stewart, of Ardvorlich, co. Perth, and Helen his wife, eldest dau. of James Maxtone, of Cultoquhey, and sister of Anthony Maxtone, *q.v. m.* Berhampore 8 Aug. 1826, Charlotte, eldest dau. of Major R. J. Debnam, H.M. 13th L.I. (*See also* Perceval Bridgman.) (She died London 24 Nov. 1860, aged 52.) Ed. Edinburgh High School.

Services : Posted to 1/11th N.I. ; transfd. to 2nd N.I. 1823 ; to 22nd N.I. (late 2/2nd) May 1824. First Burma War 1824-5 ; operations on Sylhet and Cachar borders ; Lieut. 22nd N.I. (India medal). Adjt. & Qmr. of Eur. Invalids at Chunar 1 June 1829 ; actg. Fort. Adjt. at Chunar 24 Nov. 1829 ; permanent do. 7 Jan. 1832 till 1845. Supt. of family domains of Rajah of Benares 6 Mar. 1839 till death ; A.G.G. Benares, and Supt. of ex-Rajah of Coorg 12 Nov. 1849 till death.

Refs. : Burke's *Landed Gentry,* 13th edn., p. 1673, *s.n.* Stewart, of Ardvorlich, co. Perth. *Anderson,* iii. 517. *G.M.* 1853, ii. 537. *I.M.* 20 Sept. 1853, p. 546. Will dated 7 Dec. 1846 ; proved 27 Oct. 1853. M.I. in Comrie church, and in Holy Trinity church, Chunar.

*STIBBERT, David. Ensign. Infantry. Cadet (?) Ensign (?)

Brother of Giles Stibbert, *q.v.*

Services : Was an Ensign in a Sepoy Bn. in 1764. Out of the Service before Feb. 1767.

Refs. : Broome, p. 418.

STIBBERT, Giles (*d.* 1809). Lieut. General. Infantry. Provl. C.-in-C. Bengal. Lieut. 11 Nov. 1757. Capt. 1 May 1759. Major 22 May 1764. Col. 15 Oct. 1775. Bdr. Gen. 25 Feb. 1777. Maj. Gen. 9 July 1783. Lt. Gen. 26 Nov. 1796. *d.* at his seat, Portswood House, Southampton, 21 Jan. 1809.

A native of Kent. Brother of David Stibbert and related to

John Brown (*d.* 1775), *qq.v.*[1] *m.* Calcutta 26 Dec. 1765, Sophronia Rebecca Wright. (She died London 18 Oct. 1815.)
Services: Went to sea as Capt.'s servant; enlisted in ranks of H.C.S. under the patronage of Robert Clive, *c.* 1756. (? Battle of Plassey; in the ranks. ? Storm of Masulipatam 1759.) Raised at Patna in 1761, 6th Bn. Sepoys (became 1st in 1764, 1/8th N.I. in 1796). Battle of Gheria; siege of Patna (w. 6 Nov. 1763); Capt. comdg. 6th Bn. Battle of Buxar 1764; Capt. comdg. Left Wing of Army. Capture of Chunar 1765; Major comdg. the force. On fur. to England *c.* 1769-72. Col. comdg. newly-formed Cav. Bde. 1777. Bdr. Gen. and Provl. C.-in-C., Bengal, 16 Oct. 1777 till 25 Mar. 1779, and again 27 Apr. 1783 till 21 July 1785; offg. do. during absence of Sir Eyre Coote in Madras 6 Oct. 1780 till 27 Apr. 1783. Framed the reform of the Bengal Army 1780. Embarked for Europe in the *Rodney* 15 Jan. 1786.
Refs.: *D.I.B.* *E.I.M.C.* ii. 92. *Williams,* p. 117. *B.:P.P.* lv. 216-17. *N. & Q.* 11S. iii. 324. *G.M.* 1809, i. 185. *S.M.* 1809, p. 159.[2]
[1] *Note:* His son Thomas (*b.* London 29 May 1771) is described as a nephew of this John Brown.
[2] *Note:* In both these two last he is incorrectly called 'Lt.-Gen. Hibbert, formerly C.-in-C. Bengal.'

STILES, John William (1800-1832). Captain, 30th N.I. *b.* W.I. 25 Oct. 1800. Cadet 1817. Admitted 3 Oct. 1818. Ensign 3 May 1818. Lieut. 1 Jan. 1819. Capt. 1 Nov. 1827. *d.* Almora, U.P., 4 Oct. 1832.
Nephew of Deborah Stiles, of Bermuda, wife of John Gambier, Lt. Govr. of the Bahamas. Cousin-german of James, Lord Gambier, Adm. R.N., 1st Baron Gambier (*D.N.B.*). *m.* Paris 8 Dec. 1830, Olive Ann, eldest dau. of Capt. John Mackeson, of Bath, and of Blue Mtn. Plantation, Jamaica. (She died Spanish Town, Jamaica, 21 July 1840.)
Services: Posted Lieut. to 1/15th N.I. 1819; transfd. to 30th N.I. (late 1/15th) May 1824. Fur. s.c. 14 Aug. 1828 till 5 June 1831. No record of active service.
Refs.: Burke's *Extinct Peerage* (1883 edn.), p. 226, *s.n.* Gambier, B. M.I. Almora Cantt. cemetery.

STILES, William (1815-1833). Ensign,[1] d.d. 34th N.I. *bapt.* Kilkeevin, co. Roscommon, 10 Apr. 1815. Cadet 1830. Arrived in India 5 Dec. 1831. (Ensign 9 June 1831.) *d.* Dudka, Barabhum, B. & O., 16 Feb. 1833, of jungle fever.

Son of William Barton Stiles, of Lyme Regis, Lieut. h.p. H.M. 66th Ft., and Lucy Jane his wife. Addiscombe Cadet 1829-31.
Services: Cadet d.d. 34th N.I. 13 Dec. 1831. Operations against the Kols in Chota Nagpur 28 Jan. till 9 May 1832; Cadet d.d. 34th N.I.
Refs.: A.J. N.S. xi. 132. M.I. in Barrackpore church.
¹ *Note:* Actually only a Cadet.

STIRLING, Conolly (1779-1824). Captain. 15th N.I. *b.* Tamlaght Finlagan, co. Londonderry, 3 July 1779. Cadet 1803. Arrived in India 13 Dec. 1804. Ensign 28 Sept. 1804. Lieut. 29 Sept. 1804. Capt. 25 Jan. 1815. Retired 29 Mar. 1822. *d.* in Ireland 7 June 1824.
bapt. 11 July 1779. Son of John Stirling, of Walworth, co. Londonderry, Capt. in the Derry Yeomanry (? by his 1st wife, dau. of John Blair, of Ballydivit, co. Derry). Brother (or half-brother) of William Stirling, *q.v.*
Services: Lieut. Fanne Glen Inf. Feb. 1797; Ensign Londonderry Regt. of Mil. 1 June 1799; Lieut. do. 12 Mar. 1800. Posted Lieut. to 15th N.I. 1805. Capt. 1/15th N.I. With 6th Gren. Bn. 1815-16. Transfd. to 2/15th N.I. Third Mahratta War 1819; Asirgarh; Capt. 2/15th N.I. Fur. 1 Nov. 1819 till retirement.
Refs.: Faulkner's Journal, 23 Feb. 1797.

STIRLING, Robert Gage (*c.* 1772-1825). Lieut. Colonel, 4th L.C. *b. c.* 1772. Cadet 1798. Arrived in India 15 Dec. 1799. Cornet 29 May 1800. Lieut. 5 Oct. 1800. Capt. 4 Nov. 1810. Major 1 Sept. 1818. Lt. Col. 1 May 1824. *d.* Karnal 29 Apr. 1825, aged 53.
(*Probably* son of John Stirling, of Walworth, by his 1st wife, and brother of Conolly Stirling, *q.v.*) *m.* 1st, Dinapore 18 Feb. 1807, Elizabeth Mary, dau. of Sir William Toone, *q.v.* (She died Buxar 7 Apr. 1811.) *m.* 2nd, London Sept. 1815, Miss Mary Ann Urquhart, of Ellness, Scotland. (She died 13 Mar. 1820.)
Services: Lieut. Bovevagh Yeomanry Cav., co. Londonderry, 31 Oct. 1796. Ensign d.d. 1/3rd N.I. Dec. 1799. Posted Cornet to 2nd N.C. 5 July 1800. Operations in Jumna Doab 1803; Sasni; Bijaigarh; Kachaura; Lieut. 2nd N.C. Second Mahratta War 1803-5; Koil; Aligarh; battle of Delhi; Agra; Laswari; relief of Delhi; battle and capture of Deig; Bhurtpore; Lieut. 2nd N.C. Transfd. to newly-raised 7th N.C. Apr. 1805; Adjt. do. 16 May 1805 till July 1807. Fur. 12 Dec. 1813 till June 1816. Siege and capture of Hathras 1817; Capt. 7th N.C. Third Mahratta War

1817-18; Dhamoni; Mandala; Multai; Harna; Major 7th N.C. Posted Lt. Col. to 4th L.C. June 1824.

Refs.: Burke's *Landed Gentry of Ireland*, p. 662, *s.n.* Stewart, of Horn Head, co. Donegal. *De Rhé-Philipe.* M.I. at Karnal.

STIRLING, William (1782-1842). Lieut. Colonel. 34th N.I. *b.* Farlow, psh. of Tamlaght Finlagan, 3 Feb. 1782. Cadet 1804. Arrived in India 10 Sept. 1805. Ensign 1 Sept. 1805. Lieut. 2 Sept. 1805. Capt. 11 July 1823. Major 31 May 1829. Lt. Col. 23 June 1835. Retired 7 Jan. 1836. *d.* 25 Jan. 1842. *bapt.* Walworth, co. Londonderry, 10 Feb. 1782. Son of John Stirling, of Walworth (? by his 2nd wife, sister of Alexander Knox, of Dawson St., Dublin). Brother or half-brother of Conolly Stirling, *q.v. m.* Dinapore 24 Oct. 1821, Miss Marianne Gahan, reputed dau. of Robert Gahan, *q.v.* (She died Chittagong 1 Jan. 1829.)

Services : Posted Lieut. to 23rd N.I. 1806. (? Settlement of Hariana 1809; Bhawani; Lieut. 2/23rd N.I.) Third Mahratta War 1817-19; Lieut. 2/23rd N.I. Actg. Adjt. 2/23rd N.I. 5 Jan. 1820; permanent do. 4 Dec. 1820 till 21 Oct. 1823. d.d. 2/26th N.I. 11 Feb. till 1 Nov. 1823. Fur. p.a. 24 Jan. 1824 till 6 Jan. 1827. Transfd. to 45th N.I. (late 1/23rd) May 1824. Tempy. comdg. Eur. Invalids and garr. at Chunar 23 Sept. 1833. Posted Lt. Col. to 34th N.I. 8 Sept. 1835.

STOCK, John Rodway (1792-1868). Major. 74th N.I. *bapt.* ptely. 20 Feb. 1792. Cadet 1807. Arrived in India 19 Aug. 1808. Ensign (27 Aug. 1808) 26 Nov. 1812.[1] Lieut. 13 Aug. 1815. Capt. 13 May 1825. Retired 27 Apr. 1833. Hon. Major 28 Nov. 1854. *d.* Murragh Lodge, Cheltenham, 27 Feb. 1868. Of Cheltenham; formerly of Putley Court, co. Hereford. Received into Church in Gloucester Cathedral 19 Dec. 1792. Son of Edmund Stock and Mary his wife. *m.* St. John's, Calcutta, 16 July 1825, Miss Susan Chilcott. (She died 22 Apr. 1890.)

Services : Barasat C.C. Was permitted to serve during his suspension as a Vol. with a Corps in Bengal till the Court's pleasure should be known. Posted Ensign to 2/9th N.I. Nepal War 1816; Makwanpur; Lieut. 2/9th N.I., in 4th Bde. Centre Column (India medal). Wounded at Dineah (?), 1817. With 1st Ceylon Vol. Bn. 1818-19. Transfd. to newly-formed 1/31st N.I. July 1823; Adjt. do. 1 Oct. 1823 till 12 July 1825; transfd. to newly-raised 6th Extra Regt. (became 74th N.I.) 17 July 1825. Fur. p.a. 28 Dec. 1830 till retirement. Retired on a pension of 10/6 *p.d.*

Refs.: G.M. 1868, i. 546. *The Times*, 3 Mar. 1868.

[1] *Note :* Suspended and ordered to Europe 20 Nov. 1809; restored

by C.D., but former rank cancelled, 20 Aug. 1811 ; restored to his original rank in the Service as Cadet 1st Class of 1807 ; Bt. Capt. 1 Mar. 1823. (G.O. No. 76 of 11 Mar. 1825.)

STOCKER, Abraham. Captain. 3rd Bengal Eur. Regt. Cadet 1769. Ensign 1 Oct. 1769. Lieut. 25 Mar. 1773. Capt. 23 Jan. 1781. Resigned 26 Jan. 1784.

Services : Applied in Nov. 1776 for permission to make a voyage to the Red Sea for his health ; wrote from Suez in Apr. 1777, applying to resign the Service and proceed to England on s.c. ; permitted to return to India 18 Nov. 1778, arriving in 1780. Actg. Bde. Major at Berhampore in Dec. 1780 ; Bde. Major 3rd Bde. 22 Jan. 1781 till Sept. 1782. Returned to England in the *Fox* in 1784.

STODDART, George Douglas (1792-1839). Major, 8th L.C. *b.* Old Road, Middle Island, I. of St. Kitts, 20 Oct. 1792. Cadet 1807. Arrived in India 14 Aug. 1808. Cornet 20 Aug. 1808. Lieut. 15 Feb. 1816. Capt. 13 May 1825. Major 5 Oct. 1836. *d.* Stellenbosch, S.A., 21 Jan. 1839.

Nephew of Isabel Douglas, of Walcot, Somerset.

Services : Barasat C.C. 13½ mos. Posted Cornet to 8th N.C. 1809. Third Mahratta War ; Nagpur ; Lieut. 8th N.C. A.D.C. to Bdr. J. W. Adams, *q.v.*, 3 Dec. 1825. Siege and capture of Bhurtpore ; Capt. 8th L.C., A.D.C. A.D.C. to Bdr. Adams 3 May till 1 Aug. 1828. Bde. Major on the Est. at Dacca 11 July 1828 ; do. Presdy. 28 Sept. 1829 ; D.A.A.G. on Est., Presdy., 5 Dec. 1829. 2nd A.A.G. of the Army 21 May 1832 till 6 Mar. 1835 ; offg. 1st A.A.G. 12 Mar. 1833. Dy. Paymr., Cawnpore circle, 6 Mar. 1835 ; Paymr. at Presdy. and to King's troops 9 Jan. 1836. Leave s.c. 2 yrs. to Cape 8 Mar. 1838 till death.

Refs. : A.J. N.S. xxix. 75. G.M. 1839, i. 670.

STOKES, George Warren (1808-1873). Colonel. 59th N.I. (now 4th Bn. 7th Rajput Regt.). *bapt.* St. Mary, Haverfordwest, 15 May 1808. Cadet 1825. Arrived in India 30 May 1826. Ensign 4 Feb. 1826. Lieut. 2 July 1828. Capt. 15 June 1845. Major 21 Aug. 1857. Lt. Col. 21 Feb. 1861. Retired 31 Dec. 1861. Hon. Col. 31 Dec. 1861. *d.* 8 July 1873, aged 65.

Of Netherwood, nr. Tenby. Son of Henry Stokes, coroner for co. Pembroke, and Anne his wife. *m.* Catherine Elizabeth Savery. (She died Haverfordwest 18 Jan. 1883, aged 79.)

Services : Ensign d.d. 57th N.I. 30 June 1826 ; posted to 59th N.I. 26 Sept. 1826 ; actg. Intr. & Qmr. do. 18 Feb. 1831. Fur. s.c.

20 June 1835 till 19 Sept. 1838. Actg. Adjt. 59th N.I. 15 June 1839, 14 Jan. 1841. Tempy. S.A.C.G. with Army of Reserve (for Afghanistan) 25 Nov. 1842. First Sikh War; Sobraon; Capt. 59th N.I., comdd. Regt. from Feb. 1846; operations in Jullundur Doab under Bdr. Wheeler; comdd. 59th N.I. Oct.-Dec. 1846 (Medal). Fur. 10 Jan. 1852 till 2 Apr. 1853. Was comdg. 59th N.I. as Bt. Major when the Regt. was disarmed at Amritsar, 9 July 1857, as a precautionary measure. Mutiny campaign 1857-8; comdd. Pathan Cav. Aug. 1857 till Feb. 1859; Gangari 14 Dec. 1857; operations under Lord Clyde in Oudh 1858 (Medal).
Refs.: The Times, 11 July 1873.

STOKOE, Joseph Hind (d. 1801). Bt. Captain, Engineers. Country Cadet 1782. Admitted 2 June 1782. Ensign 20 July 1782. Lieut. 12 Oct. 1794. Bt. Capt. 8 Jan. 1798. d. Penang 12 Jan. 1801.

Son of Sarah Stokoe. Brother of Sarah Wilmer, Barbara Field, Mary Tucker, and Hannah Stokoe.

Services: First Mahratta War; Asst. Field Engr. to detachment under Col. Charles Morgan, q.v. Asst. Engr. at Cawnpore in July 1787. Apptd. Engr. to Lt.-Col. Cockerell's detachment 9 Feb. 1790. Third Mysore War 1790-2; Field Engr. and Ensign comdg. a Coy. of Pioneers. Was Provision and Storekeeper in the Andamans in Apr. 1794; actg. Supt. do. 1795-6. Engr. at Penang 17 June 1796 till death.
Refs.: G.M. 1801, ii. 1211. Will dated Calcutta 5 Aug. 1796; proved 24 Feb. 1801.

STONE, Henry (1805-1838). Bt. Captain. 49th N.I. b. London 29 Jan. 1805. Cadet 1821. Arrived in India 27 May 1822. Ensign 27 Nov. 1821. Lieut. 1 May 1824. Bt. Capt. 27 Nov. 1836. Retired 11 July 1837. d. in England 29 Aug. 1838, after a long illness.

bapt. St. Luke's, Middlesex, 19 Apr. 1805. Son of Samuel Stone and Mary his wife. Brother of Samuel Stone, silkbroker.

Services: Posted to 11th N.I. 1822; transfd. to 15th N.I. (late 1/11th) May 1824; to 17th N.I. 2 Aug. 1824; actg. Intr. & Qmr. do. 6 Sept. 1824. Fur. s.c. 20 Sept. 1825 till 29 May 1829. Transfd. to 49th N.I. 11 Feb. 1826. Fur. s.c. 11 Jan. 1835 till retirement. No record of active service.
Refs.: A.J. N.S. xxvii. 123.

STONE, John (d. 1778). Captain. Artillery. (65) Cadet 1764. Fireworker 10 Mar. 1764. 2nd Lieut. 31 Jan. 1766.

Capt. Lt. 16 Sept. 1770. Capt. 31 Jan. 1774. Resigned 18 Feb. 1778. *bur.* St. Helena 7 Sept. 1778.

m. Bombay 14 Feb. 1778, Elizabeth, 3rd and youngest dau. of Capt. Thomas Ringrose, Bo. Est. (She *re-m.* Lt.-Col. Jeremiah Hawkes, Bo. Art., and died Bombay 15 July 1820, aged 56.) (? Ed. Merchant Taylors' Oct. 1756-Oct. 1758.)

Services : On recruiting duty for E.I.C. in England before proceeding to India ; apptd. Lt. F. in England 10 Mar. 1764 ; sailed for India in the *Prince of Wales* May 1764. Resigned his Commission during the " Batta mutiny " ; readmitted later. Was comdg. 2nd Coy. Art. at Berhampore in Sept. 1777. Resigned in order to proceed to Europe on s.c.

Refs. : Intest. ; admon. (Bombay) 15 May 1780.

STONEHAM, Abraham (1778-1851). Lieut. Colonel. 53rd N.I. *b.* Little Baddow, Essex, 1 June 1778. Cadet 1798. Arrived in India 26 Mar. 1800. Ensign 9 Dec. 1799. Lieut. 29 May 1800. Capt. 7 Jan. 1812. Major 11 July 1823. Lt. Col. 13 May 1825. Retired 1 Apr. 1829. *d. unm.* Trinity Sq., Newington, Surrey, 23 Apr. 1851.

bapt. 20 June 1778. 5th son of Thompson Stoneham, of Whitwells, Little Baddow, a mgte. for Essex, and Catherine Morley his wife, 2nd dau. of John Morley, Member Bo. Council. Cousin-german of the mother of Robert Steuart, *q.v.*

Services : Posted Lieut. to 1/11th N.I. 15 Apr. 1801. Operations in Jumna Doab 1802-3 ; Sasni ; Bijaigarh ; Kachaura (w.) ; Lieut. 1/11th N.I. Second Mahratta War 1803 ; Shikohabad (w. 4 Sept.) ; Lieut. 1/11th N.I., forming the garr. under Lt.-Col. Daniel Conyngham, *q.v.* Adjt. Gorakhpur Provl. Bn. 1804 till disbanded in 1807. Employed in dispersing dacoits in Dinapore district Apr. 1809. Capt. Lt. 11th N.I. 31 Aug. 1810. Reduction of Kalinjar 1812 ; Capt. 1/11th N.I. Baghelkhand 1813 ; Entauri ; Capt. 1/11th N.I. Transfd. to newly-raised 2/29th N.I. 1815. Third Mahratta War ; Capt. 2/29th N.I. Apptd. Supt. of Karim Khan and other Pindari chiefs after their surrender in 1818. Supt. of N.W. frontier from Gorakhpur to Nepal under orders of Board of Comrs. Transfd. to newly-raised 34th N.I. July 1823 ; to 67th N.I. (late 1/34th) May 1824. Fur. 1824 till Jan. 1829. Transfd. as Lt. Col. to newly-raised 1st Extra Regt. (became 69th N.I.) May 1825 ; to 53rd N.I. 21 Jan. 1829.

Refs. : Family information. *N. & Q.* 12S. vii. 7. *Pester*, pp. 157, 159, 161. *I.M.* 3 June 1851, p. 338. *Essex Herald*, 29 Apr.

THE BENGAL ARMY, 1758-1834   201

1851. Will dated 22 Jan. 1827; proved 11 Aug. 1851. M.I. Newington, Surrey.

STORY, Philip Francis (1807-1885). General, C.B. 3rd Bengal Eur. L.C. b. psh. of St. Peter, London, 22 Dec. 1807. Cadet 1824. Arrived in India 20 Oct. 1825. Cornet (30 June 1825) 20 Oct. 1825. Lieut. 10 July 1826. Capt. 28 Apr. 1832. Major 28 Oct. 1842. Lt. Col. 2 Oct. 1851. Bt. Col. 1 Feb. 1854. Maj. Gen. 13 Apr. 1855. Lt. Gen. 6 Mar. 1868. Gen. 17 Nov. 1873. Retired 31 Dec. 1877. d. Glebeside, Preston, Brighton, 13 Feb. 1885, aged 76.

Eldest son of Rev. Philip Laycock Story, of Kirkby Mallory, Leics., and Lydia his wife, sister of Alexander Baring, 1st Lord Ashburton. m. Karnal 27 Oct. 1834, Miss Ann Rich. (She died Mussoorie 6 May 1881, aged 70.)

Services: d.d. 1st L.C. 31 Mar. till 1 Oct. 1826; posted to 9th L.C. 1826. Jaipur Dec. 1835; Capt. comdg. 9th L.C. 21 Dec. 1835 till 11 June 1836. Conquest of Sind 1843; Miani (*Lond. Gaz.* 9 Mar. 1843); Hyderabad (ib. 6 June 1843); Major 9th L.C. (Medal). Fur. 1847-8. Posted Lt. Col. to 3rd L.C. Nov. 1852; to 6th L.C. Dec. 1853. Bdr. 2 cl. comdg. Cawnpore 17 Feb. 1854 till Aug. 1856. Was unemployed in India for some years. Fur. 16 Feb. 1870 till retirement. C.B. 4 July 1843.

Refs.: Burke's *Landed Gentry*, 5th edn., p. 1326, s.n. Story, of Lockington Hall, Leics. Boase. *The Times*, 16 Feb. 1885, p. 9.

STRACHAN, Alexander (1783-1818). Lieutenant, 13th N.I. b. Brechin 14 Sept. 1783. Cadet 1804. Arrived in India 10 Sept. 1805. Ensign 16 Sept. 1805. Lieut. 17 Sept. 1805. d. Almora, U.P., 31 Oct. 1818.

Son of Alexander Strachan, of Brechin, merchant, and Ann Dickson his wife.

Services: Posted Lieut. to 13th N.I. 1806. Operations against Dhundia Khan 1807; Komona; Ganauri; Lieut. 1/13th N.I. Bareilly insurrection 1816; Lieut. 1/13th N.I.

STRACHAN, Alexander Leigh (1792-1817). Cornet, 6th N.C. b. Edinburgh 15 Nov. 1792. Cadet 1810. Cornet 28 Aug. 1815. d. Kedgeree, Bengal, 11 Oct. 1817, on his way home.

bapt. St. Andrew's, Edinburgh, 19 Nov. 1792. Eldest son of James Strachan, of Dundee, merchant, later of Edinburgh, and Margaret Leigh his wife. Marlow Cadet.

Services: Cornet H.M. 6th D.G. 3 Mar. 1808. Cadet d.d. 8th

N.C. 1811-13. Fur. 12 Dec. 1813 till 1815. Posted Cornet to 6th N.C. 1815. Fur. s.c. 1817. No record of active service.

Refs.: S.M. 1818, i. 597. *G.M.* 1818, i. 568.

STRACHAN, William (*d.* 1772). Cadet, Infantry. Cadet 1771. *d.* Sultanpur 11 Aug. 1772.

Services: N.F.P.

*STRAHAN, —— (*d.* 1758). Volunteer. *bur.* Calcutta 27 Dec. 1758.

Services: N.F.P.

STREATFEILD, Frederick (1803-1829). Lieutenant, 71st N.I. *b.* Chiddingstone, Kent, 19 July 1803. Cadet 1824. Arrived in India 29 June 1825. Ensign 8 Jan. 1825. Lieut. 7 Feb. 1826. *d.* Chiddingstone 13 May 1829.

9th son (eldest by 2nd wife) of Henry Streatfeild, of Chiddingstone, high sheriff for Kent 1792, and Charlotte his 2nd wife, dau. of William Scoones, of Tonbridge. Sandhurst Cadet.

Services: Posted to newly-raised 3rd Extra Regt. (became 71st N.I.) 1825. Fur. s.c. 5 Sept. 1828 till death. No record of active service.

Refs.: Burke's *Landed Gentry*, 13th edn., p. 1688, *s.n.* Streatfeild, of Chiddingstone.

STRETTELL, Edward Francis (1791-1819). Lieutenant, 6th N.I. *b.* Calcutta Apr. 1791. Cadet 1805. Arrived in India 20 July 1807. Ensign 14 July 1807. Lieut. 10 July 1812. *d.* Saugor 3 Sept. 1819.

bapt. Calcutta 12 Sept. 1791. Son of Edward Strettell, Advocate Gen. Bengal (whose sister Anne *m.* Hon. William Williams Hewitt, son of James, 1st Viscount Lifford), and Elizabeth Child his wife. Brother of Henry Keating Strettell, *q.v.* Ed. Eton; in Remove with Percy Bysshe Shelley and T. B. Malden, *q.v.*, in 1805.

Services: Barasat C.C. Posted Ensign to 6th N.I. 1808. Nepal War 1814-15; Lieut. 1/6th N.I., in 2nd Div., d.d. Pioneers. D.A.Q.M.G. 3 cl. 1 Jan. 1817. Third Mahratta War 1817-18; Lieut. 2/6th N.I., D.A.Q.M.G. with Left Div. of Grand Army.

Refs.: Eton School Lists. M.I. St. Peter's, Saugor.

STRETTELL, Henry Keating (1798-1820). Ensign, Infantry. *b.* Calcutta 29 Mar. 1798. Cadet 1819. Ensign 31 Dec. 1819. *d.* Ballygunge, Calcutta, 10 Dec. 1820.

Son of Edward Strettell, Advocate Gen. Bengal. Brother of Edward Francis Strettell, *q.v.* Sandhurst Cadet.

THE BENGAL ARMY, 1758-1834 203

Services : 2nd Lieut. 21st Ft. (Royal N. Brit. Fus.) 7 Apr. 1814.
An unposted Ensign.

STROUD, George Forbes (1791-?). Ensign. 14th N.I. *b.*
Walcot, Bath, 22 Apr. 1791. Cadet 1808. Arrived in India
21 Oct. 1809. Ensign 11 Apr. 1810. Resigned in India 16 Oct.
1810.
bapt. Walcot 10 July 1791.¹ Ward of T. Bonar.
Services : Barasat C.C. Posted Ensign to 14th N.I. 1810.
No record of active service.
¹ *Note :* No further details in the church register.

STRUTHERS, William (1799-1848). Bt. Major, 14th N.I.
b. Glasgow 17 July 1799. Cadet 1820. Admitted 22 Aug. 1821.
Ensign 9 Mar. 1821. Lieut. 11 July 1823. Capt. 30 May 1829.
Bt. Major 9 Nov. 1846. *d.* Berhampore 10 Sept. 1848.

6th son of Robert Struthers, of Glasgow, brewer, and Euphemia
his wife, dau. of Robert Strange, of Glasgow, merchant. Ed.
Glasgow Univ. ; matric. 1814.
Services : Posted to 2/7th N.I. 1821 ; transfd. to 10th N.I.
July 1823 ; to 14th N.I. (late 1/10th) May 1824. Attached to 2nd
L.I. Bn. 1841 till broken up in Jan. 1843. First Sikh War ; Ferozshahr ; Capt. 14th N.I. (Medal).
Refs. : *I.M.* 2 Nov. 1848, p. 656.

STUART, Charles (1757/58-1828). Major General. Colonel
65th N.I. *b.* in Ireland 1757/58. Cadet 1777. Admitted
18 Dec. 1777. Ensign 4 Jan. 1778. Lieut. 12 Sept. 1778. Capt.
17 Oct. 1795. Major 31 Oct. 1799. Lt. Col. 1 Jan. 1803. Col.
4 June 1811. Maj. Gen. 4 June 1814. *d.* Calcutta 31 Mar. 1828,
aged 70.

Reputed son of Thomas Smyth, of Dublin (who was elder brother
of John Prendergast, 1st Viscount Gort). Brother of Thomas
Stuart, of Limerick, John, and Eliza, wife of Capt. Barker, Armagh
Mil. Foster brother of Denis Neale, of Quarter Town, nr. Mallow.
He lent H. R. Addison, *q.v.,* the sum of £434 to pay for the latter's
transfer to H.M.S.
Services : Sailed for India in the *Europa* 9 Feb. 1777, aged 19.
1/1st Bengal Eur. Regt. in Oct. 1779 ; apptd. Adjt. do. 22 Mar.
1780 ; Qmr. 1st Eur. Bn. in Mar. 1786 till after 1794. Capt.
2/3rd N.I. in June 1798 ; posted Major to 1/9th N.I. 15 Nov. 1799 ;
Lt. Col. to 10th N.I. 1804. Fur. 27 June 1804 till 7 Dec. 1809.
Transfd. to 19th N.I. 1810. Posted Col. to 25th N.I. 1813 ; to

16th N.I. 1815. Maj. Gen. comdg. Saugor F.F. 1819-22. Transfd. to 21st N.I. May 1824 ; to 65th N.I. 9 Feb. 1828. *Refs. : A.J.* xxvi. 487, 606-7. *G.M.* 1830, i. 470. Will dated 9 Sept. 1823 ; proved 28 Aug. 1828. M.I. in S. Park St. cemetery, Calcutta.[1]

[1] *Note :* His tomb is the model of a Hindu temple with a carved stone gate-way. (*B. : P.P.* Vol. I, pp. 74, 214 ; Vol. L, pp. 52-5— photo.) " Gen. Stuart had studied the language, manners, and customs of the natives of this country with so much enthusiasm, that his intimacy with them, and his toleration of, or rather apparent conformity to, their ideas and prejudices, obtained for him the name of *Hindoo* Stuart, by which, we believe, he is well known to many of our readers." (*Ind. Gaz.* 7 Apr. 1828.)

STUART, Charles (1776/77-1854). Major. 3rd L.C. *b.* 1776/77. Cadet 1794. Arrived in India 8 Mar. 1797. Cornet 13 Nov. 1796. Lieut. 29 May 1800. Capt. 5 Apr. 1807. Major 25 May 1816. Retired 16 July 1823. *d.* Hillingdon Grove, Middlesex, 29 Aug. 1854, aged 77.

Sometime of Iver, Bucks. Natural son of William (Stuart), 9th Baron Blantyre, by Harriet Trasdale. Brother of James Stuart, B.C.S., M.P. for Huntingdon, a Dir. E.I.C., and of Lt.-Col. John Stuart, H.M. 9th Ft. (who died of wounds received at battle of Roleia, 17 Aug. 1808). *m.* Susan ——. (She died Brighton 6 Sept. 1856.)

Services : Apptd. Cadet for Inf. ; posted Ensign to 3rd N.I. 1797, but never joined, having been transfd. same year to Cav. and posted Cornet to 2nd N.C. Transfd. to 3rd N.C. 1799 ; Adjt. do. 29 May 1800 till 1805 ; Qmr. do. 1805 till 6 June 1807. Operations in Jumna Doab 1803 ; Sasni ; Bijaigarh ; Kachaura ; Lieut. 3rd N.C. Second Mahratta War ; Koil ; Aligarh ; battle of Delhi ; Agra ; Laswari ; Rampura ; battle and capture of Deig ; Bhurtpore ; pursuit of Amir Khan ; Lieut. 3rd N.C. (India medal). Capt. Lt. 3rd N.C. 11 Mar. 1805. Operations against Dhundia Khan 1807 ; Komona ; Ganauri ; Capt. 3rd N.C. Comdd. a Sqdn. 3rd N.C. on service with detachment under Major William Cuppage, *q.v.*, 1808-9. Capture of Ajaigarh 1809 ; Capt. 3rd N.C. Comdt. Barasat C.C. Aug. 1809 till it was finally closed down 1 Sept. 1811. A.A.G. and actg. D.A.G. Presdy. 10 Dec. 1811 ; 1st D.A.G. of the Army, Presdy., 10 Mar. 1817 till 1820. Leave s.c. to Cape 1820 ; fur. s.c. from Cape 1822 till retirement.

Refs. : E.I.M.C. i. 292-6. His MS. Diary. *G.M.* 1808, ii. 964 ; 1854, ii. 413.

STUART,[1] James (1784-1859). Major General, C.B. Colonel 34th N.I. *b.* Derrykeighan, co. Antrim, 9 Jan. 1784. Cadet 1805. Arrived in India 11 July 1806. Ensign (27 Mar. 1806) 5 Sept. 1806. Lieut. 15 Feb. 1808. Capt. 11 July 1823. Major 8 Mar. 1830. Lt. Col. 6 Aug. 1835. Col. 26 Dec. 1846. Maj. Gen. 20 June 1854. *d.* in England 19 July 1859.

3rd son of James Stuart, J.P., of Gracehill, Derrykeighan, and Grace Lynd his wife, "a relative of Lord Castlestuart's family." *m.* Leckhampton, Gloucs., 30 May 1855, Maria, widow of Colin Johnston, Lieut. 21st Light Dgns., and sister of Adam Duffin, *q.v.* T.C.D.; Pensioner 7 July 1800; B.A. 1805.

Services : Posted Ensign to 17th N.I. 1807. Nepal War 1814-15; Kalanga; Lieut. 1/17th N.I., Postmr. to 2nd Div. (India medal). Intr. & Qmr. 1/17th N.I. 4 May 1815 till 4 Dec. 1820. Leave s.c. to N.S.W. 11 Apr. 1817 till 10 Jan. 1819. 4th D.J.A.G. 17 Oct. 1820 till 17 Sept. 1825. Transfd. to 35th N.I. (late 2/17th) May 1824. Asst. Sec. to Govt., Mily. Dept., 21 June 1825; actg. Dy. Sec. do. 11 Apr. 1826; permanent do. (with official rank of Major) 15 Jan. 1828. Leave s.c. to N.S.W. 25 Jan. 1828 till 5 Apr. 1829. Dy. Mily. Sec. to Govt. 21 Nov. 1834. Posted Lt. Col. to 34th N.I. 12 Jan. 1836; to 39th N.I. 6 Dec. 1838. Offg. Sec. to Govt., Mily. Dept., 14 Oct. 1837; permanent do. 16 June 1839 till 1854. Transfd. to 70th N.I. 1843. Gwalior campaign; Maharajpur (Bronze star). First Sikh War; Mudki; Ferozshahr; Lt. Col. 70th N.I., Mily. Sec. (Medal with clasp). Col. 34th N.I. 1847 till death. Fur. s.c. 31 Mar. 1854 till death. C.B. 3 Apr. 1846.

Refs. : Boase. *Three Hundred Years in Inishowen*, by Mrs. Young, pp. 306, 313. *Alumni Dub.*

[1] *Note ;* The family at various times used the spellings Stuart and Stewart.

STUART, John Lewis (1780-1827). Lieut. Colonel, 27th N.I. *b.* 27 Nov. 1780. Cadet 1798. Arrived in India 22 Dec. 1799. Ensign 27 Aug. 1799. Lieut. 28 Oct. 1799. Capt. 3 Mar. 1808. Major 1 June 1818. Lt. Col. 11 July 1823. *d.* Calcutta 3 Sept. 1827.

bapt. Abbotshall 8 Dec. 1780. Son of Lt.-Col. Hon. James Stuart (who was 2nd son of James, 8th Earl of Moray).[1] Brother of Capt. James Stuart, Maria Stuart, and Mrs. Archibald Douglas, mother of the wife of Joseph Orchard, *q.v. m.* 1st, Barnchurch, Glos., 3 Feb. 1817, Sarah, 6th dau. of Robert Morris, M.P. for Gloucester. (*See also* John Gordon (1765-1832).) (She died Calcutta 16 Sept. 1818, aged 24.) *m.* 2nd, Barrackpore 21 Aug. 1820, Gertrude, sister of Charles Thomas Gustavus Weston, *q.v.* (She died Dublin 14 Aug. 1856.)

Services : Lieut. Sutherland Regt. of Fenc. Inf., comdd. by his father, 23 May 1796. Posted to 1st Bengal Eur. Regt. 15 Apr. 1801. Second Mahratta War 1804-5 ; Lieut. Eur. Regt. Capt. Lt. Eur. Regt. 14 Nov. 1805. Expedn. to Macao 1808-9 ; Capt. Lt. Eur. Regt., A.C.G. Expedn. to Mauritius 1810; Capt. Eur. Regt., A.C.G. to the troops. A.C.G. in Java 1812-15. Fur. 1815-17. A.D.C. to Earl of Moira, the G.G., 14 July 1817 ; Agent for building public boats 1818 ; in charge of Telegraph Dept. 1821 ; Agent for army clothing, 2nd Div., 1822. Posted Lt. Col. to newly-raised 34th N.I. July 1823 ; to 68th N.I. (late 2/34th) May 1824 ; to 67th N.I. 4 Nov. 1826 ; to 27th N.I. 1827. First Burma War 1824-5 ; Lt. Col. 68th N.I.

Refs. : Burke's *Peerage*, 1923, p. 1602, *s.n.* Moray, E. *G.M.* 1817, i. 178. *S.M.* 1817, i. 239. Will dated Fatehgarh, nr. Barrackpore, 14 Nov. 1818 ; proved 21 Dec. 1827. M.I. in S. Park St. cemetery, Calcutta.

¹ *Note :* " Son of Hon. Mrs. James Stuart." (Will.)

STUART, Robert (1744-1820). Lieut. General. 2nd N.I. *bapt.* 13 May 1744. Cadet 1764. Admitted 4 June 1764. Ensign 6 Oct. 1764. Lieut. 24 Oct. 1765. Capt. Sept. 1770. Major 3 Jan. 1781. Lt. Col. 22 Dec. 1785. Col. 8 Jan. 1796. Maj. Gen. 3 May 1796. Retired on Off Reckoning fund 1 Jan. 1803. Lt. Gen. 25 Sept. 1803. *d.* Annat Lodge, nr. Perth, 18 Feb. 1820.

Of Annat. 3rd son of Alexander Steuart, Powblack of Frew, nr. Doune, co. Perth (a cadet of the Stewarts of Ardvorlich), and Isobel Miller his wife. On his return from India he bought the estate of Rait, in Kilspindie psh., co. Perth, and entailed it as Annat on his son, Kenneth Bruce Stuart, sometime a Capt. in the Mahratta service.

Services : Posted Ensign to Pioneer Coy. 25 Nov. 1764. Assault of Chunar fort Dec. 1764 ; Ensign Pioneer Coy. Raised for Nawab-Wazir of Oudh in 1776, 21st Bn. Sepoys, which became part of 12th N.I. in 1796. Apptd. to comd. 21st Bn. 27 Feb. 1778 ; do. 18th N.I. 1 Jan. 1781 ; Lt. Col. comdg. 6th Bde., and comdg. at Dinapore, in July 1787 ; comdg. 6th Bde. at Cawnpore in Dec. 1788. In 1791, whilst serving at the frontier station of Anupshahr, was taken prisoner by the Sikh army under Bhanga Singh. His release was secured 24 Oct. 1791, through the Begum Somru who, at the request of Major William Palmer, *q.v.,* paid a ransom of Rs. 15,000 which

THE BENGAL ARMY, 1758-1834

was refunded to her by Govt. The Begum herself advanced two miles to meet him and escort him to Sardhana. Comdg. troops in Purnea district in 1794 ; comdg. Fatehgarh detachment in July 1798 and in 1802. Comdd. troops in pursuit of Wazir Ali, ex-Nawab of Oudh, in 1799. Fur. 8 Mar. 1803 till death.

Refs. : Family information. *Williams*, p. 173. *Begam Samru*, by B. N. Banerji, p. 73. *A.A.R.* i. 163, etc. *S.M.* 1820, i. 295. Portrait in possession of the family ; another (artist unknown) in Govt. House, Calcutta.

STUBBINS, George (1786-1821). Bt. Captain, 25th N.I. *bapt.* St. Nicholas, Nottingham, 13 Jan. 1786. Cadet 1804. Arrived in India 10 Dec. 1805. Ensign 12 Oct. 1805. Lieut. 2 Jan. 1806. Bt. Capt. 1 Jan. 1819. *d.* Ludhiana 8 Aug. 1821. Son of John Stubbins, of Chilwell, Notts., and Frances his wife. Brother of Ann Webb.

Services : Posted Lieut. to 25th N.I. 1806. Expedn. to Mauritius 1810 ; Lieut. 1st Vol. Bn. Adjt. 1/25th N.I. 4 May 1815 till death. Siege and capture of Hathras 1817. Third Mahratta War 1817-18.

Refs. : Will dated Ludhiana, 7 Aug. 1821 ; proved 6 Sept. 1821.

STUBBS, John (*d.* 1773). Captain, Infantry. Cadet 1764. Ensign (Madras) 25 July 1765. Lieut. (Bengal) 25 Feb. 1766. Capt. 10 Apr. 1769. *d.* Dinapore 1 Oct. 1773.

Services : Apptd. in England 28 Dec. 1764, Ensign on Madras Est. ; sailed in the *Royal Charlotte* 12 Apr. 1765. Transfd. to Bengal Est. in 1766 owing to the " Batta mutiny."

STUBBS, John (1805-1881). Major. 49th N.I. *bapt.* Stratford-on-Avon 30 Jan. 1805. Cadet 1823. Arrived in India 8 Aug. 1824. Ensign (10 Feb. 1824) 7 Mar. 1825. Lieut. 27 Mar. 1826. Capt. 24 Jan. 1845. Retired 23 June 1847. Hon. Major 28 Nov. 1854. *d.* Bathampton, Bath, 3 May 1881.

Son of Walter Stubbs and Harriet his wife. Brother of Orlando Stubbs, *q.v. m.* (before 1848) ?

Services : Posted to 44th N.I. 1824. Served on Sylhet frontier with E. Div. 1824-5, during First Burma War ; Ensign 44th N.I. Transfd. to 49th N.I. 1826. Fur. s.c. 1 Feb. 1835 till 11 Dec. 1837. 2nd in comd. of Jodhpur Legion 3 May 1838 till 4 July 1843. Comdd. the Legion in a " gallant enterprise against Kot, nr. Mhairwara." (*Mily. Cons.* May 1839.)

Refs. : *Bath Chron.* 5 May 1881.

STUBBS, Orlando (1788-1846). Lieut. Colonel, 24th N.I. *bapt.* Beckbury, Salop, 20 July 1788. Cadet 1804. Arrived in India 21 June 1806. Ensign 5 Nov. 1805. Lieut. 26 June 1806. Capt. 1 Jan. 1819. Major 14 Mar. 1833. Lt. Col. 8 Oct. 1839. *d. unm.* Worcester 10 Jan. 1846.

Of Wroxeter, Salop. 2nd son of Walter Stubbs, of Beckbury Hall, and Harriet his wife. Brother of John Stubbs, *q.v.*, and nephew of John Hunt, of Stratford-on-Avon.

Services: Present as Cadet at capture of Cape, Jan. 1806. Posted Lieut. to 22nd N.I. 1806. (? Settlement of Hariana 1809 ; Bhawani ; Lieut. 1/22nd N.I. Reduction of Kalinjar 1812 ; Lieut. 1/22nd N.I.) Attached to Escort with Resdt. at Gwalior 1816-19. With Light Bn. 1817-18. Comdt. Gwalior Resdt.'s Escort 27 Mar, 1819. Transfd. to 44th N.I. (late 2/22nd) May 1824. First Burma War ; Cachar 1825 ; Capt. 44th N.I. Apptd. 2nd Ofr. Sindhia's Contingent 3 Sept. 1825 ; Comdt. do. 4 Mar. 1831 till 19 Jan. 1840. Served against Man Singh Rao Patunka Oct. 1829, also during mutiny at Gwalior in 1834. Granted a wound pension for loss of an arm. Posted Lt. Col. to 53rd N.I. 1839 ; to 8th N.I. 1840. Leave s.c. 2 yrs. to Cape 10 Mar. 1840. Transfd. to 24th N.I. 23 Nov. 1841. Gwalior campaign ; Paniar (*Lond. Gaz.* 8 Mar. 1844) ; comdg. Sipri Contingent (Bronze star). Bdr. comdg. Gwalior Contingent 13 Jan. 1844 till 25 Apr. 1845. Fur. s.c. 4 May 1845 till death.

Refs.: Mundy, ii. 91. *G.M.* 1846, i. 221. Will dated Sipri 11 Sept. 1843 ; admon. 1 May 1846.

STUDDY, Thomas Bradridge (1809-1885). Major. 8th L.C. *b.* Ipplepen, Devon, 1 Feb. 1809. Cadet 1824. Arrived in India 18 Jan. 1826. Cornet (?) Lieut. 15 Nov. 1825. Capt. 8 Nov. 1840. Invalided 29 Jan. 1847. Retired 24 Oct. 1852. Hon. Major 28 Nov. 1854. *d.* Stone House, Plymouth, 2 Aug. 1885.

bapt. Ipplepen 1 Jan. 1810. Son of Thomas Bradridge Studdy, of Coombe House, Ipplepen, Col. of the Haytor Vols., and Elizabeth his 2nd wife. *m.* 1st, Cawnpore 6 May 1834, Charlotte Louisa Elizabeth, eldest dau. of William Bishop, of Grayswood, Surrey. (*See also* W. H. Lomer.) (She died 8 Dec. 1848, aged 37.) *m.* 2nd, All Souls, Marylebone, 23 Sept. 1852, Margaret, 3rd dau. of Peter Vere, of Grosvenor Pl. (*See also* Archibald Campbell Dennistoun.)

Services: Posted to 8th L.C. 25 May 1826. Apptd. Bde. Major of Cav., Saugor Div., 4 Nov. 1842. (? Gwalior campaign ; Maharajpur *or* Paniar ; Capt. 8th L.C.) Fur. 24 Apr. 1850 till retirement.

Refs.: Burke's *Landed Gentry,* 13th edn., p. 1696, *s.n.* Studdy, formerly of Waddeston Court, Devon; 6th edn., p. 1657, *s.n.* Vere, of Carlton, Notts. *The Times,* 11 Aug. 1885.

STURGEON, Richard (*d.* 1782). Major. Infantry. Cadet 1766. Ensign 13 Dec. 1766. Lieut. 6 Apr. 1768. Capt. 2 July 1776. Major 27 Jan. 1782. Resigned 31 Jan. 1782. *bur.* Calcutta 25 June 1782.

Services: Sailed for India as a Bombay Cadet in the *Duke of Albany* 17 Mar. 1766. Transfd. to Bengal Est. 24 Sept. 1766, by permission of the Govr. of Bombay. First Rohilla War 1774; battle of St. George; Lieut. 2nd Bn. Sepoys. Apptd. to comd. Eur. Invalid Corps on its formation, and was comdg. this Corps at Calcutta in 1778; apptd. to comd. 36th Bn. Sepoys 17 Mar. 1779. Resigned owing to ill health.

Refs.: Hickey, ii. 180.

STURGES, Thomas (*d.* 1765). Lieutenant, Cavalry. Lieut. 17 May 1765. *d.* 1765.

Services: (*Perhaps* transfd. from H.M.S.) Apptd. 1st Lieut. of Cav. 12 June 1765, with effect from 17 May.

STURMER, John (1757/58-1796). Bt. Captain, Infantry. *b.* London 1757/58. Cadet 1779. Admitted 19 Aug. 1779. Ensign 10 Aug. 1779. Lieut. 2 Apr. 1781. Bt. Capt. 7 Jan. 1796. *d.* Jamudang (?), 17 Apr. 1796.

Services: Sailed for India in the *Earl Talbot* 7 Mar. 1779, aged 21. Lieut. 9th Bn. Sepoys in July 1787 and in 1792.

STURMER, William (*d.* 1797). Bt. Captain, 5th N.I. Country Cadet 1779. Ensign 30 Aug. 1779. Lieut. 17 Apr. 1781. Bt. Capt. 7 Jan. 1796. *d.* Cawnpore 14 Mar. 1797.

Son of Mrs. Ann Sturmer, of Hackney.

Services: Apptd. Cadet 19 Aug. 1779. Lieut. 23rd Bn. Sepoys in Dec. 1788 and in 1792. Third Mysore War; Lieut. Bengal Vols. Bt. Capt. 1/5th N.I. at death.

Refs.: Will dated Cawnpore, 11 Mar. 1797; proved 15 June 1797.

STURROCK, Henry (1809-1836). Lieutenant, Artillery. (572) *b.* 13 Mar. 1809. Cadet 1825. 2nd Lieut. 16 June 1825. Lieut. 28 Jan. 1832. *d.* Cawnpore 14 May 1836.

bapt. Ballintoy, co. Antrim, 21 Mar. 1809. Son of Robert Conway Sturrock, of Coulrasheskin, Lieut. R. Irish Art. (who was brother

of William Sturrock, q.v.), and Eliza Hodge his wife. Brother of Thomas Sturrock, q.v. m. Cawnpore 8 Oct. 1835, Ann Sophia Mackenzie, 4th dau. of Isaac Pereira, q.v. (She re-m. Frederick Dayot Atkinson, q.v.) Addiscombe Cadet 1823-5.
Services: Posted to 3rd Troop 1st Bde. H.A. 9 Aug. 1830; actg. Adjt. 6th Bn. Foot Art. 24 Nov. 1830; posted to 1st Coy. 6th Bn. 14 Mar. 1833; Adjt. 6th Bn. 2 Dec. 1833; actg. Adjt. Cawnpore Div. Art. 18 Feb. 1835 till death.
Refs.: A.J. N.S. xxi. 189.

STURROCK, Thomas (1814-1831). Ensign,[1] d.d. 10th N.I. b. Ballintoy, co. Antrim, 30 May 1814. Cadet 1830. Arrived in India 11 May 1831. (Ensign 21 Jan. 1831.) d. Cawnpore 25 Nov. 1831.

Son of Robert Conway Sturrock and Eliza Hodge his wife. Brother of Henry Sturrock, q.v.
Services: Cadet d.d. 33rd N.I. 2 June 1831; d.d. 10th N.I. at Cawnpore 22 Oct. 1831.
[1] Note: Really only a Cadet.

STURROCK, William (d. 1810). Bt. Major, 16th N.I. Cadet 1783. Admitted 3 Apr. 1784. Ensign 30 Jan. 1785. Lieut. 17 Mar. 1791. Capt. 30 Sept. 1803. Bt. Major 25 July 1810. d. unm. Madras 14 Aug. 1810.

Son of Ven. William Sturrock, LL.D., archdeacon of Armagh, and Harriot his wife. Uncle of Thomas Sturrock, q.v.
Services: Apptd. Cadet 8 Jan. 1783; sailed for India in H.M.S. Elizabeth. On arrival at Madras served as a Cadet with Col. T. D. Pearse's detachment during Second Mysore War. Posted to 2nd Bengal Eur. Bn. 5 Feb. 1790; to 3rd do. 1 Mar. 1790; to 5th do. 9 Sept. 1791; to 9th Bn. Sepoys 9 Nov. 1792. Lieut. 2/13th N.I. in Aug. 1798; transfd. to 16th N.I. 1798; Adjt. 2/16th N.I. in 1803. Second Mahratta War 1803-4; Agra; Laswari; (? Gwalior); Capt. 2/16th N.I. Capture of Gohad 1806; Capt. 2/16th N.I.
Refs.: Will dated Calcutta 20 Mar. 1810; proved 27 Sept. 1810.

STURT, Auchmuty Ashley (1810-1852). Captain, 6th N.I. b. Cannanore, Madras, 10 Nov. 1810. Cadet 1827. Arrived in India 14 Oct. 1828. Ensign 20 May 1828. Lieut. 11 Nov. 1837. Capt. 6 Apr. 1850. d. Cape Town 15 June 1852.

Son of John Ashley Sturt, Major H.M. 80th Regt., Col. in the Army, and Elizabeth his wife. Cousin-german of Frederick St. John Sturt, q.v., and of the wife of Sir John Grey, q.v. Ed. Eton; in 4th Form in 1826.

THE BENGAL ARMY, 1758-1834

Services: Ensign d.d. 1st N.I. 20 Nov. 1828; do. 48th N.I. 8 Jan. 1829; posted to 6th N.I. 4 Mar. 1829. Actg. Adjt. Kumaon Local Bn. 7 Nov. 1831. d.d. Assam Sebundy Corps 3 Nov. 1836; Junr. Asst. to A.G.G., N.E. frontier, 4 Feb. 1839; Principal Asst. to Comr. of Assam 18 Aug. 1840 till death. Leave s.c. to Cape and N.S.W. 8 Feb. 1841 till 24 Dec. 1842; leave s.c. to Cape 1852.

Refs.: Burke's *Peerage*, 1923, p. 94, *s.n.* Alington, B. *Eton School Lists.* M.I. in Gauhati church, Assam.

STURT, Frederick St. John (1805-1841). Captain, 10th N.I. *b.* nr. Murshidabad, Bengal, 4 Feb. 1805. Cadet 1821. Arrived in India 13 July 1822. Ensign 18 Jan. 1823. Lieut. 1 May 1824. Capt. 29 Aug. 1835. *d.s.p.* Meerut 21 May 1841.

6th son of Thomas Lennox Napier Sturt, of Buckshaw House, Dorset, sometime judge and mgte. of Murshidabad city, and Jannette his wife, dau. of Andrew Wilson, M.D. Brother of Charles Sturt, the Australian explorer (*D.N.B.*), and of John Leigh Doyle Sturt, *q.v.*

Services: Posted Ensign to 16th N.I. 1822; transfd. to 7th N.I. July 1823; to 10th N.I. (late 2/7th) May 1824; actg. Intr. & Qmr. do. 22 Oct. 1829, and 1 Mar. 1831. Fur. p.a. 10 Jan. 1833 till 6 Oct. 1834. Adjt. 10th N.I. 14 Mar. till 9 Sept. 1835. Rising in Cuttack July 1836; Capt. 10th N.I.

Refs.: Burke's *Landed Gentry*, 13th edn., p. 1697, *s.n.* Sturt, of Winterdyne, Worcs. Burke's *Colonial Gentry*, ii. 446.

STURT, John Leigh Doyle (1811-1842). Lieutenant, Engineers. *b.* Combe-Hay, Somerset, 5 Dec. 1811. Cadet 1832. Arrived in India 19 Apr. 1833. 2nd Lieut. (9 June 1831) 24 Aug. 1836. Lieut. 20 May 1839. *d.* 8 Jan. 1842: kld. in action in the Khurd Kabul Pass during the retreat from Kabul.

8th son of Thomas Lennox Napier Sturt and Jannette his wife. Brother of William Milner Neville Sturt, *q.v. m.* at the Residency, Kabul, 9 Aug. 1841, Alexandrina, dau. of Sir Robert Henry Sale, G.C.B., and sister of Robert Henry Sale, *q.v.* (*See also* Frederick Brind.) (She died 22 July 1857.) Addiscombe Cadet 16 Apr. 1829 till 9 June 1831; Chatham 13 Aug. 1831 till 31 Aug. 1832.

Services: d.d. S. & M. at Delhi 4 Oct. 1833. Shekhawat expedn. 1834. Adjt. Engrs. 24 Aug. 1836; Asst. to Supt. Doab canals 12 Dec. 1836. To comd. a Coy. of S. & M. with Army of Indus 21 Sept. 1838. First Afghan War 1838-42; Ghazni; apptd. Surveyor 28 Aug. 1839; placed at disposal of Envoy to Shah Shuja 4 Oct. 1839; outbreak at Kabul; retreat from Kabul (kld.).[1]

Refs.: Burke's *Landed Gentry*, 13th edn., p. 1697, *s.n.* Sturt, of Winterdyne, Worcs. Burke's *Colonial Gentry*, ii. 446. Burke's *Landed Gentry of Ireland*, p. 501, *s.n.* Mulock, of Kilnagarna, King's Co. Eyre's *Journal*. *The Times*, 16 Apr. 1842. Intest.; admon. (Bombay) 19 Mar. 1845. M.I. Afghan Memorial Church, Bombay.

[1] *Note:* He was stabbed in three places on face and neck in Kabul on 2 Nov. 1841, and was repeatedly wounded between that date and 25 Dec.

STURT, William Milner Neville (1800-1855). Bt. Colonel, 43rd N.I. *b.* Chapra, Bengal, 26 May 1800. Cadet 1819. Admitted 21 Aug. 1820. Ensign 9 Jan. 1820. Lieut. 28 Mar. 1822. Capt. 5 Nov. 1828. Major 23 Nov. 1841. Lt. Col. 28 Mar. 1848. Bt. Col. 28 Nov. 1854. *d.* Shahjahanpur, U.P., 10 Nov. 1855.

4th son of Thomas Lennox Napier Sturt, formerly B.C.S., and Jannette his wife. Brother of Frederick St. John Sturt, *q.v.*, and cousin-german of Auchmuty Ashley Sturt, *q.v.* *m.* Rushmere, Suffolk, 7 May 1834, Margaret, dau. of Rear-Adm. Robert Ramsay, C.B., and sister of Robert Ramsay, *q.v.* (She died 18 Feb. 1880, aged 64.) Ed. Winchester; scholar 1813-18.

Services: Posted Ensign to 1/7th N.I. 1820; Intr. & Qmr. do. 31 July 1821; do. 10th N.I. (late 2/7th) 7 June 1824 till 1828; offg. do. 1 Jan. 1829. Fur. p.a. 9 May 1831 till 1 Oct. 1834. Offg. Fort Adjt. at Ft. Wm. 21 Nov. 1834. (? Rising in Cuttack July 1836; Capt. 10th N.I.) Bde. Major in Oudh 21 Dec. 1836 till 25 Jan. 1838. Comdt. 2nd Inf., Oudh Auxy. Force, 24 Jan. 1838 till 15 May 1841. Asst. Sec. Mily. Dept. 28 Apr. 1841; Dy. do. 1846-8. Fur. s.c. 21 Feb. 1848 till 1 Jan. 1850. Posted Lt. Col. to 40th N.I. May 1848; to 62nd N.I. Dec. 1849; to 51st N.I. Oct. 1850; to 44th N.I. Jan. 1851; to 14th N.I. Aug. 1851; to 67th N.I. 15 Oct. 1851. Second Burma War 1852-3; operations against rebel chief Myat Toon 7-24 Mar. 1853; Lt. Col. 67th N.I., comdg. Left Wing of Sir J. Cheape's force (Medal). Transfd. to 43rd N.I. (now 1st Royal Bn. (L.I.) 9th Jat Regt.) Oct. 1853.

Refs.: Burke's *Landed Gentry*, 13th edn., p. 1697, *s.n.* Sturt, of Winterdyne, Worcs. Burke's *Colonial Gentry*, ii. 446. *Kirby. Boase. G.M.* 1856, i. 321. *I.M.* 2 Jan. 1856, p. 8.

SUMMERS, Henry. (*See* **SOMERS, Henry.**)

SUMNER, Edward (1760/61-1781). Lieutenant, 2/1st Bengal Eur. Regt. *b.* in Scotland 1760/61. Cadet 1777. Ensign 26 Feb. 1778. Lieut. 1 Oct. 1778. *d.* Calcutta 17 Oct. 1781.

THE BENGAL ARMY, 1758-1834

Services: Sailed for India in the *Duke of Portland* 30 Apr. 1777, aged 16. 2/1st Bengal Eur. Regt. in Oct. 1779. Second Mysore War 1781; returned sick to Calcutta and died as he was being brought ashore.

Refs.: India Gazette, 20 Oct. 1781.

SUMNER, Richard. Ensign. 2nd Bengal Eur. Regt. Cadet 1782. Arrived in India 22 Oct. 1783. Ensign 11 July 1783. Struck off 1793.

Services: Apptd. Cadet 9 Jan. 1783; sailed for India in the *Earl of Oxford* 11 Mar. 1783. Fur. 27 Sept. 1785 till struck off.

SUNDERLAND, Edward (1808-1885). Lieut. Colonel. Artillery. (568) *b.* Walsden, Lancs., 17 Dec. 1808. Cadet 1824. Arrived in India 3 Oct. 1825. 2nd Lieut. 16 Dec. 1824. Lieut. 18 Apr. 1829. Capt. 15 Jan. 1844. Bt. Major 11 Nov. 1851. Invalided 15 Sept. 1853. Retired 29 Dec. 1855. Hon. Lt. Col. 29 Dec. 1855. *d.* 1 Castle Hill Avenue, Folkestone, 9 Oct. 1885.

bapt. Ulverston, Lancs., 6 Feb. 1809. Son of Rev. John Sunderland, of Walsden, by his wife, dau. of Edward King, Vice-Chancellor of the Duchy of Lancaster. *m.* Mainpuri 12 Jan. 1831, Frances, sister of George Powell Austen, *q.v.* (*See also* Crawford Mitford Rees.) (She died Folkestone 9 Mar. 1887.) Ed. Sedbergh Aug. 1820 till June 1822. Addiscombe Cadet 1823-4.

Services: Adjt. & Qmr. 3rd Bn. Foot Art. 22 Sept. 1829 till 3 Jan. 1839. Leave s.c. to Hills 1 Mar. 1835 till 1 Nov. 1836. Adjt. & Qmr. 1st Bde. H.A. 29 Oct. 1838; do. 4th Bn. 22 July 1840 till 5 Jan. 1842. To comd. Art. at Bareilly 1 June 1842. Fur. s.c. 27 Jan. 1843 till 1846; leave s.c. 1 yr. to Simla 20 Nov. 1848; fur. p.a. 5 Jan. 1855 till retirement. No record of active service.

Refs.: Sedbergh School Register. The Times, 15 Oct. 1885.

SURDLE, John and Richard. (*See* **SARDELL.**)

SUTHERLAND, Eric (1798-1846). Lieut. Colonel, 27th N.I. Mily. Sec. to Resdt. at Hyderabad. *b.* Rosevalley, Duffus, co. Elgin, 1 May 1798. Cadet 1817. Admitted 17 Oct. 1818. Ensign (9 May 1818) 5 Oct. 1818. Lieut. 23 July 1819. Capt. 24 Sept. 1826. Major 8 Oct. 1839. Lt. Col. Jan. 1846. *d.* Hyderabad 27 Feb. 1846.

bapt. 7 May 1798. 3rd son of Eric Sutherland, in Rosevalley, and Jean Lawson his wife. Brother of Lt.-Col. John Sutherland, Bo. L.C., Alexander, of Rosevalley, and Jane Anderson.

Services: Posted to 2/13th N.I. 1819; transfd. to 27th N.I.

(late 2/13th) May 1824. Served with Nizam's army 22 Mar. 1821 till 26 Nov. 1839, and 30 Jan. 1840 till death. Siege and capture of Dandoti Jan. 1828 ; comdg. the force. Leave s.c. to Cape 31 Dec. 1829 till 10 Jan. 1831. Capt. comdg. 1st Regt. Nizam's Cav. 1832-7. Mily. Sec. to Resdt. at Hyderabad 30 Jan. 1840 till death.

Refs.: Burton, p. 111. *A.J.* N.S. xxxi. 176. *G.M.* 1846, i. 558. Will dated Hingoli 20 Apr. 1838 ; proved 5 June 1846. M.I. in Hyderabad Resdy. cemetery.

SUTHERLAND, John (1804-1846). Captain, Invalid Est. 56th N.I. *b.* Canisbay, co. Caithness, 31 May 1804. Cadet 1823. Arrived in India 28 Nov. 1824. Ensign 9 July 1824. Lieut. 19 Oct. 1826. Capt. 18 Mar. 1844. Invalided 5 Dec. 1845. *d.* Tirhut, B. & O., 18 Nov. 1846.

bapt. 9 June 1804. 5th son of George Sutherland, V of Brabster, or Brabster-Myre, and Margaret his wife and cousin, dau. of George Gibson. Cousin of John Robeson, *q.v.*

Services: Posted to 47th N.I. 1824 ; transfd. to 26th N.I. 31 Mar. 1825 ; to 69th N.I. 1825 ; to 56th N.I. 1826. Pte. Sec. and A.D.C. to V.P. in Council and Dy. Govr. of Ft. Wm. 6 Feb. 1834. Fur. p.a. 9 Feb. 1837 till 31 Jan. 1840. Gwalior campaign ; Maharajpur ; Bt. Capt. 56th N.I. (Bronze star).

Refs.: Burke's *Landed Gentry*, 11th edn., p. 1618, *s.n.* Sutherland, late of Forse, co. Caithness. *Caithness Family Hist.*, p. 95.

SUTTON, William (*d.* 1785). Ensign, Infantry. Cadet 1783. Arrived in India Oct. 1783. Ensign 4 Apr. 1785. *d.* Berhampore 23 Apr. 1785.

Services: Apptd. Cadet 18 Dec. 1782 ; sailed for India in the *Vansittart* 11 Mar. 1783.

SWAN, John (*d.* 1784). Bt. Ensign, Invalid Est. Infantry. Bt. Ensign 9 Aug. 1782. Invalided (?) *d.* Chunar 4 July 1784. *m.* Nancy.

Services: Promoted Bt. Ensign from Condr. of Ord.

SWANSTON, Anthony Lambert (1791-1828). Captain, 32nd N.I. *bapt.* Berwick-on-Tweed 12 Nov. 1791. Cadet 1806. Arrived in India 1 Aug. 1807. Ensign 8 Aug. 1807. Lieut. 6 Aug. 1810. Capt. 10 Sept. 1823. *d.* Barrackpore 30 Jan. 1828, aged 36.

2nd son of Robert Swanston and Rebecca his wife, 2nd sister of Anthony Lambert (1758-1800), *q.v.* Brother of Capt. Charles Swanston, 24th Madras N.I. *m.* (before 1814) Eleanor Wilson.

Services : Barasat C.C. Posted Ensign to 16th N.I. 1808. Operations in Bundelkhand 1810 ; Lieut. 16th N.I. Capture of Java 1811 ; Lieut. 1/16th N.I., with 5th Bengal Vol. Bn. Served with 5th Vol. Bn. till 1816. Second in comd. Mhairwara Local Bn. 1822 till death. Transfd. to 32nd N.I. (late 1/16th) May 1824. Siege and capture of Bhurtpore ; Capt. 32nd N.I. Leave s.c. 9 mos. to sea 20 Apr. 1827.

Refs. : Will dated Jellinghy, 20 Jan. 1828 ; proved 13 June 1828. M.I. Barrackpore.

SWATMAN, William (1810-1861). Bt. Colonel, 2nd Eur. Bengal Fus. *b.* King's Lynn, Norfolk, 12 Aug. 1810. Cadet 1827. Arrived in India 29 Apr. 1828. Ensign (24 Oct. 1827) 14 Aug. 1828. Lieut. 24 Aug. 1833. Capt. 17 Mar. 1840. Major 11 Mar. 1847. Lt. Col. 12 Jan. 1853. Bt. Col. 12 Jan. 1856. *d.* Landour, U.P., 9 June 1861.

Eldest son of William Swatman, of King's Lynn, collector of customs, and Elizabeth his wife, dau. of S. Lane, collector of customs at Runcton, Norfolk. Ed. Lynn Grammar School.

Services : Ensign d.d. 65th N.I. 30 May 1828 ; posted to 65th N.I. 14 Aug. 1828. S.A.C.G. 19 Nov. 1832 ; D.A.C.G. 2 cl. 12 Apr. 1837 ; 1 cl. 27 May 1842 ; A.C.G. 2 cl. 4 Oct. 1844 ; 1 cl. 3 Feb. 1846. Fur. 10 Apr. 1848 till 3 Apr. 1851. Posted Lt. Col. to 15th N.I. Mar. 1853 ; to 52nd N.I. 1 Nov. 1854 ; to 3rd Bengal Eur. Regt. Jan. 1855 ; to 60th N.I. 8 Dec. 1856. Fur. s.c. Dec. 1856 till 1860. Transfd. to 3rd Bengal Eur. Regt. 1857 ; to 2nd Eur. Bengal Fus. 13 Sept. 1859 ; Comdt. H.M. 104th (Bengal Fus.) (late 2nd Eur. Bengal Fus.) May 1861. No record of active service.

Refs. : G.M. 1861, ii. 333. *The Times,* 26 July 1861.

SWAYNE, Stephen (1789-1842). Major, 5th N.I. *bapt.* Christ Church, Bristol, 23 Mar. 1789. Cadet 1807. Arrived in India 14 Aug. 1808. Ensign 25 Aug. 1808. Lieut. 18 Aug. 1814. Capt. 13 May 1825. Major 15 Dec. 1837. *d.* Tangi Tariki, nr. Kabul, 10 Jan. 1842 : kld. in action during the retreat.

Son of Walter Swayne and Mary his wife. Brother of Charles Swayne, Bo. Est., and of Henry Swayne, Madras Est. *m.* Ghazipur, U.P., 2 Nov. 1821, Miss Harriet Maria Johnston. (She died Allahabad 6 Feb. 1855, aged 50.)

Services : Barasat C.C. 10½ mos. Posted Ensign to 2nd N.I. 1809. (? Reduction of Kalinjar 1812 ; Lieut. 2/2nd N.I.) Served in Java, latterly in Bencoolen, with 6th Vol. Bn. Mar. 1813 till 3 Jan. 1817. Transfd. to 1/2nd N.I. 1817. Lost his rt. hand by an accidental explosion at Hoshangabad. With Gorakhpur L.I.

Bn. 1819 till 1825. Transfd. to 5th N.I. (late 1/2nd) May 1824. 2nd in comd. newly-raised 8th Extra Regt. 21 May 1825 till Apr. 1826. To comd. young ofrs. 7 June 1830. Fur. p.a. 27 Mar. 1832 till 15 Aug. 1834. First Afghan War 1840-2 ; outbreak at Kabul Nov. 1842 ; operations on 3 and 13 Nov. ; expedns. to village of Bemaru, nr. Kabul, 22 and 23 Nov. (s. w.—shot through neck); retreat from Kabul (kld.) ; Major 5th N.I.

Refs. : Family information. M.I. in St. Peter's, Ft. Wm., Bengal, and St. John Evang., Bombay.

SWETENHAM, Edmund (1795-1863). Major, Invalid Est. Engineers. *b.* Chester 1 Oct. 1795. Cadet 1815. Admitted 4 Nov. 1817. Ensign 1 Sept. 1818. Lieut. 1 Mar. 1821. Capt. 28 Sept. 1827. Major 20 May 1839. Invalided 30 Sept. 1840. *d.* Dehra Dun 6 Mar. 1863.

bapt. St. Oswald's, Chester, 12 Jan. 1796. 6th son of Roger Comberbach (who assumed by R.L. 6 July 1790 the surname and arms of Swetenham, on succeeding to the estate of his great-uncle Edmund Swetenham, of Somerford Booths, co. Chester) and Anne his wife, dau. of William Archer, of co. Warwick. Brother of James Swetenham and of the wives of James Parsons and Adoniah Smith, *qq.v. m.* Mussoorie 17 May 1843, Rose Sadur, an Indian lady. (She died Mussoorie 13 Oct. 1878, aged 63.) Addiscombe Cadet 18 Nov. 1812 till 13 Nov. 1815.

Services : Siege and capture of Bhurtpore ; Lieut. Engrs. (India medal). Supt. of Delhi canals till 11 Aug. 1826 ; Garr. Engr. at Almora, and Executive Ofr. in Kumaon 27 Feb. 1826 ; Executive Engr. 10th (Agra) Div., P.W.D., 8 Aug. 1828 ; do. Meerut Div. 13 June 1833 till 24 Dec. 1838 ; comdd. S. & M. at Delhi 25 Oct. 1838 till 6 Mar. 1839 ; Executive Engr. Meerut 6 Mar. 1839. Fur. p.a. 13 Jan. 1855 till 28 Nov. 1856.

Refs. : Burke's *Landed Gentry*, 12th edn., p. 1821, *s.n.* Swetenham, of Somerford Booths, co. Chester. Ormerod's *Cheshire*, iii. 561. M.I. Dehra Dun and Christ Church, Mussoorie.

SWETENHAM, James (1802-1841). Captain, 10th N.I. *b.* Chester 10 Aug. 1802. Cadet 1818. Admitted 26 June 1819. Ensign (?) Lieut. 28 July 1820. Capt. 18 Jan. 1828. *d.* Mussoorie 17 Mar. 1841.

7th son of Roger Swetenham (formerly Comberbach) and Anne his wife. Brother of Edmund Swetenham, *q.v. m.* Karnal 18 Apr. 1829, Eliza Morrissey Roberts (*probably* grand-dau. of William Roberts (1746-1809), *q.v.*). (She died 24 Aug. 1874, aged 63.) His dau. *m.* Thomas Harvey Hunter, *q.v.*

THE BENGAL ARMY, 1758-1834

Services: Ensign d.d. 13th N.I. 1819; posted Lieut. to 2/7th N.I. 1820; transfd. to 10th N.I. (late 2/7th) May 1824. Served with 2nd L.I. Bn. in Arakan Sept. 1825 till 1826.

Refs.: Burke's *Landed Gentry*, 12th edn., p. 1821, *s.n.* Swetenham, of Somerford Booths, co. Chester. Ormerod's *Cheshire*, iii. 561. Will dated Lucknow 20 Dec. 1838; proved 24 Aug. 1841.

SWETTENHAM, Killiner [1] (1780-1829). Lieut. Colonel, Invalid Est. 9th L.C. *bapt.* St. Ann's, Dublin, 17 May 1780. Cadet 1794. Arrived in India 8 Mar. 1797. Cornet 29 Nov. 1795. Lieut. 29 May 1800. Capt. 22 Sept. 1815. Major 1 Sept. 1818. Lt. Col. 7 Oct. 1824. Invalided 26 Oct. 1827. *d.* Burdwan, Bengal, 27 Oct. 1829.

Son of Killiner Swettenham, lord mayor of Dublin, and Elizabeth his wife, sister of Sweney Toone, *q.v.* Brother of William Toone Swettenham, *q.v. m.* (before 1820) Sydney Maria, sister of Lt.-Col. Thomas Fletcher, Ceylon Rifle Regt., afterwards a coffee planter in Ceylon. (She died Dublin 23 Sept. 1877, at an advanced age.)

Services: Sailed for India in the *Pitt* 11 Aug. 1796. Lieut. 1/9th N.I. in Aug. 1798; transfd. as Cornet to 2nd N.C. Operations in Jumna Doab 1803; Lieut. 2nd N.C. Second Mahratta War 1803-5; battle of Delhi; Laswari; battle of Deig; Lieut. 2nd N.C. Capt. Lt. 2nd N.C. 15 Aug. 1809. Fur. 22 Jan. 1810 till 1813. Nepal War 1814-15; Capt. 2nd N.C., in 1st Div. Third Mahratta War; Major 2nd N.C., in Reserve Div. Posted Lt. Col. to 6th L.C.; transfd. to 5th L.C. 12 Feb. 1825. Fur. 1825-6. Transfd. to 1st L.C.; to 8th L.C. 11 Aug. 1826; to 9th L.C. 4 Nov. 1826. Comdd. Burdwan Provl. Bn. 25 Jan. 1828 till death.

Refs.: Family information. Will dated 9 Oct. 1829; proved 23 Nov. 1829.

[1] *Note:* Or Kilner.

SWETTENHAM, William Toone (1782-1802). Cornet. Cavalry. Subsequently Writer, B.C.S. *bapt.* St. Mary's, Dublin, 25 July 1782. Cadet 1798. Arrived in India 19 Sept. 1799. Cornet 12 June 1800. Resigned 18 Sept. 1800. *d.* Berhampore 9 Dec. 1802.

Son of Killiner Swettenham and Elizabeth his wife. Brother of Killiner Swettenham, *q.v.*

Services: Apptd. a Writer, B.C.S., to date from 29 Aug. 1799. Admitted to Coll. of Ft. Wm. Apr. 1801. Asst. to the Judge at Purnea 9 Jan. 1802.

SWINDELL, Benjamin Cosby (1782-1845). Major. 3rd L.C.

b. Clontarf, co. Dublin, 12 Aug. 1782. Cadet 1798. Arrived in India 14 Dec. 1799. Cornet 23 June 1800. Lieut. 11 Mar. 1805. Capt. 1 Sept. 1818. Major 16 July 1823. Invalided 11 Feb. 1825. Retired 28 Oct. 1825. *d.* 13 June 1845. Son of Charles Swindell, of Dublin, solicitor, and Elizabeth his wife, *née* Hickie.

Services : Posted Cornet to 3rd N.C. and served throughout with that Regt. Operations in Jumna Doab 1803 ; Sasni ; Bijaigarh ; Kachaura. Second Mahratta War 1803-6 ; battle of Delhi (w.) ; Rampura ; battle of Deig ; pursuit of Holkar. Operations against Dhundia Khan 1807 ; Komona ; Ganauri. Intr. & Qmr. 3rd N.C. 6 June 1807 till 10 Apr. 1819. Siege and capture of Hathras 1817. Third Mahratta War 1817-18 ; Jawad ; Bt. Capt. 3rd N.C., with Centre Div. Fur. 1822-24.

SWINEY, George (1784-1868). General, Artillery. (318) *b.* Tottenham High Cross, Middlesex, 7 Apr. 1784. Cadet 1801. Arrived in India 19 July 1802. Fireworker 19 July 1802. Lieut. 20 Aug. 1802. Capt. Lieut. 17 Sept. 1805. Capt. 23 Oct. 1811. Major 2 Aug. 1819. Lt. Col. 1 May 1824. Col. 1 Dec. 1834. Col. Comdt. 1 Dec. 1834. Maj. Gen. 28 June 1838. Lt. Gen. 11 Nov. 1851. Gen. 15 May 1859. *d.* at his residence, 5 Sandford Pl., Cheltenham, 10 Dec. 1868.

bapt. Tottenham High Cross 12 July 1789. Son of John Swiney and Mary his wife. *m.* 1st, St. George's, Bloomsbury, Oct./Nov. 1816, Julia Anne Catherine, only dau. of Rev. Hemsworth Ussher, of Templeoran, co. Westmeath, rector of Clonfadforan. (She died Calcutta 22 Apr. 1818, aged 23.) His dau. *m.* Edward Raphael Watts, *q.v. m.* 2nd, Kasim Bazar, Bengal, 7 Mar. 1823, Maria Isabella, eldest dau. of Alexander Haig, Bengal Medical Est. (*See also* William Battine.) (She died 26 Oct. 1884, aged 83.) Woolwich Cadet 12 Feb. 1800 till 13 Jan. 1802.

Services : Apptd. to Engrs. 26 Aug. 1802 ; transfd. to Art. 2 Dec. 1802. Second Mahratta War 1804-5 ; battle and capture of Deig ; Bhurtpore (w. in 3rd assault 20 Feb. 1805) ; Lieut. 1st Coy. 1st Bn., d.d. from 7th Coy. 2nd Bn. (India medal). Adjt. 3rd Bn. 1806-9 ; Adjt. & Qmr. Div. Art. at Agra 1810-11. Fur. p.a. 5 Feb. 1814 till 22 July 1817. Comy. Ord. at Ft. Wm. 2 Dec. 1817. Leave to Cape 1820-21. Dy. Principal Comy. Ord. 6 Aug. 1821 ; Principal do. 28 May 1824 till 23 Jan. 1835. Fur. s.c. 10 Mar. 1835 till death. Comdt. 19th Bde. R.A.

Refs. : Boase. *The Times,* 14 Dec. 1868. *Faulkner's Dublin Journal,* 23 Nov. 1816. M.I. Leckhampton.

SWINEY or SWEENY, George Antrobus (1761/62-1790). Lieutenant, 24th Bn. Sepoys. *b.* in Ireland 1761/62. Cadet 1778. Ensign 11 June 1779. Lieut. 5 Feb. 1781. *d.* Chittagong 22 June 1790.
Services: Apptd. Cadet 9 Dec. 1778; sailed for India in the *Ceres* 16 June 1779, aged 17. Lieut. 24th Bn. Sepoys in July 1787 and at death.
Refs.: Will proved P.C. Dublin, 1791.

SWINEY, Sidney (1792-1831). Lieutenant, Invalid Est. 18th N.I. *b.* St. Stephen's, Bristol, 28 May 1792. Cadet 1811. Ensign 6 July 1814. Lieut. 3 Apr. 1817. Invalided 1 June 1817. *d. unm.* Monghyr 20 July 1831.
Son of John Swiney, principal surveyor of tobacco office, London docks.
Services: Nepal War 1816; Ensign 1/18th N.I., in 2nd Bde., Left Column.
Refs.: A.J. N.S. vii. 42. Will dated 18 July 1831; proved 25 Feb. 1832.

SWINHOE, Samuel (1786-1866). General. Colonel 73rd N.I. *bapt.* Calcutta 4 Dec. 1786. Cadet 1803. Arrived in India 18 Mar. 1805. Ensign 18 Mar. 1805. Lieut. 27 Mar. 1805. Capt. 1 Jan. 1819. Major 14 June 1825. Lt. Col. 9 May 1830. Col. 23 June 1842. Maj. Gen. 20 June 1854. Lt. Gen. 15 Sept. 1855. Gen. 29 June 1863. *d.* Eslington House, Cheltenham, 18 June 1866, aged 79.
Son of Henry Swinhoe, atty.-at-law, of the supreme court, Calcutta, and Jane Maull his wife. His sister *m.* Sir William Nott, *q.v. m.* Calcutta 17 June 1819, Miss Emily Gillanders. (*See also* William Worsley Davis.) (She died Cheltenham 10 Feb. 1876.)
Services: Posted Lieut. to 2/14th N.I. 1806. Adjt. Mirzapur Bn. 27 Aug. 1813 till 1816; Intr. & Qmr. 2/14th N.I. 4 Nov. 1816 till 1818; 2nd Ceylon Vol. Bn. 1818-19. Transfd. as Capt. to 1/14th N.I. 11 Nov. 1819; actg. District Bk. Mr. Agra 11 Sept. 1820; transfd. to 28th N.I. (late 1/14th) May 1824. Fur. p.a. 15 Nov. 1828 till 16 Oct. 1831. Posted Lt. Col. to 61st N.I. 16 Dec. 1830; to 65th N.I. 5 Nov. 1831; to 74th N.I. 7 Jan. 1832; to 43rd N.I. 16 Jan. 1834; to 73rd N.I. 15 July 1836. Col. 73rd N.I. 21 July 1842 till death. Bdr. 2 cl. comdg. Agra District 13 Sept. 1844 till 5 Dec. 1845. Fur. s.c. 10 Mar. 1846 till death.
Refs.: Boase. *The Times,* 21 June 1866.

SWINLEY, George Henry (1806-1867). Major General, Artillery. (544) *b.* Henley, co. Oxford, 29 Mar. 1806. Cadet 1822. Arrived in India 8 Oct. 1823. 2nd Lieut. 6 June 1823. Lieut. 28 Sept. 1827. Capt. 23 Dec. 1840. Major 1 July 1853. Lt. Col. 30 May 1857. Col. 18 Feb. 1861. Maj. Gen. 22 Dec. 1865. *d.* Simla 31 May 1867.

bapt. Henley 16 May 1806. Son of George Swinley and Mary Ann his wife, 2nd dau. of Edward Bullock. Stepson of —— Cloase, of Sonning. *m.* Cawnpore 4 Mar. 1841, Sarah Jane, eldest dau. of Warren Hastings Leslie Frith, *q.v.* (*See also* Sir Archdale Wilson, Bart.) Addiscombe Cadet 9 Feb. 1821 till 6 June 1823.

Services : First Burma War ; Cachar 1824-5 ; 2nd Lieut. 6th Coy. 3rd Bn. Foot Art., with force under Maj.-Gen. T. Shuldham, *q.v.* Fur. s.c. 12 Dec. 1828 till 11 Nov. 1831. Transfd. to 4th Troop 1st Bde. H.A. 15 Feb. 1836. Adjt. & Qmr. 3rd Bde. H.A. 28 July 1838 till Dec. 1840. First Sikh War ; Mudki ; Ferozshahr ; Sobraon ; Capt. comdg. 3rd Troop 1st Bde. (Medal with 2 clasps). Second Sikh War ; Rangar Nagal ; Kalalwala ; Bt. Major 3rd Troop 1st Bde., comdg. Art. with Bdr. Wheeler's force (Medal). A.A.G. of Art. Mar. 1849 till 1 Jan. 1856. Transfd. to 1st Coy. 2nd Bn. Nov. 1849 ; posted Major to 7th Bn. July 1853 ; to 1st Bde. Apr. 1854. Fur. s.c. 8 Feb. 1856 till Jan. 1859. Bdr. Comdt. of Art. Feb. 1861 till Oct. 1862 ; transfd. to R.A. Oct. 1861 ; Insp. of Art., S. Div. at Lucknow (with rank of Bdr. Gen.), 1 Nov. 1862 till death.

Refs. : De Rhé-Philipe. *The Times,* 15 July 1867. M.I. in new cemetery, Simla.

SWINTON, Anthony Daffy (1788-1814). Ensign, 18th N.I. *b.* Sporle, Norfolk, 17 May 1788. Cadet 1808. Arrived in India 26 Jan. 1810. Ensign 22 Apr. 1811. *d.* Calcutta 8 Aug. 1814.

bapt. Sporle 20 May 1788. Son of Anthony Daffy Swinton [1] and Mary Hunt his wife. *m.* Calcutta 1 Aug. 1814, Caroline Trueman, dau. of Joseph Fletcher, *q.v.* (She *re-m.* John Edward Watson, *q.v.*)

Services : Barasat C.C. Posted to 18th N.I. 1811. No record of active service.

Refs. : M.I. S. Park St. cemetery, Calcutta.

[1] *Note :* For Peter Swinton, Anthony Daffy and "Daffy's Elixir" see *N. & Q.* clxxxviii. 227-8 (2 June 1945).

SWINTON, Archibald (1731-1804). Captain. Infantry. *b.* (*probably* at Swinton) 1731. Ensign 1 Aug. 1759. Lieut. 10 Sept. 1761. Capt. 18 Oct. 1763. Resigned 23 Jan. 1766. *d.* Bath 6 Mar. 1804.

Of Kimmerghame, co. Berwick, and Manderston. 4th son of John Swinton, of Swinton, advocate, and Mary his wife, dau. of Rev. Samuel Semple. Uncle of John Swinton, *q.v.* *m.* Edinburgh 22 Oct. 1776, Henrietta, eldest dau. of James Douglas, of Mains, afterwards Campbell, of Blythswood. (She died Edinburgh 13 Mar. 1827.)

Services : Studied surgery in Edin. ; sailed for India as Surgeon's Mate in an East Indiaman in Jan. 1752 ; arrived Madras 10 June 1752. Asst. Surg. 20 July 1752 ; apptd. an Asst. in hospital at Fort St. George. War in Carnatic 1752-7 ; Vellore 21 Apr. 1753 (w.). Left Coy.'s Service 3 Nov. 1755 ; re-engaged 8 Mar. 1756. Surgeon 1758. Applied to resign the Service 16 Nov. 1758. Commissioned as Ensign in Bengal Army 1 Aug. 1759. Resigned his rank as Surg. 4 Jan. 1761. Campaign in N. Circars 1759 ; battle of Badara 25 Nov. War with Mir Muhammad Kasim 1763 ; battle of Udhua Nullah ; capture of Monghyr (w.) ; capture of Patna (w.—lost an arm). Raised at Midnapore in 1763, 10th Bn. Sepoys. This Bn., which became 3rd N.I. in 1824 and mutinied at Phillaur 8 June 1857, was known as "*Soolteen-ki-Paltan*" after him. Apptd. Persian Intr. to Bdr.-Gen. John Carnac, *q.v.*, Jan. 1765 ; to take charge of the *Hircara* (Intelligence) Dept. with the army in the field 4 Mar. 1765. Sailed for England Jan. 1766, the bearer of a letter from Shah Alam, King of Delhi, to King George III.

Refs. : Burke's *Landed Gentry*, 13th edn., p. 1707, *s.n.* Swinton, of Swinton Bank, co. Peebles. *Swinton of Kimmerghame Records*, ptely. printed 1908. Foster's *Baronetage*, p. 106, *s.n.* Campbell, Bart., of Blythswood, co. Renfrew. *Crawford*, i. 240-1. *Roll of I.M.S.* No. M. 100. *Williams*, p. 93. M.I. in Bath Abbey. Portrait in a painting by Benjamin West in I.O.

SWINTON, Archibald Robert John (1806-1893). Colonel. 32nd N.I. *b.* Winchester 25 June 1806. Cadet 1823. Arrived in India 19 May 1824. Ensign 16 Jan. 1824. Lieut. 9 July 1825. Capt. 28 Oct. 1839. Major 2 Apr. 1856. Lt. Col. 29 Aug. 1859. Retired 10 Oct. 1859. Hon. Col. 10 Oct. 1859. *d.* 21 July 1893.

bapt. St. Thomas's, Winchester, 4 July 1806. Son of Archibald Francis William Swinton, of Warsash, Hants, Capt. E.I.C.N.S., and Louisa his wife, dau. of Rev. Henry Binfield, vicar of Albrighton. Nephew of John Swinton and cousin-german of James Wemyss, *qq.v.* Addiscombe Cadet 1822-3.

Services : Posted to 18th N.I. 1824. First Burma War ; Arakan 1825 ; Ensign 2nd L.I. Bn. (India medal). Transfd. to 32nd N.I.

1825. Siege and capture of Bhurtpore; Lieut. 32nd N.I. (clasp to India medal). Shekhawat expedn. 1834; Lieut. 32nd N.I. Fur. p.a. 3 Mar. 1837 till 1 July 1840. Attached to 2nd Vol. Regt. for China 1 Feb. 1842 till 1 Mar. 1843. First China War 1842; Capt. 2nd Vol. Regt. (Medal). He spent the remainder of his service with 32nd N.I.

Refs.: Burke's Landed Gentry, 13th edn., p. 1707, *s.n.* Swinton, of Swinton Bank, co. Peebles.

*SWINTON, Charles Vivian [1] (1807/08-1874). Lieut. Colonel. 35th N.I. *b.* 1807/08. Cadet 1828. Admitted 3 Feb. 1830. Ensign (20 June 1829) 29 July 1830. Lieut. 13 Oct. 1839. Capt. 28 Aug. 1847. Bt. Major 28 Nov. 1854. Retired 1 Mar. 1858. Hon. Lt. Col. 1 Mar. 1858. *d.* 20 May 1874.

Grandson of Sir Charles Cockerell, 1st Bart., B.C.S. *m.* 1st, Aurangabad 15 Mar. 1845, Elizabeth Anne Peel, dau. of Major Allen Roberts, 12th M.N.I., and niece of Browne Roberts, *q.v.* (She died Hingoli, Hyderabad, 28 Aug. 1845, aged 16½.) *m.* 2nd, Hingoli 29 May 1847, Fanny Rose, dau. of John Stroud.

Services: Apptd. a Local Ofr. in Nizam's service 22 Feb. 1828; passed as Cadet 3 June 1829; apptd. Actg. Ensign (having been 2 yrs. in India) 27 Feb. 1832. Posted to 35th N.I. 26 Jan. 1833, and was borne on the roll of that Regt. until his retirement, but spent the whole of his service with the Hyderabad Contingent (Nizam's Army). Served with 3rd and 7th Inf.; Comdt. 2nd Regt. 27 Jan. 1854 till 17 Sept. 1857.

[1] *Note:* The 2nd christian name appears in the marriage register but not in *E.I.R.* or Gazettes. He was *probably* son of Capt. Richard Swinton, of the Nizam's service, and nephew of John Swinton, *q.v.*; but he may have been a son of the latter by his 1st wife, as alleged in *Swintons of that Ilk.*

SWINTON, John (*d.* 1825). Lieut. Colonel, Invalid Est. 57th N.I. Cadet 1798. Arrived in India 24 Nov. 1799. Ensign 17 Sept. 1799. Lieut. 28 Oct. 1799. Capt. 1 June 1811. Major 11 July 1823. Lt. Col. 13 Jan. 1825. Invalided 12 Jan. 1825. *d.* Bhagulpur, B. & O., 27 Sept. 1825.

3rd son of Samuel Swinton, Capt. R.N., proprietor of *Le Courrier de l'Europe,* and Félicité Jeanne le Febvre his wife, dau. of an officer of the French Gds. Nephew of Archibald Swinton and cousin-german of Robert Swinton, *qq.v.* *m.* 1st, Muttra 17 May 1807, Miss Paulina Stuart or Stewart. (She died 27 Dec. 1811.) His dau. *m.* William Jervis, *q.v.* *m.* 2nd, Agra 17 June 1813, Jane, eldest natural dau. of Henry Jacques, *q.v.* (*See also* James Bourdieu.) (She re-m. Frederick Russell Moore, *q.v.*)

Services: Posted Ensign to 1/11th N.I. 1800; transfd. to 2/12th N.I. 15 Apr. 1801. Operations in Jumna Doab 1803; Sasni (w. in foot); Bijaigarh; Kachaura; Lieut. 2/12th N.I. Apptd. to newly-formed Pioneer Corps Aug. 1803, and spent the remainder of his service till invalided with the Pioneers, comdg. the Corps from 1806. Transfd. to newly-raised 21st N.I. 1803. Second Mahratta War 1803-5; Koil; Aligarh; battle of Delhi; Agra; Laswari; Gwalior; relief of Delhi; battle and capture of Deig 24 Dec. 1804 (s.w. in thigh by cannonball and lamed for life); Bhurtpore. Operations against Dhundia Khan 1807; Komona (s.w. in head by a musket-ball); Ganauri. Capt. Lt. 21st N.I. 8 Sept. 1809. Nepal War 1814-15, in 4th Div. Transfd. to newly-raised 1/29th N.I. 1815. Nepal War 1816; Makwanpur; in Centre Column. Siege and capture of Hathras 1817. Third Mahratta War 1818. Transfd. to 57th N.I. (late 1/29th) May 1824. Regulating Ofr. Invalid Jaghirdar Est. 20 May 1825 till death.

Refs.: Burke's *Landed Gentry,* 13th edn., p. 1707, *s.n.* Swinton, of Swinton Bank, co. Peebles. *E.I.M.C.* iii. 415-18. Will dated 21 June 1824; proved 15 Oct. 1825.

SWINTON, Robert (1773-1822). Major. 6th N.C. *b.* Edinburgh 16 Feb. 1773. Cadet 1794. Arrived in India 24 Sept. 1794. Cornet 1794. Lieut. 3 Oct. 1796. Capt. 13 Mar. 1803. Major 2 Oct. 1806. Resigned in India 31 Oct. 1809. *d.s.p.* Edinburgh 5 Apr. 1822.

bapt. Edinburgh 28 Feb. 1773. 4th son of John Swinton, of Swinton, Lord Swinton, one of the Senators of the Coll. of Justice, and Margaret his wife, dau. of John Mitchelson, of Middleton. Brother of William Swinton, nephew of Archibald Swinton, and cousin-german of James Anderson (1757-1833), *qq.v. m.* Anne, dau. of Alexander Elphinstone, of Glack. (She died Edinburgh 30 Oct. 1822.)

Services: Apptd. Cadet 6 Apr. 1794; sailed for India in the *Rockingham* 2 May 1794. Posted to 1st Cav. Regt. 8 Nov. 1794. Adjt. 2nd N.C. Transfd. to newly-raised 6th N.C. May 1800; Qmr. do. 29 May 1800 till 26 Jan. 1804. Operations in Jumna Doab 1803; Sasni; Bijaigarh; Kachaura; Capt. 6th N.C. Second Mahratta War 1803-6; Laswari; pursuit of Holkar; Capt. 6th N.C. Fur. 19 Feb. 1806 till 17 Sept. 1808.

Refs.: Burke's *Landed Gentry,* 13th edn., p. 1707, *s.n.* Swinton, of Swinton Bank, co. Peebles.

SWINTON, William (1784-1853). Bt. Colonel. 14th N.I. *b.* Edinburgh 10 Feb. 1784. Cadet 1798. Arrived in India 24 Nov. 1799. Ensign 6 Dec. 1799. Lieut. 29 May 1800. Capt. 16 Mar. 1814. Major 1 May 1824. Lt. Col. 16 June 1826. Bt. Col. 18 June 1831. Retired 18 June 1831. *d.* at his residence, 19 St. James's Sq., Bath, 3 Dec. 1853.

bapt. Edinburgh 10 July 1786. 6th and youngest son of John Swinton, of that ilk, Lord Swinton, and Margaret Mitchelson his wife. Brother of Robert Swinton, *q.v.*, and cousin-german of John Swinton, *q.v. m.* Calcutta 27 Mar. 1815, Elizabeth, eldest dau. of Sir Robert Blair, K.C.B., *q.v.* (*See also* Henry Clayton.) (She died Bath 17 July 1859.)

Services: Posted Lieut. to 2/8th N.I. 15 Apr. 1801. (? Operations in Jumna Doab 1803 ; Sasni ; Bijaigarh ; Kachaura ; Lieut. 2/8th N.I.) Transfd. to newly-raised 21st N.I. 1803 ; Adjt. & Qmr. do. 30 Sept. 1804 till May 1814. Capt. 1/21st N.I. Cantt. Adjt. & Qmr. at Barrackpore 1 July 1814 till July 1819. Superintended works erected at Barrackpore and constructed the aviary in the Park. Bk. Mr. at Dum-Dum 1 Aug. 1819 till 25 Oct. 1822 ; Supt. public bldgs. (title changed later to Supt. of Works) Lower Provinces 26 Oct. 1822 till 10 Apr. 1828. Transfd. to 42nd N.I. (late 2/21st) May 1824. Posted Lt. Col. to 67th N.I. 1826 ; to 69th N.I. 2 Apr. 1828 ; to 47th ; to 68th ; to 57th ; to 54th 1829 ; to 14th N.I. 7 Jan. 1832. Fur. p.a. 1 Feb. 1829 till 26 June 1833, when he retired on a pension of £1 *p.d.* with effect from 18 June 1831.

Refs.: Burke's *Landed Gentry*, 13th edn., p. 1707, *s.n.* Swinton, of Swinton Bank, co. Peebles. *Bath Chron.* 8 Dec. 1853. *G.M.* 1854, i. 109. Portrait when a Midshipman,[1] by Raeburn, in the possession of Sir E. D. Swinton.

[1] Note : Served originally in the Navy, and as a Midshipman in the *Glenmare* frigate saw the Mutiny at the Nore.

SYERS, John Drinkwater (1801-1856). Major General. Colonel 33rd N.I. *b.* Liverpool 22 Apr. 1801. Cadet 1817. Admitted 3 Oct. 1818. Ensign (27 Apr. 1818) 28 Sept. 1818. Lieut. 1 Jan. 1819. Capt. 21 Jan. 1831. Major 28 May 1837. Lt. Col. 9 Aug. 1843. Col. 1 Feb. 1854. Maj. Gen. 7 May 1855. *d.* at his residence, Grove House, Hoylake, co. Chester, 18 May 1856.

bapt. Liverpool 22 Oct. 1801. Son of George Syers, of Liverpool, merchant, and Penelope his wife. *m.* Liverpool 12 Oct. 1830, Anne, only dau. of Samuel Richardson.

THE BENGAL ARMY, 1758-1834

Services: Posted Lieut. to 2/3rd N.I. 1819; transfd. to 19th N.I. (late 2/3rd) May 1824. d.d. Ramgarh Bn. 20 Oct. 1820; Adjt. do. 7 Sept. 1821 till Feb. 1830. Fur. p.a. 1 Mar. 1830 till 20 Oct. 1831. Operations in the Kol country 1832-3; d.d. Ramgarh Bn.; tempy. comdg. do. 11 Feb. till Sept. 1832. Comdd. 19th N.I. Feb. 1837 till Mar. 1838; to comd. 4th Recruit Depot Bn. at Bareilly 7 Sept. 1839; to rejoin and comd. 19th N.I. 30 Jan. 1841. Posted Lt. Col. to 19th N.I. 24 Oct. 1843; to 59th N.I. Apr. 1847; to 74th N.I. Dec. 1853. Fur. p.a. 16 Feb. 1854 till death. Posted Col. to 33rd N.I. 20 Apr. 1854.

Refs.: Boase. *A.J.* N.S. iii. 174. *I.M.* 3 June 1856, p. 338. *G.M.* 1856, ii. 123.

*SYKES, Benjamin (*d.* 1803). Bt. Ensign, Infantry. Bt. Ensign 18 Dec. 1780. *d.* Buxar 8 Feb. 1803.

Services: Sergt. of Mil. Sepoys at Calcutta; apptd. Condr. of Ord. on the tempy. Est. 4 Apr. 1778. Was actg. Fort Adjt. at Buxar in 1799.

Refs.: Will dated Buxar 30 Sept. 1801; proved 16 Mar. 1803.

SYME, Alexander (*d.* 1783). Fireworker, Artillery. (216) Cadet 1781. Fireworker 18 Sept. 1781. *d.* Calcutta 12 Dec. 1783.

Services: Apptd. Cadet 20 Apr. 1781. Second Mysore War.

SYME, Andrew (1790-1830). Captain, 57th N.I. *b.* College Kirk psh., Edinburgh, 9 Oct. 1790. Cadet 1807. Arrived in India 19 Aug. 1808. Ensign 20 Sept. 1808. Lieut. 4 Aug. 1811. Capt. 23 Aug. 1824. *d. unm.* N.S.W. 17 Mar. 1830.

Son of James Syme, of Northfield, and Helen Knox his wife. Brother of George Syme, Lieut. R.N., and of Thomas Syme, of Edinburgh, W.S.

Services: Barasat C.C. 13 mos. Posted Ensign to 16th N.I. 1809. Operations in Bundelkhand 1810-11; Lieut. 16th N.I. Transfd. to newly-raised 2/29th N.I. 1815. Operations against the Bhattis of Hariana 1818; Lieut. 2/29th N.I. Third Mahratta War; Asirgarh; Lieut. 2/29th N.I. Comdd. a Coy. of Hill Bildars 25 Dec. 1821 till Nov. 1824. Transfd. to 57th N.I. (late 1/29th) May 1824. Fur. s.c. 19 Nov. 1824 till 13 Nov. 1827; leave s.c. to N.S.W. 20 Dec. 1828 till death.

Refs.: Will dated 16 May 1822; proved 28 Dec. 1830.

SYME, John (1792-1820). Lieutenant, 19th N.I. *bapt.* Dumfries 3 June 1792. Cadet 1810. Ensign 21 Jan. 1813.

Lieut. 16 Apr. 1815. d. Gadarwara, C.P., 16 Apr. 1820, of bilious fever.

Eldest son of John Syme, of Dumfries, collector of stamp duties.
Services: Barasat C.C. Cadet d.d. 12th N.I. 1811-13 ; posted to 1/19th N.I. 1813. Nepal War 1814-15 ; Ensign 1/19th N.I., in 1st Div. (? Nepal War 1816 ; Intr. & Qmr. 5th Gren. Bn., in 2nd Bde., Left Column.) Third Mahratta War 1817-18 ; Lieut. 1/19th N.I., offg. S.A.C.G. to detachment at Nagpur. S.A.C.G. 1819.
Refs.: *A.J.* xi. 179. M.I. Narsinghpur.

SYMES, Charles (1808-?). Lieutenant. 19th N.I. *b.* St. Peter's, Dublin, 15 Jan. 1808. Cadet 1823. Ensign 21 Feb. 1824. Lieut. 16 June 1826. Resigned in India 9 Jan. 1827.

Son of —— Symes, atty.-at-law,[1] and Eliza his wife.
Services: Posted to 19th N.I. 1824. No record of active service.
[1] *Note*: Probably son of either John or Sandham Symes.

SYMES, Jeremiah (1760-1781). Lieutenant, 35th N.I. *b.* co. Wicklow 1760. Cadet 1778. Arrived in India Mar. 1779. Ensign 12 Oct. 1778. Lieut. 10 Dec. 1788. *d. unm.* Sewalah, nr. Benares, 16 Aug. 1781 : kld. in action.[1]

Eldest son of Rev. Jeremiah Symes, of Ballybeg, co. Wicklow, rector of Kilcommon, and Jane Mead his wife, of Dublin. Uncle of William Henry Symes and cousin-german of Michael Symes, *qq.v.* T.C.D. ; Pensioner 8 Apr. 1777, aged 17.

Services: Sailed for India in the *Stafford* 27 May 1778, aged 17. Lieut. 2/2nd Bengal Eur. Regt. in Oct. 1779.

Refs.: Burke's *Landed Gentry*, 2nd edn., p. 1344, *s.n.* Symes, of Ballybeg, co. Wicklow. *Alumni Dub.* M.I. St. Mary's churchyard, Benares.

[1] *Note*: See note to Archibald Scott.

SYMES, Michael (1761-1809). Lieutenant. Infantry. Subsequently Lt. Col. 76th Ft. *b.* co. Wicklow 1761. Cadet 1780. Ensign 1780. Lieut. 24 June 1781. Resigned 2 Nov. 1788. *d.* at sea 22 Jan. 1809, on board the *Mary* transport on his passage from Corunna, in consequence of fatigue and exertion.

5th and youngest son of Richard Symes, of Ballyarthur, and Eleanor his wife, dau. of Loftus Cliffe, of Ross, co. Wexford. Cousin-german of Jeremiah Symes, *q.v. m.* Rochester 18 Feb. 1801, Jemima, dau. of Paul Pilcher, of Rochester. (She *re-m.* Sir Joseph de Courcy Laffan and died 18 Aug. 1835, aged 64.) T.C.D. ; Pensioner 2 Nov. 1778, aged 16.

THE BENGAL ARMY, 1758-1834   227

Services : See *D.N.B.* Sailed for India in the *London* 12 Feb.
1780, aged 18. Fur. 24 Jan. 1786 ; returned to India with H.M.
newly-raised 76th Ft. 1788 ; apptd. A.D.C. to Col. Musgrave, 76th
Ft., 2 Sept. 1788. Resigned his Commission in Bengal Army 2 Nov.
1788, and was apptd. Lieut. 76th Ft. same day ; Capt. do. (18 Mar.
1793) 5 June 1793 ; Lt. Col. do. 15 Feb. 1800. Left Calcutta on
an embassy to the Court of Ava 21 Feb. 1795. In England *c.*
1800-1. Returned to India and was again apptd. Ambassador to
the Court of Ava early in 1802 ; sailed from Calcutta for Rangoon
May 1802 ; returned to Calcutta Feb. 1803. Pub. 1800, " An
Account of an Embassy to the Kingdom of Ava."
Refs. : Burke's *Landed Gentry,* 2nd edn., p. 1344, *s.n.* Symes, of
Ballybeg, co. Wicklow. *Alumni Dub. D.N.B.* (incorrect in many
particulars). *G.M.* 1809, i. 185. Will proved P.C. Dublin 1809.

SYMES, William Henry (1803-1825).   Lieutenant, 40th N.I.
b. Kilcommon, co. Wicklow, 1 Apr. 1803. Cadet 1819. Ensign
4 Mar. 1820. Lieut. 23 May 1823. *d. unm.* Dublin 21 Dec.
1825.
3rd son of Rev. Richard Henry Symes, of Ballybeg, rector of
Kilcommon, and Mary Anne his wife, dau. of Rowley Heyland,
of Glenoak, co. Antrim.   Nephew of Jeremiah Symes, *q.v.* Woolwich
Cadet.
Services : Posted to 1/20th N.I. 1820 ; transfd. to 40th N.I.
(late 2/20th) May 1824. With his Regt. at Natal, Sumatra, 1824.
Fur. s.c. from Sumatra 1825 till death. No record of active service.
Refs. : Burke's *Landed Gentry,* 2nd edn., p. 1344, *s.n.* Symes, of
Ballybeg, co. Wicklow.

SYMONS, William James (1801-1863).   Major. Artillery.
(476) *b.* Croydon 12 Aug. 1801. Cadet 1817. Admitted 21 July
1818. 2nd Lieut. 1 Sept. 1818. Lieut. 30 Aug. 1819. Capt.
29 July 1833. Retired 20 Feb. 1844. Hon. Major 28 Nov. 1854.
d. Fieldhead, Hawkshead, Lancs., 28 Nov. 1863.
Of South Ferriby. *bapt.* St. Peter the Gt., Chichester, Apr.
1802. Eldest son of William John Symons, of Bury St. Edmunds,
Major 16th Light Dgns., and Letitia his 1st wife, dau. of Thomas
Cocksedge, of Bury. *m.* Knaith, Lincs., 6 Feb. 1839, Maria, 4th
dau. of William Hutton, of Gate Burton, Lincs. (She died 24 Mar.
1895, aged 86.) Ed. Bury Grammar School. Addiscombe Cadet
1816-18.
Services : Transfd. from Inf. to Art. 24 Oct. 1818. Offg. Adjt.
& Qmr. Rajputana Div. Art. 3 Mar. 1825 ; permanent do. 23 Sept.

1826; Adjt. at Nimach 9 July 1827. Fur. s.c. 8 Feb. 1828 till 13 May 1830, and 16 Dec. 1837 till 5 Jan. 1841. No record of active service.
Refs. : Burke's Landed Gentry, 13th edn., p. 959, s.n. Hutton, of Gate Burton, Lincs. Family information. A.J. N.S. xxviii. 249. G.M. 1864, i. 131. The Times, 3 Dec. 1863.

SYSONBY, Frederick (1805-1823). Ensign, Infantry. bapt. St. Mary's, Guildford, 24 Feb. 1805. Cadet 1822. Ensign May 1823. d. Calcutta 26 July 1823.

Son of Frederick Ponsonby (related to Earl of Bessborough),[1] who changed his name to Sysonby. Ed. Hertford Free Grammar School.
Services : An unposted Ensign, d.d. Bengal Eur. Regt.
Refs. : A.J. xvii. 196.

[1] Note : The 1st Earl of Bessborough was cr. a peer of Gt. Britain in 1749 as Baron Ponsonby, of Sysonby, Leics. He states on appt. as Cadet, " Col. Ponsonby is my nearest of kin, and he is on service in the Mediterranean."

T

TABBY, William James (1738/39-1763). Captain, 2nd Bn. N.I. *b.* 1738/39. Ensign (Madras) 7 Feb. 1757. Lieut. (Bengal) 1758. Capt. 8 Sept. 1759. *d.* 5th, 6th or 11th Oct. 1763: massacred at or near Patna by order of Nawab Mir Muhammad Kasim. (See note to Henry Somers.)
A native of Gibraltar.
Services: Sailed for Madras in the *Ilchester* Oct. 1753, aged 14. Sailed from Madras for Bengal as a Cadet with the detachment under Major Kilpatrick 28 July 1756. Served in Bengal under Clive 1757; battle of Plassey; Ensign in Capt. Alexander Callender's Coy. of Madras Inf. Transfd. to Bengal Est. 1758. Comdd. 2nd Bn. Sepoys and was present when it was destroyed at Manjhi in 1763.
Refs.: B.: P.P., No. 81 (Jan.-Mar. 1931). *Wilson*, i. 88. *Broome*, p. 365. *Firminger*, p. 71.
Note: (*Perhaps* son or nephew of Lieut. John Tabby (aged 44) who was a fellow-passenger in the *Ilchester*.)

TABOR, Samuel James (1806-1849). Captain, 7th L.C. *b.* London 6 Dec. 1806. Cadet 1826. Arrived in India 24 May 1827. Cornet 19 Nov. 1826. Lieut. 26 Dec. 1832. Capt. 11 Jan. 1842. *d.* Jullundur 21 Aug. 1849.
bapt. St. Dunstan's, Stepney, 7 Mar. 1807. Younger son of John Tabor, of 25 Finsbury Sq., London, notary public and banker, and Elizabeth his wife. *m.* Marylebone 15 July 1840, Emma, eldest dau. of Peter Davey, of Horton, Bucks., and sister of Sir Horace Davey, 1st Baron Davey. (She died 2 July 1903.) Ed. Charterhouse June 1819-Dec. 1822.
Services: Cornet d.d. 10th L.C. 2 June 1827; posted to 7th L.C. 19 June 1827. Offg. Intr. & Qmr. 7th L.C. June-Oct. 1832. Shekhawat expedn. 1834; Lieut. 7th L.C. Adjt. 7th L.C. 28 Nov. 1835 till Mar. 1838. Fur. p.a. 8 Mar. 1838 till 22 Feb. 1841. With Army of Reserve (for Afghanistan) Oct. 1842 till Jan. 1843; with Sind F.F. 1846. Second Sikh War; operations in Jullundur and Bari Doabs; Capt. 7th L.C., with Bdr. Wheeler's force (Medal).
Refs.: Burke's *Peerage*, 1905, p. 451, *s.n.* Davey, B. *De Rhé-Philipe. Charterhouse School List. G.M.* 1850, i. 340. M.I. at Jullundur.

TAILOUR, John (*d.* 1791). Lieutenant, Infantry. Asst. Surg. 22 May 1780. Ensign 25 Feb. 1781. Lieut. 1 Oct. 1781. *d.* Calcutta 5 Dec. 1791.[1]
Services: First Mahratta War 1780-1; with detachment under Lt.-Col. Jacob Camac, *q.v.*[2] Fur. 26 Apr. 1786 till Dec. 1788. Transfd. from 4th Bengal Eur. Bn. to 26th Bn. Sepoys 5 Feb. 1790. (? Third Mysore War 1790-1; Lieut. 26th Bn.)
Refs.: *Crawford*, i. 243-4. *Roll of I.M.S.*, No. B. 245.
[1] *Note:* There is some doubt as to actual date of death. According to some authorities this occurred on 1 Dec.; whilst the Calcutta burial registers record the burial of Lieut. John Taylor on 6 Dec. and Lieut. John Tailour on 9 *idem.*
[2] *Note:* He appears to have been serving in a medical capacity so late as 1785.

RENNY-TAILYOUR, Thomas (1812-1885). Major. Engineers. *b.* Exmouth 18 Mar. 1812. Cadet 1830. Arrived in India 8 Mar. 1831. 2nd Lieut. (12 June) 4 Nov. 1829. Lieut. 20 May 1839. Capt. 4 Nov. 1848. Retired 1 Jan. 1854. Hon. Major 28 Nov. 1854. *d.* Dubton House, Montrose, 3 Jan. 1885.

Of Borrowfield, co. Forfar, J.P. and D.L. Added the surname of Tailyour 16 Nov. 1849. 3rd son and heir of Alexander Renny-Tailyour, of Borrowfield (who added the surname of Tailyour to that of Renny in 1806), and Elizabeth his wife, eldest dau. of Sir Alexander Ramsay, Bart., of Balmain. *m.* 9 June 1847, Isabella Eliza, 2nd dau. of Major Adam Atkinson, of Lorbottle, Northumberland. (She died 16 Sept. 1896.) Addiscombe Cadet 1826 till 12 June 1829.

Services: Employed under Supt. of Foundry 11 July 1831; Asst. Grand Trig. Survey 23 July 1832 till 1844. Field Engr. with Army of Reserve (for Afghanistan) 24 Sept. 1842 till Jan. 1843. Offg. Bde. Major Engrs., with Army of Exercise, 1 Dec. 1843. Gwalior campaign; Maharajpur (*Lond. Gaz.* 8 Mar. 1844); attd. Cav. Div. (Bronze star). Fur. 17 July 1844 till 1846. 1st Asst. G.T. Survey 4 Sept. 1847; Astronomical Asst. do. 19 July 1850 till retirement. Became Hon. Col. 1st Administrative Bn. Forfarshire Rifle Vols. 4 June 1861.

Refs.: Burke's *Landed Gentry*, 12th edn., p. 1832, *s.n.* Renny-Tailyour, of Borrowfield, co. Forfar. *Walford*. *The Times*, 6 Jan. 1885.

TAIT, Craufurd (1807-1828). Ensign, 28th N.I. *b.* Harviestoun, co. Clackmannan, 9 Sept. 1807. Cadet 1826. Ensign

THE BENGAL ARMY, 1758-1834 231

(26 July 1827) 20 Feb. 1828. *d.* at sea 6 Apr. 1828, on board the *Kingston* from Calcutta.

4th son of Craufurd Tait, of Harviestoun, W.S. in Edinburgh, and Susan his wife, dau. of Sir Ilay Campbell, 1st Bart. of Succoth, Lord Succoth. Brother of Thomas Forsyth Tait, *q.v.*, and of Most Rev. Archibald Campbell Tait, archbishop of Canterbury (*D.N.B.*), and cousin-german of James Campbell (1805-1850), *q.v.* Ed. Edin. High School and Univ.

Services: Ensign d.d. 28th N.I. 22 Jan. 1828; posted to do. 20 Feb. 1828. Fur. s.c. 1828. No record of active service.

Refs.: Burke's *Landed Gentry*, 6th edn., p. 1565, *s.n.* Tait, of Blairlogie, co. Clackmannan. *A.J.* xxv. 840.

TAIT, Thomas Forsyth (1805-1859). Bt. Colonel, C.B., 28th N.I. A.D.C. to Queen Victoria. *b.* Tillicoultry 20 Aug. 1805. Cadet 1825. Arrived in India 18 Mar. 1826. Ensign 28 Sept. 1825. Lieut. 8 Apr. 1827. Capt. 24 Jan. 1845. Major 24 Nov. 1853. Lt. Col. 1 May 1858. Bt. Col. 20 June 1854. *d. unm.* London House, St. James's Sq., London, 16 Mar. 1859.

bapt. Tillicoultry 21 Sept. 1805. 3rd son of Craufurd Tait, W.S., sheriff of co. Clackmannan, and Susan his wife. Brother of Craufurd Tait, *q.v.* Ed. Edin. High School and Coll.

Services: Posted to 28th N.I. 1826. Leave s.c. to Malacca 18 June 1827 till Oct. 1828. Adjt. Burdwan Provl. Bn. 4 Mar. 1831; do. Assam L.I. 7 Sept. 1831 till 13 Aug. 1832; do. 4th Local Horse 7 Jan. 1832 till 27 Sept. 1838. Bde. Major to Bde. of Local Horse with Army of Indus Sept. till 22 Dec. 1838, when dissolved. 2nd in comd. 3rd Local Horse 27 Sept. 1838; Comdt. do. 2 Aug. 1839 till 17 Mar. 1851. This Regt. of Irreg. Cav. was known as "Tait's Horse." Transfd. to newly-raised 2nd Bengal Eur. Regt. 8 Oct. 1839. First Afghan War 1842; forcing of Khyber; Mamu Khel; Koochee Khel (w.) (*Lond. Gaz.* 8 and 24 Nov. 1842); reoccupation of Kabul; Tazin; Lieut. comdg. Tait's Horse (Medal). First Sikh War; Ferozshahr; Capt. comdg. Tait's Horse (Medal). Second Sikh War; Ramnagar; Chilianwala; Gujerat; Bt. Major comdg. Tait's Horse (Medal with 2 clasps). Fur. s.c. 9 Mar. 1851 till 3 Feb. 1856. Offg. Comdt. 14th Irreg. Cav. 17 May 1856. Fur. s.c. 3 yrs. Mar. 1857 till death. Posted Lt. Col. to 28th N.I. 24 July 1858. C.B. 21 May 1846. A.D.C. to Queen Victoria 23 Nov. 1855 till death.

Refs.: Burke's *Landed Gentry*, 6th edn., p. 1565, *s.n.* Tait, of Blairlogie, co. Clackmannan. Foster's *Baronetage*, p. 102, *s.n.* Campbell, Bart., of Succoth. Boase. *I.M.* 22 Mar. 1859, p. 255.

G.M. 1859, i. 429. *The Times,* 18 Mar. 1859. Portrait in oils in possession of Gen. Pitman.

TALBOT, Edmund (1809-?). Captain. 53rd N.I. *b.* Catton, Norfolk, 20 Aug. 1809. Cadet 1825. Arrived in India 16 May 1826. Ensign 5 Nov. 1825. Lieut. 31 May 1831. Capt. 22 Dec. 1842. Resigned in India 1 Oct. 1843.

bapt. Catton 10 Sept. 1809. 4th son of Rev. Thomas Sugden Talbot, of Sprowston Hall, Norfolk, rector of Tivetshall, and Ann his wife, late Hill. *m.* 1st, Calcutta 7 Nov. 1832, Eliza Augusta, dau. of George Sunbolf, Lieut. h.p. 33rd Ft., by Bertha Russell his wife, dau. of Robert Pott, B.C.S.[1] (*See also* Jasper Trower.) (She died Etawah 13 Nov. 1835, aged 25.) *m.* 2nd, Jersey 4 Sept. 1839, Anna Margaret, youngest dau. of Rev. William Perry, vicar of Stone, nr. Aylesbury. *m.* 3rd, Caroline (who predeceased him, Oct. 1866, aged 43). Ed. Winchester.

Services : Posted to 53rd N.I. 1826 ; Adjt. do. 21 Nov. 1834 till 9 Nov. 1837. Fur. p.a. 14 Oct. 1837 till 14 Feb. 1840.[2] First Afghan War 1842 ; retreat from Ali Masjid in Jan. ; forcing of Khyber Pass in Apr. ; Bt. Capt. 53rd N.I. (Medal).

Refs. : *A.J.* N.S. xxx. 169.

[1] *Note :* The "Bob Pott" of Hickey's *Memoirs.*

[2] *Note :* He was wrecked in the *Duke of Buccleugh* on his passage back to India.

TALBOT, George Richard (1801-1853). Lieut. Colonel, 2nd Eur. Bengal Fus. *b.* Calcutta 18 July 1801. Cadet 1818. Admitted 27 Mar. 1820. Ensign 20 Sept. 1819. Lieut. 11 July 1823. Capt. 8 Oct. 1839. Major 21 July 1848. Lt. Col. 24 Nov. 1853. *d.* at sea 24 Dec. 1853, on board the *Lady Jocelyn.*

bapt. Calcutta 9 Aug. 1801. Son of John Talbot, Conductor of Ord.,[1] and Elizabeth Ann his wife, widow of —— Saunders. Brother of John Robert Talbot, *q.v.* *m.* Hansi 11 May 1833, Miss Fanny Plumbe. (She died 5 Pierrepont St., Bath, 17 July 1881, aged 73.)

Services : Posted Ensign to 1/30th N.I. ; transfd. to 9th N.I. July 1823 ; to 8th N.I. (late 1/9th) May 1824 ; Adjt. do. 23 Aug. 1825 till 20 Nov. 1839. Operations against the Kols Jan.-June 1832 ; d.d. Ramgarh Bn. Transfd. to newly-formed 2nd Eur. Regt. 21 Oct. 1839. Fur. s.c. 12 Feb. 1842 till 2 Dec. 1843. Second Sikh War ; Chilianwala ; Gujerat ; Major 2nd Eur. Regt. (Medal with 2 clasps). Fur. s.c. 1853 till death.

Refs. : *A.J.* N.S. viii. 67, *seq.* *I.M.* 1 Mar. 1854, p. 99.

[1] *Note :* An Irishman who rose from the ranks of the Bengal Art. and became eventually a Dy. Comy. of Ord.

TALBOT, Henry Christian (1805-1868). Major, Invalid Est. 61st N.I. *b.* Stone, Kent, 14 Mar. 1805. Cadet 1823. Arrived in India 22 May 1824. Ensign 17 Jan. 1824. Lieut. 13 May 1825. Capt. 11 Oct. 1838. Major 11 Apr. 1851. Invalided 1 Aug. 1851. *d.* Mussoorie 22 Nov. 1868.

Youngest son of Robert Talbot, of Stone Castle, Kent, barr.-at-law, and Elizabeth Sophia his wife, dau. of J. Savary, of Greenwich, Kent. Cousin-german of J. T. Savary, *q.v.* *m.* St. John's, Calcutta, 20 Aug. 1825, Miss Julia Anderson.

Services : Posted Ensign to 61st N.I. ; actg. Adjt. Magh Levy 20 July till 30 Aug. 1826. Fur. s.c. 31 Jan. 1831 till 25 June 1832. Shekhawat expedn. 1834 ; Lieut. 61st N.I. S.S.O. at Hansi 7 Dec. 1835. On service in Bundelkhand 1843-5 ; Capt. 61st N.I.

Refs. : *The Times,* 16 Jan. 1869. M.I. Christ Church and old cemetery, Mussoorie.

TALBOT, John Robert (1799-1853). Major, Invalid Est. 59th N.I. *b.* Calcutta 29 Sept. 1799. Cadet 1819. Admitted 17 July 1820. Ensign 14 Feb. 1820. Lieut. 17 June 1822. Capt. 3 Mar. 1832. Major 23 Dec. 1844. Invalided 15 June 1845. *d.* Calcutta 18 Nov. 1853.

Son of John Talbot, Dy. Comy. of Ord., Bengal, and Elizabeth Ann his wife. Brother of George Richard Talbot, *q.v.* *m.* 1st, (?) (She died 25 June 1824.) *m.* 2nd, St. John's, Calcutta, 6 Aug. 1825, Miss Sarah Gillanders. (*See also* William Worsley Davis.) (She died Dinapore 18 Jan. 1832.) *m.* 3rd, Fatehgarh 11 Apr. 1851, Emilia, widow, an Indian Christian.

Services : Posted to 1/30th N.I. ; transfd. to 59th N.I. (late 1/30th) May 1824 ; Intr. & Qmr. 2nd Gren. Bn. 7 Sept. 1824 till 7 June 1825. (? First Burma War ; Arakan 1825 ; Lieut. 2nd Gren. Bn.) Intr. & Qmr. 59th N.I. 7 June 1825 till 3 Apr. 1832.

Refs. : *I.M.* 13 Jan. 1854, p. 2.

TALLEMACHE, William (1786-1818). Captain, Artillery. (346) *b.* Kingston-on-Thames 2 Feb. 1786. Cadet 1804. Arrived in India 12 July 1805. Lieut. 6 May 1805. Capt. Lt. 12 July 1811. Capt. 25 Sept. 1817. *d.* Dum-Dum 26 Jan. 1818.

bapt. 3 Mar. 1786. Son of Richard Tallemache and Mary his wife. Brother of Richard, Maria, Ann and Sophia. Woolwich Cadet 9 June 1802 till 10 Jan. 1805.

Services : Siege and capture of Hathras 1817 ; Capt. Lt. 7th Coy. 3rd Bn. Foot Art.

Refs. : *G.M.* 1818, ii. 372. Will dated Dum-Dum 25 Jan. 1818 ; proved 5 Feb. 1818. M.I. at Dum-Dum.

TALLEY, James (*d.* 1765). Lieutenant, Infantry. Lieut. 9 Mar. 1764. *d.* 1765.

Services : N.F.P. (*Perhaps* transfd. from H.M.S.)

TANDY, James (1764-1847). Lieutenant. Artillery. (182) *b.* in Ireland 1764. Cadet 1781. Fireworker 13 June 1781. Lieut. 19 Dec. 1782. Retired on Lord Clive's fund. *d.* in Ireland 8 Jan. 1847, aged 82.

Services : Apptd. Cadet 2 Feb. 1781, aged 16 ; sailed for India in the *Hinchinbrooke* 13 Mar. 1781. Transfd. from Inf. to Art. Fur. 20 Oct. 1786. " In early life he entered E.I.C.S. and after a series of important services he was apptd. to the comd. of the body guard of the Vizier of Lucknow, and subsequently became A.D.C. to the Marquess Cornwallis. He retired on pension, 1836." (*G.M.*) Left India in 1796.

Refs. : *G.M.* 1847, i. 678.

TANDY, John O'Brien (1785-1827). Ensign. 1st N.I. Subsequently a merchant in Calcutta. *b.* Drogheda 5 Jan. 1785. Cadet 1809. Arrived in India 2 Aug. 1810. Ensign 25 Aug. 1811. Resigned in India 14 Oct. 1814. *d.* Serampore, Bengal, 20 Feb. 1827.

bapt. St. Peter's, Drogheda, 12 Jan. 1785. Son of Henry Tandy and Anna Maria Braddell his wife, of Waterford. *m.* Calcutta 23 July 1817, Sarah, 3rd dau. of Thomas Young, of Carlisle.

Services : Ensign 11th (Forfar & Kincardine) Regt. of Mil. 22 Mar. 1808. (? Barasat C.C. 1810-11.) Posted Ensign to 1st N.I. 1811. No record of active service. Joined firm of Mercer & Co., Calcutta.

Refs. : Family information. *A.J.* xxiv. 274. Will dated 21 Jan. 1827 ; proved 7 Mar. 1827. M.I. Serampore Mission burial ground.

TANNER, Henry (1781-1854). Captain, Invalid Est. 24th N.I. *b.* Berwick 17 Jan. 1781. Cadet 1796. Arrived in India 31 Jan. 1798. Ensign 12 Oct. 1797. Lieut. 10 Sept. 1798. Capt. 8 June 1806. Invalided 18 Feb. 1815. *d.* Monghyr 29 May 1854.

bapt. Berwick 28 Jan. 1781. Son of William Tanner and Isabel his wife. *m.* Calcutta 10 Oct. 1800, Miss Catherine Driver, natural dau. of William Driver, of Calcutta, merchant. (She died Howrah, nr. Calcutta, 23 Jan. 1851.)

Services : Posted to 1st N.I. 1798 ; transfd. as Lieut. to 19th N.I. Second Mahratta War 1803-4 ; operations in Cuttack ; capture of

Balasore; Lieut. 1st Vol. Bn. Transfd. to newly-raised 21st N.I. 1803; to 2/24th N.I. 1804. Employed on survey of Daman-i-Koh, Santal Parganas, 1827-30.
Refs.: *I.M.* 28 July 1854, p. 422. *G.M.* 1854, ii. 408. Will dated Monghyr 9 Feb. 1851; proved 15 June 1854. M.I. Monghyr.

TANNER, Samuel (1756/57-1789). Lieutenant, 17th Bn. Sepoys. *b.* Devon 1756/57. Cadet 1781. Ensign 22 July 1782. Lieut. 18 Jan. 1785. *bur.* St. Mary's cemetery, Madras, 12 Jan. 1789.[1]
m. Madras 31 Aug. 1781, Miss Mary D'Auvergne. (She died Calcutta 13 Feb. 1783.)
Services: Served in E. Devon Mil.; Ensign in 1779; Lieut. do. 6 Apr. 1779. Sailed for India in the *Valentine* 13 Mar. 1781, aged 24. (? Second Mysore War 1781-5.) Supy. Lieut., unposted, in July 1787; 17th Bn. Sepoys in Dec. 1788.
[1] *Note*: Died at sea on his passage to Madras.

TAPLEY, Richard (1791-1815). Lieutenant, 27th N.I. *b.* Gt. Torrington, Devon, 5 Sept. 1791. Cadet 1806. Arrived in India 1 Aug. 1807. Ensign 5 Aug. 1807. Lieut. 1 Nov. 1814. *d.* 25 Apr. 1815: kld. in action at Almora.
bapt. 6 Sept. 1791. Son of Richard Tapley, druggist, and Mary his wife.
Services: Barasat C.C. Posted Ensign to 27th N.I. 1808. Nepal War 1814-15; capture of Almora (kld.); Lieut. 2/27th N.I., with Light Bn.
Refs.: Name on cenotaph on Sitoli Hill.

TAPP, Horatio Thomas (1785-1849). Major General. Colonel 64th N.I. Comdg. Dinapore Div. *bapt.* ptely. Gorleston, Suffolk, 29 Aug. 1785. Cadet 1800. Arrived in India 22 Aug. 1801. Ensign 12 Sept. 1801. Lieut. 13 July 1803. Capt. 22 Mar. 1814. Major 1 May 1824. Lt. Col. 2 June 1826. Col. 9 Mar. 1837. Maj. Gen. 23 Nov. 1841. *d.* Kaltu, nr. Sabathu, 9 Apr. 1849.[1]
Son of William Tapp and Eliza his wife, *née* Barr. *m.* Mehindee Khanum. Brother of Capt. Hammond Astley Tapp.
Services: Posted Ensign to 1st Bengal Eur. Regt. 8 Oct. 1801; transfd. to 1/1st N.I. Apr. 1802. Second Mahratta War; operations in Bundelkhand 1803-6; Lieut. 1/1st N.I. Pursuit of Roshan Khan Apr. 1810. Third Mahratta War 1817-18; Rampur; Jawad; Capt. 1/1st N.I. Transfd. as Major to 4th N.I. (late 2/1st) May 1824. Apptd. to raise and comd. 8th Extra Regt. 21 May 1825

till disbanded Apr. 1826. Posted Lt. Col. to 1st N.I. 7 Dec. 1826. P.A. at Sabathu and comdd. Nassiri Bn. 24 Feb. 1836 till 2 June 1841. Transfd. to 15th N.I. 26 Mar. 1836. Posted Col. to 64th N.I. July 1837. Declined appt. of Bdr. 2 cl. 3 June 1840. Apptd. to Divl. Staff of Army and posted to Dinapore Div. 27 Aug. 1847, but never joined this appt. owing to ill health.
Refs.: De Rhé-Philipe. Will dated 25 Nov. 1847; proved 25 June 1849. M.I. at Sabathu.
[1] *Note*: A promontory at Kasauli is known as "Tapp's Nose," presumably in his memory; and a sauce is named after him.

TATAM, John (1724/25-1765). Captain, Infantry. *b.* 1724/25. Cadet (?) Ensign (?) Lieut. (?) Capt. (?) *d.* Fort Marlbro' 25 June 1765, of consumption, aged 40.
Services: N.F.P.

TATTERSON, John (*d.* 1779). Lieutenant, Infantry. Cadet 1770. Ensign 6 Dec. 1771. Lieut. 13 Aug. 1776. *d.* Calcutta 16 Jan. 1779.
Nephew of Rev. Trevor Benson, archdeacon of Down. (*Probably* son of —— Tatterson by Anne, 3rd dau. of Rev. Edward Benson, preby. of St. Andrew's in Down cathedral.)
Services: N.F.P.
Refs.: Will dated Barrackpore 16 July 1778; proved 19 Mar. 1779.

TAYLER, Arthur William (1807-1843). Captain, 1st Bengal Eur. L.I. *b.* Wanstead, Essex, 24 May 1807. Cadet 1825. Arrived in India 19 Mar. 1826. Ensign 9 Sept. 1825. Lieut. 7 Aug. 1826. Capt. 25 Feb. 1837. *d.* Ludhiana 25 Dec. 1843. *bapt.* Wanstead 26 Apr. 1809. Son of John Tayler and Elizabeth his wife. Brother of Edward Tayler, *q.v. m.* Radakissenpore 5 Apr. 1837, Eliza, youngest dau. of William Jones, of Sibpore. (She died Boulogne 1846.) Addiscombe Cadet 1823-4.
Services: Posted Ensign to 1st Bengal Eur. Regt. Extra A.D.C. to C.-in-C., Madras (Lt.-Gen. Sir G. T. Walker, G.C.B.), 5 Jan. 1829 till 26 Oct. 1830. Fur. s.c. 14 Feb. 1833 till 27 May 1836. Apptd. Bde. Major 4th Bde., Army of Indus, 10 Sept. 1838. First Afghan War 1838-40; Ghazni (w.—*Lond. Gaz.* 30 Oct. 1839); posted to Shah Shuja's force and apptd. Inspr. 1st Jan-baz Horse 27 Aug. 1839; Capt. 1st Bengal Eur. Regt. (Medal). Leave s.c. to India 15 Dec. 1840; s.c. to sea 21 Apr. till 6 Sept. 1841. Comdd. 4th Inf. Levy at Cawnpore 31 Jan. till 1 Oct. 1842. With Army of

Reserve (for Afghanistan) Oct. 1842 till Jan. 1843 ; Capt. 1st Bengal Eur. L.I. Durani 3 cl.
Refs. : *I.M.* 9 Mar. 1844, p. 339.

TAYLER, Edward (1810-1834). Cornet, 6th L.C. *b.* Bishopsgate 2 July 1810. Cadet 1826. Arrived in India 27 Oct. 1827. Cornet (28 May 1828) 13 Jan. 1829. *d.* Hodnet rectory, Salop, 18 Aug. 1834.

bapt. St. Botolph, Bishopsgate, 12 Dec. 1812. Son of John Tayler and Elizabeth his wife. Brother of Arthur William Tayler, *q.v.*

Services : Posted Cornet to 5th L.C. 25 Nov. 1828 ; transfd. to 6th L.C. 13 Jan. 1829. Fur. s.c. 23 July 1832 till death. No record of active service.

Refs. : *A.J.* N.S. xv. 124. *G.M.* 1834, ii. 557.

TAYLER, Thomas (1778-1809). Captain, 7th N.I. *b.* Devizes, Wilts., 18 Apr. 1778. Cadet 1794. Arrived in India 20 Apr. 1797. Ensign 16 Oct. 1795. Lieut. 19 Feb. 1797. Capt. 21 Sept. 1804. *d.* Calcutta 23 Oct. 1809.

bapt. St. John the Baptist, Devizes, 10 May 1778. Son of Samuel Tayler, six times mayor of Devizes, who formed and comdd. the " Devizes Loyal Vols.," and Sarah his wife, dau. of Joseph Needham, M.D. Brother of Joseph Needham Tayler, Rear Adm. R.N. (*D.N.B.*).

Services : Apptd. Cadet 6 July 1796 ; sailed for India in the *Princess Mary* 25 Oct. 1796. Lieut. 1/9th N.I. in Aug. 1798 ; transfd. to 7th N.I. 1798.

TAYLOR, Charles (1785-1826). Captain, 4th N.I. *b.* Kew Green, Surrey, 7 Nov. 1785. Cadet 1804. Arrived in India 10 Sept. 1805. Ensign 8 Aug. 1805. Lieut. 9 Aug. 1805. Capt. 1 Aug. 1818. *d. unm.* at sea 1826, on board the *Mary Anne.*

bapt. 8 Nov. 1785. Son of Simon Taylor, of Richmond, and Anne his wife.

Services : A survivor from the wreck of the *Earl of Abergavenny* 5 Feb. 1805. (See note to Charles Davis or Davies.) Posted Lieut. to 1st N.I. 1806. (? Operations in Bundelkhand 1806-7 ; Chamir ; Sehlehuganj ; Lieut. 2/1st N.I. Bundelkhand 1809 ; Rajaoli ; Ajaigarh ; Lieut. 2/1st N.I.) Capture of Java 1811 ; Lieut. 5th Vol. Bn. Intr. & Qmr. 2/1st N.I. 1 July 1814 till 4 May 1815. Nepal War 1814-15 ; Lieut. 2/1st N.I., in 1st Div. Capt. Lt. 2/1st N.I. 5 Dec. 1815. Siege and capture of Hathras 1817 ; Capt. 2/1st N.I. Third Mahratta War. Bde. Major Rajputana F.F. 1818 till Aug. 1826. Transfd. to 4th N.I. (late 2/1st) May 1824. Fur. 25 Aug. 1826 till death.

Refs.: *A.J.* xxi. Will dated on board his budgerow on the Ganges, nr. Cawnpore, 5 Feb. 1825; proved 13 Feb. 1827.

TAYLOR, John (1788-1841). Lieut. Colonel. 15th N.I. *b.* Lauder, co. Berwick, 19 Mar. 1788. Cadet 1804. Arrived in India 2 June 1806. Ensign 23 Oct. 1805. Lieut. 12 Apr. 1806. Capt. 11 July 1823. Major 21 Jan. 1831. Lt. Col. 22 Sept. 1836. Retired 26 Mar. 1840. *d.* St. Andrews 26 July 1841. *bapt.* 29 Mar. 1788. Son of John Taylor, schoolmaster and burgess of Lauder, and Sarah Falconar his wife. *m.* Bombay 17 July 1823, Miss Sarah Falconer Graham, dau. of William Graham, of Haddington. (She died N.Z. 11 Aug. 1871.)

Services: Posted Lieut. to 3rd N.I. 1806. (? Operations in Bundelkhand 1809; Rajaoli; Ajaigarh; Lieut. 1/3rd N.I.) d.d. Resdt.'s escort at Delhi 1812; Adjt. 1/3rd N.I. 1813-14; do. 2/3rd N.I. 1815. Tempy. S.A.C.G. in the field 27 Oct. 1814; permanent do. 22 Dec. 1815 till 1824. Nepal War 1814-15; S.A.C.G., in 1st Div. Comst. Ofr. with Nimach F.F. in Rajputana, comdd. by Lt. Col. John Ludlow, *q.v.*, June 1820. D.A.C.G. 1824; A.C.G. 2 cl. 27 May 1825; 1 cl. 2 July 1828 till 12 Apr. 1837. Sent to Chittagong on outbreak of war with Ava. First Burma War; A.C.G. Posted Lt. Col. to 29th N.I. 29 Apr. 1837; to 15th N.I. 14 Feb. 1838. Fur. p.a. 22 Jan. 1838 till retirement.

Refs.: *I.N.* No. 17, p. 398. Will dated Cupar 13 Oct. 1840; admon. 26 July 1842.

TAYLOR, John (1802-1822). Ensign, 18th N.I. *b.* Townhead, Lancs., 8 Feb. 1802. Cadet 1818. Ensign 16 Aug. 1819. *d. unm.* nr. Patna 23 Aug. 1822: drowned.

bapt. Staveley-in-Cartmel, Lancs., 8 Feb. 1802. 3rd son of Harry Taylor, of Townhead, and of Abbot Hall, Westmorland, M.C.S., and Charlotte his wife, 4th dau. of Rev. Robert Andrews, rector of Ealing. Brother of Robert Taylor and of the wife of Charles Graham (1788-1858), *qq.v.* Nephew of Col. John Bladen Taylor, Madras Est., M.P. for Hythe and Dir. E.I. Co., cousin-german of Henry Clerk, *q.v.*, and related to Thomas Montgomerie, *q.v.* Addiscombe Cadet 1818-19.

Services: Ensign d.d. Bengal Eur. Regt. 1819; posted to 1/18th N.I. Leave to Madras 1821-2. No record of active service.

Refs.: *Misc. Gen. et Her.* N.S. iii. 181.

TAYLOR, John Lewis (1806-1879). Major General. 32nd N.I. *b.* London 27 Aug. 1806. Cadet 1824. Arrived in India 5 June

1825. Ensign 23 Jan. 1825. Lieut. 26 Dec. 1826. Capt. 12 Jan. 1837. Major 18 June 1850. Lt. Col. 10 Feb. 1856. Bt. Col. 14 Mar. 1857. Retired 31 Dec. 1861. Hon. Maj. Gen. 31 Dec. 1861. *d.* Mussoorie, U.P., 23 June 1879.

Of Dehra Dun, U.P. *bapt.* Allhallows the Gt., London, 23 Sept. 1806. Son of John Thomas Taylor, of Upper Thames St., iron merchant. *m.* Meerut 26 June 1838, Eliza, youngest dau. of Capt. William Williams, Paymr. H.M. 16th Lrs. (*See also* Henry Lloyd.) (She died Brighton 25 Jan. 1897, aged 77.)

Services : Posted Ensign to 64th N.I. 1825 ; to 32nd N.I. 1825. Siege and capture of Bhurtpore ; Ensign 32nd N.I. (India medal). Transfd. to 26th N.I. 1826 ; Adjt. do. 3 May 1832 till 13 Feb. 1837. Postmr. to Gen. McCaskill's Bde. proceeding to Afghanistan 5 Jan. till 16 Apr. 1842. First Afghan War 1842 ; comdd. 2 Coys. 26th N.I., ½ Coy. H.M. 9th Ft., and 40 Sappers in action at Koochee Khel 24 Aug. (*Lond. Gaz.* 11 Nov. 1842) ; reoccupation of Kabul ; Istalif ; Capt. 26th N.I., with Pollock's force (Medal). Comdt. Recruit Depot at Ferozepore 7 Apr. 1843. First Sikh War ; Mudki ; Ferozshahr ; Sobraon ; Capt. 26th N.I., Bde. Major 5th Inf. Bde. (Medal with 2 clasps). Fur. 1849 till Jan. 1852. Posted Lt. Col. to 26th N.I. 1856. Fur. s.c. Feb. 1857 till 6 Oct. 1859. Transfd. to 32nd N.I. 7 Nov. 1859.

Refs.: *The Times,* 2 July 1879. M.I. Dehra Dun.

TAYLOR, John William (1782-1824). Lieut. Colonel, 20th N.I. *bapt.* St. Katherine's nr. Tower of London 7 May 1782. Cadet 1797. Arrived in India 14 Sept. 1798. Ensign 15 Sept. 1798. Lieut. 1 Nov. 1798. Capt. 17 Sept. 1807. Major 4 Nov. 1817. Lt. Col. 11 July 1823. *d.* Saugor 30 July 1824.

Son of James Taylor, of Lavender Hill, and Christian his wife. *m.* Calcutta 27 Nov. 1810, Miss Emma Gould, dau. of Blissett William Gould, of Calcutta, merchant, and half-sister of Frederick Robert Turnbull, *q.v.* (She died 10 June 1844.)

Services : Posted Ensign to 2nd Bengal Eur. Regt. Oct. 1798 ; transfd. to 14th N.I. 1798. Second Mahratta War 1803-6 ; Lieut. 14th N.I. Professor of Hindustani at Coll. of Ft. Wm. 22 Feb. 1808 till Nov. 1823. Capt. 2/14th N.I. Sec. to Board of Superintendence for improving the breed of cattle 21 Jan. 1817 ; afterwards Member of do. Major 1/14th N.I. Offg. J.A.G. May 1822 till death, but retained his professorship. Lt. Col. 20th N.I. May 1824.

Refs.: Will undated ; proved 21 Aug. 1824.

TAYLOR, John William (1792-1815). Lieutenant, 13th N.I. *b.* Halifax, Nova Scotia, 10 Oct. 1792. Cadet 1807. Arrived in

India 19 Aug. 1808. Ensign 19 Aug. 1808. Lieut. 7 Aug. 1814. *d.s.p.* Bareilly, U.P., 4 Sept. 1815.

Eldest son of William Taylor (of the Pennington family), C.J. of Jamaica, and Eliza his wife, dau. of Col. Philip Van Cortlandt. *Services:* Barasat C.C. Posted Ensign to 13th N.I. 1809; Lieut. 1/13th N.I. Adjt. Dacca Provl. Bn. 1813-14. No record of active service.

Refs.: Burke's *Landed Gentry*, 11th edn., p. 1445, *s.n.* Pringle-Taylor, of Pennington, Hants. *A.J.* i. 605.

TAYLOR, Joseph (1765/66-1811). Bt. Major. Artillery. (269) *b.* 1765/66. Cadet 1783. Admitted 28 Aug. 1783. Fireworker 13 May 1785. Lieut. 23 Jan. 1794. Capt. Lt. 24 Feb. 1802. Capt. 12 Nov. 1804. Bt. Major 25 July 1810. Retired 12 July 1811. *d.* Llangenny, co. Brecon, 8 Aug. 1811, aged 45.[1]

Of Court Duff and Blomtherstown, nr. Dublin. Elder son of Joseph Taylor, of Dunkerron, co. Kerry, by his wife, " dau. of an Indian rajah." Brother of Thomas Taylor (1757-1804), *q.v. m.* (before 1785) Poor Begum. Father of Thomas Taylor, M.D. (*D.N.B.*), and grandfather of the wife of Robert Henry Seale, *q.v.*

Services: Apptd. Cadet 3 Dec. 1782; sailed for India in the *Barwell* 11 Mar. 1783. Posted Lieut. to 1st Bn. Art. 30 Jan. 1794. Apptd. Asst. to Agent for manufacture of gunpowder 8 Nov. 1794; Agent to new Gunpowder Agency at Allahabad on a salary of Rs. 1,000 *p.m.*, plus pay, batta, and gratuity of his rank, 1800 till Apr. 1808. Fur. 1808 till retirement. No record of active service.

Refs.: Burke's *Landed Gentry*, 4th edn., p. 1486, *s.n.* Taylor, of Dunkerron, co. Kerry. *The E.I. Co.'s Arsenals and Manufactories.* Will dated 12 Feb. 1811; proved 15 Dec. 1817.

[1] *Note:* ? *d.* Clifton, of water on the chest. (*G.M.*)

TAYLOR, Joseph (1790-1835). Lieut. Colonel, Engineers. *bapt.* Bishops Castle, Salop, 27 Jan. 1790. Cadet 1806. Arrived in India 2 Oct. 1807. Ensign 6 Oct. 1807. Lieut. 4 Oct. 1808. Capt. 1 Sept. 1818. Major 20 Sept. 1827. Lt. Col. 18 June 1831. *d.* Agra 20 Apr. 1835, of apoplexy.

Son of Joseph Taylor and Margaret his wife. *m.* 1st, Agra 30 Aug. 1811, Anne, eldest dau. of Rev. Jonathan Bourchier, of Epsom. (She died Agra 11 July 1814.) His daus. *m.* W. E. M. R. Hay and Johnson Phillott, *qq.v. m.* 2nd, Calcutta 1 May 1819, Frances Henrietta, of Yatton, Wilts., 3rd dau. of R. H. Colebrooke, *q.v.* Woolwich Cadet 1 Feb. 1804 till 27 Feb. 1807.

Services: Permitted to join Engrs. as Actg. Ensign 2 Nov.

1807; recommended by Col. Alexander Kyd, *q.v.*, for permanent appt. to Engrs. (*Cons.* 29 Apr. 1809). Asst. to Garr. Engr. at Agra; repaired the Taj at Agra and Akbar's tomb at Sikandra 1810-11. Leave s.c. 6 mos. 1 Mar. 1815. Siege and capture of Hathras 1817, and subsequently superintended its demolition. Third Mahratta War; Asst. Field Engr. 1st Div. Apptd. to construct a lighthouse on Saugor I. Jan. 1820. Garr. Engr. & Executive Ofr. Agra 18 Oct. 1821; Executive Engr. Agra Div., P.W.D., 19 Apr. 1825; do. Dinapore 26 Oct. 1825. Siege and capture of Bhurtpore (s.w.). Garr. Engr. & Executive Ofr. at Ft. Wm., and Civil Architect at Presdy. 14 Feb. 1829; Suptg. Engr. N.W.P. 16 July 1830 till death.
Refs.: *D.I.B.* *Bengal Obit.*, p. 378. Will dated 18 Jan. 1833; proved 26 May 1835. M.I. at Agra.

TAYLOR, Robert (1800-1843). Captain, 65th N.I. *b.* Marylebone 17 Nov. 1800. Cadet 1816. Admitted 13 June 1817. Ensign (?) Lieut. 1 Aug. 1818. Capt. 31 Jan. 1832. *d.* Darjeeling 21 June 1843.

bapt. 8 Dec. 1800. 2nd son of Harry Taylor, M.C.S., and Charlotte Andrews his wife. Brother of John Taylor (1802-1822), *q.v.* *m.* 1st, Dinapore 15 Nov. 1824, Miss Sarah Keys. (She died Mhow 7 Apr. 1833.) *m.* 2nd, Bath 16 Jan. 1838, Charlotte Helen, youngest dau. of Samuel Delpratt, of Bath, and of the psh. of St. David, Jamaica. Ed. Warminster. Addiscombe Cadet 1816-17.

Services: Ensign d.d. 11th N.I. 1817; posted Lieut. to 1/11th N.I. 1818; transfd. to newly-raised 33rd N.I. July 1823; to 65th N.I. (late 1/33rd) May 1824; Intr. & Qmr. do. 7 July 1825 till 14 Oct. 1829; actg. Adjt. Agra Provl. Bn. 22 Oct. 1829. Fur. s.c. 21 July 1835 till 21 Oct. 1838. Leave s.c. 2 yrs. to Darjeeling 15 Sept. 1841. No record of active service.
Refs.: *Misc. Gen. et Her.* 2S. iii. 346. *G.M.* 1838, i. 312.

TAYLOR, Thomas (*d.* 1773). Lieutenant, 6th Bn. Sepoys. Cadet 1769. Ensign 4 Sept. 1769. Lieut. 29 Jan. 1773. *d.* Chichacotta, Cooch Behar, 25 Mar. 1773.

Services: Operations against the Bhutias in Cooch Behar 1772-3; storm and capture of Cooch Behar; Lieut. 6th Bn. Sepoys.

TAYLOR, Thomas (1757-1804). Lieut. Colonel, 11th N.I. *b.* 1757. Cadet 1777. Arrived in India 18 Dec. 1777. Ensign 5 Feb. 1778. Lieut. 15 Sept. 1778. Capt. 7 Jan. 1796. Major 21 Apr. 1800. Lt. Col. 13 July 1803. *d.* Gwalior 24 May 1804. Younger son of Joseph Taylor, of Dunkerron. Brother of Joseph

Taylor (d. 1811), q.v. Owned property in Mountrath St., Dublin, and in Kilmore. m. Nooran Begum.

Services: Sailed for India in the *Egmont* 1 Jan. 1777, aged 19. First Mahratta War; retreat down the Bhor Ghaut 24 Apr. 1781 (w.). Lieut. 1st Bn. Sepoys in July 1787; 6th Eur. Bn. in Feb. 1796; Capt. 2/3rd N.I. in June 1798; transfd. to 11th N.I. 1798. Operations in Jumna Doab 1803; Sasni; Major 2/11th N.I. Second Mahratta War; Bundelkhand 1803; Kapsa; Kalpi; capture of Gwalior 1804; Lt. Col. 2/11th N.I.

Refs.: Burke's *Landed Gentry*, 4th edn., p. 1486, *s.n.* Taylor, of Dunkerron, co. Kerry. *Pester*, p. 296. Will dated 24 Oct. 1798; proved 2 July 1804.

TAYLOR, Thomas (1784-1869). Lieutenant. 26th N.I. *b.* London 27 Sept. 1784. Cadet 1800. Arrived in India 19 Aug. 1801. Ensign 2 Nov. 1801. Lieut. 30 Sept. 1803. Resigned in England 1812. *d.* Clifton, Glos., 16 Nov. 1869.

Of Valetta Lodge, Clifton, and The Mythe, Glos. *bapt.* Marylebone 28 Nov. 1785. Son of Thomas Taylor and Eleanor his wife. *m.* 27 Mar. 1820, Mary, 3rd dau. of Sir John Geers Cotterell, 1st Bart., of Garnons, co. Hereford. (She died 26 Aug. 1868, aged 73.)

Services: Ensign d.d. 16th N.I. in 1802. Second Mahratta War 1803-5; Agra; Laswari; capture of Tonk; Monson's retreat; capture of Deig; Bhurtpore (w. in 3rd assault 20 Feb. 1805); Lieut. 1/12th N.I. (India medal). Transfd. to newly-raised 26th N.I. 1805. Fur. s.c. 1806-12. Resigned owing to ill health. Comdd. for many yrs. a Coy. in N. Glos. Mil. (Capt. 30 Mar. 1813).

Refs.: Burke's *Peerage*, 1923, p. 593, *s.n.* Cotterell, Bart. M.I. Arno's Vale cemetery, Bristol.

TAYLOR, Thomas (1785-1860). Colonel. 6th N.I. *bapt.* Overton, Hants, 9 Apr. 1785. Cadet 1799. Arrived in India 12 Jan. 1801. Ensign 14 Oct. 1800. Lieut. 21 Jan. 1803. Capt. 16 Dec. 1814. Major 13 May 1825. Lt. Col. 1 Apr. 1829. Retired 17 Jan. 1834. Hon. Col. 28 Nov. 1854. *d.* 22 Edward St., Portman Sq., London, 13 Aug. 1860, aged 75.

Son of Thomas Taylor and Hannah his wife.

Services: Posted Ensign to 1/3rd N.I. 17 Apr. 1801. (? Operations in Bundelkhand 1809; Rajaoli; Ajaigarh; Lieut. 1/3rd N.I.) Comdd. Resdt.'s escort at Delhi 1811. Capt. Lt. 3rd N.I. 19 Aug. 1814. Capt. 1/3rd N.I. Transfd. to Pension Est. on account of ill health 15 Apr. 1816; restored to effective branch as Supy. Capt.

THE BENGAL ARMY, 1758-1834 243

2/3rd N.I., without loss of rank, 15 Nov. 1816; brought on est. of 3rd N.I. 15 Dec. 1817. Actg. Fort Adjt. at Agra 26 Feb. 1824. Transfd. to 6th N.I. (late 1/3rd) May 1824. Siege and capture of Bhurtpore; Major 6th N.I. (India medal). Posted Lt. Col. to 6th N.I. 1829; to 19th N.I. 24 Sept. 1831; to 12th N.I. 27 Oct. 1832; to 6th N.I. 7 Dec. 1833. Fur. p.a. 3 Jan. 1831 till 10 Dec. 1833.

Refs.: *I.M.* 22 Aug. 1860, p. 632. *The Times*, 18 Aug. 1860.

TAYLOR, Thomas Matthew (1791-1871). General. 1st Bengal Eur. L.C. *b.* Clogher, co. Tyrone, 12 May 1791. Cadet 1807. Arrived in India 21 Mar. 1809. Cornet (27 Mar. 1809) 30 Apr. 1811. Lieut. 1 Sept. 1818. Capt. 13 May 1825. Major 1 Mar. 1836. Lt. Col. 5 Aug. 1839. Col. 22 Aug. 1855. Maj. Gen. 28 Nov. 1854. Lt. Gen. 17 Apr. 1863. Gen. 8 Feb. 1870. *d.* Granville Hotel, Ramsgate, 2 Sept. 1871.

bapt. 22 May 1791. Son of James Taylor, of Springfield, Clogher (of Cranbrook, co. Fermanagh), and Elizabeth his wife. Grandson of Thomas Taylor, lord mayor of Dublin 1750.

Services: Barasat C.C. 8 mos. Posted Cornet to 5th N.C. 1811. Attached to Java L.C. 1814-15. Third Mahratta War 1817-19; specially mentioned for gallantry in action against the Pindaris in May 1817 (*Lond. Gaz.* 24 Mar. 1823); Lieut. 5th N.C. Fur. s.c. 24 Dec. 1825 till 1 Oct. 1829. Asst. Sec. to Govt., Mily. Dept., 22 Jan. 1831 till 12 Feb. 1832. Mily. Sec. to Lord William Bentinck, the G.G., 4 Sept. 1833 till 20 Mar. 1835. Town & Fort Major Ft. Wm. 23 Jan. 1835; M.M.B. 6 Mar. 1837 till 1844. Posted Lt. Col. to 7th L.C. 1839; to 11th L.C. 1841; to 5th L.C. 3 Apr. 1844. Leave s.c. to Cape and N.S.W. 13 Feb. 1840 till Dec. 1841; do. 12 Feb. till 31 Dec. 1844; fur. s.c. 22 Feb. 1845 till 7 Dec. 1849; p.a. 3 Mar. 1851 till 1 Dec. 1853. Transfd. to 6th L.C. Nov. 1853; to 3rd L.C. Dec. 1853. Bdr. 2 cl. comdg. Peshawar 13 Dec. 1853 till Jan. 1855. Fur. s.c. 4 Jan. 1855 till death. Posted Col. to 1st L.C. Apr. 1856; Col. 1st Eur. L.C. May 1858 till 1859.

Refs.: Burke's *Peerage*, 1923, p. 2269, *s.n.* Waterford, M. Burke's *General Armory.* *List of Mily. Secs. to G.G.* Boase. *The Times,* 5 Sept. 1871.

TAYLOR, William Cheke (*d.* 1778). Captain, 2nd Bengal Eur. Regt. Cadet 1767. Ensign 13 July 1767. Lieut. 12 Apr. 1769. Capt. 5 Apr. 1777. *d.* Calcutta 5 Feb. 1778.

(*Probably* natural son of Cheke Taylor, Surg. in the *Success* Indiaman, 1764. Cousin-german of the mother of Edward Allingham, *q.v.*)

Services : Operations against the Saniyasis in the Rajshahi district 1771 ; Lieut. comdg. a detachment of Sepoys under James Rennell, *q.v.*
Refs. : (? Berry's *Berks. Peds.*, p. 45.) *B. : P.P.* x. 151.

TEASDALE, John (*d.* 1784). (See **TISDALE, John.**)

TEASDALE, John (*d.* 1796). Captain, Infantry. Cadet 1772. Admitted 1 Aug. 1772. Ensign 23 July 1776. Lieut. 9 July 1778. Capt. 6 Mar. 1793. *d. unm.* Kasipur, B. & O., 6 Sept. 1796.
Brother of Eleanor Crosby.
Services : (? First Rohilla War ; battle of St. George ; Cadet in the Select Picket.) Lieut. 24th Bn. Sepoys in July 1787 and in Dec. 1792 ; posted Capt. to 1st Bengal Eur. Bn. 22 Mar. 1793.
Refs. : Will dated 25 Oct. 1789 ; proved 19 Oct. 1796.

TEBBS, George (1810-1852). Bt. Major, 33rd N.I. Comdt. Regt. of Ferozepore. *b.* Chelsea 10 June 1810. Cadet 1826. Arrived in India 22 Sept. 1827. Ensign 8 Feb. 1827. Lieut. 4 Aug. 1832. Capt. 24 Jan. 1840. Bt. Major 11 Nov. 1851. *d.* at sea 14 Mar. 1852, on board the *Agincourt* on the voyage to England.
bapt. St. Luke's, Chelsea, 15 July 1810. Son of William Tebbs, of Chelsea and of Doctor's Commons, proctor, and Mary his wife, *née* Virtue. Grandson of Sir Benjamin Tebbs, Kt., sheriff of London. *m.* Landour 18 July 1843, Charlotte, youngest dau. of Capt. Richard Phillips, Madras Eur. Regt.,. and niece of Owen Phillips, *q.v.* (*See also* Thomas Quin.) (She died 22 June 1882.)
Services : Posted Ensign to 12th N.I. 19 June 1827 ; transfd. to 33rd N.I. 29 Nov. 1828. Fur. s.c. 20 Nov. 1830 till 18 Nov. 1833. First Afghan War 1842 ; forcing of Khyber ; reoccupation of Kabul ; Capt. 33rd N.I., with Pollock's force (Medal). First Sikh War ; Ferozshahr ; Sobraon ; Capt. 33rd N.I. (Medal with clasp). Comdt. newly-raised Regt. of Ferozepore 1 Aug. 1846 till 13 Jan. 1852. Fur. s.c. 1852.
Refs. : I.M. 18 May 1852, p. 306. *G.M.* 1852, i. 632.

TELFER or TILFER, James Thomas. (*See* **TILFER.**)

TEMPLER, Charles (1788-1806). Cadet, Infantry. *b.* Teingrace, Devon, 14 Jan. 1788. Cadet 1805. Never arrived in India. *d.* Dec. 1806, on his passage to India, in the wreck of the *Skelton Castle.* Struck off with effect from 5 Nov. 1806. (See note to David Allan.)

Son of James Templer, of Stover Lodge, Devon, and Mary his wife, 3rd dau. of James Buller, of Morval, Cornwall. Uncle of William Buller, q.v., and cousin-german of James Templer Parlby and George Templer, qq.v. Ed. Blundell's 2 Feb. 1798 till 16 Dec. 1802.

Refs.: Burke's *Landed Gentry*, 12th edn., p. 1846, *s.n.* Templer, of Lindridge, Devon. *Blundell's School Register.* *G.M.* 1808, i. 371.

TEMPLER, George (1798-1848). Bt. Major, 22nd N.I. *bapt.* Teingrace, Devon, 26 July 1798. Cadet 1818. Arrived in India 16 Sept. 1819. Ensign (?) Lieut. 25 June 1821. Capt. 3 May 1830. Bt. Major 9 Nov. 1846. *d.s.p.* Ambala 1 Nov. 1848.

4th and youngest son of Henry Line Templer, of Teignmouth, Col. 10th Hrs., and Mary his wife, eldest dau. of Sir Frederick Leman Rogers, 5th Bart. Brother of Henry Templer and cousin-german of Charles Templer, *qq.v.* *m.* 1st, Teignmouth Nov. 1831, Elizabeth Louisa, dau. of Henry Disney Roebuck. (She died Lucknow 24 Jan. 1834, aged 20.) *m.* 2nd, Colney, Norfolk, 30 May 1843, Harriet Rose, dau. of Laurence Gwynne, LL.D., of Teignmouth. (She *re-m.* 27 Dec. 1849, Lt.-Col. James Robert Young, H.M. 25th Regt.)

Services: d.d. Bengal Eur. Regt. 1819-20; posted to 1/2nd N.I. Jan. 1821. Fur. 5 Feb. 1822 till 5 Apr. 1825. Transfd. to 2/2nd N.I. Dec. 1823; to 22nd N.I. (late 2/2nd) May 1824. Leave s.c. May 1827 till July 1829; fur. 3 July 1829 till 25 June 1832. Jodhpur demonstration and Shekhawat expedn. 1834; Capt. 22nd N.I. Fur. s.c. 25 Jan. 1841 till 24 Nov. 1843. A.D.C. to Maj.-Gen. Sir W. R. Gilbert, *q.v.*, comdg. Sirhind Div., Sept. 1846 till Oct. 1848.

Refs.: Burke's *Landed Gentry*, 12th edn., p. 1846, *s.n.* Templer, of Lindridge, Devon. *De Rhé-Philipe. A.J.* 3S. i. 330. *G.M.* 1834, ii. 222; 1849, i. 222. M.I. at Ambala.

TEMPLER, Henry (1796-1875). Major General. 6th Bengal Eur. Inf. *bapt.* Teingrace, Devon, 26 Aug. 1796. Cadet 1813. Admitted 9 Dec. 1814. Ensign 16 Dec. 1814. Lieut. 1 Aug. 1818. Capt. 2 Jan. 1831. Major 6 Nov. 1848. Lt. Col. 7 May 1854. Bt. Col. 7 May 1857. Retired 24 Aug. 1859. Hon. Maj. Gen. 24 Aug. 1859. *d.* 1 Grove Villas, Teignmouth, 18 Apr. 1875, aged 78.

2nd son of Col. Henry Line Templer, D.L. co. Devon, and Mary his wife. Brother of George Templer, *q.v.* *m.* Cawnpore 15 Dec. 1823, Emma Frances, 2nd dau. of John Fombelle, B.C.S. (*See also* Colin Campbell (1775-1819).) (She died 3 Dec. 1868.)

Services: Nepal War 1816; Ensign 2/4th N.I., in 4th Bde. Centre Column (India medal). Actg. Adjt. Left Wing 2/4th N.I. 9 Oct. 1820. Transfd. to 7th N.I. (late 1/4th) May 1824; Intr. & Qmr. do. 17 June 1824; Adjt. do. 29 July 1825 till 6 July 1831. Offg. Bde. Major Cawnpore 25 Jan. 1838. Fur. s.c. 3 Mar. 1842 till 6 Nov. 1843. Posted Lt. Col. to 7th N.I. 20 May 1854, and was comdg. the Regt. at Dinapore when it mutinied 25 July 1857. Transfd. to newly-raised 6th Eur. Inf. 1858. Fur. s.c. 22 July 1858 till retirement. Transfd. to 1st Eur. Bengal Fus. 21 Oct. 1859, before the report of his retirement had reached India.

Refs.: Burke's *Landed Gentry*, 12th edn., p. 1846, *s.n.* Templer, of Lindridge, Devon. Foster's *Families of Royal Descent*, i. 69. *The Times*, 21 Apr. 1875.

TENNANT, Sir James (1789-1854). Colonel, K.C.B., Artillery. (359) *b.* Ayr 21 Apr. 1789. Cadet 1804. Arrived in India 4 Aug. 1806. Lieut. 29 Mar. 1806. Capt. Lt. 1 Oct. 1816. Capt. 1 Sept. 1818. Major 3 Mar. 1831. Lt. Col. 18 Jan. 1837. Lt. Col. Comdt. 3 July 1845. Col. 9 Nov. 1846. *d.* Mian Mir 6 Mar. 1854.

bapt. Ayr 25 Apr. 1789. Son of William Tennant, merchant in Ayr, and Wilhelmina Ramsay his wife, dau. of Dr. William Dalrymple. Brother of William Tennant and of Susan Gardner. *m.* Calcutta 7 Apr. 1828, Elizabeth Louisa, eldest sister of Charles Pattenson, *q.v.* (*See also* Richard Horsford.) (She died Ulcombe Place, Kent, 4 Apr. 1882, aged 78.) Marlow Cadet; Woolwich Cadet 25 Jan. 1804 till 26 July 1805.

Services: See *D.N.B.* Capture of the Cape Jan. 1806. Operations in Bundelkhand and Oudh 1808-11. Reduction of Kalinjar 1812; actg. Adjt. & Qmr. Art. Nepal War 1814-15; Ramgarh; Taragarh; Capt. 6th Coy. 1st Bn., in 1st Div. (India medal). Apptd. Bde. Major Art., Centre Div. of Grand Army, 14 Dec. 1817. Third Mahratta War 1817-18; Capt. 2nd Coy. 1st Bn., Bde. Major. Bde. Major to Art. in the field 1818 till Dec. 1823. A.A.G. of Art. May 1824 till Aug. 1834. Siege and capture of Bhurtpore; A.A.G. of Art. (clasp to India medal). Offg. Agent for manufacture of gunpowder at Ishapur 27 Apr. 1835; permanent do. 27 July 1835 till Feb. 1837. Posted Lt. Col. to 4th Bn. Art. 21 Mar. 1837. Leave s.c. to Cape Feb. 1838 till Dec. 1839. Gwalior campaign; Maharajpur; Bdr. comdg. Foot Art. (Bronze star). Leave s.c. to Simla Jan. 1845 till Jan. 1847. Second Sikh War; passage of Chenab; Chilianwala; Gujerat; Bdr. Gen. comdg. Art. (Medal with 2 clasps). Comdd. Meywar F.F. Mar.-Dec. 1849; comdd.

THE BENGAL ARMY, 1758-1834

troops at Lahore Dec. 1849 till death. Col. 9th Bn. July 1848 ; 8th Bn. Aug. 1851. C.B. 9 Apr. 1849 ; K.C.B. 6 Apr. 1852.
Refs. : D.N.B. De Rhé-Philipe. D.I.B. Boase. I.M. 28 Apr. 1854, p. 227. *G.M.* 1854, i. 664 ; ii. 103. M.I. Lahore Cantt.

TENNISON, Richard (1751/52-1795). Lieutenant, Infantry.
b. in Ireland 1751/52. Cadet 1778. Admitted 10 Dec. 1778. Ensign 1778. Lieut. 10 Oct. 1778. *d.* Buxar 24 Sept. 1795.
Services : Ensign H.M. 46th Ft. Sailed for India in the *Nassau* 1 Mar. 1778, aged 26. Removed from Inf. to Cav. Bde. 18 Feb. 1779 ; retransfd. to Inf. Lieut. 7th Bn. Sepoys in July 1787 and in 1792.

***TERRANEAU, Charles** (1808-1835). Lieutenant, 5th N.I.
b. Rangpur, Bengal, 23 Nov. 1808. Cadet 1824. Admitted 27 Mar. 1826. Ensign 22 Sept. 1825. Lieut. 16 Mar. 1827. *d.* Saugor 13 Nov. 1835.

Son of William Terraneau, of Rangpur, indigo planter,[1] and Elizabeth his wife, dau. of Capt. Mitchell, of the Madras Est. Brother of William Henry Terraneau, *q.v.*, and cousin-german of Lucius Horton Smith, *q.v.* His sister *m.* Thomas Fisher (1798-1847), *q.v.*

Services : Was already in India when apptd. Cadet. Posted Ensign to 5th N.I. 1826. No record of active service.
Refs. : A.J. N.S. xx. 47.

[1] *Note :* He *d.* Rangpur 19 Apr. 1850, aged 87. He was probably son of Charles Cossard de Terraneau, *q.v.* The following details are extracted from a letter recommending Charles for a Cadetship. He (William) was born in Bengal, educated in London, and went out again to India as an officer in H.M. 42nd Regt. He resigned and went into business in Calcutta, which failing, he became an indigo planter. " It is uncertain whether he is Swiss, German, or Portuguese." He was undoubtedly of French extraction.

***TERRANEAU, Charles Cossard de** [1] (*d.* 1765). Capt. Lieutenant, Artillery. *d.* in India 1765 : hanged himself.
m. 1st, (?) (*Probably* grandfather of Charles Terraneau, *q.v.*)
m. 2nd, Anne.
Services : A French Ofr. of Art. serving in Chandernagore during the siege of that fort by Clive in Mar. 1757 ; quarrelled with the Govr. of Chandernagore and deserted to the British 19 Mar. Given a Commission in Coy.'s (? Madras) Art. (? to rank as Lieut. from 1756). " The romantic story of the French officer who deserted to the English, revealed to them the weakness of Chandernagore, and

then hanged himself, bequeathing a tarnished fortune to his family who indignantly refused to accept it, is familiar and apocryphal. M. Cossard de Terraneau bore the recollection of his treachery very well for at least eight years, rising to the rank of Capt. Lt. in the Coy.'s Art., and at last hanged himself owing to the misconduct of his wife ; . . ." (*Dodwell*) " Being now ordered on an expedition against Cossim Ally Cawn." (Will)

Refs.: The Nabobs of Madras, by H. Dodwell, London, 1926, p. 43. (? *Leslie*, No. 28.) *Forrest's Clive*, i. 389, 391. Will dated Calcutta 3 Sept. 1763 ; filed and proved 12 Feb. 1765.

[1] *Note :* His name is also given as Etienne Charles Cossard de Terraneau.

TERRANEAU, William Henry (1791-1843). Bt. Major, 24th N.I. b. Calcutta 17 Dec. 1791. Cadet 1810. Arrived in India 22 Oct. 1811. Ensign 6 Aug. 1813. Lieut. 20 Sept. 1816. Capt. 1 Aug. 1825. Bt. Major 28 June 1838. d. Garaunda, nr. Karnal, 11 Oct. 1843.

bapt. Calcutta 2 Feb. 1792. 2nd son of William Terraneau, indigo planter, and Elizabeth his wife. Brother of Charles Terraneau, *q.v.* *m.* Barrackpore 9 Jan. 1823, Sophia, dau. of Charles Christiana, Asst. in Accountant Gen.'s Dept., Board of Trade. (*See also* Birnie Browne.) (She died Calcutta 23 Nov. 1881, aged 71.)

Services : Cadet d.d. 1/12th N.I. 1811 till Oct. 1813 ; posted Ensign to 1/8th N.I. 8 Oct. 1813 ; d.d. Rangpur Local Bn. 8 Oct. 1813 till Nov. 1820. Nepal War 1814-15 ; Ensign Rangpur Local Bn., with force under Major B. R. W. Latter, *q.v.* Supt. public bldgs. at Rangpur 1817 till Nov. 1820. Bk. Mr. Dacca Div. 16 July 1821 ; Executive Ofr., P.W.D., Dacca Div. 1824 ; do. Benares Div. 6 Apr. 1835 ; do. Agra Div. 12 Oct. 1835 till Nov. 1841. Transfd. to 24th N.I. (late 2/8th) May 1824. Leave s.c. to Hills Nov. 1841 till death. He never did a single day's duty with his own Regt. during a service of 32 yrs.

Refs.: De Rhé-Philipe. *I.M.* No. 9, p. 272. M.I. at Karnal.

TERRELL, James Bates (1792-1816). Lieutenant, 20th N.I. b. Deptford, Kent, 2 Aug. 1792. Cadet 1806. Arrived in India 15 May 1808. Ensign 30 Mar. 1808. Lieut. 3 Jan. 1813. d. unm. Makwanpur 28 Feb. 1816 : kld. in action.

bapt. St. Nicholas, Deptford, 11 Nov. 1792. Son of Gabriel Terrell, of Union St., Deptford, and Elizabeth his wife.

Services : Barasat C.C. Ensign d.d. 21st N.I. 1810-12 ; posted Ensign to 1/20th N.I. 1812. Served at P.W.I. till Apr. 1814. Adjt. 1/20th N.I. 27 Oct. 1814 till death. Nepal War 1816 ;

THE BENGAL ARMY, 1758-1834   249

Makwanpur (kld.); Lieut. 1/20th N.I., attached to 2/25th N.I., in 3rd Bde. Centre Column. A collector of Malayan MSS.
Refs.: A.J. iv. 187. Will dated Barrackpore 9 Oct. 1815; proved 14 May 1816.

TERRY, Thomas (*d.* 1772). Cadet. Infantry. Cadet 1770. Resigned 27 Sept. 1771. *bur.* Calcutta 7 Mar. 1772. *m.* Elizabeth.
Services: Sailed for India in the *Northumberland* 12 Apr. 1770. After resignation became a free merchant in Calcutta in partnership with Stair Hathorn Stewart.
Refs.: Will dated Calcutta, 28 Feb. 1772; proved 10 Mar. 1772.

TETLEY, James (*d.* 1820). Colonel, 4th N.I. Country Cadet 1778. Admitted 12 Oct. 1778. Ensign 28 Mar. 1779. Lieut. 31 Jan. 1781. Capt. 30 Oct. 1797. Major 27 Jan. 1804. Lt. Col. 27 Sept. 1807. Col. 21 Mar. 1819. *d. unm.* Allahabad 11 Nov. 1820.

Father of George Tetley (see Appendix A). His sister Elizabeth *m.* as 2nd wife George, 4th son of Capt. Peter Garric by Arabella Clough, and youngest brother of David Garrick, the actor (*D.N.B.*); his sister Alice *m.* as 3rd wife Henry Wedderburn, *q.v.*; and his niece *m.* James Murray (1779-1847), *q.v.*

Services: Recommended for a Cadetship by Warren Hastings 12 Oct. 1778. He stated in 1781, when applying for transfer to B.C.S. as a Writer, that he was employed by the Board of Trade. Apptd. Adjt. 23rd Bn. Sepoys 22 Mar. 1780; was Adjt. 20th Bn. in Mar. 1786 and for many years after. Second Rohilla War 1794; battle of Bitaurah; Lieut. 20th Bn. Lieut. in the Cav. in 1795. A.D.C. to Maj.-Gen. William Jones (1740-1818), *q.v.*, 1796-7. Capt. 1/13th N.I. in Aug. 1798. Apptd. 29 Oct. 1798 to comd. newly-raised 2nd Bn. Bengal Vols. This Bn., which in June 1800 was brought into the Line as 1/19th N.I., was known as " *Titteelee-ki-Paltan.*" Fourth Mysore War 1798-1800; Seringapatam; service on N. frontier of Mysore; Capt. comdg. 2nd Vol. Bn. (Medal). Transfd. to Marine Regt. (became 20th N.I. in 1803). Second Mahratta War; operations in Cuttack 1803; capture of Barabati fort; Capt. 20th N.I.; relief of Shamli; action at Deoband 1804; pursuit of Holkar 1805-6; Major newly-raised 21st N.I. Posted Lt. Col. to 2/21st N.I. 1807. Operations in Rewah 1811; unsuccessful attack on Bhapawi fort (w.); Lt. Col. comdg. the force, consisting of his own Bn., unsupported by any guns. Transfd. to 2/24th N.I. 1812. Comdg. at Lucknow in 1815; at Agra in 1818. Posted Col. to 4th N.I. in 1819.

Refs.: *E.I.M.C.* ii. 303. *Cardew*, p. 111. Will dated 23 Apr. 1816; proved 23 Nov. 1820.

TEULON, George (1793-?). Ensign. 14th N.I. Subsequently Col. in H.M.S. *b.* St. Anne's, Cork city, 8 Nov. 1793. Cadet 1808. Admitted 29 July 1809. Ensign 1 Sept. 1809. Struck off 21 Mar. 1810. Restored 1812. Ensign 21 Sept. 1812. Struck off 25 Sept. 1813.

Son of John Teulon, of a Huguenot family, and Mary his wife, eldest dau. of Rev. G. Wood, of Bandon, Cork. Brother of Peter Teulon, *q.v.*, and nephew of Mary Whitesmith.

Services: Barasat C.C. Struck off by order of C.D., having obtained his appt. by improper means (M.C. 21 Mar. 1810); restored, and finally struck off, having entered H.M.S., 25 Sept. 1813. Ensign 30th Ft. 17 Aug. 1809; Lieut. do. 14 July 1811; Capt. (Army rank) 13 Mar. 1817, 30th Ft.; h.p. 1818. Capt. 35th Ft. 12 Oct. 1820; Major do. 17 Oct. 1826; Lt. Col. do. 12 Apr. 1831 till exchanged to h.p. Bt. Col. 16th Ft. 9 Nov. 1846. Sold out (retired) 10 Mar. 1848. Inspecting Field Ofr. of Mil. in N. America and Ionian Is. 31 Dec. 1833 till 1848. His name appears in *Hart's A.L.* down to 1895 as "late 16th Ft." He probably died long before that year.

Refs.: Agnew's *French Protestant Exiles*, iii. 255.

TEULON, Peter (1788-1866). Lieut. Colonel. 1st N.I. *b.* Cork 18 Oct. 1788. Cadet 1804. Arrived in India 6 Apr. 1806. Ensign 7 Apr. 1806. Lieut. 26 Aug. 1806. Capt. 1 Jan. 1819. Major 14 Nov. 1832. Retired 20 June 1833. Hon. Lt. Col. 28 Nov. 1854. *d.* 30 July 1866.

Son of John Teulon and Mary his wife. Brother of George Teulon, *q.v.*

Services: Barasat C.C. Posted Lieut. to 12th N.I. 1807. Operations in Oudh 1808; Lieut. 12th N.I. Adjt. 1/12th N.I. 29 July 1815 till 20 Nov. 1818. Fur. p.a. 18 Feb. 1822 till 11 Oct. 1824. Transfd. to 1st N.I. (late 2/12th) May 1824. Tempy. comdg. Delhi Palace Gds. Oct. 1830; offg. Comdt. do. 19 May 1831. Fur. p.a. 14 Feb. 1833 till retirement.

THACKERAY, Thomas (1789-1814). Lieutenant, 26th N.I. *b.* Monken Hadley, Middlesex, 26 July 1789. Cadet 1803. Arrived in India 17 Mar. 1805. Ensign 1 Apr. 1805. Lieut. 2 Apr. 1805. *d. unm.* 27 Dec. 1814: kld. in action at Jampta, nr. Jaithak fort.

bapt. Monken Hadley 3 Sept. 1789. 4th son of William Make-

THE BENGAL ARMY, 1758-1834 251

peace Thackeray, B.C.S. ("Sylhet Thackeray"), and Amelia his wife, dau. of Lt.-Col. Richmond Webb. Uncle of John Dowdeswell Shakespear, *q.v.*, and of William Makepeace Thackeray, the novelist. Ed. Cheam School.

Services : d.d. 1/10th N.I. 6 Oct. 1805. Second Mahratta War 1805-6 ; Lieut. d.d. 1/10th N.I. Posted to newly-raised 2/26th N.I. 14 Jan. 1806. Operations in Bundelkhand 1807-10 ; Sehlehuganj ; Hirapur ; Rajaoli ; Ajaigarh ; operations against Gopal Singh ; Lieut. 2/26th N.I. Apptd. to newly-formed Light Bn., and to comd. the Light Coy. 2/26th N.I., Oct. 1814 ; Intr. & Qmr. do. 20 Oct. 1814. Nepal War 1814 ; Kalanga (s.w.) ; Jaithak (kld.) [1] ; Lieut. 2/26th N.I., with Light Bn. in 2nd Div.

Refs. : Burke's *Landed Gentry*, 4th edn., p. 1493, *s.n.* Thackeray, of Clenchwarton. Burke's *Family Records*, p. 593, *s.n.* Thackeray. *De Rhé-Philipe. The Thackerays in India*, by Sir W. W. Hunter, pp. 137-40. *Stubbs*, ii. 13. M.I. at Nahan.

[1] *Note :* He and Lieut. W. McM. Wilson, *q.v.*, as well as 57 sepoys of the Light Coy. 2/26th, fell whilst covering with the greatest gallantry the retreat of the column under Major (afterwards Gen. Sir William) Richards, *q.v.*

THATCHER, Robert (1812-1899). Lieut. Colonel. 9th N.I. *bapt.* Hastings 29 July 1812. Cadet 1828. Arrived in India 15 Sept. 1829. Ensign (1 Apr. 1829) 5 June 1829. Lieut. 31 Mar. 1835. Capt. 24 Jan. 1845. Major 21 Nov. 1860. Retired 31 Dec. 1861. Hon. Lt. Col. 31 Dec. 1861. *d.* 11 Oct. 1899.

Son of Robert Thatcher and Mary Ann his wife, of All Sts. Cottage, Hastings.

Services : Posted Ensign to 9th N.I. 2 Aug. 1832. Placed tempy. under Lieut. W. Swatman, *q.v.*, for suptg. *keddah* operations in Chittagong 1 Oct. 1838, with a gratuity of Rs. 50 per elephant caught. Actg. Adjt. 9th N.I. 27 Jan. 1842 ; permanent do. 2 Feb. 1842 till 7 Mar. 1845. With Army of Reserve (for Afghanistan) Oct. 1842 till Jan. 1843 ; Lieut. 9th N.I. Sub-Asst. in Stud Dept. 11 June 1850 ; Asst. 2 cl. do. Apr. 1853 ; 1 cl. 16 Aug. 1853 ; Dy. Supt., N.W.P., 24 Mar. 1855 till retirement. No record of active service.

THELLUSSON, Thomas Robarts (1801-1869). Lieutenant. 3rd L.C. *b.* 19 June 1801. Cadet 1817. Cornet (?) Lieut. 4 Nov. 1818. Resigned 28 May 1824. *d.* 23 Wilton Cresc., London, 29 Mar. 1869.

bapt. Addington, Surrey, 19 July 1801. 2nd son of Charles

Thellusson, M.P. for Evesham, and Sabine his wife, eldest dau. of Abraham Robarts. Nephew of 1st Baron Rendlesham. *m.* 17 Aug. 1822, Maria, 6th sister of John Dunkin Macnaghten, *q.v.* (She died 23 Jan. 1881.) Ed. Rugby; admitted 1814. *Services:* Posted Lieut. to 3rd L.C. Fur. 1821 till resignation. No record of active service.

Refs.: Burke's *Landed Gentry*, 13th edn., p. 1731, *s.n.* Thellusson, of Brodsworth Hall, Yorks. Foster's *Peerage*, p. 560, *s.n.* Rendlesham, B. *The Times*, 1 Apr. 1869.

THELWALL, Watkin (1747/48-1814). Major. Artillery. (47) *b.* 1747/48. Fireworker (Madras) 16 Jan. 1764. Transfd. to Bengal Art. 20 Nov. 1765. Lieut. 25 Nov. 1765. Capt. Lt. 15 Sept. 1767. Capt. 8 May 1772. Major 18 Nov. 1780. Resigned 18 Mar. 1782. *d.* Chester 6 Oct. 1814, aged 76.

Services: Arrived in Madras Dec. 1764. Was comdg. 1st Coy. Art. at Dinapore in Sept. 1777, when he was reported unfit for field duty, having lost the use of his limbs.

Refs.: Leslie, No. 54. *Wilson*, ii. 337. *G.M.* 1814, ii. 501.

THOMAS, Charles Henry (1804-1866). Major. 11th N.I. *b.* Berhampore 23 Feb. 1804. Cadet 1822. Arrived in India 16 Jan. 1824. Ensign 18 Aug. 1823. Lieut. 13 May 1825. Capt. 16 Dec. 1839. Retired 10 Nov. 1847. Hon. Major 28 Nov. 1854. *d.* 26 Henrietta St., Bath, 5 Jan. 1866.

bapt. Berhampore 31 Mar. 1804. Eldest son of Lewis Thomas, *q.v.*, and Maria Frances his wife. Brother of George Powell Thomas, *q.v. m.* 1st, Bath 18 Mar. 1841, Leonora Elizabeth, youngest dau. of Capt. Clotworthy Gillmor, R.N., of Brock St., Bath. (*See also* George Powell Austen.) (She died Cawnpore 17 Aug. 1844, aged 24.) *m.* 2nd, Weston-super-Mare 23 July 1850, Mary Hurst, eldest dau. of J. W. S. Crutwell, formerly Lieut. H.M. 83rd Regt. (She died Bath 24 Oct. 1904.) Addiscombe Cadet 23 Aug. 1820 till 12 June 1823.

Services: Posted Ensign to 11th N.I. Siege and capture of Bhurtpore; Lieut. 11th N.I. (India medal). Fur. u.p.a. 17 Jan. 1829 till 20 Dec. 1830. Asst. in *Thagi* Dept. 29 Sept. 1835 till 1839; actg. Supt. of Hapur Stud 26 Apr. 1836; Joint Mgte. in Chittoor district, Madras, May 1838. Fur. p.a. 13 Sept. 1839 till 29 Sept. 1841. (? Disturbances in Bundelkhand 1842; Capt. 11th N.I.) First Sikh War; Ferozshahr; Capt. 11th N.I. (Medal).

Refs.: *G.M.* 1866, i. 296. *The Times*, 16 Jan. 1866.

THOMAS, Charles Thynne (1798-1874). Lieut. Colonel. 15th N.I. *b.* Walton, nr. Wells, Somerset, 15 Jan. 1798. Cadet

1813. Admitted 3 Dec. 1814. Ensign (16 Dec. 1814) 5 June 1815. Lieut. 20 Jan. 1817. Capt. 9 Mar. 1826. Major 5 Nov. 1841. Retired 1 Feb. 1843. Hon. Lt. Col. 28 Nov. 1854. *d.* Motueka, Nelson, N.Z., 23 June 1874, from an accident causing instantaneous death.

bapt. Walton 14 May 1798. 2nd son of Rev. Josiah Thomas, rector of Walton, and Susanna Isabella his wife, only dau. of Henry Harington, M.D., of Bath. Brother of George Hudleston Thomas, *q.v. m.* Meerut 2 June 1829, Anne Armstrong, dau. of Lt.-Col. James Dunbar Tovey, 31st Ft.

Services: Posted to 1/11th N.I. 1815 ; Lieut. 1/11th N.I. Apptd. to 1st Ceylon Vols. 1818, but never joined. Leave s.c. to Mauritius 7 Nov. 1820 till Mar. 1822. Actg. Intr. & Qmr. 2/11th N.I. 30 Dec. 1823. Transfd. to 15th N.I. (late 1/11th) May 1824 ; Intr. & Qmr. do. 13 July 1824 till 12 July 1825. Siege and capture of Bhurtpore ; Lieut. 15th N.I.[1] Sub-Asst. in Stud Dept. 11 June 1825 ; 2nd Asst. Central Stud 12 Apr. 1837 ; actg. Supt. do. Mar. 1838. Leave s.c. to Cape 8 Jan. 1839 till 6 Jan. 1840. 1st Asst. Central Stud 30 Dec. 1840 ; Supervisor Hissar Stud 7 Apr. 1841 (joined in Oct.) till retirement.

Refs.: Family information. *Memoranda . . . relating to the parish of Kelston,* by F. J. Poynton, pt. iv. pp. 53, 54, 56. *The Times,* 21 Sept. 1874.

[1] *Note:* Name included in Bhurtpore P.R. but not in India M.R.

THOMAS, David (1791-1825). Captain, 10th N.I. *b.* Llandilo Vawr, co. Carmarthen, 1 Sept. 1791. Cadet 1807. Arrived in India 16 Nov. 1808. Ensign 4 Dec. 1808. Lieut. 26 July 1813. Capt. 1825. *d.* on his way from Saugor 9 Dec. 1825.

Son of D. Thomas. *m.* Calcutta 1 Sept. 1814, Elizabeth, dau. of George Foulis, *q.v.* (She died Edinburgh 25 Mar. 1836, aged 38.)

Services: Barasat C.C. Posted to 1/7th N.I. 1809. Fur. 9 Dec. 1809 till 1811. (? Reduction of Kalinjar 1812 ; Ensign 1/7th N.I. ? Nepal War 1814-15 ; Lieut. 1/7th N.I., in 2nd Div.) With Rangpur Local Bn. 1816-17. Third Mahratta War 1817-19 ; Lieut. 1/7th N.I. Fort Adjt. at Buxar 1819 ; Bk. Mr. 10th (Agra) Div. 1820-5. Transfd. to 2/7th N.I. ; to 10th N.I. (late 2/7th) May 1824. First Burma War ; Arakan 1825 ; Capt. 2nd L.I. Bn. Svptg. Ofr. of Gent. Cadets at Ft. Wm. 3 June 1825.

THOMAS, Francis (1803-1842). Captain, 73rd N.I. *b.* Sidmouth, Devon, 2 Nov. 1803. Cadet 1820. Arrived in India 5 Nov. 1821. Ensign 4 July 1821. Lieut. 16 Jan. 1824. Capt. 17 Sept. 1841. *d. unm.* Delhi 30 June 1842.

4th son of Lt.Gen. William Thomas, of Bluehayes House (of Brockhill House), nr. Exeter, Lt. Govr. of Tynemouth Castle, and Nevillia his wife, elder dau. of Ascanius William Senior, of Pilewell, Hants, and Cannon Hill House, Berks. Cousin-german of William Hickey, *q.v.*, and of the wife of Robert Rayner Young, *q.v.* Ed. Blundell's 18 Aug. 1815 till 29 June 1820.

Services : Ensign d.d. 2/23rd N.I. Jan.-July 1822 ; posted to 2/22nd N.I. Apr. 1822 and joined in Dec. Transfd. to 2/18th N.I. Sept. 1823 ; to 36th N.I. (late 1/18th) May 1824 ; to 50th N.I. Feb. 1825 ; to newly-raised 5th Extra Regt. (became 73rd N.I.) 1 July 1825. Actg. Intr. & Qmr. 73rd N.I. July 1828 till July 1829 ; Adjt. do. 21 July 1829 till 2 Jan. 1837. Fur. s.c. 8 Mar. 1838 till Nov. 1841. No record of active service.

Refs. : Foster's *Families of Royal Descent,* i. 17. *Blundell's School Register. De Rhé-Philipe. G.M.* 1842, ii. 558. M.I. in Rajpura cemetery, Delhi.

THOMAS, George (*d.* 1772). Captain, Infantry. Cadet (?) Ensign 10 July 1763. Lieut. 2 Feb. 1764. Capt. 8 July 1766. *d. unm.* Rangpur, Bengal, 29 Dec. 1772 : kld. in action against the Saniyasis.

Cousin of Maria Thomas.

Services : Comdd. a detachment of sepoys from the Parganna Bns., sent to Rangpur in Dec. 1772 against the Saniyasis, which was disgracefully defeated and almost destroyed.

Refs. : Cardew, p. 37. Will dated 5 Dec. 1772 ; proved 15 Jan. 1773.

THOMAS, George Hudleston (1801-1839). Cadet. Infantry. Subsequently Capt. 7th Madras L.C. *b.* Walton, Somerset, 1 Apr. 1801. Cadet 1817. Transfd. to Madras Est. 1818. *d.* Bellary, Madras, 5 Mar. 1839 : kld. by a fall from his horse.

bapt. Walton 23 June 1801. Youngest son of Ven. Josiah Thomas, archdeacon of Bath, and Susanna Isabella his wife, only dau. of Henry Harington, M.D., of Bath, and cousin of John Hudleston, a Dir. E.I. Co. Brother of Charles Thynne Thomas, *q.v. m.* Walcot church, Bath, 22 Sept. 1825, Mary Anne, youngest dau. of Rev. Thomas Broadhurst, of Belvedere House, Bath. (She died Weston-super-Mare 16 Feb. 1895, aged 89.)

Services : Lieut. 7th Madras L.C. 1 Sept. 1818 ; Capt. do. 7 Feb. 1832. Was comdg. this Regt. at death.

Refs. : Family information. *Memoranda . . . relating to the parish of Kelston,* by F. J. Poynton, pt. iv. pp. 53, 54, 56. *A.J.* N.S. xxix. 145. M.I. Bellary Cantt. cemetery.

THE BENGAL ARMY, 1758-1834   255

THOMAS, George Powell (1808-1857). Major, 3rd Bengal Eur. Regt. b. Bairamghat, nr. Lucknow, 26 Aug. 1808. Cadet 1825. Arrived in India 24 Feb. 1826. Ensign 6 Sept. 1825. Lieut. 11 Apr. 1828. Capt. 24 Apr. 1842. Major 21 Jan. 1857. d. Agra fort 4 Aug. 1857, of wounds received in action on 5 July, and dysentery.

bapt. Calcutta 31 Dec. 1809. 2nd son of Lewis Thomas, q.v., and Maria Frances his wife. Brother of Charles Henry Thomas, q.v. m. Dacca 1 Aug. 1831, Albina Grace, sister of James Richard Benson Andrews, q.v. (She died 14 Dec. 1889.)

Services: Posted to 9th N.I. 1826; transfd. to 64th N.I. 2 Dec. 1829; actg. Intr. & Qmr. do. 10 June 1830; permanent do. 22 May 1833 till Dec. 1835. Asst. in *Thagi* Dept. 21 Feb. 1835; Asst. to Comr. in Saugor 24 Aug. 1835; Principal Asst. at Hoshangabad 14 Oct. 1835 till Dec. 1839. Adjt. 64th N.I. 23 June 1840; Intr. & Qmr. do. 14 Sept. 1840 till 1843. First Afghan War 1842; retreat from Ali Masjid; action in mouth of Khyber 24 Jan.; Bde. Qmr. to Bdr. Wild's Bde. 24 Feb. till 7 Apr. 1842; comdd. newly-raised Regt. of Afghan Levies at Landi Khana May 1842; reoccupation of Kabul; Capt. 64th N.I., with Pollock's force (Medal). Pol. employ in Bhawalpur 8 Apr. 1843; do. in Sind 21 July 1843. Fur. s.c. 21 Feb. 1845 till 18 Dec. 1847. Offg. Fort Adjt. Allahabad 13 Oct. 1848. Transfd. to newly-raised 3rd Bengal Eur. Regt. 15 Nov. 1853. Fur. Feb. 1854 till 1856. Crimean War; Local Lt. Col. in Turkey 27 Mar. 1855 (Medal). Mutiny campaign; action at Shahganj 5 July 1857 (s.w.); Major 3rd Bengal Eur. Regt. Pub. 1846, " Views of Simla," 24 lithos. with descriptions, folio.

Refs.: Boase. *I.M.* 1 Oct. 1857, p. 646. *G.M.* 1857, ii. 385.

THOMAS, John (1783-1821). Captain, 9th N.I. b. London 22 Oct. 1783. Cadet 1803. Arrived in India 2 Dec. 1804. Ensign 12 Nov. 1804. Lieut. 12 Nov. 1804. Capt. 1 Jan. 1819. d. Chittagong 1 July 1821, of spasmodic cholera.

bapt. St. Martin-in-the-Fields 10 Nov. 1783. Son of John Thomas, of Kidwelly, co. Carmarthen, and Mary his wife, dau. of Christopher Cooper, of Middlesex. Brother of Lejonier (? Ligonier) Thomas. m. 14 Nov. 1812, Mary Catherine, dau. of George Dick, q.v. (*See also* James Sissmore.) (She re-m. 3 Aug. 1831, Edward Bricklade.)

Services: Posted Lieut. to 9th N.I. 1805. Intr. & Qmr. 2/9th N.I. 1 July 1814 till 17 June 1819. Nepal War 1816; Makwanpur; Lieut. 2/9th N.I., in 4th Bde. Centre Column. Bk. Mr. and Executive Ofr. 18th (Dacca) Div. P.W.D. 1819 till death.

Refs. : A.J. xiii. 96. Will dated Chittagong 9 Aug. 1820; proved 18 July 1821. M.I. Chittagong.

THOMAS, Lewis (*d.* 1824). Major General, C.B. Colonel 3rd N.I. Comdg. at Cawnpore. Country Cadet 1778. Admitted 9 Mar. 1778. Ensign 1778. Lieut. 6 Sept. 1779. Capt. 3 Oct. 1796. Major 4 Feb. 1803. Lt. Col. 21 Sept. 1804. Col. (4 June 1813) 1 Mar. 1818. Maj. Gen. 12 Aug. 1819. *d.* Cawnpore 2 May 1824.

Son of Lewis Thomas, of Brookhill, co. Kilkenny, and Mary his wife, eldest dau. of Rt. Hon. Sir Edward Lovett Pearce (*D.N.B.*). Brother of Pearce Thomas, *q.v.*, Lloyd Henry Thomas, of Upper Gardiner St., Dublin, solicitor to the Ordnance, and of Henrietta Dorothea, wife of Rev. James Slator, of Townend, co. Longford. *m.* in Ireland 16 Sept. 1802, Maria Frances, 3rd dau. of Henry Thomas Houghton, of Kilmannock House, co. Wexford. (*See also* Charles Caesar Pigott and Goddard Richards.) Father of Charles Henry Thomas, *q.v.*, and of George Powell Thomas, *q.v.*

Services : Lieut. 2/3rd Bengal Eur. Regt. in Oct. 1779. Second Mysore War 1781-5; Pollilur; Sholingarh; Vellore; Cuddalore (w.); Lieut. 13th N.I. Adjt. 13th N.I. *c.* 1785-94. Third Mysore War 1790-2; Bangalore; Arikera; Nandidrug; Savandrug; Seringapatam; Lieut. 13th Bn. Sepoys. Second Rohilla War 1794; battle of Bitaurah (s.w.); Lieut. 13th Bn.—the only survivor amongst the Ofrs. Capt. 14th N.I. in 1798. Fur. 9 Mar. 1800 till 2 Sept. 1803. Second Mahratta War; Agra (w. 10 Oct. 1803); operations against Sher Singh Dec. 1804; Major 1/14th N.I. Posted Lt. Col. to 2/14th N.I. 1804; transfd. to 2/16th N.I. 1807. Operations in Bundelkhand 1809-11; Lt. Col. 2/16th N.I., comdg. a detached force in 1811. Transfd. to 2/7th N.I. 1812. Fur. 12 Jan. 1812 till 1816. Transfd. to 13th N.I. 1816; to 2/30th N.I. 1817. Posted Col. to 3rd N.I. 1818. Actg. on Staff as Maj. Gen. comdg. Presdy. 1820-2; comdg. Cawnpore Div. 1822 till death. C.B. 4 June 1815.

Refs. : Burke's *Landed Gentry*, 4th edn., p. 726, *s.n.* Houghton, of Kilmannock House. Burke's *Landed Gentry of Ireland*, p. 642, *s.n.* Wilson-Slator. *E.I.M.C.* ii. 306-8. *Hickey*, iii. 351; iv. 122. Will dated Cuttack 30 Nov. 1818; proved 31 May 1824. M.I. in St. David's church, Naas, co. Kildare.

THOMAS, Mills (1784-1828). Lieut. Colonel, 46th N.I. *b.* Edinburgh 17 Feb. 1784. Cadet 1800. Arrived in India 4 Feb. 1802. Ensign 2 Sept. 1801. Lieut. 13 July 1803. Capt.

THE BENGAL ARMY, 1758-1834   257

1 Oct. 1815. Major 1 May 1824. Lt. Col. 30 Sept. 1827. d. Kasipur, nr. Calcutta, 10 May 1828.

bapt. Edinburgh 25 Feb. 1784. Son of Mills [1] Thomas, merchant in Edinburgh, and Isabella his wife, dau. of George Wright, tailor. Brother of William Thomas, q.v. m. Farrukhabad, U.P., 11 Aug. 1805, Susan Hollings. (She died 27 Nov. 1826.)

Services : Lieut. 13th N.I. (? Second Mahratta War 1803-4 ; Lieut. 13th N.I.) Transfd. to newly-raised 27th N.I. in 1805. Fort Adjt. at Allahabad 27 Jan. 1807 till 1824. Capt. 1/27th N.I. Transfd. to 54th N.I. (late 2/27th) May 1824. Posted Lt. Col. to 46th N.I. 3 Apr. 1828. Granted fur. s.c. 9 May 1828.

Refs. : A.J. xxvi. 487. M.I. in S. Park St. cemetery, Calcutta.

[1] Note : His name is given as Miles in the register of licences to marry.

THOMAS, Osburn Boydell (1803-1834). Lieutenant, 19th N.I. b. St. Asaph 22 July 1803. Cadet 1821. Arrived in India 20 Aug. 1822. Ensign 7 May 1822. Lieut. 1 May 1824. d. 15 Sept. 1834 on board H.C. flat *Experiment*, whilst comdg. the treasure escort on board.

bapt. St. Helens, Lancs., 27 Jan. 1804. Son of John Thomas, of St. Asaph, surgeon.

Services : Posted to 12th N.I. 1822 ; transfd. to 3rd N.I. 1823 ; to 6th N.I. (late 1/3rd) May 1824 ; to 19th N.I. (late 2/3rd) 1825 ; actg. Adjt. do. 20 Oct. 1829. No record of active service.

Refs. : A.J. N.S. xvi. 196. M.I. in old Residency graveyard at Jangpur, Murshidabad district, washed away by the river in 1847.

THOMAS, Pearce (1762/63-1782). Lieutenant, Infantry. b. in Ireland 1762/63. Cadet 1780. Never arrived in India. Ensign 1780. Lieut. 2 Aug. 1781. d. at sea 1782, on the voyage to India.

Son of Lewis Thomas, of Brookhill, co. Kilkenny. Brother of Lewis Thomas, q.v.

Services : Sailed for India in the *Hinchinbrooke* [1] 13 Mar. 1781, aged 18.

[1] Note : This ship was captured by the French whilst at anchor in Porto Praya Bay, S. Iago, Cape Verde Is., 16 Apr. 1781. She was retaken by H.M.S. *Juno* the following day, reached Madras Mar. 1782, and was lost in the Hooghly R. 10 Apr. 1783.

THOMAS, Philip (1786-1832 ?). Captain. 32nd N.I. b. Llanboidy, co. Carmarthen, 4 Oct. 1786. Cadet 1805. Arrived in India 11 July 1806. Ensign 24 Aug. 1806. Lieut. 30 May

1808. Capt. 22 Feb. 1822. Retired 12 July 1824. (? d. 1832.[1])
Son of Walter Thomas and Mary his wife.

Services : Barasat C.C. Posted Ensign to 16th N.I. 1807. Operations in Bundelkhand against Gopal Singh 1810-11 ; Lieut. 1/16th N.I. Adjt. 1/16th N.I. Apr. 1818 till 1822. Fur. 1822 till retirement. Transfd. to 32nd N.I. (late 1/16th) May 1824.

[1] *Note :* His name disappears from *E.I.R.* after May 1828, but he continued to draw his pension till 1832.

THOMAS, Robert Arding (1789-1860). Lieut. Colonel. 48th N.I. *b.* Bristol 2 Mar. 1789. Cadet 1804. Arrived in India 10 Sept. 1805. Ensign 27 Sept. 1805. Lieut. 1 Oct. 1805. Capt. 18 Jan. 1823. Major 27 June 1835. Retired 1 Mar. 1840. Hon. Lt. Col. 28 Nov. 1854. *d.* at his residence, Slough, Bucks., 10 Jan. 1860.

bapt. St. Augustine the Less, Bristol, 2 Sept. 1789. Son of Robert Thomas, M.D., of Salisbury, and Anna Maria his wife. *m.* 1st, Brading, I.W., Aug. 1812, Caroline, 2nd dau. of J. Gilbert, of Newport. (She died Dinapore 7 Nov. 1824.) His daus. *m.* George Newbolt, *q.v.*, and **Henry** Davis Van Homrigh, *q.v. m.* 2nd, Marylebone 12 July 1827, Dorothy Georgiana, youngest sister of Henry Shadwell, *q.v.* (She died 15 Dec. 1881.)

Services : Posted Lieut. to 24th N.I. 1806. Fur. s.c. 30 July 1811 till 3 Dec. 1814. Third Mahratta War 1817-19 ; Lieut. 1/24th N.I. Fur. s.c. 19 Sept. 1826 till 7 Oct. 1829. Wahabi rising 1831 ; Capt. 48th N.I. First Afghan War 1838-40 ; Ghazni ; Major 48th N.I. (Medal). Durani 3 cl. 15 Aug. 1840.

Refs. : Howard & Crisp (Notes), v. 22, *s.n.* Shadwell. *G.M.* 1860, i. 416. *The Times*, 18 Jan. 1860.

THOMAS, William (1778-1826). Lieut. Colonel Comdt., 10th N.I. *b.* Edinburgh 17 Dec. 1778. Cadet 1795. Arrived in India 8 Mar. 1797. Ensign 4 Oct. 1796. Lieut. 30 Oct. 1797. Capt. 19 Apr. 1805. Major 16 Dec. 1814. Lt. Col. 6 July 1820. Lt. Col. Comdt. 1 May 1824. *d.* Nimach 28 Nov. 1826.

bapt. Edinburgh 30 Dec. 1778. Son of Mills Thomas and Isabella Wright his wife. Brother of Mills Thomas, *q.v. m.* Cheltenham Aug. 1812, Ann, eldest dau. of Thomas Hunter, of Cumberland Pl. (She *re-m.* Calcutta 31 May 1828, Thomas Ferguson.)

Services : Apptd. Lieut. in the Loyal Brit. Fenc. Inf., comdd. by Col. Sir Robert Stuart, Bart., in 1795 ; transfd. to Northumberland Regt. of Fenc. Inf. 1796. Posted Ensign to 2/5th N.I. Mar. 1797 ; transfd. as Lieut. to 2/1st N.I. Oct. 1797. Adjt. 1st Gren.

THE BENGAL ARMY, 1758-1834   259

Bn. 1799 ; transfd. to 13th N.I. 1799. Second Mahratta War ; operations in Baghelkhand 1803 ; reduction of Chaukandi fort ; Lieut. 2/13th N.I. Fur. 17 Feb. 1808 till 15 Mar. 1813. Third Mahratta War 1818-19 ; Mandala ; Asirgarh ; Major 2/13th N.I. Posted Lt. Col. to 1/22nd N.I. in 1820 ; transfd. to 2/7th N.I. 1823 ; to 10th N.I. (late 2/7th) May 1824.
Refs. : *E.I.M.C.* i. 162-7. *G.M.* 1827, i. 647. Will dated 9 Apr. 1825 ; proved 1 May 1827. M.I. Nimach.

THOMPSON, Alexander (*d.* 1804). Captain. Infantry. Cadet 1770. Ensign 31 Dec. 1772. Lieut. 25 Mar. 1777. Capt. 25 Mar. 1781. Struck off 1793. *d.* Putney, Surrey, 1 July 1804. (? Ed. Merchant Taylors' Oct. 1758-Apr. 1764. If so, *b.* 2 Jan. $17\frac{50}{51}$.)
Services : Adjt. 2nd Bengal Eur. Regt. ; apptd. Adjt. 1st do. 27 Feb. 1778. Lieut. 1/1st Eur. Regt. in Oct. 1779 ; Qmr. 2/1st do. 22 Mar. 1780 till Jan. 1781 ; apptd. Bde. Major 1st Bde. 27 Feb. 1781 ; Capt. comdg. Chittagong Regt. in Jan. 1783. Fur. 3 yrs. on h.p. 24 July 1786 till struck off. Pensioned on Lord Clive's fund 2 Feb. 1796.
Refs. : (? *Robinson.*) *S.M.* 1804, p. 647. *G.M.* 1804, ii. 695.

THOMPSON or THOMSON, Charles. Captain. Infantry. Lieut. 22 Nov. 1764. Capt. 31 May 1767. Resigned 4 Feb. 1775.
Services : Probably an ofr. in H.M.S. ; apptd. in England 2 Mar. 1764, Lieut. on Bengal Est. ; sailed for India in the *Fort William* 17 May 1764. Posted to 1st Bengal Eur. Regt. 13 Aug. 1765 ; Qmr. 3rd Eur. Bn. in 1766. Was Dy. Judge Advocate to 3rd Bde. 1771-3 ; Capt. in 3rd Bde. on resignation.

THOMPSON, David (1799-1865). Lieut. Colonel. 56th N.I. *b.* Clonfin, co. Longford, 13 Sept. 1799. Cadet 1818. Admitted 26 June 1819. Ensign (?) Lieut. 12 Aug. 1820. Capt. 7 May 1827. Bt. Major 23 Nov. 1841. Retired 4 July 1845. Hon. Lt. Col. 28 Nov. 1854. *d.* 7 Jan. 1865.
4th son of William Thompson, of Clonfin, Major Longford Mil., and Mary his wife, dau. of John Garnet, of Hollywoodrath. *m.* 1st, Meerut 17 Aug. 1822, Miss Sophia MacMahon. *m.* 2nd, Clonbroney 24 Oct. 1843, Harriette, dau. of J. Montgomery. Woolwich Cadet.
Services : Posted Lieut. to 1/28th N.I. ; transfd. to 56th N.I. (late 2/28th) May 1824 ; Adjt. do. 10 Aug. 1825 till 14 Mar. 1827. Apptd. Bde. Major on the Est. 2 Mar. 1827 ; posted to Berhampore

14 Apr. 1827; do. Rajputana F.F. 30 Apr. 1827; do. Agra and Muttra frontiers 19 May 1828; do. Cawnpore 9 July 1832; D.A.A.G. of Div. 16 July 1832; posted to Dinapore 31 July 1832; A.A.G. of Div. at Dinapore 3 Apr. 1838; do. Meerut 6 Oct. 1839; do. Dinapore 7 Dec. 1839. Fur. s.c. 15 Jan. 1843 till 14 Nov. 1844. Placed on special duty at Presdy. in order to compile a Code of Mily. Regulations 13 Dec. 1844. No record of active service.

Refs. : Burke's *Landed Gentry of Ireland*, p. 688, *s.n.* Thompson, of Clonfin, co. Longford.

THOMPSON, Emanuel M—— (*d.* 1780). Ensign, Infantry. Cadet 1780. Ensign 1780. *d.* Calcutta 1 July 1780.

Services : N.F.P.

Note : Included on the authority of *D. & M.*, but not traced elsewhere.

THOMPSON, George (1741/42-?). Major. Infantry. *b.* London 1741/42. Cadet 1762. Ensign 9 July 1762. Lieut. 2 Feb. 1764. Capt. 23 July 1766. Major 22 Jan. 1777. Resigned 19 Feb. 1777.

Services : Sailed for India in the *Chesterfield* 1760, aged 18. Served as a Vol. 1761-2. Resigned 21 Apr. 1763, owing to ill health; readmitted 10 July 1763. Battle of Buxar 23 Oct. 1764 (s.w.—lost a leg); Lieut. Bengal Eur. Regt. Did not take part in the " Batta mutiny." Capt. comdg. 18th Bn. Sepoys in Jan. 1777. Pensd. on Lord Clive's fund 14 Mar. 1781.

Refs. : *Broome*, p. 480. *Williams*, p. 51.

*THOMPSON, James. Cadet. Artillery. Cadet 28 Mar. 1783. Declined coming out.

Note : Not identical with John Thompson (II), *q.v.*

THOMPSON, James (1813-1850). Captain, 19th N.I. *b.* Walcot, Somerset, 10 June 1813. Cadet 1832. Arrived in India 15 Feb. 1834. Ensign (15 Aug. 1833) 15 Feb. 1834. Lieut. 23 July 1835. Capt. 22 Nov. 1843. *d. unm.* Benares 31 Dec. 1850.

2nd son of Henry Thompson, of Walcot. Ed. Shrewsbury 1826-7. B.N.C., Oxon.; matric. 17 Mar. 1831.

Services : Ensign d.d. 55th N.I. 25 Feb. 1834; posted to 19th N.I. 5 Nov. 1834. Rising in Cuttack July 1836; Lieut. 19th N.I. Adjt. 19th N.I. 10 Dec. 1842 till 3 Jan. 1844. Fur. s.c. 10 Mar. 1848 till 1849.

Refs. : *Shrewsbury School Register*. *Alumni Oxon*. *I.M.* 18 Feb.

1851, p. 99. *The Times*, 1 Mar. 1851. Will dated Benares, 6 Dec. 1850; admon. 9 Mar. 1852. M.I. Benares.

THOMPSON, James Stewart [1] (*d.* 1780). Lieutenant, 12th Bn. Sepoys. Cadet 1771. Ensign 19 Mar. 1773. Lieut. 17 May 1778. *d.* Chunar 18 Dec. 1780.
Services: Apptd. Adjt. 12th Bn. Sepoys 22 Mar. 1780.
[1] *Note:* Or Stewart James Thompson.

THOMPSON, John. Ensign. Infantry. Cadet 1782. Ensign 22 Mar. 1783. Struck off 1788.
Services: Apptd. Cadet 2 May 1782. Was on fur. in July 1787. Probably never arrived in India. Possibly identical with the next.

THOMPSON, John. Cadet. Artillery. (III.-21) Cadet 28 Mar. 1783. Declined coming out.
Note: Not identical with James Thompson (I), *q.v.*

THOMPSON, John (1790-1846). Captain. 68th N.I. *b.* Cuckney, Notts., 20 Feb. 1790. Cadet 1806. Arrived in India 17 Mar. 1808. Ensign 11 Sept. 1808. Lieut. 15 Sept. 1814. Capt. 13 May 1825. Retired 3 Oct. 1832. *d.* 28 July 1846.
Son of John Thompson and Dorothy his wife, eldest dau. of Rev. Edward Otter, vicar of Cuckney.
Services: Barasat C.C. 8 mos. Posted Ensign to 10th N.I. 1809. (? Operations in Rewah 1813-14; Entauri; Ensign 2/10th N.I.) Third Mahratta War 1817-18; Chanda; Lieut. 2/10th N.I. With 3rd Ceylon Vols. 1818-19. Transfd. to newly-raised 34th N.I. July 1823; to 68th N.I. (late 2/34th) May 1824. First Burma War; Arakan 1825; Capt. 68th N.I. Actg. Bde. Major in Arakan 11 Feb. 1828; offg. S.A.C.G. in Arakan 31 Dec. 1828; tempy. charge of Comst. office at Dinapore 18 Sept. 1829. Fur. s.c. 20 Nov. 1830 till retirement. Retired on pension of 10/6 *p.d.*
Refs.: *Misc. Gen. et Her.* N.S. iii. 302.

THOMPSON, John Armston (1798-1866). Colonel, C.B. 19th N.I. *bapt.* St. Martin's, Leicester, 11 Jan. 1798. Cadet 1817. Admitted 5 Sept. 1818. Ensign 1 Mar. 1818. Lieut. 1 Aug. 1818. Capt. 21 June 1826. Major 27 Sept. 1837. Lt. Col. 10 Nov. 1843. Retired 18 Mar. 1847. Hon. Col. 28 Nov. 1854. *d.* Clifton 16 Mar. 1866.
Son of William Thompson and Elizabeth his wife. Ward of Francis Burgess.
Services: Posted Lieut. to Bengal Eur. Regt. 1818; to newly-raised 2nd Bengal Eur. Regt. May 1824. First Burma War;

Arakan 1825; Lieut. 2nd Bengal Eur. Regt. Actg. Adjt. 2nd Bengal Eur. Regt. 10 Oct. 1826. Fur. p.a. 25 Mar. 1829 till 14 Sept. 1832. Posted to Left Wing Bengal Eur. Regt. Jan. 1830. First Afghan War 1838-9; Ghazni; Major 1st Bengal Eur. Regt. (Medal). Leave s.c. 2 yrs. to Tasmania 28 July 1840. Posted Lt. Col. to 20th N.I. 11 Feb. 1844; to 59th N.I. 16 Nov. 1844. First Sikh War; Sobraon; Lt. Col. 59th N.I. (Medal). Transfd. to 19th N.I. 1846. C.B. 27 June 1846. Durani 3 cl. 15 Aug. 1840.
Refs.: *G.M.* 1866, ii. 771. *The Times*, 10 Apr. 1866.

THOMPSON, John Chetwood (1810-?). Ensign. 63rd N.I.
b. Cork 14 Apr. 1810. Cadet 1827. Arrived in India 15 Oct. 1828. Ensign (16 Apr. 1828) 4 Mar. 1829. Name removed from *A.L.* 1 Jan. 1834. (? Living in Chepstow Villas, Bayswater, in 1856.)
bapt. St. Peter's, Cork, 24 Apr. 1810. Son of Ven. Archibald William Thompson, archdeacon of Cork, and Mary Frances his 2nd wife, dau. of Rev. John Chetwood, preby. of Cahirlag, Cork. Ed. Charterhouse; admitted 1823, left Dec. 1826.
Services: Ensign d.d. 7th N.I. 20 Nov. 1828; d.d. 63rd N.I. 21 Jan. 1829; posted to 63rd N.I. 4 Mar. 1829. Granted leave to Calcutta preparatory to resigning the Service 1 Oct. 1833 till 1 Jan. 1834. Suspended 26 Mar. 1834 for quitting India in the *London* without leave on 17 Jan. 1834. Name removed from *A.L.* by C.D. from the date his leave expired.
Refs.: *Charterhouse School List.*

THOMPSON, Lancelot (1760/61-?). Lieutenant. 10th N.I.
b. Westmorland 1760/61. Cadet 1778. Ensign 1778. Lieut. 12 Nov. 1778. Dismissed by C.M. 21 Sept. 1784.
Services: Sailed for India in the *Norfolk* 7 Mar. 1779, aged 18. Lieut. 1/10th N.I., in 2nd Bde. Dismissed for Neglect of Duty, Disrespect, and Drunkenness on Duty.

THOMPSON, Primrose (*d.* 1778). Captain, Cavalry. Cadet 1766. Ensign 9 Dec. 1766. Lieut. 3 Apr. 1768. Capt. 12 Sept. 1774. *d.* Cawnpore 21 Oct. 1778: kld. by a fall from his horse.
Services: Ensign H.M. 31st Ft. 19 Feb. 1766. Apptd. Lieut. in England 13 Dec. 1769. Served with the Bombay Army *c.* 1772-3; on fur. in England 1773-5. Q.M.G. to the Nawab-Wazir's troops and was responsible for laying out the new camp or cantt. at Fatehgarh in May 1777, for the reception of his troops preparatory to their transfer later in the year to the Coy. Apptd. by C.D. in England, 7 Jan. 1779, to comd. 3rd Regt. Cav.

Refs.: *S.M.* 1779, p. 510 (where the name is given as Thomson).
G.M. 1779, p. 470 (where the name is given as Thornton).

THOMPSON, Richard (*d.* 1764). Ensign, Bengal Eur. Bn.
Cadet 1764. Ensign 4 Oct. 1764. *d.* 23 Oct. 1764 : kld. in action at the battle of Buxar.
Services: Battle of Buxar (kld.); Ensign with Grenadiers of Bengal Eur. Bn.
Refs.: Broome, p. 480. Cardew, p. 26.

THOMPSON, Robert (1812-1841). Lieutenant. 34th N.I.
b. Epsom 9 Dec. 1812. Cadet 1828. Arrived in India 4 Dec. 1829. Ensign 24 Nov. 1829. Lieut. 8 Oct. 1839. Resigned 13 Oct. 1841. *d.* Moradabad 2 Nov. 1841.
Son of Henry Thompson, of Woodcote, Epsom, controller of customs, and Emma Elizabeth his wife.
Services: Ensign d.d. 50th N.I. 31 Dec. 1829; Cadet d.d. 7th N.I. 18 Oct. 1831. Apptd. Actg. Ensign (having been 2 yrs. in India) 12 Mar. 1832. Posted Ensign to 34th N.I. 14 Mar. 1833; transfd. to 68th N.I. 24 Sept. 1835; to 34th N.I. 28 June 1836. No record of active service.

THOMPSON, William Augustus (*d.* 1822). Lieut. Colonel, C.B., 28th N.I. Cadet 1783. Admitted 16 Oct. 1783. Ensign 4 Jan. 1785. Lieut. 8 Nov. 1790. Capt. 10 May 1802. Major 3 May 1806. Lt. Col. 22 Dec. 1811. *d.* Delhi 1 Sept. 1822.
Brother of Charles Thompson, Lt. Col. H.M. 27th Ft.
Services: Lieut. H.M. 48th Ft. 12 Apr. 1780. Apptd. Cadet 6 Dec. 1782; sailed for India in the *Atlas* 11 Mar. 1783. Posted to 5th Bengal Eur. Bn. 5 Feb. 1790; 32nd Bn. Sepoys in 1792; Capt. 1/4th N.I. in Dec. 1802. Second Mahratta War 1803-4; Capt. 4th N.I. Fur. 25 Aug. 1805 till 30 Oct. 1808. (? Operations in Bundelkhand 1809; Rajaoli; Ajaigarh; Major 1/4th N.I.) Posted Lt. Col. to 2/3rd N.I. Nepal War 1814-15; capture of Malaun; Lt. Col. comdg. 2/3rd N.I., in 1st Div. Transfd. to newly-raised 28th N.I. 1815. Third Mahratta War 1818; capture of Madhurajpura; Lt. Col. 1/28th N.I., comdg. the force. Lt. Col. comdg. 3rd Ceylon Vol. Bn. 1818-19. Transfd. to 2/28th N.I. C.B. 8 Dec. 1815.
Refs.: Will dated 29 Aug. 1822; proved 20 Nov. 1822.

THOMPSON, William John (1800-1858). Bt. Colonel, C.B., 12th N.I. *b.* London 15 Jan. 1800. Cadet 1816. Admitted 19 Aug. 1817. Ensign 14 Aug. 1817. Lieut. 1 Aug. 1818. Capt.

12 Sept. 1825. Major 10 Apr. 1843. Lt. Col. 10 Oct. 1849. Bt. Col. 20 June 1854. *d.* Dacca 18 May 1858.

bapt. Marylebone 5 Mar. 1816. Son of William Thompson and Mary Ann his wife. *m.* Karnal 18 Apr. 1829, Caroline, 2nd dau. of John Littledale Gale, *q.v.* (*See also* F. W. S. Chapman.) (She died Dulwich 22 Oct. 1892, aged 82.)

Services: Ensign d.d. Bengal Eur. Regt. 1817; posted Lieut. to 1/12th N.I. 1818; transfd. to 12th N.I. (late 1/12th) May 1824. Supy. S.A.C.G. 17 Dec. 1823; S.A.C.G. 3 Feb. 1824; D.A.C.G. 2 cl. 30 Dec. 1826; 1 cl. 12 Dec. 1829; A.C.G. 2 cl. 14 Sept. 1831; 1 cl. 12 Apr. 1837; Dy. Comy. Gen. 24 Dec. 1847 till 9 May 1853. First Afghan War 1842; Tazin (*Lond. Gaz.* 24 Nov. 1842); A.C.G. with Pollock's force (Medal). First Sikh War; Sobraon; A.C.G. (Medal). Posted Lt. Col. to 12th N.I. 1849; to 50th N.I.; to 52nd, 73rd, 43rd, 63rd; to 1st Eur. Bengal Fus. 2 Feb. 1854; to 39th N.I. 14 Oct. 1854; to 19th N.I. 15 Nov. 1854; to 12th N.I. Sept. 1855 till death. Fur. p.a. 11 Sept. 1856 till 1857. C.B. 24 Dec. 1842.

Refs.: Howard & Crisp, i. 278, *s.n.* Gale. Boase. *I.M.* 19 July 1858, p. 605. *G.M.* 1858, ii. 312. *The Times,* 15 July 1858. M.I. Dacca cemetery.

THOMS, James (*d.* 1766). Captain, 3rd Bengal Eur. Regt. Ensign (Madras) 11 May 1763. Lieut. (Bengal) 9 Mar. 1764. Capt. 20 Dec. 1764. *d.* 4 Nov. 1766.

m. Jacobina.

Services: 2nd Lieut. 125th Coy. Marines 28 Nov. 1759; h.p. 1763. Apptd. in England 11 May 1763, Ensign on Madras Est., but was permitted to remain in England till the following year; apptd. Lieut. on Bengal Est. 9 Mar. 1764. Raised several recruits for the Coy. in England and sailed with them in the *Success* 17 May 1764. Posted to 3rd Eur. Regt. 5 Aug. 1765. Resigned his Commission during the " Batta mutiny "; later restored.

THOMSON, Alexander (1795-1825). Lieutenant, Artillery. (457) *bapt.* Foveran, co. Aberdeen, 6 Aug. 1795. Cadet 1814. Fireworker 2 Apr. 1817. Lieut. 1 Sept. 1818. *d.* Prome, Burma, 11 May 1825.

Eldest son of George Thomson (of Culter House, Foveran), of Fairley, co. Aberdeen, and Agnes Dingwall his wife. Brother of George Thomson (1799-1886), *q.v.*, and cousin-german of John Orrok, *q.v.* Addiscombe Cadet 1813-14.

Services: Third Mahratta War; Lieut. 1st Troop H.A.; after-

THE BENGAL ARMY, 1758-1834   265

wards 2nd Troop. First Burma War; Ava 1824-5; Lieut. H.A., with Sir A. Campbell's force.
Refs.: S.M. 1826, i. 256.

THOMSON, George (1799-1886). Lieut. Colonel, C.B. Engineers. Subsequently H.E.I.C. recruiting officer in the Cork district. *b.* Fairley, co. Aberdeen, 19 Sept. 1799. Cadet 1815. Arrived in India 18 Sept. 1818. Ensign 1 Sept. 1818. Lieut. 10 May 1823. Capt. 28 Sept. 1827. Bt. Major 23 July 1839. Retired 25 Jan. 1841. Major (local) 24 July 1844. Hon. Lt. Col. 28 Nov. 1854. *d.* 33 Leeson Park, Dublin, 10 Feb. 1886.

Of Culter House, Aberdeen. 2nd son of George Thomson, of Fairley, and Agnes Dingwall his wife. Brother of John Thomson (1801-1840), *q.v. m.* Aberdeen 4 Feb. 1830, Anna, dau. of Alexander Dingwall, of Rannieston, postmaster of Aberdeen. (*See also* John Anderson (1810-1857).) (She died 1 Nov. 1900, aged 87.) Addiscombe Cadet 30 Mar. 1814 till 14 Oct. 1816.

Services: See *D.N.B.* Adjt. S. & M. 29 May 1823. First Burma War 1824-6; Chittagong; conquest of Arakan 1825 (*Lond. Gaz.* 1 Oct. 1825); Field Engr. to Bdr. Morrison's force (India medal). Executive Engr. S.E. Div., P.W.D., 7 May 1825; do. Nimach 7 Oct. 1826; do. Rohilkhand Div. 21 Feb. 1828. Fur. p.a. 12 Feb. 1829 till 11 Nov. 1831. Comdd. Corps of S. & M. 11 Apr. 1837 till retirement. Supt. construction of Hindaun bridge 9 Oct. 1837; apptd. Chief Engr. Army of Indus 13 Sept. 1838. First Afghan War 1838-9; Ghazni (*Lond. Gaz.* 30 Oct. 1839); Chief Engr., comdg. 2 Coys. S. & M. (Medal). Returned to India Nov. 1839. Recruiting Ofr. in Cork district 24 July 1844 till 1861, and Paymr. of soldiers' pensions 24 July 1844 till 1877, when he resigned and settled in Dublin. Dir. Gt. S. & W. Rly. Co., Ireland, 1846. C.B. 20 Dec. 1839. Durani 2 cl. 15 Aug. 1840. Author of " The Storming of Ghazni."

Refs.: D.N.B. Vibart. D.I.B. Boase. The Times, 15 Feb. 1886, p. 7. *Genealogies of an Aberdeen Family 1540-1913,* by Rev. James Smith (Abd. 1913), p. 69 (portrait).

THOMSON, George (1801-1852). Bt. Lieut. Colonel, 40th N.I. *b.* Dalhousie, Edinburgh, 31 Mar. 1801. Cadet 1818. Admitted 10 Feb. 1820. Ensign 16 Aug. 1819. Lieut. 19 Apr. 1822. Capt. 13 Apr. 1830. Major 18 June 1850. Bt. Lt. Col. 7 June 1849. *d.* Calcutta 26 July 1852.

Owned estate of Charlieshope, New Norfolk, Tasmania. *bapt.* Cockpen 28 Apr. 1801. Son of George Thomson, farmer at Annan, co. Dumfries, and Elizabeth Montague Alves his wife. *m.* Mhow

2 Nov. 1830, Ellinor Crawfurd, dau. of Alexander Graham, of Milton Pl., Glasgow. (*See also* S. F. Hannah and G. A. S. Fullarton.)
Services: Posted Ensign to 1/20th N.I.; Intr. & Qmr. do. (became 25th N.I.) 26 Feb. 1824 till May 1827. Served at P.W.I. 1821-6. Transfd. to 40th N.I. (late 2/20th) May 1827; Intr. & Qmr. do. 27 May 1827 till 20 Nov. 1830. S.A.C.G. 10 Dec. 1834; D.A.C.G. 2 cl. 27 May 1842. Leave s.c. 2 yrs. to Cape and N.S.W. 26 Dec. 1842. D.A.C.G. 1 cl. 8 Jan. 1844; A.C.G. 2 cl. 3 Feb. 1846; 1 cl. 10 Feb. 1848 till 9 Sept. 1850. Second Sikh War; Chilianwala; Gujerat; A.C.G. (Medal with 2 clasps). Leave s.c. 1 yr. to Hills Dec. 1849. Second Burma War 1852; Bt. Lt. Col. 40th N.I. (Medal).
Refs.: *A.J.* N.S. iv. 215. *I.M.* 20 Sept. 1852, p. 516. *G.M.* 1852, ii. 546.

THOMSON, Harry (1780-1878). General. Colonel 1st Bengal Eur. L.C. *bapt.* Lewisham, Kent, 9 May 1780. Cadet 1798. Arrived in India 31 Aug. 1799. Cornet 20 June 1800. Lieut. 22 Dec. 1803. Capt. 15 Apr. 1816. Major 27 Oct. 1818. Lt. Col. 29 Apr. 1825. Col. 1 Dec. 1829. Maj. Gen. 28 June 1838. Lt. Gen. 11 Nov. 1851. Gen. 21 Feb. 1861. *d.* 3 Park Sq. W., Regent's Pk., London, 27 June 1878, aged 98.

Son of David Thomson and Elizabeth his wife. *m.* Millburn, co. Sutherland, 31 Aug. 1812, Jane, 2nd dau. of Rev. Thomas Burns, minister of Renfrew 1790-1830.

Services: Operations in Jumna Doab 1803; Sasni; Bijaigarh; Kachaura; Cornet 6th N.C. Second Mahratta War 1803-5; Laswari; battle of Delhi; capture of Deig; Bhurtpore; Afzalgarh 2 Mar. 1805; pursuit of Holkar; Lieut. 6th N.C. (India medal). Adjt. 6th N.C. 1808-10. Operations in Hariana 1809; Bhawani. Fur. p.a. 25 Jan. 1811 till 20 Nov. 1813. Actg. Qmr. 6th N.C. in 1816. Leave s.c. to sea 26 Aug. 1817 till 28 Feb. 1819; fur. s.c. 19 Nov. 1824 till 23 Sept. 1828. Posted Lt. Col. to 10th L.C. May 1825; to 7th L.C. 4 Nov. 1826. Posted Col. to 6th L.C. 11 May 1830; to 7th L.C. 2 Apr. 1833; to 3rd L.C. 22 Aug. 1833; to 6th L.C. 24 Dec. 1833; to 1st L.C. 24 Nov. 1834. To comd. troops in Oudh tempy. 26 Mar. 1834; Bdr. 2 cl. to comd. 1st Cav. Bde. for service in Rajputana 1 Nov. 1834, but did not take up the appt. owing to ill health. Fur. s.c. 22 Dec. 1834 till death. Col. 6th L.C. 22 Apr. 1835; 4th L.C. 1839; 3rd L.C. 1849; 1st Eur. L.C. 1859-69.

Refs.: *Boase.* Scott's *Fasti*, iii. 187. *The Times*, 2 July 1878, p. 5; 9 Jan. 1928, p. 15d.

THE BENGAL ARMY, 1758-1834 267

THOMSON, John (1786-1839). Lieut. Colonel, 31st N.I. *b.* Orwell, co. Kinross, 7 July 1786. Cadet 1807. Arrived in India 21 Mar. 1809. Ensign 8 Feb. 1809. Lieut. 12 Jan. 1813. Capt. 1 May 1824. Major 14 May 1832. Lt. Col. 20 Dec. 1838. *d.* Gurhee Kasim, nr. Shikarpur, Sind, 19 Apr. 1839, of heat stroke. Son of William Thomson, portioner of Ballingal, co. Kinross, and Catherine Beveridge his wife. *m.* (before 1813) Bathurst Burrel. (She died 7 Apr. 1847.) Father of William Beveridge Thomson, *q.v.*
Services : Barasat C.C. Posted Ensign to 2/15th N.I. July 1811. Nepal War 1814-15 ; led a party of 90 sepoys in the attack on post of Burhurwa 24 Nov. 1814 (*Lond. Gaz.* 17 June 1815) ; Lieut. 2/15th N.I., in 4th Div. Adjt. Chittagong Provl. Bn. 1815 ; do. 2/15th N.I. 3 Nov. 1815 till 1818 ; do. Champaran L.I. 1818 till 25 June 1823. Dy. Paymr. Dinapore 7 June 1823 till Sept. 1829. Transfd. to 31st N.I. (late 2/15th) May 1824. In charge of 68th N.I. 16 Sept. 1829 till July 1830. Dy. Paymr. Dinapore 7 July 1830 till 1 Jan. 1833. Offg. Comdt. Bengal Eur. Regt. 30 Mar. 1833 ; rejoined 31st N.I. 21 Dec. 1833. Fur. s.c. 7 Jan. 1835 till 30 Jan. 1838. Posted Lt. Col. to 31st N.I. 10 Jan. 1839, and was marching with his Regt. to take part in First Afghan War when his death occurred.
Refs. : A.J. N.S. xxix. 306. M.I. Afghan Memorial Church, Bombay.

THOMSON, John (1795-?). Ensign. Infantry. *b.* Kilmore, co. Down, end of June 1795. Cadet 1807. Arrived in India 21 Mar. 1809. Ensign 23 Mar. 1808. Dismissed by G.C.M. 29 July 1809.
Son of James Thomson.
Services : Dismissed whilst at Barasat C.C.

THOMSON, John (1801-1840). Captain, Engineers. *b.* Ythan Lodge, Foveran, Aberdeen ; *bapt.* 17 Feb. 1801. Cadet 1819. Admitted 30 May 1820. 2nd Lieut. (?) Lieut. 1 May 1824. Capt. 9 May 1829. *d.* Ghazipur 12 Aug. 1840.
Son of George Thomson, of Culter House, Aberdeen, formerly Purser E.I.C.S., and Agnes his wife, 2nd dau. of Bailie John Dingwall, of Rannieston. Brother of Alexander Thomson, *q.v.* Addiscombe Cadet 1 Feb. 1816 till 22 July 1818.
Services : Posted to S. & M. at Allahabad 22 July 1820 ; Field Engr. Malwa F.F. 3 Oct. 1823 ; Adjt. S. & M. 28 June 1825 till 8 Feb. 1827. Siege and capture of Bhurtpore ; Lieut. S. & M. Executive Engr. 3rd (Dinapore) Div. 8 Jan. 1827. Fur. p.a. 4 Jan. 1830 till 25 Jan. 1833. Agent for construction of iron suspen-

sion bridges, and Supt. Circular and E. canals 15 May 1833 till Oct. 1838; Executive Engr. 5th (Benares) Div. 24 Oct. 1838 till death. Author of " Essay on Suspension Bridges," Jan. 1840.
Refs.: Misc. Gen. et Her. 4S. v. 4-5. I.N. Vol. i., p. 127.

THOMSON, Thomas (d. 1786). Captain, Invalid Est. Capt. Feb. 1784. Invalided Feb. 1784. d. at sea Sept. 1786, on his passage to England.

Services: Capt. in Scots Bde. in service of Holland; resigned on outbreak of war with that State. Purchased a Lieutenancy in newly-raised 98th (Fullarton's) Ft. 29 Dec. 1780. Expedn. against the Cape under Gen. William Medows; Lieut. 98th Ft., A.Q.M.G. Proceeded to India with his Regt. 1782; served in three engagements under Adm. Sir Edward Hughes in the *Superb* against the French fleet between Madras and Trincomali 1782; Fort Major at Trincomali under Col. Fullarton. Lost a limb in a fourth engagement under Hughes 1782. Served under Maj.-Gen. James Stuart, Madras Est., at siege of Cuddalore 1783; recommended by Stuart and Hughes to H.M. for rank of Capt. in the Army.[1] Admitted by the Board in Calcutta to the Bengal Invalid Est., with rank of Capt., in recognition of his good service.[2] Leave s.c. to sea June 1784; fur. s.c. 3 yrs. July 1785.

Refs.: S.M. 1786, p. 467. G.M. 1786, ii. 908.

[1] *Note:* 98th Ft. was disbanded in 1785, and he was placed on h.p. as Capt. till death. Capt. 9 July 1783.

[2] *Note:* There is no record of any other similar case.

THOMSON, William. Captain. Infantry. Capt. Sept. 1768. Resigned 17 Jan. 1776.

Services: Ensign 79th Ft. 20 May 1759; Lieut. do. 29 Jan. 1760; h.p. Lieut. late 79th Ft. from 1763 or 1764; do. in 1780; not in 1781. Transfd. as Capt. to Bengal Army (M.C. 1 Sept. 1768); permitted to embark as a Capt. 23 Dec. 1768; sailed for India in the *Prince of Wales* 24 Mar. 1769. Apptd. to comd. the Select Picket 3 Feb. 1771; resigned comd. 24 June 1773 on appt. as Dy. Judge Advocate, 1st Bde.

Refs.: Macpherson, pp. 59, 137.

THOMSON, William Beveridge (1809-1863). Major General, C.B. 57th N.I. Comy. Gen. Bengal. b. Edinburgh 21 May 1809. Cadet 1825. Arrived in India 7 Dec. 1826. Ensign 30 June 1826. Lieut. 8 Apr. 1828. Capt. 3 Aug. 1837. Major 21 Sept. 1854. Lt. Col. 13 July 1858. Bt. Col. 29 May 1857. Retired 31 Dec. 1861. Hon. Maj. Gen. 31 Dec. 1861. d. at his residence, 22 St. Peter's Sq., Hammersmith, 21 Jan. 1863.

bapt. St. Cuthbert's, Edinburgh, 30 May 1809. Son of John Thomson (1786-1839), *q.v.*, and Bathurst his wife. *m.* Karnal 18 Feb. 1841, Selina Maria, 5th dau. of George Christopher, of Morton House, Chiswick, and of Grangefield, co. Durham. (*See also* George Cautley.) (She died 15 Dec. 1896, aged 81.)

Services: Ensign d.d. 67th N.I. 4 Jan. 1827 ; posted to 67th N.I. 19 May 1827 ; Intr. & Qmr. do. 8 Oct. 1828 till 1835. S.A.C.G. 16 Mar. 1835 ; D.A.C.G. 2 cl. 23 Nov. 1842 ; 1 cl. 4 Oct. 1844 ; A.C.G. 2 cl. 13 Sept. 1847 ; 1 cl. 9 Sept. 1850 ; Dy. Comy. Gen. 9 May 1853 ; Comy. Gen. 9 Nov. 1858 till retirement. First Sikh War ; Ferozshahr ; Capt. 67th N.I., D.A.C.G. (Medal). Mutiny campaign 1857-8 ; siege and capture of Delhi ; Bt. Col. 3rd Bengal Eur. Regt., Dy. Comy. Gen. (Medal with clasp). Transfd. from 67th N.I. to newly-raised 3rd Bengal Eur. Regt. 15 Nov. 1853 ; posted Lt. Col. to 57th N.I. 13 Sept. 1859. C.B. 18 June 1858.

Refs.: Burke's *Landed Gentry*, 13th edn., p. 337, *s.n.* Christopher, of Norton. *I.M.* 30 Jan. 1860, p. 66. *G.M.* 1863, i. 391. *The Times*, 24 Jan. 1863.

THORESBY, Charles (1793-1862). Colonel. 18th N.I. *bapt.* Barton Mills, Suffolk, 11 Jan. 1793. Cadet 1808. Arrived in India 27 Oct. 1809. Ensign 29 Mar. 1810. Lieut. 16 Dec. 1814. Capt. 2 Jan. 1826. Major 26 Aug. 1842. Lt. Col. 10 Mar. 1849. Retired 1 Apr. 1850. Hon. Col. 28 Nov. 1854. *d.* Waldron Castle, Torquay, 16 Aug. 1862, aged 69.

Son of Thomas Thoresby and Anna Maria his wife.

Services: Barasat C.C. 7 mos. Posted Ensign to 19th N.I. 1810. Capture of Mauritius 1810-11 ; Ensign d.d. 2nd Bengal Vols. Nepal War 1814-15 ; Lieut. 19th N.I. (India medal). Transfd. to newly-raised 29th N.I. 1815. Siege and capture of Hathras 1817 ; Lieut. 1/29th N.I. Third Mahratta War 1817-18 ; Lieut. 1/29th N.I. Adjt. 1/29th N.I. 10 Jan. 1819 till 1823. Transfd. to newly-raised 2/34th N.I. Sept. 1823 ; actg. Adjt. do. 30 Sept. 1823 ; permanent do. 16 Dec. 1823 till 21 Apr. 1824. Transfd. to 68th N.I. (late 2/34th) May 1824. Sec. to committee of management, Hindu Coll. at Benares, 12 Apr. 1824 till 1836. Actg. P.A. Murshidabad 31 Oct. 1833 till 18 Feb. 1834. P.A. Shekhawat 1836-7 ; Supt. Bhatti territory 18 June 1837 till 7 Sept. 1842 ; P.A. Jaipur 7 Sept. 1842 ; Pol. employ in Rajputana 16 Sept. 1843 ; Resdt. in Nepal 29 Dec. 1846 till retirement. Posted Lt. Col. to 52nd N.I. Mar. 1849 ; to 18th N.I. Dec. 1849.

Refs.: The Times, 23 Aug. 1862.

THORNE, James (1782-1813). Captain, 10th N.I. Dy. Mily. Auditor Gen. *bapt.* St. Mary Major, Exeter, 22 Aug. 1782. Cadet 1797. Arrived at Madras 12 Apr. 1799. Ensign 16 Sept. 1798. Lieut. 1 Nov. 1798. Capt. 13 Sept. 1809. *d.* Calcutta 4 Mar. 1813, in consequence of a fall from his horse.

Son of Lt.-Col. Peregrine Francis Thorne, of Hills Court, Exeter, Mily. Auditor Gen. Ceylon, and Euphemia his wife, half-sister of James Hanson Salmond, *q.v.* Brother of Bt. Lt.-Col. Peregrine Francis Thorne, K.H., Major 44th Ft.

Services : On arrival in Madras as a Cadet he joined the Bengal Vols., then before Seringapatam. Fourth Mysore War ; capture of Seringapatam. Was Adjt. 2/10th N.I. in 1803 ; Adjt. & Qmr. 10th N.I. 1804 till 18 Sept. 1810. (? Second Mahratta War 1805-6 ; Lieut. 10th N.I.) Asst. Mily. Auditor Gen. 1811 ; Dy. Mily. do. 1812 till death. Capt. 1/10th N.I.

Refs. : Burke's *Landed Gentry*, 13th edn., p. 1545, *s.n.* Salmond, of Waterfoot. *G.M.* 1813, ii. 499. Will dated Rewari 19 Jan. 1810 ; admon. 23 Mar. 1813.

THORNTON, George (1788-1866). Lieut. Colonel. 1st L.C. *b.* London 4 Dec. 1788. Cadet 1805. Arrived in India 11 July 1806. Cornet 17 July 1806. Lieut. 1 Sept. 1818. Capt. 13 May 1825. Major 27 Apr. 1833. Retired 12 Jan. 1834. Hon. Lt. Col. 28 Nov. 1854. *d.* 28 Royal Cresc., Bath, 4 May 1866.

bapt. St. Olave's, Hart St., 7 Dec. 1788. Son of Thomas Thornton and Ann Christian his wife. Brother of John Thornton, *q.v.* *m.* Sultanpur, Benares, 6 May 1824, Miss Jane Satterthwaite, 5th dau. of John Satterthwaite, of Plymouth. (*See also* John Holt White.) (She died 11 Apr. 1889.)

Services : Posted Cornet to 1st N.C. 1807. Operations in Bundelkhand 1810-11 ; Bichaund ; Cornet 1st N.C. Fur. p.a. 14 Feb. 1817 till 25 Feb. 1821 ; wrecked during his return voyage in the *Brilliant.* Adjt. 1st L.C. 3 Apr. 1821 till 6 Oct. 1825. Tempy. attached to G.G.B.G. 6 Apr. till 16 July 1821. Operations against the Larka Kols in Singhbhum district ; Lieut. d.d. G.G.B.G. Rejoined 1st L.C. Oct. 1821. Operations in Oudh 1822 ; actg. Staff Ofr. to detachment in Jaunpur district under Lt.-Col. Richard Clarke, *q.v.* Fur. p.a. 9 July 1832 till retirement.

Refs. : *V.B.G. G.M.* 1866, i. 924. *The Times*, 8 May 1866.

THORNTON, John (1790-1808). Ensign, 7th N.I. *b.* London 2 Apr. 1790. Cadet 1805. Arrived in India 11 July 1806. Ensign 3 Aug. 1806. *d.* 20 Nov. 1808 : lost at sea in the *Glory,* and struck off from 24 Jan. 1809.

bapt. St. Olave's, Hart St., 29 Apr. 1790. Son of Thomas Thornton and Ann Christian his wife. Brother of George Thornton, *q.v.*

Services : Barasat C.C. Posted Ensign to 7th N.I. 1807. Fur. 13 Aug. 1808 ; struck off from 24 Jan. 1809, " being a passenger on one of the missing ships." No record of active service.

THORNTON,[1] **Joseph** (*d.* 1809). Major, 4th N.I. Cadet 1782. Admitted 12 Nov. 1782. Ensign 28 Jan. 1783. Lieut. 9 Oct. 1789. Capt. 6 Aug. 1801. Major 19 Dec. 1805. *d.* Rampur-Boalia, Bengal, 18 Dec. 1809.

m. Stepney 18 June 1803, Miss Clara Wilkin Nash, of Finsbury Sq. (She *re-m.* Alexander Hind, *q.v.*)

Services : Apptd. Cadet 24 Oct. 1781 ; sailed for India in the *Norfolk* 6 Feb. 1782. Posted to 3rd Bengal Eur. Regt. 28 Feb. 1783. Ensign 4th Bengal Eur. Bn. in July 1787 ; transfd. to 30th Bn. Sepoys Feb. 1790 ; Lieut. 4th N.I. in 1798 ; Capt. Lt. do. 4 June 1801. Fur. 31 Jan. 1802 till 15 Mar. 1804. Major 2/4th N.I.

Refs. : Will dated 5 Oct. 1809 ; proved 6 Feb. 1810.

[1] *Note :* He describes himself in his Will as " Joseph Lind, commonly known by the name of Joseph Thornton," and his children as " Lind, *alias* Thornton."

THORNTON, Samuel Lowis [1] (1792-1860). Lieut. Colonel, Invalid Est. 48th N.I. *b.* Calcutta 17 Dec. 1792. Cadet 1807. Arrived in India 1 Nov. 1808. Ensign 9 Oct. 1808. Lieut. 16 Jan. 1812. Capt. 13 May 1825. Major 25 Nov. 1842. Lt. Col. 19 Mar. 1849. Invalided 1 Mar. 1850. *d.* Meerut 14 Aug. 1860.

bapt. Calcutta 14 Oct. 1793. Eldest son of Thomas Thornton, of Calcutta, formerly Asst. in Board of Revenue, afterwards indigo planter at Koil, and Harriet Frances his wife, dau. of Samuel Skardon, *q.v.* Cousin-german of Thomas Ramsay Wharton, *q.v.*

m. St. James's, Calcutta, 6 Dec. 1845, Mary Sarah Lamb.

Services : Barasat C.C. 9 mos. Posted Ensign to 7th N.I. 1809. Operations in Bundelkhand against Gopal Singh 1810-11 ; Ensign 1/7th N.I. Reduction of Kalinjar 1812 ; Lieut. 1/7th N.I. Nepal War 1814-15 ; Nahan ; Kalanga ; Lieut. 1/7th N.I., in 2nd Div. (India medal). Actg. Adjt. 1/7th N.I. 1815. Third Mahratta War 1817-18 ; Lieut. 1/7th N.I. Actg. Adjt. 1/7th N.I. 16 May 1820 ; permanent do. 16 Oct. 1823 till 14 July 1825. Transfd. to 13th N.I. (late 1/7th) May 1824. Actg. Bde. Major in Rohilkhand Apr. 1833, Mar. 1834, 18 Mar. 1835. On service in Bundelkhand

1841; Bt. Major 13th N.I. Posted Lt. Col. to 13th N.I. Mar. 1849; to 71st N.I. Dec. 1849; to 48th N.I. Jan. 1850.

Refs.: *I.M.* 6 Oct. 1860, p. 742. Will dated 9 Apr. 1860; proved 28 Sept. 1860.

[1] *Note:* Although his second name appears invariably in *A.L.* as Lewis, it is given as Lowis in the bapt. register; and one of the sons mentioned in his Will is John Lowis Thornton. (*See also* John Thornton Lowis.) John Lowis signed the register as a witness at the marriage of his parents.

THOROLD, Charles (1807-1868). Ensign. 49th N.I. *b.* Rauceby, Lincs., 7 Apr. 1807. Cadet 1825. Arrived in India 3 Feb. 1827. Ensign 9 Sept. 1826. Resigned 8 Feb. 1832. *d.* Tunbridge Wells 3 Feb. 1868.

Of Dacre House, Lee. 3rd son of Rev. George Thorold, rector of Hougham-cum-Marston, and Elizabeth his wife, only dau. of Benjamin Baugh. Grandson of Sir John Thorold, 9th Bart. *m.* 25 May 1830, his cousin-german Sophia, 3rd dau. of Rev. Edward Thorold. (She died 19 Mar. 1892.)

Services: Ensign d.d. 49th N.I. 20 Feb. 1827; posted to 49th N.I. 10 May 1827; transfd. to 61st N.I. 3 Jan. 1828; to 49th N.I. 28 Jan. 1828. Fur. s.c. 21 Aug. 1829 till Dec. 1832, when he resigned with effect from 8 Feb. 1832. No record of active service.

Refs.: Burke's *Peerage*, 1923, p. 2174, *s.n.* Thorold, Bart., of Marston, Lincs. Burke's *Landed Gentry*, 15th edn., p. 2242, *s.n.* Thorold, of Marston Hall. *The Times*, 5 Feb. 1868.

THOROLD, William Hardy (1794-1816). Cornet, 3rd N.C. *b.* Gt. Grimsby 29 June 1794. Cadet 1808. Cornet 18 Aug. 1814. *d.* at sea 10 Mar. 1816, on board the *Charles Mills*, on his passage to England.

bapt. Gt. Grimsby 12 Aug. 1794. Son of Rev. William Thorold, of Weelsby House, Lincs., rector of Cuxwold and Ravendale, and vicar of Kirmington, and Frances his wife.

Services: Barasat C.C. Cadet d.d. 4th N.I. 1811; posted Cornet to 3rd N.C. 1814. Fur. 14 Jan. 1816 till death. No record of active service.

Refs.: Burke's *Landed Gentry*, 13th edn., p. 1744, *s.n.* Grant-Thorold, of Weelsby House, Lincs. Will dated 27 Dec. 1815; proved 30 Nov. 1816.

THORPE, Ralph (1799-1864). Major, Invalid Est. 14th N.I. *b.* London 19 Aug. 1799. Cadet 1817. Admitted 19 Aug. 1818. Ensign 14 Mar. 1818. Lieut. 21 Aug. 1818. Capt. 23 May 1828.

THE BENGAL ARMY, 1758-1834

Major 23 Nov. 1841. Invalided 10 June 1842. *d.* Wells, Somerset, 4 June 1864.

2nd son of Hon. Robert Thorpe, LL.D., barr.-at-law, C.J. of Sierra Leone, and Sarah his wife, dau. of Sir Ralph Fetherston, Bart., of Ardagh. *m.* Meerut 28 Feb. 1833, Mussamat Ameerun, " dau. of H.H. the Maharajah of Kashmir." (*Burke*) Ed. Charterhouse Sept. 1809-Aug. 1814.

Services : Offg. Intr. & Qmr. 1/10th N.I. 24 Sept. 1821 ; Intr. & Qmr. 2/10th N.I. 1 Oct. 1823 ; do. 14th N.I. (late 1/10th) 17 June 1824 till 9 Aug. 1828. Postmr. at Sabathu 10 Apr. 1843. Fur. p.a. 10 Jan. 1845 till 1846. Postmr. at Fatehgarh 31 Oct. 1849 till 1851. Fur. s.c. 30 Jan. 1855 till 4 Mar. 1857. No record of active service. Became a Dir. of Eastern Bank of India.

Refs. : Burke's *Landed Gentry*, 13th edn., p. 1745, *s.n.* Thorpe, of Choisi, Guernsey. *Charterhouse School List. G.M.* 1864, ii. 124. *The Times*, 8 June 1864.

THRING, John (1746/47-1766). Ensign, Infantry. *b.* Southampton 1746/47. Cadet 1764. Ensign 27 Dec. 1764. *d.* 9 June 1766.

Services : Sailed for India in the *Devonshire* 20 Feb. 1764, aged 17. Posted to Bengal Eur. Bn. 25 Nov. 1764 ; to 1st Eur. Regt. 13 Aug. 1765.

THUILLIER, Sir Henry Edward Landor (1813-1906). General, Kt., C.S.I., Artillery. (660) Col. Comdt. R.A. Surveyor Gen. of India. *b.* Bath 10 July 1813. Cadet 1832. Arrived in India 19 Oct. 1833. 2nd Lieut. 14 Dec. 1832. Lieut. 1 Sept. 1840. Capt. 2 Feb. 1851. Lt. Col. 18 Feb. 1861. Col. 20 Sept. 1865. Col. Comdt. 1 Jan. 1883. Maj. Gen. 1 Oct. 1877. Lt. Gen. 10 July 1879. Gen. 1 July 1881. *d.* Richmond, Surrey, 6 May 1906.

Of Tudor House, Richmond. *bapt.* Bath 5 July 1822. Youngest son of John Pierre Thuillier, merchant of Cadiz and Bath, Baron de Malapert, of France, and Julia his wife, dau. of James Burrow, of Exeter. *m.* 1st, Calcutta 21 Dec. 1835, Susanne Elizabeth, sister of Ambrose Cardew, *q.v.*, and widow of Henry William Steer, of Bengal (who was brother of William Frederick Steer, *q.v.*). (She died Calcutta 7 Jan. 1844.) *m.* 2nd, Calcutta cathedral 8 Apr. 1847, Annie Charlotte, eldest dau. of George Gordon Macpherson, Bengal Medical Est. (*See also* William Augustin John Mayhew.) Addiscombe Cadet 4 Feb. 1831 till 14 Dec. 1832.

Services : See *D.N.B.* Employed on survey work from June

1836; apptd. to Revenue Survey 7 Jan. 1837. Fur. s.c. 16 Feb. 1844 till 1846. Offg. Dy. Surveyor Gen. Jan. 1847; Revenue Surveyor in Tirhut 30 Aug. 1847; Dy. Surveyor Gen. and Supt. Revenue Surveys 13 Apr. 1849 till Mar. 1861; Surveyor Gen. 12 Mar. 1861 till 1878. C.S.I. May 1870. Kt. 26 June 1879. F.R.S. 1869. Good Service Pension July 1876. No record of active service. Joint author of a "Manual of Survey for India."
Refs.: Walford (1900 edn.). *D.N.B. D.I.B. The Times*, 8 May 1906, p. 12. Portrait in oils by G. G. Palmer (1885) in Surveyor Gen.'s office, Calcutta.

THURSBY, Walter (1808-1829). Lieutenant, 5th N.I. *bapt.* Abington, Northants, 20 Mar. 1808. Cadet 1823. Ensign May 1824. Lieut. 13 May 1825. *d. unm.* Delhi 23 June 1829, of spasmodic cholera, aged 21.

6th and youngest son of John Harvey Thursby, of Abington Abbey, high sheriff Northants 1803, and Emma his wife, dau. of William Pigott, of Doddershall, Bucks., J.P.

Services: Posted Ensign to 5th N.I. 31 Mar. 1825. No record of active service.

Refs.: Burke's *Peerage*, 1923, p. 2179, *s.n.* Thursby, Bart., of Ormerod House, Lancs. *Howard & Crisp (Notes)*, x. 13. *A.J. N.S.* i. 33.

THWAITES, John (1789-1824). Lieutenant. 25th N.I. *bapt.* St. Lawrence's, Appleby, 1 Mar. 1789. Cadet 1804. Arrived in India 11 July 1805. Ensign 7 Aug. 1805. Lieut. 8 Aug. 1805. Retired 23 June 1817. *d.* Paris 7 Mar. 1824.

Son of John Thwaites, of Appleby, and Elizabeth his wife, *née* Harrison.

Services: A survivor of the wreck of the *Earl of Abergavenny*. (See note to Charles Davis or Davies.) Posted Lieut. to 25th N.I. 1806. Capture of Mauritius 1810; Lieut. 2/25th N.I., with 1st Vol. Bn. Fur. 1815 till retirement.

TICKELL, Richard (1785-1855). Lieut. General, C.B. Engineers. *b.* Tallagh, co. Waterford, 10 Sept. 1785. Cadet (Art. -300) 1802. Admitted 20 Oct. 1803. Lieut. (Art.) 31 Aug. 1803. Ensign (Engrs.) 21 Sept. 1804. Lieut. 10 May 1807. Capt. 23 Dec. 1812. Major 28 Sept. 1827. Lt. Col. 9 May 1829. Col. 22 Jan. 1834. Maj. Gen. 3 Nov. 1841. Lt. Gen. 11 Nov. 1851. *d.* Ravensworth, Cheltenham, 3 Aug. 1855; *bur.* Leckhampton.

Of Ravensworth, Cheltenham. 4th son of Thomas Tickell, of

Carnolway, co. Kildare, Capt. 5th R. Irish Dgns., high sheriff of Kildare 1803, and Sarah his wife, only dau. of Luke Sparks, H.E.I.C.S. Cousin-german of Samuel Tickell, *q.v.* *m.* 1st, Cawnpore 1 Feb. 1808, Mary Anne, dau. of Richard Proctor, M.D., of Leominster, Surg. in the Army (*probably* aunt of Richard Proctor, *q.v.*). Father of Richard Samuel Tickell, *q.v.* (She died Calcutta 28 Sept. 1833, aged 44.) *m.* 2nd, St. George's, Bloomsbury, 18 June 1840, Margaret Scott, 2nd dau. of Adam Walker, Surg. E.I.C.N.S., and sister of John Pascal Walker, *q.v.* (She died Cheltenham 15 Feb. 1882, aged 66.)

Services: Transfd. from Art. to Engrs. (G.O. 14 Sept. 1804). Second Mahratta War 1804-5; battle and capture of Deig; Lieut. Art.; Bhurtpore; Ensign Engrs. (India medal). Actg. Adjt. Engrs. 1807-8. Operations in Bundelkhand 1807. Surveyor with Hon. Mountstuart Elphinstone's mission to Kabul till 23 Apr. 1809, and surveyed the route as far as Dera Ismail Khan. Settlement of Hariana 1809; Bhawani; comdg. Engrs. Garr. Engr. & Executive Ofr. at Allahabad 21 Dec. 1810. Reduction of Kalinjar 1812. Operations in Baghelkhand 1813-14; Entauri. Apptd. Field Engr. 4th Div. for Nepal 15 Nov. 1814. Nepal War 1815-16; Capt., Field Engr. (clasp to India medal). Siege and capture of Hathras 1817. Third Mahratta War 1817-18; Mandala (*Lond. Gaz.* 7 Dec. 1818); Field Engr. 6th Inf. Bde., 3rd Div. Tempy. Bk. Mr. Allahabad Div. 31 July 1819. Supt. of canals in Delhi territory 19 July 1821 till 22 Jan. 1827; Suptg. Engr., P.W.D., S.W. Provs. 13 Nov. 1826; do. Lower Provs. 10 Apr. 1828 till Dec. 1837. Fur. p.a. 16 Dec. 1837 till death. C.B. 27 Sept. 1831.

Refs.: Burke's *Landed Gentry of Ireland*, p. 691, *s.n.* Tickell, of Carnolway, co. Kildare. Family information. *Misc. Gen. et Her.* N.S. ii. 473. *Vibart*, pp. 26-30. *Boase. Memoirs of John Shipp* (1890 edn.), p. 297. *I.M.* 16 Aug. 1855, p. 442. *The Times*, 2 Sept. 1927. M.I. Christ Church, Cheltenham.

TICKELL, Richard Samuel (1809-1860). Major. 72nd N.I. *bapt.* Calcutta 11 Feb. 1809. Cadet 1825. Arrived in India 22 Oct. 1826. Ensign 21 May 1826. Lieut. 27 Feb. 1833. Capt. 11 July 1841. Retired 19 Feb. 1851. Hon. Major 28 Nov. 1854. *d.s.p.* Brighton 24 Oct. 1860, of diphtheria, aged 51; *bur.* Kensal Green.

Eldest son of Richard Tickell, *q.v.*, and Mary Anne his 1st wife. *m.* Calcutta 12 June 1833, Jessey Eliza, dau. of Maj.-Gen. Sir Robert Bartley, K.C.B. (She died 27 Apr. 1901, aged 86.) Ed. Charterhouse and Eton.

Services : Posted to 4th Extra Regt. (became 72nd N.I.) 9 Nov. 1826. Actg. Intr. & Qmr. H.M. 16th Ft. 10 Apr. 1832 ; do. 64th N.I. 7 Apr. 1835 ; Intr. & Qmr. 72nd N.I. 23 Sept. till 31 Oct. 1835. To accompany Ramgarh L.I. for the performance of a special duty 5 Nov. 1835. S.A.C.G. 4 Jan. 1836. Attached as S.A.C.G. to 4th Inf. Bde., Army of Reserve (for Afghanistan) 20 Nov. 1842. D.A.C.G. 2 cl. 8 Feb. 1843 ; 1 cl. 2 May 1845 ; A.C.G. 2 cl. 5 Feb. 1848 till retirement.

Refs. : Burke's *Landed Gentry of Ireland*, p. 691, *s.n.* Tickell, of Carnolway, co. Kildare. *Charterhouse School List.* *I.M.* 3 Nov. 1860, p. 805. *G.M.* 1860, ii. 98.

TICKELL, Samuel (1785-1817). Captain, 8th N.I. *b.* London 31 Jan. 1785. Cadet 1800. Arrived in India 24 Oct. 1801. Ensign 19 Sept. 1801. Lieut. 13 July 1803. Capt. 16 Dec. 1814. *d.* on the river 5 Oct. 1817, between Ghazipur and Berhampore ; *bur.* Berhampore.

bapt. Marylebone 3 Mar. 1785. 2nd son of Richard Tickell, Comr. of Stamps (*D.N.B.*), and Mary his 1st wife, dau. of Thomas Linley, of Bath. Cousin-german of Richard Tickell, *q.v. m.* Calcutta 9 June 1810, Mary, dau. of Lawrence Burke Morris, *q.v.* (She *re-m.* George King, Suptg. Surgeon, Bengal Est.) Father of Samuel Richard Tickell, *q.v.*, and of the wife of William Edward John Hodgson, *q.v.*

Services : (? Operations in Jumna Doab 1803 ; Sasni ; Bijaigarh ; Kachaura ; Ensign 8th N.I.) Second Mahratta War 1803-5 ; Laswari ; Rampura 1804 ; operations nr. Tonk Rampura Jan.-Mar. 1805 ; Lieut. 2/8th N.I. Storm of Badekh 1806 ; Lieut. 2/8th N.I. Adjt. 2/8th N.I. 11 June 1808 till 28 Nov. 1811. Nepal War 1814-15 ; Capt. 1/8th N.I., in 4th Div. D.J.A.G. Dinapore and Benares Divs. 1815 till death.

Refs. : Burke's *Landed Gentry of Ireland*, p. 691, *s.n.* Tickell, of Carnolway, co. Kildare. Will dated 18 Nov. 1816 ; proved 21 Oct. 1817.

TICKELL, Samuel Richard (1811-1875). Colonel. 2nd N.I. *b.* Cuttack 19 Aug. 1811. Cadet 1828. Arrived in India 9 Feb. 1830. Ensign (12 June 1829) 7 Nov. 1829. Lieut. 4 Aug. 1836. Capt. 25 Dec. 1847. Major 18 Feb. 1861. Lt. Col. 18 Feb. 1863. Retired 24 Jan. 1865. Hon. Col. 24 Jan. 1865. *d.* Cheltenham 20 Apr. 1875.

bapt. Calcutta 16 Jan. 1812. Elder son of Samuel Tickell, *q.v.*, and Mary his wife. 2nd cousin of Richard Samuel Tickell, *q.v.*

THE BENGAL ARMY, 1758-1834 277

m. Bankura, Bengal, 11 July 1844, Maria Georgiana, 2nd dau. of John William Templer (who was cousin-german of George Templer, *q.v.*). Addiscombe Cadet 1827-9.

Services : d.d. 68th N.I. 22 Apr. 1830; d.d. 72nd N.I. 3 Sept. 1830. Actg. Ensign (having been 2 yrs. in India) 12 Mar. 1832. d.d. 31st N.I. 13 Mar. 1832; posted to 22nd N.I. 23 Dec. 1832; to 31st N.I. 22 Feb. 1833. Operations against Kols and Chuars 1832-3; Ensign 31st N.I.; and 1835-7; d.d. Ramgarh L.I. Employed on survey work in Kol country 1835-6. Asst. to Resdt. in Nepal, and comd. escort 27 May 1840; Asst. to A.G.G., S.W. frontier, 17 Feb. 1841. Leave s.c. to Cape 13 May 1842 till 5 Feb. 1843. Junior Asst. to A.G.G., S.W. frontier, 11 Mar. 1843; 1 cl. Asst. to Comr. Chota Nagpur 13 Nov. 1843; Asst. to Comr. Arakan 13 Jan. 1847; Principal do. 12 June 1849; Principal Asst. to Comr. Tenasserim and Martaban provinces 30 Dec. 1852; D.C. do. 14 Feb. 1855; Comr. Pegu Div., Brit. Burma, 22 Apr. 1863. Fur. s.c. 15 mos. Jan. 1857. Transfd. to Staff Corps 18 Feb. 1861; transfd. to 2nd N.I. (late 31st) May 1861. Author and illustrator of " Game Birds and Fishes of India."

Refs. : Burke's *Landed Gentry of Ireland*, p. 691, *s.n.* Tickell, of Carnolway, co. Kildare. Family information. *The Times*, 26 Apr. 1875.

TIDEMAN, John Arnold (1785-1809). Lieutenant, 2nd N.I.
b. Leghorn, Italy, 14 June 1785. Cadet 1804. Arrived in India 10 Dec. 1805. Ensign 9 Nov. 1805. Lieut. 17 Sept. 1806.
d. Midnapore, Bengal, 21 May 1809 : drowned in the Kossye nullah whilst crossing on horseback.
bapt. English Factory, Leghorn. Son of J. Arnold Tideman and Elizabeth his wife.
Services : Posted Lieut. to 2nd N.I. 1806. No record of active service.
Refs. : *Calcutta Monthly Journal*, May 1809.

TIERNEY, Edward Thomas (1808-1872). Lieut. Colonel. 28th N.I. *b.* Rathkeale, co. Limerick, 2 Feb. 1808. Cadet 1823. Arrived in India 3 Sept. 1824. Ensign 13 Apr. 1824. Lieut. 13 May 1825. Capt. 26 Mar. 1840. Major 22 Aug. 1852. Retired 15 Nov. 1852. Hon. Lt. Col. 28 Nov. 1854. *d.* Cheshunt Cottage, S. Norwood, 25 Dec. 1872.

3rd and youngest son of Thomas Tierney, Paymr. H.M. 43rd L.I., and Elizabeth his wife, relict of John Fitzgerald, of Rathkeale. Brother of John Tierney, *q.v.*, nephew of Sir Matthew John Tierney, 1st Bart., of Brighton, and cousin-german of Henry McMahon, *q.v.*

m. 1st, Christina Rathay (? Rattray). (She died Dehra Dun 5 Apr. 1838, aged 28.) *m.* 2nd, Calcutta 26 Dec. 1842, Jane, sister of John Howard Rice and widow of Joseph Whiteford, *qq.v.* (She died London 14 Feb. 1885, aged 82.) Sandhurst Cadet.
Services : Posted Ensign to 28th N.I. and served throughout with that Regt. Intr. & Qmr. 1 Feb. 1838 till 1840. Second Sikh War ; Jullundur Doab 1848–9 ; Capt. 28th N.I. (? Medal).
Refs.: Burke's *Peerage*, 1859, p. 995, *s.n.* Tierney, Bart., of Brighton. *The Times*, 27 Dec. 1872.

TIERNEY, John (1806-1829). Lieutenant, 40th N.I. *b.* Rathkeale, co. Limerick, 3 Aug. 1806. Cadet 1821. Ensign 11 Feb. 1823. Lieut. 17 May 1824. *d. unm.* Mhow 24 May 1829, of spasmodic cholera.

2nd son of Thomas Tierney and Elizabeth his wife. Brother of Edward Thomas Tierney, *q.v.* Addiscombe Cadet 1820-2.
Services : Posted Ensign to 30th N.I. 1823 ; transfd. to 25th N.I. May 1824 ; to 40th N.I. 1827. Served at P.W.I. with his Regt. 1824-5. No record of active service.
Refs.: Burke's *Peerage*, 1859, p. 995, *s.n.* Tierney, Bart., of Brighton. *A.J.* xxviii. 604.

TILFER, James Thomas (*d.* 1794). Fireworker, Artillery. (265) Country Cadet (Inf.) 1783. Ensign (Inf.) 11 Apr. 1785. Fireworker (Art.) 11 Apr. 1785. *d.* 26 Oct. 1794 : kld. in action at battle of Bitaurah.

Son of William Tilfer, of Belgona, co. Fife. Nephew of Rev. John Telfer, minister of Kilsyth 1754-89.
Services : Second Mysore War 1783 ; served as a Volunteer with detachment under Col. T. D. Pearce, *q.v.* Apptd. Cadet 21 July 1783. Posted Ensign to 6th Eur. Bn. 15 Feb. 1790 ; transfd. to Art. 3 Dec. 1790. Second Rohilla War 1794 ; battle of Bitaurah (kld.) ; Lieut. F. 2nd Coy. 3rd Bn. Art.
Refs.: Will dated camp on banks of the Sanyka Nulla 26 Oct. 1794 ; proved 7 May 1795.

TILLOTSON, John James (1789-1831). Captain, 2nd N.I. *bapt.* Takeley, Essex, 2 July 1789. Cadet 1808. Arrived in India 27 Oct. 1809. Ensign 1 July 1810. Lieut. 16 Dec. 1814. Capt. 13 May 1825. *d.* Dinapore 7 Apr. 1831.

Son of Rev. John Tillotson and Elizabeth his wife.
Services : Barasat C.C. Posted Ensign to 1st N.I. 1810. Third Mahratta War 1817-18 ; Rampur ; Jawad ; Lieut. 1/1st N.I.,

in Left Div. Actg. Intr. & Qmr. 1/1st N.I. 1819-22. Transfd. to 2nd N.I. (late 1/1st) May 1824.
Refs.: *A.J.* N.S. vi. 138.

TILSON, James Henry. (*See* CHOWNE, James Henry.)

TIMBRELL, Thomas (1791-1875). Lieut. Colonel, C.B. Artillery. (395) *b.* Stepney 16 Jan. 1791. Cadet 1807. Arrived in India 16 Nov. 1808. Fireworker 25 Sept. 1808. Lieut. 28 Oct. 1811. Capt. 12 Dec. 1821. Major 7 Mar. 1838. Retired 2 Jan. 1843. Hon. Lt. Col. 28 Nov. 1854. *d.* Reading 25 Mar. 1875.

bapt. St. Dunstan's, Stepney, 10 Mar. 1799. Only child of Thomas Timbrell, E.I.C.N.S., and Maria his wife, dau. of Capt. Joseph Richardson, of Limehouse. Cousin-german of William Timbrell, *q.v. m.* Ann Paris. (She died Englefield Green 24 Nov. 1869.) Woolwich Cadet.

Services: Operations in Bundelkhand against Gopal Singh 1810; action at Parari 18 Feb. (slight contusion from a matchlock ball); Lieut. comdg. a detachment of 6th Coy. 3rd Bn., with force under Capt. E. P. Wilson, *q.v.* (? Reduction of Kalinjar 1812.) Nepal War 1814-15; Lieut. 7th Coy. 3rd Bn., in 1st Div. (joined after capture of Nalagarh 5 Nov. 1814) (India medal). Siege and capture of Hathras; Lieut. 7th Coy. 3rd Bn. Third Mahratta War 1817-19; Lieut. 7th Coy. 3rd Bn., Adjt. Foot Art. in Centre Div. Fur. p.a. 19 Feb. 1820 till 12 Nov. 1821. Comdd. a flotilla of gunboats on Brahmaputra R. Nov. 1822 till Mar. 1823. First Burma War; Ava 1824; to comd. Bengal Div. Art. at Rangoon 1 Apr. 1824; Kemmendine; Kamarut; Dalla; Martaban 8 & 9 Oct. 1824 (*Lond. Gaz.* 22 & 25 Mar. 1825); returned sick to Bengal Dec. 1824; Capt. 3rd Coy. 5th Bn. (clasp to India medal). Offg. Supt. and Dir. of Foundry 27 Feb. 1826. Fur. s.c. 22 Dec. 1829 till 24 Jan. 1833. In charge of Expense Mag. at Dum-Dum 2 Aug. 1834 till Feb. 1835. Capt. comdg. 4th Troop 3rd Bde. H.A. 1835-6. Comdd. Meywar Div. Art. 26 Jan. till 17 Apr. 1836. Agent for manufacture of gunpowder at Ichapur 5 May 1837 till 2 Jan. 1843. C.B. 20 July 1838.

Refs.: *The Times*, 27 Mar. 1875.

TIMBRELL, William (1813-1844). Bt. Captain, Artillery. (627) *b.* Hampstead 3 Feb. 1813. Cadet 1828. Arrived in India 9 Feb. 1830. 2nd Lieut. 12 June 1829.[1] Lieut. 16 Oct. 1837. Bt. Capt. 12 June 1844. *d.* Shikarpur, Sind, 18 Sept. 1844.

bapt. St. John's, Hampstead, 11 Nov. 1816. Son of James

Timbrell, E.I.C.N.S., Capt. H.C. Ship *Exeter*, and Harriet his wife, *née* Armstrong. Cousin-german of Thomas Timbrell, *q.v.* *m.* Agnes Ann ——. (She died 17 Nov. 1893, aged 69.) Addiscombe Cadet 1827-9.

Services : Posted to 4th Coy. 2nd Bn. Foot Art. 28 Feb. 1834 ; to 3rd Troop 3rd Bde. H.A. 17 Mar. 1838 ; to 3rd Troop 2nd Bde. 6 Oct. 1838 ; to 4th Troop 1st Bde. 2 Nov. 1841. A.D.C. to Maj. Gen. W. Battine, *q.v.*, comdg. 2nd Inf. Div., Army of Reserve (for Afghanistan) 14 Oct. 1842 till May 1843. No record of active service.

Refs.: *G.M.* 1845, i. 222.

[1] *Note :* Rank cancelled and reduced to Cadet (G.G.O. 31 May 1830) under instructions from C.D. Apptd. Actg. 2nd Lieut. (G.G.O. 27 Feb. 1832) ; service afterwards allowed to count for brevet rank.

TIMINGS, Henry (1798-1839). Captain, Artillery. (465) *bapt.* St. Helen's, Worcester, 18 Feb. 1798. Cadet 1815. Admitted 16 Aug. 1816. Fireworker 14 Aug. 1817. Lieut. 1 Sept. 1818. Capt. 2 Sept. 1832. *d.* in camp nr. Kabul 12 Sept. 1839, aged 42.

Youngest son of John Timings, of Worcester, cabinet maker, and Mary his wife. *m.* Ambassador's Chapel, Paris, Feb./Mar. 1834, Charlotte, youngest dau. of Robert Crump, late of Charlton Kings. (*See also* C. J. C. Davidson and Z. H. Turton.) Addiscombe Cadet 1813-16.

Services : Served with 1st Troop H.A. 1820-9. First Burma War 1824-6 ; operations in Ava ; Lieut. H.A., with Sir A. Campbell's force. Apptd. Adjt. & Qmr. detachment of H.A. in Ava 11 June 1825. Adjt. Malwa Div. Art. 22 Jan. 1829. Transfd. from 2nd Troop 2nd Bde. H.A. to 4th Troop 3rd Bde. 22 Mar. 1832. Fur. s.c. 13 Feb. 1833 till 10 Dec. 1834. Posted to 4th Troop 2nd Bde. 20 Feb. 1835 ; to 4th Troop 3rd Bde. 6 Feb. 1837 till death. First Afghan War 1838-9 ; Ghazni ; Capt. comdg. 4th Troop 3rd Bde.

Refs.: *Bath Chron.* 25 Mar. 1834. *G.M.* 1840, i. 223. Will dated Lucknow 11 Dec. 1835 ; admon. 11 Aug. 1840. M.I. Afghan Memorial Church, Bombay.

TIMINS, George (1809-1875). Colonel. 34th N.I. *b.* Newton Flotman, Norfolk, 1 Feb. 1809. Cadet 1824. Arrived in India 12 June 1825. Ensign 25 Jan. 1825. Lieut. 7 Apr. 1828. Capt. 10 Jan. 1845. Major 19 May 1858. Lt. Col. 5 Mar. 1859. Retired 31 Dec. 1861. Hon. Col. 31 Dec. 1861. *d.* 2 Mar. 1875, at his residence, Newstead, Torquay.

bapt. St Anne's, Liverpool, 13 Aug. 1809. Son of George Timins, of Liverpool, Comdr. R.N., and Mary his wife, late Sayer. Nephew of John Timins, E.I.C.N.S., Comdr. of the *Royal George* East Indiaman. *m.* Mehidpur 4 Oct. 1842, Jane, eldest dau. of Frederick Hervey Sandys, *q.v.* (*See also* Samuel John Becher.)

Services : Ensign d.d. 16th N.I. 23 June 1825 ; posted to 34th N.I. 1825. Operations against the Kols and Chuars 1832-3 ; Lieut. 34th N.I. Fur. s.c. 29 July 1833 till 20 Aug. 1836. 2nd in comd. Malwa Contingent 19 Feb. 1838 ; Comdt. do. 15 Sept. 1841 ; Comdt. United Malwa Contingent 15 Dec. 1841 till 1857, when it mutinied. Fur. 1859 till retirement.

Refs. : The Times, 12 Mar. 1875.

TINDAL, Joseph (1803-1826). Lieutenant, Engineers. *b.* Skipton, Yorks., 23 Mar. 1803. Cadet 1822. Ensign (?) Lieut. 1 May 1824. *d.* Bhurtpore 1 Jan. 1826 : kld. in action.

bapt. Skipton 8 May 1803. Son of William Tindal, of Skipton, atty.-at-law, and Ann his wife. Nephew of Thomas Chippendale, of the Inner Temple, barr.-at-law. Addiscombe Cadet 1818-20.

Services : First Burma War ; Lieut., Field Engr. Garr. Engr. at Almora and Executive Ofr. in Kumaon 11 Feb. 1825. Siege and capture of Bhurtpore (kld.) ; Lieut., Field Engr.

Refs. : Will dated camp nr. Bhurtpore, 12 Dec. 1825 ; proved 30 June 1826.

TIPPETT, Charles Edward (1791-1821). Lieutenant, 22nd N.I. *b.* Falmouth, Cornwall, 13 Apr. 1791. Cadet 1807. Arrived in India 16 Nov. 1808. Ensign 20 Nov. 1808. Lieut. 1 Sept. 1814. *d.* at sea 28 Apr. 1821, on board the *Lord Hungerford*.

bapt. Falmouth 22 Apr. 1791. Son of James Tippett, of Falmouth, atty.-at-law, and Harriot his wife, *née* Bell. Ed. Blundell's 18 Aug. 1806 till 15 Dec. 1807.

Services : Barasat C.C. Posted Ensign to 22nd N.I. 1809. (? Reduction of Kalinjar 1812 ; Ensign 1/22nd N.I.) Lieut. 1/22nd N.I. With 7th Gren. Bn. 1815-16. Third Mahratta War 1817 ; Nagpur ; Lieut. 1/22nd N.I. Fur. 1821 till death.

Refs. : Blundell's School Register.

TIPPETT, William Hornby [1] (1782-1824). Lieutenant. 3rd N.I. Subsequently B.C.S. *b.* Bombay 21 Nov. 1782. Cadet 1798. Admitted 16 Oct. 1800. Ensign 1 Dec. 1799. Lieut. 29 May 1800. Transfd. to B.C.S. 14 July 1803. *d.* at sea 11 July 1824, on board the *Berwickshire*.

bapt. Bombay 29 Apr. 1783. Son of Capt. James Tippett, Bo. Est., and Mary Ann his wife, sister of Lt.-Col. William Mason, 7th Bo. N.I., of Wobern Hill, Chertsey.

Services : Posted Lieut. to 3rd N.I. No record of active service. Judge and mgte. of Patna city 17 Dec. 1816 till death.

[1] *Note :* Qy. Henry.

TISDALE, John (*d.* 1784). Captain, Infantry. Cadet 1769. Ensign 12 Apr. 1770. Lieut. 17 Mar. 1773. Capt. 13 Jan. 1781. *d.* Monghyr [1] 11 May 1784.

Services : Nominated for comd. of a Sepoy Bn. 1 Jan. 1781.

[1] *Note :* Qy. *d.* at Plassey.

TITCHER, Jeremiah (1782-1809). Lieutenant, 22nd N.I. *bapt.* Gosport, Hants, 17 Jan. 1782. Cadet 1798. Arrived in India 26 Mar. 1800. Ensign 14 Jan. 1800. Lieut. 29 May 1800. *d.* Lucknow 29 May 1809.

Son of Philip Titcher and Elizabeth his wife.

Services : Posted Lieut. to 2/5th N.I. 15 Apr. 1801. Transfd. to newly-raised 22nd N.I. 1804. Second Mahratta War 1804-5 ; battle and capture of Deig ; Bhurtpore (w. in 1st assault 9 Jan. 1805) ; Lieut. 2/22nd N.I.

Refs. : Will dated 1 Jan. 1802 ; admon. 22 Aug. 1809.

TOD, Alexander (1779-1817). Captain, 26th N.I. *b.* Beley, co. Banff, 13 Dec. 1779. Cadet 1798. Arrived in India 24 Feb. 1800. Ensign 30 Aug. 1799. Lieut. 28 Oct. 1799. Capt. 29 Nov. 1809. *d.* Kaitha, U.P., 31 Jan. 1817.

bapt. Beley 21 Dec. 1779. Eldest son of Robert Tod, of Tipperty, co. Banff, and Margaret his wife.

Services : Posted to 1/3rd N.I. 15 Apr. 1801. Transfd. to newly-raised 26th N.I. 1805. Adjt. Patna Provl. Bn. 1805-9. Capt. Lt. 27 Apr. 1809. Capt. 1/26th N.I.

Refs. : S.M. 1817, ii. 98. *G.M.* 1817, ii. 281. Will dated Kytah 13 Jan. 1817 ; proved 5 Mar. 1817. M.I. Kaitha.

TOD, James (1782-1835). Lieut. Colonel. 2nd Bengal Eur. Regt. *b.* Islington 19 Mar. 1782. Cadet 1798. Arrived in India 26 Aug. 1799. Ensign 9 Jan. 1800. Lieut. 29 May 1800. Capt. 26 Oct. 1813. Major 1 May 1824. Lt. Col. 2 June 1826. Retired 28 June 1825. *d.* London 17 Nov. 1835, as the result of an apoplectic stroke.

bapt. Islington 5 May 1782. Son of James Tod and Mary his wife, sister of Patrick Heatly, *q.v.* Brother of Suetonius Henry

Tod and cousin-german of Alexander Douglas and Patrick Young Waugh, qq.v. m. St. George's, Hanover Sq., London, 16 Nov. 1826, Julia, 3rd dau. of Henry Clutterbuck, M.D., of Bridge St., Blackfriars, London. (She died nr. Lucerne 18 Aug. 1850, aged 41.)

Services: See D.N.B. Posted Ensign to 2nd Bengal Eur. Regt. ; Lieut. to 14th N.I. ; transfd. to 2nd Eur. Regt. 15 Apr. 1801 ; to Marine Regt. 1803 ; to newly-raised 25th N.I. 1805. Attached to escort with embassy to Sindhia 1805 ; comdd. do. 25 Feb. 1812 till 1817. Surveying in Chambal district 1811. Capt. Lt. 25th N.I. 13 Aug. 1812 ; Capt. 2/25th N.I. 2nd Asst. to Resdt. at Gwalior Oct. 1815 ; 1st do. 1816. In charge of Intelligence Dept. in Pindari War 1817. P.A. Western Rajput States 1818-22. Fur. Feb. 1823 till retirement. Posted Major to 49th N.I. (late 1/25th) May 1824 ; Lt. Col. to 51st N.I. 30 Oct. 1826. Retired in 1827 with effect from 28 June 1825, but with his rank as Lt. Col. Librarian to R. Asiatic Soc. Pub. London, 1829-32, " Annals and Antiquities of Rajasthan . . .," 2 vols. 4to, etc.

Refs.: D.N.B. D.I.B. Ency. Brit. G.M. 1836, i. 202. A.J. N.S. xviii. 261.

TOD,[1] **Suetonius Henry** (1780-1861). General. Colonel 60th N.I. b. Islington 19 Dec. 1780. Cadet 1798. Admitted 3 Apr. 1800. Ensign 14 Sept. 1799. Lieut. 28 Oct. 1799. Capt. 26 Feb. 1813. Major 11 July 1823. Lt. Col. 12 Jan. 1825. Col. 5 Apr. 1834. Maj. Gen. 28 June 1838. Lt. Gen. 11 Nov. 1851. Gen. 30 Jan. 1861. d. Whitehouse, Edinburgh, 1 Sept. 1861.

bapt. Islington 14 Jan. 1781. Son of James Tod and Mary his wife. Brother of James Tod, q.v. m. New Norfolk, Tasmania, 5 July 1825, Mary, youngest dau. of Capt. Ewen Macdonald, Griminish, N. Uist.

Services: Ensign H.M. 78th Ft. 15 Oct. 1798. Posted Lieut. to 2/10th N.I. 15 Apr. 1801. Capt. Lt. 10th N.I. 14 Sept. 1809. (? Operations in Rewah 1813-14 ; Entauri ; Capt. 2/10th N.I.) Transfd. to newly-raiscd 2/30th N.I. 1815. Leave s.c. 10 mos. to Cape 10 Sept. 1815 ; shipwrecked on the voyage. Suptg. civil bldgs. at Allahabad ; do. Murshidabad 28 Mar. 1817 till Aug. 1819. Transfd. as Major to 32nd N.I. July 1823. Leave s.c. 8 mos. to Presdy. 21 Aug. 1823 ; s.c. to N.S.W. 7 May 1824 till 25 Jan. 1826. Transfd. to 63rd N.I. (late 1/32nd) May 1824 ; as Lt. Col. to 19th N.I. 1825 ; to 30th N.I. 1826 ; to 55th N.I. 28 Aug. 1829 ; to 3rd 5 Dec. 1829 ; to 8th 11 Mar. 1832 ; to 72nd 22 Aug. 1833.

Leave s.c. to N.S.W. 21 Nov. 1829 till 16 Jan. 1832; fur. s.c. 19 Sept. 1832 till death. Posted Col. to 41st N.I. 4 Oct. 1834; 60th N.I. 2 Apr. 1856 till death.

Refs.: *Clan Donald,* p. 543, *s.n.* Macdonald, of Aird and Vallay. Boase. *G.M.* 1861, ii. 456.

¹ *Note:* The name is often spelt Todd in *A.L.* and official documents.

TODD, Elliott D'Arcy (1808-1845). Captain, Artillery. (555) *b.* London 28 Jan. 1808. Cadet 1823. Arrived in India 22 May 1824. 2nd Lieut. 18 Dec. 1823. Lieut. 28 Sept. 1827. Capt. 13 May 1842. *d.* 21 Dec. 1845: kld. in action at battle of Ferozshahr.

bapt. 6 Mar. 1808. 3rd and youngest son of Fryer Todd, of Chancery Lane, accountant, of a Yorkshire family, and Mary Evans his wife. Brother of Fryer Bowes Todd, *q.v.* *m.* Calcutta 22 Aug. 1842, Marian, eldest dau. of Backshall Lane Sandham, M.D., Surg. 16th Lrs. (She died Ambala 9 Dec. 1845, aged 23.) Addiscombe Cadet 1 Jan. 1822 till 18 Dec. 1823.

Services: See *D.N.B.* Siege and capture of Bhurtpore; Lieut. 4th Coy. 3rd Bn. Foot Art. Served with H.A. May 1826 till Aug. 1833. Selected 9 July 1833 to serve with disciplined troops of Shah of Persia, and served in Persia (latterly with local rank of Major) till July 1838, when he returned to India. Mily. Sec. to Sir H. L. Bethune, comdg. Shah's disciplined troops, 1836; accompanied Sir John McNeill to Persian camp at Herat, as Sec. to the Legation, Apr. 1838. Apptd. Mily. Sec. and Pol. Asst. to Sir W. H. Macnaghten Oct. 1838; despatched on a special mission to Herat June 1839; P.A. at Herat Jan. 1841; removed from Pol. employ and recalled to India by Lord Auckland Apr. 1841. Posted to comd. 2nd Troop 1st Bde. H.A. Sept. 1845. First Sikh War; Mudki; Ferozshahr (kld.); Capt. comdg. 2nd Troop 1st Bde. Persian Order of the Lion and Sun. Durani 2 cl. 26 Mar. 1841.

Refs.: *D.N.B.* *De Rhé-Philipe.* *D.I.B.* *Stubbs,* iii. 21-3 (portrait). *Calcutta Review,* vii. (1847), pp. 304-5. M.I. at Ambala and St. Andrew's, Ferozepore.

TODD, Fryer Bowes (1800-1847). Captain, Invalid Est. 11th N.I. *b.* London 25 Nov. 1800. Cadet 1819. Admitted 9 Oct. 1820. Ensign 5 Apr. 1820. Lieut. 11 July 1823. Capt. 1 Dec. 1836. Invalided 20 Jan. 1841. *d.* Mirzapur, U.P., 7 Oct. 1847.

bapt. St. James's, Westminster, 10 Dec. 1800. 2nd son of Fryer Todd, of Chancery Lane, and Mary his wife. Brother of Elliott

THE BENGAL ARMY, 1758-1834 285

D'Arcy Todd, *q.v. m.* Koil, U.P., 15 Mar. 1824, Miss Charlotte Tilney Long.[1]
Services : Was already in India as a Vol. in the Pilot service when apptd. Cadet. Posted Ensign to 1/29th N.I.; transfd. as Lieut. to 5th N.I. July 1823; to 11th N.I. (late 1/5th) May 1824. Served with 2nd L.I. Bn. in Arakan from Sept. 1825. Fur. p.a. 12 Jan. 1832 till 4 Jan. 1834. Served with Invalid Bn. at Chunar 1 Nov. 1841 till 1846. No record of active service.
Refs. : I.M. 6 Dec. 1847, p. 712. M.I. Mirzapur cemetery.
[1] *Note :* Probably dau. of William Long (see Appendix A).

TODD, Hugh (1803-1832). Lieutenant, 21st N.I. Sec. to Council, Coll. of Ft. Wm. *bapt.* Ballymoney, co. Armagh, 30 May 1803. Cadet 1820. Arrived in India 18 Dec. 1821. Ensign 1 June 1821. Lieut. 1 May 1824. *d.* Calcutta 21 Mar. 1832, aged 28.
Eldest son of Gabriel Todd, of Ballygan, Ballymoney, gentleman farmer. Nephew of David Ruddell, *q.v.*, and of James Ruddell Todd, of Ballintaggart, co. Armagh.
Services : Posted to 1/10th N.I. 1822; transfd. to 1/9th N.I. 1823; to 21st N.I. (late 2/9th) May 1824. Offg. Examiner, Coll. of Ft. Wm., 6 Apr. 1825; permanent do. 30 June 1825 till 1831. Siege and capture of Bhurtpore; Lieut. 21st N.I. Offg. Sec. to Committee of Examiners in Sanskrit and Arabic Jan. 1827. Leave s.c. to Malacca and Java 5 Apr. till 9 Nov. 1831; s.c. 2 yrs. to Cape Mar. 1832, but died before embarking. A great scholar in Arabic, Hindi, Persian, Bengali and Hindustani.
Refs. : B. : P.P., No. 48, p. 137. *A.J.* N.S. ix. 36. *Belfast Newsletter*, 28 Sept. 1832.

TODD, John (*d.* 1770). Lieutenant, Infantry. Cadet 1767. Ensign 15 Sept. 1767. Lieut. 25 Sept. 1769. *d.* Monghyr 19 Jan. 1770.
Services : Sailed for India in the *Calcutta* 31 Dec. 1766.

TODD, Joseph (1785-1825). Captain. 26th N.I. *b.* Chester-le-Street, co. Durham, 1 June 1785. Cadet 1805. Arrived in India 20 July 1807. Ensign 6 July 1807. Lieut. 1 Sept. 1809. Capt. 1 May 1824. Retired 25 May 1825. *d.* 13 Dec. 1825.
bapt. 22 Aug. 1785. Son of William Todd, of Lumley Castle, and Elizabeth his wife. Brother of William Todd, *q.v.*, and half-brother of Miss Barbara Coxon.
Services : Barasat C.C. Posted Ensign to 13th N.I. 1808.

Bareilly insurrection 1816; Lieut. 1/13th N.I. Fur. 1823 till retirement. Transfd. to 26th N.I. (late 1/13th) May 1824.

TODD, William (1787-1823). Bt. Captain, 10th N.I. *b.* Chester-le-Street, co. Durham, 7 July 1787. Cadet 1805. Arrived in India 20 July 1807. Ensign 7 July 1807. Lieut. 6 Mar. 1812. Bt. Capt. 6 Dec. 1821. *d.* Saharanpur, U.P., 16 Nov. 1823.

bapt. 24 July 1787. Son of William Todd, of Lumley Castle, and Elizabeth his wife. Brother of Joseph Todd, *q.v.*

Services: Barasat C.C. Posted Ensign to 10th N.I. 1808. (? Settlement of Hariana 1809; Bhawani; Ensign 1/10th N.I. Nepal War 1814-15; Lieut. 1/10th N.I.) Adjt. newly-raised Sirmoor Bn. 27 July 1815 till death. Transfd. to 2/10th N.I.

Refs.: Will dated 13 Nov. 1823; proved 7 Feb. 1824.

TOLFREY, John (1757-1779). Ensign, Infantry. *bapt.* St. Pancras, Soper Lane, London, 22 June 1757. Cadet 1778. Ensign 1778. *d.* Patna 18 Apr. 1779.

Son of Samuel Tolfrey and Margaret his wife, dau. of Nathaniel Stackhouse. Brother of Peter Tolfrey, *q.v.*, and of Stackhouse Tolfrey, Coy.'s atty. in Calcutta.

Services: Was already in India when apptd. Cadet 27 Feb. 1778.

TOLFREY, Peter. Bt. Captain. Infantry. Pensioner on Lord Clive's fund. Country Cadet 1781. Ensign 2 Aug. 1782. Lieut. 24 Jan. 1785. Bt. Capt. 7 Jan. 1796. Pensioned 23 May 1798.

Son of Samuel Tolfrey and Margaret his wife. Brother of John Tolfrey, *q.v.*

Services: Apptd. Cadet 28 Nov. 1781. Fur. on h.p. 20 Nov. 1786 till 1790. Lieut. 4th Bengal Eur. Bn. Third Mysore War; Lieut. Bengal Vols. Transfd. from 4th to 6th Eur. Bn. 27 Mar. 1792; to 3rd Eur. Regt. June 1796.

TOLLEMACHE, William (1810-1886). Ensign. 22nd N.I. *b.* 7 Nov. 1810. Cadet 1827. Arrived in India 10 Oct. 1828. Ensign (10 May 1828) 4 Mar. 1829. Resigned 13 Sept. 1832. *d.* Victoria St., Westminster, 17 Mar. 1886.

bapt. Edmondthorpe, Leics., 25 Dec. 1810. 5th (3rd by 2nd wife) son of Hon. Charles Tollemache (formerly Manners), of Harrington, Northants (of Huntsmoore Park, nr. Uxbridge), and Gertrude Florinda his 2nd wife, dau. of Gen. William Gardiner, and relict of Charles John Clarke. *m.* 1st, 13 Sept. 1838, Anna

THE BENGAL ARMY, 1758-1834   287

Maria, dau. of Edward Adolphus, 11th Duke of Somerset, K.G. (She died 23 Sept. 1873.) *m.* 2nd, 11 May 1875, Emma, dau. of James Sidney, and widow of Maj.-Gen. Sir Herbert Edwardes, K.C.B. (She died 28 Aug. 1904.)
Services : Ensign d.d. 51st N.I. 5 Nov. 1828 ; posted to 22nd N.I. 4 Mar. 1829. No record of active service.
Refs. : Burke's *Peerage*, 1923, p. 802, *s.n.* Dysart, E. *The Times*, 19 Mar. 1886.

TOLLY, John (*d.* 1776). Lieutenant, Infantry. Cadet 1769. Ensign 5 Mar. 1769. Lieut. 1 Apr. 1771. *d.* Chittagong (? April) 1776.
m. Frances.
Services : N.F.P.
Refs. : Will dated Luckypore 17 May 1775 ; proved 22 Apr. 1776.

TOLLY,[1] William (*d.* 1784). Lieut. Colonel. Artillery. (46) Capt. 24 Jan. 1767. Major 27 Jan. 1773. Lt. Col. 9 Dec. 1782. Resigned 23 Jan. 1784. *d.* at sea 1784, on board the *Dutton*, on his passage to England.
(*Perhaps* son of William Tolley, " free inhabitant," who died at Fort Marlbro', Sumatra, 24 May 1766.) Brother of Mary Burgess. *m.* 1st (in England before 1764) ——. *m.* 2nd, Calcutta 11 Apr. 1768, Miss Anna Maria Theresa Hintz. (She *re-m.* Calcutta 12 Jan. 1788, William Johnson, Clerk of the Crown, and died London 27 Oct. 1797.) Father of 4 Minor Cadets (see Appendix C).
Services : Ensign Corps of Engrs. (H.M.S.) 23 Dec. 1759. Belleisle 1761 ; Ensign Engrs. Resigned his Commission 17 Nov. 1763. Apptd. in England 12 Oct. 1763, Principal Engr. at Fort Marlbro', and to succeed to comd. of Art. Coy. there when a vacancy occurs ; sailed for Bencoolen in the *Earl of Elgin* 4 May 1764. Comdd. Train of Art. at Fort Marlbro' 1765-6. Transfd. from Bencoolen to Bengal Est. as Capt. 1767 ; apptd. Bk. Mr. at Monghyr 1772 ; Insp. of Works *c.* 1779. Maker of "Tolly's nullah" between Calcutta and Alipore, 1775, and founder of Tollygunge.
Refs. : D.I.B. Will dated 9 Feb. 1784 ; proved P.C.C. 1 Sept. 1784 ; filed at Calcutta 28 Jan. 1788 ; admon. 20 Dec. 1799.

[1] *Note :* His name usually appears as Tolley in early records, as "Tolly, otherwise Tolley" in his Will.

TOMBS, John (1777-1848). Major General. Colonel 6th L.C. *bapt.* St. Paul's, Covent Gdn., 22 May 1777. Cadet 1796. Arrived in India 8 Mar. 1797. Cornet 26 Nov. 1797. Lieut. 29 May 1800. Capt. 1 Feb. 1806. Major 1 Sept. 1818. Lt. Col.

1 May 1824. Col. 26 Mar. 1829. Maj. Gen. 28 June 1838. d. Malta 30 Oct. 1848, aged 71.

Owned property at New Yatt, nr. Witney, Oxon. Son of Joseph Tombs and Elizabeth his wife. m. Calcutta 6 Mar. 1812, Miss Mary Remington. (She died 27 Dec. 1876, aged 84.) Father of William Henry Tombs and the wife of Rowland Money, qq.v.

Services: Cornet 1st N.C.; Adjt. do. 29 May 1800 till 1806. Operations in Jumna Doab 1803; Sasni; Bijaigarh; Kachaura. Second Mahratta War 1803-5; Koil; Aligarh; Delhi; Agra; Laswari; capture of Deig; Bhurtpore. Capt. Lt. 1st N.C. 11 Mar. 1805. Fur. p.a. 16 Feb. 1808 till 16 Aug. 1811. Third Mahratta War 1817-18; Capt. 1st N.C., in Rt. Div. Operations against the Bhattis of Hariana 1818. Leave 10 Feb. 1820 till Feb. 1822. Siege and capture of Bhurtpore; Lt. Col. 3rd L.C. Transfd. to 6th L.C. 18 Sept. 1826; apptd. Bdr. on the Est. 16 Apr. 1829; posted Col. to 6th L.C. 15 Aug. 1829. Fur. p.a. 28 Feb. 1830 till 7 Feb. 1833. Transfd. to 3rd L.C. 24 Dec. 1833; to 8th L.C. 30 Dec. 1834. To comd. Rajputana F.F. with rank of Bdr. 2 cl. 8 Aug. 1833; Bdr. 2 cl. comdg. Rohilkhand 20 Dec. 1834 till May 1840. Transfd. to 4th L.C. 26 Feb. 1838; Col. 6th L.C. 1839 till death. On Gen. Staff of Army, comdg. Saugor Div., 25 June 1842 till 25 June 1847. Apptd. to chief comd. of troops to be employed against insurgents in Saugor and Bundelkhand district 20 Jan. 1843. Fur. Jan. 1848 till death.

Refs.: *I.M.* 5 Dec. 1848, p. 730. *G.M.* 1849, i. 223. Will dated 6 July 1846; proved 12 Dec. 1848.

TOMBS, William Henry (1814-1842). Lieutenant, 5th N.I. b. Muttra 31 Mar. 1814. Cadet 1832. Arrived in India 18 June 1833. Ensign (14 Dec. 1832) 18 June 1833. Lieut. 4 May 1837. d. nr. Kabul (? 13) Jan. 1842: kld. in action during the retreat.

Son of John Tombs, q.v., and Mary his wife. Brother of Maj. Gen. Sir Henry Tombs, K.C.B. (*D.N.B.*). Addiscombe Cadet 4 Feb. 1831 till Dec. 1832.

Services: Cadet d.d. 31st N.I. 29 July 1833; Ensign d.d. 55th N.I. 19 Dec. 1833; posted to 5th N.I. 24 May 1834. Actg. Adjt. 4th Depot Bn. 27 Nov. 1839; rejoined 5th N.I. 1841. First Afghan War 1841-2; outbreak at Kabul; retreat from Kabul (kld.); Lieut. 5th N.I.

Refs.: M.I. Afghan Memorial Church, Bombay.

***TOMKINS or TOMKYNS, A—— (or G——).** Lieutenant. Infantry. Cadet 1778. Ensign 22 July 1779. Lieut. 13 Mar. 1781.

Services : Probably never arrived in India. In *A.L.* for Jan. 1781, not in July 1787.

TOMKINS, John William (1810-1834). Ensign, 1st N.I. *bapt.* Holybourne, Hants, 30 Oct. 1810. Cadet 1828. Arrived in India 4 May 1829. Ensign (8 Jan. 1829) 14 Sept. 1829. *d.* Fatehgarh 31 May 1834, aged 23.

Son of Benjamin Tomkins, of 42 Upper Thames St., maltfactor, and Sarah his wife.

Services : Ensign d.d. 33rd N.I. 10 June 1829 ; posted to 1st N.I. 14 Sept. 1829. No record of active service.

Refs. : G.M. 1835, i. 221. M.I. at Fatehgarh.

TOMKYNS, George (1790-1873). General. Colonel 19th N.I. *bapt.* Bromyard, co. Hereford, 15 July 1790. Cadet 1806. Arrived in India 1 Aug. 1807. Ensign (28 Feb. 1807) 24 Aug. 1807. Lieut. 5 Jan. 1811. Capt. 1 May 1824. Major 5 Mar. 1835. Lt. Col. 23 Nov. 1841. Col. 16 Oct. 1851. Maj. Gen. 28 Nov. 1854. Lt. Gen. 29 Apr. 1866. Gen. 25 June 1870. *d.* 31 Arundel Gdns., Notting Hill, London, 16 Nov. 1873, aged 83.

Son of Rev. Pakington George Tomkyns, D.C.L., of Buckinghill Park, Hereford, and Margaret his wife. *m.* St. John's, Calcutta, 6 Nov. 1823, Jessie, 2nd dau. of Capt. Alexander Nash, of Gravel Hill House, Chalfont St. Peter, Bucks. (She died Worcester 11 Jan. 1900, aged 95.) Ed. Winchester ; K.S. 1802.

Services : Barasat C.C. 8 mos. Posted Lieut. to 7th N.I. 1808. (? Reduction of Kalinjar 1812 ; Lieut. 1/7th N.I.) Nepal War 1814-15 ; Lieut. 1/7th N.I., in 2nd Div. (India medal). Actg. Intr. & Qmr. 1/7th N.I. 14 Oct. 1817 till 1819. Third Mahratta War 1817-19. Served in Nizam's army 20 Dec. 1819 till Mar. 1849 with only one short break. Transfd. to 13th N.I. (late 1/7th) May 1824 ; to 10th N.I. (late 2/7th) 17 Sept. 1824. Comdt. 2nd Bn. Ellichpur Bde. 1820 ; do. Nizam's 6th Inf. Regt. 20 Apr. 1831 ; Bdr. comdg. Hingoli Div. 3 Aug. 1835 ; do. Hyderabad Div. 21 Aug. 1837 till 1848 ; do. Aurangabad Div. Insurrection in Shorapur 1842 ; Bdr. comdg. the force ; also engaged in several other minor operations. Fur. s.c. 15 Mar. 1849 till 1851. Posted Lt. Col. to 22nd N.I. Nov. 1841 ; to 31st N.I. 15 Nov. 1843 ; to 9th N.I. 17 Apr. 1845 ; to 61st N.I. 1849 ; to 21st N.I. 30 July 1851. Col. 19th N.I. 13 Jan. 1852 till 1869. Fur. s.c. 1853 till 17 Nov. 1856 ; do. Feb. 1859 till death.

Refs. : Boase. Burton. *Calcutta Review,* xi. 183. *The Times,* 22 Nov. 1873.

TOMKYNS, John (*d.* 1830). Lieut. Colonel. Artillery. (188) Country Cadet 1778. Admitted 14 Sept. 1778. Fireworker 4 Nov. 1778. Lieut. 17 Feb. 1784. Capt. 27 Oct. 1794. Major 21 Sept. 1804. Lt. Col. 12 Nov. 1804. Retired 29 May 1805. *d.* Budleigh Salterton, Devon, 20 Jan. 1830.

2nd son of Rev. Chichester Tomkyns (originally Tomkins), formerly of St. Winnow, Cornwall.

Services : Second Mysore War 1781-5 ; Pollilur ; Sholingarh ; Vellore ; Cuddalore ; Lt. F. 5th Coy. 2nd Bn. Third Mysore War 1790-2 ; Bangalore ; Uskata ; Utradrug ; Nandidrug ; Savandrug ; Seringapatam ; Lieut. 3rd Coy. 2nd Bn. Apptd. to tempy. charge of 3rd Coy. 1st Bn. 27 Nov. 1794. Fourth Mysore War 1798-1800 ; Seringapatam ; operations on N. frontier of Mysore 1800 ; Capt. 1st Coy. 3rd Bn. Fur. 19 Jan. 1803 till 6 May 1806, when he retired with effect from 29 May 1805.

Refs. : *E.I.M.C.* i. 109-10. *Bath Chron.* 4 Feb. 1830. M.I. in St. Paul's church, Exeter.

TOMLINSON, John (1792-1826). Bt. Captain, 61st N.I. *b.* London 2 Jan. 1792. Cadet 1808. Arrived in India 27 Oct. 1809. Ensign 18 May 1810. Lieut. 16 Dec. 1814. Bt. Capt. 24 Apr. 1824. *d. unm.* Arakan 2 May 1826.

bapt. Christ Church, Middlesex, 10 Feb. 1792. Son of John Tomlinson and Catherine his wife (who *re-m.* James Philipps). Marlow Cadet.

Services : Posted to 2/29th N.I. 1810. Nepal War 1816 ; Makwanpur ; Lieut. 2/9th N.I., in 4th Bde. Centre Column. Operations in Oudh 1822 ; capture of Bardgaon ; Lieut. 2/9th N.I. Fur. 1823-4. Transfd. to 31st N.I. July 1823 ; to 61st N.I. (late 1/31st) May 1824 ; Adjt. do. 12 July till 18 Nov. 1825.

Refs. : Will dated 9 Feb. 1822 ; proved 31 May 1826.

TOMMS, James. (*See* **THOMS, James.**)

TOONE, James Hastings (1801-1822). Lieutenant, 6th L.C. *b.* London 18 Oct. 1801. Cadet 1817. Cornet (?) Lieut. 31 Aug. 1819. *d.* Ghazipur 30 Nov. 1822.

bapt. Marylebone 12 Nov. 1801. Youngest son of Sweney Toone, *q.v.*, and Sarah Frances his wife.

Services : Posted Lieut. to 6th L.C. 1819. 2nd in comd. Gardner's Horse 1822. No record of active service.

TOONE, James Hastings Lindsay Metcalfe (1816-1886). Major. 2nd L.C. *b.* Ghazipur, U.P., 8 Jan. 1816. Cadet 1832. Arrived in India 19 June 1833. Cornet 27 Feb. 1833. Lieut.

16 Nov. 1841. Capt. 7 Feb. 1851. Retired 1 May 1854. Hon. Major 28 Nov. 1854. *d.* suddenly at Quinta Ribeiro Secco, Madeira, 15 Dec. 1886.

Of Madeira; formerly of Richmond, Surrey. Son of William Thomas Toone, B.C.S., and Maria Helen his wife, dau. of Jonah Hogg, of Scarth House, Rathkeale. Grandson of William Toone and cousin-german of Robert William Hogg, *qq.v. m.* Hampton, Middlesex, 15 Oct. 1861, Emma, 2nd dau. of T. Healey, of the Manor House, Hampton. (She died Biarritz 12 July 1888, aged 41.)

Services: Cadet d.d. 8th L.C. 24 July 1833; posted to 2nd L.C. 9 June 1836. First Afghan War 1838-40; Ghazni (Medal); Parwandara; Cornet 2nd L.C. Adjt. 7th Irreg. Cav. 28 Apr. 1841 till 5 Mar. 1842. Posted to newly-raised 11th L.C. (became 2nd in 1850) on disbandment of 2nd L.C. for misconduct in Afghanistan; Adjt. do. 8 Feb. 1842 till 1 Aug. 1846; Intr. & Qmr. do. 27 Aug. 1847 till Apr. 1851. Gwalior campaign; Paniar; Lieut. 11th L.C. (Bronze star). Second Sikh War; Multan; Suraj Khund; Bt. Capt. 11th L.C. (Medal with clasp).

Refs.: The Times, 31 Dec. 1886.

TOONE, Sweney[1] (1746-1835). Lieut. Colonel. G.G.B.G. Dir. E.I. Co. *b.* Finglas, nr. Dublin, 1746. Cadet 1764. Ensign 4 Aug. 1765. Lieut. 24 Dec. 1766. Capt. 20 Oct. 1769. Major 10 Jan. 1781. Lt. Col. 17 Jan. 1785. Resigned 28 Jan. 1785. *d.* at his residence, Keston Lodge, Kent, 2 Nov. 1835, aged 89.

2nd son of William Toone, of Finglas, and Mary his wife, dau. of Owen Sweney. Brother of William Toone, *q.v. m.* London 27 Oct. 1787, Sarah Frances, dau. of Francis Grey, of Lehena, co. Cork. (She died Keston 31 Jan. 1848, aged 84.) Father of James Hastings Toone, *q.v.,* and of Maria Elizabeth, 8th Countess of Dysart.

Services: Apptd. in England 9 Nov. 1764, Ensign on Bengal Est.; sailed in the *Falmouth* 10 May 1765; wrecked on Saugor bank 13 June 1766. Bde. Major 1st Bde. in 1770. Apptd. A.D.C. to Govr. of Bengal 10 June 1771; do. to Warren Hastings May 1772. Selected by Hastings in 1773 to raise and discipline a troop of cav. to act as his body guard. Raised the "Governor's Troop of Moguls" at Benares in Sept. 1773 and comdd. till 24 Jan. 1777. Operations against the Saniyasis 1773-4. First Rohilla War 1774; battle of St. George. Fur. 19 Feb. 1777 till 1783. Apptd. 4 Aug. 1781 by C.D. to inspect and report on the Bn. of Swiss Inf. raised for E.I. Co. at Rheinau, nr. Schaffhausen, by Col. James Francis Erskine (father of Francis Tell Erskine, *q.v.*). Apptd. to comd.

Sebundy Corps at Murshidabad 30 Jan. 1784 ; comdd. Hastings's escort up country 1784. Left India with Hastings in the *Berrington* 1785. Dir. E.I. Co. 6 Mar. 1798 till 23 Feb. 1831.

Refs.: Family information. *Grier. V.B.G. Macpherson.* Burke's *Peerage*, 1923, p. 802, *s.n.* Dysart, E. *G.M.* 1836, i. 202. *A.J.* N.S. xix. 88. M.I. St. John's church, St. John's Wood Rd., London.

[1] *Note*: His name often appears as Sweny or Sweeny.

TOONE, Sir William (1749-1822). Major General, K.C.B. Colonel 7th and 8th L.C. Comdg. Dinapore Div. *b.* Finglas, nr. Dublin, 1749. Cadet 1780. Admitted 6 Mar. 1781. Cornet 1780. Lieut. 2 June 1781. Capt. 29 May 1800. Major 5 Oct. 1800. Lt. Col. 1 May 1804. Col. 4 June 1813. Maj. Gen. 12 Aug. 1819. *d.* Dinapore 16 Aug. 1822.

Of Lilliput, Hornchurch. 3rd son of William Toone and Mary his wife. Brother of Sweney Toone, *q.v.*, and of Elizabeth, mother of Killiner Swettenham, *q.v. m.* 1st, 26 June 1776, Anne, dau. of Thomas Hill, of Noak Hill, Hornchurch, Essex. (She died 10 Aug. 1811.) Father of the wife of Robert Gage Stirling, *q.v.*, and grandfather of James Hastings Lindsay Metcalfe Toone, *q.v. m.* 2nd, Dinapore 1 Aug. 1812, Mary, widow of Thomas Malone. (She died at sea on board the *Rose*, from Bengal, 19 July 1829.)

Services: Ensign H.M. 11th Foot 12 Aug. 1779. Sailed for India in the *Bellmont* 3 Apr. 1780, when he gave his age as 25. Campaign against the Rajah of Benares Aug. 1781 ; action at Bamnagar 19 Sept. 1781 ; Lieut. comdg. a party of 47 men of G.G.B.G. With Murshidabad Sebundy Corps in 1784. Lieut. 5th Bengal Eur. Bn. in July 1787 and Dec. 1788 ; transfd. to 30th Bn. Sepoys 9 Sept. 1791. Apptd. to 3rd N.C. 2 June 1797 ; Capt. Lt. 2nd N.C. 1 Nov. 1798. Operations in Jumna Doab 1803 ; Major 2nd N.C. Second Mahratta War 1803 ; battle of Delhi ; Laswari ; Major 2nd N.C. Posted Lt. Col. to 1st N.C. 1804. To comd. Corps of Hill Rangers 6 June 1805. Comdt. of Buxar fort 2 Oct. 1806 till 1819 ; also, in addition, for some yrs. Regulating Ofr. of Invalid Tannah Ests. at Shahabad. Transfd. to 2nd N.C. 1807 ; to 7th N.C. 1810 ; to 4th N.C. 1812. Tempy. comdg. troops at Dinapore 1817-19. Maj. Gen. on Gen. Staff comdg. Dinapore Div. 22 May 1820 till death. Col. of a Bde. from 29 Aug. 1821 ; Col. 7th and 8th L.C. 29 Apr. 1821. C.B. 7 Apr. 1815 ; K.C.B. 26 Nov. 1819.

Refs.: Family information. *V.B.G.* Will dated 3 July 1821 ; proved 26 Sept. 1822.

TOPPIN, John (*d.* 1825). Bt. Captain. Artillery. (231)
Cadet 1781. Admitted 26 Nov. 1781. Fireworker 11 Aug. 1782.
Lieut. 25 Mar. 1790. Capt. Lt. 8 Jan. 1796. Bt. Capt. 7 Jan.
1796. Retired 5 July 1799. *d.* Newcastle 23 Mar. 1825.
Cousin of James Griffith Hoare and Nathaniel Leonard, *qq.v.*
m. Calcutta 10 Apr. 1787, Miss Elizabeth Hunter.
Services : Came out to India as 4th Ofr. in the *Valentine* which
sailed 13 Mar. 1781. Lieut. 3rd Bn. Art. in July 1787 ; transfd.
to 2nd Bn. 8 Feb. 1790. Third Mysore War 1790-1 ; Bangalore ;
Lieut. 5th Coy. 1st Bn. Returned sick to Bengal Sept. 1791.
Apptd. Dy. Comy. Ord. 23 Jan. 1792. Fur. 19 June 1797 till
retirement. Pensd. on Lord Clive's fund 5 July 1799.

*TORCKLER, Matthew Godfrey (1807-1824). Ensign, Infantry. *b.* Calcutta 9 Sept. 1807. Cadet 1824. Ensign Dec.
1824. *d.* Calcutta 7 Dec. 1824.
bapt. Calcutta 11 Oct. 1807. Son of Adolph Peter (or Peter
Adolphus) Torckler and Eleanor his wife. Brother of Peter Arnold
Torckler, *q.v.*
Services : An unposted Ensign.
Refs. : M.I. S. Park St. cemetery, Calcutta.

TORCKLER, Peter Arnold (1802-1842). Captain, Artillery.
(490) *b.* Calcutta 8 Dec. 1802. Cadet 1818. Admitted 30 Oct.
1819. 2nd Lieut. 17 Apr. 1819. Lieut. 25 Aug. 1821. Capt.
2 July 1835. *d.* Sikraul, Benares, 13 May 1842, of small-pox.
bapt. Calcutta 16 Jan. 1803. Son of Adolph Peter Torckler,
of Calcutta, merchant, and Eleanor his wife, widow of —— Isacke.
Brother of William Young Torckler, *q.v.*, and of the wife of Joshua
Wilcox, *q.v. m.* Calcutta 16 Mar. 1835, Mary Georgiana, 2nd dau.
of William McQuhae, *q.v.* (*See also* James Tobin Bush.) (She died
Dum-Dum 13 Aug. 1838.) Addiscombe Cadet 1818-19.
Services : Siege and capture of Bhurtpore ; Lieut. 1st Coy.
(Field Batty.) 3rd Bn. Offg. Comy. Ord. 5 June till 21 Sept. 1835.
Leave s.c. 2 yrs. to Cape 8 Aug. 1839.
Refs. : Will dated 13 Nov. 1838 ; admon. 25 July 1842. M.I.
Benares.

TORCKLER, William Young (1804-?). Lieutenant. 4th N.I.
b. Calcutta 15 Aug. 1804. Cadet 1820. Admitted 25 Feb. 1821.
Ensign 26 Sept. 1820. Lieut. 11 July 1823. Discharged the
Service 19 Nov. 1829. (Living in 1851.)[1]
bapt. Calcutta 11 Nov. 1804. Son of Peter Adolph Torckler and
Eleanor his wife. Brother of Matthew Godfrey Torckler, *q.v. m.*

a dau. of Hon. Jacob Jordan, Paymr. Gen. of Brit. Forces and Speaker to Upper House of Assembly, Canada.

Services: Wrecked 25 Feb. 1821 on the voyage out to India. Posted Ensign to Bengal Eur. Regt.; transfd. to 1st N.I. July 1823; to 4th N.I. (late 2/1st) May 1824. Siege and capture of Bhurtpore; Lieut. 4th N.I., d.d. Rt. Wing 41st N.I. (India medal). Intr. & Qmr. 4th N.I. 8 Feb. 1827 till 23 May 1828. d.d. 48th N.I. 27 July 1829. Tried by G.C.M. at Cawnpore 19 Nov. 1829 for firing a pistol at Lieut. Philip Goldney, *q.v.*; sentenced to be hanged; sentence remitted by C.-in-C. 25 Mar. 1830. Suspended from his Commission pending a reference to C.D. 24 July 1830. Fur. p.a. (under suspension) 28 Feb. 1831 till discharged. Granted a pension of £70 *p.a.* 30 Nov. 1831. Brought an action against Lord Dalhousie, C.-in-C., for injuries Jan. 1836. Pub. an account of his trial, Calcutta, 1830.

Refs.: *A.J.* N.S. iii. 72-3.

[1] *Note:* Believed to have been living at Sydney, N.S.W., 1859.

TORRENS, Frederick (1812-1866). Ensign. 52nd N.I. Subsequently Capt. 23rd Ft. (R.W.F.). *b.* Fulham, London, 1 Sept. 1812. Cadet 1828. Arrived in India 3 July 1829. Ensign (5 June 1829) 7 Jan. 1830. Resigned 17 Sept. 1832. *d.* Birkenhead 4 Aug. 1866.

bapt. Fulham 24 Sept. 1812. Son of Maj. Gen. Henry Torrens, K.C.B., Adjt. Gen. H.M.S. (*D.N.B.*), and Sarah his wife, dau. of Robert Patton (1742-1812), *q.v.* Cousin-german of James Lumsdaine Walker, *q.v.* Ed. Naval Coll., Portsmouth.

Services: Ensign d.d. 29th N.I. 16 July 1829; posted to 52nd N.I. 7 Jan. 1830 and joined in July. Fur. u.p.a. 1 yr. without pay 7 Oct. 1831 till resignation. 2nd Lieut. 23rd Ft. 17 Dec. 1830; 1st Lieut. do. 11 Dec. 1835; Capt. do. 16 Nov. 1841.

Refs.: *The Times*, 8 Aug. 1866.

TOTTENHAM, John Loftus (1804-1847). Bt. Major, 3rd L.C. *bapt.* St. Mary's, New Ross, 24 May 1804. Cadet 1819. Arrived in India 21 Nov. 1820. Cornet 5 June 1820. Lieut. 1 Oct. 1823. Capt. 30 Dec. 1833. Bt. Major 9 Nov. 1846. *d.* Ferozepore 29 May 1847.

2nd son of Henry Loftus Tottenham, of MacMurrough, co. Wexford, Collector of New Ross, and Sarah his wife, dau. of Rev. John Cliffe, of New Ross. His sister *m.* James Gordon (1807-1875), *q.v. m.* Edinburgh 14 Oct. 1833, Isabella, 2nd dau. of Alexander Gordon, of Edinburgh. (She died 26 June 1875.)

Services: Cadet d.d. 3rd L.C. Nov. 1820; posted to 3rd L.C. Jan. 1821. Operations in Jodhpur 1823; capture of Lamba; Cornet 3rd L.C. Intr. & Qmr. 3rd L.C. 23 Aug. 1825 till Oct. 1827. Siege and capture of Bhurtpore; Lieut. 3rd L.C. Fur. p.a. 11 Jan. 1831 till 17 Apr. 1834. First Afghan War 1838-9; Ghazni; occupation of Kabul; Capt. 3rd L.C. (Medal). With Army of Reserve (for Afghanistan) at Ferozepore Oct. 1842 till Jan. 1843. Offg. D.J.A.G. Punjab Div. at Lahore Mar. 1846 till May 1847. Leave s.c. 6 mos. to Mussoorie May 1847.

Refs.: Burke's *Landed Gentry of Ireland*, p. 697, *s.n.* Tottenham, of Ballycurry, co. Wicklow. *De Rhé-Philipe.* I.M. 3 Aug. 1847, p. 453. Will dated Ferozepore 18 June 1843; proved 24 Aug. 1847. M.I. at Ferozepore.

TOTTINGHAM, John (1738/39-1802). Colonel. Infantry. *b.* 1738/39. Capt. 27 July 1764. Major 1 Apr. 1768. Lt. Col. 19 Sept. 1770. Col. Jan. 1782. Resigned 23 Mar. 1782. *d.* London 3 June 1802, aged 63.

Related to Nathaniel Smith, Chairman E.I. Co. *m.* Theresa. (She died Berners St., London, 17 May 1833.) Father of John James Tottingham, *q.v.*

Services: Formerly an officer on the Bombay Est.; served in Bengal under Clive from Mar. 1757; battle of Plassey; Ensign Bo. Est. Resigned his Commission at Calcutta Oct. 1757, and returned to Europe. Ensign H.M. 37th Ft. 21 Mar. 1759; Lieut. h.p. 37th Ft. 1763 till death. Apptd. in England 2 Mar. 1764, a Capt. on the Bengal Est. in consideration of his having raised recruits; arrived in India 27 July 1764, and was granted rank as Capt. from that date. Posted to 3rd Bengal Eur. Regt. 5 Aug. 1765; Bde. Major 3rd Bde. in 1766. Lt. Col. comdg. 2/2nd Bengal Eur. Regt. in Sept. 1777 and in Oct. 1779. Comdg. at Chunar 1780-1.

Refs.: B.: P.P. vii. 123. M.I. in Marylebone church.

*TOTTINGHAM, John James (1774-?). Cadet. Infantry. *b.* Dinapore 27 Oct. 1774. Cadet 1791. Resigned 14 Dec. 1791. *bapt.* Berhampore 23 Dec. 1775. Son of John Tottingham, *q.v.*, and Theresa his wife.

Services: Apptd. a Minor Cadet 29 Mar. 1782; struck off 2 May 1786.

TOULMIN, Charles Clark (1809-1842). Lieutenant. 33rd N.I. *b* London 14 Feb. 1809. Cadet 1825. Arrived in India

16 May 1826. Ensign 5 Nov. 1825. Lieut. 13 Jan. 1828. Invalided 9 Sept. 1831. Retired 2 Sept. 1835. *d.* 28 June 1842.
bapt. St. James's, Clerkenwell, 11 Oct. 1816. Son of Samuel Wilton Toulmin, of Smith St., Hackney, and Maria Wright his wife. Ed. Christ's Hospital.
Services: Posted to 33rd N.I. 1826. Leave s.c. to Calcutta 26 Sept. 1827 till Dec. 1828; fur. s.c. 14 Jan. 1833 till retirement. No record of active service. Retired on h.p. of Ensign with addl. allowance of £25 *p.a.* (M.C. 2 Sept. 1835).
Refs.: Burke's *Landed Gentry*, 15th edn., p. 2264, *s.n.* Toulmin, *formerly* of Hackney. *A.J.* N.S. xxxviii. 349. *G.M.* 1842, ii. 217. *The Times*, 30 June 1842.

TOULMIN, Samuel (1809-1848). Bt. Captain, 63rd N.I. *b.* London 8 June 1809. Cadet 1828. Arrived in India 29 May 1829. Ensign 20 Jan. 1829. Lieut. 20 Jan. 1835. Bt. Capt. 20 Jan. 1844. *d.* Mirzapur, U.P., 30 Apr. 1848.
bapt. St. Mary Woolchurch, London, 19 Sept. 1809. Son of Joseph Petty Toulmin, of Clapham Common, banker, and Harriot Bill his wife. *m.* Tirhut, B. & O., 6 Oct. 1830, Laura Emily, eldest dau. of Thomas Barlow, of Tirhut. (She died 24 Sept. 1875, aged 65.)
Services: Ensign d.d. 65th N.I. 13 July 1829; d.d. 72nd N.I. 4 Aug. 1829; posted to 65th N.I. 14 Sept. 1829; transfd. to 63rd N.I. 27 Aug. 1831. Reduction of Jhansi 1838-9; Lieut. 63rd N.I. With Army of Reserve (for Afghanistan) Oct. 1842 till Jan. 1843; Lieut. 63rd N.I. Fur. 5 Jan. 1845 till 20 Sept. 1847.
Refs.: Burke's *Landed Gentry*, 15th edn., p. 2264, *s.n.* Toulmin, *formerly* of Hackney. *I.M.* 4 July 1848, p. 394.

TOWERS, John (1763/64-1797). Bt. Captain, 3rd Bengal Eur. Regt. *b.* in Ireland 1763/64. Cadet 1779. Admitted 2 May 1781. Ensign 1780. Lieut. 23 Aug. 1781. Bt. Capt. 7 Jan. 1796. *d.* Berhampore 7 July 1797.
Brother of James Towers, Capt. H.M. 8th Light Dgns.
Services: Apptd. Cadet 20 Apr. 1779; sailed for India in the *Bellmont* 3 Apr. 1780, aged 16. Lieut. 2nd Bn. Sepoys in July 1787 and in Dec. 1792. Posted to 3rd Bengal Eur. Regt. June 1796.
Refs.: Will dated July 1786; proved 23 Nov. 1797.

TOWGOOD, Joseph (1810-1858). Lieut. Colonel. 35th N.I. *b.* London 17 Oct. 1810. Cadet 1827. Arrived in India 26 Oct. 1828. Ensign (19 May 1828) 4 Mar. 1829. Lieut. 17 Feb. 1837. Capt. 11 Mar. 1847. Bt. Major 1854. Retired 10 July 1854.

THE BENGAL ARMY, 1758-1834 297

Hon. Lt. Col. 28 Nov. 1854. *d.* Ben Rhydding, Yorks., 24 Oct. 1858.

Of Arborfield, Reading. 5th son of Matthew Towgood, of St. Neots, Hunts., paper manufacturer, and Ann his wife, dau. of Samuel Gibson. *m.* 1st, Moradabad 29 May 1837, Amelia Augusta Woodmason, 2nd dau. of George Moore (1789-1848), *q.v.* (*See also* William Blackwood.) (She died Agra 28 June 1844, aged 29.) *m.* 2nd, Thornhill, Yorks., 27 Apr. 1854, Adelaide Mary Anne, 2nd dau. of William Stansfeld, of Flockton Manor House, nr. Wakefield. (She *re-m.* Rev. Edward Macfarlane and died Chesterfield 15 June 1900, aged 81.) Ed. Elizabeth Coll., Guernsey, 1825-7.

Services: Ensign d.d. 33rd N.I. 20 Nov. 1828; posted to 35th N.I. 4 Mar. 1829. First Afghan War 1839-40; Ghazni; Lieut. 35th N.I. (Medal). Actg. Adjt. 4th Depot Bn. 2 Oct. 1840; returned to Afghanistan with a convoy Jan. 1841. First Afghan War 1841-2; operations in Nazian valley Feb. 1841; S.A.C.G.; offg. Field Paymr. Army of Indus 15 Oct. 1841; defence of Jalalabad 1841-2 (Medal); reoccupation of Kabul; Lieut. 35th N.I. (Medal). Adjt. 35th N.I. 16 June 1841 till 11 Jan. 1845. Fur. 13 Dec. 1844 till 5 Feb. 1848; s.c. 10 Jan. 1852 till retirement.

Refs: Burke's *Landed Gentry*, 2nd edn., p. 1285, *s.n.* Stansfeld, of Burley Wood, co. York. *Elizabeth Coll. Register. G.M.* 1858, ii. 649.

TOWNLEY, Henry. Lieutenant. Infantry. Cadet (?) Ensign 16 Aug. 1765. Lieut. 28 May 1767. Resigned 4 May 1769.

Services: Resigned his Commission during the " Batta mutiny "; readmitted 1766.

TOWNSEND, Edward Nelson (1801-1836). Captain, 31st N.I. *b.* Honiton, Devon, 2 Apr. 1801. Cadet 1818. Admitted 1 Jan. 1820. Ensign 24 July 1819. Lieut. 29 Mar. 1822. Capt. 8 June 1827. *d.* on the river nr. Allahabad 15 Feb. 1836.

bapt. Honiton 11 Aug. 1801. Son of James Townsend, solicitor, and Mary his wife. *m.* Axminster 14 Mar. 1833, Miss Elizabeth Steer, niece of Rev. Charles Steer, vicar of Axminster.

Services: Ensign d.d. Bengal Eur. Regt. 1820; posted to 2/15th N.I.; transfd. to 31st N.I. (late 2/15th) May 1824. Fur. s.c. 6 Nov. 1822 till 4 Oct. 1825. Adjt. Bundelkhand Provl. Bn. 2 Nov. 1825 till 25 Feb. 1826. Siege and capture of Bhurtpore; Lieut. 31st N.I. Actg. Adjt. Rampura Local Bn. 7 Nov. 1826; Adjt. Sirmoor Bn. 14 June 1827 till 16 Apr. 1828. Leave s.c. 12 mos. to Hills 10 June 1828; fur. s.c. 16 Aug. 1830 till 18 Nov. 1833. His death took place while he was on sick leave.

Refs.: *A.J.* N.S. x. 178; N.S. xx. 178. M.I. Kydganj cemetery, Allahabad.

TOWNSEND, Thomas (1758/59-1795). Lieutenant, Infantry. *b.* London 1758/59. Cadet 1780. Admitted 26 Aug. 1780. Ensign 1780. Lieut. 18 June 1781. *d.* Monghyr 28 Nov. 1795. *Services*: Sailed for India in the *Lascelles* 12 Feb. 1780, aged 21. Lieut. 33rd Bn. Sepoys in July 1787 and in 1792.

TOWNSHEND, Edward Du Pré (1805-1883). Colonel. 9th N.I. *b.* Beaconsfield, Bucks., 11 Oct. 1805. Cadet 1821. Arrived in India 19 Aug. 1822. Ensign 10 Mar. 1822. Lieut. 3 June 1824. Capt. 15 Feb. 1842. Major 24 Dec. 1853. Bt. Lt. Col. 22 Aug. 1855. Retired 4 Apr. 1857. Hon. Col. 4 Apr. 1857. *d.* Annefield, Gresford, 18 May 1883.

bapt. Beaconsfield 13 Nov. 1805. 2nd son of Edward Venables Townshend, of Wincham, co. Chester, and Cornelia Anne his wife, dau. of Josias du Pré, of Wilton Park, Berks., sometime Govr. of Madras. Cousin-german of W. H. Massie, *q.v. m.* 1847, Mary, dau. of Major Hunter.

Services: Posted to 30th N.I. 1822; transfd. to 8th N.I. 1823; to 9th N.I. (late 1/8th) May 1824; 2nd in comd. Sylhet L.I. 2 Apr. 1828 till 1836. Operations against the Khasias Jan. 1831. Fur. p.a. 15 Mar. 1836 till 14 Oct. 1839. Adjt. 3rd L.I. Bn. 21 Nov. 1840 till 12 Mar. 1842. With Army of Reserve (for Afghanistan) Oct. 1842 till Jan. 1843; Capt. 9th N.I. D.C. Sukkur, Sind, 26 Oct. 1843 till June 1847; Mily. Sec. to Dy. Govr. of Bengal July 1847; A.D.C. do. 11 Dec. 1847; Comdt. Bhopal Contingent 3 Mar. 1848 till 1855. Fur. p.a. 6 Aug. 1855 till retirement.

Refs.: Burke's *Landed Gentry*, 12th edn., p. 1879, *s.n.* Townshend, of Wincham Hall, co. Chester. *The Times*, 26 May 1883.

*****TRACY, Anthony** (1738/39-?). Ensign. Infantry. *b.* London 1738/39. Cadet 1765. Ensign 19 Aug. 1765.

Services: Sailed for India in the *Fort William* 17 May 1764, aged 25. To be Ensign from 5 Mar. 1765 till his rank is settled by the date of his Commission. Not in list of 1 Feb. 1767.

Refs.: B.M. Add. MS. 6050.

TRAFFORD, George Leigh (1803-1836). Captain, 10th L.C. *b.* 30 May 1803. Cadet 1819. Arrived in India 6 Jan. 1821. Cornet 16 July 1820. Lieut. 21 Feb. 1823. Capt. 3 May 1829. *d.* Muttra 7 (? 17) Feb. 1836, of an apoplectic attack.

bapt. Middlewich, co. Chester, 20 June 1803. 2nd son of Trafford

Leigh (who assumed the surname and arms of Trafford only, by sign-manual, 5 Dec. 1791), of Oughtrington Hall, co. Chester, and Henrietta his wife, dau. of Rev. Sir Thomas Broughton, Bart., of Doddington Park. Brother of William Leigh Trafford, *q.v.* m. Calcutta 15 Dec. 1834, Anna Maria, dau. of G. Wilkinson, of Dublin. (She died 1842.)
Services: Posted Cornet to 2nd L.C.; transfd. to newly-raised 10th L.C. 17 June 1825. Siege and capture of Bhurtpore; Lieut. 10th L.C. Actg. Intr. & Qmr. 10th L.C. 20 June 1826 till 16 July 1829. Fur. p.a. 10 Jan. 1832 till 4 Dec. 1834.
Refs.: Burke's *Landed Gentry*, 5th edn., p. 1403, *s.n.* Trafford, of Oughtrington Hall, co. Chester. Ormerod's *Cheshire* (1882 edn.), i. 588-9. *A.J.* N.S. xx. 242.

TRAFFORD, William Leigh (1808-1835). Ensign, 74th N.I. *b.* Lymm, co. Chester, 7 Apr. 1808. Cadet 1826. Arrived in India 2 Oct. 1827. Ensign (23 Mar. 1827) 3 Jan. 1828. *d.* Muttra 23 May 1835.
bapt. Lymm 3 Oct. 1808. 3rd son of Trafford Trafford (formerly Leigh) and Henrietta his wife. Brother of George Leigh Trafford, *q.v.* Haileybury 1824-6.
Services: Posted Ensign to 6th Extra Regt. (became 74th N.I.) 3 Jan. 1828. Was on leave at Muttra from Bareilly when his death occurred. No record of active service.
Refs.: Burke's *Landed Gentry*, 5th edn., p. 1403, *s.n.* Trafford, of Oughtrington Hall, co. Chester. Ormerod's *Cheshire* (1882 edn.), i. 588-9. *G.M.* 1836, i. 102.

TRAHERNE, John (1777-1800). Lieutenant, 12th N.I. *bapt.* Llantrisant, co. Glam., 17 Nov. 1777. Cadet 1793. Arrived in India 16 Oct. 1794. Ensign 25 Sept. 1794. Lieut. 8 Jan. 1796. *d.* Cawnpore 29 Nov. 1800.
3rd son of Edmund Traherne, of Castellau, Llantrisant, collector and controller of customs, and Frances Popkin his 2nd wife, sister and heiress of John Popkin, of Coytrahen.
Services: Apptd. Cadet 5 Mar. 1794; sailed for India in the *Airly Castle* 2 May 1794. Posted to 4th Bengal Eur. Bn. 8 Nov. 1794; Ensign 31st Bn. Sepoys in Jan. 1796.
Refs.: Burke's *Landed Gentry*, 13th edn., p. 1760, *s.n.* Traherne, of Coedarhydyglyn, co. Glam.

TRAIL, John (1811-1854). Bt. Captain. Engineers. *b.* Panbride, co. Forfar, 30 July 1811. Cadet 1831. Arrived in India 8 June 1832. 2nd Lieut. (11 June 1830) 15 Sept. 1837. Lieut.

20 May 1839. Bt. Capt. 11 June 1845. Retired 5 June 1846. *d.* 25 June 1854.

bapt. 13 Aug. 1811. 4th and youngest son of Rev. David Trail, minister of Panbride 1798-1844, and Catherine his wife, dau. of John Biss, of Deptford, co. Durham. St. Andrews Univ. 1827-8. Addiscombe Cadet 15 Aug. 1828 till 11 June 1830; Chatham 13 Aug. 1830 till 23 July 1831.

Services: d.d. S. & M. at Delhi 28 June 1832; surveyed Agra and Muttra Cantts. 7 Apr. till 1 Oct. 1834. Fur. s.c. 15 Jan. 1836 till 30 Jan. 1840. Executive Engr. Barisal Div., P.W.D., 3 June 1840. Fur. s.c. 5 Dec. 1843 till retirement. No record of active service.

Refs.: Burke's *Landed Gentry of Ireland*, p. 703, *s.n.* Traill, of Ballyclough, co. Antrim. Scott's *Fasti*, v. 448.

TRAVERS, Henry Millett (1817-1842). Lieutenant, 8th N.I. *bapt.* St. Botolph, Bishopsgate, London, 15 Oct. 1817. Cadet 1834. Arrived in India 8 June 1835. Ensign (21 Jan. 1835) 13 Mar. 1835. Lieut. 8 Oct. 1839. *d.* Ferozepore 16 Aug. 1842, aged 26.

3rd son of Benjamin Travers, of 12 Bruton St., London, surgeon H.E.I.C. warehouse dept. (*D.N.B.*), and Caroline his 2nd wife, dau. of George Millett, Dir. E.I.C. Brother of Eliza Mary, wife of Daniel Burges, of Bristol. Ed. Felsted Jan. 1827-June 1828; Harrow 1829-33.

Services: Ensign d.d. 57th N.I. 12 June 1835; posted to 8th N.I. 24 Sept. 1835. Offg. Adjt. 2nd Local Horse 7 Oct. till Nov. 1839. Attached to 1st L.I. Bn. Oct. 1841 till death. No record of active service.

Refs.: De Rhé-Philipe. *Alumni Felstedienses. Harrow School Register.* G.M. 1843, i. 554. *The Times,* 10 Nov. 1842. Will dated 27 Aug. 1841; admon. 3 Jan. 1843. M.I. at Ferozepore.

TRAVERS, Thomas Otho (1785-1844). Captain. 20th N.I. Subsequently H.E.I.C. recruiting ofr. in Cork district. *b.* Patrick St., Cork, 25 Sept. 1785. Cadet 1803. Arrived in India 2 Sept. 1804. Ensign 10 Sept. 1804. Lieut. 21 Sept. 1804. Capt. 27 May 1818. Retired 16 Jan. 1822. *d.* 9 July 1844.

Of Lee Mount, co. Cork. *bapt.* Holy Trinity, Cork, 26 Sept. 1785. 3rd son of Robert Travers, late of Cork, banker. Brother of Boyle Travers, Lt. Col., late 114th Regt. *m.* 4 Oct. 1817, Mary Peacocke, 2nd dau. of Charles Henry Leslie, of Wilton, Cork, and grand-niece of Matthew Leslie, *q.v.* (She died 2 Apr. 1882, aged 93.)

THE BENGAL ARMY, 1758-1834

Services: Posted Lieut. to 20th N.I. At P.W.I. in 1807. Capture of Java 1811; Lieut. 1/20th N.I. Town Major of Batavia 1812. Expedn. to Palembang 1812; Actg. Comy. Arrived in England on duty from Java Sept. 1814; fur. from Java 1816-18. Capt. Lt. 1/20th N.I. 3 June 1816. At Bencoolen in 1819. 2nd Asst. to Lt. Govr. of Fort Marlbro' 1819. Fur. from Fort Marlbro' 2 Dec. 1820 till retirement. Recruiting ofr. in Cork district 1822 till death.

Refs.: Burke's *Landed Gentry*, 15th edn., p. 1362, *s.n.* Leslie, *late* of Courtmacsherry, co. Cork. M.I. Cork cathedral.

TRAVIS, James Hardy (1790-1821). Lieutenant, 18th N.I. *b.* East Bergholt, Suffolk, 11 Dec. 1790. Cadet 1808. Admitted 15 Dec. 1809. Ensign 5 July 1811. Lieut. 16 Dec. 1814. *d.* at sea 20 Aug. 1821, on board the *Brailsford*, on the voyage to England. *bapt.* ptely. 7 Feb. 1791; publicly 23 Sept. 1791. 3rd son of William Travis, of East Bergholt, surgeon, and Susanna his wife, *née* Hardy.

Services: Barasat C.C. Posted to 18th N.I. 1811. Nepal War 1816; Lieut. 1/18th N.I., in 1st Bde. Rt. Column. Cuttack insurrection 1816; Khurda; Lieut. 1/18th N.I. Third Mahratta War; Jawad; Lieut. 1/18th N.I. Fur. 27 Dec. 1820 till death.

Refs.: G.M. 1821, ii. 475. M.I. E. Bergholt churchyard.

TREADWELL, James (*d.* 1763). Captain, Infantry. Cadet (?) Ensign 19 Jan. 1758. Lieut. 30 Apr. 1759. Capt. 1763. *d.* Patna 25 June 1763: kld. in action in the assault of the *kila*. Of Magdalen psh., Oxford. Brother of Sarah Treadwell and of Mary Leveret, of Oxford, and of Thomas Treadwell.

Services: N.F.P.

Refs.: Orme MSS., vol. xxi, Bengal, p. 129. Will dated Calcutta 4 Aug. 1760; proved 14 Aug. 1764.

TRELAWNY, Jonathan (1785-1855). Colonel. 7th N.I. *bapt.* Pelynt, Cornwall, 31 Aug. 1785. Cadet 1804. Arrived in India 10 Dec. 1805. Ensign 18 Sept. 1805. Lieut. 19 Sept. 1805. Capt. 1 Jan. 1819. Major 3 Nov. 1831. Lt. Col. 18 Feb. 1838. Retired 20 Dec. 1838. Hon. Col. 28 Nov. 1854. *d. unm.* Trelawny, Cornwall, 13 Sept. 1855, aged 70.

4th and youngest son of Rev. Sir Harry Trelawny, Bart., preby. of Oxford, and Anne his wife, dau. of Rev. James Brown, rector of Portishead, Somerset. Ed. Westminster 1796-8. St. Mary Hall, Oxon.; matric. 1 Mar. 1803, aged 17.

Services: Posted Lieut. to 26th N.I. 1806. Operations in

Bundelkhand 1807 ; Sehlehuganj ; Lieut. 26th N.I. Intr. & Qmr. 2/26th N.I. 1 July 1814 till 1818. Nepal War 1814-15 ; Lieut. L.I. Bn. (India medal). Capt. 2/26th N.I. ; Bk. Mr. (afterwards styled Executive Ofr.) Rajputana Div., P.W.D., 23 June 1818 till Sept. 1828 ; transfd. to 51st N.I. (late 1/26th) May 1824. Fur. s.c. 22 Sept. 1828 till 30 Nov. 1832 ; p.a. 23 Feb. 1834 till 31 Oct. 1837. Posted Lt. Col. to 7th N.I. 13 Nov. 1838.

Refs.: Burke's *Peerage*, 1923, p. 2193, *s.n.* Salusbury-Trelawny, Bart., of Trelawny, Cornwall. Vivian's *Visitations of Cornwall*, p. 578. *Westminster School List (Supplt.). Alumni Oxon. G.M.* 1855, ii. 554.

TREMAMONDO, Anthony Angelo Malevolti (1747-1829). Lieutenant. Cavalry. *b.* in Italy 1747. Cadet 1777. Arrived in India 1778. Ensign 1778. Lieut. 10 Dec. 1778. Resigned 20 Feb. 1785. *d.* Newman St., London, 2 Oct. 1829, aged 82.

(*Probably* son of John Xavier Tremamondo, of Edinburgh, and Francisca di Pescara his wife.) Nephew of Domenico Angelo, the fencing-master (*D.N.B.*). *m.* St. Pancras, London, 27 July 1787, Elizabeth Martha, dau. of Edward Bland, and cousin of Dorothea Bland (Mrs. Jordan) (*D.N.B.*). Father of the Angelo brothers, *qq.v.*, and of the wives of George Richard Pemberton, William Simonds, and James Steel, *qq.v.*

Services: Apptd. Cadet 12 Nov. 1777 ; sailed for India in the *Gatton* 27 Apr. 1778. Served in G.G.B.G. 1780-1 ; apptd. Riding Master to the Army 13 Oct. 1780 on a monthly salary of Rs. 1,500, and was granted a site in Calcutta for a riding-school. This appt. was abolished 28 July 1783.

Refs.: *The Ancestor*, viii. (1904), pp. 1 *sqq.* ; x. (1904), p. 223. *Misc. Gen. et Her.* 4S. ii. 282. *The Mansell and Angelo Families*, by Col. R. F. Angelo, Simla, p.p., June 1914. *V.B.G. G.M.* 1829, ii. 379. Will dated 21 Jan. 1828 ; proved in London 10 Oct. 1829. Portrait by Zoffany, *c.* 1787.

TREMENHEERE, George Borlase (1809-1896). Major General. Engineers. *b.* Woolwich 9 Nov. 1809. Cadet 1826. Arrived in India 11 June 1827. 2nd Lieut. 16 Dec. 1825. Lieut. 28 Sept. 1827. Capt. 20 May 1839. Major 4 Nov. 1848. Lt. Col. 1 Aug. 1854. Col. 2 Apr. 1856. Retired 15 Apr. 1856. Hon. Maj. Gen. 15 Apr. 1856. *d.* Treneere, Torquay, 19 Dec. 1896.

Of Spring Grove, Middlesex, J.P. 3rd son of Maj. Gen. Walter Tremenheere, K.H., and A.D.C. to William IV, and Frances his

THE BENGAL ARMY, 1758-1834 303

wife, 2nd dau. of Thomas Apperley, of Plasgronow. Cousin-german of William Wynne Apperley, *q.v.* *m.* Moulmein, Burma, 16 Mar. 1844, Sarah Swaine, widow of John Richard Lumsden, *q.v.* (She died 24 Apr. 1900, aged 85.) Addiscombe Cadet 13 Feb. 1824 till 16 Dec. 1825; Chatham 30 Jan. till 20 Dec. 1826.

Services: Posted to S. & M. 23 July 1827; Adjt. do. 25 Apr. 1829 till 6 Jan. 1836, and comdd. do. June 1835 till 20 Dec. 1836. Fur. p.a. 4 Mar. 1837 till 23 Dec. 1840. Supt. Tenasserim Div., P.W.D., 20 Jan. 1841; Suptg. Engr. Punjab circle 1 Nov. 1847; do. 3rd (Pegu) circle 2 May 1854 till Feb. 1855. Second Sikh War; passage of Chenab; Chilianwala; Gujerat; Senior Field Engr. (Medal with 2 clasps). Against Kohat Pass Afridis 9 Feb. 1850 (Medal). Fur. s.c. 6 Feb. 1855 till retirement. Capt. 1st Cornwall Rifle Vols. 10 Sept. 1859; Lt. Col. do. 20 Apr. 1860; Hon. Col. do. 7 July 1875 till death. A.I.C.E. 8 May 1838. Geologist. Executed two views of church at Delhi.

Refs.: Burke's *Landed Gentry*, 13th edn., p. 1766, *s.n.* Tremenheere (*now* Monro), of Tremenheere, Cornwall. Vivian's *Visitations of Cornwall*, p. 622. *The Tremenheeres*, by S. G. Tremenheere (1925). Boase. *The Times*, 22 Dec. 1896, p. 4; 23 Dec. p. 4. *Black and White*, 2 Jan. 1897, p. 4 (portrait).

TRENCH, Frederick (*d.* 1819). Bt. Lieut. Colonel, Invalid Est. 3rd N.I. Cadet 1782. Admitted 21 Aug. 1783. Ensign 7 Mar. 1783. Lieut. 19 Feb. 1790. Capt. 21 Jan. 1803. Major 15 May 1810. Bt. Lt. Col. 4 June 1814. Invalided 15 May 1815. *d.* Calcutta 2 Jan. 1819.

His dau. *m.* Robert Rich, *q.v.*

Services: Apptd. Cadet 29 May 1782, but was permitted to remain in England till the following year. Ensign 3rd Eur. Bn.; transfd. to 18th Bn. Sepoys Feb. 1790. Adjt. & Qmr. 3rd N.I. in 1802; Capt. 3rd N.I. Operations in Bundelkhand 1809; Rajaoli; Ajaigarh; Bt. Major 1/3rd N.I. Major 2/3rd N.I. Comdg. Invalids at Monghyr 1815-18.

TRENCH, Hon. Luke Henry (1775-1798). Lieutenant, Infantry. *b.* 1775. Cadet 1794. Arrived in India 23 Feb. 1795. Ensign 19 Oct. 1794. Lieut. 14 Sept. 1796. *d.* at sea 24 July 1798, on board the *Hawke*.

bapt. Stretton 17 Jan. 1776. 6th son of William Power Keating Trench, 1st Earl of Clancarty, and Anne his wife, eldest dau. of Rt. Hon. Charles Gardiner and sister of Luke, 1st Lord Mountjoy. Cousin-german of Frances, mother of Nicholas Power Palmer, *q.v.*

Services : Fur. 2 May 1798 till death. N.F.P.
Refs. : Burke's *Peerage*, 1923, p. 516, *s.n.* Clancarty, E.

*TREVANION, John (d. 1764). Captain. Comdg. 6th N.I. Cadet (?) Ensign Jan. 1758. Lieut. 1 May 1759. Capt. Oct. 1763. Dismissed Nov. 1764. *d.* Monghyr 25 Dec. 1764.

Services : War with Mir Muhammad Kasim 1763; battle of Gheria (w.); capture of Patna. Given comd. of newly-raised 12th Bn. Sepoys at end of 1763. This Bn., which became 6th in 1764, 10th N.I. in May 1824, and mutinied at Fatehgarh 18 June 1857, was for a time called " *Teerbanis-ki-Paltan* " after him. Battle of Buxar 23 Oct. 1764 ; Capt. comdg. 6th Bn.
Refs. : *Williams*, pp. 104, 106, appendix A.

TREVES, Pellegrin (1762-1825). Ensign. Infantry. Subsequently B.C.S.; P.M.G. Bengal. *b.* London 1762. Cadet 1781. Ensign 19 July 1781. Resigned 5 Aug. 1782. *d.* Lucknow 22 Aug. 1825.

Son of Pellegrin Treves, a London moneylender (originally from Venice),[1] and Bathsheba his wife, dau. of Moses de Paiba, a rich Jew broker, and niece of Sampson Gideon, the capitalist (*D.N.B.*). *m.* Calcutta 7 Sept. 1785, Miss Hetty Stokes. St. John's Coll., Camb. ; admitted 5 Dec. 1779 ; name off 29 Nov. 1780.

Services : Apptd. Cadet 22 Dec. 1780, aged 18 ; sailed for India in the *Queen* 13 Mar. 1781. Returned to England Aug. 1782. Apptd. Writer B.C.S., through the influence of the Prince of Wales, 15 Oct. 1784. P.M.G. 23 Jan. 1820.

Refs. : *Hickey*, ii. 280. *G.M.* 1817, ii. 91. Will dated 11 Nov. 1823 ; proved 9 Sept. 1825.

[1] *Note :* " the companion of royalty and the wit of society." (*G.M.*)

TREVOR, Alexander Charles (1784-1823). Bt. Captain, Invalid Est. 16th N.I. *b.* Newtownards, co. Down, 16 Mar. 1784. Cadet 1804. Arrived in India 10 Sept. 1805. Ensign 18 Oct. 1805. Lieut. 22 Feb. 1806. Bt. Capt. 1 Jan. 1819. Invalided 1 May 1819. *d.* Alipore, Calcutta, 30 July 1823.

Son of John Trevor, of Dublin, and Mary his wife. Brother of Ann Callwell and of Frances, wife of William Grounds. Brother-in-law of John Brunton.

Services : Posted Lieut. to 16th N.I. 1806. (? Operations in Bundelkhand 1807 ; capture of Chamir fort ; Lieut. 1/16th N.I.) Fur. 8 Dec. 1807 till 17 Oct. 1810, and 1815-17. Transfd. to 2/16th N.I.

THE BENGAL ARMY, 1758-1834

Refs.: Will dated 3 May 1817 ; codicil 7 July 1823 ; proved 5 Aug. 1823. M.I. in Bhowanipore cemetery, Calcutta.

TREVOR, Henry Robert Æneas (1812-1839). 2nd Lieutenant, Artillery. (644) *b.* Chelsea 4 July 1812. Cadet 1829. Arrived in India 18 Feb. 1831. 2nd Lieut. (11 June 1830) 18 Feb. 1831. *d.* Cape Town 16 June 1839.
bapt. St. Luke's, Chelsea, 6 Apr. 1817. Son of Henry Trevor, of 3 Robinson Pl., Little Chelsea, and Elizabeth his wife. Addiscombe Cadet 1828-30.
Services: Cadet d.d. 3rd Troop 2nd Bde. H.A. 13 Apr. 1832 ; Actg. 2nd Lieut. 20 Feb. 1833 ; d.d. 1st Troop 3rd Bde. 16 Sept. 1834 ; posted to do. 24 June 1835. Fur. s.c. 20 Feb. 1839 till death. No record of active service.

TREVOR, Robert Salusbury (1802-1841). Bt. Captain, 3rd L.C. *b.* Chester 30 Dec. 1802. Cadet 1823. Arrived in India 9 June 1824. Ensign (Inf.) 7 Jan. 1824. Transfd. to Cav. 1825. Lieut. 13 May 1825. Bt. Capt. 11 Dec. 1839. *d.* Kabul 23 Dec. 1841 : assassinated at a Conference.[1]
bapt. ptely. 31 Dec. 1802 ; *bapt.* in Chester cathedral 31 May 1804. 3rd son of Rev. Thomas Trevor Trevor (formerly Humphreys), LL.D., preby. of Chester, and Elizabeth his wife, eldest dau. of Rev. John Briggs. *m.* Cawnpore 22 June 1829, Mary, youngest dau. of William Spottiswoode, laird of Glenfernate, co. Perth. (*See also* Robert Bruce (1789-1819).) (She died London 11 Oct. 1889, aged 79.) Ed. Rugby ; admitted 1813.
Services: Posted Ensign to 32nd N.I. ; transfd. to Cav. 2 June 1825 (G.O. 166 of 31 May 1825) ; Cornet d.d. 1st Extra Cav. 11 June 1825 ; posted to 3rd L.C. 1825. Siege and capture of Bhurtpore ; Lieut. 3rd L.C. Actg. Intr. & Qmr. 3rd L.C. 11 Feb. 1828 ; permanent do. 9 Feb. 1829 till 5 Aug. 1834 ; actg. do. 6 July 1836 till 5 Mar. 1837 ; permanent do. 4 July 1838 till 1839. Operations against the Kols 1832 ; Lieut. 3rd L.C. Posted to Shah Shuja's force 27 Aug. 1839. First Afghan War 1838-41 ; Ghazni ; apptd. Supt. of Afghan Cav. in Kabul ; forcing of Khurd Kabul 12 Oct. 1841 ; outbreak at Kabul, comdg. *Hazirbash*, or King's Life Gds. ; expedn. against Bemaru village 23 Nov. 1841 ; taken as hostage, and was present at both conferences on 11 and 23 Dec. 1841 between Sir W. Macnaghten and Akber Khan and other chiefs.
Refs.: Burke's *Landed Gentry*, 13th edn., p. 947, *s.n.* Davenport-Handley-Humphreys, of Clipsham Hall, co. Rutland. *Rugby School Register.* M.I. Afghan Memorial Church, Bombay.

[1] *Note:* It was stated at the time that he had fired at the Sirdar,

but this was denied by Capt. Colin Mackenzie, Madras Est., who was present.

TRIMMER, Francis (1801-1848). Bt. Major, 50th N.I. *b.* Ealing 4 Dec. 1801. Cadet 1821. Arrived in India 13 Apr. 1822. Ensign 24 Oct. 1821. Lieut. 1 May 1824. Capt. 29 Oct. 1838. Bt. Major 9 Nov. 1846. *d.* Simla 9 May 1848.

bapt. Ealing 3 Feb. 1802. Son of William Kirby Trimmer, of Brentford, Middlesex, and Jane his wife. *m.* Battersea 28 Mar. 1843, Laura Isabella, 3rd dau. of Henry Thompson, of Chiswick. (She died Ventnor, I.W., 24 June 1875.)

Services: Posted Ensign to Bengal Eur. Regt. 31 May 1822; transfd. to 2/25th N.I. Sept. 1823; to 50th N.I. (late 2/25th) May 1824. Adjt. Cawnpore Provl. Bn. 2 Oct. 1827 till disbanded Jan. 1831. Operations against Kols and Chuars 1832; Lieut. 50th N.I. With 3rd L.I. Bn. at Cawnpore Oct. 1840 till Feb. 1841. Fur. p.a. 26 July 1841 till 28 Aug. 1843. Comdd. Left Wing of 50th N.I. at Moradabad Dec. 1845 till Oct. 1846. Leave s.c. to Simla Apr. 1848.

Refs.: De Rhé-Philipe. *I.M.* 26 July 1848, p. 424. M.I. in Cart Road cemetery, Simla.

TRIPE, Richard (*d.* 1772). Ensign (? Major), Infantry. (? Ensign 2 Oct. 1769.[1]) *d.* Benares 2 June 1772.

Services: N.F.P.

[1] *Note:* Dodwell & Miles give him as a Cadet of 1770; Major 2 Oct. 1769. This is obviously incorrect.

TRIPP, Charles Upton (1808-1840). Bt. Captain, 36th N.I. *b.* Rewe, Devon, 30 Dec. 1808. Cadet 1824. Arrived in India 17 Nov. 1825. Ensign 13 May 1825. Lieut. 14 June 1833. Bt. Capt. 13 May 1840. *d.* Jamalpur, Bengal, 6 July 1840.

bapt. Rewe 10 Apr. 1809. 4th son of Rev. Robert Tripp, rector of Rewe, and afterwards of Kentisbeare, and Mary his 2nd wife, elder dau. of Robert Leigh, of Bardon, Somerset.

Services: Posted to 36th N.I. 1825; Adjt. do. 29 Sept. 1831 till death. Shekhawat expedn. 1834; Lieut. 36th N.I.

Refs.: Burke's *Landed Gentry*, 12th edn., p. 1442, *s.n.* Owen, of Huntspill and Sampford Brett, Somerset. *Howard & Crisp*, xvi. 79, *s.n.* Leigh, of Bardon. *G.M.* 1840, ii. 675.

TRIST, Thomas (1788-1832). Bt. Captain. 5th N.I. *b.* 31 July 1788. Cadet 1804. Arrived in India 13 May 1806. Ensign 2 Apr. 1806. Lieut. 31 Mar. 1807. Bt. Capt. 1 Jan. 1818. Retired 16 July 1823. *d.* 4 Apr. 1832.

THE BENGAL ARMY, 1758-1834

bapt. Veryan, Cornwall, 3 Aug. 1788. Elder son of Rev. Jeremiah Trist, of Parc Behan, J.P., vicar of Veryan, and Elizabeth Charlotte his wife, only child of Richard Fincher, of Carneggan. *m.* Dec. 1819, Frances, eldest sister of George Grose, *q.v.* (She died 6 May 1873.)

Services : Barasat C.C. Posted Ensign to 5th N.I. 1807. Capture of Java 1811; Lieut. 3rd Vol. Bn. Adjt. 3rd Vol. Bn. 1813-14. Capture of Sambas, Borneo, 1813 (s.w.). (? Nepal War 1815; operations in Kumaon; capture of Almora; Lieut. 2/5th N.I.) Fur. 1817-20, and 3 Feb. 1821 till retirement.

Refs. : Burke's *Landed Gentry*, 13th edn., p. 1770, *s.n.* Trist, of Tristford, Devon. Burke's *Royal Descents*, ped. ci.

TRITTON, William (1799-1838). Bt. Captain, 41st N.I. *b.* Hythe 13 June 1799. Cadet 1820. Arrived in India 12 Nov. 1821. Ensign 4 July 1821. Lieut. 1 Nov. 1823. Bt. Capt. 4 July 1836. *d.* Benares 22 Apr. 1838, of bilious fever.

bapt. St. Leonard's, Hythe, 11 July 1799. Son of William Tritton, of Hythe, and Elizabeth his wife. *m.* Calcutta 10 Aug. 1833, Mary Anne, only dau. of Henry James, *q.v.*

Services : Posted to 15th N.I.; transfd. to 2/18th N.I. 23 Oct. 1822; to 21st N.I. July 1823; to 41st N.I. (late 1/21st) May 1824. First Burma War; Arakan 1825; Lieut. 1st L.I. Bn. Siege and capture of Bhurtpore; Lieut. Rt. Wing 41st N.I. Fur s.c. 19 Mar. 1834 till 20 Dec. 1836.

Refs. : *A.J.* N.S. xxvi. 244. M.I. Benares.

TRITTON, William Mills (1805-1861). Major, Invalid Est. 26th N.I. *b.* Cawnpore 23 May 1805. Cadet 1821. Arrived in India 14 Apr. 1822. Ensign 24 Oct. 1821. Lieut. 1 May 1824. Capt. 30 Jan. 1830. Major 22 Nov. 1843. Invalided 14 Dec. 1843. *d.* Mussoorie 16 Feb. 1861.

bapt. Cawnpore 2 May 1806. Son of John Tritton, of Lacton House, nr. Ashford, Kent, Capt. 24th Light Dgns., and Mary his wife. His sister *m.* W. C. Carleton, *q.v.* *m.* Mussoorie 14 Sept. 1847, Ellen Georgiana, dau. of Robert Centlivre Nuthall, *q.v.* Addiscombe Cadet 1819-21.

Services : Posted to 2/21st N.I. 31 May 1822; transfd. to 13th N.I. July 1823; to 27th N.I. (late 2/13th) May 1824; to 26th N.I. 3 June 1825. First Burma War; Arakan 1825; Lieut. 26th N.I. Actg. Intr. & Qmr. 26th N.I. 1 Nov. 1825 till 1827. First Afghan War 1842; forcing of Khyber Pass 5 Apr. (*Lond. Gaz.* 7 June 1842); Kabul; Istalif; Capt. 26th N.I., with Pollock's force (Medal).

Posted to Eur. Invalids and Veteran Coy. at Chunar 30 May 1848. Resided at Mussoorie, or in the vicinity, 1849 till death.

*TROOP (or TROUP), William (d. 1800). Bt. Ensign, Pension Est. Bt. Ensign 4 Oct. 1779. d. Fraserburgh, co. Aberdeen, 23 Aug. 1800.

m. 1st, Edinburgh 14 Oct. 1789, Sophia, dau. of William Pery, manufacturer in Fraserburgh. m. 2nd, Ann, dau. of Alexander Leslie, in Banff.

Services : Enlisted 1760, and saw much active service in the ranks ; w. at Pondicherry, Manila 1762, Madura. Invalided as Sergt. Appt. Ensign of Mil. " in consideration of long service and wounds," 4 Oct. 1779. Fur. h.p. 20 Dec. 1786 till death. Granted a pension of 2/- *p.d.* from Lord Clive's fund 17 Sept. 1787. Capt. Fraserburgh Vols.

Refs. : *G.M.* 1800, ii. 903.

TROTTER, Alexander (1784-1828). Major, Invalid Est. 26th N.I. b. Glasgow 3 Feb. 1784. Cadet 1800. Arrived in India 22 Aug. 1801. Ensign 15 Oct. 1801. Lieut. 30 Sept. 1803. Capt. 3 Sept. 1818. Major 11 Oct. 1824. Invalided 28 Jan. 1825. d. *unm.* Allahabad 27 Aug. 1828.

Eldest son of John Trotter, of Myrtlemount, *alias* Ibrox, and of Glasgow, merchant, and Elizabeth Rolland his wife. Glasgow Univ. ; matric. 1795.

Services : Ensign 13th N.I. Second Mahratta War ; operations in Bundelkhand ; Lieut. 13th N.I. Operations against Dhundia Khan 1807 ; Komona ; Ganauri ; Lieut. 1/13th N.I. Intr. & Qmr. 1/13th N.I. 1 July 1814 till 17 Aug. 1819. Bareilly insurrection 1816. Transfd. as Capt. to 2/13th N.I. On leave to Cape in 1822. Transfd. to 26th N.I. (late 1/13th) May 1824. Comdd. 1st Bn. Native Invalids at Allahabad 25 Apr. 1827 till death.

Refs. : Will dated 1 Nov. 1822 ; proved 9 Sept. 1828. M.I. Kydganj cemetery, Allahabad.

TROTTER, Robert Archibald (1814-1894). Lieut. Colonel. 43rd N.I. b. Calcutta 13 Feb. 1814. Cadet 1832. Arrived in India 14 July 1834. Ensign (10 Mar. 1834) 14 July 1834. Lieut. 10 Oct. 1839. Capt. 14 July 1853. Retired 31 Dec. 1861. Hon. Major 31 Dec. 1861. Hon. Lt. Col. 1868. d. 72 Redcliffe Gdns., London, 5 May 1894.

Of Bush, Castlelaw, and Dryden, Midlothian, J.P. *bapt.* Calcutta 15 July 1814. Eldest son of Archibald Trotter, of Dryden, Castlelaw, and Bush, J.P., formerly B.C.S., commercial resdt. at Patna;

THE BENGAL ARMY, 1758-1834 309

and Laura Maria his wife, 2nd dau. of Thomas Chase, M.C.S. His sister *m.* Steuart Bayley Hare, *q.v.* Ed. Edin. Acad. 1824-30.

Services: Ensign d.d. 56th N.I. 24 July 1834; posted to 27th N.I. 5 Nov. 1834; transfd. to 43rd N.I. 28 Jan. 1835. First Afghan War 1839-42; Ghazni 1839 (Medal); reoccupation of Kalat 1840; defence of Kalat-i-Ghilzai 1841-2 (Medal); capture of Istalif; Lieut. 43rd N.I. Gwalior campaign; Maharajpur; Lieut. 43rd N.I. (Bronze star). Fur. s.c. 22 Feb. 1845 till 1847.

Refs.: Burke's *Landed Gentry*, 12th edn., p. 1895, *s.n.* Trotter, of Bush, Midlothian. *The Times*, 8 May 1894.

TROUP, Colin (1804-1876). Lieut. General, C.B. 68th N.I. *b.* 1 Apr. 1804. Cadet 1819. Arrived in India 6 Jan. 1821. Ensign 16 July 1820. Lieut. 11 July 1823. Capt. 8 Oct. 1839. Major 24 July 1847. Lt. Col. 5 June 1853. Bt. Col. 28 Nov. 1854. Maj. Gen. 26 May 1864. Lt. Gen. 21 Mar. 1872. *d.* Mussoorie 19 Mar. 1876.

4th son of John Troup, of Fir Hall, co. Nairn, and Jane his wife, sister of Hugh Rose, *q.v.* Brother of Hugh Troup and of the wife of James Bedford, *qq.v. m.* 1st, Cawnpore 12 Mar. 1845, Katherine Maria, eldest dau. of Birnie Browne, *q.v.* (She died Bareilly 21 May 1854, aged 26.) *m.* 2nd, 28 Mar. 1862, Elizabeth Mary, 2nd dau. of Birnie Browne, *q.v.*, and widow of Lieut. Frederick William Birch, 59th B.N.I. (She died 27 Dec. 1912.)

Services: Posted to 1/11th N.I.; transfd. to 24th N.I. July 1823; to 47th N.I. (late 1/24th) May 1824; to 48th N.I. 24 June 1824. On service against the freebooter Diraj Singh Dec. 1824, with 2 Coys. 48th N.I., under Capt. H.M. Wheeler, *q.v.* Operations against the Bhils 1827; Lieut. 48th N.I. Adjt. 48th N.I. 1 Jan. 1836 till 16 Feb. 1838. 2nd in comd. 2nd Inf., Oudh Auxy. Force, 27 Dec. 1837; rejoined his Regt. for service Sept. 1838. Apptd. Baggage Mr. with Army of Indus 10 Sept. 1838; apptd. Bde. Major to Shah Shuja's force 6 Apr. 1839. First Afghan War 1838-42; Ghazni; retreat from Kabul; w. in Khurd Kabul Pass 8 Jan. 1842; taken prisoner; released Sept. 1842; Capt. 48th N.I. (Medal). D.A.A.G. Cawnpore Div. 8 Dec. 1843; A.A.G. do. 19 Mar. 1846 till 1847. First Sikh War; Aliwal; Capt. comdg. 48th N.I. (Medal). Posted Lt. Col. to 22nd N.I. 4 Aug. 1853; to 59th N.I. Dec. 1853; to 45th N.I. Mar. 1854; to 18th N.I. 1 Dec. 1854; to 68th N.I. May 1855, and was comdg. this Regt. when it mutinied at Bareilly 31 May 1857. Bdr. 2 cl. comdg. at Bareilly 9 June 1858; do. at Multan 1859; do. at Agra 1861-3. Maj. Gen. comdg. Meerut Div. 5 Aug. 1865 till 5 Aug. 1869. C.B. 28 Feb. 1861.

Refs.: Boase. *D.I.B.* Eyre's *Journal. The Times,* 8 Oct. 1842. *Pioneer Mail* (Allahabad), 1 Apr. 1876.

TROUP, Hugh (1803-1879). General. Colonel 6th Bengal Eur. Inf. *b.* Nairn 9 Feb. 1803. Cadet 1819. Arrived in India 6 Jan. 1821. Ensign 16 July 1820. Lieut. 11 July 1823. Capt. 27 June 1830. Major 16 May 1844. Lt. Col. 13 Aug. 1850. Col. 11 Sept. 1859. Maj. Gen. 10 June 1862. Lt. Gen. 25 July 1870. Gen. 1 Oct. 1877. *d.* Perth 2 Nov. 1879.
3rd son of John Troup and Jane Rose his wife. Brother of John Rose Troup, *q.v. m.* Hazaribagh, B. & O., 18 June 1840, Lucy Maria, 3rd sister of M. E. Sherwill, *q.v.* (She died 12 Oct. 1891.)
Services: Posted Ensign to 1/30th N.I.; transfd. to newly-raised 33rd N.I. July 1823; to 66th N.I. (late 2/33rd) May 1824. Adjt. newly-raised 9th Extra Regt. 21 May 1825 till 1826, when disbanded. Actg. Adjt. 66th N.I. 13 May 1826; permanent do. 26 May 1829 till 21 Dec. 1830. Fur. s.c. 25 June 1832 till 3 Nov. 1835. Offg. Bde. Major at Cawnpore 9 Mar. 1839, and 25 July 1840 till 26 Oct. 1841. Transfd. to 66th (or Gurkha) Regt. (late Nassiri Bn., now 1st K.G.O. Gurkha Rifles) Feb. 1850 on disbandment of 66th N.I. for mutiny; posted Lt. Col. do. 21 Oct. 1850. Operations on N.W.F. 1851-2; against Mohmands; Swatis; Utman Khel 11 May 1852; Punjpoo Ishakot 15 May 1852; Lt. Col. comdg. 66th (Gurkha) Regt. (Medal). Transfd. to 45th N.I. 2 Nov. 1855; to 8th, 31st, 37th N.I. Feb. 1856; to 47th N.I. Aug. 1856. Fur. s.c. 12 Feb. 1856 till 13 Nov. 1858. Transfd. to 62nd N.I. 24 July 1858; to newly-raised 6th Bengal Eur. Inf. 1858; Col. do. 1859-69. Bdr. 2 cl. comdg. Delhi Bde. 17 May 1859. Fur. 14 Aug. 1860 till death.
Refs.: Boase.

TROUP, John Rose (1802-1862). Lieutenant. 36th N.I. *b.* Nairn 19 Feb. 1802. Cadet 1817. Admitted 3 Oct. 1818. Ensign 27 Apr. 1818. Lieut. 30 Dec. 1818. Resigned in India 19 Aug. 1831. *d.* London 2 July 1862.
bapt. Nairn 22 Feb. 1802. 2nd son of John Troup and Jane his wife. Brother of Robert Troup, *q.v. m.* 1st, Dacca 10 Dec. 1820, Caroline Georgiana, 2nd dau. of Charles Stopford, of Chiplinton Park, Oxon. *m.* 2nd, Sardhana, Punjab, 3 Oct. 1831, Ann May, dau. of " Col." George Alexander David Dyce, agent to the Begum Somru, grand-dau. of David Dyce, *q.v.*, and half-sister of David Ochterlony Dyce-Sombre *(D.N.B.).*[1] (She died in Italy 18 Mar. 1867.)

THE BENGAL ARMY, 1758-1834 311

Services: Posted to 2/18th N.I. 1818; Adjt. 1/18th N.I. 1 Oct. 1823; transfd. to 37th N.I. (late 2/18th) May 1824; Intr. & Qmr. do. 17 June 1824; transfd. to 36th N.I. 1825; Intr. & Qmr. do 28 June 1825 till resignation. Siege and capture of Bhurtpore; Lieut. 36th N.I. (India medal).[2] In June 1831, the Begum Somru applied for his services, stating that she wished "to have him by her, as he was highly qualified and intelligent and well versed in the Hindoostanee language." On this request being refused by Govt. he resigned his Commission and entered her service.

Refs.: Begam Samru, by Brajendranath Banerji, Calcutta, 1925. *N. & Q.* 8S. vii. 309; clxi. 458. *A.J.* xii. 89. Will dated 8 May 1862.

[1] *Note:* The ceremony was performed in the cathedral of Sancta Maria, and was afterwards celebrated a second time in the Begum's palace by the Protestant chaplain of Meerut.

[2] *Note:* He is styled "Maj. Gen." in the India M.R.

TROUP, Robert (1811-1867). Colonel, 63rd N.I. *b.* Nairn 1 Sept. 1811. Cadet 1827. Arrived in India 29 Apr. 1828. Ensign 24 Oct. 1827. Lieut. 5 Apr. 1834. Capt. 1 Oct. 1848. Major 31 Dec. 1855. Lt. Col. 19 Aug. 1859. Col. 1867. *d.* Sim Tola, nr. Almora, U.P., 21 Oct. 1867.

bapt. Nairn 12 Nov. 1811. 5th and youngest son of John Troup, of Fir Hall, Nairn, and Jane his wife. Brother of William Alexander Troup, *q.v. m.* Berhampore 21 Oct. 1833, Emma Deborah, 2nd dau. of Nathaniel Henry Hart, of Berhampore, merchant. (She died 16 Nov. 1866, aged 53.)

Services: Ensign d.d. 66th N.I. 26 May 1828; posted to 63rd N.I. 1828; Adjt. do. 10 Jan. 1837 till 1845; do. 1st Oudh Local Inf. 29 Aug. 1845 till 28 Feb. 1846. Rejoined 63rd N.I. in Sind Oct. 1845. First Sikh War; Ferozshahr; Sobraon; Bt. Capt. 63rd N.I. (Medal with clasp). Adjt. Nassiri Bn. 28 Feb. 1846; 2nd in comd. 1st Regt. Inf., N.W.F. Bde., 14 Dec. 1846; Comdt. 2nd Regt. Oudh Local Inf. 3 Dec. 1847 till 1 Apr. 1856. Comdg. 9th B.N.I. (late 63rd N.I., now 9th Gurkha Rifles) 1861; Comdt. do. 1 Jan. 1864 till 20 Aug. 1866. Was a tea planter at Ranikhet at death.

TROUP, William. (*See* **TROOP, William.**)

TROUP, William Alexander (1800-1846). Major, 15th N.I. *b.* Fir Hall, co. Nairn, 3 Nov. 1800. Cadet 1817. Arrived in India Sept. 1818. Ensign (?) Lieut. 29 Dec. 1818. Capt. 20 Dec. 1826. Major 1 Feb. 1843. *d.* in camp, Dinanagar, Bari Doab, 5 Oct. 1846.

bapt. Nairn 12 Nov. 1800. Eldest son of John Troup, of Fir Hall, and Jane his wife. Brother of Colin Troup, *q.v.* *m.* Barrackpore 13 June 1837, Mary, dau. of John Ward. (She *re-m.* 27 Apr. 1859, Rev. Alexander Bunn Haden, and died 21 July 1905.)
Services : Ensign d.d. 1/11th N.I. Oct. 1818 ; posted Lieut. to 1/11th N.I. Mar. 1819 ; transfd. to 15th N.I. (late 1/11th) May 1824. Intr. & Qmr. 15th N.I. 29 June 1824 ; Adjt. do. 13 July 1824 till Dec. 1826. Action at Patan, nr. Kotah, against Rajah Balwant Singh, 7 Nov. 1824 ; Lieut. 15th N.I. Siege and capture of Bhurtpore ; Lieut. 15th N.I. His death occurred whilst he was proceeding on service to Jammu with his Regt. against Sheikh Imam-ud-Din.
Refs. : *De Rhé-Philipe.* M.I. at Mukerian.

TROUTBACK,[1] **Samuel.** Fireworker. Artillery. (79) Cadet (?) Fireworker Feb. 1767. Resigned 1767.
N.B.—The following is conjectural only : (? Son of Samuel Troutback, of Madras, free merchant, and Susannah his wife, *née* Morgan. *b.* Madras 6 Apr. 1729 ; bapt. there 16 Apr. 1729. Samuel Troutback, senr., was *bur.* Madras 24 July 1785.)
Services : Apptd. Conductor of Art. Stores 24 May 1765.
[1] *Note :* Both *Dodwell & Miles* and *Stubbs* give the name as Troutbeck.

TROWER, Charles Farquhar (1811-1846). Captain, 33rd N.I. Nizam's army. *b.* Calcutta 19 Apr. 1811. Cadet 1827. Arrived in India 30 Sept. 1828. Ensign (22 May 1828) 3 June 1829. Lieut. 13 May 1833. Capt. 14 July 1842. *d.* Mominabad, Hyderabad, 11 May 1846, of cholera.
bapt. Calcutta 6 May 1812. Son of Charles Trower, B.C.S., civil auditor, Calcutta, and Amelia Catherine his 2nd wife, sister of Roger Keys Erskine, *q.v.* Brother of Gordon Perceval Trower and of the wife of Charles Henry Wintour, and cousin-german of the wife of Alfred Jackson, *qq.v.* *m.* (before 1845) ?
Services : Ensign d.d. 59th N.I. 28 Oct. 1828 ; posted to 48th N.I. 4 Mar. 1829 ; to 25th N.I. 3 June 1829. Fur. 1 yr. without pay 22 Mar. 1829 till 1 May 1830. d.d. 59th N.I. 1 June 1830 till 1 Jan. 1831 ; transfd. to 33rd N.I. 2 Aug. 1832. Placed at disposal of Resdt. at Hyderabad 6 Oct. 1835 and served in Nizam's army 17 May 1836 till death ; Capt. in do. 22 May 1840. Rejoined 33rd N.I. tempy. for service Feb. 1842. First Afghan War 1842 ; comdd. convoy proceeding to Jalalabad June 1842 ; Capt. 33rd N.I., with Pollock's force (Medal). Rejoined Nizam's army 1843.

Capt. 4th Cav., Bde. Major and Paymr. of Cav. Div. at Mominabad. Author of "Hints on Irregular Cavalry," 1845.
Refs.: Family information. M.I. Mominabad.

*TROWER, Gordon Perceval (1813-?). Cadet. *bapt.* Chinsura, Bengal, 3 Sept. 1813. Cadet 1829. Resigned May 1830. Son of Charles Trower, B.C.S., and Amelia Catherine his 2nd wife. Brother of Charles Farquhar Trower, *q.v.* Addiscombe Cadet 1829.
Services: Probably never went to India.

TROWER, Jasper (1806-1845). Captain, Artillery. (563) *b.* London 2 Apr. 1806. Cadet 1824. Arrived in India 6 May 1825. 2nd Lieut. 13 Oct. 1824. Lieut. 1 Jan. 1828. Capt. 8 Oct. 1843. *d.* in camp 18 Dec. 1845, of wounds received earlier in the day at the battle of Mudki.

bapt. St. Peter-le-Poor, London, 5 June 1806. 3rd son of George Trower, of Russell Sq., London, merchant, and Mary his 1st wife, eldest dau. of George Griffin Stonestreet, of Halton, Sussex, and Stondon Hall, Essex. Nephew of William Trower, *q.v.* *m.* Calcutta 3 July 1832, Charlotte, dau. of George Sunbolf, Lieut. h.p. 33rd Ft., and grand-niece of George Cruttenden, *q.v.* (*See also* Edmund Talbot.) (She *re-m.* 5 Oct. 1850, Octave Delpierre, Sec. to Belgian Legation.) Ed. Rugby.[1] Addiscombe Cadet 1822-4.

Services: Posted to Foot Art. June 1825; served with H.A. May 1826 till Oct. 1834. Fur. s.c. 21 Oct. 1834 till 9 Jan. 1837. In charge of revenue survey, S. Div. of Cuttack, 3 Oct. 1837 till Dec. 1839; transfd. to 3rd Coy. 5th Bn. Nov. 1837; comdd. Art. Coy. of Oudh Auxy. Force (became 9th Coy. 7th Bn. in Mar. 1842) 18 Jan. 1840 till Nov. 1844; transfd. to 3rd Coy. 4th Bn. July 1845. First Sikh War; Mudki (s.w.); Capt. comdg. 3rd Coy. 4th Bn. (No. 7 Heavy Field Batty.).

Refs.: *Howard & Crisp*, xxi. 101, *s.n.* Trower. Burke's *Landed Gentry*, 2nd edn., p. 1311, *s.n.* Stonestreet, of Halton, Sussex. De Rhé-Philipe. Will dated 25 July 1845; proved 24 Feb. 1846. M.I. in St. Andrew's, Ferozepore.

[1] *Note:* Not in *Rugby School Register*.

TROWER, William (1782-1825). Lieutenant. 9th N.I. Subsequently B.C.S. *bapt.* St. John, Hackney, 24 Jan. 1782. Cadet 1798. Arrived in India 24 Nov. 1799. Ensign 14 Nov. 1799. Lieut. 29 May 1800. Transfd. to B.C.S. 21 Aug. 1801. *d.* Calcutta 24 Sept. 1825.

Son of Thomas Trower, of Clapton, Middlesex, and Elizabeth his

wife, dau. of John Smith, of Fleet St., London. Uncle of Jasper Trower, q.v. m. Calcutta 26 Mar. 1805, Miss Louisa Anne Fleming. Ed. Eton; admitted 1794; K.S. 1796.
Services: Sailed for India in the *Asia* 1799. Posted to 1/9th N.I. 15 Apr. 1801. 3rd Member of Board of Revenue, Lower Provinces, 23 Jan. 1823 till death.
Refs.: Etoniana, p. 683.

*TRUEMAN, William Louis (1791-1824). Captain, 40th N.I. *b.* Camberwell 7 Nov. 1791. Cadet 1806. Arrived in India 25 Nov. 1807. Ensign 31 Oct. 1807. Lieut. 1 June 1812. Capt. 14 Mar. 1823. *d. unm.* Ramu, Burma, 17 May 1824: kld. in action.

bapt. Camberwell 13 Dec. 1791. Son of Robert Trueman and Sarah his wife. (? His sister *m.* James Plumer, *q.v.*)
Services: Barasat C.C. Posted Ensign to 20th N.I. 1808. Capture of Java 1811; Ensign 20th N.I. Lieut. 2/20th N.I. at Bencoolen 1814-15; transfd. to 1/20th; retransfd. to 2/20th; to 40th N.I. (late 2/20th) May 1824. First Burma War; Chittagong 1824; disaster at Ramu (kld.); Capt. 40th N.I.
Refs.: Will dated 11 Oct. 1823; proved 10 June 1824.

TRUSCOTT, John (1779-1865). General. Colonel 74th N.I. *b.* 29 (? 28) Feb. 1779. Cadet 1798. Arrived in India 22 Nov. 1799. Ensign 13 Oct. 1799. Lieut. 28 Oct. 1799. Capt. 4 Mar. 1812. Major 6 Nov. 1818. Lt. Col. 1 Mar. 1824. Col. 4 Mar. 1830. Maj. Gen. 28 June 1838. Lt. Gen. 11 Nov. 1851. Gen. 27 Jan. 1858. *d.* Dawlish, Devon, 12 June 1865.

bapt. W. Teignmouth 26 Mar. 1779. 4th son of Rear-Adm. William Truscott, R.N., of St. Sidwell's, Exeter, and Mary his wife, dau. of Robert Croucher, of Didmarton, Gloucs. *m.* Newton St. Cyres, Devon, 17 Jan. 1805, Mary Lambert, dau. of William Lambert Gorwyn, of Drewsteignton, Devon. (She died Dawlish 18 Jan. 1857, aged 75.)
Services: Midshipman R.N. Posted Lieut. to 1/17th N.I. 15 Apr. 1801. Fur. s.c. 10 Dec. 1801 till 8 Oct. 1805. Transfd. to newly-raised 27th N.I. 1805. (? Operations against Dhundia Khan 1807; Komona; Ganauri; Lieut. 27th N.I.) Adjt. & Qmr. at Ghazipur in 1810; Bk. Mr. do. 15 Jan. 1811; Cantt. Adjt. & Bk. Mr. do. 1813-19; Capt. 1/27th N.I. Leave s.c. to Cape 8 July 1819; fur. s.c. from Cape Aug. 1821 till 1 June 1824. Major 2/27th N.I. Posted Lt. Col. to 45th N.I. May 1824; to 46th N.I. 26 Oct. 1828. Posted Col. to 45th N.I. 15 Mar. 1830. Fur. s.c.

THE BENGAL ARMY, 1758-1834 315

24 Jan. 1831 till death. Transfd. to 6th N.I. 14 June 1842 ; to 40th N.I. 19 Dec. 1842 ; to 74th N.I. 11 Mar. 1847 till death.

Refs. : Howard & Crisp, iv. 100, *s.n.* Truscott (portrait). Boase. The Times, 15 June 1865.

TUCKER, Auchmuty (1803-1891). General, C.B. 4th Bengal Eur. L.C. *b.* Ospringe, Kent, 24 June 1803. Cadet 1826. Arrived in India 4 Feb. 1827. Cornet 12 Sept. 1826. Lieut. 9 Jan. 1829. Capt. 23 Dec. 1839. Major 28 Nov. 1854. Lt. Col. 1 Jan. 1862. Bt. Col. 2 Apr. 1856. Maj. Gen. 9 Apr. 1865. Lt. Gen. 14 Dec. 1873. Gen. 1 Oct. 1877. Retired under R.W. of 25 June 1881. *d.* at his residence, Shilston House, Leamington, 6 Mar. 1891.

bapt. 18 July 1803. Eldest son of John Goulston Price Tucker, Col. 5th W.I. Regt., and Ann his wife, dau. of Maj.-Gen. Frederick George Mulcaster, R.E. Brother of Henry Tod Tucker, *q.v.*, and of the wife of William Cookson, *q.v.* Nephew of Henry St. George Tucker, Chairman E.I. Co., and cousin-german of Henry St. George Tucker, *q.v. m.* Brighton 16 Nov. 1837, Sarah, eldest sister of William Cookson, *q.v.* (She died 20 Nov. 1890, aged 80.) Woolwich Cadet.

Services : 2nd Lieut. 1/60th Rifles 10 Apr. 1825 ; Lieut. H.M. 41st Ft. 17 Mar. 1826. Cornet d.d. 10th L.C. 20 Feb. 1827 ; posted to 9th L.C. 10 May 1827 ; Intr. & Qmr. do. 4 Nov. 1828 till 22 Mar. 1834. Fur. s.c. 6 Feb. 1836 till 20 Jan. 1840. Served in Mily. Auditor Gen.'s Dept. 24 Feb. 1840 till Oct. 1842. Conquest of Sind 1843 ; Miani (s.w. in 5 places—*Lond. Gaz.* 11 Apr. and 4 July 1843) ; Capt. 9th L.C. (Medal). Fur. s.c. 5 Apr. till 15 Nov. 1844. Agent for army clothing, 1st Div., 30 May 1845 till Apr. 1853. Fur. 1853 till 3 Jan. 1856, and 12 Jan. 1856 till 13 Nov. 1858. Posted to newly-raised 4th Bengal Eur. L.C. May 1858. Bdr. comdg. Rawal Pindi Bde. 31 Jan. 1862 till 1865. Transfd. to Staff Corps 12 Sept. 1866. Fur. 24 Jan. 1867 till retirement. C.B. 4 July 1843.

Refs. : Boase. The Times, 9 Mar. 1891.

*TUCKER, Henry St. George (1813-1840). Cadet. Infantry. Subsequently Factor, B.C.S. *b.* 23 Jan. 1813. Cadet 1827. Resigned 22 July 1829. *d.* Meerut 11 Dec. 1840.

Eldest son of Thomas Tudor Tucker, of Dunkerque, Rear Adm. R.N. (*D.N.B.*), and Anne Byam Wyke his wife, eldest dau. of Daniel Hill, of Antigua, merchant. Brother of Thomas Tudor Tucker and cousin-german of Henry Tod Tucker, *qq.v. m.* Allahabad 10 Mar. 1836, his cousin-german Maria Juliana Frances, eldest sister of Auchmuty Tucker, *q.v.* (*See also* William Cookson.) (She died Torquay 25 Dec. 1899, aged 89.) Addiscombe Cadet 1827-29 ; Haileybury 1829-31.

Services : Resigned whilst at Addiscombe and went to Civil Coll., Haileybury. Apptd. Writer 30 Apr. 1831. Offg. Mgte. and Collector of Jaunpur 2 May 1839 till death.

TUCKER, Henry Tod (1808-1896). Major General, C.B. 8th N.I. Adjt. Gen. Bengal. A.D.C. to Queen Victoria. *b.* Edinburgh 8 Mar. 1808. Cadet 1823. Arrived in India 31 Mar. 1825. Ensign 10 Sept. 1824. Lieut. 20 July 1832. Capt. 13 Mar. 1844. Major 20 Feb. 1856. Bt. Lt. Col. 7 June 1849. Bt. Col. 20 June 1854. Retired 6 May 1856. Hon. Maj. Gen. 6 May 1856. *d.* 51 Glos. Gdns., Hyde Pk., London, 6 Aug. 1896.

bapt. St. Andrew's, Edinburgh, 2 Apr. 1808. Son of Col. John Goulston Price Tucker and Ann Mulcaster his wife. Brother of Auchmuty Tucker, *q.v. m.* St. James's, Piccadilly, 2 May 1857, Harriet Maria, 2nd dau. of Sir Henry Allen Johnson, 2nd Bart., of Bath. (She died 14 May 1900.)

Services : Posted to 8th N.I. 1825 ; actg. Adjt. do. 23 Nov. 1829, 5 Jan. 1831, 20 Sept. 1831 till 2 July 1832. d.d. Assam Sebundy Corps 11 June 1835 ; Junr. Asst. to Comr. of Assam 20 Oct. 1835 till 27 Feb. 1837 ; d.d. Ramgarh Bn. and in charge of two *risalas* of Local Horse attached to the Bn. 14 Nov. 1837. Fur. s.c. 17 May 1839 till 22 Nov. 1843. Orderly Ofr. at Addiscombe 28 Oct. 1840 till 1843. Bde. Major at Barrackpore 13 Sept. 1844 till Mar. 1846. First Sikh War ; Sobraon (horse kld.) ; Capt. 8th N.I., A.A.G. (Medal). 1st A.A.G. of Army 28 Mar. 1846. Second Sikh War ; Ramnagar ; Chilianwala (w.—horse kld.) ; Gujerat (slew 3 enemy horsemen in single combat) ; Bt. Major 8th N.I., D.A.G. (Medal with 2 clasps). D.A.G. 13 Jan. 1849 ; A.G. 6 May 1850 till retirement. C.B. 17 Aug. 1850. A.D.C. to Queen 20 June 1854. Hon. A.D.C. to G.G. July 1851 and Mar. 1856. Author of " A Glance at the Past and Future, in connection with the Indian Revolt," London, 1857.

Refs. : Burke's *Peerage,* 1859, p. 559, *s.n.* Johnson, Bart., of the city of Bath. *D.I.B. I.M.* 2 Apr. 1850, p. 210. *The Times,* 8 Aug. 1896.

TUCKER, John. Ensign, Infantry. Cadet 1766. Ensign 1 Jan. 1767. *d.* (date not known).

Services : Sailed for India as a Bombay Cadet in the *Duke of Albany* 17 Mar. 1766. Transfd. to Bengal Est. 12 Oct. 1766, by permission of the Govr. of Bombay.

TUCKER, Thomas Tudor (1817-1857). Bt. Lieut. Colonel, 8th L.C. Clothing Agent, 1st Div. b. Tenby 28 Jan. 1817. Cadet 1832. Arrived in India 16 Sept. 1833. Ensign 28 Jan. 1833. Cornet 17 Jan. 1836. Lieut. 21 Jan. 1839. Capt. 10 Aug. 1850. Bt. Major 11 Aug. 1850. Bt. Lt. Col. 28 Nov. 1854. d. Fatehgarh 29 June 1857 : kld. in the defence of the fort.
bapt. Tenby 26 Feb. 1817. 2nd son of Thomas Tudor Tucker, Rear Adm. R.N., and Anne Byam Wyke his wife. Brother of Henry St. George Tucker, q.v. m. Simla 5 June 1851, Louisa Isabella, widow of Alexander Humfrays, q.v. (She and her four children, after escaping from Fatehgarh, were massacred at Cawnpore 15 July 1857.) Addiscombe Cadet 4 Feb. 1831 till 14 Dec. 1832.
Services : Supy. Ensign d.d. 66th N.I. 12 Dec. 1833 ; posted to 39th N.I. 24 May 1834 ; to 74th N.I. 6 Nov. 1835. Transfd. to Cav. 27 Jan. 1836 ; d.d. 5th L.C. 6 June 1836 ; posted to 8th L.C. 3 Jan. 1837. Actg. Adjt. 8th L.C. 8 Oct. 1839 ; actg. 2nd in comd. 8th Irreg. Cav. 30 Apr. 1842 till 6 Apr. 1843. Insurrection in Bundelkhand 1842-3 ; with Bundelkhand F.F. Gwalior campaign ; Paniar ; Lieut. 8th L.C. (Bronze star). Adjt. G.G.B.G. 7 Jan. 1846 ; 2nd in comd. do. 5 Mar. till June 1846. First Sikh War ; Aliwal ; Sobraon ; Lieut. 8th L.C., with G.G.B.G. (Medal with clasp). Leave s.c. 1 Mar. 1846 till 1 May 1847. Second Sikh War ; Ramnagar ; Chilianwala ; Gujerat ; Bt. Capt. 8th L.C., D.A.Q.M.G. Cav. Div., Army of Punjab (Medal with 2 clasps). D.A.Q.M.G. of the Army, 2 cl., 8 Feb. 1850 ; A.Q.M.G. 11 June 1852 ; Agent for army clothing, 1st Div., at Fatehgarh 23 Apr. 1853 till death.
Refs. : V.B.G. G.M. 1857, ii. 566. M.I. Fatehgarh fort cemetery.

TUDMAN, James (d. 1770). Ensign, Infantry. Cadet (?) Ensign 25 Sept. 1769. d. Berhampore 15 July 1770.
Services : N.F.P.

TUDOR, George Cowley (1783-1813). Lieutenant, 25th N.I. bapt. Abergavenny, co. Monmouth, 18 July 1783. Cadet 1800. Arrived in India 22 Aug. 1801. Ensign 18 Sept. 1801. Lieut. 8 Apr. 1803. d. Nadia, Bengal, 14 June 1813.
Son of Thomas Tudor and Eliza Grizel his wife. Related to Eliza Maria, 2nd wife of Rawson Hart Boddam, formerly Govr. of Bombay (? and brother of Thomas Tudor, q.v.). His niece m. William Lisle Hall, q.v.

Services : Ensign d.d. 1st N.I. in 1802 ; transfd. as Ensign to 7th N.I. Second Mahratta War 1803-4 ; operations in Cuttack ; capture of Balasore ; Lieut. 2/7th N.I., with 1st Vol. Bn. Transfd. to newly-raised 25th N.I. 1805. Operations against the Rana of Gohad 1806 ; capture of Gohad ; Lieut. 25th N.I. Lieut. 2/25th N.I.

TUDOR, James Colley (1801-1854). Lieut. Colonel, C.B., 8th N.I. *b.* Walton, Lancs., 9 May 1801. Cadet 1819. Admitted 9 Oct. 1820. Ensign 17 Apr. 1820. Lieut. 11 July 1823. Capt. 1 Apr. 1828. Major 18 Sept. 1844. Lt. Col. 8 Oct. 1850. *d.* C.G.H. 5 Aug. 1854.

bapt. St. James's, Walton, 29 Sept. 1801. 2nd child of John Kindersley Tudor, of Liverpool, merchant, and Kitty his wife, formerly Duckle. *m.* Calcutta 28 July 1830, Harriet Jane, youngest dau. of Charles Becher, B.C.S., *q.v.* (She died Simla 9 May 1849, aged 38.)

Services : Posted Ensign to 1/12th N.I. 1820 ; transfd. as Lieut. to 23rd N.I. 1823. First Burma War ; Assam 1824 ; Lieut. 2/23rd N.I. (India medal). Transfd. to 46th N.I. (late 2/23rd) May 1824. Leave s.c. 6 mos. to Mauritius 22 Nov. 1824 ; fur. s.c. thence 5 Dec. 1824 till 24 Sept. 1827. d.d. 51st N.I. 1 Oct. 1828. S.A.C.G. 19 Dec. 1831 ; D.A.C.G. 2 cl. 18 Jan. 1837 ; 1 cl. 14 Aug. 1837. Leave s.c. to Cape 23 Sept. 1839 till 5 Nov. 1841. A.C.G. 2 cl. 8 Jan. till 25 Oct. 1844. Second Sikh War ; Ramnagar ; Sadulapur ; Chilianwala ; Gujerat ; Major 46th N.I. (Medal with 2 clasps). Posted Lt. Col. to 46th N.I. Jan. 1851 ; to 1st Eur. Bengal Fus. Sept. 1852. Second Burma War 1852 ; capture of Pegu ; Lt. Col. comdg. 1st Eur. Bengal Fus. (Medal). Transfd. to 30th N.I. Feb. 1853 ; to 8th N.I. 1 Mar. 1853. Leave to Cape 1854. C.B. 9 Dec. 1853.

Refs. : Will dated 3 Aug. 1854 ; admon. 15 Dec. 1858.

TUDOR, Thomas (1787-1813). Lieutenant, Invalid Est. 6th N.I. *b.* Shrewsbury 8 May 1787. Cadet 1805. Arrived in India 13 Dec. 1806. Ensign 7 Dec. 1806. Lieut. 12 May 1811. Invalided 26 Nov. 1811. *d.* Chunar 23 Jan. 1813.

Son of Thomas Tudor and Elizabeth his wife. Brother of William and Owen Tudor (? and of George Cowley Tudor, *q.v.*). Ed. Shrewsbury ; admitted 1 Oct. 1798.

Services : Barasat C.C. Posted Ensign to 6th N.I. 1807. Served with Eur. Invalids at Chunar. No record of active service.

Refs. : Shrewsbury School Register. M.I. in old cemetery below Chunar fort.

THE BENGAL ARMY, 1758-1834 319

TULLIKEN,[1] **James Jones** (1758/59-1791). Lieutenant, 14th Bn. Sepoys. *b.* in Ireland 1758/59. Cadet 1779. Ensign 12 Feb. 1780. Lieut. 2 Feb. 1781. *bur.* Madras 17 Oct. 1791.

(*Probably* grandson of Col. Tullekens (who came from Holland with William, Prince of Orange), whose dau. Jemima was mother of Arnoldus Jones Skelton, *q.v.*, and son of Lt. Col. Comdt. John Tullikens, h.p. 94th Ft., who *d. c.* 1785.)

Services : Ensign of Addl. Coy. H.M. 14th Ft. 15 Aug. 1775 ; Lieut. 14th Ft. 7 Aug. 1777. Sailed for India in the *Fox* 7 Mar. 1779, aged 20. Lieut. 32nd Bn. Sepoys in July 1787 ; Adjt. 14th Bn. in 1788-91. Third Mysore War 1790-1 ; Bangalore ; Arikera ; Lieut. 14th Bn., with detachment under Lt. Col. Cockerell, *q.v.*

[1] *Note :* The name sometimes appears as Tullican or Tullikan. One John Tulliken was naturalized in 1800.

TULLOCH, John (1790-1862). Lieut. General, C.B. Colonel 51st N.I. *b.* London 9 Feb. 1790. Cadet 1804. Arrived in India 16 May 1806. Ensign 23 Nov. 1805. Lieut. 2 Feb. 1807. Capt. 11 July 1821. Major 24 Jan. 1829. Lt. Col. 30 Apr. 1834. Col. 23 Oct. 1845. Maj. Gen. 20 June 1854. Lt. Gen. 11 Sept. 1859. *d.* 25 Dawson Pl., Notting Hill, 13 Apr. 1862.

bapt. St. James's, Westminster, 8 Mar. 1790. Son of Alexander Tulloch, of Charles St., Westminster, and Margaret his wife, *née* Munro. *m.* Jacobina Maria Coúperús. Father of John Samuel Drury Tulloch, Stamford William Raffles Tulloch, and Maria, wife of George Palmer Whish, *qq.v.*

Services : Served as Cadet at capture of Cape Jan. 1806. Barasat C.C. Posted to 22nd N.I. 1807. Settlement of Hariana 1809 ; Bhawani ; Lieut. 1/22nd N.I. Bundelkhand 1810. Actg. Adjt. Bengal L.I. Vol. Bn. 8 Feb. 1811. Capture of Java 1811 ; Lieut. L.I. Vol. Bn. (Medal). Third Mahratta War ; Nagpur ; Lieut. 1/22nd N.I. (India medal). Transfd. to 43rd N.I. (late 1/22nd) May 1824. First Burma War ; Arakan 1825 ; Capt. 1st L.I. Bn. (clasp to India medal). Posted Lt. Col. to 30th N.I. 4 Oct. 1834 ; to 60th N.I. 6 Dec. 1834. Mutiny in camp of Baiza Bai at Fatehgarh 9 Sept. 1835 ; comdg. the troops. First Afghan War 1842 ; forcing of Khyber in Jan. ; Lt. Col. comdg. 60th N.I. ; Bdr. 2 cl. to comd. 2nd Inf. Bde. of Pollock's force 7 Apr. 1842 ; Mamu Khel ; Tazin ; reoccupation of Kabul ; Istalif (*Lond. Gaz.* 7 June, 8 and 24 Nov. 1842, 7 Feb. 1843) (Medal). Transfd. to 39th N.I. 27 Mar. 1844 ; to 62nd N.I. ; to 52nd N.I. 10 Oct. 1844. Posted Col. to 52nd N.I. 1845 ; to 10th N.I. 1846 ; to 51st N.I. 5 June 1853 till death.

Bdr. 2 cl. comdg. Mhow 5 Jan. 1847 till 1850. Fur. 3 Mar. 1850 till death. C.B. 24 Dec. 1842.

Refs.: Boase. *G.M.* 1862, i. 657. *The Times,* 18 Apr. 1862.

TULLOCH, John Samuel Drury (1815-1899). General. 28th Punjab N.I. *b.* Batavia 22 July 1815. Cadet 1832. Arrived in India 19 Apr. 1833. Ensign 14 June 1832. Lieut. 9 July 1840. Capt. 15 Nov. 1853. Major 18 Feb. 1861. Lt. Col. 18 Feb. 1863. Col. 18 Feb. 1866. Maj. Gen. 1 Oct. 1877. Lt. Gen. 1 July 1881. Gen. 22 Jan. 1889. *d.* in England 25 Feb. 1899.

Son of John Tulloch, *q.v.*, and Jacobina Maria his wife. Brother of Stamford William Raffles Tulloch, *q.v. m.* Meerut 5 Apr. 1841, Catherine, sister of J. C. Murphy. Addiscombe Cadet 20 Aug. 1830 till 6 Nov. 1832.

Services: Cadet d.d. 55th N.I. 18 May 1833; d.d. 43rd N.I. 5 Sept. 1833; posted Ensign to 17th N.I. 11 Feb. 1834. Actg. Intr. & Qmr. 62nd N.I. 4 Jan. 1836; do. 4th L.C. 21 Aug. 1839. Adjt. 17th N.I. 8 Nov. 1841 till 5 Oct. 1853. Second Sikh War; Bt. Capt. 17th N.I., with Army of Reserve at Jagraon. Transfd. to Staff Corps 18 Feb. 1861. Comdt. 28th Punjab N.I. (now 4th Bn. 15th Punjab Regt.) 8 Feb. 1868 till Feb. 1873. Fur. p.a. 23 Mar. 1873 till death. Transfd. to *u.s.l.* 1 July 1881. No record of active service.

TULLOCH, Stamford William Raffles (1813-1845). Lieutenant, 22nd N.I. *b.* Batavia 31 May 1813. Cadet 1831. Arrived in India 22 Dec. 1832. Ensign 7 Nov. 1832. Lieut. 21 Sept. 1837. *d.* Barrackpore 29 July 1845, of wounds received in a duel on 26 July.[1]

Son of John Tulloch, *q.v.*, and Jacobina Maria his wife. Brother of John Samuel Drury Tulloch, *q.v.* Addiscombe Cadet 6 Aug. 1830 till 14 Dec. 1832.

Services: Cadet d.d. 43rd N.I. 8 Jan. 1833; d.d. 38th N.I. 31 Jan. 1834; posted Ensign to 23rd N.I. 11 Feb. 1834; to 22nd N.I. 28 June 1834. Shekhawat expedn. 1834; Ensign 22nd N.I. Fur. s.c. 5 Mar. 1842 till 1844.

Refs.: I.M. 25 Sept. 1845, p. 546; 4 Nov. 1845, pp. 642-7. M.I. at Barrackpore.

[1] *Note:* Charles Nelson, of the P. & O. Co., the other principal, and the two seconds were all tried before the Supreme Court in Calcutta 19 Aug. 1845 on a charge of wilful murder. All were acquitted.

THE BENGAL ARMY, 1758-1834 321

TULLOH, Robert (1763/64-1802). Bt. Captain, Artillery. (252) *b.* 1763/64. Cadet 1783. Admitted 29 Sept. 1783. Fireworker 11 Feb. 1785. Lieut. 7 Sept. 1791. Bt. Capt. 8 Jan. 1798. *d.* Calcutta 6 May 1802, aged 38.

(*Probably* son of Robert Tulloh, of Bogton, Forres.)

Services: Apptd. Cadet 7 Jan. 1783; sailed for India in the *Stormont* 11 Mar. 1783. Lieut. F. 1st Bn. Art. in July 1787. Third Mysore War; Bangalore; Lieut. 5th Coy. 1st Bn. Fur. 6 June 1797 till 9 Feb. 1802.

Refs.: M.I. S. Park St. cemetery, Calcutta.

TURNBULL, Frederick Robert (1785-1805). Lieutenant, 8th N.I. *b.* 13 Nov. 1785. Cadet 1800. Arrived in India 24 Aug. 1801. Ensign 9 Oct. 1801. Lieut. 30 Sept. 1803. *d.* Rampura 24 Oct. 1805.

bapt. Monghyr 5 Apr. 1787. Son of Peter Turnbull, Surg. Bengal Est., and Elizabeth Wallace his wife. His half-sister *m.* John William Taylor (1782-1824), *q.v.*

Services: Ensign d.d. 5th N.I. in 1802; posted Ensign to 8th N.I. Operations in Jumna Doab 1803; Sasni; Bijaigarh; Ensign 1/8th N.I. Second Mahratta War 1804-5; capture of Deig; Bhurtpore (w. in 1st assault 9 Jan. 1805); Lieut. 1/8th N.I.

TURNBULL, James (1755-1787). Lieutenant, Infantry. *b.* in Scotland 1755. Cadet 1781. Arrived in India 28 May 1782. Ensign 14 July 1781. Lieut. 13 Oct. 1782. *d.* Barrackpore 2 Mar. 1787.

m. Calcutta 24 June 1784, Miss Anne Porterfield.

Services: Apptd. Cadet 29 Dec. 1780, aged 25; sailed for India in the *Hinchinbrooke* 13 Mar. 1781, aged 25. Was on fur. in Mar. 1786.

TURNBULL, Robert Harvey (1807-1833). Lieutenant, 24th N.I. *bapt.* St. Nicholas, Worcester, 18 Oct. 1807. Cadet 1823. Arrived in India 19 May 1824. Ensign 16 Jan. 1824. Lieut. 25 Feb. 1825. *d.* Bandi 2 Jan. 1833, from an arrow wound received the previous day in action against the Chuars.[1]

Son of William Turnbull, of St. James's Pl., London, mariner, and Eliza his wife. Ed. in Paris.

Services: Posted Ensign to 24th N.I. in 1824, and served throughout with that Regt. Actg. Adjt. 10 July 1828; permanent do. 14 Jan. 1830 till death. Operations against the Chuars 1832-3 (kld.); Lieut. 24th N.I., with the Jungle Mehals F.F.

Refs.: G.M. 1833, ii. 93. M.I. in St. John's, Calcutta.

[1] *Note:* (? *d.* in camp, Chulleana, Jungle Mehals.)

TURNER, Augustus (1816-1897). General. 4th Bengal Eur. Inf. b. Liverpool 29 June 1816. Cadet 1834. Arrived in India 10 Feb. 1835. Ensign 13 June 1834. Lieut. 28 June 1837. Capt. 14 Nov. 1849. Major 18 Feb. 1861. Lt. Col. 18 Feb. 1863. Col. 18 Feb. 1866. Maj. Gen. 1 Oct. 1877. Lt. Gen. 1 July 1881. Gen. 22 Jan. 1889. d. St. Brannocks, Eastbourne, 19 June 1897.

bapt. St. George's, Liverpool, 16 Aug. 1816. 6th son of Charles Turner, Official Assignee, Bankruptcy Court, and Maria his wife, dau. of Samuel B. Athill, of Antigua. Nephew of Thomas Turner, M.D., Phys. Extraord. to William IV. m. 1st, 11 May 1841, Matilda, dau. of Rev. Richard Pain, rector of Wigborough, Essex. (She died Barrackpore 20 Sept. 1843, aged 24.) m. 2nd, Jullundur 8 Aug. 1850, Helen Marion Jessie, dau. of James Remington, q.v. m. 3rd, Rawal Pindi 18 Nov. 1852, Ellen, dau. of Rev. Richard Pain. Addiscombe Cadet 3 Aug. 1832 till 13 June 1834.

Services : Posted to 1st N.I. 2 Mar. 1835. Fur. s.c. 9 Apr. 1838 till 24 Oct. 1841, and 10 Jan. 1845 till 1847. Second Sikh War ; no actions ; Bt. Capt. 1st N.I. (Medal). D.J.A.G. Peshawar Div. 7 Jan. 1853 ; do. Dinapore Div. 1856 till 1863 ; do. Benares Div. 1863-4. Posted to newly-raised 4th Bengal Eur. Inf. 1858. Offg. Civil Engr., N.W.P., 1867-8. Transfd. to u.s.l. 1881.

Refs. : Oliver's Hist. of Antigua, iii. 164. Boase. The Times, 23 June 1897, p. 14.

TURNER, Charles Exuperius [1] (1786-1825). Captain, 24th N.I. b. London 10 Apr. 1786. Cadet 1805. Arrived in India 11 July 1806. Ensign 17 Aug. 1806. Lieut. 22 July 1807. Capt. 3 Jan. 1820. d. Delhi 25 Feb. 1825.

bapt. Marylebone 31 Aug. 1788. Son of Exuperius Turner and Susannah his wife. Half-brother of Exuperius Robert Turner, q.v.

Services : Barasat C.C. Posted Lieut. to 8th N.I. 1807. Capture of Mauritius 1810 ; Lieut. 2nd Vol. Bn. Nepal War 1814-15 ; Lieut. 1/8th N.I., in 4th Div. Nepal War 1816 ; Lieut. 1/8th N.I., in 2nd Bde. Left Column. Third Mahratta War 1818-19 ; Lieut.1/8th N.I. Capt. 1/8th N.I. Transfd. to 24th N.I. (late 2/8th) May 1824.

[1] Note : His 2nd name is sometimes given as Experius or Exuperious. Other variants of this name—not found in I.O. records—are, Euxperius and Exsuperius. (Cf. N. & Q. cli. 225.) A Bill to dissolve the marriage of Exuperius Turner and Elizabeth Louisa Minshull was passed 33 Geo. II.

TURNER, Charles Walshingham (1790-1821). Lieutenant, 28th N.I. bapt. St. Mary's, Truro, 2 Sept. 1790. Cadet 1808.

Arrived in India 27 Oct. 1809. Ensign 25 Aug. 1810. Lieut. 16 Dec. 1814. *d.* Vizagapatam, Madras, 5 May 1821.

Son of Edmund Turner and Joanna his wife, dau. of William Ferris.

Services: Barasat C.C. Posted to 7th N.I. 1810; mily. student at Coll. of Ft. Wm. 1814. Nepal War 1814-15; Kalanga; Lieut. 1/7th N.I., in 2nd Div. Transfd. to newly-raised 1/28th N.I. 1815; apptd. 2nd in comd. 1st Rohilla Cav. 1816. Siege and capture of Hathras 1817; Lieut. 1st Rohilla Cav. Transfd. as 2nd in comd. to 2nd Rohilla Cav. 5 May 1817 till disbanded 10 Mar. 1820. Third Mahratta War 1817-18; Lieut. 2nd Rohilla Cav., with Left Div. under Maj.-Gen. Dyson Marshall, *q.v.*

TURNER, Exuperius Robert (1789-1820). Lieutenant, 28th N.I. *b.* London 4 Oct. 1789. Cadet 1806. Arrived in India 25 Nov. 1807. Ensign 11 Oct. 1807. Lieut. 13 Aug. 1810. *d.* Nomillah (?), nr. Agra, 2 Sept. 1820.

bapt. St. James's, Westminster, 11 Jan. 1790. Son of Exuperius Turner and Harriott his wife. Half-brother of Charles Exuperius Turner, *q.v.*

Services: Barasat C.C. Posted Ensign to 12th N.I. 1808. Capture of Mauritius 1810; Lieut. 1st Vol. Bn. Transfd. to newly-raised 28th N.I. 1815. Third Mahratta War 1818; Madhurajpura; Lieut. 1/28th N.I.

TURNER, Sir Frank (1813-1890). General, K.C.B., Artillery. (639) Col. Comdt. R.A. *b.* London 29 Jan. 1813. Cadet 1829. Arrived in India 8 Mar. 1831. 2nd Lieut. 11 June 1830. Lieut. 11 Mar. 1839. Capt. 7 Jan. 1848. Bt. Major 22 Aug. 1855. Lt. Col. 11 Oct. 1858. Col. 10 Mar. 1863. Col. Comdt. 14 Jan. 1882. Maj. Gen. 18 Jan. 1867. Lt. Gen. 4 May 1877. Gen. 1 Oct. 1877. *d.* 12 Cromwell Houses, Southsea, 19 Dec. 1890.

Younger son of Michael Turner, of Fleet St., London, merchant, and Mary Elizabeth Fülling his wife. *m.* 1st, Dinapore 19 Aug. 1845, Mary Jane, 5th dau. of James Gibbon, indigo planter. (*See also* William Nisbett.) (She died 25 Jan. 1862, aged 36.) *m.* 2nd, Calcutta 13 Apr. 1864, Marianne Thérèse, dau. of Richard Leyburn Burne. (She died 1869.) Addiscombe Cadet 1828-30.

Services: Actg. 2nd Lieut. 25 Mar. 1833; d.d. 2nd Bde. H.A. 20 June 1833; posted to 2nd Troop 2nd Bde. 8 Nov. 1834. To comd. 2nd Troop Shah Shuja's H.A. 23 Sept. 1838. First Afghan War 1838-42; Ghazni (Medal); operations at Kandahar; Baba-Wali 25 Mar. 1842 (*Lond. Gaz.* 4 Sept. 1842); Goaine (*ib.* 4 Dec.

1842); Lieut. comdg. Shah's 2nd Troop (Medal). Adjt. Nimach Div. Art. 21 Jan. 1843; Bde. Major Gwalior Contingent 26 Jan. 1844; Comdt. 1st Coy. Art., Gwalior Contingent, 31 Mar. 1845 till 18 Feb. 1848. Mutiny campaign 1857-8; Delhi; relief and capture of Lucknow; operations in Oudh; Bt. Major 3rd Troop 3rd Bde. H.A. (Medal with clasps). Agent for gun carriages at Fatehgarh 18 Jan. 1858; I.G. Ord. and Magazines 8 Mar. 1864 till 1874. Placed on Retired List 1 Jan. 1881. C.B. 24 Mar. 1858; K.C.B. 29 May 1886. Good Service Pension 11 Jan. 1865.

Refs.: Boase. *D.I.B. The Times*, 23 Dec. 1890, p. 4.

TURNER, George (1806-1863). Major. 38th N.I. *b.* Kidderminster 3 May 1806. Cadet 1823. Arrived in India 6 Oct. 1824. Ensign 16 Apr. 1824. Lieut. 22 Apr. 1827. Capt. 18 Feb. 1840. Invalided 10 Oct. 1846. Retired 30 Mar. 1852. Hon. Major 28 Nov. 1854. *d.* Eastbourne 22 Dec. 1863.

bapt. Kidderminster 16 May 1806. 6th son of Jacob Turner, of Park Hall, nr. Kidderminster, and Ann his wife, only dau. of Alderman Thomas Farley, of Henwick, nr. Worcester. Cousingerman of William Johnson Farley, *q.v.*

Services: Posted Ensign to 38th N.I. 1824; d.d. 23rd N.I. 12 Dec. 1825. Siege and capture of Bhurtpore; Ensign 38th N.I., d.d. 23rd N.I. (India medal). Actg. Adjt. 38th N.I. 24 Apr. 1828. Fur. s.c. 15 Mar. 1836 till 17 Apr. 1839.[1] First Afghan War 1841; returned sick from Kandahar to Ferozepore 1841; Capt. 38th N.I. Leave s.c. to Cape and N.S.W. 17 Mar. 1844 till 1846. Fur. s.c. Jan. 1850 till retirement.

Refs.: Burke's *Landed Gentry*, 5th edn., p. 1421, *s.n.* Turner-Farley, of Marnhull, co. Dorset. *A.J.* N.S. xix. 93, 168. *G.M.* 1864, i. 264. *The Times*, 25 Dec. 1863.

[1] *Note*: His skull was fractured by a rock falling on him whilst shooting nr. Mussoorie. *G.M.* (1836, i. 445) reported that he had "died lately whilst shooting at Landeur, nr. Calcutta [*sic*]. He was killed by a monkey throwing a large stone at him, and striking him on the temple."

TURNER, James William Hickey (1799-1854). Captain. 59th N.I. *b.* Calcutta 30 Nov. 1799. Cadet 1816. Admitted 9 Sept. 1817. Ensign (?) Lieut. 1 Aug. 1818. Capt. 10 June 1826. Invalided 4 Feb. 1833. Retired 2 Mar. 1852. *d.* Clifton, Bristol, 15 Apr. 1854.

bapt. Calcutta 24 May 1800. Son of Benjamin Turner, atty. of the Supreme Court in Calcutta (sometime partner with William

THE BENGAL ARMY, 1758-1834

Hickey, the diarist), and Finella his wife, née Davidson. Brother of Peregrine Powell Turner, q.v., and of the wife of Francis Roberts Evans, q.v. Addiscombe Cadet 1816-17.

Services : Ensign d.d. 2/20th N.I. 1817 ; posted Lieut. to 2/30th N.I. 1818 ; transfd. to 59th N.I. (late 1/30th) May 1824. Leave s.c. to Singapore 14 May 1823 ; fur. s.c. 5 Nov. 1823 till 25 Nov. 1825, and 22 Mar. 1829 till 17 Nov. 1832. Apptd. to charge of *sudder* bazar at Barrackpore 12 Aug. 1835. Fur. 1849 till retirement. No record of active service.

Refs. : Will dated 8 Jan. 1849 ; admon. 18 Jan. 1858. M.I. in Clifton churchyard.

TURNER, John (1813-1853). Captain, 51st N.I. *b.* London 30 Mar. 1813. Cadet 1832. Arrived in India 7 Feb. 1833. Ensign 7 Nov. 1832. Lieut. 3 Oct. 1840. Capt. 14 June 1847. *d.* Calcutta 20 Jan. 1853.

bapt. Christ Church-in-Surrey, Blackfriars Rd., 8 June 1813. Son of Thomas Turner, of Nelson Sq., London, stationer, afterwards consul at Ragusa, and Mary his wife. *m.* Calcutta 11 Feb. 1841, Pamela, 5th dau. of Peter Jeremie, q.v. (*See also* Henry Walter Bellew.) Addiscombe Cadet 6 Aug. 1830 till 14 June 1832.

Services : Cadet d.d. 2nd N.I. 23 Feb. 1833 ; posted Ensign to 51st N.I. 11 Feb. 1834 ; to 2nd N.I. 24 Sept. 1835 ; to 51st N.I. 28 June 1836. (? Shekhawat expedn. 1834 ; Ensign 51st N.I.) Actg. Adjt. 51st N.I. 19 Sept. 1840 and 9 Apr. 1842 ; Adjt. 2nd Inf. Levy 21 June till 8 Oct. 1842 ; actg. Adjt. 51st N.I. 14 Dec. 1843 ; permanent do. 1 May 1844 till 28 Feb. 1845. Gwalior campaign ; Paniar ; Lieut. 51st N.I. (Bronze star). Intr. & Qmr. G.G.B.G. 22 July 1846 till Mar. 1847. S.A.C.G. 3 Mar. 1847 ; D.A.C.G. 2 cl. 8 Dec. 1850 ; 1 cl. 19 Jan. 1853. Second Sikh War ; Gujerat ; Capt. 51st N.I., S.A.C.G. (Medal with clasp).

Refs. : *V.B.G.* M.I. Lower Circular Rd. cemetery, Calcutta.

TURNER, Peregrine Powell (1806-1848). Captain. 61st N.I. *b.* Calcutta 9 Apr. 1806. Cadet 1821. Arrived in India 12 Jan. 1823. Ensign 7 Feb. 1823. Lieut. 13 May 1825. Capt. 13 Oct. 1834. Retired in India 25 Jan. 1843. *d.* Saharanpur, U.P., 10 Jan. 1848.

bapt. Calcutta 23 Feb. 1807. Son of Benjamin Turner, atty., and Finella his wife. Brother of James William Hickey Turner, q.v., and of Amelia Darby, of Breutry Lodge, nr. Bristol. *m.* 1st, Hansi 28 Apr. 1841, Louisa, 2nd dau. of Col. James Skinner, C.B. (see Appendix A). (*See also* Radclyffe Haldane.) (She died Delhi

31 Jan. 1844, aged 22.) m. 2nd, Mussoorie 15 June 1846, Jane Mary, dau. of Christopher Dixon Wilkinson, q.v.
Services: Posted to 31st N.I. 1823; transfd. to 61st N.I. (late 1/31st) May 1824; actg. Intr. & Qmr. do. 17 May 1826; offg. S.S.O. at Akyab 6 July 1826. Actg. Intr. & Qmr. 61st N.I. 27 June 1827; permanent do. 27 Aug. 1828 till July 1833; Adjt. do. 16 July 1833 till 8 Nov. 1834. Shekhawat expedn. 1834; Capt. 61st N.I. 2nd in comd. Ramgarh L.I. 25 Nov. till 10 Dec. 1836; do. Hariana L.I. Bn. 22 July 1839 till 10 Dec. 1842.
Refs.: Will dated 9 Jan. 1848; proved 21 Mar. 1848.

TURNER, Richard (d. 1767). Lieutenant, Infantry. Cadet (?) Ensign 22 Nov. 1765. Lieut. 28 May 1767. d. 1767.
Services: N.F.P.

TURNER, Samuel (1759/60-1802). Captain, 10th N.I. b. 1759/60. Cadet 1780. Arrived in India Feb. 1781. Ensign 1780. Lieut. 8 Aug. 1781. Capt. 18 Mar. 1799. d. London 2 Jan. 1802, of a paralytic stroke, aged 42.

Son of John Turner and Anne his wife, dau. of Thomas Warren, of Stubhill, yeoman. His sister m. Rev. Dr. Joseph White, the orientalist (D.N.B.). Cousin-german of Warren Hastings.
Services: See D.N.B. Apptd. Cadet 10 Apr. 1780; sailed for India in the Bellmont Apr. 1780, aged 22. Apptd. A.D.C. to Warren Hastings 27 Mar. 1781, having joined him at Bankipore earlier in the month. Applied unsuccessfully for transfer to B.C.S. May 1781. Was with the G.G. at Benares on the outbreak of Rajah Cheyt Singh's rebellion and accompanied him on his flight to Chunar on the night of 21/22 Aug. 1781. Comdt. G.G.B.G. 1782 till Feb. 1797. Sent by Hastings on a special embassy to Tibet 9 Jan. 1783 till Mar. 1784. Third Mysore War 1790-2; Seringapatam; Lieut. comdg. G.G.B.G. Deputed as ambassador to Mysore. Fur. 28 Feb. 1797 till death. Bt. Capt. 3rd Bengal Eur. Regt. in 1798; transfd. as Capt. Lt. to 10th N.I. 1798. Pub. "An Account of an Embassy to the Court of the Teshoo Lama in Tibet," London, 1800. D.C.L., Oxon., 7 July 1800. F.R.S. 15 Jan. 1801.
Refs.: D.N.B. Grier. V.B.G. D.I.B. G.M. 1802, i. 87. M.I. St. James's church, Piccadilly.

TURNER, Thomas Joseph (1786-1866). Captain. 11th N.I. b. Gt. Yarmouth 23 May 1786. Cadet 1800. Arrived in India 6 Feb. 1802. Ensign 23 Sept. 1801. Lieut. 30 Sept. 1803. Capt. 5 Aug. 1816. Retired 30 Mar. 1819. d. Little Olivers, Colchester, 26 Aug. 1866.

THE BENGAL ARMY, 1758-1834

Of Little Olivers, J.P. and D.L. Essex, alderman and mayor of Colchester 1840-1. *bapt.* Gt. Yarmouth 5 June 1786. 3rd son of Rev. Richard Turner, vicar of Gt. Yarmouth, and Elizabeth his 2nd wife, elder dau. of Thomas Rede, of Beccles, Suffolk. *m.* 13 Apr. 1820, Jane, dau. of John Bawtree, of Colchester. (She died 23 Aug. 1872.)

Services: Posted Ensign to 11th N.I. 1802. Second Mahratta War 1803-5; Bundelkhand 1803; Kapsa; Kalpi; Gwalior 1804; Lieut. 2/11th N.I. Adjt. 2/11th N.I. 28 Sept. 1804 till 22 Apr. 1811. Operations against the Rana of Gohad 1806; capture of Gohad. Adjt. & Qmr. 11th N.I. 22 Apr. 1811 till 1 July 1814. Reduction of Kalinjar 1812. Intr. & Qmr. 2/11th N.I. 1 July 1814 till 20 Nov. 1815. Fur. 1816 till retirement.

Refs.: Burke's *Family Records*, p. 606, *s.n.* Turner. *G.M.* 1866, ii. 557.

TURNER, Valpy Francis Thomas (1808-1898). Major. 1st L.C. *b.* London 27 Mar. 1808. Cadet 1826. Arrived in India 29 Oct. 1827. Cornet 26 Feb. 1828. Lieut. 12 Nov. 1838. Capt. 3 June 1842. Retired 20 Feb. 1853. Hon. Major 28 Nov. 1854. *d.* at his residence, 10 Park Cresc., Brighton, 14 Oct. 1898.

bapt. St. George the Martyr, Middlesex, 25 June 1808. Son of Rev. John Turner, D.D., of Chiswick, and Elizabeth his wife, *née* Cort. Peterhouse Coll., Cambs.; Pensioner 9 Oct. 1825.

Services: Cornet d.d. 6th L.C. 15 Jan. 1828; posted to 1st L.C. 25 Nov. 1828. Fur. s.c. 26 July 1828 till 11 Jan. 1831, and 28 Mar. 1837 till 22 Nov. 1839. First Afghan War 1842; reoccupation of Kabul; Bt. Capt. 1st L.C., with Pollock's force (Medal). First Sikh War; Aliwal; Bt. Capt. 1st L.C. (Medal).

Refs.: *The Times*, 19 Oct. 1898.

TURNER, William (*d.* 1763). Captain, Infantry. Vol. 1757. Ensign 4 June 1757. Lieut. 1 July 1758. Capt. 18 Sept. 1761. *d.* Monghyr 1763, of a flux, whilst a prisoner of the Nabob.

Son of —— Turner and Sarah his wife. Brother of John Turner.

Services: Siege of Chandernagore 14 Mar. 1757 (w.); Vol. under Clive.

Refs.: *Orme MSS.*, vol. xxi, Bengal, p. 129. Will dated 9 June 1758; proved 21 Feb. 1764.

TURNER, William (1778-1806). Lieutenant, 4th N.I. *bapt.* St. Margaret's chapel, Durham, 19 May 1778. Cadet 1798. Admitted 9 Jan. 1800. Ensign 2 Jan. 1800. Lieut. 29 May 1800. *d.* Agra 6 June 1806.

Son of Charles Turner and Hannah his wife.
Services: Lieut. Northants Mil. 28 Mar. 1799. Posted Lieut. to 2/4th N.I. 15 Apr. 1801. Second Mahratta War 1803-4; Aligarh; defence of Delhi; Lieut. 2/4th N.I.
Refs.: M.I. Agra Cantt. cemetery.

TURNER, William (1784-?). Lieutenant. 15th N.I. *b.* Warrington, Lancs., 26 Mar. 1784. Cadet 1803. Arrived in India 17 Mar. 1805. Ensign 27 Mar. 1805. Lieut. 28 Mar. 1805. Struck off in England 30 June 1809.

bapt. Trinity church, Warrington, 7 May 1784. Son of William Turner, solicitor at Warrington, and Mary his wife. Ed. Rugby; admitted Jan. 1798.
Services: Posted Lieut. to 15th N.I. Fur. 22 Jan. 1807 till struck off. No record of active service.
Refs.: Rugby School Register.

TURNER, William (1791-1871). Lieut. Colonel. 54th N.I. *b.* London 11 Feb. 1791. Cadet 1807. Arrived in India 16 Nov. 1808. Ensign 3 Dec. 1808. Lieut. 16 Dec. 1814. Capt. 1 May 1824. Major 24 Feb. 1835. Retired 26 Jan. 1837. Hon. Lt. Col. 28 Nov. 1854. *d.* Wimbledon 2 Feb. 1871.

bapt. St. Mary's, Lambeth, 30 Sept. 1792. Son of George Mathias Turner and Frances his wife. *m.* Bareilly 24 Jan. 1816, Annette, natural dau. of Richard Mabert, *q.v.* (She died 13 Aug. 1871, aged 72.)
Services: Barasat C.C. 8 mos. Posted Ensign to 27th N.I. 1809. Nepal War 1814-15; Lieut. 27th N.I. (India medal). Adjt. 2/27th N.I. 5 May 1815 till 17 Aug. 1819. Fur. s.c. 19 June 1818 till 23 June 1821. Fort Adjt. at Delhi 31 Dec. 1821; do. Agra 21 June 1823 till Apr. 1829. Transfd. to 54th N.I. (late 2/27th) May 1824. Bde. Major Agra 10 Apr. 1829; D.A.A.G. Saugor Div. 14 May 1830; 2nd A.A.G. of the Army 16 Feb. 1831.; Dy. Paymr. at Muttra 18 Feb. 1832. Leave s.c. to Cape 5 Jan. till 19 Nov. 1833. Offg. Agent for family money and Paymr. of Native Pensioners at Barrackpore 8 Feb. 1834; permanent do. 11 Feb. till 5 June 1835. Fur. s.c. 25 Nov. 1835 till retirement. Apptd. agent in England for Bengal Mily. Orphans Soc. 21 Oct. 1836; removed from the appt. Mar. 1839; reapptd. Jan. 1841 till 1856, when he was succeeded by Lt.-Col. H. B. Henderson, *q.v.* Retired on a pension of 16/- *p.d.*
Refs.: The Times, 3 Feb. 1871.

TURNER, William (1791-1827). Bt. Captain, 58th N.I. *bapt.* Westmeston, Sussex, 30 Dec. 1791. Cadet 1808. Arrived in

THE BENGAL ARMY, 1758-1834 329

India 15 Dec. 1809. Ensign 13 Aug. 1811. Lieut. 15 Apr. 1815.
Bt. Capt. 13 Aug. 1826. *d.* Agra 8 June 1827, of apoplexy.

Son of Rev. Richard Turner, of Hartfield, Sussex, and Jane his wife. *m.* Muttra 7 Apr. 1817, Frances, eldest dau. of Sir Thomas Brown, *q.v.* (*See also* James Franklin.) (She died Calcutta 5 Jan. 1853, aged 62.) His dau. *m.* James Don Kennedy, *q.v.*
Services: Barasat C.C. Posted to 11th N.I. 1811. Reduction of Kalinjar 1812; Ensign 11th N.I. Transfd. to newly-raised 1/29th N.I. 1815. Siege and capture of Hathras 1817; Lieut. 1/29th N.I. Third Mahratta War 1817-18; Lieut. 1/29th N.I., tempy. A.D.C. to his father-in-law. Transfd. to 58th N.I. (late 2/29th) May 1824. Adjt. Benares Provl. Bn. 1824-5. Siege and capture of Bhurtpore; Lieut. 58th N.I. Intr. & Qmr. 58th N.I. 6 Feb. 1826 till death.
Refs.: A.J. xxiv. 792. *G.M.* 1827, ii. 647. Will dated Benares 30 July 1825; proved 11 Aug. 1828. M.I. at Agra.

TURNER, William Donaldson (1784-1813). Capt. Lieutenant, 15th N.I. *b.* Menie, Belhelvie, co. Aberdeen, 26 Feb. 1784. Cadet 1800. Arrived in India 23 Aug. 1801. Ensign 3 Jan. 1802. Lieut. 2 Nov. 1803. Capt. Lt. 19 Feb. 1812. *d.* Mirzapur, U.P., 24 June 1813.

5th son of Robert Turner, of Menie, and Euphemia his wife, dau. of David Simpson, of Hazelhead. Younger brother of Sir George Turner, K.C.B., Gen. R.A. Ed. Aberdeen Grammar School 1795-8.
Services: Ensign d.d. 4th N.I. in 1802. Operations in Jumna Doab 1803; Sasni; Bijaigarh; Kachaura; Ensign 1/15th N.I. Second Mahratta War 1803-5; battle of Delhi; Agra; Laswari; battle of Deig (w.); Bhurtpore (w. in 3rd assault 20 Feb. 1805); Lieut. 1/15th N.I. Adjt. 1/15th N.I. 26 Aug. 1804 till 29 June 1813. Capture of Mauritius 1810-11; Lieut. & Qmr. 1st Vol. Bn.
Refs.: Burke's *Landed Gentry,* 5th edn., p. 1421, *s.n.* Turner, of Menie, Aberdeen. Temple's *Thanage of Fermartyn,* p. 640. M.I. at Mirzapur.

TURNOUR, Hon. George (1768-1813). Ensign. Infantry. Subsequently H.M. Ceylon C.S. *b.* Shillinglee Park, Sussex, 4 Feb. 1768. Cadet 1783. Arrived in India 22 Oct. 1783. Ensign 9 Feb. 1785. Transfd. to H.M.S. 1789. *d.* Ceylon 19 Apr. 1813.

3rd son of Edward Turnour Garth, 1st Earl Winterton (who assumed the surname and arms of Turnour 1744), and Anne his 1st wife, dau. of Thomas, Lord Archer. *m.* (before 1803) Marie Emilie de Beausset, niece of the Cardinal Duc de Beausset. (She died Pondicherry 20 Aug. 1846, aged 68.) Ed. Harrow; in School list for 1776.

Services: Apptd. Cadet 29 Nov. 1782; sailed for India in the *Atlas* 11 Mar. 1783. Ensign H.M. 76th Ft. 3 Nov. 1788; Lieut. 73rd Ft. (23 Feb. 1789) 6 Oct. 1789; Qmr. do. 5 Nov. 1793 (? till 25 Aug. 1798). Lieut. 19th Ft. 29 Aug. 1796. Fort Adjt. at Jaffna, Ceylon, in 1795; Comdt. of Manaar 1797-1800. Retired 18 Nov. 1801. Was at one time a tobacco merchant at Jaffna. Apptd. to Ceylon C.S. 1807; "Collector of the Wanny" till Jan. 1813.

Refs.: Burke's *Peerage*, 1923, p. 2349, *s.n.* Winterton, E. *Officers of the Green Howards*, by Major M. L. Ferrar. *N. & Q.* 9S. xi. 373. *G.M.* 1813, ii. 699. M.I. in Jaffna church.

TURTON, John (*d.* 1790). Lieutenant, 5th Bengal Eur. Bn. Cadet 1781. Ensign 1 Sept. 1781. Lieut. 15 June 1783. *d.* Barrackpore 31 May 1790.

Services: Apptd. a Vol. by Sir Eyre Coote 6 Mar. 1781, and served as such with the Bengal detachment during Second Mysore War. Lieut. 5th Bengal Eur. Bn. in July 1787; transfd. to 6th Eur. Bn.; to 5th do. 5 Feb. 1790.

TURTON, John (1780-1803). Lieutenant, 4th N.I. *b.* Sugnall, Staffs., 28 Oct. 1780. Cadet 1798. Arrived in India 14 Apr. 1800. Ensign 12 Dec. 1799. Lieut. 29 May 1800. *d. unm.* 4 Sept. 1803: kld. in action at the storm of Aligarh.

bapt. Eccleshall, Staffs., 28 June 1781. Eldest son of John Turton, of Sugnall, nr. Eccleshall, and of the Inner Temple, and Mary his wife, dau. and co-heir of Rev. Thomas Meysey, Fellow of Wadham Coll., Oxon. Brother of William, the father of John Turton (1809-1868), *q.v.*, and of Marianne, wife of Sir Thomas Plumer, Master of the Rolls (*D.N.B.*). Ed. Charterhouse; Scholar 22 Jan. 1793; Exhibitioner 19 Apr. 1798. Univ. Coll., Oxon.; matric. 31 May 1797.

Services: Posted Lieut. to 2/4th N.I. 15 Apr. 1801. Second Mahratta War 1803; Aligarh (kld.); Lieut. 1/4th N.I.

Refs.: *Pedigree of Turton*, by F. A. Homer and C. S. James, privately printed 1924. *Alumni Carthusiani*. *Alumni Oxon*. M.I. at Aligarh.

TURTON, John (1809-1868). Major. 3rd N.I. *bapt.* Kidderminster 11 June 1809. Cadet 1826. Arrived in India 2 June 1827. Ensign 3 Feb. 1827. Lieut. 25 Aug. 1836. Capt. 19 Apr.

1842. Retired 20 Sept. 1853. Hon. Major 28 Nov. 1854. d. Guernsey 8 Sept. 1868.

Son of William Turton, of Sheen House, Mortlake, and of the Middle Temple, one of the Six Clerks of the King's High Court of Chancery, and Penelope his wife, dau. of —— Parsons, of Bewdley. Nephew of John Turton (1780-1803), q.v. m. Berhampore 7 Nov. 1840, Jane, eldest dau. of James Robson, of Berhampore. (She died Richmond, Surrey, 16 May 1885, aged 64.)

Services: Posted Ensign to 3rd N.I. 19 June 1827. Shekhawat expedn. 1834; Ensign 3rd N.I. Fur. p.a. 8 Mar. 1838 till 2 Aug. 1839. Served with 2nd Vol. Regt. for China 11 Feb. 1842 till 1 Mar. 1843. First China War 1842; Capt. 2nd Vol. Regt. (Medal). Second Sikh War; Jullundur Doab 1848-9; heights of Dalla; Capt. 3rd N.I., with Bdr. Wheeler's force (Medal). Fur. s.c. 20 Mar. 1851 till retirement.

Refs.: Pedigree of Turton. I.M. 7 Mar. 1844, pp. 108-9. *The Times,* 17 Sept. 1868.

TURTON, Joseph (1803-1858). Bt. Colonel, Artillery. (510) b. Chepstow 2 Sept. 1803. Cadet 1820. Arrived in India 11 Feb. 1822. 2nd Lieut. 16 June 1820. Lieut. 1 May 1824. Capt. 16 Oct. 1837. Major 1 Dec. 1847. Lt. Col. 17 May 1854. Bt. Col. 9 Dec. 1856. d. at sea 17 Aug. 1858, on board the *Hindostan* in the Red Sea, on the voyage to England.

bapt. 1 Mar. 1804. 3rd son of Zouch Turton and Mary Ann his wife, only dau. of Stephen Bayley, of Chepstow. Brother of Zouch Henry Turton, q.v., nephew of William Turton, of Swansea, the conchologist (D.N.B.), and distant cousin of John Turton, q.v. m. Simla 20 Aug. 1846, Marie, dau. of Horace Watson. (*See also* Edward Griffith Austin.) (She died London 5 Mar. 1875, aged 51.) Addiscombe Cadet 1818 till 16 June 1820.

Services: Sailed for India in the *Emma* 1 Oct. 1820 and was wrecked in Table Bay 4 Jan. 1821; delayed at the Cape till 12 Sept. 1821. Adjt. & Qmr. Div. Art. at Benares 24 Jan. 1824. First Burma War; Cachar 1824-5; Lieut. Foot Art. Asst. Surveyor under Suptg. Engr. P.W.I. Jan. 1827; Adjt. & Qmr. 5th Bn. 31 Oct. 1827 till 1837. Shekhawat expedn. 1834; actg. Bde. Major Art. Fur. p.a. 1 Dec. 1837 till 25 Oct. 1840. Transfd. from 1st Coy. 2nd Bn. to 1st Troop 2nd Bde. H.A. 16 Jan. 1843. First Sikh War; Badhowal; Aliwal (horse shot under him); Sobraon; Capt. 1st Troop 2nd Bde. (Medal with clasp). Fur. s.c. 10 Feb. 1849 till Nov. 1851. Second Burma War 1852-3; capture of Martaban; capture of Rangoon (w.); comdg. Art. of Gen. Godwin's force; comdd. Bengal Art. throughout operations in Pegu 1852-3 (Medal). Posted Lt. Col. to 5th Bn. June 1854; to 2nd Bn. May 1855; to 2nd Bde. H.A. 25 July 1856. Fur. 1858.

Refs.: Pedigree of Turton. Turton family MSS. *The Times*, 13 Sept. 1858. M.I. in St. Arvan's churchyard.

TURTON, Robert (1760-1817). Lieut. Colonel. Artillery. (195) *b.* Limerick 1760. Country Cadet 1778. Admitted 17 Dec. 1778. Fireworker 28 Dec. 1778. Lieut. 5 Aug. 1784. Capt. 26 Nov. 1795. Major 21 Sept. 1804. Lt. Col. 7 May 1806. Retired 5 Dec. 1809. *d.* Dublin 23 Nov. (? Dec.) 1817.

Son of Francis Turton, atty., and Elizabeth his wife. Brother of Frances Anne, wife of Rev. George William Cotton. *m.* Frances, elder dau. of Edward Rowland Jackson, *q.v.* T.C.D.; Pensioner 4 Nov. 1776, aged 16.

Services: Recruited in Ireland as a gentleman vol., "being a young gentleman of Family and Education"; sailed for India in the *Calcutta* 27 Apr. 1778. Second Mysore War 1781-5; Lt. F. 4th Coy. 2nd Bn., with detachment under Col. T. D. Pearse, *q.v.* Lieut. 3rd Bn. Art. in July 1787; Qmr. 1st Bn. *c.* 1790-4. Fur. 31 Jan. 1796 till 22 Dec. 1798, and 4 Mar. 1800 till 20 Feb. 1804. Operations in Bundelkhand 1805-6. Operations against the Rana of Gohad 1806; capture of Gohad; Capt. 1st Coy. 3rd Bn. Fur. 24 May 1808 till retirement.

Refs.: Burke's *Landed Gentry*, 8th edn., p. 1056, *s.n.* Jackson, of Ahanesk, co. Cork. *Alumni Dub.* M.I. St. Anne's, Dublin (where age is given as 52).

TURTON, Zouch Henry (1799-1835). Captain, 15th N.I. *b.* Chepstow 2 Apr. 1799. Cadet 1817. Arrived in India 30 Jan. 1819. Ensign 6 Aug. 1818. Lieut. 12 Feb. 1820. Capt. 3 May 1832. *d.* Simla 29 Sept. 1835.

bapt. Chepstow 25 July 1799. Eldest son of Zouch Turton and Mary Ann his wife. Brother of Joseph Turton, *q.v. m.* Asirgarh, Khandesh district, 11 Oct. 1823, Anne, dau. of Robert Crump, of Cheltenham, formerly of Calcutta. (*See also* Henry Timings.) (She died Stoke Newington 24 Aug. 1866.)

Services: d.d. Bengal Eur. Regt. Feb. 1819; d.d. 2/4th N.I. Oct. 1819; posted to 1/11th N.I. June 1820; transfd. to 15th N.I. (late 1/11th) May 1824. Siege and capture of Bhurtpore; Lieut. 15th N.I. Actg. Adjt. Left Wing 15th N.I. 11 Oct. 1828 till Feb. 1829. Leave s.c. to Simla 15 Dec. 1833 till death.

Refs.: Pedigree of Turton, Ped. iv. De Rhé-Philipe. A.J. N.S.

xix. 206. M.I. Mall cemetery, Simla; inside Christ Church, Cheltenham; and St. Arvan's churchyard.

TWEEDALE, Alexander (1806-1907). Lieutenant. 4th Extra N.I. Subsequently Capt. 1st Bo. L.C. *b.* 19 June 1806. Cadet 1822. Ensign 11 July 1823. Lieut. 13 May 1825. Resigned in England 16 May 1827. *d.* 81 Duke St., Grosvenor Sq., London, 7 Dec. 1907, aged 101.[1]
bapt. St. Mary's, Lambeth, Surrey, 18 Nov. 1806. Son of James Tweedale, of Brighton, Comdr. E.I.C.N.S. Brother of Farquharson Tweedale, *q.v. m.* Sardinian Ambassador's Chapel, London, 6 Nov. 1858, Maria Katharine, youngest dau. of John Rorke, of Tyrelstown and Upper Temple St., Dublin.
Services: Posted to 3rd N.I. 1824; transfd. to 24th N.I. 31 Mar. 1825; to newly-raised 4th Extra Regt. May 1825. Fur. 1825 till resignation. Bo. Cav. Cadet 1826; Cornet 3 June 1828; Lieut. 2 Nov. 1833; Capt. 6 Mar. 1841; retired 5 Feb. 1849.
Refs.: The Times, 10 Dec. 1907, p. 10 f.
[1] *Note:* The only known centenarian in this *List.*

TWEEDALE, Farquharson (1802-1873). Lieut. Colonel. 8th L.C. *bapt.* St. Mary's, Lambeth, 14 July 1802. Cadet 1819. Admitted 30 Aug. 1820. Cornet 21 Feb. 1820. Lieut. 1 May 1824. Capt. 21 July 1835. Major 21 Nov. 1848. Retired 10 Aug. 1850. Hon. Lt. Col. 28 Nov. 1854. *d.* 18 Feb. 1873.
Son of James Tweedale, of Brighton, Comdr. E.I.C.N.S., and Caroline his wife. Brother of James Charles Tweedale, *q.v.,* and related to George Moore (1789-1848), *q.v.*
Services: Posted Cornet to 8th L.C. and served throughout with that Regt. Actg. Post Adjt. at Lohargaon 3 Aug. 1825. Siege and capture of Bhurtpore; Lieut. 8th L.C. (India medal). Fur. s.c. 16 Dec. 1835 till 31 Dec. 1839. (? Insurrection in Bundelkhand 1842-3; Capt. 8th L.C.) Fur. s.c. 10 Feb. 1848 till retirement.

TWEEDALE, James Charles (1798-1826). Lieutenant, 3rd N.I. *b.* Calcutta 20 Dec. 1798. Cadet 1817. Ensign (?) Lieut. 1 Aug. 1818. *d.* Akyab 8 May 1826.
Son of James Tweedale, of Brighton, Comdr. E.I.C.N.S. Brother of William Hutton Tweedale, *q.v.* R.M.C., Sandhurst.
Services: Ensign H.M. 67th Ft. 21 Feb. 1816; h.p. do. 24 May 1817. Posted Lieut. to 1/6th N.I.; transfd. to 3rd N.I. (late 1/6th) May 1824. First Burma War; Arakan 1825; Lieut. 2nd L.I. Bn. S.A.C.G. in Arakan 1825 till death.

334 LIST OF THE OFFICERS OF

Refs. : Will dated " Uckeeop I., nr. Arakan " (Akyab), 7 Feb. 1826 ; proved 25 Oct. 1826.

TWEEDALE, William Hutton (1804-1882). Captain, Invalid Est. 8th L.C. *bapt.* St. Mary's, Lambeth, 8 Mar. 1804.[1] Cadet 1825. Arrived in India 24 June 1826. Cornet (5 Feb. 1826) 20 Dec. 1826. Lieut. 5 Oct. 1836. Capt. 1849. Invalided 1 Sept. 1849. *d.* Dehra Dun, U.P., 12 Dec. 1882. Son of James Tweedale, of Brighton, Comdr. E.I.C.N.S., and Caroline his wife. Brother of Alexander Tweedale, *q.v.*
Services : Cornet d.d. 8th L.C. 8 July 1826 ; d.d. 6th L.C. 26 Sept. 1826 ; posted to 8th L.C. 20 Dec. 1826. Leave s.c. to Hills 15 Oct. 1832 till 15 Oct. 1834 ; fur. s.c. 14 Feb. 1837 till 22 Nov. 1840, and 9 Oct. 1845 till 1847. Second Sikh War ; Chilianwala ; Gujerat ; Bt. Capt. 8th L.C. (Medal with 2 clasps). Fur. 1854 till 16 Jan. 1855.
[1] *Note :* His age is given as 82 in the bur. register.

TWEMLOW, George (1795-1877). Lieut. General. Artillery. (441) *b.* Hanley, Stoke, Staffs., 29 Nov. 1795. Cadet 1811. Admitted 22 Aug. 1812. Fireworker 6 Aug. 1812. Lieut. 1 Aug. 1818. Capt. 16 Sept. 1829. Major 15 Jan. 1844. Lt. Col. 1 July 1847. Col. Comdt. 6 Mar. 1854. Col. 28 Nov. 1854. Maj. Gen. 17 May 1859. Lt. Gen. 25 May 1870. Retired List 1 Oct. 1877. *d.* at his residence, Poyle Lodge, Guildford, 2 Oct. 1877.

bapt. Hanley chapel 5 Nov. 1797. Eldest son of John Twemlow, of Lawton, co. Chester, and Sarah his wife, dau. of John Twiss. Brother of Samuel Twemlow, *q.v.*, and nephew by marriage of Elizabeth, sister of William Hamilton (1779-1818), *q.v. m.* Dum-Dum 30 Mar. 1825, Anna Maria Hannah, 2nd sister of Thomas D'Oyly, *q.v.* (*See also* William Geddes.) (She died 6 Dec. 1872.) Addiscombe Cadet 1810-11.
Services : Nepal War 1814-15 ; Lt. F. 5th Coy. 2nd Bn., in 4th Div. Nepal War 1816 ; Lt. F. 5th Coy. 2nd Bn. (India medal). Third Mahratta War ; Chanda ; Asirgarh ; Lieut. 6th Troop H.A. Served in Nizam's army 26 Oct. 1820 till Feb. 1853. To comd. 1st Coy. Nizam's Art. 21 Aug. 1837. Insurrection in Jalgaon 1841 ; capture of Jamod fort 5 Dec. 1841. Capture of Barud fort 27 Jan. 1842 ; Bairugarh 13 Feb. 1842. Fur. 1844 till 9 May 1845. Bdr. comdg. Ellichpur, afterwards Aurangabad, Div. Fur. s.c. 22 Feb. 1853 till retirement.
Refs. : Burke's *Landed Gentry*, 13th edn., p. 1788, *s.n.* Twemlow, of Peatswood, Staffs. Burke's *Family Records*, p. 608, *s.n.* D'Oyly-

Twemlow. Ormerod's *Cheshire*, iii. 118. Burton. Boase. *The Times*, 5 Oct. 1877.

TWEMLOW, Samuel (1802-1825). Lieutenant, 68th N.I. b. 23 Mar. 1802. Cadet 1819. Arrived in India Jan. 1821. Ensign 16 July 1820. Lieut. 11 July 1823. d. Barrackpore 15 July 1825. *bapt.* Church Lawton, co. Chester, 17 Aug. 1802. 3rd son of John Twemlow and Sarah his wife. Brother of George Twemlow, *q.v.*
Services: Posted Ensign to 1/24th N.I. 1821; transfd. as Lieut. to newly-raised 34th N.I. July 1823; to 68th N.I. (late 2/34th) May 1824. No record of active service.
Refs.: Burke's *Landed Gentry*, 13th edn., p. 1788, *s.n.* Twemlow, of Peatswood, Staffs. Burke's *Family Records*, p. 608. M.I. at Barrackpore.

TWISS, John. Ensign. Infantry. Cadet (?) Ensign 1766. Resigned 8 Feb. 1767.
Services: N.F.P.

TYLEE, George (1807-1865). Major General. 41st N.I. b. Broadleaze, nr. Devizes, 30 Apr. 1807. Cadet 1823. Arrived in India 10 Aug. 1824. Ensign 18 Feb. 1824. Lieut. 13 Oct. 1825. Capt. 4 Mar. 1839. Major 15 Dec. 1849. Lt. Col. 24 Apr. 1855. Bt. Col. 1858. Retired 23 Nov. 1858. Hon. Maj. Gen. 23 Nov. 1858. d. Rome 8 May 1865.

3rd son of John Tylee, of Broadleaze, banker at Devizes, and Mary Anne his wife, only child of Samuel Napper, of London. *m.* Catholic Church, Clifton, 23 July 1857, Katherine Elizabeth, 3rd dau. of Seth Stephen Ward, of Camberwell. (She died Clifton 1 Aug. 1897.)
Services: Posted Ensign to 53rd N.I.; actg. Adjt. do. 9 Feb. 1828. Fur. s.c. 3 Dec. 1831 till 5 Dec. 1836. First Afghan War 1842; Ali Masjid; operations of Bdr. Wild's Bde.; forcing of Khyber; engagement in Mazina valley; Capt. 53rd N.I., with Pollock's force (Medal). Bde. Major at Meerut 27 Oct. 1843. Fur. s.c. 22 Feb. 1845 till 1847. Bde. Major at Mhow 3 June 1848; do. Multan Dec. 1849 till 1850. Second Sikh War; Capt. 53rd N.I. (Medal). Fur. p.a. 19 Jan. 1855 till retirement. Posted Lt. Col. to 27th N.I. Dec. 1855; to 41st N.I. 1857.
Refs.: Burke's *Landed Gentry*, 13th edn., p. 1789, *s.n.* Tylee, of The Chantry, nr. Frome, Somerset. *G.M.* 1865, i. 805. *The Times*, 15 May 1865.

TYSON, Peter Thomas (1780-1804). Lieutenant, 15th N.I. b. I. of St. Kitts, W.I., 10 Sept. 1780. Cadet 1798. Arrived in

India 8 Dec. 1800. Ensign 24 Nov. 1799. Lieut. 29 May 1800. *d.* Biana, Rajputana, 2 Jan. 1804 : murdered by Mewatties whilst shooting outside the outposts.

(*Perhaps* son of Richard Tyson, of St. George's, Basseterre, who *m.* Mary Cooke 27 July 1776.)

Services : Posted Lieut. to 2/15th N.I. 15 Apr. 1801. Operations in Jumna Doab 1803 ; Sasni ; Bijaigarh ; Kachaura ; Lieut. 2/15th N.I. Second Mahratta War 1803 ; battle of Delhi ; Agra ; Laswari ; Lieut. 2/15th N.I.

Refs. : Thorn's *War in India, 1803-6,* p. 328.

TYSSEN, Samuel (1781-1817). Bt. Captain, 29th N.I. *b.* St. Pancras, Middlesex, 30 Mar. 1781. Cadet 1800. Arrived in India 25 Oct. 1801. Ensign 19 Dec. 1801. Lieut. 8 Sept. 1803. Bt. Capt. 8 Jan. 1816. *d.* in camp at Salleia, C.I., 24 Nov. 1817.

bapt. St. Pancras 1 Apr. 1782. Son of Francis John Tyssen, of Maidstone, and Eleanor his wife.

Services : Ensign 6th N.I. Transfd. to newly-raised 27th N.I. 1804. Operations against Dhundia Khan 1807 ; Komona ; Ganauri ; Lieut. 27th N.I. Transfd. to newly-raised 1/29th N.I. 1815. Actg. Bde. Major Delhi and Rewari in 1816. (? Siege and capture of Hathras 1817 ; Bt. Capt. 1/29th N.I.)

Refs. : Will dated Rewari 10 Aug. 1814 ; cod. camp Salleia 22 Nov. 1817 ; admon. 7 Mar. 1818.

TYTLER, Robert Christopher (1818-1872). Bt. Colonel. 38th N.I. *b.* Allahabad 25 Sept. 1818. Cadet 1834. Arrived in India 24 Feb. 1835. Ensign (13 Dec. 1834) 16 Feb. 1835. Lieut. 25 Sept. 1837. Capt. 26 Feb. 1846. Major 16 May 1858. Lt. Col. 7 Jan. 1862. Bt. Col. 18 Feb. 1866. *d.* Simla 10 Sept. 1872.

bapt. Cawnpore 1 Feb. 1819. 2nd son of Robert Tytler, M.D., Bengal Medical Est., and Elizabeth his wife, dau. of Count Schneeberg. His sister *m.* John Macdonald (1807-1872), *q.v. m.* 1st, Meerut 21 Jan. 1843, Isabella, eldest dau. of Dr. Francis Neilson, of Glasgow. (She died Landour, U.P., 6 Jan. 1847, aged 21.) *m.* 2nd, Lucknow 2 Mar. 1848, Harriet Christina, 2nd dau. of John Lucas Earle, *q.v.* (*See also* William Young Siddons.) (She died Simla 24 Nov. 1907.) Ed. Edin. Univ.

Services : d.d. 34th N.I. 11 Mar. 1835 ; posted to 38th N.I. 24 Sept. 1835. First Afghan War 1840-2 ; Kalat Nov. 1840 ; operations against the Ghilzais May 1841 ; operations in vicinity of Kandahar ; relief of Kalat-i-Ghilzai ; Goaine ; Ghazni ; reoccupation of Kabul ; Lieut. 38th N.I., with Nott's force (Medal). Actg. Intr. & Qmr. 2nd N.I. 3 Aug. 1842 till Dec. 1844. Gwalior campaign; Maharajpur; Lieut. 38th N.I., with 2nd N.I. (Bronze star). Fur. Oct. 1852 till 16 Dec. 1854. Was present with 38th N.I. when it mutinied at Delhi 11 May 1857, but succeeded in escaping to Karnal. Mutiny campaign; siege and capture of Delhi; in charge of mily. treasure chest of Delhi F.F. (Medal with clasp). Fur. May 1860 till Nov. 1861. Offg. Supt. of Port Blair, Andaman Is., Apr. 1862 till Feb. 1864.

Refs.: Misc. Gen. et Her. 5S. ii. 251. *De Rhé-Philipe. I.M.* 20 July 1860, p. 551. *N. & Q.* 4S. ix. 393. M.I. in new cemetery, Simla.

FRASER-TYTLER, Alexander (1803-1832). Lieutenant, 33rd N.I. *b.* Edinburgh 24 Mar. 1803. Cadet 1823. Arrived in India 10 Oct. 1824. Ensign 9 May 1824. Lieut. 13 May 1825. *d.* Akyab, Burma, 4 Aug. 1832.

Eldest son of William Fraser Tytler, of Balnain, co. Inverness, sheriff of Inverness, and Margaret Cussans Grant his wife, only dau. of George Grant, of Sanquhar, co. Moray. Brother of George Fraser-Tytler and of the 1st wife of Sir Patrick Grant, *qq.v.* Lincoln's Inn; admitted 7 Dec. 1822.

Services: Posted Ensign to 33rd N.I. 31 Mar. 1825. Siege and capture of Bhurtpore; Lieut. 33rd N.I. Adjt. Kumaon Local Bn. 9 Aug. (joined 3 Nov.) 1831 till 18 May 1832; Junr. Asst. to Comr. in Arakan 12 Mar. 1832 till death.

Refs.: Family information. Burke's *Landed Gentry*, 12th edn., p. 1917, *s.n.* Fraser-Tytler, of Aldourie and Balnain, co. Inverness. *Frasers of Lovat*, p. 572. *Family of Seton*, i. 571-3.

FRASER-TYTLER, George (1807-1836). Lieutenant. 16th N.I. Afterwards Lieut. 4th Foot. *b.* Aldourie, Dores, Inverness, 11 Apr. 1807. Cadet 1823. Ensign 9 May 1824. Lieut. 24 Sept. 1826. Resigned in India 8 Dec. 1826. *d. unm.* at sea 12 Mar. 1836.[1]

2nd son of William Fraser Tytler, of Balnain, and Margaret Cussans his wife. Brother of Alexander Fraser-Tytler, *q.v.* Addiscombe Cadet 1823-4.

Services: Posted to 45th N.I. 31 Mar. 1825; transfd. to 16th N.I. 6 Apr. 1825. Ensign 4th (King's Own) Ft. 17 July 1828; Lieut. do. 14 Dec. 1832; out of the Service in 1835.

Refs.: See Alexander Fraser-Tytler. *A.J.* N.S. xx. 205.

[1] *Note:* He was washed overboard during a storm while on his return from Australia, together with the captain, some of the officers and several of the crew of the *Hercules*. His name sometimes appears as George Grant Fraser Tytler.

U

UNDERWOOD, James (*d.* 1789). Lieutenant, Infantry. Cadet 1772. Ensign 4 July 1776. Lieut. 25 June 1778. *d.* at sea 1789, on his passage to Europe.
Son of Mary Scobie, of Walthamstow, Essex.
Services: Lieut. 1/3rd Bengal Eur. Regt. in Oct. 1779. Campaign against the Rajah of Benares 1781; Bijaigarh. Lieut. 30th Bn. Sepoys in July 1787. On fur. in Dec. 1788.
Refs.: Will dated 1 Mar. 1788; proved 13 June 1789.

UPTON, John (*d.* 1780). Lieut. Colonel. 1st Bengal Eur. Regt. Capt. 27 July 1764. Major 2 Dec. 1767. Lt. Col. 2 Oct. 1769. Resigned 13 Nov. 1780. *d.* Contai, Bengal, 9 Dec. 1780.
(? Related to Clotworthy Upton, 1st Baron Templetown, to whom he bequeathed the sum of £10,000.)
Services: 2nd Lieut. 2nd Bn. 23rd R.W.F. 4 Oct. 1757; converted into 68th Ft. 22 Apr. 1758; Lieut. 68th Ft. 12 Oct. 1760. Capt. newly-raised 109th Ft. 19 Oct. 1761; h.p. do. on disbandment 1763 till death. Sailed for India in the *Prince of Wales* 16 May 1764. Posted to 1st Bengal Eur. Regt. 5 Aug. 1765. Lt. Col. (H.M.S.) in E.I. 14 Mar. 1777. Posted Lt. Col. to a Bde. May 1772. Comdd. garr. at Allahabad 1 Feb. till 6 May 1773. Comdg. a division of the Bde. at Berhampore in 1774-5. Deputed to Poona in 1775 to negotiate a treaty with the Regency. The treaty with the Mahrattas was signed 1 Mar. 1776, and the Mission reached Calcutta 1 July 1777.[1] Comdg. at Chunar in Nov. 1777 and 1779; comdg. 1/1st Bengal Eur. Regt. in Oct. 1779. Left Calcutta for England in the *Walpole* Dec. 1780.
Refs.: (? Burke's *Peerage*, 1923, p. 2161, *s.n.* Templetown, V.) *Macpherson, passim. India Gazette*, 16 Dec. 1780. Will dated 26 May 1779; proved 15 Dec. 1780.
[1] *Note:* His " Journal of the Road, travelled by Col. Upton from Kalpee . . . in the years 1775 and 1776 " is in B.M. (*Add. MS.* 29, 213).

URMSTON, William John (1789-1809). Cornet, 4th N.C. *b.* Chigwell, Essex, 30 Oct. 1789. Cadet 1806. Arrived in India 21 July 1807. Cornet 28 July 1807. *d.* Karnal 8 Dec. 1809.
bapt. Chigwell 29 Nov. 1789. 3rd son of James Urmston, of

LIST OF OFFICERS OF THE BENGAL ARMY 339

Rath House and of Chigwell House, Essex, J.P., high sheriff co. Essex 1806, sometime R.N. and afterwards H.E.I.C.N.S., and Elizabeth his wife, dau. of George Lawrence, R.N.
Services: Barasat C.C. Posted Cornet to 4th N.C. 1808. No record of active service.
Refs.: Burke's *Landed Gentry*, 12th edn., p. 1921, *s.n.* Urmston, of Glenmorven, co. Argyll.

URQUHART, Charles Farquharson (1791-1856). Major, Invalid Est. 54th N.I. *b.* Fearn, co. Ross, 4 July 1791. Cadet 1810. Admitted 3 Dec. 1811. Ensign 10 Nov. 1813. Lieut. 29 Nov. 1816. Capt. 11 Feb. 1827. Major 26 Jan. 1837. Invalided 23 July 1838. *d.* Meerut 17 Feb. 1856.
bapt. 11 July 1791. 4th and youngest son of Rev. John Urquhart, of Mount Eagle, minister of Fearn 1771-1800, and Katherine his wife, dau. of Alexander Houston, provost of Fortrose. Brother of John Urquhart, clerk in the Ordnance office, and cousin of Rev. Alexander Wood, minister of Rosemarkie, co. Ross.
Services: Cadet d.d. 12th N.I. 1811-13 ; posted to 1/25th N.I. 1813 ; transfd. to 2/27th N.I. 24 May 1816 ; to 1/27th N.I. 30 Apr. 1818. Third Mahratta War 1818 ; Madhurajpura ; Lieut. 1/27th N.I. Transfd. to 54th N.I. (late 2/27th) May 1824 ; Adjt. do. 17 June 1824 till 14 Mar. 1827 ; comdd. do. 14 June till 9 Nov. 1833.
Refs.: Scott's *Fasti*, vii. 56. *I.M.* 3 Apr. 1856, p. 188. Will dated Meerut 17 Aug. 1854 ; admon. 27 June 1856.

URQUHART, George (1802-?). Lieutenant. 65th N.I. *b.* London 17 Dec. 1802. Cadet 1822. Arrived in India 6 July 1823. Ensign 29 June 1823. Lieut. 13 May 1825. Resigned 29 Feb. 1836.
bapt. St. Pancras 23 May 1803. Son of Walter Urquhart, of Gt. Baddow, Essex, and Sarah his wife. Nephew of Alexander Urquhart, of Long Ditton. *m.* Barrackpore 23 June 1827, Cecilia Mary, youngest dau. of Col. George Torrane, Govr. at Cape Coast, Africa, 1805-7. Ed. Winchester.
Services: Posted to newly-raised 33rd N.I. 1823 ; transfd. to 65th N.I. (late 1/33rd) May 1824 ; Adjt. do. 28 Dec. 1827 till 22 Oct. 1831. Fur. p.a. 30 Aug. 1833 till resignation. No record of active service.

V

VALLÉ, Lewis (or Lazarus) (*d.* 1793). Lieutenant, 1st N.I. Cadet 1781. Admitted 10 Apr. 1781. Ensign 10 Sept. 1781. Lieut. 21 June 1783. *d.* Chunar 5 Aug. 1793.
Father of Bartholomew Vallé. (See Appendix A)
Services: Lieut. 1st Bn. Sepoys in July 1787.

VALLOTTON,[1] **J——** (*d.* 1767). Cadet, Infantry. Cadet 1767. *d.* 1767.
Services: N.F.P.
[1] *Note:* Name given in *D. & M.* as Valatoon. One Francis Valotton or Vallotton (*d.* 1772) was Dy. Librarian to George II. Nowell Leny Vallotton, Esq., of Rutland Lodge, Addison Rd., Kensington, *d.* 28 Feb. 1858, aged 69. (*G.M.* 1858, i. 451.)

VAN,[1] **Thomas.** Lieutenant. Infantry. Cadet 1778. Ensign 1778. Lieut. 10 Dec. 1778. Resigned 19 Nov. 1779.
Services: Apptd. Cadet 17 Apr. 1778 ; sailed for India in H.M.S. *Asia*.
[1] *Note:* (*Probably* the Thomas Van, son of Charles Van (? of Llanwern, Mon.), ed. Eton 1771-4 ; admitted fellow commoner at King's Coll., Camb., 11 Mar. 1775, aged 17. One of this name *m.* Miss Wewitzer (Qy. the actress—*D.N.B.*) 28 Oct. 1784.)

VANAS, William (*d.* 1803). Colonel, 4th N.I. Country Cadet 1767. Admitted 14 Sept. 1767. Ensign 20 Aug. 1767. Lieut. 8 Oct. 1769. Capt. 4 Jan 1778. Major 22 Sept. 1781. Lt. Col. 1 Mar. 1794. Col. 31 Oct. 1799. *d.* at sea 20 (or 25) Apr. 1803, on board the *Lady Castlereagh*, on his return to India.
Brother-in-law of Bdr.-Gen. Simon Fraser, of Balnain, who was kinsman of Andrew Fraser (*d.* 1812), *q.v. m.* (? at the Cape) Catharina Dorothea Antonitta ——. (She died 23 Apr. 1821.) His dau. *m.* Gregory Hickman, *q.v.*
Services: Fur. 20 Jan. 1778 till Jan. 1781. On return from fur. he served for a year at Madras under Sir Eyre Coote, during Second Mysore War, before returning to Bengal. Battles of Sholingarh and Virakandalur ; Major comdg. 24th N.I. from Aug. 1781, after the death of Samuel Kilpatrick, *q.v.* To comd. 16th Sepoys 10 May 1782 ; comdg. 20th Bn. Sepoys in July 1787 ; comdg. 4th Bengal Eur. Bn. in Dec. 1788 ; transfd. to 2nd Bde. Sepoys 7 Nov. 1793 ; Lt. Col. 1/8th N.I. till 15 Nov. 1799, when posted Col. to 4th N.I.

LIST OF OFFICERS OF THE BENGAL ARMY 341

Comdd. in 1800 a detachment which disbanded ten of the Nawab of Oudh's Bns. Fur. 5 Mar. 1802 till death.
Refs.: *Macpherson*, p. 5. *E.I.M.C.* iii. 415. *Wilson*, ii. 50 *n*. *G.M.* 1803, i. 596. Will dated 15 Feb. 1802; proved 13 Sept. 1803.

VANDERHEYDEN, Randolphus Philip (*d.* 1783). Ensign, Infantry. Country Cadet 1781. Ensign 5 Aug. 1782. *d.* Berhampore 14 Jan. 1783.
Services: Apptd. Cadet 28 Nov. 1781. N.F.P.

*VANDERSTEEN or VANDERSTEIN, Anthony (*d.* 1782). Ensign, Engineers. Ensign 6 Oct. 1781. *d.* Bombay 31 Oct. 1782.
Services: Sergt. on Bombay Est.; commissioned as Lt. F. in Bo. Art. 19 June 1781. Apptd. Ensign in Bengal Engrs. (M.C. 24 June 1782) and served with Bengal detachment under Col. Charles Morgan, *q.v.*, during First Mahratta War.
Refs.: *Spring*, No. 143. Intest.; admon. 23 Dec. 1782.

VANGREEN, John (*d.* 1760/61). Capt. Lieutenant, Artillery. (9) Fireworker 11 Nov. 1757. 2nd Lieut. 11 Dec. 1758. Capt. Lt. 13 Mar. 1760. *d.* between Sept. 1760 and Apr. 1761.
Services: N.F.P.
Refs.: Will dated Calcutta 22 Sept. 1760; proved 3 Apr. 1761.

VANHAMMUT, Francis. (*See* **VAN HEMERT.**)

VAN HEMERT, Francis ($174\frac{5}{6}$-1818). Ensign. Infantry. *b.* London 4 Mar. $174\frac{5}{6}$. Cadet 1769. Ensign 12 Sept. 1769. Resigned 1770. *d.* London 9 May 1818, aged 73.

bapt. St. Dionis Backchurch, London, 12 Mar. $174\frac{5}{6}$. Only son of John van Hemert, of Amsterdam, later of Broad St., London, merchant, and Elizabeth his wife. *m.* ——, dau. of Roger Walshman, of Lancaster. (She died 23 Mar. 1818, aged 67.)
Services: N.F.P.
Refs.: Oliver's *Hist. of Antigua*, i. 88. *G.M.* 1818, i. 572.
Note: Francis Van Hemert was naturalized 6 Geo. I (1717-20). One of this name was Lieut. in Middlesex (Westminster) Mil. 24 Feb. 1780.

VAN HEYTHUYSEN, Gerard Edward William Delamé (1804-1879). Major. 24th N.I. *bapt.* St. Giles-in-the-Fields,

London, 18 July 1804. Cadet 1821. Arrived in India 29 Sept. 1822. Ensign 17 Oct. 1822. Lieut. 30 July 1824. Capt. 8 Oct. 1839. Retired 1 Apr. 1845. Hon. Major 28 Nov. 1854. *d.* Coombe Bury, Kingston Hill, 16 May 1879, aged 75.

Son of Gerard Levinge Van Heythuysen, of 5 Southampton St., Strand, barr.-at-law, of the Six Clerks Office, and Marianne his wife, dau. of Rev. Dr. Holte, rector of N. Repps, Norfolk. *m.* 1st, St. James's, London, 9 May 1831, Zillah, eldest dau. of Thomas L. Holt, of Lower Bedford Pl., Russell Sq., London. (She died Barrackpore 29 Oct. 1834, aged 30.) *m.* 2nd, Marian, dau. of John Seck, of Chiswick. (She died 21 Nov. 1864, aged 51.) *m.* 3rd, Georgina Sophia ——. (She died 13 Oct. 1876.) Ed. St. Paul's; admitted 29 Apr. 1815, aged 11.

Services: Posted to 23rd N.I. 1822; transfd. to 8th N.I. July 1823; to 24th N.I. (late 2/8th) May 1824; actg. Intr. & Qmr. do. 30 Aug. 1826. Leave s.c. 12 mos. to Hills 17 Jan. 1829; fur. s.c. 14 June 1830 till 11 Dec. 1832. Adjt. 24th N.I. 11 Aug. 1835 till 10 Oct. 1836. (? Rising in Cuttack July 1836; Lieut. 24th N.I.) Leave s.c. to Cape 4 Nov. 1836 till 24 Dec. 1838. Attached to 3rd L.I. Bn. at Cawnpore 1841 till 1 Nov. 1842, when broken up. Leave 1844 till retirement.

Refs.: Gardiner. *G.M.* 1831, i. 463. *The Times*, 20 May 1879.

VAN HOMRIGH, Henry Davis (1809-1845). Captain, 48th N.I. *b.* St. Thomas's, Dublin, 12 Aug. 1809. Cadet 1830. Arrived in India 9 Mar. 1831. Ensign 9 Mar. 1831. Lieut. 18 July 1836. Capt. 28 Apr. 1841. *d.* 19 Dec. 1845, of wounds received in action at the battle of Mudki.

Son of Peter Van Homrigh, barr.-at-law, M.P. for Drogheda, Recorder of Drogheda. *m.* Sitapur, U.P., 15 Apr. 1836, Caroline Louisa, dau. of Robert Arding Thomas, *q.v.* (*See also* George Newbolt.)

Services: Cadet d.d. 63rd N.I. 7 Apr. 1831. Apptd. Actg. Ensign (having been 2 yrs. in India) 26 Mar. 1833; Ensign 2 July 1833, subsequently antedated to 9 Mar. 1831. Posted to 48th N.I. 19 Oct. 1833. First Afghan War 1838-9; Ghazni (w.) (*Lond. Gaz.* 30 Oct. 1839); occupation of Kabul; Lieut. 48th N.I. (Medal). In charge of Haji Khan, Kakar, a State prisoner from Afghanistan, 10 Feb. till 18 Nov. 1840. First Sikh War; Mudki (s.w.); Capt. 48th N.I., actg. A.D.C. to Sir Harry Smith, comdg. 1st Div. (Medal).

Refs.: De Rhé-Philipe. M.I. in St. Andrew's, Ferozepore.

VANRENEN (*recte* **van RENEN**), **Jacob** (1762-1828). Colonel, 37th N.I. Bdr. Gen. comdg. in Rohilkhand. *b.* C.G.H. 20 Feb.

THE BENGAL ARMY, 1758-1834   343

1762. Cadet 1780. Ensign 24 May 1781. Lieut. 6 Sept. 1782. Capt. 29 May 1800. Major 11 Oct. 1804. Lt. Col. 1 Aug. 1810. Col. 12 Aug. 1819. Bdr. Gen. 7 Nov. 1822. *d.* on board a boat on the Ganges nr. Cawnpore 8 Feb. 1828.

bapt. 28 Feb. 1762. Only son of Daniel van Renen, of the Cape, and Catharina Christina his wife, dau. of Johann Zacharias Beck. Brother of the wife of Thomas Hawkshaw, *q.v.*, and of Johanna, mother of Francis Robert Baumgardt, *q.v.* Nephew of the wife of Alexander Grant (*d.* 1768), *q.v. m.* 25 Mar. 1792, Johanna Adriana, dau. of —— Bogaardt, Dutch Govr. of Chinsura, Bengal. (She died Southampton 5 Sept. 1854, aged 79.) Father of John Heyning Vanrenen, *q.v.*, Tunus Augustus Vanrenen, *q.v.*, and of the wives of James Blair, Christopher Godby, William Conway-Gordon, Charles Griffiths, and John Satchwell, *qq.v.*

Services : Apptd. Cadet 13 Dec. 1780 ; sailed for India in the *Osterley* 13 Mar. 1781. Lieut. 20th Bn. Sepoys in July 1787. Second Rohilla War 1794 ; battle of Bitaurah ; Lieut. 20th Bn. Capt. Lt. 2/13th N.I. 21 Apr. 1800. Transfd. as Capt. to newly-raised 2/18th N.I. 29 May 1800. Second Mahratta War 1803-4 ; operations in Bundelkhand 1803 ; Kapsa ; Kalpi ; Gwalior 1804 ; Jaitpur ; Capt. 2/18th N.I. Bundelkhand 1809 ; Rajaoli ; Ajaigarh ; Major 1/18th N.I. Comdg. at Fatehgarh 1810-11. Posted Lt. Col. to 18th N.I. 1810 ; to 2/12th N.I. 1812 ; to newly-raised 2/29th N.I. 1815 ; to 2/12th N.I. 1816. Siege and capture of Hathras 1817 ; Lt. Col. 2/12th N.I. Transfd. to 1/18th N.I. 1818. Third Mahratta War 1817-18 ; comdg. 4th Inf. Bde., Rt. Div. of Grand Army. Comdg. in Bundelkhand 1819. Transfd. to 13th N.I. 1820 ; to 2/25th N.I. 1821. Col. 11th N.I. 7 Nov. 1822 ; 37th N.I. (late 2/18th) May 1824 till death. Comdg. in Rohilkhand 1820 till death. Served in India continuously for 46 yrs. with only one period of sick leave to Cape for 9 mos.

Refs. : De La Ferté. *A.J.* xxvi. 128. Codicil to Will dated Bareilly 5 Jan. 1828 ; proved 29 Apr. 1828.

VANRENEN, John Heyning (1804-1867). Captain. 25th N.I. *b.* Bengal 26 Apr. 1804. Cadet 1820. Admitted 22 Aug. 1821. Ensign 9 Mar. 1821. Lieut. 11 July 1823. Capt. 3 July 1831. Resigned 15 May 1837. *d.* 4 Jan. 1867.

bapt. Ghazipur 12 Oct. 1807. 2nd son of Jacob Vanrenen, *q.v.*, and Johanna Adriana his wife. Brother of Tunus Augustus Vanrenen, *q.v. m.* Cape Town 16 July 1830, Yda Johanna, only dau. of Adrian Christian Deneys (de Nys), of Roode Bloem, Cape Town. (She died 25 Oct. 1896.)

Services: Posted to 2/29th N.I. 1821; d.d. 2/15th N.I.; d.d. 2nd Nassiri Bn. 13 Mar. 1822 till 1824; actg. Adjt. do. 31 Oct. 1823. Transfd. to 20th N.I. July 1823; to 40th N.I. (late 2/20th) May 1824. First Burma War; Chittagong 1824; Lieut. 40th N.I. Adjt. 40th N.I. 30 Dec. 1824 till May 1827. Transfd. to 25th N.I. 1827; Adjt. do. 21 May 1827 till 28 Apr. 1831. Leave s.c. to Cape 7 Jan. 1829 till 21 Nov. 1830; u.p.a. 1 yr. to Cape 22 Aug. 1831; p.a. to Cape 22 Mar. 1834 till 23 Apr. 1837.

Refs.: De La Ferté. A.J. N.S. v. 154.

VANRENEN, Tunus[1] **Augustus** (1793-1836). Captain, Artillery. (434) *b.* Chunar 12 Aug. 1793. Cadet 1810. Admitted 27 Aug. 1811. Fireworker 20 Aug. 1811. Lieut. 25 Sept. 1817. Capt. 28 Sept. 1827. *d.* Meerut 7 Oct. 1836. *bapt.* Chunar 23 Aug. 1793. Eldest son of Jacob Vanrenen, *q.v. m.* Midnapore 14 Oct. 1819, Harriot Catherine, his cousin-german, elder dau. of Adm. Donald Campbell, R.N. (She died 31 July 1878, aged 78.) Addiscombe Cadet 1810.

Services: Nepal War 1814-15; Lt. F. 2nd Coy. 2nd Bn., in 4th Div. Siege and capture of Hathras 1817; Lt. F. 3rd Coy. 2nd Bn. Third Mahratta War; Lieut. 3rd Coy. 2nd Bn., detached with Rt. Div. from Agra Dec. 1817. Adjt. & Qmr. 2nd Bn. 17 Dec. 1822; do. 5th Bn. 22 July 1825 till 31 Oct. 1827. Leave s.c. 2 yrs. to Cape 7 Jan. 1829. Tempy. charge of expense mag. at Dum-Dum 21 Feb. till 5 June 1835; actg. Comy. Ord. 6 May 1835; transfd. to H.A. 5 June 1835.

Refs.: De La Ferté. A.J. N.S. xxii. 212. Will dated 25 Aug. 1820; proved 13 Dec. 1836.

[1] *Note:* The name is usually given as Tuneus, but incorrectly so according to *De La Ferté.*

VAN RIXTELL,[1] **Charles** (*d.* 1795). Captain, Infantry. Cadet 1771. Ensign 18 Mar. 1773. Lieut. 16 May 1778. Capt. 12 Jan. 1784. *d.* Rajmahal, B. & O., 13 Mar. 1795.[2]

(*Probably* son of John Van Rixtell, of St. Mary Aldermary, London, a Dutch merchant, by his wife Dorothy, and brother of Alexander Van Rixtel, B.C.S., Member of the Board of Trade.)

Services: Apptd. Adjt. 32nd Bn. Sepoys 22 Mar. 1780. Second Mysore War 1781-5; Lieut. comdg. 1/25th N.I., with Col. T. D. Pearse's detachment. Fur. 25 Oct. 1785, and was still on fur. in Dec. 1788. Posted to 4th Bengal Eur. Bn. 8 Mar. 1790; transfd. to 2nd do. 8 Apr. 1793.

Refs.: M.M. 1809, i. 124.

[1] *Note:* It is not easy to determine the correct form of this name

THE BENGAL ARMY, 1758-1834 345

which appears variously in contemporary official documents as Van Rextell, Vanrixtel, Vanrestell, Vanrisdell and, in the official casualty lists, as Ristell. One John Van Rextell was naturalized 24 Apr. 1724.

² *Note :* He was leaning on some wooden railings in front of the palace, admiring the view over the river, when they gave way. He fell forty feet down a *khud* and his head was dashed to pieces on the rocks below. He was buried in a garden adjoining the palace.

VAN SANDAU, Lewis (1793-1827). Lieutenant, 68th N.I. Rangpur L.I. *b.* St. Michael Bassishaw, London, 20 Sept. 1793. Cadet (1809) 1813. Ensign 16 Aug. 1813. Lieut. 19 Nov. 1817. *d.* Bishnath, Assam, 12 Aug. 1827 : accidentally shot by a sepoy sentry.[1]

Son of Bernard Van Sandau, of Pentonville, formerly of the Royal Exchange, notary public. *m.* Calcutta 23 Feb. 1814, Mary, dau. of John Forbes (*d.* 1808), *q.v.* (*See also* John Paton (1763-1824).) (She died Ludhiana 8 Dec. 1847, aged 50.) Ed. Merchant Taylors' July-Oct. 1807.

Services : Restored to his original rank as Cadet 5th cl. of 1809 (G.O. 76 of 11 Mar. 1825). Barasat C.C. Cadet d.d. 8th N.I. 1811 ; posted to 20th N.I. 1813 ; transfd. to newly-raised 1/28th N.I. 1815 ; as Lieut. to 11th N.I. Nov. 1817 ; to 2/8th N.I. 1817. Third Mahratta War 1817-19 ; Lieut. 2/8th N.I. Transfd. to newly-raised 34th N.I. July 1823 ; to 67th N.I. (late 1/34th) May 1824 ; to 68th N.I. Oct. 1824 ; Intr. & Qmr. do. 26 Oct. 1824 till 28 Dec. 1826. First Burma War ; Arakan 1825 ; Lieut. 68th N.I. 2nd in comd. Rangpur L.I. Bn. 9 Oct. 1826 till death.

Refs. : Robinson. Bengal Chron., 4 Sept. 1827. M.I. at Bishnath.

[1] *Note :* " The unfortunate officer was dressed in a white jacket, and in the darkness of the night the superstitious and alarmed sipahi took him for a ghost and fired his piece with too fatal precision." (*Bengal Chron.*)

VAN SWINDEN, Philip Simeon (Peter) (1785-1820). Bt. Captain, Bengal Eur. Regt. *b.* St. George's, Hanover Sq., London, 19 Aug. 1785. Cadet 1803. Arrived in India 12 Dec. 1804. Ensign 30 Sept. 1804. Lieut. 30 Sept. 1804. Bt. Capt. 1 Jan. 1818. *d.* Dinapore 17 June 1820.

bapt. 24 Oct. 1785. Son of Rev. Dr. Philip Van Swinden, D.D. (Leyden), of Prince's Row, Pimlico, for 30 yrs. one of the Dutch

ministers to George III, and Elizabeth his wife. Ed. St. Paul's; admitted 2 Apr. 1798.
Services : Posted Lieut. to Bengal Eur. Regt. 1805 ; actg. Qmr. do. 1810. Bde. Major at Amboyna 1812-16.
Refs. : Gardiner.

VANZANDT, James (1755-1823). Lieutenant. 9th Bn. Sepoys. *b.* in America 1755. Cadet 1781. Ensign 19 Mar. 1781. Lieut. 10 July 1782. Resigned 3 Dec. 1792. *d.* at his residence, Netherclay House, 26 Oct. 1823.
Of Netherclay House, Bishop's Hull, Somerset. Son of Jacobus Vanzandt, of New York. Brother of Catherine, wife of James Homer Maxwell. *m.* Hannah.
Services : Had been an Ofr. in the standing Mil. of New York. Apptd. Cadet 14 Mar. 1781, aged 25 ; sailed for India in the *Northumberland* 26 June 1781, aged 26. Lieut. 9th Bn. Sepoys in July 1787. Became an auctioneer in firm of Dring & Co., Calcutta. Sheriff of Calcutta 1798. Resigned his Commission as Lieut. in Calcutta Native Mil. 29 Nov. 1799.
Refs. : *G.M.* 1823, ii. 574. Will dated 29 May 1823 ; P.C.C. 1 Dec. 1823 ; admon. granted in Calcutta 4 Oct. 1826.

VANZETTI, George Lewis (1798-1834). Captain, 5th N.I. *b.* St. Mary Newington, Surrey, 23 May 1798. Cadet 1817. Admitted 19 Sept. 1818. Ensign 25 May 1818. Lieut. 13 Sept. 1819. Capt. 20 Dec. 1834. *d.* Saugor 25 Dec. 1834.
bapt. St. Mary Newington 28 June 1798. Son of Angelo Lewis Vanzetti and Maria his wife. Ward of Dr. Emanuel Pacifico. *m.* Stoke Newington 23 Aug. 1831, Emma, youngest dau. of George Pringle, of Stoke Newington. (She died 12 Mar. 1895, aged 84.)
Services : Posted to 2/2nd N.I. 1819. Mily. student at Coll. of Ft. Wm. 1819-20. Intr. & Qmr. 1/2nd N.I. (became 5th N.I.) 1 Oct. 1823 till 24 Jan. 1826 ; d.d. Ramgarh Bn. 24 Jan. 1826 ; do. Kumaon Local Bn. 3 Mar. 1826 till 26 Sept. 1827. Fur. p.a. 22 Sept. 1828 till 25 June 1832. No record of active service.
Refs. : *A.J.* N.S. vi. 43. M.I. Saugor.

VARDON, Charles (1807-1825). Ensign, 56th N.I. *b.* London 8 June 1807. Cadet 1824. Arrived in India 21 May 1825. Ensign 7 Dec. 1824. *d.* Etmadpur, Agra, 11 Nov. 1825, of brain fever.
bapt. St. Mary's, Battersea, 9 July 1807. Son of Charles Vardon, of Ramsgate, and Marian his wife. Ed. Eton 1820-3.
Services : Ensign d.d. 2nd Bengal Eur. Regt. 10 June 1825 ;

posted to 56th N.I., and was on his way to join when his death occurred.

Refs.: Eton School Lists.

*VAUGHAN, Charles (1725/26-1760). Ensign, Infantry. *b.* co. Monmouth 1725/26. Cadet 1757. Ensign 13 Oct. 1757. *d.* in India 1760.

Services: Sailed for India in the *Bombay Castle* in 1758, aged 32. Storm of Masulipatam Apr. 1759, and was apptd. one of the four prize agents after its capture.[1]

Refs.: Orme MSS.—India, xiii, p. 3639. Will dated 28 Mar. 1760; proved 13 June 1760.

[1] *Note:* Said to have been tried by C.M. for accepting bribes and dismissed the Service: if so, he was apparently reinstated.

*VAUGHAN, Charles (*d.* 1767). Ensign, Infantry. Cadet 1766. Ensign 1 Sept. 1766. *d.* Monghyr 31 Mar. 1767.

Son of —— Vaughan, of Bristol, banker. Brother of John Vaughan.

Services: Apptd. Cadet in England 16 Dec. 1765. N.F.P.

Refs.: B.M. Add. MS. 6050, p. 90. *G.M.* 1767, p. 524. *Farley's Bristol Journal*, 3 Oct. 1767. Will dated Monghyr, 27 Mar. 1767; proved 1767.

VAUGHAN, Edward. Cadet, Infantry. Cadet 1772. *d.* Allahabad (?)

Services: N.F.P.

VAUGHAN, Gwynne (*d.* 1788). Ensign. 1st Bengal Eur. Regt. Cadet 1781. Ensign 1 Feb. 1783. Dismissed by C.M. 21 Apr. 1785. *bur.* Calcutta 25 Nov. 1788.

Services: Apptd. Cadet 28 Nov. 1781; sailed for India in the *Norfolk* 6 Feb. 1782. Posted to 1st Eur. Regt. 28 Feb. 1783. Found Guilty by C.M. at Berhampore, 1-18 Apr. 1785, of Conduct unbecoming the character of an ofr. and a gentleman, and sentenced to be dismissed with infamy.

VAUGHAN, John (*c.* 1780-1830). Colonel, 37th N.I. Town Major of Ft. Wm. *b.* Bristol *c.* 1780. Cadet 1795. Arrived in India 16 Feb. 1797. Ensign 4 Nov. 1796. Lieut. 30 Oct. 1797. Capt. 19 Nov. 1807. Major 1 Feb. 1818. Lt. Col. 11 July 1823. Lt. Col. Comdt. 1 Nov. 1827. Col. 5 June 1829. *d.* Calcutta 1 Nov. 1830.

Son of Robert Walter Vaughan, of Bristol, salesman, and Catherina Byrne his wife. Brother of Capt. Thomas Vaughan, Royal N. Glos. Mil., Mary Anne, and Sylvia.

Services: Operations in Jumna Doab 1803; Sasni; Lieut. 2nd N.I. Transfd. to newly-raised 21st N.I. 1804. Second Mahratta War 1805-6; pursuit of Holkar; Lieut. 1/21st N.I. Capt. 1/21st N.I. Fur. 9 Mar. 1811 till 3 Oct. 1815. A.D.C. to G.G. 1816. 2nd A.A.G. of the Army at H.Q. (with official rank of Major) 16 June 1817. Major 1/21st N.I. Town Major of Ft. Wm. 1818 till death. Lt. Col. 18th N.I. May 1824; posted Lt. Col. Comdt. to 37th N.I. 3 Apr. 1828; Col. do. June 1829 till death. Supy. A.D.C. to G.G. 26 Sept. 1828.
Refs.: A.J. N.S. v. 36. *G.M.* 1831, i. 382. Will dated 12 May 1815; proved 8 Nov. 1830.

VAZEILLE, John Anthony (*d.* 1771). Captain, Infantry. Ensign 11 Aug. 1765. Lieut. 21 Dec. 1766. Capt. 11 Oct. 1769. *d.* Calcutta 15 Jan. 1771.

(*Perhaps* son of Anthony Vazeille who was naturalized 13 Geo. II.)

Services: Ensign H.M. 12th Ft. 22 Mar. 1757; in Germany in 1758; resigned 9 Feb. 1759. Apptd. in England 9 Nov. 1764, Ensign on the Bengal Est.; sailed in the *Grenville* 4 Mar. 1765.

VEITCH, James (1783-1814). Lieutenant, 15th N.I. *b.* Selkirk 6 Aug. 1783. Cadet 1803. Arrived in India 18 Mar. 1805. Ensign 6 May 1805. Lieut. 7 May 1805. *d.* Rangpur 14 May 1814.

bapt. Selkirk 10 Aug. 1783. Son of John Veitch, vintner in Selkirk, and Barbary Anslie (*sic*) his wife. *m.* Calcutta 21 Dec. 1810, Miss Sarah Bird, dau. of Shearman Bird, senr., B.C.S. (*See also* William Midwinter.)

Services: Posted Lieut. to 15th N.I. 1806. Served with Rangpur Bn. 1813 till death. No record of active service.

VENABLES, George Henry (1809-1835). Ensign, 29th N.I. *b.* Machynlleth, co. Montgomery, 13 Apr. 1809. Cadet 1827. Arrived in India 10 Feb. 1829. Ensign (23 Aug. 1828) 3 June 1829. *d.* Mirzapur 9 Sept. 1835.

Son of Rev. George Venables, rector of Machynlleth, and Mary his wife, dau. of J. Lloyd, of Cardigan. Ed. Shrewsbury 1819-20.

Services: Posted to 29th N.I. June 1829. No record of active service.

Refs.: Burke's *Landed Gentry*, 13th edn., p. 1104, *s.n.* Dillwyn-Venables-Llewellyn, of Llysdinam Hall, co. Brecon. *Shrewsbury School Register. A.J.* N.S. xix. 206. M.I. at Mirzapur.

THE BENGAL ARMY, 1758-1834 349

*VERELST, John (*d.* 1760). Ensign, Infantry. Ensign Feb. 1757. *bur.* Calcutta 27 Aug. 1760.

(*Probably* son or brother of Henry Verelst, Govr. of Bengal 1767-9, who was grandson of Cornelius Verelst.)

Services : Was in Calcutta during the siege, June 1756. Battle of Plassey ; Ensign under Capt. Alexander Grant, *q.v.* He states in his petition for appt. as Writer in 1760, that he was " aged 16 yrs. and upwards," and that, " he proceeded to Bengal with license in 1754, and was employed as an Officer in your forces in those parts on the Exigency of Affairs there."

Refs. : *Hill's Calcutta*, p. 92. *Orme MSS.*—India, xiii. 3639. Writers' Petitions, Vol. IV, No. 13 of 1760.

VERNER, George (1809-1885). Lieut. General. 9th N.I. *b.* 20 Nov. 1809. Cadet 1829. Arrived in India 22 Nov. 1830. Ensign 24 July 1830. Lieut. 20 Apr. 1835. Capt. 4 Mar. 1848. Major 18 Feb. 1861. Lt. Col. 18 Feb. 1863. Bt. Col. 18 Feb. 1866. Maj. Gen. 1 Oct. 1877. Retired 1 Jan. 1880. Hon. Lt. Gen. 1 Jan. 1880. *d.* Pau, France, 26 Feb. 1885.

bapt. Belfast 3 Jan. 1810. 4th and youngest son of Thomas Verner, of Churchill, co. Armagh, sovereign of Belfast, high sheriff Armagh 1800, and Elizabeth his wife, 2nd dau. of Sir Edward May, Bart., of Mayfield, co. Waterford. Brother of James Edward Verner, *q.v.*, and nephew of James Verner, *q.v.* *m.* 8 May 1845, Johanna Hillegonda, youngest dau. of Oloff Godlief de Wet, of Cape Town. (She died Pau 9 June 1884.)

Services : Cadet d.d. 50th N.I. 5 Jan. 1831 ; d.d. 69th N.I. 27 Feb. 1832 ; Actg. Ensign 5 Dec. 1832 ; posted Ensign to 9th N.I. 18 Oct. 1833. Fur. u.p.a. 15 Jan. 1833 till 24 Feb. 1835. Actg. Adjt. Sylhet L.I. 15 Oct. 1838 ; permanent do. 18 June 1839 till Dec. 1847. Offg. Asst. to P.A. Khasi Hills 16 Dec. 1840 and 1 Dec. 1841. To rejoin his Regt. at Sukkur May 1843. Leave s.c. to sea 22 Mar. 1844 till 1845. Offg. Supt. of Cachar 23 July 1847 ; 2nd in comd. Sylhet L.I. 11 Dec. 1847 ; Supt. of Cachar 20 June 1849 ; offg. Comr. of Arakan Mar. 1857 ; permanent do. 6 Dec. 1858 ; Comr. Arakan Div., Brit. Burma, 31 Jan. 1862 till 1869. Transfd. to Staff Corps 18 Feb. 1861. Fur. m.c. 1863-4, Apr. 1867 till Sept. 1868, and 24 Oct. 1872 till retirement.

Refs. : Burke's *Peerage*, 1923, p. 2227, *s.n.* Verner, Bart., of Verner's Bridge, co. Armagh. *The Times*, 4 Mar. 1885.

VERNER, James (1778-1816 ?). Lieutenant. 3rd N.C. Afterwards Capt. 19th Light Dgns. *b.* co. Dublin 1778. Cadet 1798. Arrived in India 22 Dec. 1799. Cornet 29 May 1800.

Lieut. 13 Nov. 1800. Resigned 9 May 1803. *d. unm.* (? 7 Sept. 1816).

2nd son of Col. James Verner, M.P., high sheriff for cos. Armagh, Meath, Monaghan, Dublin and Tyrone, and Jane his wife, dau. of Rev. Henry Clarke, of Anasammery, co. Armagh, rector of Clonfeacle. Brother of Sir William Verner, K.C.H., 1st Bart., and uncle of George Verner, *q.v.*

Services : Ensign R. Tyrone Regt. of Mil. 24 May 1798. Cornet 19th Light Dgns. 23 Sept. 1802 ; Lieut. do. 1 June 1803 ; Capt. do. 10 Dec. 1812.

Refs. : Burke's *Peerage*, 1923, p. 2227, *s.n.* Verner, Bart., of Verner's Bridge, Armagh.

VERNER, James Edward (1804-1865). Lieut. Colonel. 60th N.I. *b.* 26 Oct. 1804. Cadet 1828. Arrived in India 22 Mar. 1829. Ensign (12 Sept. 1828) 3 June 1829. Lieut. 7 Jan. 1836. Capt. 10 Aug. 1849. Bt. Major 20 June 1854. Retired 22 Mar. 1861. Hon. Lt. Col. 22 Mar. 1861. *d.* Belfast 25 Mar. 1865.

bapt. Belfast 20 Jan. 1808. Eldest son of Thomas Verner, of Dresden, and Elizabeth his wife. Brother of George Verner, *q.v. m.* Allahabad 27 Feb. 1843, Frances Constantia, 3rd dau. of John Camin Carne, *q.v.* (She died at sea off Cape Town 16 Apr. 1848, aged 27.) Ed. Eton ; in Lower Div. in 1820. T.C.D. ; Fellow Commoner 4 Dec. 1821. B.N.C., Oxon. ; matric. 21 May 1823.

Services : Ensign d.d. 59th N.I. 10 June 1829 ; posted Supy. Ensign to 50th N.I. ; transfd. to 69th N.I. 21 Sept. 1831 ; to 70th N.I. 2 Aug. 1832 ; to 60th N.I. 10 Nov. 1832. Adjt. 5th (Bhopawar) Local Horse 15 Dec. 1836 till Jan. 1839. Expedn. against Panch Mehal Naikras June 1838 ; Adjt. 5th Local Horse. Rejoined 60th N.I. Jan. 1839. Comdt. Cav. of Bundelkhand Legion (became 10th Irreg. Cav. in 1847) 30 Jan. 1840 till 1859.[1] Operations in Bundelkhand 1841 ; Chirgaon ; comdg. Cav. of Bundelkhand Legion. First Afghan War 1842 ; Lieut. 60th N.I., with Pollock's force (Medal). Operations on N. Sind frontier against Hill tribes 1844-5 ; Bt. Capt. comdg. Cav. of Bundelkhand Legion. Fur. 1860 till retirement. Major 28th Middlesex Rifle Vols.

Refs. : Burke's *Peerage*, 1923, p. 2227, *s.n.* Verner, Bart., of Verner's Bridge, co. Armagh. *Eton School Lists. Alumni Dub. Alumni Oxon. I.N.* No. 17, p. 382. *The Times*, 31 Mar. 1865.

[1] *Note :* This Regt. was disarmed at Nowshera and Peshawar in 1857 and disbanded, but the roll of officers of the corps was retained in *E.I.R.* down to 1859.

VERNON, Charles (*d.* 1785). Lieutenant, Artillery. (169) Country Cadet 1778. Fireworker 25 Sept. 1778. Lieut. 17 Apr. 1781. *d.* Ramgarh, B. & O., 29 Oct. 1785.

Services: Apptd. Cadet from Condr. of Ord. 11 Aug. 1778. Campaign against the Rajah of Benares 1781 ; action at Ramnagar 20 Aug. (w.).

*VERNON, Robert (or Richard) (*d.* 1787/88). Bt. Ensign, Infantry. Bt. Ensign 31 Dec. 1781. *d.* in India 1787/88.

Services: Promoted Bt. Ensign from Sergt. " for long and faithful service."

VERNON, Winthrop (1798-1838). Captain, 33rd N.I. *bapt.* White Ladies, Aston, Worcs., 7 May 1798. Cadet 1817. Admitted 5 Sept. 1818. Ensign 21 Apr. 1818. Lieut. 9 Dec. 1818. Capt. 21 Mar. 1831. *d.* Calcutta 12 Feb. 1838.

2nd son of James Baillie Vernon, Capt. R.N., sometime A.D.C. to Govr. of Jamaica, and Elizabeth his wife, dau. of Adm. G. Dorril, sometime Govr. of Newfoundland. *m.* 1st, Benares 18 Apr. 1823, Mrs. Sarah Beswick. (She died Barrackpore 3 May 1832.) *m.* 2nd, Calcutta 29 Dec. 1836, Mary, dau. of Bernard Reilly, late Civil Surg. at Fatehgarh. (*See also* Charles Elliot Goad.) Ed. in Jamaica.

Services: Posted Supy. Lieut. to 23rd N.I. 1819 ; posted Lieut. to 1/16th N.I. 18 Nov. 1820 ; transfd. to 33rd N.I. (late 2/16th) May 1824 ; actg. Intr. & Qmr. do. 18 Aug. 1824. Posted to 1st Gren. Bn. at Chittagong 5 Sept. 1825. First Burma War ; Arakan 1825-6 ; Lieut. 1st Gren. Bn. Fur. s.c. 23 Jan. 1834 till 25 Nov. 1836 ; leave s.c. to Calcutta 6 Nov. 1837 till death.

Refs.: Family information. *A.J.* N.S. xxvi. 46.

VERTUE, William (*d.* 1779). Lieutenant. 18th Bn. Sepoys. Country Cadet 1764. Ensign 6 June 1764. Lieut. 21 Aug. 1765. Cashiered by G.C.M. 29 Aug. 1766. *bur.* Calcutta 15 Nov. 1779.

Services: Was an Ofr. in R.N. in 1760 ; sailed for India as a Free Mariner in the *Pitt* 21 Mar. 1763. Battle of Buxar Oct. 1764 ; Ensign comdg. 4 Coys. Sepoys in the village. Was Adjt. of 2nd Bde. at Allahabad in 1766. Placed under close arrest 7 June 1766 for his active participation in the " Batta mutiny," tried by G.C.M. in July and sentenced to be cashiered.[1] He was further ordered to quit India, but was back in Calcutta in Sept. 1775, when he applied for a copy of the proceedings of his trial.

Refs.: Broome, p. 598. *Proc. of Select Committee,* 11 Jan. 1767.

[1] *Note:* On 16 July 1766 he addressed to the Presdt. of the C.M. which was to try him a protest against the treatment he had received,

claiming that he had "never at any time been a contracted officer or soldier in the service of the E.I. Co. It being a certain and known truth that I only acted voluntarily while I was employed in the said service, receiving an allowance for subsistence at the rate of 12 Rs. per day for my trouble."

"He was found guilty of the crimes of disobedience of orders and desertion, and sentenced to be cashiered with infamy, by having a sword and espontoon broke over his head, and a sash cut in pieces before him, at the head of all the troops cantoned at Bankipore." (Strachey's *Narrative*.)

VETCH, George Anderson (1786-1873). Lieut. Colonel. 54th N.I. *b.* Haddington 30 Nov. 1786. Cadet 1805. Arrived in India 19 Sept. 1806. Ensign 21 Sept. 1806. Lieut. 29 Aug. 1810. Capt. 20 Aug. 1823. Major 18 May 1833. Retired 24 Feb. 1835. Hon. Lt. Col. 28 Nov. 1854. *d.* Hawthornbank 10 Oct. 1873; *bur.* psh. churchyard at Haddington.

bapt. 12 Dec. 1786. 2nd son of Robert Vetch, of Hawthornbank (now Caponflat), nr. Haddington, and Agnes Sharp his wife. Brother of Hamilton Vetch, *q.v.*, and of James Vetch (*D.N.B.*). *m.* 1st, Bellevue, Edinburgh, 25 Jan. 1820, Helen, youngest dau. of George Hoggan, of Waterside, and sister of John Hoggan, *q.v.* (She died Edinburgh.) *m.* 2nd, 1837, Jane, dau. of William Anderson, of Edinburgh, solicitor, and of Colinton House, Midlothian.

Services : Ensign 1st (Berwickshire) Regt. of Brit. Mil. Posted Ensign to 2/27th N.I. 1806. Operations against Dhundia Khan 1807; Komona (w.); Ensign 2/27th N.I. Nepal War 1814-15; Jaithak; Lieut. 2/27th N.I., with L.I. Bn. in 2nd Div. (India medal). Actg. Adjt. 2/27th N.I. in 1815. Bareilly insurrection 1816.[1] Fur. u.p.a. 5 Jan. 1818 till 3 Oct. 1820. Supt. new road Benares to Allahabad 6 Nov. 1821; do. N. Div. of Cuttack road 17 Apr. 1826; do. Berhampore road 11 Aug. 1826; do. new Burdwan road 1831 till 1 Jan. 1835. Transfd. to 54th N.I. (late 2/27th) May 1824. Author of, *inter alia*, "Dara, or the Minstrel Prince," a dramatic poem pub. *c.* 1848-50; "The Gong: or Reminiscences of India," Edin., 1852.

Refs. : Family information. *D.I.B. A.A.R.* x. 21. *Haddingtonshire Courier*, 17 Oct. 1873. *The Times*, 18 Oct. 1873.

[1] *Note :* For his services on this occasion he was presented in 1816 by the inhabitants of Bareilly with a handsome sword and massive silver scabbard, now (1929) in the possession of his son, Mr. W. W. Vetch, of London.

THE BENGAL ARMY, 1758-1834

VETCH, Hamilton (1804-1865). Major General. 54th N.I.
b. Hawthornbank 30 Apr. 1804. Cadet 1822. Arrived in India
21 June 1823. Ensign 15 June 1823. Lieut. 13 May 1825.
Capt. 13 Jan. 1842. Major 29 Aug. 1854. Lt. Col. 6 June 1858.
Col. 31 Dec. 1861. Retired 31 Dec. 1861. Hon. Maj. Gen.
31 Dec. 1861. *d.* Dacca 11 June 1865.
bapt. Haddington 12 June 1804. 6th son of Robert Vetch, of
Hawthornbank, Haddington, and Agnes Sharp his wife. Brother
of Robert Vetch, *q.v.* *m.* Calcutta 31 Aug. 1842, Louisa Colebrooke,
dau. of Colin Campbell, Physician Gen. Bengal. (*See also* L. P. D.
Eld.) (She died Edinburgh 1851.)
Services: Posted to 2/27th N.I. 1823; transfd. to 54th N.I.
(late 2/27th) May 1824. First Burma War; Arakan 1825-6;
Lieut. 2nd Gren. Bn. (India medal). Actg. Adjt. 2nd Gren. Bn.
21 Dec. 1825. Operations against Khasias 1829-30; action nr.
Nongkhlao July 1830; d.d. Assam L.I. Actg. Adjt. Assam L.I.
24 Dec. 1830 and 24 Feb. 1831; actg. 2nd in comd. do. 9 Feb. 1833;
rejoined 54th N.I. May 1834. Junior Asst. to Comr. of Assam
30 Mar. 1835; Principal Asst. to A.G.G. and Comr., N.E. frontier,
11 Oct. 1838 till Feb. 1852. Served as a Vol. with detachment of
Assam Sebundy Corps under Lieut. H. W. Matthews, *q.v.*, in action
against Bhutias at Subankhata, 8 Mar. 1836, when he personally
captured a standard. D.C. of Assam 21 Feb. 1852 till Apr. 1857.
Fur. s.c. Apr. 1857 till 7 Mar. 1860. Posted Lt. Col. to 54th N.I.
1858. Placed tempy. at disposal of Govt. of Bengal 29 May 1860.
Refs.: Family information. *G.M.* 1865, ii. 391. M.I. in Dacca
cemetery.

VETCH, Robert (1791-1818). Lieutenant, 26th N.I. *b.* Haddington 5 Feb. 1791. Cadet 1806. Arrived in India 3 Oct. 1807.
Ensign 14 Oct. 1807. Lieut. 1 Jan. 1811. *d. unm.* Gwalior
23 Aug. 1818.
5th son of Robert Vetch and Agnes Sharp his wife. Brother of
George Anderson Vetch, *q.v.*
Services: Lieut. 1st (Berwickshire) Mil. in Mar. 1807. Posted
Ensign to 26th N.I. 1808. Operations in Bundelkhand against
Lachman Dawa 1809; Rajaoli; Ajaigarh; Ensign 26th N.I., with
4th L.I. Bn. Served with 4th L.I. Bn. till broken up May 1811.
Suptg. contract for bldgs. at Kaitha 1817. Third Mahratta War
1818; Dhamoni; Satanwara; Lieut. 1/26th N.I. Asst. to Resdt.
with Sindhia.
Refs.: Family information. Will dated Keitah 20 July 1817;
proved 5 Mar. 1819. M.I. Sagar Tal cemetery, Old Gwalior.

VEVERS, Spencer Edmund (1785-1815). Lieutenant, 7th N.C. *b.* Fillingham, Lincs., 8 Sept. 1785. Cadet 1800. Arrived in India 22 Aug. 1801. Cornet 13 Mar. 1803. Lieut. 24 Oct. 1805. *d.* Calcutta 30 Dec. 1815.

bapt. Fillingham 8 Oct. 1785. 2nd son of Rev. Richard Vevers, rector of Saxby, Leics., and Theodosia Dorothy his wife, 3rd dau. of Rev. Sir William Anderson, Bart., of Lea, Lincs. His sister *m.* Thomas Denman, 1st Baron Denman, of Dovedale, co. Derby. Ed. Eton 1796-9.

Services : Cornet d.d. 6th N.C.; posted Cornet to 1st N.C. 1803. Second Mahratta War 1803; Laswari; Cornet 1st N.C. Transfd. as Lieut. to newly-raised 7th N.C. 1805. Operations in Oudh 1808; Lieut. 7th N.C. Settlement of Hariana 1808-10. Fur. 1812 till 22 Sept. 1815.

Refs. : Foster's *Families of Royal Descent*, ii. 651. Burke's *Peerage*, 1859, p. 21, *s.n.* Anderson, Bart., of Broughton, Lincs. *Eton School Lists.* Will dated 3 Nov. 1815; proved 2 Jan. 1816.

VEYSIE, William (1801-1883). Lieut. Colonel. 7th L.C. *bapt.* Plymtree, Devon, 27 Oct. 1801. Cadet 1817. Admitted 5 Sept. 1818. Cornet 21 Apr. 1818. Lieut. 1 Oct. 1819. Capt. 13 June 1827. Major 10 Mar. 1841. Invalided 26 July 1841. Retired 18 Oct. 1843. Hon. Lt. Col. 28 Nov. 1854. *d.* Plymtree 10 June 1883.

Son of Rev. Daniel Veysie, rector of Plymtree, preby. of Exeter 1812, and Anne his wife. *m.* Mhow 6 Nov. 1832, Charlotte, 3rd dau. of Isaac Pereira, *q.v.* (See also F. D. Atkinson.) Ed. Exeter.

Services : Posted Cornet to 1st N.C.; transfd. as Lieut. to 7th L.C. 1819. Operations against the Bhils 1822-3; Lieut. 7th L.C. Suspended from rank and pay for 5 mos. 6 Apr. 1832. Shekhawat expedn. 1834; Capt. 7th L.C. Fur. p.a. 11 Jan. 1842 till retirement.

Refs. : *A.J.* N.S. ix. 137. *The Times*, 13 June 1883.

VIBART, Edward (1807-1857). Bt. Major, 2nd L.C. *b.* Amberd House, Pitminster, 15 Nov. 1807. Cadet 1823. Arrived in India 27 July 1824. Cornet 1 May 1824. Lieut. 13 May 1825. Capt. 16 Feb. 1849. Bt. Major 11 Nov. 1851. *d.* (? Sheorajpur, U.P., ? 1 July) of wounds received at Cawnpore 28 June 1857.[1]

bapt. 6 Oct. 1808. Youngest son of James Meredith Vibart, *q.v. m.* Bishop's Hull 4 June 1833, Emily, 2nd dau. of Edward Coles, of Paul's House, Taunton, clerk of the peace, co. Somerset. (She was massacred at Cawnpore July 1857.)

Services : Posted Cornet to 2nd L.C. Fur. u.p.a. 17 Feb. 1829 till 8 Aug. 1831 ; p.a. 10 Jan. 1833 till 11 Feb. 1834. Actg. Adjt. 2nd L.C. 10 Feb. 1839. First Afghan War 1839-40 ; Ghazni ; Bt. Capt. 2nd L.C. (Medal). Leave to India 15 Sept. 1840. d.d. 1st L.C. 6 May 1841 ; d.d. 3rd L.C. 14 Jan. 1842 ; posted to newly-raised 11th L.C. (became 2nd L.C.) 1842. Gwalior campaign ; Paniar ; Bt. Capt. 11th L.C. (Bronze star). Fur. 5 June 1846 till 1849. Was comdg. 2nd L.C. at Cawnpore when it mutinied 4 June 1857.

Refs. : Blunt's *Tombs in U.P.*, pp. 112, 125. *G.M.* 1857, ii. 685. M.I. All Sts. Memorial Church, Cawnpore.

[1] *Note :* He was the last man to leave the entrenchments at Cawnpore, and his was the only boat that escaped.

VIBART, James Meredith (*d.* 1827). Lieut. Colonel. 1st Bengal Eur. Regt. Cadet 1769. Admitted 26 July 1769. Ensign 26 July 1769. Lieut. 19 Nov. 1772. Capt. 14 Nov. 1780. Major 1 Mar. 1794. Lt. Col. 1 June 1796. Retired 26 Sept. 1798. *d.* 12 May 1827.

Of Amberd House, Pitminster, Somerset. *m.* Calcutta 4 Apr. 1785, Juliana, dau. of Capt. John Williams, E.I.C.N.S., Comdr. of the *Hector* East Indiaman, and sister of Capt. Robert Williams, E.I.C.N.S., Dir. E.I. Co. 1809-20. (*See also* J. H. Bellasis.) Father of Edward Vibart, *q.v.*

Services : Posted to Cav. 6 Apr. 1778 ; Capt. of Cav. in Jan. 1781 ; 1st Bengal Eur. Bn. in July 1787 ; apptd. to comd. 24th Bn. Sepoys 31 Oct. 1787. Posted Lt. Col. to 1st Bengal Eur. Regt. June 1796. Fur. 3 June 1797 till retirement.

Refs. : Will dated 28 Dec. 1824 ; proved 16 Oct. 1829.

VICARY, Nathaniel (1805-1863). Major. 2nd Eur. Fus. *bapt.* St. Peter's, Dublin, 29 July 1805. Cadet 1824. Arrived in India 23 July 1825. Ensign 20 Mar. 1825. Lieut. 25 June 1826. Capt. 24 Jan. 1845. Retired 15 Nov. 1849. Hon. Major 28 Nov. 1854. *d.* 13 Sept. 1863.

Son of Benjamin Vicary, of Wexford, solicitor, and Margaret his wife. *m.* Anne. (She died Ghazipur 18 July 1838, aged 38.) Ed. Wexford.

Services : Posted to 4th N.I. 1825. Leave s.c. to N.S.W. 17 Mar. 1836 till 7 May 1838. Transfd. to newly-raised 2nd Bengal Eur. Regt. 8 Oct. 1839. Executive Ofr. Allahabad-Goorhshaiganj Div. of Grand Trunk Road 18 Dec. 1841 till 6 May 1842. Second Sikh War ; Ramnagar ; passage of Chenab ; Chilianwala ; Gujerat ; Capt. 2nd Bengal Eur. Regt. (Medal with 2 clasps).

VICKERS, Charles Robert (1809-?). Ensign. 52nd N.I. *bapt.* St. Helier, Jersey, 5 Apr. 1809. Cadet 1827. Arrived in India 28 May 1828. Ensign (25 Dec. 1827) 4 Nov. 1828. Struck off 1 Nov. 1834.

Son of Charles Vickers, Lieut. h.p. H.M.S., and Helen Marie his wife. Stepson of Thomas Clifton Wheat, Lieut. h.p. H.M. 81st Ft.

Services: Posted to 52nd N.I. 4 Nov. 1828. Suspended from the Service for violence towards natives (G.O. 16 Oct. 1833); struck off by C.D. from 1 Nov. 1834 (G.O. 6 Nov. 1834), and embarked for England Apr. 1835. No record of active service.

VICKERS, John (*d.* 1799). Ensign, Invalid Est. Infantry. Bt. Ensign 24 Sept. 1782. Ensign 12 Apr. 1783. Invalided (?) *d.* Calcutta 10 Jan. 1799.

Father of Joseph, John Springer, Thomas Augustus, and Elizabeth, wife of William Hastings, *q.v.*

Services: Transfd. as Sergt. from Bengal Eur. Bn. to the Risala of Black Cav. 25 Feb. 1765. Promoted Ensign from Bt. Ensign in Feb. 1787, to rank from 12 Apr. 1783. Was serving at death with Calcutta Mil.

Refs.: Will dated 10 June 1797; admon. 7 Mar. 1799.

***VICKERS, Thomas.** Cadet. Infantry. Cadet 1782. Never arrived in India.

Services: Apptd. Cadet 10 May 1782; to sail in the *Busbridge;* did not proceed; struck off by C.D. Feb. 1783.

VIGNE, Edward (1784-1816). Lieutenant, Pension Est. 18th N.I. *b.* psh. of St. Bridget, Dublin, June 1784. Cadet 1804. Arrived in India 10 Sept. 1805. Ensign 4 Sept. 1805. Lieut. 5 Sept. 1805. Pensioned 13 June 1809. *d.* Chunar 21 July 1816.

Son of James Vigne, of College Green, Dublin, jeweller.

Services: Posted Lieut. to 18th N.I. 1806. No record of active service.

Refs.: M.I. old cemetery below Chunar fort.

VIGOGNE, William (1799-?). Lieutenant. 26th N.I. *bapt.* Bray, co. Wicklow, 14 Apr. 1799. Cadet 1817. Ensign (?) Lieut. 1 Jan. 1819. Dismissed in England without trial 27 Feb. 1822.

Eldest son of Charles Augustus Vigogne, of Little Cork, an ofr. in the Brit. Army, and Mary his wife, only dau. of Clotworthy

THE BENGAL ARMY, 1758-1834 357

Rowley, and sister of Adm. Sir Josias Rowley, Bart., G.C.B., G.C.M.G. (*D.N.B.*). His sister *m*. Sir Gilbert King, 3rd Bart., of Charlestown, co. Roscommon.
Services : Posted Supy. Lieut. to 1/26th N.I. 1819. Suspended 1821 ; dismissed by C.D. and sent home 1822.
Refs. : Hough's *Courts-Martial* (2nd edn.), p. 427.

VILLARS, Thomas. Lieutenant, Infantry. Country Cadet 1778. Ensign 1778. Lieut. 6 Aug. 1780. (*d.* before July 1787.)
Services : Apptd. Cadet 27 Feb. 1778. Ensign 2/1st Bengal Eur. Regt. in Oct. 1779.

VINCENT, George Frederick Frank (1794-1865). Lieut. Colonel. 8th N.I. *b.* St. Anne's, Limehouse, London, 31 Aug. 1794. Cadet 1810. Ensign 15 June 1813. Lieut. 21 Feb. 1816. Capt. 18 June 1830. Major 23 Nov. 1841. Retired 23 Feb. 1842. Hon. Lt. Col. 28 Nov. 1854. *d.* at his residence, 21 Kensington Pl., Bath, 27 Sept. 1865, after a short illness resulting from paralysis.

Son of Elizabeth Vincent. *m.* Bathwick, Somerset, 4 Sept. 1823, Mary Amelia, 3rd dau. of Rev. John Amyatt Chaundy, of Charlinch, Somerset.
Services : Cadet d.d. 9th N.I. 1811-13 ; posted Ensign to 1/9th N.I. 1813. Fur. p.a. 6 Dec. 1821 till 16 Apr. 1824. Transfd. to 8th N.I. (late 1/9th) May 1824. Adjt. Chittagong Provl. Bn. 17 June 1824 ; do. Dacca 28 Jan. 1825 ; do. Burdwan 20 May 1826 till 1831. Jodhpur demonstration 1834 ; Capt. 8th N.I. Actg. Dy. Paymr. Rajputana 4 Nov. 1835.
Refs. : *G.M.* 1823, ii. 552 ; 1865, ii. 658. *Bath Chron.* 28 Sept. 1865. *The Times*, 29 Sept. 1865.

VINCENT, Henry (*d.* 1767 ?). Lieutenant. Infantry. Cadet (?) Ensign 4 Apr. 1764. Lieut. 13 Aug. 1765. (? *d.* 1767.)[1]
Services : Posted to Bengal Eur. Bn. 25 Nov. 1764. (*Probably* dismissed in 1766 for implication in the " Batta mutiny.")

[1] *Note :* Was sick in Calcutta in Feb. 1767 when under orders to return to England.

VINCENT, Henry (*d.* 1797). Lieut. Colonel, Infantry. Cadet 1769. Admitted 12 Sept. 1769. Ensign 27 Dec. 1769. Lieut. 23 Mar. 1773. Capt. 6 Jan. 1781. Major 1 Mar. 1794. Lt. Col. 14 Sept. 1796. *d.* at sea 24 Dec. 1797.
m. 1st (before 1782), (?). *m.* 2nd, Calcutta 1 Jan. 1797, Miss Harriet Albina Turner.

Services : Capt. 4th Bengal Eur. Bn. in July 1787 and in Dec. 1788. Fur. 12 Jan. 1789 till 13 July 1791. Posted to 4th Eur. Bn. 16 Aug. 1791 ; to comd. 25th Bn. Sepoys 21 Nov. 1792 ; transfd. to 2nd Eur. Regt. June 1796. Fur. 27 July 1797 till death.

VINCENT, Orlando (1809-1831). Ensign, 29th N.I. *b.* Constantine, Cornwall, 14 Apr. 1809. Cadet 1827. Arrived in India 10 June 1828. Ensign (20 Feb. 1828) 4 Nov. 1828. *d.* Meerut 3 Nov. 1831 : murdered by his sirdar bearer.[1]

Son of Rev. John Vincent, chaplain Bengal Est., and Mary his wife.

Services : Ensign d.d. 60th N.I. 25 July 1828 ; posted to 29th N.I. 4 Nov. 1828. No record of active service.

Refs. : A.J. N.S. viii. 41.

[1] *Note :* He was found murdered in his bed : the bearer appears to have committed suicide immediately after the assassination of his master.

VINCENT, William (1781-1859). Lieut. General. 8th N.I. *bapt.* Waterford cathedral 29 Oct. 1781. Cadet 1801. Arrived in India 13 Feb. 1804. Ensign 5 July 1802. Lieut. 29 Mar. 1804. Capt. 9 Apr. 1816. Major 2 Oct. 1824. Lt. Col. 30 May 1828. Col. 8 Oct. 1839. Maj. Gen. 23 Nov. 1841. Lt. Gen. 11 Nov. 1851. *d.* Mussoorie 28 Aug. 1859, aged 75 yrs. 10 mos.

Son of William Vincent and Mary his wife. *m.* 1st, St. Andrew's, Calcutta, 12 July 1827, Elizabeth, widow of William Pickersgill, *q.v.* (She died Meerut 22 Oct. 1838.) *m.* 2nd, Meerut 6 Apr. 1847, Phoebe Letitia Cecilia, widow of G. R. P. Becher, *q.v.*, and grand-dau. of H. N. L. Berkeley, *q.v.*

Services : Held a provisional Commission in Marine Bn. during expedn. to Ternate in 1801, under Lieut. William Gill, *q.v.* Posted Ensign to 20th N.I. (late Marine Bn.) 1803. Capture of Java 1811 ; Lieut. 1/20th N.I. (Medal). Capt. Lt. 2/20th N.I. 1 Oct. 1815. Fort Adjt. Malacca 1815-16. Served in Ceylon with 2/20th N.I. Oct. 1818 till Feb. 1819. At Singapore in 1821. First Burma War 1824 ; at Ramri I. ; Capt. 2/20th N.I. (India medal). Transfd. to 25th N.I. (late 1/20th) May 1824. Posted Lt. Col. to 25th N.I. 10 Sept. 1828. Fur. p.a. 3 Jan. 1830 till 11 Nov. 1831. Transfd. to 26th N.I. 27 Oct. 1832 ; to 68th N.I. 29 Mar. 1839. Posted Col. to 46th N.I. 1839. Fur. p.a. 16 Apr. 1840 till 24 Sept. 1841. Col. 8th N.I. 21 Sept. 1841 till 1858. Bdr. 2 cl. comdg. Agra 5 Jan. 1842 ; Dinapore 30 Sept. 1842 ; Ferozepore 6 July 1843 ; Delhi

Bde. 27 Apr. 1845; Rohilkhand and Kumaon 1846. Maj. Gen. comdg. Cawnpore Div. 4 Feb. 1848 till 9 Apr. 1852. Fur. 1858-9.
Refs.: Boase. I.M. 22 Oct. 1859, p. 870. M.I. Mussoorie old cemetery.

VITALIS, Henry Thomas (*d.* 1774). Cadet, Infantry. Cadet 1772. *d.* in camp at Bisauli, U.P., 25 Oct. 1774.
Son of Mary Vitou (*sic*—? Vitalis).. Brother of Mary Magdalen Vitalis.
Services: First Rohilla War 1774; battle of St. George; Cadet, with 2nd Bn. Sepoys.
Refs.: Will dated camp, 30 Sept. 1774; proved 29 Apr. 1775.

VIZETTE, Lewis (*d.* 1768). Lieutenant, Infantry. Cadet (?) Ensign 24 Apr. 1765. Lieut. 17 Dec. 1766. *d.* 1768.
Services: N.F.P.

VOLHAM, John (*d.* 1769). Lieutenant, Artillery. (63) Cadet (?) Fireworker 29 Sept. 1764. 2nd Lieut. Feb. 1767. Lieut. 8 Aug. 1768. *d.* Calcutta 18 Jan. 1769.
Brother of Richard and Thomas Volham, of St. George-in-the-East, and of Sarah, wife of James Forster.
Services: Dy. Comy. of Ord. at Patna in 1765; posted to Calcutta 17 Feb. 1765.
Refs.: Will dated 13 Jan. 1769; proved 20 Jan. 1769.

VOLHAM, Lewis (*d.* 1765). Lieutenant, Infantry. Cadet (?) Ensign (?) Lieut. 1764. *d.* Jaunpur, U.P., 18 Jan. 1765: kld. in action.
Services: N.F.P. (*Possibly* a Comy. of Ord.)
Refs.: Broome, p. 504.

VOULES, Herbert Poulton (1809-1869). Lieutenant. 3rd L.C. Subsequently one of H.M. Inspectors of Prisons, Northern district. *bapt.* Windsor 27 July 1809. Cadet 1825. Arrived in India 25 June 1826. Cornet 16 Feb. 1826. Lieut. 24 July 1828. Retired 30 June 1838. *d.* Sea View, I.W., 28 Sept. 1869.
Of Uffington, nr. Stamford, Lincs. Son of William Voules, of Windsor, and Elizabeth his wife. *m.* Ballina 25 Jan. 1848, Maria, 3rd dau. of William Malley, of Ballivary, co. Mayo. (She died London 14 Nov. 1887.) Ed. Eton 1817-25.
Services: Cornet d.d. 9th L.C. 8 July 1826; posted to 3rd L.C. 26 Sept. 1826; actg. Adjt. do. 7 Mar. 1831 and 7 Dec. 1832. Operations against the Kols 1832; actg. Adjt. to detachment of 3rd L.C. under Capt. John Angelo, *q.v.*, from 23 Jan. 1832.

Leave s.c. to Hills 15 Feb. 1833 till 15 Nov. 1834. Adjt. 3rd L.C. 6 Sept. 1834 till Dec. 1835. Fur. s.c. 30 Dec. 1835 till retirement. Retired on pension of 4/- p.d.

Refs. : Eton School Lists. The Times, 1 Oct. 1869.

VOYLE, Elliot (1765-1834). Lieut. Colonel. 10th N.I. b. 20 May 1765. Cadet 1782. Admitted 15 Nov. 1782. Ensign 9 Feb. 1783. Lieut. 1 Feb. 1790. Capt. 2 Dec. 1802. Major 26 Feb. 1813. Bt. Lt. Col. 4 June 1814. Invalided 1 Mar. 1816. Retired 1 Aug. 1820. d. Norton Cottage, Tenby, 28 July 1834, of spasmodic gout.

bapt. Lawrenny, co. Pembroke, 1 June 1765. Son of Rev. John Voyle, rector of Lawrenny (who was son of William Voyle, of Greengrove, by Elizabeth, sister of Rev. John Grant, of Fenton), and Lettice his wife, eldest dau. of Rev. Philip Elliot, of St. Botolph, co. Pembroke. First cousin once removed of Cornelius Davies and Henry Grant, qq.v. m. London 10 Nov. 1806, his kinswoman Elizabeth, elder dau. of George Elliot, q.v. (iii. 722) (She died Tenby 4 Oct. 1856, aged 68.) Father of Francis Elliot Voyle, q.v. Friend and schoolfellow of Richard Parry (1760/61-1794), q.v.

Services : Posted to 3rd Bengal Eur. Regt. 28 Feb. 1783. Ensign 1st Eur. Bn. in July 1787 ; transfd. from 5th Eur. Bn. to 33rd Bn. Sepoys 5 Feb. 1790 ; to 34th Bn. 25 Feb. 1790. On service with a detachment in Chittagong against the Burmese 1794. A.D.C. to Maj.-Gen. Charles Morgan, q.v., 1795 ; Qmr. of one of the Eur. Regts. 1796 ; Lieut. 10th N.I. in 1798 ; Adjt. & Qmr. do. in 1802 ; Capt. 10th N.I. Fur. 28 Jan. 1805 till 19 July 1809. Operations in Rewah 1813-14 ; Major comdg. 2/10th N.I. Apptd. Dec. 1814 to raise and discipline 28th N.I. ; returned to 2/10th N.I. July 1815. Comdd. Benares Provl. Bn. 1816 till Nov. 1820. Fur. 26 Jan. 1821. Subsequently retired with effect from 1 Aug. 1820.

Refs. : Family information. E.I.M.C. i. 349-50. G.M. 1834, ii. 334. Will dated 3 Nov. 1830 ; proved 22 Oct. 1836. M.I. in St. Mary's, Tenby.

VOYLE, Francis Elliot (1815-1877). Major General. 39th N.I. b. Cawnpore 11 Apr. 1815. Cadet 1830. Arrived in India 5 Dec. 1831. Ensign (9 June 1831) 5 Dec. 1831. Lieut. 17 Oct. 1838. Capt. 18 Nov. 1846. Major 4 June 1855. Lt. Col. 18 Feb. 1861. Col. 18 Feb. 1866. Maj. Gen. 11 May 1871. d. Norton Cottage, Tenby, 23 Apr. 1877.

bapt. Cawnpore 21 May 1815. Son of Elliot Voyle, q.v., and Elizabeth his wife. m. 1st, Simla 20 July 1840, Anne, 2nd dau. of Mossom Boyd, q.v. (She died Simla 14 Nov. 1841.) m. 2nd,

THE BENGAL ARMY, 1758-1834

St. Mary's, Bryanston Sq., 25 Apr. 1844, Caroline Sarah, youngest dau. of Vice-Adm. James Noble. (She died 14 Oct. 1852.) *m.* 3rd, Prestbury 13 Sept. 1855, Elizabeth, dau. of John Nichols, of Kempsey, Worcs. (She died Penally, nr. Tenby, 11 Apr. 1915, aged 84.) Addiscombe Cadet 1829-31.

Services: Cadet d.d. 55th N.I. 17 Jan. 1832; posted Ensign to 39th N.I. 19 Oct. 1833; Intr. & Qmr. do. 18 Sept. 1834 till Jan. 1841. Operations against the Bhils 1837; Ensign 39th N.I., with Nimach F.F. under Lt.-Col. C. R. Skardon, *q.v.* Offg. Executive Engr. 21 Dec. 1838. Adjt. W. Meywar Bhil Corps 27 Jan. till 26 May 1841. Intr. & Qmr. 39th N.I. 29 May 1841 till 2 May 1843. With Army of Reserve (for Afghanistan) Oct. 1842 till Jan. 1843. Fur. s.c. 1 Apr. 1843 till 6 Nov. 1844. Adjt. 39th N.I. 16 Oct. 1845 till 20 Jan. 1847. Asst. Comr. in Punjab 13 Apr. 1849; Jhelum Div. 1852; Asst. Comr. 2 cl., Peshawar Div., 10 May 1853; D.C. 2 cl., Leiah Div., 30 May 1854; 1 cl. in Oudh 13 May 1857; D.C. Punjab (1 Apr. 1858) 4 Feb. 1859 till 1869. Mutiny campaign 1857-8 (Medal). Fur. Apr. till 23 Oct. 1859, and 24 Apr. 1867 till death. Transfd. to Staff Corps 18 Feb. 1861.

Refs.: Family information. *G.M.* 1844, i. 645. *The Times,* 28 Apr. 1877. M.I. in St. Mary's, Tenby.

VYSE, James (1784-1824). Captain, 57th N.I. *b.* Eton 17 Feb. 1784. Cadet 1804. Arrived in India 10 Sept. 1805. Ensign 15 Sept. 1805. Lieut. 16 Sept. 1805. Capt. 11 July 1823. *d.* Rangpur 23 Aug. 1824.

Son of John Vyse.

Services: Posted Lieut. to 25th N.I. 1806. Capture of Mauritius 1810; Lieut. 25th N.I., with 1st Vol. Bn. Transfd. to newly-raised 29th N.I. 1815. Siege and capture of Hathras 1817; Lieut. 1/29th N.I. Actg. Intr. & Qmr. 1/29th N.I. 1818. Transfd. to 57th N.I. (late 1/29th) May 1824. First Burma War 1824; Assam; Capt. 57th N.I.

Refs.: Will dated Calcutta 7 Sept. 1810; proved 10 Sept. 1824. M.I. at Rangpur.

www.ingramcontent.com/pod-product-compliance
Lightning Source LLC
Chambersburg PA
CBHW061930220426
43662CB00012B/1858